Fiscal Policy

Fiscal Policy

Lessons from Economic Research

edited by Alan J. Auerbach

The MIT Press
Cambridge, Massachusetts
London, England

This book was set in Palatino on the Monotype "Prism Plus" PostScript Imagesetter by Asco Trade Typesetting Ltd., Hong Kong.

Printed and bound in the United States of America.

Library of Congress Cataloging-in-Publication Data

Fiscal policy : lessons from economic research / edited by Alan J. Auerbach.
p. cm.
Includes bibliographical references and index.
ISBN 0-262-01160-3 (hc : alk. paper)
1. Fiscal policy—Congresses. 2. Fiscal policy—United States—Congresses.
I. Auerbach, Alan J.
HJ192.5.F573 1997
336.3'0973—DC21 96-53456
CIP

Contents

Acknowledgments

Any undertaking of this type requires contributions beyond those that appear in print. The conference that gave rise to this book could not have occurred without the generous support of Robert D. Burch. I would also like to thank Tara Kerwin for her help in planning the conference and in shepherding the manuscript into its current state.

Contributors

Henry J. Aaron
Brookings Institution

Alan J. Auerbach
University of California, Berkeley

B. Douglas Bernheim
Stanford University

David M. Cutler
Harvard University

Nada Eissa
University of California, Berkeley

Jeffrey Frankel
University of California, Berkeley

William G. Gale
Brookings Institution

Roger H. Gordon
University of Michigan

Edward M. Gramlich
University of Michigan

Bronwyn H. Hall
University of California, Berkeley

Kevin A. Hassett
Board of Governors
Federal Reserve System

James R. Hines, Jr.
Harvard University

Hilary Williamson Hoynes
University of California, Berkeley

R. Glenn Hubbard
Columbia University

Robert P. Inman
University of Pennsylvania

Laurence J. Kotlikoff
Boston University

Robert A. Moffitt
Johns Hopkins University

Joseph P. Newhouse
Harvard University

James M. Poterba
Massachusetts Institute of Technology

John M. Quigley
University of California, Berkeley

Robert D. Reischauer
Brookings Institution

David Romer
University of California, Berkeley

Daniel L. Rubinfeld
University of California, Berkeley

John B. Shoven
Stanford University

Jonathan S. Skinner
Dartmouth College

Joel Slemrod
University of Michigan

John B. Taylor
Stanford University

1 Introduction

Alan J. Auerbach

The chapters and comments in this book were presented originally at a conference sponsored by the Robert D. Burch Center for Tax Policy and Public Finance at the University of California, Berkeley, in February 1996. The conference brought together economists who have been leading contributors to the public finance literature and the public policy debate. Its immediate objective was to provide a sense of the policy-relevant lessons from the literature to date in eight important areas of economic research. This information should be useful to policymakers, who are often hard-pressed to understand what economists have to say on policy issues, and to students and scholars, who wish to know what we have learned to date and what questions remain unanswered. Although much of the research cited deals with the U.S. experience, there is little that will not be of use to those in other developed countries as well.

The chapters are broad in their scope, but they are not, and were not intended to be, neutral and comprehensive surveys of the literature. Authors and discussants were encouraged to offer their views and to focus on the issues they found most important or interesting. The conference confirmed that on some questions there is a broad consensus among leading economists and that on other questions there is strong disagreement. Because perspectives do differ, this book presents, after each chapter the comments of two discussants offering their own views on the material and the subjects more generally. Probably more so than is typical in conference volumes, these comments should be seen as an integral part of the presentation on each subject.

The eight chapters that follow divide into three subject areas. The first two chapters deal with issues of government budget management and control, with one considering the impact of restrictive budget rules and another the impact of changes in the intergovernmental allocation of resources and responsibilities. The next three deal with the three major federal entitlement program areas: poverty alleviation, health care, and retirement. The last three deal with notable areas of tax code management, where policymakers have attempted to influence private sector behavior: private saving, business fixed investment, and international finance, investment, and production decisions.

In a federal system, different levels of government have different responsibilities and sources of revenue. The literature on fiscal federalism through the years has considered the impact of alternative federal fiscal structures and the optimal design of such structures to take account of such matters as competition, spillover effects, and differences in preferences across lower-level jurisdictions. In chapter 2, John Quigley and Daniel Rubinfeld consider the likely impact of a devolution of program responsibilities to state and local governments, an approach many policymakers have advocated as a means of enforcing budget discipline. Quigley and Rubinfeld suggest that the United States is entering a period of increasing state responsibility for programs historically provided at least in part at the federal level. This shift in responsibilities may well lead to a reduction in the size of these programs, though not necessarily because of the added flexibility afforded states with respect to program design, a proposition that Quigley and Rubinfeld label dubious. Rather, the elimination of federal control may result in a "race to the bottom," with jurisdictions seeking (presumably without ultimate success) to foist their social problems off on one another.

Struggles with the federal deficit and debates over measures to restrict it, from the Gramm-Rudman-Hollings Act of 1985 to a balanced budget amendment to the U.S. Constitution, have raised the questions of whether such measures are effective and, if so, whether they are advisable. In chapter 3, James Poterba focuses on the first of these questions, relying primarily on the empirical evidence from the individual states that have implemented measures to restrict deficits. A serious theoretical challenge to such rules is that they may have no impact, either because they are superfluous or because the ambiguity of deficit measurement makes them ineffective. Poterba's review of the evidence, though, suggests that budget restrictions have placed considerable restrictions on the abilities of states to establish and maintain large budget deficits.

Many view the alleviation of poverty as a central task of government. However, the sense that many of the poor have become dependent on welfare programs, notably Aid to Families with Dependent Children, and that such programs have contributed to undesirable changes in family structure, has led to consideration of alternative policies to deal with poverty, such as the earned income tax credit, "workfare," and time limits on the receipt of welfare benefits. In her review of the relevant research in chapter 4, Hilary Williamson Hoynes concludes that the effects of such policy reforms on teenage pregnancies, female headship of households, and overall work effort are likely to be small. However, she also cautions that these predictions involve considerable uncertainty, because many potential policy changes lie well outside past experience.

In chapter 5, David Cutler considers the role of government in the provision of health care. He suggests two distinct roles for policy intervention. First, governments can alter individual behavior to promote health, through education and through policies to discourage unhealthful activities such as smoking. Second, government can make the health care and insurance markets function better. There is considerable scope for such intervention, because many of the assumptions needed to ensure efficient market outcomes are violated. In particular, there is incomplete information about individual health status on the part of insurers and about the benefits of treatment among individuals. However, Cutler finds that government policy responses have introduced their own considerable distortions, most notably the overuse of medical resources. He argues that some of these inefficiencies can be alleviated by moving to a market structure with more emphasis on the individual, but that in doing so we must develop ways to deal with the greater separation of individuals by health status and risk that are likely to result.

The largest program in the U.S. federal budget is the social security retirement system. As this system's obligations expand with the aging of the U.S. population and the approaching retirement of the baby boom generation, many observers have grown concerned about the system's impact on the level of private saving and individual labor force participation decisions. Spurred by recent reforms in other countries, notably Chile, some economists have argued in favor of converting the U.S. social security system into a private old-age pension scheme. Others have countered that privatization offers few benefits not available through reform of the existing system, while still others have expressed concern that a private system would fail to meet the current system's distributional objectives. In chapter 6, Laurence Kotlikoff argues that privatization would represent a major change from the current social security system and that its benefits would include a reduced labor supply distortion and a clearer public perception of the program's costs.

Whether one looks at national saving or saving by the private sector, the U.S. saving rate is low by international standards, and has become lower in the past two decades. To encourage private saving, the federal government has experimented with a variety of tax incentives, including Individual Retirement Accounts (IRAs) and employer-based contributory schemes known as 401(k)s, in reference to the relevant section in the Internal Revenue Code. In chapter 7, Douglas Bernheim reviews the literature on the effects of these schemes, arguing that the evidence to date on IRAs is inconclusive but that the impact of 401(k)s is more clearly positive. He also argues that too little attention has been paid to the institutional differences between these approaches and simpler, more broadly based reductions in the taxation of capital income. While the basic life cycle model of household behavior ignores such considerations, Bernheim suggests the potential relevance of institutional channels, such as the involvement of employers in organizing and encouraging saving. This issue is of central importance in evaluating the potential effects of a major change in the tax treatment of saving, such as a shift to consumption taxation.

One reason for promoting saving is to increase the rate of accumulation of fixed capital by U.S. businesses. The U.S. government has also engaged in more direct policy actions to influence the level and composition of business fixed investment, beginning with the introduction of accelerated depreciation schedules in 1954 and the investment tax credit (repealed in 1986) in 1962. The frequent changes in tax policy toward investment have encouraged researchers to study their effectiveness. In chapter 8, Kevin Hassett and Glenn Hubbard consider the evidence from these studies, emphasizing recent work that has found a significant effect of tax changes on investment behavior. They argue that these studies overcome econometric difficulties of earlier work that caused such work to understate the impact of taxation. Based on this evidence and an evaluation of the impacts on different policies on the incentive to invest, Hassett and Hubbard go on to argue that more effective control of inflation or a shift to consumption taxation significantly would stimulate investment.

As international trade and capital flows expand with improvements in technology, the tax treatment of multinational corporations takes on greater importance as a public policy issue. This is a complex area, because it necessarily involves the tax codes of at least two countries and their impact on a number of interrelated business decisions regarding where to obtain funds, invest, and produce. Based on a detailed survey of the empirical evidence, James Hines concludes in chapter 9 that the activities of multinational corporations are quite sensitive to their tax treatment. Thus, countries wishing to impose taxes on such enterprises must either coordinate their activities or rely on complex and possibly quite distortionary tax rules that prevent significant shifting away from taxation. Hines emphasizes the need to develop and distinguish empirically among alternative theoretical explanations for the observed behavior of multinationals. He notes that the sensitivity of behavior to taxation implies that tax policy can exert potentially large effects on economic efficiency, the magnitude of which depends on the precise nature of firm decisions.

As all of these chapters illustrate, public policy decisions can benefit from better information about the behavioral effects of existing and prospective policies. They also illustrate, alas, how many questions remained unanswered. Nevertheless, much is known, and it is important that this be recognized. Moreover, identifying what is yet unknown is a necessary first step toward an answer.

2 Federalism as a Device for Reducing the Budget of the Central Government

John M. Quigley and
Daniel L. Rubinfeld

The U.S. Constitution incorporates built-in tensions of economic federalism, enumerating certain powers for the central government while reserving others for the state. The historical resolution of these tensions has a complex political and economic history. Given the substantial inertia that is built into the U.S. federalist system, it is not surprising that the current set of economic responsibilities has evolved only slowly during the past two centuries.

The historian Harry Scheiber (1966) has identified four stages in the development of federalism in the United States: (1) a period of dualism (1790–1860) in which the states and the central government had comparable responsibilities; (2) a period of centralizing federalism (1860–1933), when federal responsibilities grew; (3) a time of cooperative federalism (1933–1964), which marked a substantial growth in social programs arising out of the Great Depression; and (4) a period of creative federalism (since 1964) in which the federal government has taken an active role in the problems of state and local governments.

The period of creative federalism was spurred by the support for programs of revenue sharing from the federal government to the states by economists Walter Heller and Joseph Pechman (Perloff and Nathan 1968). In today's environment of large budgetary deficits, it is difficult to imagine that a crucial argument for a broad-based program of unrestricted grants to states was the fear of "fiscal drag"—that the automatic growth of federal revenues under a progressive personal income tax would otherwise lead to excessive fiscal surpluses. The Heller-Pechman plan, substantially modified by Congress and the executive, ultimately became the General Revenue Sharing Program, the heart of President Nixon's New Federalism in 1972.

A decade later, in January 1982, it appeared that a new period in federal relations would begin when the Reagan administration proposed to reverse the trend toward the centralization of financing of government services.

The Reagan proposal sought to return to states and localities all financial responsibility for income redistribution (Aid to Families with Dependent Children, i.e., AFDC, and food stamps) as well as control over more than sixty federal programs targeted to low-income households, including education, community development (e.g., water and sewer programs), transportation, and social services. This was to be accomplished in part by a cut in specific grant programs and in part by the consolidation of other programs into a single block grant program.

Perhaps most important, the Reagan federalism initiatives forced a serious rethinking of the evolutionary path of the public economy, which had moved financial and managerial responsibility for public goods and services steadily up to the national level. Although the core reforms of Reagan's New Federalism proposal never became law, the Reagan budgets significantly curtailed the levels of federal support for state and local governments. This curtailment was bifurcated: federal support for spending on local goods and services declined dramatically, but support for distributional programs, especially those involving health care, increased substantially over the past decade.

The issues that have divided the Clinton administration and the 104th Congress mirror those of the Reagan initiative in many ways. Rather than marking a reversion to the New Federalism of the 1980s, the current debate may well signify the beginning of a new period of retrenchment in American federalism. The debate puts the presumptions of our entire federalist system under scrutiny and asks whether the current structure of responsibilities is appropriate now.

A coherent discussion of the issues that surround the federalism debate requires a well-articulated view of the goals of a federalist economy. Section 2.1 provides an economist's perspective of the essential ingredients. On the basis of economic efficiency, we suggest that governmental functions should be centralized if the decentralized alternative would create substantial spillovers that are unlikely to be remedied through bargains reached among the affected governments. Further, to the extent that externality-creating competition rather than cooperation is the rule, the imposition of national standards can be desirable. Finally, we suggest that a third nonefficiency criterion can be important. When a substantial portion of the population believes that certain fairness principles should apply to all, the imposition of centralized national norms, affecting all citizens, may be appropriate.

Section 2.2 discusses some normative implications of our federalism perspective for intergovernmental fiscal relations. We explain why federalism principles suggest a strong, but not necessarily exclusive, role for the central government in overseeing distributional programs. We believe that the current federalism debates involve two distinct but related features. In section 2.3 we discuss the first issue: the growth of mandates and the opportunity that a change in mandates provides for the federal government to cut its budget. The second issue—the structural changes in intergovernmental grant programs corresponding to a shift in responsibilities from the federal government to the states—is the focus of analysis in section 2.4.

2.1 The Normative Theory of Economic Federalism

The accepted model of federalism, summarized in Wallace Oates's 1972 book *Fiscal Federalism*, gives to the central government responsibility for financial oversight of those public activities distinguished by significant externalities involving spatially dispersed populations, while leaving to local governments responsibility for those public activities for which spatial spillovers are limited or absent. The guiding principle is to internalize all economic externalities at the smallest level of government possible, a principle formalized by Oates in his "decentralization theorem."[1] Decentralization to small collectives is favored since taste differences can best be accounted for by the political process if decision makers most closely represent their constituents. As Oates put it more recently (1994, p. 130), "The tailoring of outputs to local circumstances will, in general, produce higher levels of well-being than a centralized decision to provide some uniform level of output across all jurisdictions.... And such gains do not depend upon any mobility across jurisdictional boundaries."

The consensus at the time of Oates's book was that regulation of markets, national defense, public health, economic stabilization, and redistribution policies are best handled at the centralized, or national, level of government, while education and the maintenance and protection of private and public property are best left to decentralized state or local levels of government. The current political debate questions this view. As a prelude to commenting on this debate, it will be useful to review the underpinnings of the basic theory.

In our multilevel federalist economy, two separate but related efficiency issues arise. The first is interjurisdictional efficiency, involving the appropriate allocation of people and capital among jurisdictions. Interjurisdictional efficiency is achieved when the level of publicly provided goods and services is sufficient to satisfy individuals' demands at minimum cost.

The second is intrajurisdictional efficiency; this is achieved when the choice of government activities in each jurisdiction maximizes the sum of all residents' willingness to pay for those activities net of any cost.

In a federal system, both interjurisdictional and intrajurisdictional inefficiencies can arise, the former because the decisions and actions of individuals within one jurisdiction generate spillovers that affect individuals located in other jurisdictions, and the latter because the political process may not produce wealth-maximizing outcomes within a jurisdiction. In a broad sense, the choice of the appropriate jurisdiction to be responsible for a government activity involves a trade-off: the larger the jurisdiction, the less likely it is that there will be spillovers from one jurisdiction to the next, but the more likely that the political process will lead to a misallocation of resources within the jurisdiction.

The public economy differs importantly from the private economy in that the number of households that benefit from public provision is likely to vary for different activities. In the extreme case of a pure public good, the additional cost of providing the good is zero, so larger communities are more efficient. However, in the more realistic case of a congested public good, the marginal cost of producing the good will increase (after some point) as the number of households in the community increases. When public goods are congested, a jurisdiction reaches its optimal size when the average cost per household of public service provision is equal to the marginal cost of adding another household to the community (Buchanan 1965). Were the average cost higher, the population of the community would be too small; more residents would allow the community to take advantage of economies of scale in producing public goods, and average cost would fall.

The Tiebout model comes closest to making the case for a decentralized system of local governments. In this framework of numerous jurisdictions and a mobile population, each jurisdiction may offer a different tax expenditure and regulation package. By assumption, a sufficient number of jurisdictions will allow each household to choose the one that supplies its desired public sector package. With perfect information and costless mobility, each individual will reveal his or her preference for public services simply by moving into the community of choice. If some other jurisdiction provided a better public service or the same service at a lower cost, there would be nothing to stop the individual from relocating. As a result of this "fiscally motivated" migration, local head taxes would allow competitive governments to allocate public sector packages among individuals in a manner similar to the way in which the competitive private market allocates its goods among individuals. If no community provided the exact bundle of public services that a household wanted, a new community that provided those services at minimum average cost would be established.

In the simplified Tiebout model, there are no spillovers across jurisdictional boundaries. When a government decides to engage in an activity such as primary education, the benefits are obtained only by the residents of the jurisdiction. When benefits and costs do extend beyond the local boundaries, the "optimal" fiscal unit may be a higher (state or federal) level of government. And when governments are deciding how to spend or to regulate, those decisions are determined on the basis of the desires of current residents only.

These spillovers can create competitive incentives that lead to further and more significant inefficiencies. For example, states might be encouraged to relax their environmental controls to encourage business migration. The net result is a race to the bottom, leading to regulatory standards that vary from state to state and that could be significantly more lax than states would prefer if common national standards were set (Revesz 1992).

A further case for a national standard can be made on nonefficiency grounds. To the extent that there is widespread support for a particular national norm, a centralized policy that reflects that viewpoint may be appropriate, whether or not there are significant spillovers. Thus, "fairness" may require that all individuals receive equal access to public services and, more generally, equal treatment under the law. Alternatively, fairness can involve a judgment about the appropriate allocation of entitlements to the nation's output, pointing, for example, to the possibility of an ideal progressive distribution of income or wealth.

It would be wrong to conclude that the presence of spillovers by itself is sufficient to undo the efficiency of a Tiebout economy. For example, in a world with zero transactions costs and full information, a cooperative allocation might emerge from bargaining among governments that are affected by spillovers (Inman and Rubinfeld 1997). Thus, if a public good benefits two or more Tiebout communities (e.g., transportation that requires a large public infrastructure), a Coasian bargain might arise in which joint production internalizes the externality. With costly bargaining, a higher level of government can facilitate and enforce the Coasian bargain (e.g., a county government for water and air quality, a state for roadways, and a national government for defense). The mechanisms established to internalize these cross-community externalities can involve regulation (e.g., direct provision of the overlapping public good), taxes, or subsidies (e.g., an internally financed matching grant).

Seen from this bargaining perspective, the central government has an important role to play in regulating the activities of local communities. This may involve direct constraints on the provision of services (e.g., minimum levels of provision); it could suggest the use of taxes and subsidies, including matching grants-in-aid; it could involve the monitoring and enforcement of agreements reached among states; and it could involve programs to discourage the competitive race to the bottom. To the extent that spillovers include utility interdependence among households across jurisdictional lines, central government transfers to households—as either lump-sum payments or commodity-specific transfers—are appropriate.

This perspective may be appealing to those who support the Contract with America as well as those who do not. This perspective could form the foundation for a fifth period in our federalism history: one of restrained federalism. In this more limited federalist economy, a primary function for the central government would be to enforce interjurisdictional contracts. Beyond this, the central government's role would be limited to the provision of a few goods or services that are produced nationally by unanimous agreement—for example, military defense and the guarantee of free trade across regions. In the extreme, under a policy of restrained federalism, we could see a minimalist national government responsible for enforcing contracts, ensuring free trade, and providing national defense; a network of ever-changing special districts, state, and county governments controlling specific intercommunity spillovers via regulations, taxes, and transfers, with local communities producing most public goods.

We believe, however, that a more realistic role for the central government would also include the assumption of responsibility for failed Coasian bargains between communities—as an arbitrator of last resort when agreements falter or as the permanent, direct provider when agreements are not reached. Although national provision may not balance benefits and costs perfectly in each locality, communities may still prefer some provision to no agreement at all. Examples include the national supervision of environmental policy, the provision of national parks, or the maintenance of a national highway system.

Perhaps the two most important examples of the failure of Coasian bargaining in a decentralized public economy are the agreement to redistribute income to needy households and the agreement to manage jointly the overall macroeconomic performance of the economy. Mark Pauly and others have argued that redistributive preferences can have an important geographical dimension. Proximity causes familiarity, and familiarity breeds concern. If so, redistribution policy should allow for regional differences, yet regional agreements, particularly interconnected regional agreements, may not emerge because of strategic bargaining. If so, a national redistribution policy that explicitly grants some degree of local choice may be the second-best compromise. Similarly, strategic bargaining between localities would most certainly prevent the design of a coordinated macroeconomic policy—as it did during the days of the Articles of Confederation. The only recourse, when a voluntary agreement cannot be reached, is a coercive, nationally directed fiscal policy.

Further, we believe that there is a national consensus that poor and elderly U.S. residents should have access to minimum levels of health care. On the basis of this national norm alone, centralized regulation of health care is desirable. Further, however, harmful competition among states could lead to the underprovision of both health and welfare benefits. As a result, there is a presumptive case for minimum national standards for both programs, leaving management and the possibility of program augmentation to the states.

An alternative possibility is for the central government to find constitutionally acceptable mechanisms for allowing states to encourage locational neutrality by requiring new residents to "pay" for some or all of the costs that they impose on current residents when they move into a state. The European Union has residency requirements that restrict new residents' ability to receive the benefit of social programs, but similar requirements were deemed to violate the fundamental "right to travel" as interpreted by the U.S. Supreme Court in *Shapiro v. Thompson.*[2] A state program that allows new residents to receive the benefit levels of their old state for several years may move us closer to locational neutrality within our constitutional confines.[3]

2.2 Implications for Intergovernmental Fiscal Relations

Allocation of Economic Activity

The decentralization theorem suggests that publicly provided programs should be offered by the jurisdiction that covers the smallest area over which benefits are distributed. An examination of expenditure data

Table 2.1
Expenditures by level of government incurring the expenditure, 1992 (millions of dollars)

Category	Federal	State	Local
Intergovernmental expenditure[a]	$ 186,036	$201,314	$ 7,355
Direct expenditure	1,341,275	498,640	647,970
Defense and general expenditure	886,545	409,132	562,842
Education	26,821	86,650	240,120
Elementary and secondary education	12,402	2,221	226,696
Higher education	11,268	70,904	13,424
Public welfare	47,722	125,500	28,734
Health and hospitals	30,679	41,643	46,469
Highways	813	40,266	26,211
Police protection	6,703	4,863	29,682
Fire protection	0	0	14,358
Corrections	2,411	18,306	10,300
Natural resources	51,501	9,022	3,127
Sewerage and sanitation	0	2,235	30,163
Housing and community development	15,482	1,606	15,461
Governmental administration	16,845	19,847	30,488
Parks and recreation	1,984	2,688	13,040
Interest on general debt	199,713	24,622	30,633
Utility and liquor store expenditure	0	9,613	74,748
Insurance trust expenditure	454,730	79,895	10,381
Total	$1,527,311	$699,954	$655,325

Source: U.S. Bureau of the Census, *Government Finances*, Series GF, No. 5, annual. See also *Budget of the United States*, Fiscal Year 1996, Historical Tables, Table 3.2.
[a] Aggregates exclude duplicative transactions between levels of government.

confirms this expectation; programs that are widely dispersed, such as national defense and redistribution, are provided primarily at the national level, while programs with more localized benefits, such as education, police, and fire services, are provided locally. Table 2.1 summarizes government expenditures on various programs by the level of government incurring the expenditure. As the table indicates, expenditures on programs with localized benefits such as education, police, and highways are made disproportionately at the state and local level. Expenditures for the protection of natural resources and social insurance are made disproportionately at the federal level. Despite this, the possibility of Coasian bargains and the potential for political inefficiencies associated with centralized provision raises a question as to whether the decentralization theorem should necessarily apply to all programs with spatially diverse benefits.

Distributional Programs

Although most economists would support the view that distributional programs are best designed centrally, there remains disagreement as to whether certain programs can be more effectively managed at the state or local level. For example, the potential for local redistribution programs to be effective is limited by the possibility of individuals' or households' migrating in response to differential benefit levels.

An alternative view, that of Boadway and Wildasin (1984), provides a rationale that more closely explains U.S. distributional arrangements. Boadway and Wildasin believe that potential donors obtain benefits from redistributional programs that go beyond the boundaries of their jurisdictions but that these donors wish to choose the appropriate level of redistribution. Such a view can be accommodated by a system of federal matching grants, as is currently done in the cases of AFDC and Medicaid.

A third view, supported by Gramlich (1985) among others, argues that a national minimum standard that is higher than the levels of Medicaid or AFDC offered in many states is required. According to his view, allowing states to make redistributional choices ensures that the overall level of distributional effort will be substantially reduced. This position is supported implicitly by Inman (1985, p. 17), who suggests that AFDC and food stamp spending would fall by 70 percent if these programs were transferred to the state and local sector.

Simple productive efficiency may also vary with the level of government actually managing any economic activity. There are many allegations, though not much hard evidence, that nationally run programs stifle the initiative of states and localities. These arguments are made with special force in considering the design and execution of distributional programs.

Intergovernmental Grants

Just as spillovers associated with public programs can create the need for programs that are centrally financed, so can intergovernmental programs be used to overcome inefficiencies and inequities associated with decentralized taxation.[4] In fact, as envisioned by Break (1980) among others, grant programs can be useful in achieving two distinct goals: the reduction in the inequalities among (or the equalization of) tax bases, and the control of tax and benefit competition among states.

Grants can be matching (price reducing) or nonmatching, categorical or general purpose. The latter, which do not alter the price of local spending, can be used to equalize tax bases and incomes among local and state jurisdictions. Given the empirical findings (Quigley and Smolensky 1992) of a "flypaper effect," these programs can also be used to stimulate spending by state and local governments—governments that would otherwise be restrained by an atmosphere of tax competition. In the alternative competitive environments, governments compete by offering financial incentives to attract new business and keep the old (to stimulate investment and economic growth). The result could be suboptimal levels of state and local spending (Feldstein 1970).[5] Matching categorical programs, on the other hand, can be effective in reducing the inefficiencies described. Matching terms would be set to induce state and local governments to internalize the spillovers provided to other jurisdictions. By far the largest intergovernmental transfers have been categorical matching grants in such areas as transportation, education, community services, and environmental protection.

One particular source of inequity is the disparity in tax bases that result from location-specific resource advantages. As Boadway and Flatters (1982) explain, taxing these resources centrally and distributing them to states and localities is appropriate. When the source of inequity is a local political bias against low-income residents, however, a central grant that penalizes the use of regressive taxes and subsidizes progressive taxes can be beneficial. The U.S. General Revenue Sharing Program, in force between 1972 and 1982, provides a clear example (see Reischauer 1975 for a discussion).

Central government grant policies can also be used to mute the adverse congestion effects from the relocation of economic activity (as when an appealing public program induces migration). The imposition of a charge based on the states whose population creates the congestion, or a subsidy to the states that are adversely affected by the congestion, can be effective. (See Wildasin 1986 and Rivlin 1992, chap. 8.)

While the normative theory of intergovernmental grants is reasonably clear, there is little doubt that government policies have not generally been consistent with these theoretical goals. As Oates (1994) points out, many matching grant programs have very high matching rates—80 to 90 percent. These rates seem inconsistent with the likely fraction of external benefits generated by state and local programs. Further, many of the programs are closed-ended with relatively modest limits, so that the matching terms have no incentive effects on the margin. More generally, Inman (1988) finds that the structure of U.S. direct grants to states does little to control tax spillovers on the margin, nor does it provide appreciably greater assistance to low-income or resource-poor states. In effect, such programs have become lump-sum transfers to residents (or to the governments serving those residents) financed by national taxes.

2.3 The Growth of Mandates: Opportunities for Federal Budget Cutting?

Federal mandates—directives to state governments—are a built-in feature of America's federal structure. Mandates reflect the constitutional division between the enumerated responsibilities of national government and those reserved to the states by the Bill of Rights (in the Tenth Amendment).

At one level, the appropriate use of mandates encompasses fundamental questions in fiscal federalism. Where in the system of governments should a policy be made? Who should be charged with the execution and implementation of a given policy? How much flexibility in execution should be afforded? Who should bear the costs of compliance?

These philosophical and normative issues once dominated the budgeting policy debate. However, a narrower and more recent focus on "unfunded federal mandates" presupposes answers to these questions and invites the conclusion that central government directives have been used to save federal dollars by imposing expenditure responsibilities on state and local governments.

Federal mandates include a variety of distinct forms, encompassing differing rationales, costs, and levels of direction of state activity by central authorities. One indirect form of federal control, through conditional grants, is considered in section 2.4 below. In this section, we consider other more direct forms.

Direct orders by the federal government to the states can be enforced with civil or criminal penalties, or both. Direct orders are relatively rare. One example is the Equal Employment Opportunity Act of 1972, which bars job discrimination by state and local governments. Other examples are the Asbestos Hazard Emergency Response Act of 1986 and the Fair Labor Standards Act.

More common are the kinds of rules that condition state participation in federal programs. Thus, Congress has passed a series of *crosscutting requirements* that apply to state participation in a range of federally sponsored programs. For example, the Civil Rights Act of 1964 bars specific discriminatory acts in a broad range of federally assisted local programs. The Davis-Bacon Act sets specific requirements for procedures and standards in all federally assisted construction activities. A variety of laws require that estimates of environmental impacts be made for many classes of federally assisted projects.

Crossover sanctions imposed by the federal government specify that the failure to comply with one federal requirement will result in the loss of funds from a federal program that need not be related to the purpose of the requirement. For example, the federal requirement for a 55 mph speed limit, imposed until November 1995, was accomplished by a national law denying federal highway funding to states not in compliance. The same sanction was used to require that states impose a minimum drinking age of twenty-one years.

Program-specific *matching requirements and grant conditions* include federal rules about the populations served by state programs that are partly financed by the federal government. These also include matching requirements and nonsupplant clauses in federal legislation.

Statutory preemptions involve the assertion by the federal government of full or partial regulatory authority over a particular governmental function. This preemption may be total, as in the case of the Ocean Dumping Ban of 1988, which asserts federal regulatory control over the continental shelf. (This preemption thus prohibits any use of the continental shelf for the deposit of municipal and state wastes.) A more common preemption is partial in nature. The federal government establishes minimum regulatory standards in some program, while permitting states to administer the federal standards or to choose stricter state standards. Many environmental programs are mandated in this way, under, for example, the Clean Air Act, the Clean Water Act, and the Safe Drinking Water Act.

An economic taxonomy of federal government mandates is somewhat elusive. Table 2.2 presents a categorization of mandates by their economic rationale and the type of activity regulated. Objectives for federal mandates include the reduction of spillovers across states, the imposition of national standards, and the reflection of national norms. The first two are clearly efficiency-enhancing rationales: air and water quality standards encourage concerted action by adjoining states on efficiency grounds. The requirement that highway access be provided uniformly for forty-ton trucks ensures a market for these vehicles. The prohibition against automotive fuel economy regulations by the states protects scale economies in auto design. In addition, many federal mandates are imposed on the basis of the third criterion, fairness, to ensure equal treatment of citizens across states (in antidiscrimination mandates or in drinking rules), equal access to

Table 2.2
Economic taxonomy of federal mandates

	Rationale		
Type of state activity	A. To reduce spillovers	B. To impose national standards	C. To reflect national norms
I. Produce some good	Clean air	Highways appropriate for large trucks	Unemployment insurance
II. Produce in a specified way	Specific tests for drinking water		Union wages in construction
III. Regulate firms and consumers (or refrain from regulation)	Handgun waiting period	Refrain from regulating fuel economy	Drinking age at 21

mandated services (unemployment insurance), or other forms of equal treatment (as in the removal of asbestos from schools).[6]

The growth in the number of federal mandates, their complexity, and their costs to state and local governments were pointed out forcefully at the beginning of the Reagan administration (see Koch 1980 for a characteristically sharp statement). In response, much more systematic information about the fiscal dimensions of proposed mandates has been gathered. Beginning in 1983, the State and Local Government Cost Estimate Act required that the Congressional Budget Office (CBO) estimate the intergovernmental fiscal effects of proposed federal legislation. Between 1983 and the end of the decade, the CBO produced cost estimates for state and local governments on over 3,500 proposed pieces of legislation, including estimates for 457 bills that were enacted into law (Gullo 1990).

Increased attention to the existence of mandates and their costs during the 1980s did little, however, to reduce the growth of federal mandates. For example, one count of conservatively defined statutory mandates reported that Congress enacted only one mandate in the 1930s, one in the 1940s, none in the 1950s, nine in the 1960s, and twenty-five in the 1970s. According to this definition, Congress enacted twenty-seven more statutory mandates during the 1980s (U.S. ACIR 1995). Another study reported that more than half of all federal preemption statutes enacted since the founding of the republic had been passed since 1970 (Conlan 1991). Table 2.3 lists some of the most important statutory mandates passed during the 1980s, the so-called era of deregulation.

A comprehensive listing of federal government mandates to the states has been prepared by the National Conference of State Legislatures (1994). The latest compilation from this database lists 192 separate mandates

Table 2.3
Major new statutory mandates affecting state and local governments, 1981–1990

Measure	Public Law	Type
Surface Transportation Assistance Act of 1982	97-424	Crossover
Voting Rights Act Amendments of 1982	97-205	Direct order
Social Security Amendments of 1983	98-21	Direct order
Child Abuse Amendments of 1984	98-457	Crossover
Hazardous and Solid Waste Amendments of 1984	98-616	Partial preemption
Highway Safety Amendments of 1984	98-363	Crossover
Voting Accessibility for the Elderly and Handicapped 1984	98-435	Direct order
Age Discrimination of Employment Act Amendments of 1986	99-592	Direct order
Asbestos Hazard Emergency Response Act of 1986	99-519	Direct order
Commercial Motor Vehicle Safety Act of 1986	99-570	Crossover
Consolidated Omnibus Budget Reconciliation Act 1986	99-272	Direct order
Education of the Handicapped Act Amendments of 1986	99-457	Crossover
Emergency Planning and Community Right-to-Know 1986	99-499	Partial preemption
Handicapped Children's Protection Act of 1986	99-372	Crossover
Safe Drinking Water Act Amendments of 1986	99-339	Partial preemption, direct order
Civil Rights Restoration Act of 1987	100-259	Crosscutting
Water Quality Act of 1987	100-4	Preemption, direct order, crosscutting
Drug-Free Workplace Act of 1988	100-690	Crosscutting
Fair Housing Act Amendments of 1988	100-430	Direct order
Lead Contamination Control Act of 1988	100-572	Direct order
Ocean Dumping Ban Act	100-688	Direct order
Americans with Disabilities Act	101-327	Crosscutting, direct order
Clean Air Act Amendments of 1990	101-549	Partial preemption
Education of the Handicapped Act Amendments of 1990	101-476	Crossover

Sources: See Conlan (1991); Musso and Quigley (1996).

and federal preemptions, 20 of which were passed by the most recent legislature, the 103d Congress. Table 2.4 lists some significant mandates reported by the NCSL that are currently in force. Note that a substantial fraction of these important mandates have been imposed to reflect national norms, not necessarily to increase economic efficiency.

The increase in the number of mandates during the 1980s and 1990s raises the possibility that the federal government has been "saving" money by imposing fiscal burdens on lower levels of government. There is some documentation supporting the second part of the statement, about the increased financial burden on lower levels of government. An early systematic study of mandates (Lovell et al. 1979) concluded that significant costs were shifted. However, the authors refrained from making any cost estimates because available data were not systematic and therefore were quite fragile. A contemporaneous study by Muller and Fix (1980) obtained cost estimates by analyzing intensively a small number of jurisdictions. For the time period studied (the late 1970s), the authors concluded that the cost of federal mandates was roughly an offset to the general revenue-sharing funds received by lower levels of government. Specifically, the authors estimated that the local costs of federal requirements averaged about 19 percent of all federal aid received. The authors also noted that mandates imposed very different costs across jurisdictions.

A more recent study prepared for the U.S. Environmental Protection Agency (EPA) attempted to measure the cumulative costs of regulations imposed during the 1980s (Singh et al. 1988). This research examined the fiscal effects of twenty-two federal environmental regulations on a sample of 270 local governments. The analysis was confined to measuring the effect of environmental regulations at the local level. However, these regulations included many of the more costly provisions, reported in table 2.3, which were enacted by Congress during the 1980s.

The EPA study was intended to analyze directly the combined effects of multiple regulations and to examine the ability of affected jurisdictions to finance their regulatory compliance. The study identified a variety of new requirements that affect local government finances, but it considered the fiscal effects of only a few for which credible cost estimates could be made. Despite these limitations, the cumulative effects of environmental regulations on local governments were estimated to be quite substantial. The authors estimated that local governments would need to generate approximately $22 billion in capital expenditures to comply with pending and previously promulgated rules, along with $2.8 billion in annual expenses for operations and maintenance. To finance these expenditures,

Table 2.4
Some important federal mandates cataloged in 1994

Law	Description	Category[a]
Vehicle Weight Limitations Highway Improvement	Interstate highways must accommodate big trucks	IB
Voting Rights Language Assistance Act	Mandates aid to non–English speaking voters	IA
Anti-Car Theft Act	States must verify cross-state title transfers	IA
Migratory Bird Conservation Act	States must sell land to the federal government	IA
Clean Air Act	States must meet air quality standards	IA
Safe Drinking Water Act	State must take a number of specific actions	IA
AFDC	Welfare mandated; states set level	IC
Education for All Handicapped Children	Education requirements	IC
Welfare Reform Act	Requires job training; expand AFDC & Medicaid	IC
Americans with Disabilities Act	Disabled accessibility	IC
Unemployment Insurance	Mandated; states can choose level	IC
Medicaid and extensions	Medicaid mandated; states set level	IC
Asbestos Hazard Emergency Response Act	Asbestos must be removed from schools	IC
National Environmental Policy Act of 1969	Environmental impact statements for state projects	IIA
Professional and Amateur Sports Protection Act	States may not operate sports lotteries	IIC
Fair Labor Standards Act	Overtime and minimum wage for state employees	IIC
Davis-Bacon Act	Union wages for state construction	IIC
Motor Vehicle Information and Cost Savings Act	States may not regulate fuel efficiency	IIIB
Commercial Motor Vehicle Driver's License	Requires minimum standards and reciprocity	IIIB
Federal National Mortgage Charter Act	States must allow Ginnie/Fannie Mae to operate	IIIB
Interstate Banking Efficiency Act	Restricts state regulation; allows interstate banking	IIIB
United States Grain Standards Act	Imposes federal standards on grain exports	IIIB
Minimum Drinking Age	Minimum age to drink	IIIC

Control of Outdoor Advertising and Junkyards	Highway beautification	IIIA
Brady bill	Handgun waiting period and background check	IIIA
Endangered Species Act of 1973	States must implement conservation programs	IIIA
National Maximum Speed Limit[b]	55, 65 mph	IIIC
National Voter Registration Act	Motor voter; easier registration	IIIC

Source: National Conference of State Legislatures (1994).
[a] Category as defined in table 2.2, I, II, and III refer to the type of state activity; A, B, and C to the rationale for that activity.
[b] Repealed in 1995.

the study concluded that about 15 percent of local jurisdictions would have to double their current fees charged for environmental services. Given the magnitude of these costs, the study estimated that about a fifth of the nation's water and sewer systems could ultimately find it difficult to issue revenue bonds or to obtain bank loans to finance required capital improvements.[7]

The CBO routinely estimates the cost imposed on state and local governments by significant bills that are reported out of congressional committees. These cost estimates are intended to be made available to members of the House and Senate prior to consideration of legislation on the floor, and they are generally included with committee reports. Supporters of this process of provision of fiscal notes on pending legislation believe that a major source of excessive regulatory costs is inadequate information (see Barr 1990).[8]

CBO's own analysis of its costs estimates (Gullo 1990) indicates that the vast majority of the legislation reported from committee imposes no financial costs on state and local governments. Only 382 of the fiscal notes prepared between 1983 and 1988—11 percent of the total—indicated any financial impact on states and localities. The number of bills the CBO estimated would impose substantial costs of $200 million or more was even smaller. By CBO's estimates, only eighty-nine bills would have produced these major financial impacts.

As reported by Gullo and also by Barr (1990), there are a variety of limitations on the accuracy of CBO's cost estimates—limitations that arise from the hurried nature of the legislative process and the opportunity for substantial amendment in floor debate. In addition, CBO cost estimates are not always completed or made available for inclusion in committee reports. For example, no cost estimates were provided for several bills that ultimately proved to be very costly, including the Asbestos Hazard Emergency Response Act of 1986 and the Water Quality Act of 1987.

There have been several recent efforts to increase the salience of federal mandates and to make their costs more transparent. For example, the National Conference of State Legislatures maintains and publicizes a catalog of federal mandates imposed on the states. In addition, recent legislation (the Unfunded Mandates Reform Act of 1995) provides a more carefully constructed definition of those mandates that "impose an enforceable duty" on lower levels of government. This legislation requires CBO to prepare timely cost estimates for mandates expected to cost as little as $50 million.

Several credible cost estimates are available for the most important mandates imposed on state and local governments. EPA has produced

Table 2.5
Cost estimates for major unfunded mandates (thousands of 1994 dollars)

Type	Federal	State and Local	Example
Annual cost			
Air quality	$1,202	$ 1,318	Clean Air Act, Radon Gas
Water quality	8,437	19,974	Clean Water Act, Safe Drinking Water, Marine Protection
Land conservation	1,765	8,226	RCRA, Comprehensive Environmental Response
Chemical requirements	413	125	
Multimedia	1,175	18	
Education of disabled	—	643	
Asbestos	—	164	
Disabilities act	—	664	
Fair labor standards	—	484	
Aggregate cost to cities, 1994–1998			
Underground storage tanks		$ 1,040	
Clean water and wetlands		29,303	
Clean air		3,652	
Resource Recovery and Conservation Act		5,476	
Safe drinking water		8,644	
Asbestos		746	
Lead paint		1,628	
Endangered species		189	
Disabilities act		2,196	
Fair labor standards		1,121	

Sources: Environmental Protection Agency (1991, p. 8-51, Table 8-12A (estimates are for 1988 in 1994 dollars); U.S. Advisory Commission on Intergrovernmental Relations (September 1994, pp. 13, 15 (estimates are for 1991 in 1994 dollars); Price Waterhouse (1994, p. 4).

estimates of the magnitude of costs imposed on central and lower-level governments by the most important environmental mandates of the 1980s. These are summarized in table 2.5. Clean air, water, and land conservation, together with chemical requirements and multimedia mandates, impose costs of about $13 billion annually on the federal government and about $31.6 billion on state and local governments. (Other costs to households and private firms, not shown, are estimated to add $76 billion to the bill.)

The ACIR has calculated that mandates relating to the education of the disabled, together with the Americans with Disabilities Act, imposed costs of $1.3 billion annually on state and local governments. The Fair Labor Standards Act is estimated to impose annual costs of slightly less than half a billion dollars. Price Waterhouse has surveyed city governments about the costs imposed by federal mandates. The firm estimated that the ten most important mandates will increase the costs borne by city governments by about $54 billion during the next five years.

These expenditures are certainly substantial, and they may be quite burdensome to the state and local governments required to undertake them. Nevertheless, from the viewpoint of the federal budget process, the numbers are quite small indeed. The cost estimates, $30 billion or more annually, are on the order of 2 percent of federal expenditures. We must conclude that although "mandates" may provide a battle cry for states' rights, they have not provided a substantial opportunity for offloading federal expenditures to the states.

2.4 Reversing the Trend in Intergovernmental Grants: Reform or Budget Cutting?

Federal edicts can require expenditures by state and local governments, which can substitute directly for federal outlays. Consequently, these edicts can be used to reduce the central government deficit. While also making certain stipulations on states and localities as conditions of receipt, federal grants-in-aid involve substantial central government expenditures. As a result, federal deficit reductions can be achieved by enforcing mandates on state spending and cutting grant-in-aid programs. Moreover, if these programs are cut or modified in form, the conditions of receipt will change, as will the incentives of state and local governments to continue the provision of the affected public services.

Even general revenue sharing, in effect between 1972 and 1982, imposed some relatively modest restrictions on recipient governments (Nathan et al. 1975). Most restrictions on grants-in-aid apply explicitly to categories of expenditure by lower-level governments, and many involve matching programs. As a result, these programs stimulate the provision of state and local services.

Reforms in the intergovernmental grant system can therefore have two significant effects. First, changes in regulations governing federal programs may provide ample opportunity for intergovernmental grants to be cut in magnitude and changed in form; the result could be a substantial

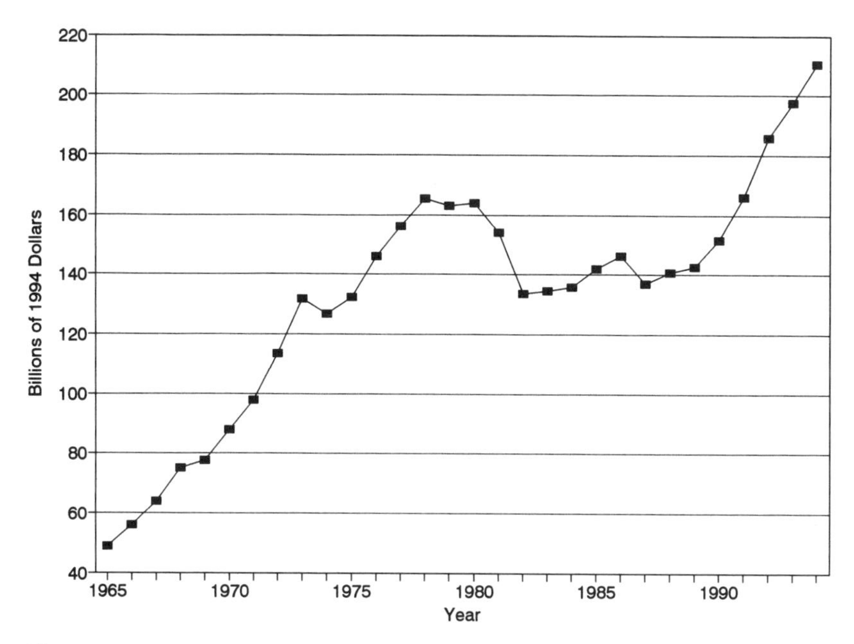

Figure 2.1
Grants to state and local governments. Source: Executive Office of the President, Office of Management and Budget, *Budget of the United States Government*, Fiscal Year 1996, Historical Tables, Tables 10.1, 12.1.

budget reduction by the central government. Second, both cuts and reformulations of grant programs may lead to substantial reductions in state and local spending on programs such as health and welfare. We treat each of these issues in turn.

Reversing the Trend: An Opportunity for Deficit-Reducing Budget Cuts?

Figure 2.1 reports the trend in federal government grant activity during the past three decades. In real terms, federal grants-in-aid quadrupled during the period, from under $50 billion to more than $210 billion (in current dollars). Importantly, more than one-fourth of this substantial increase has been registered in the past five years. Between 1989 and 1994, federal grants-in-aid to state and local governments increased by more than $68 billion.

The pattern of federal grants as a fraction of gross domestic product (GDP) follows this recent trend. Since 1989, grants to states and localities

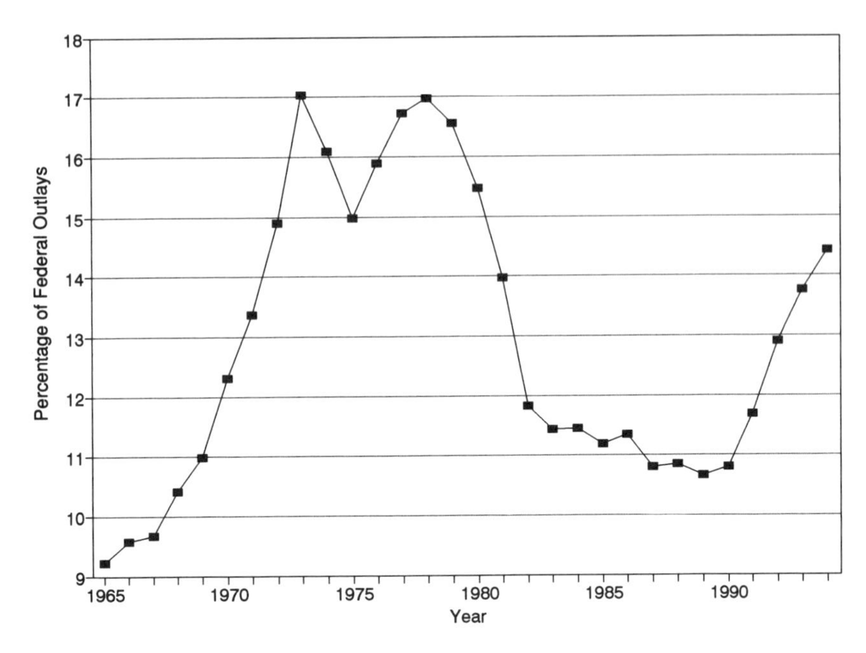

Figure 2.2
Grants as a fraction of federal outlays. Source: *Budget of the United States Government*, Fiscal Year 1996, Historical Tables, Tables 3.1, 12.1.

have increased from about 2.4 percent to 3.2 percent of GDP. Figure 2.2 shows the trend in grants as a fraction of federal government spending. As the figure indicated, spending on grants exceeded 17 percent of federal spending in 1974 and was almost as high in 1979. The Reagan years saw a steady drop in grants as a fraction of federal spending. However, since 1989 grants have climbed from less than 11 percent of federal outlays to about 14.4 percent of outlays.

Figure 2.3 reports trends in grants to state and local governments for the four largest expenditure categories: transportation, education and training, health, and income security.[9] As the figure indicates, there has been little change in the pattern of federal grants for transportation. The pattern of grants for education and training is more complex, but the current level of grant expenditures is substantially lower, in real terms, than it was in the late 1970s. The same cannot be said for federal grants for income security and for health. Grants to state and local governments for income security have risen steadily, from $15.7 billion in 1965 to $38 billion in 1989 (in current dollars). Since 1989, federal grants have risen sharply by $13.5 billion, or by more than one-third.

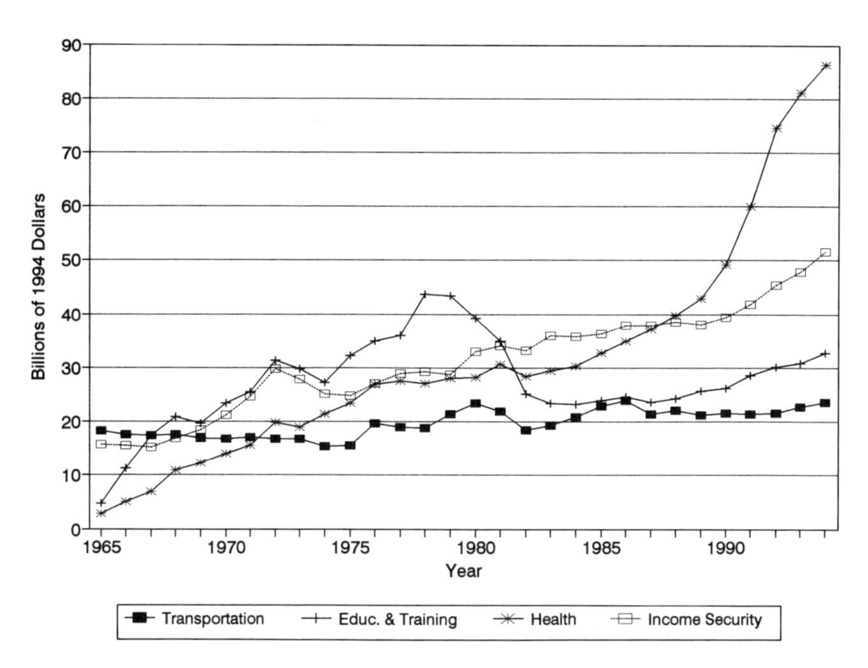

Figure 2.3
Major categories of federal grants. Source: *Budget of the United States Government,* Fiscal Year 1996, Historical Tables, Tables 10.1, 12.2.

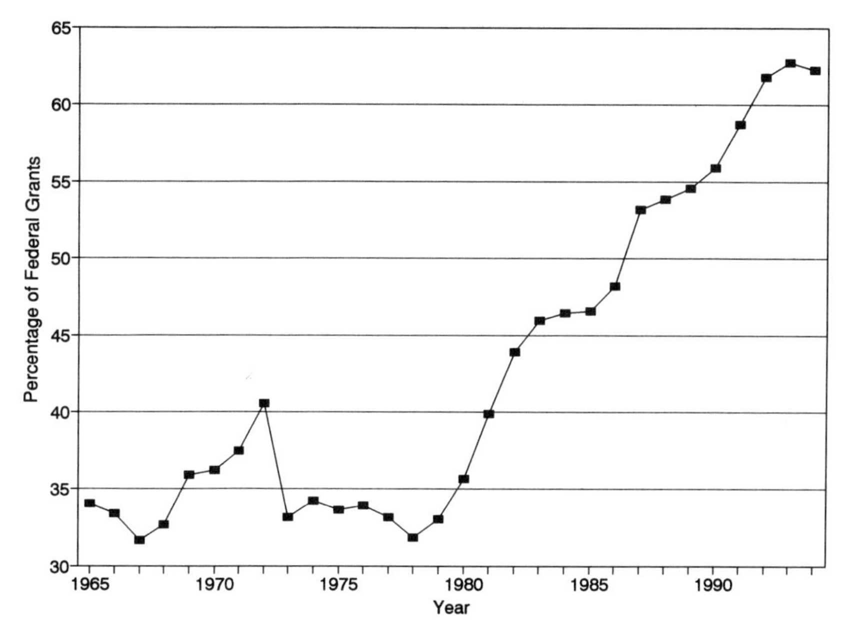

Figure 2.4
Grants to lower-level governments for payments to individuals (as a percentage of all grants). Source: *Budget of the United States Government,* Fiscal Year 1996, Historical Tables, Table 12.1.

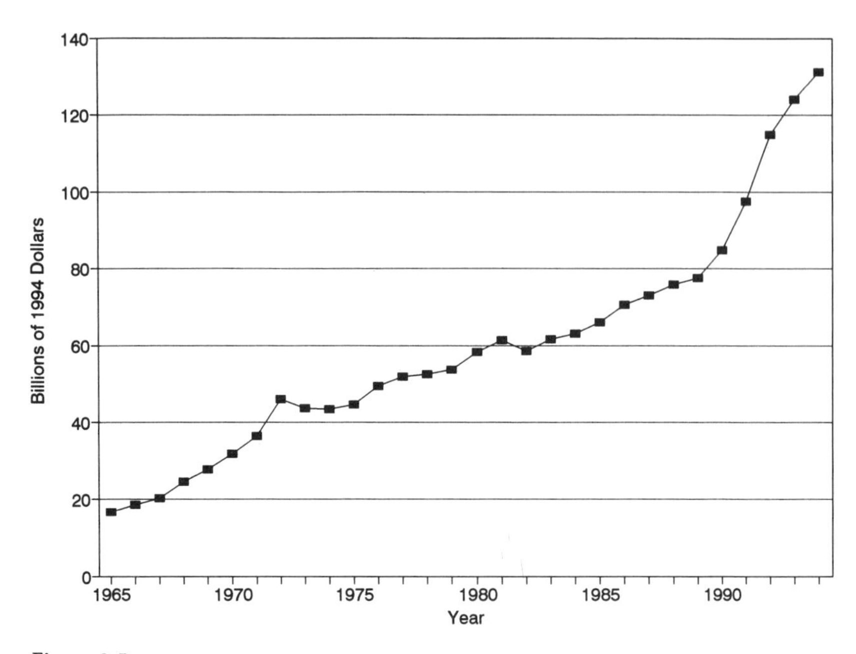

Figure 2.5
Grants to lower-level governments for individuals (billions of dollars). Source: *Budget of the United States Government*, Fiscal Year 1996, Historical Tables, Tables 10.1, 12.1.

The increases in grants for health have been nothing short of explosive. Federal government grants to state and local governments increased from \$2.8 billion in 1965 to more than \$32.8 billion by 1985 (again, in current dollars). During the past decade, however, grants for health care have almost tripled, to \$86.3 billion. The exponential growth of health care grants has continued; health care grants have doubled in the past five years alone.

Figure 2.4 reports the trend in federal grants to local governments for payments to individuals. Chief among these are, in order, medical care (chiefly Medicaid), public assistance (chiefly AFDC), housing assistance, and nutrition programs (not including food stamps). As the figure indicates, the trend between 1965 and 1980 is flat; grants for payments to individuals were something less than 35 percent of the total. The explosion since 1980 has almost doubled the fraction of grants to lower levels of government, which are passed through as payments to individuals.

Figure 2.5 shows the trend in dollar expenditures for grant payments to individuals. Again, there is a steady growth until 1989 and then an

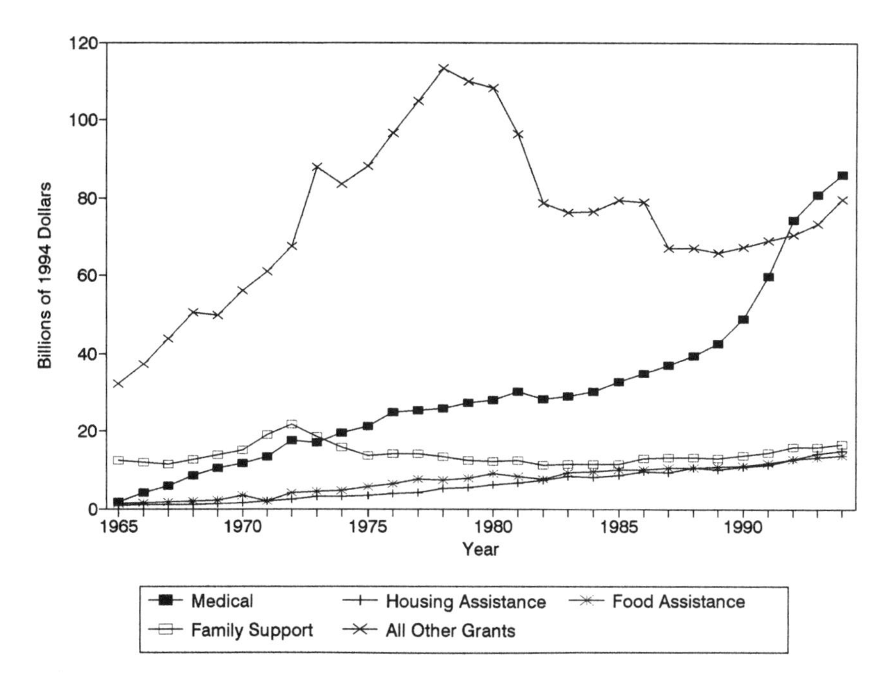

Figure 2.6
Grants to lower-level governments for individuals, by type. Source: *Budget of the United States Government*, Fiscal Year 1996, Historical Tables, Tables 10.1, 11.3, 12.1.

explosive increase. These grants have increased by $53.4 billion in the past five years.

Figure 2.6 compares the trends in federal grants to state and local governments for payments to individuals with other types of grants in aid to lower-level governments. As the figure shows, the trend since the mid-1970s has been a decline in programmatic grants for education, transportation, and the production of local services and an increase in the extent of grants for payments to individuals, principally for medical care. Since 1991, grants for medical care have exceeded all grants for goods and services at the state and local level.

For comparison, figure 2.7 reports direct federal payments to individuals under the largest programs: food stamps and direct housing assistance. Food stamp expenditures by the federal government have increased by more than 25 present since 1989, but current expenditures on this direct federal transfer program are less than $20 billion.

The debate over whether the grant levels of the 1970s or even the 1980s were reasonable and appropriate will certainly continue for many years

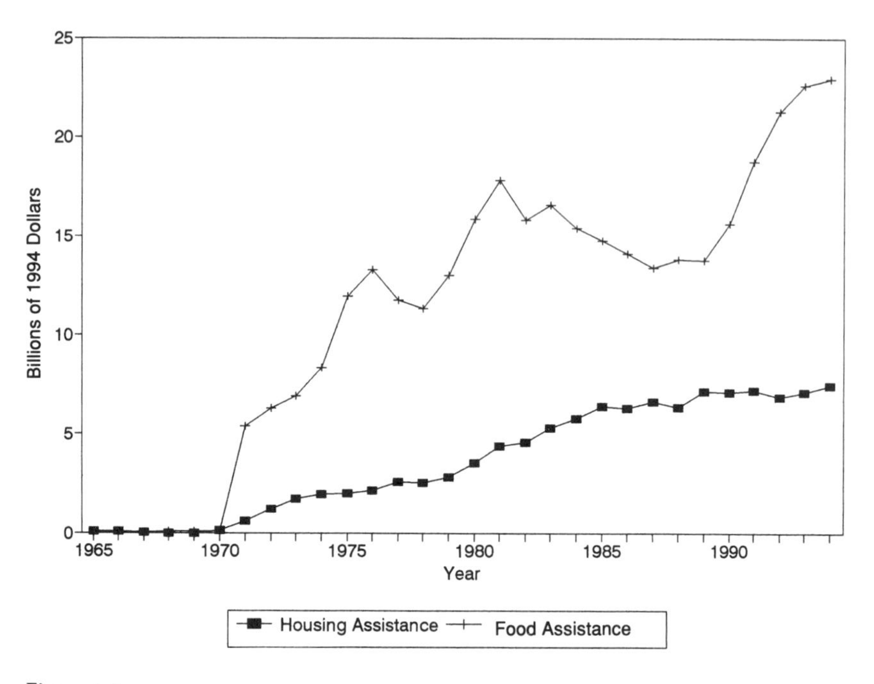

Figure 2.7
Federal direct payments to individuals. Source: *Budget of the United States Government*, Fiscal Year 1996, Historical Tables, Tables 10.1, 11.3.

to come as the specific public programs supported are evaluated and reevaluated. Whatever one's view on the merits of specific programs, a serious commitment to deficit reduction implies some cuts in federal expenditures on these programs. Indeed, much of the current rhetoric for reform of health care and AFDC is explicitly motivated by deficit-reduction efforts. No picture of budgetary reform can be complete, however, without some commentary on the implications for the programs themselves of proposed changes in the federal system of intergovernmental aid. We now turn briefly to the possible effects that changes in grant programs will have on the state and local public sectors.

How Will State and Local Governments Respond?

Most state and local governments operate under balanced budget constraints. It is not surprising, therefore, that the aggregate of state and local budgets is in modest surplus rather than deficit. More to the point, however, the aggregate surplus has generally been declining for a decade.[10]

Seen in this context, we should expect many states would choose not to provide equivalent services when they are given responsibility for health and welfare programs without the funding to support the programs.

At this time, the outcome of budgetary debates between the Republican Congress and the Democratic executive is unclear. It does seem clear, however, that the current health and welfare programs, heavily subsidized by the federal government through a system of open-ended matching grants, will be reformed, or perhaps replaced, by block grants of fixed size. For example, AFDC is currently an open-ended matching program in which the price subsidy varies inversely with state income, ranging from 50 percent to 78.6 percent; Medicaid matches state spending at the same rate as AFDC.[11] Even without any change in federal funding or other regulations, a switch from matching programs with price and income effects to block grants without price effects will lead to a reduction in state and local spending.

The state and local government responses to the policy changes will clearly vary substantially depending on current budgetary pressures and preferences. Depending on the regulations governing program change, it is quite possible that cuts in current programs could be substantial. A review of the evidence on price and income elasticities of demand for transfer programs suggests the reasons; recent work by Chernick (1996) provides some estimates of the responses of state and local governments to a programmatic change in which AFDC and Medicaid were converted to block grants. He suggests that the shift would raise the price of a dollar of AFDC benefits and Medicaid outlays from forty-five cents to one dollar.[12]

The magnitude of the spending response of lower levels of government will depend heavily on the size of the relevant elasticities and the course of reductions in federal spending on block grants. Even if federal budgetary cuts were small initially, they would almost certainly grow over time. Current proposals cap future increases in program expenditures at the federal level. The response magnitude also depends on the extent to which states alter their benefit levels to compete with other states; a decline in one state's benefits could lead (through a race to the bottom) to substantial decreases in benefits offered by other states. At the high end in terms of predicted responses are Gramlich (1985) and Craig and Inman (1986), whose work suggests reductions in AFDC spending of from 70 to 85 percent. At the other extreme are Moffitt (1984, 1990) and Craig (1993), who suggest that substitution effects will reduce AFDC benefit levels by about 9 percent.

A large body of econometric evidence on state welfare spending and state AFDC benefit levels suggests that price elasticities are rather large, income elasticities are relatively small, and there is little substitution of food stamps for other forms of public welfare. Thus, studies by Gramlich (1982, 1985), Gramlich and Laren (1984), and Craig and Inman (1986) all find that the form and level of federal matching programs have substantial effects on the amount of redistribution undertaken by the states. These studies are consistent with declines in benefit levels or state welfare spending of 70 to 85 percent. In contrast, two papers by Moffit (1984, 1990) find smaller price elasticities and somewhat larger income elasticities, both of which would moderate the disastrous effects predicted by the others in moving to block grants.

The views of Gramlich and Laren (1984) and others are based in part on the evidence that states responded to court-mandated increases in beneficiaries (arising from the "right to travel" rulings) by restricting benefits. This suggests that there will be a race to the bottom in the provision of welfare benefits as each state reacts to the cuts in welfare levels proposed in neighboring states by cutting their own benefit levels. To the extent, however, that states are able to create constitutionally acceptable devices for restricting benefit levels of new entrants, or more generally that states do not respond closely to the choices of benefit levels of neighboring states, the race may not be as extreme as suggested by Gramlich and Laren.

There is much less econometric evidence on the determinants of state spending on Medicaid. (An early review is by Inman 1985. Chernick provides a more recent review.) Chernick (1996) concludes that "the small number of studies of Medicaid price responses suggest that the absolute magnitude of the income and price elasticities is greater than for AFDC." If true, these findings imply even larger estimates of the effect of block granting on Medicaid spending and public medical care spending by the state.

This evidence is not conclusive. But given that many states have become more fiscally conservative and given the tightness of their budgets, the conclusion that the effects would be substatial seems appropriate.

From our normative perspective, there is a strong case to be made for centralized control of distribution programs involving health and welfare. Apparently only one factor could mitigate the substantial reductions in aggregate spending on transfer programs that would accompany the termination of current federally supervised matching grants: a large increase in x-efficiency accompanying a shift in control to state governments. Indeed, there are extravagant claims that the states are more creative and innovative in designing welfare programs, and that they are better managers of these programs. These claims are made more forcefully about transfer programs than about other government activity. There is little doubt that a shift to state-administered block grants will involve less bureaucracy and will give more flexibility to states.[13] Beyond this, there is little or no systematic evidence about creativity or innovation.

Anecdotal evidence is not reassuring. It is reported that efforts to computerize child support and welfare payments in Maryland have been disastrous; the system will be two years late and 67 percent over budget. News accounts have estimated that Florida lost $170 million on food stamp errors, and state officials have acknowledged $28 million in mistakes in the Medicaid program. California's new welfare computer system is now estimated to be $455 million over budget—about 90 percent—and will not accommodate the volume of transactions.

As far as management is concerned, one state secretary of human services suggests that passage of these federalism initiatives will be like "flying blind into a fog."[14]

2.5 Conclusion

It is clearly too early to know with much certainty the direction in which U.S. federalism will move. However, the current budgetary debate suggests strongly that we are entering a new period in fiscal federalism, one marked by restrained federalism. In this more limited federalist economy, the federal government will mandate state responsibilities for a number of public regulatory and spending programs.

This review of the linkages between federal and lower levels of government does suggest three conclusions. First, an increasing burden of federal mandates for expenditures has been placed on the state and local governments by the central government. Despite increasing attention to this issue during the past decade, the level and extent of unfunded mandates continue to grow. However, the evidence also indicates that these mandates provide only limited opportunities for budget reduction at the federal level. Cumulative state and local expenditures engendered by preemptions, direct orders, and crossover mandates are significant and large from the local perspective but rather small in comparison with expenditures from the federal budget.

Second, the rapid rise in federal grants to local governments does provide a significant opportunity to reduce the budget of the central government by appealing to federalist principles. The federalist principles are dubious. They involve the assertion that benefit levels in transfer programs are better decided locally and that program operations and standards are better managed locally. We have seen no systematic evidence suggesting a better management capacity by local government. Further, although we believe that there are gains to be had from state experimentation with new programs and new ways to administer old programs, we recognize that states already have substantial flexibility to experiment.

The budget opportunity arises from the shift from open-ended matching grants for substantial programs to block grants of fixed size whose increase can be controlled centrally. We are persuaded by the evidence that there are moderate price elasticities and small income elasticities at the local level. Given the real possibility of a race to the bottom as well, this suggests that budget savings at the federal level will be achieved by drastically reducing the aggregate size of these programs. This reduction, could be put off temporarily by the addition of a "hold-harmless" clause to any new block grant programs; that is, a condition of receipt of a block grant would be that the state maintain nominal benefits at current levels.

Third, since budgetary savings arise from capping the future growth of these programs, the savings arise in some part from the elimination of federally imposed rules for eligibility and program participation. It is elimination of the entitlement aspects of the programs that permits them to be devolved to the states. Removal of this "mandate" imposed on states and localities can generate substantial budgetary savings to the central government (at the expense of low-income people), but it will substantially change the nature of federalism in the United States.

Notes

We are grateful to Scott Susin for research assistance. Financial support for this research has been provided by the Fisher Center for Real Estate and Urban Economics, University of California, Berkeley.

1. This theorem is closely related to the concept of "subsidiarity," which appears frequently in the current debates over the governmental structure of the European Union. See also Breton (1965).

2. 394 U.S. 618 (1969). In this case the state could not, because of the fundamental right to travel, impose welfare assistance waiting periods on new entrants. The Court did not claim that budgetary considerations were irrelevant; rather, it stated that the specific budgetary arguments made by the state were "utterly devoid of evidence of use of the one-year requirement as a means to predict the number of people who will require assistance in the budget year." The Court also struck down a one-year residency requirement for receipt of indigents of nonemergency hospitalization and medical care at county expense in *Memorial Hospital v. Maricopa County*, 415 U.S. 250 (1974).

3. The law is unclear whether a state's attempt to discriminate in any form against new entrants may itself violate *Shapiro v. Thompson.*

4. See Gordon (1983) and Inman and Rubinfeld (1996) for details.

5. Tax competition was essentially the argument that Heller and Pechman had raised in the 1960s.

6. Unfunded mandates have been attacked as inappropriately clouding the link between funding and decision making. See, for example, Rivlin (1992, p. 109). However, they are supported for many of the reasons given above by Dana (1995).

7. EPA research also indicated that the costs of recent environmental regulations are likely to vary widely across jurisdictions.

8. For example, in retrospect, one of the most costly intergovernmental regulations enacted during the 1970s was the Rehabilitation Act of 1973, which prohibited discrimination against disabled persons in federally assisted programs. In public transportation programs alone, the CBO estimated in the late 1970s that this law would require transit authorities to spend $6.8 billion over thirty years to equip buses with wheelchair lifts, install elevators in subway systems, and take other measures to expand access to public transit systems by the physically disabled.

9. These are gross categories. For example, the category "income security" includes substantial expenditures by the Departments of Agriculture and Housing and Urban Development, as well as expenditures by the Department of Health and Human Services.

10. See Gramlich (1991, figure 1). The National Income Accounts Surplus began to decline in 1983, while the operating surplus has generally fallen since 1972.

11. Specifically, the federal matching rate is: $1 - .45(S^2/N^2)$, where S is state per capita income and N is national per capita income. See ACIR (1992) for an extensive discussion.

12. The price would be higher than one dollar if the food stamp program were to continue to tax AFDC benefits.

13. Gold (1995) develops these points.

14. These anecdotes are reported in *Business Week* (1995) and Babington (1995) among other popular sources.

References

Babington, Charles. 1995, October 23–29. "Overloading the States." *Washington Post,* National Weekly Edition.

Barr, Calvaresi. 1990. "Cost Estimation as an Anti-Mandate Strategy." In Michael Fix and Daphne Kenyon, eds., *Coping with Mandates: What Are the Alternatives?* pp. 49–56. Washington, DC: Urban Institute.

Boadway, Robin W., and Frank Flatters. 1982. "Efficiency and Equalization Payments in a Federal System of Government: A Synthesis and Extension of Recent Results." *Canadian Journal of Economics* 15:613–633.

Boadway, Robin W., and David E. Wildasin. 1984. *Public Sector Economics.* Boston: Little, Brown.

Break, George. 1980. *Financing Government in a Federal System.* Washington, DC: Brookings Institution.

Breton, Albert. 1965. "A Theory of Government Grants." *Canadian Journal of Economics and Political Science* 31:175–187.

Buchanan, James. 1965. "An Economic Theory of Clubs." *Economica* 32:1–14.

Business Week. 1995, August 7. "Power to the States: Are They Ready?"

Chernick, Howard. 1996, January. "Fiscal Effects of Block Grants for the Needy: A Review of the Evidence." New York: Department of Economics, Hunter College and Graduate Center, City University of New York.

Conlan, Timothy J. 1991. "And the Beat Goes On: Intergovernmental Mandates and Preemption in an Era of Deregulation." *Publius* 21:43–57.

Craig, Steven G. 1993, September. "Redistribution in a Federalist System: Can the Federal Government Alter State Government Behavior?" Houston: Department of Economics, University of Houston.

Craig, Steven G., and Robert P. Inman. 1986. "Education, Welfare, and the New Federalism: State Budgeting in a Federalist Public Economy." In H. Rosen, ed., *Studies in State and Local Public Finance.* Chicago: Chicago University Press.

Dana, David A. 1995. "The Case for Unfunded Environmental Mandates." *Southern California Law Review* 69:1–45.

Environmental Protection Agency. 1991. *Environmental Investments: The Costs of a Clean Environment.* Washington, DC: Island Press.

Feldstein, Martin. 1970. "Comment on 'An Efficiency Bias for Federal Fiscal Equalization'." In Julius Margolis, ed., *The Analysis of Public Output,* pp. 159–163. New York: National Bureau of Economic Research.

Gold, Steven D. 1995, Summer. "Impacts of the Revolution in Federal Policies on State and Local Governments." *NTA Forum,* no. 22.

Gordon, Roger A. 1983. "An Optimal Taxation Approach to Fiscal Federalism." *Quarterly Journal of Economics* 95:567–586.

Gramlich, Edward M. 1991. "The 1991 State and Local Fiscal Crisis." *Brookings Papers on Economic Activity* 2:249–287.

Gramlich, Edward M. 1987. "Federalism and Federal Deficit Reduction." *National Tax Journal* 40:299–313.

Gramlich, Edward M. 1985. "Reforming U.S. Fiscal Arrangements," In J. M. Quigley and D. L. Rubinfeld, eds., *American Domestic Priorities,* pp. 34–69. Berkeley: University of California Press.

Gramlich, Edward M. 1982. "An Econometric Examination of the New Federalism." *Brookings Papers on Economic Activity* 2:327–360.

Gramlich, Edward M., and Deborah Laren. 1984. "Migration and Income Distribution Responsibilities." *Journal of Human Resources* 19(4):489–511.

Gullo, Theresa A. 1990. "Estimating the Impact of Federal Legislation on State and Local Governments." In Michael Fix and Daphne Kenyon, eds., *Coping with Mandates: What Are the Alternatives?* pp. 41–48. Washington, DC: Urban Institute.

Inman, Robert P. 1988. "Federal Assistance and Local Services in the United States: The Evolution of a New Federalist Fiscal Order." In H. Rosen, ed., *Fiscal Federalism*, pp. 33–74. Chicago: University of Chicago Press.

Inman, Robert P. 1985. "Fiscal Allocations in a Federalist Economy." In J. M. Quigley and D. L. Rubinfeld, eds., *American Domestic Priorities*, pp. 34–69. Berkeley: University of California Press.

Inman, Robert P., and Daniel L. Rubinfeld. 1996. "Designing Tax Policy in Federalist Economies: An Overview." *Journal of Public Economics* 60:307–344.

Inman, Robert P., and Daniel L. Rubinfeld. 1997. "The Political Economy of Federalism." In D. Mueller, ed., *Perspectives on Public Choice*, pp. 73–105. Cambridge: Cambridge University Press.

Koch, Edward I. 1980, Fall. "The Mandate Millstone." *Public Interest*, 42–57.

Lovell, Catherine H., et al. 1979. *Federal and State Mandating on Local Governments: An Exploration of Issues and Impacts*. Riverside, CA: University of California, Riverside.

Moffitt, Robert. 1990, June. "Has State Redistribution Policy Grown More Conservative?" *National Tax Journal* 43(2):123–142.

Moffitt, Robert. 1984. "The Effects of Grants-in-Aid on State and Local Expenditures: The Case of AFDC." *Journal of Public Economics* 23:279–306.

Muller, Thomas, and Michael Fix. 1980. "The Impact of Selected Federal Actions on Municipal Outlays." In U.S. Congress, Joint Economic Committee, *Government Regulation: Achieving Social and Economic Balance*, Vol. 5. Washington, DC: U.S. G.P.O.

Musso, Juliet, and John M. Quigley. 1996. "Intergovernmental Fiscal Relations in California: A Critical Evaluation." In D. Batten, ed., *Infrastructure, Economic Growth, and Regional Development*. New York: Springer Verlag.

Nathan, Richard P., et. al. 1975. *Monitoring Revenue Sharing*. Washington, DC: Brookings Institution.

National Conference of State Legislatures. 1994, December. *1994 Mandate Catalog*. Hall of the States Mandate Monitor Database. Special Edition. Washington, DC: The National Conference of State Legislatures.

Oates, Wallace, E. 1994. "Federalism and Government Finance," In John M. Quigley and Eugene Smolensky, eds., *Modern Public Finance*. Cambridge: Harvard University Press.

Oates, Wallace. 1972. *Fiscal Federalism*. New York: Harcourt Brace Jovanovich.

Pauly, Mark. 1973. "Income Distribution as a Local Public Good." *Journal of Public Economics* 2:35–58.

Perloff, Harvey S., and Richard P. Nathan, eds. 1968. *Revenue Sharing and the City*. Baltimore: Johns Hopkins University Press.

Price Waterhouse. 1994, December. *Impact of Unfunded Federal Mandates on US Cities*. Washington, DC: Price Waterhouse.

Quigley, John M., and Eugene Smolensky. 1992. "Conflicts among Levels of Government in a Federal System." *Public Finance* 47:202–215.

Reischauer, Robert 1975. "General Revenue Sharing—The Program's Incentives." In W. Oates, ed., *Financing the New Federalism*, pp. 40–87. Baltimore, Maryland: Johns Hopkins University Press.

Revesz, Richard. 1992. "Rehabilitating Interstate Competition: Rethinking the 'Race to the Bottom' Rationale for Federal Environmental Regulation," *New York University Law Review* 67:1210.

Rivlin, Alice. 1992. *Reviving the American Dream*. Washington, DC: Brookings Institution.

Scheiber, Harry N. 1966, October 15. "The Condition of American Federalism: An Historian's View." Subcommittee on Intergovernmental Relations to the Committee on Governmental Operations, U.S. Senate.

Singh, Jasbinder, et al. 1988, September. *Municipal Sector Study: Impacts of Environmental Regulations on Municipalities*. Prepared by Policy Planning and Evaluation for the U.S. Environmental Protection Agency. Washington, DC.

U.S. Advisory Commission on Intergovernmental Relations. 1992, June. *Medicaid: Intergovernmental Trends and Options*. A-119. Washington, DC: ACIR.

U.S. Advisory Commission on Intergovernmental Relations. 1994, September. *Federally Induced Costs Affecting State and Local Governments*. M-193. Washington, DC: ACIR.

U.S. Advisory Commission on Intergovernmental Relations. 1995, January. *Federal Mandate Relief for State, Local, and Tribal Governments*. A-129. Washington, DC: ACIR.

Wildasin, David. 1986. *Urban Public Finance*. New York: Harwood.

Comment

Roger H. Gordon

John Quigley and Dan Rubinfeld have emphasized the sharp changes in views over time in the United States regarding the appropriate division of fiscal responsibilities among federal, state, and local governments. Currently the U.S. Congress strongly favors a shift away from federal toward state and local responsibilities for many activities. This debate about the appropriate design of a federalist system is not confined to the United States. The current debate in the European Union (EU) is at least as intense. There the pressure is toward increasing rather than decreasing the extent of central control within the EU, given the fears that decentralized policies are resulting in a misallocation of resources within the EU and leading to an undermining of the extensive social welfare policies that have developed in most member countries in the postwar period. Another related trend is increasing attempts to establish international agreements over trade policies, environmental regulations, and defense policies. As Quigley and Rubinfeld emphasize, these are just the functions that a minimalist view would assign to a central government.

What can economics contribute to this debate about the qualitative and quantitative implications of alternative federal structures for both economic efficiency and the equilibrium distribution of income? Although the existing academic literature certainly provides some useful guidelines to help in answering these questions, on net surprisingly little is really known about the economic implications of alternative federal structures, in either theory or practice. Although the degree of central control differs substantially across different nations and across time, to my knowledge little or no attempt has been to test empirically the effects of the degree of centralization on economic efficiency or distribution.[1]

Certainly a number of attempts have been made to model these issues theoretically. But important aspects of the problem have been glossed over. What factors, for example, prevent centralized allocations from being efficient, how large are the resulting inefficiencies, and how do they vary across types of government activities? In my own attempt to model the problem (Gordon 1983), I imposed the assumption that centralized provision must be uniform across locations, while the efficient provision could well vary by location. In practice, central government expenditures on goods or services often vary by locality. What then prevents a central authority from pursuing any activity that yields a Pareto improvement, including building a new middle school, say, in Berkeley?

Part of the answer may be diseconomies to scale in eliciting information about individual preferences: any given national election at best can reveal voter preferences over a few key issues, whereas local elections have the potential to reveal much more information. Individual representatives should have many more sources of information than just electoral outcomes, however.

Another explanation for why a central government will not in practice undertake all Pareto-improving projects may be a lack of flexibility in the range of tax instruments. If benefit taxes are unavailable, then any project necessarily entails distributional as well as efficiency implications, complicating the decision making substantially and certainly undermining the forecast that any efficient project will be undertaken. Given this lack of flexibility in tax instruments, it is also difficult for any given representative to reveal credibly the value of a given project in his or her district, since the district would not end up having to pay most of the added cost if the project is approved. This lack of flexibility in tax instruments may be an essential feature of any government, however, since a government would choose to impose this constraint on itself in order to prevent the majority of voters from imposing arbitrary losses on any given minority of voters.

Given this inflexibility in tax instruments available to any government and in particular to the central government, what alternatives exist? One response might well be greater use of mandates rather than direct provision by the central government. With mandates, financing of the resulting expenditures occurs locally, eliminating any interregional redistribution that inevitably would occur with centralized funding. If optimal expenditure levels are reasonably uniform across localities and financing is entirely local, then the national Congress would have the incentive to approve all efficiency-enhancing projects. For example, if past use of asbestos in schools occurred primarily in a few regions, then the U.S. Congress would not likely approve a nationally financed program to eliminate existing asbestos since most regions would lose on net from the program. If the efficient policy is to remove asbestos from all schools, however, a mandate to do so should gain universal approval in the Congress. Quigley and Rubinfeld note the rapid growth in the use of mandates, and this story may be one explanation for the role of mandates.

Certainly decentralization provides an effective alternative to central government mandates and would be particularly attractive when the regional pattern of benefits for a program differs substantially from the regional pattern of costs under national taxes *and* when the efficient level of expenditures varies substantially by location. Decentralized decision making has the added advantage that residents can convey their preferences through "exit" as well as "voice," imposing more pressures on public officials to take voter preferences into account. Tiebout-type sorting combined with zoning restrictions should lead to relatively homogeneous communities, minimizing distributional considerations when setting local expenditure policies. Without distributional considerations as a complication, local governments would be expected to approve projects if and only if they raise efficiency.

Decentralized decision making has its own drawbacks, however. The literature has focused heavily on spillovers across communities, but this is not the only problem with decentralization. To begin with, the Tiebout-type sorting that generates homogeneous communities comes at a cost. The original Tiebout article for simplicity ignored any costs of sorting by assuming a featureless plain and only dividend income. It is surprising, though, to what degree the literature since then has continued to ignore these costs. In fact, individuals can have strong preferences over their residential location unrelated to local fiscal policies due to their job location, the location of their friends and family, and the characteristics of the neighborhood and the neighbors more generally.[2] Residential patterns would likely be very different if the financial incentives to form homogeneous communities were eliminated.[3] Partly these efficiency costs of sorting are justified in order to facilitate the efficiency gains from tailoring local public good provision more closely to each individual's tastes. When the costs of sorting are incurred in order to avoid redistribution within the community, however, this sorting results in both less efficiency and less redistribution so would be hard to justify on social welfare grounds. It would be of value to measure these costs when considering decentralization, particularly to local rather than state governments.

Another possible cost of decentralized provision that has been ignored in the literature but may be nontrivial is the cost that individuals and companies considering locating in a community face in assessing the attractiveness of the community. The larger the number of dimensions along which communities can differ, the more time and effort potential residents must expend to investigate a particular location, and as a result the greater the barriers to mobility of economic activity. Will their children be exposed to asbestos in the schools or toxic chemicals in the soil? How much debt does the community have that new residents would have to help repay? And so forth. National boundaries certainly restrict the flow of economic activity, even ignoring tariffs, as clearly documented by Helliwell (1995). Likely the explanation for the limited amount of cross-border activity is asymmetric information about the economic environment at home versus abroad. Asymmetric information may also potentially reduce the flow of economic activity *within* a country and would likely become worse as more government functions are decentralized. Although communities can attempt to provide information about their debt or the amount of asbestos in the schools, how credible would this information be?[4] One effective way to reassure potential residents about these local characteristics is to have a higher level of government constrain the policies of the local government, for example, by setting uniform regulations on asbestos or preventing local government from borrowing except for investment projects. The more uniform the economic environment is, the less room there is for asymmetric information to restrict the flow of economic activity across jurisdictions.

The most contentious issue in the federalism debate seems to concern redistributional programs rather than expenditures on goods and services. Here the theory states clearly that a small jurisdiction cannot successfully redistribute across income groups when individuals can shift location without charge.[5] Although a property tax does succeed at seizing the assets of the person who owns a piece of land at the date potential owners first recognize the possibility of the tax, this type of redistribution has little appeal on equity grounds. (See, e.g., Feldstein, 1976.)

What, therefore, underlies the arguments for decentralizing redistributional programs in the United States—or for not centralizing these programs within the EU? Certainly those opposed to redistribution may attempt to eliminate redistribution by pushing for decentralization. But can there be economic justification for such decentralization? Quigley and Rubinfeld argue, for example, that individual voters like more direct control over how much redistribution they undertake. Even if decisions would not change due to decentralization, perhaps the warm glow that results may differ depending on the size of the decision-making unit. Personally I find this argument farfetched.

Another possible argument is that the amount of redistribution that occurs through the political process simply reflects the vagaries of majority rule decision making and has no relation to either the amount of altruism of the rich (see, e.g., Hochman and Rodgers 1969) or the amount of social insurance desired by those at risk. While state governments would be as subject as the national government to the vagaries of majority rule, at least the Feldstein-Vaillant (1994) results suggest that redistribution would not be feasible at the state level. The question is then a second-best comparison of little or no redistribution under state control versus the arbitrary pattern that arises under national control.

There may also be economic arguments for variation in the extent of redistribution across locality, variation that presumably could not occur if redistribution policies are set at the national level. Viewing redistributional programs as a form of social insurance, one can easily construct arguments for why the nature of the optimal social insurance program should differ by locality. For example, the moral hazard costs limiting the scope of welfare programs arise in large part because the availability of welfare benefits reduces the incentive to work. For a given level of benefits, the number of people whose behavior will be affected will depend heavily on the local wage rate. If wage rates in Mississippi, for example, are lower than those available elsewhere, then the optimal welfare benefits would also be lower in Mississippi. The optimal extent of social insurance also likely varies between urban and rural areas, since the observed income in rural areas does not include home-grown agricultural products, which help cushion the potential fall in consumption. In addition, the benefits from social insurance (and therefore the optimal scale of the program) will differ by location because of variation across a region in the volatility of the economic base; manufacturing jobs may be more insecure, for example, than jobs in the service sector. National policies likely cannot reflect these desired variations in structure across locality. For decision making about social insurance to be efficient, it would be important to separate efficiency from ex ante redistributional consequences of the program. If local communities are more homogeneous, then the political decision making there can focus more easily on the efficiency consequences of the programs.

How can this desired variation in social insurance provisions by location be achieved if policies enacted by the national government must be uniform across locations?[6] Decentralization by itself would simply eliminate any social insurance if individuals can move without cost ex post to the jurisdiction paying the most generous benefits. The current response in the United States is to provide national subsidies to local social insurance provisions, though this approach may be highly imperfect since the size of the externalities would likely be a highly nonlinear function of the differences in benefits paid across locations.

Other alternatives exist, however, particularly if individuals incur some fixed costs of changing locations to get higher benefits. If the national government sets a minimum level of benefits, for example, then local jurisdictions can raise their benefits by up to this fixed cost above the stated minimum without inducing migration. The incentive to migrate can be reduced further by imposing residency requirements to qualify for benefits in a new location, particularly if migration causes a loss of benefits in the previous location. The longer this residency requirement is, the greater the difference in benefits can be across location without inducing migration, though the greater the loss from discouraging efficiency-enhancing migration.[7] This is the approach that a number of EU countries have taken to prevent their social insurance programs from being undermined by migration. It would be of value to compare the potential efficiency losses from discouraged migration with the efficiency and equity gains from the resulting increase in the variability in social insurance benefits across location to judge the appropriate trade-off better.

Given that the United States will likely experiment with a substantial decentralization of government functions during the next few years, further academic research is needed to analyze the economic implications of this decentralization and to explore possible approaches to mitigate any efficiency losses that result.

Notes

1. In France, for example, both tax and expenditure policies are highly centralized; in Germany tax authority alone is highly centralized; and in Switzerland and Canada both functions are quite decentralized compared to the United States.

Quigley and Rubinfeld document the changes in policy over time in the United States, while the changes in the EU over time can in principle provide additional evidence.

2. As emphasized, for example, by Benabou (1994), individuals may care about whom their children go to school with, even given the expenditures per pupil within the school.

3. Residential patterns seem to be very different in countries such as France where expenditure decisions are more centralized.

4. See Auerbach, Gokhale, and Kotlikoff (1991), for example, for a discussion of the myriad ways available to hide government debt.

5. See Feldstein and Vaillant (1994) for evidence that state income taxes fail to redistribute income, due to compensating changes in the pretax wage distribution.

6. The same problem is being faced more acutely in the EU currently, given the greater variation in social insurance provisions across locations within the EU.

7. States would have the incentive to set residency requirements on their own but would tend to impose barriers that are too high since they would ignore the fiscal implications for other jurisdictions.

References

Auerbach, Alan, Jogadeesh Gokhale, and Laurence Kotlikoff. 1991. *Social Security and Medicare Policy from the Perspective of Generational Accounting.* NBER Working Paper 3915.

Benabou, Roland. 1994. *Education, Income Distribution, and Growth: The Local Connection.* NBER Working Paper 4798.

Feldstein, Marian S. 1976. On the Theory of Tax Reform. *Journal of Public Economics* 6:77–104.

Feldstein, Martin S., and Marian Vaillant. 1994. *Can State Taxes Redistribute Income?* NBER Working Paper 4785.

Gordon, Roger H. 1983. "An Optimal Taxation Approach to Fiscal Federalism." *Quarterly Journal of Economics* 98:567–586.

Helliwell, John. 1995. *Do National Borders Matter for Quebec's Trade?* NBER Working Paper 5215.

Hochman, Hal, and James Rodgers. 1969. "Pareto Optimal Redistribution." *American Economic Review* 59:542–557.

Comment

Robert P. Inman

Federal, state, and local fiscal relationships in the United States are undergoing a fundamental reevaluation by policymakers concerned with meeting taxpayer demands for a less burdensome public sector and by academics seeking a richer understanding of the effects of fiscal institutions on fiscal policy. John Quigley and Daniel Rubinfeld provide a concise survey of contemporary federalism facts and theory and offer new and provocative insights for future research.

President Reagan's fiscal revolution aimed at shrinking the influence of the national government on the U.S. economy contained as a key component a New Federalism agenda. As originally advertised, Reagan's New Federalism policies were to return historically important federal policy responsibilities—AFDC, food stamps, education, community development, and transportation—to state and local governments. In return, Washington would take full responsibility for Medicaid spending. Quigley and Rubinfeld's analysis shows that this New Federalism agenda, although not fully implemented, had a significant effect on the long-run path of federal assistance to state and local governments.[1] The observed downward shift may be temporary, however. As Quigley and Rubinfeld show, alongside the cut in grants spending as a means of fiscal control was the concurrent expansion of unfunded federal mandates (see table 2.3). Although federal regulations attached to the receipt of federal dollars have always been commonplace, *unfunded* mandates—mandates unattached to grants—appear to be a 1980s fiscal innovation. Further, the fiscal costs of these unfunded mandates seem roughly equal to the cut in federal aid—both approximately $30 billion.

When seen side by side, as the Quigley-Rubinfeld analysis allows, the grants-to-mandates shift suggests that perhaps Reagan's New Federalism was less about shifting the *policy* responsibility for public spending and more about shifting the *political* responsibility for raising taxes from

Washington to the states. This cannot be a long-run political equilibrium for a decentralized central legislature driven by incentives to maximize the net fiscal benefits for the folks back home. Decentralized legislatures seek to concentrate the benefits of fiscal policies on local residents and to spread the costs over a national tax base. The 1980s shift from grants to unfunded mandates under Reagan does just the opposite: it concentrates costs and in many cases diffuses the benefits. The post-Reagan return of grants funding to its old growth path and the nearly unanimous passage of the Unfunded Mandates Reform Act of 1995 may be congressional efforts to restore the old federalist fiscal order. Seen in the light of the Quigley-Rubinfeld analysis, today's political struggle over the federal budget is at its core a federalism issue. Today's policymakers are trying to decide what level of government should provide what services and who should pay for them.

Politicians are not the only ones struggling to make sense of today's federalist fiscal structure. As Quigley and Rubinfeld point out, public finance economists also have come to question familiar notions of federal, state, and local responsibilities. In setting distribution policy, Mark Pauly (1973) has raised the possibility that income distribution might more plausibly be seen as a local public good best assigned to local or (at most) state governments.[2] When deciding macropolicy Edward Gramlich (1987) has suggested that state government fiscal policy might have real effects on state employment levels; if so, perhaps annual balanced budget rules should be relaxed to accommodate local deficit policies. Setting such local deficit rules is now a (perhaps, the) central issue as Europe moves toward a monetary union (Bayoumi and Eichengreen 1995). Finally, in deciding regulatory and spending policies, Dan Rubinfeld and I (1996) have argued that interjurisdictional Coasian agreements might be preferred to central government grants as a means to control interstate spillovers, a point shown formally in the case of intercommunity tax competition by Gordon Myers (1990).

Implicit in all of this new federalism research is a more careful balancing of the benefits and costs of centralizing economic policymaking. Upper-level governments encompassing more people within their jurisdictions are more likely to internalize all relevant externalities; this is the benefit of centralization. Offsetting this benefit are the costs of centralization. Three have been identified. First, larger governments allow greater diversity of preferences, creating well-known problems of preference aggregation and cycling. Second, larger governments may make monitoring of elected representatives more difficult, increasing agency costs. Third, perhaps because of the increased cycling and the higher agency costs with centralization, larger governments may discourage political participation and threaten personal liberties (Inman and Rubinfeld 1997). How one assesses and then measures these gains and losses from centralization of policy responsibilities is at the core of federalism's new research agenda. As Quigley and Rubinfeld's review makes clear, public finance scholars are also asking what levels of government should provide what services and who should pay.

There remains a final issue for both policymakers and public finance scholars. Whatever the new order of fiscal hierarchies and fiscal assignments, it must be enforced by a stable, long-run coalition of political forces. Announcing a governmental structure and an assignment of fiscal activities and having that structure and assignment respected by the pressures of annual fiscal politics are two separate matters. Quigley and Rubinfeld see the United States leaving what Harry Scheiber has called the "creative federalism" of the past thirty years and entering a new era of "restrained federalism." Will restrained federalism last? The answer depends on whether the new political forces now seeking a smaller central government and more responsibilities and financing at the local levels will prove successful over the long term. Their short-term successes—the Reagan presidency and the first year of the 104th Congress—have been closely tied to the ability of strong Republican presidential and congressional leadership to fashion a stable majority in Congress. If, and (I suspect) only if, that majority coalition holds together over the long run can we expect a stable period of restrained federalism. If not, then for reasons I have outlined elsewhere (Inman 1988) Scheiber's era of creative federalism is likely to continue.

Today both the policies and the theory of fiscal federalism are in flux, motivated by a growing appreciation that a strongly centralized public sector is not likely to be optimal. As public finance scholars searching for richer theory of fiscal federalism, we must carefully articulate and then measure the comparative benefits and costs of alternative federalist structures. How many state and local governments should there be, and what should be the allocation of policy responsibilities across the federal and state-local levels? To be useful as either a normative guide to policymakers or as a prediction as positive theory, our answers must move beyond the narrow economic spillover theories of the past and consider explicitly the ability of centralized and decentralized democratic institutions to make their necessarily political decisions. The Quigley-Rubinfeld survey puts us on the right path.

Notes

1. Although President Reagan coined the phrase "New Federalism" it is clear from Quigley-Rubinfeld's figures 2.1 to 2.3 that something was afoot even before Reagan took office. The downturn in federal aid to state and local governments, notably education and transportation grants, began under Carter and a Democratic Congress in FY (fiscal year) 1980. Whether this downturn was due to an explicit cancellation of federal programs or to the interaction of growing state and local fiscal conservatism with federal matching formulas remains to be seen. In any case, Reagan consolidated the downturn with an explicit reduction of federal aid in all major categories in the FY 1981 and 1982 budgets. With the exception of health care's Medicaid grants, there reductions held until FY 1989, the last Reagan budget. All grants categories have been rising in real terms ever since, approximately on trend with their real growth over the period FY 1965 to FY 1979.

2. Indeed, today's budget debate over federal welfare reform and Medicaid spending might well be characterized as an application of Pauly's insight. In today's fiscal climate, Medicaid and AFDC transfers to low-income households are an obvious target for budget savings to fund middle-class tax relief. To justify this federal fiscal reform, federalism arguments favoring local control over redistributive policies have been invoked. As Quigley and Rubinfeld point out, one way to control redistributive spending is to substitute an equal-cost block grant for the current open-ended (or "entitlement") matching aid and to allow interstate fiscal competition to provide a check of future spending increases. If income redistribution is truly a local public good, then this proposed federalism reform is correct, both economically and politically. But as Quigley and Rubinfeld suggest, there may well be national minimum standards for redistribution, which set a floor for local redistributive efforts. These national floors should be financed by federal grants, but not (as now) using open-ended entitlement support.

References

Bayoumi, Tamin, and Barry Eichengreen. 1995. "Restraining Yourself: The Implications of Fiscal Rules for Economic Stabilization." *IMF Staff Papers* 42:32–48.

Gramlich, Edward. 1987. "Subnational Fiscal Policy." *Perspectives on Local Public Finance and Public Policy* 3:3–27.

Inman, Robert. 1988. "Federal Assistance and Local Services in the United States: The Evolution of a New Federalist Fiscal Order." In H. Rosen, ed., *Fiscal Federalism*, pp. 33–74. Chicago: University of Chicago Press.

Inman, Robert, and Daniel Rubinfeld. 1997. "Making Sense of Antitrust State Action Doctrine: Resolving the Tension Between Political Participation and Economic Efficiency." *Texas Law Review*. Forthcoming.

Inman, Robert, and Daniel Rubinfeld. 1996. "The Political Economy of Federalism." In Dennis Mueller, ed., *Perspectives on Public Choice*. New York: Cambridge University Press.

Myers, Gordon M. 1990. "Optimality, Free Mobility, and the Regional Authority in a Federation." *Journal of Public Economics* 43:107–123.

Pauly, Mark. 1973. "Income Redistribution as a Local Public Good." *Journal of Public Economics* 2:35–58.

3 Do Budget Rules Work?

James M. Poterba

Many public finance economists have historically viewed budget rules as institutional details that do not warrant substantial research attention. With several notable exceptions, including Musgrave (1939), Colm and Wagner (1963), and Kotlikoff (1986), the discussion of budget policy has focused on optimal levels of expansionary or contractionary policy, or the design of tax and expenditure programs, as though an all-powerful social planner could modify policy precisely in accord with economists' recommendations. The potential role for budget institutions in affecting policy outcomes has received relatively little investigation.

In the social planner paradigm, arbitrary budget restrictions such as balanced budget rules or tax and expenditure limits represent constraints that cannot improve, and may reduce, social welfare. One positive theory of government deficits, formalized by Barro (1979), views deficits and surpluses as the outcome of a social planner's tax-smoothing problem. In this setting, a balanced budget rule that requires taxes to equal spending would reduce welfare by preventing the social planner from choosing the optimal time path of taxes.

Actual budget deliberations may deviate in critical ways, however, from the stylized setting of the social planner paradigm. For example, if democratic budget processes exhibit a bias toward excessive spending and deficit finance, then the welfare cost of suboptimal tax timing must be weighed against the welfare gains associated with constraining policy outcomes along other dimensions. It is precisely this possibility that is advanced by many of those who support the enactment of various types of fiscal limits. Alternatively, if the budget process is myopic and places too much weight on the current cost of a project, regardless of its benefit stream, then long-lived capital projects may face more difficult political battles than short-run projects. This possibility is suggested by those who advocate adopting a separate capital and operating budget for the U.S. federal government.

Although theoretical models that permit detailed analysis of the impact of budget reforms have yet to be developed, there has been much speculation and some empirical research on the potential effects of different fiscal institutions. Blue ribbon panels, such as the President's Commission on Budget Concepts (1967), have periodically considered the nature of existing budget rules and made suggestions for reform. A substantial volume of academic research has focused on defining "the" appropriate budget concept. Static, cash accounting measures of budget deficits are widely recognized as imperfect measures of government fiscal stance, and a number of alternatives to current deficit measures have been developed. Among the modifications considered are distinguishing between capital and operating expenditures with an explicit capital budget, recognizing implicit liabilities and more generally treating budget accruals as well as cash transactions, and expanding the budget horizon to provide information on fiscal balance over horizons longer than a single year.

Another line of research does not focus on the definition of the budget as much as on the process by which the budget is enacted. This work, which is based on research in positive political economy, implies that changes in the structure of the budget process, such as enactment of a line item veto or requirement of a supermajority in Congress to enact budgets with deficits of a given size, implicitly or explicitly suggest that reforms to the budget process could affect policy outcomes.

The central issue for economic policy is whether changing the yardstick used to assess fiscal policy, or the rules of the budget enactment process and the relative political power of those who participate in it, would affect budget outcomes such as the level of government spending or the fiscal deficit. It is difficult to bring convincing empirical evidence to bear on this issue for at least two reasons. First, some proposals under debate at the federal level involve budgetary innovations that have not been tried on a national or subnational scale before. Second, there is relatively little variation over time within nations in the nature of budget processes or in the set of summary statistics that are the center of budget debates. It is therefore difficult to compare fiscal policy before and after significant institutional reforms of the type that are under discussion.

In spite of these difficulties, there are some opportunities to study the effect of budget rules. One is the U.S. experience with Gramm-Rudman-Hollings (GRH), the antideficit legislation enacted in the mid-1980s. Another is provided by the variation in budget rules across states within the United States. Yet a third possible source of evidence arises from differences across nations in budget outcomes and budget policies, particularly within otherwise homogeneous groups of nations. Some analysts are understandably hesitant to draw strong conclusions from cross-national comparisons because of the difficulty in holding constant other factors that might affect fiscal institutions.

One potential difficulty confronting research in this area is that the term *budget rules* refers to a wide range of fiscal institutions. Examples include, but are not limited to, tax and expenditure limits at the local or state level in the United States, antideficit rules that restrict the power of state governments to borrow and carry over budget shortfalls from one year to the next, and restrictions on the type of debt that can be issued without voter approval. Even the institutions that legislatures use to prepare budgets, and the structure of committees through which budget deliberations must proceed, can be viewed as budget rules. The wide variation in budget rules makes it difficult to draw any uniform conclusions about the effect of such rules on policy outcomes.

This chapter draws together the limited evidence that has emerged from various research programs on the impact of budget rules. The preponderance of this evidence suggests that these rules mater, although the results do not permit refined judgments about the impact of specific provisions in budget policy. The chapter is divided into five sections. The first provides a framework for discussing budget institutions and considers the fundamental question of whether budget institutions can be viewed as anything more than a summary statistic for voter preferences. I argue that with careful attention to the source of budget rules, it is possible to find exogenous variation in these rules and to use this variation as a source of information on how rules affect policy outcomes.

The second section discusses the U.S. experience since the enactment of federal antideficit legislation in the mid-1980s and early 1990s. It considers both the effect of this legislation on the level of taxes, spending, and deficits and evidence on how the budget enactment and evaluation process has been affected by this legislation. Section 3.3 presents related evidence based on the experience of the states with antideficit rules and tax and expenditure limits. The fourth section discusses international evidence on the effect of budget rules and other fiscal institutions on deficits and the level of government indebtedness, referring to both developed and developing nations. A brief conclusion suggests a number of points about the research agenda on budget institutions.

3.1 A Framework for Analyzing Budget Rules

Two recent development have stimulated growing interest in fiscal institutions. First, there are evident differences in the size and persistence of budget deficits across nations. These do not seem obviously related to short-term spending needs, such as wars, or to intertemporal variation in the marginal cost of raising revenue, as theories of optimal debt policy such as Barro (1979) would suggest. The inability to explain cross-national differences solely in terms of economic factors has led to a search for other factors, notably politicoeconomic explanations for deficit policies. Roubini and Sachs (1989) wrote one of the first studies in the modern revival to explore how political institutions such as the presence or absence of divided government affect fiscal policy outcomes.

The second factor driving recent interest in fiscal institutions is the rise of large peacetime budget deficits in the United States during the late 1970s and even more during the 1980s. The possibility that fiscal policy is biased toward deficit finance, and toward spending that yields concentrated benefits and diverse costs that nevertheless exceed the benefits, has been recognized for decades. Buchanan and Wagner (1977) and Weingast, Shepsle, and Johnsen (1981) are relatively recent statements of these central points. Yet until the early 1980s, fiscal deficits in the United States and most other developed nations had been relatively small except during wars or deep economic downturns. As Poterba (1994a) and others have noted, the substantial tax cuts of 1981 and the failure to achieve the spending reductions that President Reagan had promised would coincide with these tax reductions led to unprecedented peacetime deficits. The rise of such deficits was the proximate cause of the discussion, beginning in the mid-1980s, of a federal balanced budget amendment and of the related enactment of the Gramm-Rudman-Hollings antideficit legislation. To evaluate the potential effects of such fiscal rules, public finance and macroeconomists have embarked on new research programs that draw substantially on previous work in positive political theory and in public administration.

What Role Do Budgets Play?

Economic research on budget institutions has taken three forms. The oldest line of inquiry asks, What are budgets for? and considers issues of budget measurement and definition. Budgets can serve at least three functions: to inform the fiscal policy debate, to structure the debate on government programs, and to affect fiscal policy outcomes. With respect to information provision, it is possible to envision budgets defined over various horizons, with the nearest-term measuring the government's expenditures and revenues in only the current period and the longest-horizon measure describing the present discounted value of government outlays and revenues under current or projected policies. The current horizon for most aspects of the federal budget process is five years, although political maneuvering in 1996 involved promises of budget balance by 2002. There are examples, such as the annual report produced by the trustees of the social security system, of much longer budget horizons. In the social security case, projections of cash flows and account balances for seventy-five years are presented each year.

With regard to structuring debate, the budget has important effects along many dimensions. Many features of actual budgets, such as the distinction between on- and off-budget programs, the categorization of spending into mandatory and discretionary, the "pay as you go" requirement that certain programs be fully funded when enacted, and even the sequencing of approval of overall budget targets (the budget resolution) and individual appropriation measures, affect the debate on government programs and revenue sources. The information provision and debate-structuring role of budgets are clearly linked together, in that with multi-year budgets it is possible to consider a wider range of budget balance concepts than with a single year's account.

The final role of budgets, to affect fiscal policy outcomes, has attracted the most attention in recent policy discussions of balanced budget rules. The central objective of such reforms is to affect the relative likelihood of some budget outcomes rather than others. Tax limitation laws and requirements for popular approval of debt issues at the state level are examples of similar budgeting rules that are explicitly designed to reduce spending and tax levels relative to the size of the private economy.

How Do Budget Rules Affect Outcomes?

A second line of research on budgets has built on the recent advances in positive political economy to provide theoretical insights into the effect of budget institutions. This literature is directed toward a range of questions relating to the "industrial organization" of the legislature and the budget process, such as whether it matters if legislators vote first on the size of the budget and then on its allocation across spending programs, or vice versa. The findings of this literature are often sensitive to modeling assumptions. Ferejohn and Krehbiel (1987) illustrate this difficulty with respect to the timing of votes on budget size and allocation. They show that provided legislators form rational expectations about the allocative stage of the budget game, reversing the timing of the budget votes will not have any effect on fiscal policy outcomes. Masia (1995) presents a related analysis of how budget institutions can alter the political power of the executive and thus affect the nature of budgetary bargains.

One explanation of the role of budget rules, which has not been emphasized in the political economy literature to date, is that these rules provide a form of "self-control" for political actors. If society exhibits dynamically inconsistent preferences with respect to fiscal policy, always preferring a larger budget deficit in the current period than it would have agreed to in previous periods, then budget rules may provide a mechanism for constraining the discretion of future budget deliberators. Laibson (1994) discusses a similar set of issues with respect to individual saving behavior. He suggests that in the presence of hyperbolic discounting, individual preferences with respect to saving will be time inconsistent and that individuals may develop institutions that restrict their future ability to consume. Formal analysis of budget rules in a framework such as this, while promising, remains an issue for future research.

Empirical Evidence on the Effects of Budget Rules

The final strand of research on budget institutions has taken an empirical tack, analyzing how various rules for developing, enacting, and enforcing budgets affect the nature of fiscal policy. This work has exploited differences across nations, across states within nations, and within nations over time to search for effects of budget rules on fiscal outcomes. A number of studies in this tradition have identified substantial effects of fiscal rules; this is the primary subject of this chapter.

The central empirical problem in the research program on fiscal institutions and their effects is the potential endogeneity of budget institutions. Riker (1980) argues that essentially all political institutions reflect the "congealed preferences" of the electorate. In this view, institutions that no longer suit a majority of the electorate will be overturned, and the institutional structure of a nation or state contains no information other than some aggregation of information on current voter preferences. Skidmore and Alm (1994) demonstrate that state fiscal conditions, notably the level of state taxes, are related to the probability that voters will pass a tax limitation law; this finding underscores the institutional endogeneity problem for budget rules.

The institutional endogeneity problem with respect to budget deficits is similar to the problem that has plagued the macroeconomic research program on the effects of central bank independence. Posen (1995) argues that whether a central bank is independent is largely explained by the degree of opposition to inflation in the financial community within a nation. This suggests that the independence of the central bank cannot be viewed as an exogenous variable for explaining outcomes such as a nation's inflation rate.

With respect to budget institutions, the counterargument to the institutional endogeneity view emphasizes the difficulty of changing these institutions and the costs of revising fiscal rules. Alesina and Perotti (1996) argue that at least some of the international differences in budget rules should be viewed as exogenous. The difficulty associated with changing the federal budget process is evidence for this view, as is the fact that in many of the U.S. states, the current budget institutions are those that were established when the state joined the union.

There are at least two ways to reduce, if not solve, the problem of endogenous fiscal institutions. One strategy is to control for some measure of voter preferences, such as the political party of elected officials, or an objective index of voter preferences on the political spectrum. This reduces the potential for observed correlations between budget rules and fiscal outcomes to reflect a correlation of both of these variables with an omitted third variable, voter tastes for fiscal outcomes. The difficulty with this approach is that any set of control variables may not completely capture the potential omitted variables that underlie spurious findings.

A second approach involves modeling the evolution of budget rules and using variables that affect budget rules but not fiscal policy as instrumental variables in a simultaneous equations econometric framework. The difficulty with this approach is finding valid instruments. Although it is unlikely that any instruments will be beyond dispute, this approach provides a potentially promising method of addressing the institutional endogeneity problem. Exploiting these strategies represents an important part of the empirical agenda for research on budget institutions.

3.2 U.S. Federal Experience with Deficit Limitation Laws

The U.S. experience with antideficit rules in the mid-1980s and early 1990s represents one of the clearest cases of change in budget institutions at a national level and therefore provides one of the best opportunities for learning about the potential effects of such reform. This section considers the impact of these antideficit rules. It begins with a brief overview of the time path of federal deficits, then describes the experience since the enactment of Gramm-Rudman-Hollings in the mid-1980s and the Budget Enforcement Act (BEA) of 1990.

Federal Deficit Experience: The Postwar Period

Table 3.1 shows federal budget deficits for the postwar period. The table includes both "on-budget" deficits, which exclude the net surplus or deficit in the social security and postal service trust fund accounts, as well as the total deficit. The total deficit as a share of gross domestic product (GDP) averaged 0.7 percent between 1950 and 1974 and then increased to 3 percent of GDP between 1975 and 1979. One of the many potential explanations for this apparent shift in the level of the deficit was a change in the internal organization of Congress in the late 1960s and early 1970s. A variety of institutional reforms reduced the power of committee chairs and central party leadership, "democratizing" Congress and granting increased power to individual members. The Budget and Impoundment Act of 1974 is the most extreme example of this type with respect to budget process, since it altered the relative power of the chairs of committees concerned with appropriations and the chairs of the Appropriations and Ways and Means committees. This may have resulted in growing support for spending programs with specific benefits but diffuse costs.

Deficits became substantial in the late 1970s, but in the aftermath of the tax reductions in the Economic Recovery Tax Act of 1981 and the Reagan defense buildup, they became even more pronounced in the early 1980s. The federal deficit peaked at 6.3 percent of GDP in fiscal year 1983. The total deficit as a share of GDP has declined since then, falling to 2.9 percent of GDP in 1989 and, after increasing again during the recession of the early 1990s, to 3.1 percent for fiscal 1994. Table 3.1 also shows that the on-budget deficit has not declined as sharply as the total deficit, which reflects the substantial surplus (0.8 percent of GDP for fiscal 1995) in the social security trust fund account.

The apparent reduction in deficits that the data in table 3.1 suggest is often cited as an illustration of the difficulties posed by annual budget measures. Auerbach (1995) explains that changing demographics, coupled with the rising relative costs of many of the services that governments in the United States are committed to purchase, imply a rising path of defi-

Table 3.1
Federal surpluses and deficits, 1950–1995 (percentage of GDP)

Fiscal Year	Total Deficit	On-Budget Deficit	Fiscal Year	Total Deficit	On-Budget Deficit
1950	−1.2	−1.8	1974	−0.4	−0.6
1951	1.9	1.4	1975	−3.5	−3.7
1952	−0.4	−1.0	1976	−4.4	−4.2
1953	−1.8	−2.3	1977	−2.8	−2.6
1954	−0.3	−0.8	1978	−2.7	−2.5
1955	−0.8	−1.1	1979	−1.7	−1.6
1956	0.9	0.6	1980	−2.8	−2.8
1957	0.8	0.6	1981	−2.7	−2.5
1958	−0.6	−0.7	1982	−4.1	−3.8
1959	−2.7	−2.5	1983	−6.3	−6.3
1960	0.1	0.1	1984	−5.0	−5.0
1961	−0.6	−0.7	1985	−5.4	−5.6
1962	−1.3	−1.1	1986	−5.2	−5.6
1963	−0.8	−0.7	1987	−3.4	−3.8
1964	−0.9	−1.0	1988	−3.2	−4.0
1965	−0.2	−0.2	1989	−2.9	−4.0
1966	−0.5	−0.4	1990	−4.0	−5.1
1967	−1.1	−1.6	1991	−4.7	−5.7
1968	−3.0	−3.3	1992	−4.9	−5.8
1969	0.4	−0.1	1993	−4.1	−4.8
1970	−0.3	−0.9	1994	−3.1	−3.9
1971	−2.2	−2.5	1995 (est.)	−2.7	−3.6
1972	−2.0	−2.3	1996 (est.)	−2.7	−3.5
1973	−1.2	−1.2	1997 (est.)	−2.7	−3.6

Source: U.S. Office of Management and Budget, *Historical Tables: Budget of the United States Government, Fiscal Year 1996.*
Note: The 1976 entry excludes a transition quarter associated with a change in fiscal years.

cits as a fraction of GDP prospectively, even though current period and near-term deficit projections suggest some improvement in the fiscal situation. Focusing on longer-term measures of budget policy could thus reverse the conclusions suggested by short-term trends.

One way to avoid the short-term focus that occurs with annual deficit statistics is explicitly to project the present discounted value of future outlays that are implied by currently legislated programs, to add this to the value of outstanding debt, and to compare this with the value of salable government assets. This is essentially the procedure that underlies the projection component of the "generational accounts" algorithms developed by Auerbach, Gokhale, and Kotlikoff (1991). These algorithms use available information on projected economic and demographic conditions to evaluate the long-term evolution of government spending. The precise assumptions underlying any set of generational accounts may be open to question, but the general finding that these accounts provide additional insight on the budget process is difficult to refute.

The Balanced Budget Amendment and the Passage of Gramm-Rudman-Hollings

The shift from near balance in fiscal policy to persistent peacetime federal deficits starting in the mid-1970s led to emerging policy concern about fiscal policy. This concern first reached a critical juncture in August 1982, when the Senate passed the balanced budget amendment (BBA) by a 69–31 margin, two votes more than the two-thirds majority needed for a constitutional amendment. The proposed amendment required Congress to adopt a balanced budget before the start of each fiscal year, although it incorporated limited override provisions for deficits in wartime or if approved by 60 percent of Congress. Despite support from the White House, the BBA did not pass the House of Representatives by the required two-thirds majority.

Although the BBA could not command sufficient legislative support for passage, it indicated a desire to alter the budget process in ways that would reduce the chance of future deficits. As chronicled in Poterba (1994a), this desire surfaced again in late 1985, when the Senate took up legislation to raise the federal debt limit from $1.8 trillion to $2.1 trillion. The expansion in debt authority was needed to avoid a federal financial crisis, since increased borrowing was required to make federal interest payments. During the debate on the debt ceiling bill, Senators Phil Gramm, Ernest Hollings, and Warren Rudman took the initiative on broad deficit issues and introduced a bill requiring a phased-in program of deficit reduction, leading to budget balance in fiscal 1991.

The Gramm-Rudman-Hollings (GRH) bill that passed the Senate by a wide majority had two components. The first altered the timing of the federal budget process, accelerating budget discussions and placing deadlines earlier in the calendar year in an effort to permit more deliberation before the start of the fiscal year. The second objective was to introduce a set of deficit targets and a mechanism for ensuring that actual deficits did not exceed them. There were five central provisions in the bill:

1. The president would be required to submit budgets with forecast deficits no greater than the target for a given year.

2. The Office of Management and Budget (OMB) and Congressional Budget Office (CBO) would prepare estimates of the projected deficit from the enacted budget and tax legislation.

3. If the average of the CBO and OMB deficit computations exceeded the target, then the president would have two weeks to issue a sequester order, requiring permanent reductions in budget authority for all outlays other than a set of exempt programs, which included means-tested entitlement programs, interest on the federal debt, government pensions, and existing contractual obligations.

4. Half of the sequester cuts would come from entitlement programs with automatic spending increases, such as Medicaid, Aid to Families with Dependent Children, and food stamps, while the other half would come from other discretionary programs.

5. A suspension clause rendered the need for spending cuts inoperative if the economy was in recession. This would occur if actual economic growth fell below 1 percent for two consecutive quarters, or if the CBO or OMB projected negative growth for two quarters. The suspension clause would also apply in periods when there was a war declared by Congress or whenever a three-fifths majority of Congress voted for such suspension.

The Gramm-Rudman-Hollings bill represented a substantial change in the rules governing budgetary politics in the United States. The conference bill that President Reagan signed called for a deficit target of $171.9 billion in fiscal 1986, declining to zero by fiscal 1991. Half of the automatic cuts would come from defense and half from nonexempt nonmilitary programs, including AFDC, Medicaid, and social security. All programs would have to be cut proportionally, thereby limiting presidential discretion. A key provision required the General Accounting Office (GAO) to calculate the average of the OMB and CBO deficit estimates and transmit an estimate of the needed sequester to the president. AFDC, Medicaid, and social security were excluded from the sequestration process.

The GAO provision was the basis for a constitutional challenge to GRH. In July 1986, the Supreme Court declared GRH unconstitutional, on the grounds that because Congress can dismiss the head of the GAO, the bill provided executive authority to an organization under legislative control. The Supreme Court decision derailed the first GRH deficit limitation plan. A year later, the Senate passed new legislation, sponsored by

Senators Gramm, Chiles, and Domenici, in which the final step in the sequester process required GAO to submit its report to OMB, an executive agency. OMB would review the GAO report, and the president would then issue an order based on it to enforce spending cuts. The deficit targets were loosened from levels in the previous year's legislation to require a deficit of $144 billion in fiscal 1988, declining to zero in fiscal 1993. In addition, the law permitted a $10 billion margin of error in all years until 1993. President Reagan signed this bill in September 1987. Although it was technically different from the original Gramm-Rudman-Hollings bill, this legislation is frequently referred to as Gramm-Rudman or Gramm-Rudman-Hollings, and it shall be referred to as GRH in what follows.

Deficit Experience Under Gramm-Rudman-Hollings

When GRH was enacted, many analysts predicted that it would have no effect on tax and spending outcomes, because Congress and the president could always agree to modify the targets. Others noted that it would be straightforward to circumvent the budget targets with a series of budgeting gimmicks, such as the postponement of some expenditures until the first day of the next fiscal year or the acceleration of some receipts. Both of these concerns proved correct to some degree, but at least some studies conclude that in spite of these issues, GRH did affect budgetary outcomes.

The initial experience with GRH supported those who doubted that it would matter. In 1987, when congressional leaders concluded that the fiscal 1988 deficit target specified by GRH was unattainable, the timetable for deficit elimination was extended, and the near-term deficit targets were increased. A similar strategy was invoked in 1988. Much of the budget "savings" in these years was achieved through a variety of accounting manipulations and one-time revenue raisers, including asset sales and moving some agencies, such as the postal service, off budget. These factors, coupled with other shocks such as rapid growth of medical care costs during the late 1980s and the expenses associated with the savings and loan bailout, led to deficits substantially above the initial GRH targets. This failure to achieve the hoped-for deficit reduction led to further budgetary reform in the 1990 Budget Enforcement Act. Yet it may be inappropriate to dismiss GRH as ineffectual simply because substantial deficits remained at the end of the 1980s.

Gramlich (1990), Hahm et al. (1992), and Reischauer (1990) present careful analyses of deficit reduction and GRH. The first and last of these studies were prepared by participants in the budget process. Gramlich begins by observing the decline in average federal deficits between the years immediately before and the years after the enactment of GRH. He cautions that although this pattern provides superficial support for the effectiveness of the deficit legislation, the disaggregate pattern of spending and revenues suggests that not all of the deficit reduction could be attributed to antideficit legislation. He calculates that there was a 2.8 percent of GDP decline in the primary deficit between the 1983–1986 period and 1989, and he attributes this change among various factors as follows:

Nondefense baseline drift	1.2 percent
Defense base calculation	0.8
Higher taxes	1.0
Other factors	−0.2
Total	2.8 percent

The most important factor in deficit reduction, nondefense baseline drift, reflects the declining GDP share of entitlement programs as productivity and other factors lead to increases in real GDP. The next largest component, the increase in taxes, was due in roughly equal parts to the increase in payroll taxes in the 1983 social security compromise and the increase in corporate taxes under the Tax Reform Act of 1986. The latter could have been affected by the GRH budget rules, since some of the provisions, such as less generous depreciation schedules for some assets, would raise revenue in the short term but reduce it in the longer term.

The changing defense baseline spending was proximately the result of GRH, which replaced the previous practice of projecting the growth rate of defense outlays on the basis of some earlier budget agreement with the practice of projecting current real level of outlays into the future. This change, adopted as part of the sequester procedure in GRH, had the effect of reducing the projected level of defense outlays, and thus the base from which contributions to the deficit were assessed. But Gramlich (1990) argues that the change in defense projections probably reflected changing political support for defense spending rather than a revision in the principles of budgeting. After dissecting the budget components, he concludes, "The fact that GRH was instituted just as primary deficits were dropping seems largely coincidental ... changes in the process due to GRH seemed to have little to do with the improvement" (p. 80).

Hahm et al. (1992) reach a somewhat different conclusion. They present the most disaggregate analysis of how GRH affected the outcome of the budget process. They rely on a multisector model of federal spending, which relates spending on each of sixty subcategories of federal spending to a set of variables that are plausibly related to spending choices, such as the fraction of households in poverty and the presence or absence of a war. They use their model to simulate spending in the late 1980s in the absence of GRH and compare the findings with the actual spending levels observed during this period. They conclude that there was no systematic change in spending levels for programs that were exempt from sequestration, but that spending for programs subject to sequestration did decline after GRH was enacted. Their central estimates suggest that GRH reduced spending on these programs by nearly $60 billion in fiscal 1989.

Whether Gramlich's (1990) investigation or Hahm et al.'s (1992) analysis represents a better assessment of the impact of GRH is unclear. The difficulty of performing the counterfactual experiment of observing spending in the absence of GRH makes it hard to evaluate observed budget outcomes, and the lessons from the GRH experience may simply be too subtle to interpret with confidence.

Reischauer (1990) provides evidence on the importance of several budgetary "gimmicks" used to reduce measured deficits. First, he notes that the CBO estimates that approximately half of the deficit reduction during the GRH period was achieved through one-shot fiscal measures, such as asset sales. Although this suggests that concerns about budget manipulation are not without basis, it also suggests that approximately half of the deficit reduction was not due to these factors. Second, Reischauer presents evidence on the increasingly optimistic economic assumptions OMB used in projecting future deficits. Table 3.2 shows the time profile of CBO's economic and technical adjustments to the president's budget for each fiscal year from 1983 to 1992. The average correction rises from $8 billion in the four years before GRH took effect to $36 billion in the six years afterward. This pattern, confirmed by Auerbach's (1994) evidence on various sources of revision to budget estimates, suggests that one of the important consequences of GRH was to place greater pressure on forecasters to use optimistic assumptions that would make deficit reduction easier.

This example of endogenous forecast optimism illustrates the difficulty of controlling budget outcomes on any multiyear basis. It is almost always possible to predict a balanced budget over some horizon if the budget forecaster has enough discretion in setting the underlying economic assumptions. Because GRH did not place restrictions on this aspect of the budget process, some of the deficit reduction generated by GRH was the result of adjustment along this margin.

Table 3.2
CBO economic and technical adjustments to the president's budget

Fiscal year	Economic	Technical	Total adjustments
1983	4	25	29
1984	−11	−2	−13
1985	8	3	11
1986	7	−1	6
Average, 1983–1986	2	6	8
1987	−1	17	16
1988	15	12	27
1989	25	11	36
1990	10	17	27
1991	9	30	39
1992	26	44	70
Average, 1987–1992	14	22	36

Source: Reischauer (1990); author's calculations.

The Budget Enforcement Act of 1990

The inability to achieve the GRH deficit targets led to renewed discussion of deficit reduction only three years after the GRH was enacted. The result was the 1990 Budget Enforcement Act, which added two new features to budgeting procedures. The first is a series of annual caps on discretionary spending, which require real reductions in outlays on these programs. The second is a pay-as-you-go (PAYG) rule for entitlement spending excluding social security. This requires a nonnegative net revenue effect in each fiscal year of all mandatory and revenue legislation approved since the 1990 budget act. The effect was to require any proponent of a policy that would increase spending on one program to propose cuts in another program or a specific mechanism for raising revenues. Social security, although excluded from the overall entitlement program pay-as-you-go rules, is subject to a separate but similar set of rules. The 1990 BEA applied to fiscal years from 1990 to 1995, but the central provisions have been extended through fiscal 1998 by the Omnibus Budget Reconciliation Act of 1993.

The 1990 BEA differs from GRH in a critical respect. Although GRH specified numerical deficit targets on a year-by-year basis, the BEA specifies only that enacted policies cannot raise deficits relative to initial projected levels. Thus, if existing programs expand prospectively, existing revenue sources coutract, or economic conditions are such that deficits are projected to grow, the BEA would not limit these deficits in any way. BEA is thus an example of a reform in budget process, while GRH was in large part a stipulation of budget targets.

Auerbach (1994) formalizes this important difference between GRH and the 1990 BEA. He notes that under GRH if the deficit target for year t had been set at D_t^*, and the deficit projection at the end of the previous fiscal year was ${}_{t-1}D_t$, then the deficit consequences of policy changes in year $t(P_t)$ are constrained by the rule

$$P_t < D_t^* - {}_{t-1}D_t.$$

This implies that the actual deficit for fiscal year t will deviate from the deficit target only by the amount of "technical projection errors" for the fiscal year.

Under the 1990 BEA, policies cannot be predicted to raise the deficit in any of the next five fiscal years. In this case, Auerbach (1994) shows that the realized deficit in year t will equal the projected deficit in that year from five fiscal years earlier, plus any revisions in the deficit projection due to economic or technical errors in the ensuing five years.

The BEA rules create strong incentives for enacting policies that will not affect deficits during the next five fiscal years, or whatever the budget window is, but will expand deficits further in the future. For example, a bill that promised to eliminate the federal income tax and balloon the deficit in six years would not be identified as deficit enhancing by the BEA, since its deficit expansion would occur outside the BEA window. Such a policy would show up as a large projected baseline deficit in fiscal year $t+6$. All BEA requires is that policies enacted in the next five years do not increases that projected deficit relative to what it was when first forecast.

Auerbach (1994) presents evidence that the shifting budget process of the past decade has led to changes in the relative importance of various factors that contribute to deficits. In particular, he shows that between 1987 and 1990, there was some tendency to reduce deficits in the current fiscal year at the expense of deficits in near-term future years. Because the 1990 BEA restricted the possibility of raising deficits in the next five years to reduce current fiscal year deficits, it has led to less near-term deficit retiming but potentially more long-term retiming. A key factor behind the slow decline in federal budget deficits appears to be a continuing flow of "forecast errors" that have raised deficits relative to previous expectations. These errors can be due to changes in policy, changes in economic assumptions, or technical factors, and the relative importance of different

Table 3.3
Distribution of outlays by Budget Enforcement Act category, 1965–1998 (percentages of GDP)

	Discretionary			
Fiscal year	Defense (%)	Other (%)	Mandatory (%)	Net interest (%)
1965	7.6	4.6	5.4	1.3
1970	8.3	4.3	7.2	1.4
1975	5.8	4.9	9.7	1.5
1980	5.1	5.4	9.9	2.0
1985	6.4	4.1	10.1	3.3
1986	6.5	3.9	9.8	3.3
1987	6.3	3.6	9.4	3.2
1988	6.1	3.6	9.3	3.2
1989	5.9	3.6	9.4	3.2
1990	5.5	3.6	10.3	3.4
1991	5.6	3.7	10.5	3.4
1992	5.1	3.9	10.9	3.4
1993	4.7	4.0	10.7	3.2
1994	4.3	4.0	10.7	3.2
1995 (est.)	3.9	4.0	10.7	3.3
1996 (est.)	3.5	3.9	10.9	3.5
1997 (est.)	3.3	3.7	11.1	3.4
1998 (est.)	3.1	3.4	11.2	3.4

Source: U.S. Office of Management and Budget, *Historical Tables: Budget of the United States Government, Fiscal Year 1996.*

types of errors seems to have been affected by changes in budgetary rules.

The enactment of the 1990 BEA coincided with the acceleration of a long-standing trend in the composition of federal outlays. Tables 3.3 and 3.4 present information on federal spending by BEA category, discretionary versus nondiscretionary, for the period 1965 through 1998 (projected). The tables show a sharp decline in discretionary spending as a share of GDP, from 9.2 percent in 1990 to a projected 6.6 percent in 1998. This decline is nearly as large as the drop between 1970 and 1990 (12.6 percent to 9.2 percent) and is primarily the result of a projected decline in defense outlays. The GDP share devoted to mandatory programs is projected to increase during the 1990s, from 10.3 percent in 1990 to 11.2 percent in 1998. This increase is largely the result of a growing GDP share allocated to means-tested entitlement programs, which include

Table 3.4
Distribution of outlays by Budget Enforcement Act category, 1965–1998 (percentages of total outlays)

Fiscal year	Discretionary		Mandatory (%)	Net interest (%)
	Defense (%)	Other (%)		
1965	43.2	26.0	23.5	7.3
1970	41.9	21.8	29.0	7.4
1975	26.4	22.5	44.1	7.0
1980	22.8	24.0	44.3	8.9
1985	26.7	17.3	42.3	13.7
1986	27.7	16.7	41.9	13.7
1987	28.1	16.2	41.9	13.8
1988	27.3	16.4	42.0	14.3
1989	26.6	16.3	42.4	14.8
1990	24.0	16.1	45.2	14.7
1991	24.2	16.3	44.9	14.7
1992	21.9	16.9	46.7	14.4
1993	20.8	17.7	47.4	14.1
1994	19.3	18.0	48.8	13.9
1995 (est.)	17.7	18.3	48.8	15.2
1996 (est.)	16.3	17.8	50.0	15.9
1997 (est.)	15.3	17.2	51.4	16.0
1998 (est.)	14.6	16.4	52.8	16.2

Source: U.S. Office of Management and Budget, *Historical Tables: Budget of the United States Government, Fiscal Year 1996.*

Medicaid, food stamps, AFDC, social security, child nutrition programs, veterans' pensions, and the earned income tax credit. Spending on these means-tested entitlements equaled 1.7 percent of GDP in 1990 and had increased very little in the previous fifteen years. It is projected to rise to 2.8 percent of GDP by 1998.

The changing GDP shares accounted for by different types of spending can be placed in stark relief by calculating the shares of the federal budget accounted for by various expenditure items. Discretionary spending, which was more than half of the federal budget as recently as 1974, declines from 40.1 percent in 1990 to 31.0 percent in 1998. Mandatory spending rises from 45.2 percent (1990) to 52.8 percent (1998), and net interest increases by 1.5 percent of the total budget. These statistics suggest that the share of the federal budget that is directly controllable by changes in current program outlays, without manipulation of entitlement rules, is small and declining. The open question is whether the trend toward reduced discretionary spending was accelerated by the spending caps in the 1990 Budget Enforcement Act; anecdotal evidence suggests that this may be the case.

If Antideficit Rules Work, Why Do They Work?

Although the experience with GRH is difficult to interpret, evidence on the shifting composition of federal spending since the passage of BEA 1990 and Auerbach's (1994) findings on the changes in the source of "errors" in the budget process suggest that changes in the budget process during the past decade have coincided with changes in fiscal policy outcomes. The fundamental difficulty in evaluating antideficit rules is the institutional endogeneity problem. The passage of GRH and later BEA may signal shifting voter preferences, as reflected in the political process, for high deficits, tax reductions, and spending increases. If so, then the budget outcomes observed since the enactment of these reforms may not be due to these laws per se but may reflect changing fiscal tastes more generally. It may be impossible to reject this view given the short data samples since the passage of these laws.

If one were to subscribe to the view that these institutional changes affected policy outcomes, however, what would the mechanism for such effects be? There are two channels through which deficit targets like those in GRH and BEA may affect fiscal policy. First, they provide a benchmark for budget deliberations, an objective standard against which the president's budget proposal or congressional modifications can be evaluated. Media discussions of whether particular proposals meet the deficit targets appear to score different proposals and may encourage frugality by both the president and the legislature. Gramlich (1990) argues that although his statistical analysis does not suggest a large direct effect of GRH, it may still be possible that GRH changed the terms of budget policy debate. In particular, GRH introduced the notion of "revenue-neutral" and "deficit-neutral" policies, thereby setting the ground rules for many of the tax and spending policy debates of the late 1980s and early 1990s. Provided it is not costless to manipulate reported budget numbers, policies that attach costs to failure to report particular deficit values will have real effects.

Second, in the case of GRH, the sequestration procedures through which cutbacks occur enable current legislators to shirk some responsibility for spending reductions, blaming the cuts on the Congress that enacted the budget targets. Although Congress and the president may opt to circumvent this process if the cuts are too painful, a sequester that is perceived as an equitable reduction in expenditures might be allowed to take effect. In any case, the threat of a painful sequester probably does provide some pressure for budget compromise. Developing theoretical positive political economy models that explain how power is allocated in budgetary deliberations is an important future research issue.

3.3 The Effect of Budget Institutions: U.S. State Evidence

Although the federal budget policy reforms of the past decade provide a potentially valuable source of information on how budget rules affect policy outcomes, it can be difficult to evaluate the evidence from a single episode of policy reform. To expand the base of variation in budget rules available for study, it is helpful to consider information from other jurisdictions or time periods. Data from the U.S. states provide one promising source of evidence on the impact of budget rules.

This section, which draws on Poterba (1995a), focuses on state balanced budget rules, most of which are substantially different from those being discussed at the federal level. In particular, virtually all states allow some types of borrowing to be used in budget balancing, most states apply the balanced budget rule to only part of their budget, and there are virtually no formal provisions for enforcing state balanced budget rules. Thus the states do not provide evidence on whether sequesters or other devices are particularly effective in reducing budget deficits. These limitations notwithstanding, evidence on the effect of state balanced budget institutions is relevant for the broader question of whether fiscal institutions can affect fiscal policy outcomes.

State Balanced Budget Rules

Most state constitutions preclude deficits in state operating budgets, but the nature and scope of these limits vary widely. Detailed summaries of state budget practices may be found in National Association of State Budget Officers (NASBO) (1992) and the U.S. General Accounting Office (1993). Only Vermont does not have a balanced budget requirement. The balanced budget requirements in the forty-nine states with such requirements can be broadly categorized into three groups, depending on the stage in the budget process at which balance is required.

First, in forty-four states, the governor must submit a balanced budget. This is the weakest of the various balanced budget requirements. Second, thirty-seven states impose a stricter standard, requiring that the legislature enact a balanced budget. These balanced budget rules nevertheless allow for actual revenues and expenditures to diverge from balance if realizations differ from expectations. In many states that require passage of a balanced budget, the actual budget may be in deficit, and the state can borrow to carry this deficit forward to future years.

The third and strictest type of balanced budget rule combines a requirement that the legislature enact a balanced budget with a prohibition on deficit carry-forward. This is the situation in twenty-four of the thirty-seven states that require the legislature to enact a balanced budget. Such stringent antideficit rules are more common in small than large states; seven of the ten largest states allow deficits to be carried forward to subsequent years.

An important difference between existing state balanced budget rules and recent proposals at the federal level is that state rules frequently apply to only part of the budget. The general fund, or state operating budget, is almost always subject to a balanced budget rule. In forty-eight of the forty-nine states classified by NASBO (1992) as having balanced budget rules, these rules apply to the general fund. Such rules are less likely to apply to special funds (thirty-four states), such as those with earmarked tax receipts or used to fund particular programs such as intergovernmental aid, capital spending funds (thirty-three states), and trust funds (thirty states) such as those for highways or some social insurance programs. In some cases, particularly with respect to the capital account, funds raised by issuing long-term debt can be included in the revenue flow that balances the budget.

There is substantial variation across states in the fraction of state spending that is likely to be affected by balanced budget rules. In the NASBO (1992) survey, three states reported that between 25 and 50 percent of their spending was affected by these rules, nine states reported that 50 to 75 percent of spending was affected, and the remaining states with balanced budget rules indicated that these rules applied to at least 75 percent of their state spending.

States that face budget deficits at some stage of their budget process have three options for closing such deficits: raise taxes, reduce spending, or change budget execution to close the apparent deficit. Some actions that fall in the last category might be labeled cosmetic budgetary changes, such as deferring payments across fiscal years or accelerating receipts. The General Accounting Office's (1985) study provides several examples of the changes that were used to satisfy budgetary targets in the early 1980s. California transferred oil extraction royalty tax revenues from a trust fund to the general fund; New York enacted a new payroll system to shift its last payroll payment from fiscal year 1983 into the next fiscal year; Minnesota accelerated tax collections to move receipts across fiscal years. The state experience suggests that although some cosmetic changes are used to meet balanced budget requirements, these changes are quantitatively less important than tax increases and spending cuts.

The GAO's (1993) survey of state budgeting collected information on the dollar value of various accounting changes that states used to meet balanced budget targets. Twenty-five states reported that they had faced prospective deficits during a recent budget enactment period and had taken actions to close these deficits. Nearly half (49 percent) of the deficit reduction was achieved through spending cuts, another 32 percent through revenue increases, and the remaining 19 percent through other actions, such as accounting changes. In addition, thirty-two states reported that they had faced prospective deficits after budget enactment and had taken actions to close these deficits. Spending cuts accounted for 60 percent of the within-fiscal-year deficit reduction, revenue increases 4 percent, and other actions accounted for 36 percent. These other actions included drawing down rainy-day funds (32 percent of the total deficit reduction), interfund transfers (22 percent), short-term borrowing (17 percent), and deferred payments (13 percent). Accounting changes and related actions thus appear to account for a substantial part of fiscal adjustment within the budget cycle, but they are not the primary source of longer-term state deficit reduction.

The GAO (1993) findings provide important support for the possibility that changing the definition of the budget deficit would affect real fiscal outcomes, at least when antideficit rules are in place. They suggest that states take actions to achieve a balanced budget, even in the absence of stringent enforcement provisions. Gold (1992) notes that most states have no formal enforcement mechanisms for their balanced budget requirements, and the GAO (1993) reports that there have never been lawsuits to challenge state budgeting outcomes, although there have been instances when budgets failed to balance. According to the GAO's (1985) survey, state policymakers appear to view tradition, or a history of balanced budgets, as the primary factor encouraging them to maintain budget balance. It is not clear how such experience can be translated to analyze the potential effects of federal antideficit rules.

Balanced Budget Rules, Taxation, and Expenditures

A number of research studies have considered the effects of balanced budget rules on the size and persistence of state budget deficits, and on state tax and expenditure levels more generally. A substantial literature, exemplified by Preston and Ichniowski (1991) and Dye and McGuire (1995), suggests that local property tax limitation laws have important effects on the level of local taxes. The evidence on state-level budget institutions is more limited.

Simple cross-sectional comparisons of state institutions and spending levels provide inconclusive evidence on the impact of such institutions on fiscal outcomes. Abrams and Dougan (1986) conclude that such limits do not have substantial effects. Other studies, such as Eichengreen's (1992) analysis of the effect of limits on state debt and spending and Crain and Miller's (1990) of how such limits affect spending growth rates rather than levels, do report that tax limits constrain government size or growth.

Two recent studies represent important advances in the analysis of tax and expenditure limits. Shadbegian (1996) estimates regression models for both the level and the growth rate of state government spending, as a function of both the presence of tax and expenditure limits and the interaction between these limits and the state's personal income growth rate. He finds that the interaction effect is particularly important, because many tax and expenditure limits are specified as a limit on state spending as a fraction of personal income. In states with slow income growth rates, limitation laws have had a more restrictive effect on government growth than in fast-growth states.

A second recent study, Rueben (1995), presents the most careful control to date for the endogeneity of fiscal institutions, and it therefore generates the most compelling evidence on how these institutions affect policy outcomes. Rueben uses both historical variation in state institutions and differences in the political process that may facilitate the passage of tax limits to model and attempt to correct for the endogeneity of budget rules. Her empirical findings show that although ordinary-least-squares regressions of spending levels on fiscal institutions lead to statistically insignificant findings, after the presence of these institutions is treated as endogenous, the explanatory power of the institutional variables rises markedly and the estimated effects become negative.

In addition to the substantial body of research on the impact of tax and expenditure limits on state or state and local government spending, several studies have considered the effect of antideficit rules, possibly in conjunction with limits on borrowing or other fiscal limits. Three recent empirical studies provide important support for the real effects associated with fiscal rules.

Alt and Lowry (1994) analyze data from the Census of Governments for the period 1968 through 1987. They model state revenue and expenditures as a function of current state income, current federal grants, lagged values of state revenue, state expenditures, the lagged difference between revenues and expenditures, and a set of indicator variables for state political circumstances. They compare fiscal policy reactions to disparities between revenues and expenditures, which can exist even in states with balanced budget requirements. They find that a one-dollar state "deficit" in the current year triggers a seventy-seven-cent response, through tax increase or spending reduction, for states that are Republican controlled and prohibit deficit carryovers, compared with a thirty-four-cent reaction in states that are Democrat controlled and have such limits. In states that do not restrict deficit carryovers, the adjustments are thirty-one cents and forty cents, respectively, for Republican and Democratic states. This empirical evidence suggests that state politics is an important influence on deficit reduction and that at least in some political configurations, variation in antideficit rules is associated with variation in fiscal actions.

Bohn and Inman (1995) explore the effect of fiscal institutions in a panel data set that includes information on forty-seven states for twenty-two years. They find that balanced budget rules that restrict end-of-year budget deficits have a statistically significant effect in reducing state general fund deficits, with an average deficit-reducing effect of approximately $100 per capita. "Soft" constraints on proposed budgets do not affect deficits. The deficit reduction in states with tight antideficit rules appears to result from lower levels of spending, not higher taxes, in these states.

Poterba (1994b) presents evidence on how state balanced budget rules affect the way state fiscal policies respond to unexpected deficits or surpluses. This study considers both within-fiscal-year adjustment, through spending cuts or tax increases, and adjustment in the next fiscal year. It focuses on how an indicator variable for states with "weak antideficit rules," as classified in the Advisory Council on Intergovernmental Relations (ACIR) (1987) study on fiscal stringency, is related to state reactions to fiscal shocks. The results, based on the twenty-seven continental states with annual budget cycles, suggest that states with weak antideficit rules adjust spending less in response to unexpected deficits than do their counterparts with strict antideficit rules. A $100 deficit overrun leads to only a $17 expenditure cut in a state with a weak antideficit law and to a $44 cut in other states. There is no evidence that antideficit rules affect the magnitude of tax changes in the aftermath of an unexpected deficit.

The cumulative evidence from these three studies, using different time periods and data samples, suggests that budget rules do affect deficit policies. These studies do not provide much guidance on the long-term issue of whether tighter antideficit rules reduce spending or taxes but, rather, emphasize the high-frequency effect of fiscal institutions on the conduct of fiscal policy.

Balanced Budget Rules and State Borrowing

In addition to the evidence on how balanced budget rules affect tax and spending policies, there is also some evidence on how these rules, and related debt limitation laws, affect the level of state indebtedness. Von Hagen (1991) compares the level of state general obligation debt, per capita and relative to state income, in states with and without stringent balanced budget requirements. His findings suggest that general obligation indebtedness is substantially lower in states with stringent balanced budget amendments than in other states. He also explores the effect of stringent balanced budget rules on the ratio of non–full faith and credit to full faith and credit debt across states. States with more stringent deficit limits, as well as states with lower general obligation debt limits, exhibit higher levels of revenue debt and other debt that is not backed by the full faith and credit of the state. These results are consistent with Bunch's (1991) demonstration that states with tighter debt limits or balanced budget rules are more likely to use public authorities and other alternatives to state-backed borrowing to finance various projects.

Kiewiet and Szakaly (1996) present a related analysis of the real effects of antideficit rules and related limits on state borrowing. They study whether state constitutional debt limits have any effect on total state indebtedness or on the composition of this debt. The only institution that the authors find to be highly negatively correlated with state indebtedness is a requirement that state debt be approved by popular referendum. This suggests that a combination of a stringent antideficit rule and a requirement that debt be approved by the voters is likely to bring pressure for tax increases or spending cuts, rather than debt finance, in response to state deficits. This evidence is also consistent with the findings reported above on the effect of tax limitation laws. Constitutional or legislative provisions that make it more costly to balance the budget in a given fashion, by raising taxes or by issuing long-term debt, appear to have real effects in discouraging these fiscal actions.

Most research on the real effects of budget rules has focused on how these rules affect deficits or the level of taxation and spending. An intriguing alternative perspective on these rules is developed in Goldstein and Woglom (1992), Bayoumi and Woglom (1995), and Lowry and Alt (1995). These studies focus on the interest rates at which states can borrow funds and how these borrowing rates are related to fiscal rules. Goldstein and Woglom relate the interest rate on general obligation debt to the ACIR index of state limits on deficits. Their results, which also control for the level of state indebtedness and the observed state deficit, suggest that a state with the most restrictive set of fiscal limits faces an interest rate 0.05 percentage points lower than a state with an average set of limits.

Lowry and Alt show that the bond market reaction to a state deficit projection depends on whether the state has a balanced budget requirement. States with these rules experience smaller increases in their borrowing costs for a given deficit. These results are a first step toward a normative analysis of whether states benefit from adopting antideficit rules. They are important in the current context because they suggest that capital market participants, who have strong incentives to monitor and evaluate state fiscal performance, consider the presence of antideficit rules in evaluating state fiscal conditions.

These finding on budget rules and borrowing behavior provide important confirmation for the earlier results on how budget rules affect reported deficits. The substantial empirical literature on state budgeting and fiscal policy provides clear support for the view that budget rules matter, and for the idea that changing the rules that govern the taxation and expenditure process can alter the outcomes of this process.

What Can Be Learned from State Experience?

One key question that arises in evaluating the state experience with antideficit rules and tax limitation laws concerns the difference in fiscal equilibrium processes between states and national governments. Voters can move between states and other subfederal jurisdictions; this may limit the fiscal behavior of states but not national governments. Consider, for example, the consequences of a state choosing to transfer funds from its pension account to the current account, thereby balancing the current budget at the expense of future fiscal balance. If residents and potential residents recognize the future tax liability associated with such a transaction and if future taxes are lump-sum levies on landowners, then the price of land in the state should decline to offset exactly the future tax burden. Such capitalization effects are not likely to operate at the federal level.

There are also important differences in the constraints that ultimately affect state and federal policymakers in the United States. Because the federal government, but not the states, can resort to printing money as a means of financing a deficit, states may face tighter limits on fiscal actions. States may also differ from the federal government in their degree of access to credit markets. As the New York City fiscal crisis of 1975 and some of Philadelphia's fiscal difficulties of the early 1990s demonstrate, subfederal borrowers can be denied access to credit. Such credit market factors may discipline state policymakers but not impose the same restraints on federal decision makers.

Another potential difference between states and the federal government concerns information. In Washington, numerous watchdog groups provide commentary and analysis on budget proposals and outcomes, often drawing on quite sophisticated analytical frameworks. There is less external oversight in many state capitals. The role of the federal budget document in describing federal fiscal policy may therefore be less central than the analogous role of budget documents in the states. Whether this limits the application of state-level findings in federal policy discussions is an open issue.

3.4 The Effect of Budget Institutions: International Evidence

Cross-sectional comparison of state budget outcomes and budget rules is one way of exploiting jurisdictional variation in budget institutions; international comparisons of the same type represent another research opportunity. A number of studies have pursued this research direction and found effects of fiscal institutions as well as related variables that describe political circumstances. Although this research is more likely than cross-state analysis to be affected by omitted variables that are correlated with both fiscal tastes and budget institutions, it is nevertheless valuable to summarize the primary findings.

The differences in budget processes across countries are much greater than those between states within the United States or between the United States in 1984 and 1988. It is therefore necessary to develop a typology for categorizing budget rules. The two aspects of budget process that have proved most important in previous analyses are the degree of centralization of authority in the budget process, and the degree of budget transparency. With respect to centralization, at one extreme are authoritarian institutions, which centralize power in the hands of a treasury minister or another small group of decision makers. At the other extreme are collegial institutions, which disperse power and require substantial consensus at one or several stages of the budget enactment process. Alesina and Perotti (1996) discuss institutions along this spectrum, and von Hagen (1992) provides summary information on the budget process in European Community nations.

Budget transparency is more difficult to categorize. There are important differences in the way budgets are prepared, debated, and ultimately approved by the legislature indifferent nations. Von Hagen (1992) interviewed policymakers involved in the budget process in a range of European nations, and he constructed indexes of transparency based on the number and significance of "special accounts" in the budget, whether all budget information was presented in a single document, and related measures. On the basis of these responses and other information on the nature of the budget process, he constructed indexes of government budget rules. The Organization for Economic Cooperation and Development (1995) provides a more recent survey of detailed budgetary practices in a sample of developed nations, but this report does not distill the information to summary statistics that can be used for standardized international comparisons.

Von Hagen's (1992) indexes of budget stringency are extremely valuable for studying international differences in budget outcomes, but they must be viewed with some caution. Essentially these indexes are constructed by adding together a set of categorical variables, thus implicitly assuming that various indicators for the restrictiveness of the budget process operate as perfect substitutes. A country with a weak prime minister, and hence a low score on one dimension of budget practice, can nevertheless achieve the same score on the budget process index as another nation with a strong prime minister if the weak-minister nation has fewer special accounts in the budget process. Ideally one would like to distinguish separate effects for various budget rules, but this may be impossible in analysis of data from a small set of countries with little intertemporal variation in budget rules.

Von Hagen and Harden (1995) use these indexes of budget process to estimate simple cross-sectional regression models relating budget structure to fiscal outcomes such as the debt-to-GDP and deficit-to-GDP ratios. The results suggest that tighter budget rules are associated with lower budget deficits and reduced levels of government borrowing. The authors also note some regularities about the countries that have modified their budget process in an effort to reduce fiscal deficits. Procedural reforms, as opposed to budget target reforms, have succeeded in all of the large European Union nations that have successfully reduced budget deficits in recent years (France, Britain, and Germany). This finding bolsters the tentative U.S. evidence suggesting that the Budget Enforcement Act of 1990 may have a greater effect on fiscal policy outcomes than GRH did.

Subsequent studies have confirmed the presence of fiscal effects correlated with budget structure. Alesina and Perotti (1995), in related empirical work, find that coalition governments are much less likely to pursue tight fiscal policies, or successful "fiscal adjustments," than are single-party governments. This evidence supports the key role of strong decision making in promoting fiscal restraint and may be extrapolated to suggest that strengthening the role of a central player in any budget negotiation can impose discipline on the fiscal policy process.

One of the most intriguing empirical studies to date is Alesina et al.'s (1995) analysis of budget rules and fiscal outcomes in a sample of Latin American economies. This study develops separate indexes for the presence of constitutional constraints on borrowing, for the importance of the finance minister or other key participant in the budget process, and for the relative power of the legislature and the executive in budget deliberations. The empirical results suggest that stronger finance ministers are systematically correlated with smaller primary deficits. This research also suggests an important effect for the relative power of the legislature and the executive: a more powerful executive leads to smaller primary deficits.

None of the foregoing studies addresses the problem of institutional endogeneity, which raises some questions about the interpretation of their findings. One important subject for future analysis should be the careful modeling of the origin of budget institutions in an international context.

3.5 Conclusions

What conclusions, if any, can we draw from the existing literature on budget institutions and fiscal policy outcomes? First, fiscal institutions do matter. Although the evidence is not conclusive, the preponderance of studies suggests that institutions are not simply veils pierced by voters but are important constraints on the nature of political bargaining. Studies of the demand for public spending, by state and local governments or by nations, should recognize that this demand is mediated through a set of fiscal and budgeting rules. The evidence from empirical studies of fiscal institutions and budget outcomes suggests that tightly drawn antideficit rules, especially when coupled with limits on government borrowing, induce smaller deficits and more rapid adjustment of taxes and spending to unexpected fiscal shortfalls. It is not unreasonable to interpret this evidence as suggesting that modifying the federal budget process could affect federal fiscal policy.

Yet in spite of this emerging body of empirical evidence, much remains to be learned about budget processes and budget outcomes. Two central issues have not yet been resolved and require further research attention. First, there is no agreement on the underlying politicoeconomic model that should be used to predict the effect of changes in fiscal institutions. There are both basic and applied issues unresolved in this vein. For example, to what degree are legislative bodies organized to facilitate log-rolling and other types of coalition formation? How should one model the conflict between an executive with ostensible commitment to the interests of the nation, and legislators whose interests lead them to support projects that benefit their own districts? How important are information flows between various actors in the budget process, and is information or the power to threaten painful cuts in programs the more important mechanism for changing the budget process?

Political scientists and economists have proposed various models of how legislative bodies such as the Congress operate (Weingast and Marshall 1988), but the models have not yet reached a degree of sophistication that permits strong answers to detailed questions. Budget rules that restrict the discretion of budget actors, by either constraining current actors to achieve budget targets that were enacted in the past or limiting the ability of individual committees within Congress to control their appropriations, entail a trade-off. They may promote desirable aggregate budget objectives, but at the cost of reducing the amount of information that can be brought to bear on particular budget decisions. Models of information flows in legislatures, and the effects of changing such flows, therefore seem potentially relevant in assessing fiscal limit laws.

While empirical research has explored the correlations between some rather specific aspects of budget policy and observed spending outcomes, with examples being Holtz-Eakin's (1988) study of state line item veto provisions or my own (1995b) study of capital budgeting rules, there is little theory to guide the empirical researcher in choosing covariates or control variables in such models. Given the tremendous interest in political economy models and deficit issues in the past decade, however, and the progress during this period, it is not unrealistic to expect future progress on this front.

Second, the existing body of empirical research has not been very successful at disentangling the components of various budget policies. For example, is the sequester provision or the change in the timing of the budget functions more important in the 1986 GRH legislation? Which feature of the various budget institutions that are considered in cross-country studies like von Hagen's (1992) analysis is the most important for influencing fiscal policy? This is a problem that may prove very difficult to solve, because there is little distinct variation in budget rules across jurisdictions. It is virtually impossible to distinguish the effect of a number of particular budget rules in the U.S. states because the set of states with one institution but not another is often very small.

The absence of information on detailed budget rules is an important limitation for advising policymakers, because actual debates hinge on precise rules. The existing literature cannot provide very helpful answers to questions such as how a balance-budget rule should be enforced or how high a supermajority requirement one needs to impose on passing revenue bills in order to hold down the growth of taxes.

Yet these shortcomings of the existing research should not detract from the substantial agreement that modifying the budget process can affect fiscal policy outcomes. The literature to date suggests that reforms that centralize power in a small set of budget actors, increase the transparency of the budget process, and make it more difficult to issue long-term debt are likely to reduce the level of government spending. Policies that are designed to reduce deficits in the U.S. states do appear to rein in the practice of rolling over short-term debt and thereby using deficit finance. Although these findings cannot be carried over completely to analyzing the case of federal budget policy in the United States, they create a presumption that altering the budget process can affect budget outcomes.

Acknowledgments

I am grateful to Alan Auerbach, Doug Bernheim, David Cutler, Robert Reischauer, and David Romer for helpful comments and discussions and to the National Science Foundation for research support.

References

Abrams, B. A., and W. R. Dougan. 1986. "The Effects of Constitutional Restraints on Government Spending." *Public Choice* 49:101–116.

Advisory Council on Intergovernmental Relations. 1987. *Fiscal Discipline in the Federal System: National Reform and the Experience of the States*. Washington, DC: Advisory Council on Intergovernmental Relations.

Alesina, Alberto, and Roberto Perotti. 1996, May. *Budget Deficits and Budget Institutions*. NBER Working Paper 5556.

Alesina, Alberto, Ricardo Hausmann, Rudolf Hommes, and Ernesto Stein. 1995. "Budget Institutions and Fiscal Performance in Latin America." Mimeo. International Development Bank.

Alesina, Alberto, and Roberto Perotti. 1995, October. "Fiscal Adjustment: Fiscal Expansions and Fiscal Adjustments in OECD Countries." *Economic Policy* 21:207–240.

Alt, James E., and Robert C. Lowry. 1994. "Divided Government, Fiscal Institutions, and Budget Deficits: Evidence from the States." *American Political Science Review* 88:811–828.

Auerbach, Alan J. 1994. "The U.S. Fiscal Problem: Where We Are, How We Got Here, and Where We Are Going." In S. Fischer and J. Rotemberg, eds., *NBER Macroeconomics Annual, vol. 9.* Cambridge, MA: MIT Press.

Auerbach, Alan J. 1995. "Budget Deficits and Debt: Solutions for Developed Economics." In Federal Reserve Bank of Kansas City, *Budget Deficits and Debt: Issues and Options*. Kansas City: Federal Reserve Bank of Kansas City.

Auerbach, Alan J., Jegadeesh Gokhale, and Laurence Kotlikoff. 1991. "Generational Accounts: A Meaningful Alternative to Deficit Accounting." In D. Bradford, ed., *Tax Policy and the Economy, vol. 5.* Cambridge, MA: MIT Press.

Bayoumi, Tamim, and Geoffrey Woglom. 1995. "Do Credit Markets Discipline Sovereign Borrowers: Evidence from U.S. States." *Journal of Money Credit and Banking* 27:1046–1059.

Barro, Robert. 1979. "On the Determination of the Public Debt." *Journal of Political Economy* 87:940–971.

Bohn, Henning, and Robert P. Inman. 1995, December. *Constitutional Limits and Public Deficits: Evidence from the U.S. States.* Carnegie-Rochester Conference Series on Public Policy.

Buchanan, James, and R. Wagner. 1977. *Democracy in Deficit*. New York: Academic Press.

Bunch, Beverly S. 1991. "The Effect of Constitutional Debt Limits on State Governments' Use of Public Authorities." *Public Choice* 68:57–69.

Colm, G., and P. Wagner. 1963. "Some Observations on the Budget Concept." *Review of Economics and Statistics* 45:122–126.

Crain, W. Mark, and James C. Miller III. 1990. "Budget Process and Spending Growth." *William and Mary Law Review* 31:1021–1046.

Dye, Richard F., and Therese J. McGuire. 1995. "The Effect of Property Tax Limitation Measures on Local Government Fiscal Behavior." Mimeo University of Illinois, Institute of Government and Public Affairs.

Eichengreen, Barry J. 1992. *Should the Maastrict Treaty Be Saved?* International Finance Section Working Paper 74. Princeton: Princeton University.

Ferejohn, John, and Keith Krehbiel. 1987. "The Budget Process and the Size of the Budget." *American Journal of Political Science* 31:296–320.

Gold, Steven D. 1992, May 13. "State Government Experience with Balanced Budget Requirements: Relevance to Federal Proposals." In U.S. House of Representatives, Committee on the Budget, *The Balanced Budget Amendment*, Washington, DC: U.S. Government Printing Office. 2:202–210.

Goldstein, Morris, and Geoffrey Woglom. 1992. "Market-Based Fiscal Discipline in Monetary Unions: Evidence from the U.S. Municipal Bond Market." In M. B. Canzoneri, V. Grilli, and P. R. Masson, eds., *Establishing a Central Bank: Issues in Europe and Lessons from the United States*. Cambridge: Cambridge University Press.

Gramlich, Edward M. 1990. "U.S. Federal Budget Deficits and Gramm-Rudman-Hollings." *American Economic Review* 80:75–80.

Hahm, Sung D., Mark S. Kamlet, David C. Mowery, and Tsai-Tsu Su. 1992. "The Influence of the Gramm-Rudman-Hollings Act on Federal Budgetary Outcomes, 1986–1989." *Journal of Policy Analysis and Management* 11:207–234.

Holtz-Eakin, Douglas. 1988. "The Line Item Veto and Public Sector Budgets: Evidence from the States." *Journal of Public Economics* 36:269–292.

Kiewiet, D. Roderick, and Kristin Szakaly. 1996. "The Efficacy of Constitutional Restrictions on Borrowing, Taxing, and Spending: An Analysis of State Bonded Indebtedness, 1961–90." *Journal of Law, Economics, and Organization* 12:62–97.

Kotlikoff, Laurence J. 1986. "Deficit Delusion." *Public Interest* 84:53–65.

Laibson, David. 1994. "Self-Control and Saving." Mimeo. Harvard University, Department of Economics.

Lowry, Robert C., and James E. Alt. 1995. "A Visible Hand? Intertemporal Efficiency, Costly Information, and Market-Based Enforcement of Balanced Budget Laws." Mimeo. Harvard University, Department of Government.

Masia, Neal. 1995. "Essays on the Political Economy of Government Spending." Ph.D. diss. University of Rochester, Department of Economics. Washington, DC: Congressional Budget Office.

Musgrave, Richard A. 1939. "The Nature of Budgetary Balance and the Case for the Capital Budget." *American Economic Review* 29:260–271.

National Association of State Budget Officers. 1992. *State Balanced Budget Requirements: Provisions and Practice*. Washington, DC: National Association of State Budget Officers.

Organization for Economic Cooperation and Development. 1995. *Budgeting for Results: Perspectives on Public Expenditure Management*. Paris: OECD.

Posen, Adam S. 1995. "Declarations Are Not Enough: Financial Sector Sources of Central Bank Independence." In B. Bernanke and J. Rotemberg, eds., *NBER Macroeconomics Annual 1995*. Cambridge: MIT Press.

Poterba, James M. 1994a. "American Fiscal Policy in the 1980s." In M. Feldstein, ed., *American Economic Policy in the 1980s*. Chicago: University of Chicago Press.

Poterba, James M. 1994b. "State Responses to Fiscal Crises: The Effects of Budgetary Institutions and Politics." *Journal of Political Economy* 102:799–821.

Poterba, James M. 1995a. "Balanced Budget Rules and Fiscal Policy: Evidence from the States." *National Tax Journal* 48:329–337.

Poterba, James M. 1995b. "Capital Budgets, Borrowing Rules, and State Capital Spending." *Journal of Public Economics* 56:165–187.

President's Commission on Budget Concepts. 1967. *Report of the President's Commission on Budget Concepts*. Washington, DC: U.S. Government Printing Office.

Preston, Anne E., and Casey Ichniowski. 1991. "A National Perspective on the Nature and Effects of the Local Property Tax Revolt, 1976–1986." *National Tax Journal* 44:123–146.

Reischauer, Robert D. 1990. "Taxes and Spending Under Gramm-Rudman-Hollings." *National Tax Journal* 43:223–232.

Riker, William. 1980. "Implications for the Disequilibrium of Majority Rule for the Study of Institutions." *American Political Science Review* 74:432–446.

Roubini, Nouriel, and Jeffrey Sachs. 1989. "Government Spending and Budget Deficits in the Industrialized Countries." *Economic Policy* 8:99–132.

Rueben, Kim S. 1995. "Tax Limitations and Government Growth: The Effect of State Tax and Expenditure Limits on State and Local Government." Mimeo. MIT, Department of Economics.

Shadbegian, Ronald J. 1996. "Do Tax and Expenditure Limitations Affect the Size and Growth of State Government?" *Contemporary Economic Policy* 14:22–35.

Skidmore, Mark, and James Alm. 1994. "Voting on Tax and Expenditure Limitations." Mimeo. Northern Illinois University, Department of Economics.

U.S. General Accounting Office. 1985. *Budget Issues: State Balanced Budget Practices*. GAO/AFMD-86-22BR. Washington, DC: General Accounting Office.

U.S. General Accounting Office. 1993. *Balanced Budget Requirements: State Experiences and Implications for the Federal Government*. GAO/AFMD-93-58BR. Washington, DC: General Accounting Office.

von Hagen, Jurgen. 1991. "A Note on the Empirical Effectiveness of Formal Fiscal Restraints." *Journal of Public Economics* 44:199–210.

von Hagen, Jurgen. 1992. *Budgeting Procedures and Fiscal Performance in the European Communities*. Economic Paper 96. Commission of the European Communities DG for Economic and Financial Affairs.

von Hagen, Jurgen, and Ian J. Harden. 1995. "Budget Processes and Commitment to Fiscal Discipline." *European Economic Review* 39:771–779.

Weingast, Barry R., and William J. Marshall. 1988. "The Industrial Organization of Congress: or Why Legislatures, Like Firms, Are Not Organized As Markets." *Journal of Political Economy* 96:132–163.

Weingast, Barry R., Kenneth Shepsle, and C. Johnsen. 1981. "The Political Economy of Benefits and Costs: A Neoclassical Approach to Distributive Politics." *Journal of Political Economy* 89:642–664.

Comment

Robert D. Reischauer

"Do Budget Rules Work?" presents a balanced and useful summary of the evidence concerning the extent to which institutional restraints affect fiscal policy outcomes. James Poterba's conclusion that such restraints do make some difference is reassuring considering the tremendous amount of effort that has gone into changing federal budgetary institution over the past quarter of a century. The fruits of this effort have been embodied in the Congressional Budget and Impoundment Control Act of 1974 (CBA), the Balanced Budget and Emergency Deficit Control Act of 1985 (GRH-I), the Balanced Budget and Emergency Deficit Control Reaffirmation Act of 1987 (GRH-II), the Budget Enforcement Act of 1990 (BEA), and the Federal Credit Reform Act of 1990 (CRA).

From the standpoint of procedure, the changes brought about by these laws have been sweeping; the federal budget process has been restructured so profoundly since 1973 that a participant from the pre-1974 era would not recognize much of what is routine practice now. Whether these institutional changes have altered fiscal outcomes significantly, modestly, marginally, or not at all, however, is another question, which will be debated and analyzed for years to come. Certainly the gap between fiscal promises and aspirations on the one hand and fiscal results on the other remains as great as, if not greater than, ever and this is deeply unsettling to many. Those who are most disturbed by this gap feel that the political system contains such a strong bias toward a fiscal profligacy that is not reflective of the underlying preferences of the citizenry that even more radical institutional changes are needed. At the top of the list of these radical changes is the constitutional amendment requiring that the federal budget be balanced except during wars or when deficits are approved by supermajorities of both chambers of the Congress. There are also proposals to limit the growth of overall spending to the growth of the economy or the increase in the price level, to require that supermajorities approve any increases in taxes, to allow taxpayers to designate up to 10 percent of their tax payments to reduce the federal debt, and to cap the spending on some or all entitlement programs. If policymakers do not succeed in their effort to reduce the deficit substantially over the next few years, one or more of these more radical institutional changes will probably be adopted.

As Poterba correctly emphasizes, it is extremely difficult to measure even crudely the impact of budget institutions and rules on fiscal policy outcomes. One core problem is that of endogeneity. Are, as some have argued, budget rules and institutions no more than a reflection of the underlying or congealed fiscal preferences of the voters? If that is the case, fiscal institutions might be irrelevant to fiscal outcomes. It is impossible to resolve this question without conducting a controlled experiment, which is, of course, impossible. One reason that the issue is unresolvable relates to the formation of fiscal policy preferences. Unlike more basic issue areas such as family, food, shelter, or transportation, fiscal policy is an abstract concept to most citizens, who have no independent or experiential way of gaining fiscal policy knowledge. It is likely that fiscal policy preferences are shaped by the way budget information, issues, and decisions are presented to the public. But the way information is presented and issues are framed, in turn, are determined by a nation's budget rules and institutions.

No doubt the discussions that the public and policymakers would be having today would be quite different if our federal budget rules had focused on measures of standardized employment outlays and revenues, the primary deficit, or the operating budget excluding investment activities. Similarly, the debate would be quite different if the pension systems for government workers and the social security system had been run for the past sixty years by quasi-governmental corporations whose accounts were isolated from the normal budget process.

A second problem that arises in trying to estimate the independent impact that changes in rules and institutions have on the fiscal policy outcomes of a single jurisdiction is the issue of selecting the appropriate counterfactual against which the impact should be measured. One can not simply compare measures of fiscal outcomes before and after a change in budget regimes unless one is certain that the structural underpinnings of the fiscal system have not shifted. This has not been the case over the course of the last quarter of a century in the United States.

Deficits as a percentage of GDP rose fairly steadily from the mid-1950s through the 1980s (see the table shown here). Poterba's brief discussion of this trend points to two possible explanations for the fiscal deterioration,

Table 3C.1
Standardized employment and actual surplus, fiscal years 1955 to 1995

	Standardized employment surplus as a percentage of potential GDP		Actual surplus as a percentage of GDP	
Year	Annual	5-year average	Annual	5-year average
1955	−0.8		−0.8	
1956	−0.2		0.9	
1957	−0.1		0.8	
1958	−0.2		−0.6	
1959	−2.4	−0.7	−2.7	−0.5
1960	0.0		0.1	
1961	0.4		−0.6	
1962	−1.0		−1.3	
1963	−0.6		−0.8	
1964	−1.3	−0.5	−0.9	−0.7
1965	−1.0		−0.2	
1966	−2.3		−0.5	
1967	−2.7		−1.1	
1968	−4.3		−2.9	
1969	−1.2	−2.3	0.3	−0.9
1970	−0.9		−0.3	
1971	−2.0		−2.1	
1972	−2.1		−2.0	
1973	−2.3		−1.1	
1974	−1.3	−1.7	−0.4	−1.2
1975	−2.2		−3.4	
1976	−3.0		−4.3	
1977	−2.3		−2.7	
1978	−2.9		−2.7	
1979	−2.1	−2.5	−1.6	−3.0
1980	−2.1		−2.7	
1981	−1.7		−2.6	
1982	−1.9		−4.0	
1983	−3.4		−6.1	
1984	−4.1	−2.6	−4.9	−4.1
1985	−4.8		−5.2	
1986	−4.7		−5.1	
1987	−2.8		−3.2	
1988	−3.0		−3.1	
1989	−2.8	−3.6	−2.8	−3.9
1990	−2.9		−3.9	

Table (*cont.*)
Standardized employment and actual surplus, fiscal years 1955 to 1995

	Standardized employment surplus as a percentage of potential GDP		Actual surplus as a percentage of GDP	
Year	Annual	5-year average	Annual	5-year average
1991	−3.1		−4.6	
1992	−3.5		−4.7	
1993	−3.5		−3.9	
1994	−2.8		−3.0	
1995	−2.7	−3.1*	−2.3	−3.7*

Source: Congressional Budget Office, *The Economic and Budget Outlook: Fiscal Years 1997–2006*. Table E-1, May 1996, page 133.
*6-year average

both of which reflect a political system losing its fiscal self-control. One was the reforms that democratized Congress in the late 1960s and early 1970s. These reforms undercut the power of the leadership and the fiscally conservative barons who controlled the committees responsible for appropriations and taxes. The second explanation for the increase in the deficit is the policy excesses—the tax cuts and defense buildup—of the early 1980s.

But part, possibly the bulk, of the explanation for the increase in the size of deficits during the 1970s and 1980s lies in several unanticipated changes in underlying structural conditions over which policymakers exercised little direct control. One of these was the slowdown in economic growth. During the period from the end of World War II through 1973, real per capita growth averaged 2.5 percent a year; since then, growth has averaged 1.5 percent per year. The program and tax structures that seemed to be sustainable when the economy was growing rapidly proved to be unsustainable when growth slowed. With the confusion caused by two oil price shocks, the deep recessions of 1974–1975 and 1981–1982, and the high inflation of this period, it took political leaders some time to realize and then accept that the nation had entered a new era of slower growth, one that required a more parsimonious fiscal posture.

Another piece of the explanation for the increasing deficits lies in the commitment the government made in 1965 to finance health insurance for the elderly, disabled, and poor through the Medicare and Medicaid programs. This commitment turned out to be much more expensive than policymakers anticipated at the time because of the revolution in medical technology. But as costs exploded, policymakers found it difficult to scale back their promises. They were not alone. Employers were also caught off guard and were slow to respond to the surge in health care costs by cutting back their health insurance commitments to their employees.

A third piece of the story can be found in the cyclical performance of the economy. The average gap between actual and potential output increased over the period in question. According to CBO estimates (December 1995), the economy operated at or above its potential in twelve of the twenty fiscal years between 1955 and 1974 and nine of the eleven fiscal years in the 1964 to 1974 period (see table 3C.1). That has been the case in only four of the twenty-two fiscal years since 1974. The economy's strong performance between 1955 and 1974 probably gave policymakers an unrealistic impression of the program spending that was sustainable over the long run. It certainly masked the sharp deterioration in the standardized employment deficit that took place during the second half of the 1960s (see the table in this Comment). The comparatively poor performance of the economy during the following two decades not only brought the reality that the spending programs were unsustainable to light but also added to the debt service burden. Possibly one-fifth of the increase in debt service costs, which rose from 1.5 percent of GDP in fiscal 1974 to 3.3 percent of GDP in fiscal 1995, can be pinned on the economy's cyclical failings.

Clearly, significant, unanticipated, and poorly understood changes took place in the structural conditions that underlay the nation's fiscal system during the past twenty-five years. Even larger deficits were not just the result of a political system that was beginning to lose its sense of fiscal self-discipline. More likely than not, deficits would have begun to increase even if the political power structure that controlled fiscal policy during the two decades immediately after World War II had not begun to crumble. The underlying structural challenge would have been too much for even its parsimonious instincts to contend with. Moreover, it is highly likely that the deficit situation would have been significantly worse had Congress and the president been forced to operate under the pre-1974 budget rules and institutions during the past two decades. In short, the fact that the CBA, GRH-I, GRH-II, and BEA procedures did not produce declining deficits does not mean that these institutional changes did not reduce deficits significantly from where they would have been had the budget rules not changed.

But this is not to say that all of the major procedural reforms of the past twenty-five years have been effective at holding down the deficit. Some did not have that as an objective. For example, the CBA was intended to organize and rationalize Congress's work on the budget and increase the legislative branch's budget power relative to that of the executive. It was not designed to curb spending or reduce deficits. Nevertheless, the CBA may have had some impact in that direction because it established debating and decision-making frameworks that focused congressional attention on the deficit and required Congress in its budget resolution to vote on a deficit number for the first time. The multiyear perspective of the CBA also might have acted to curb deficits because it revealed the future budgetary implications of current decisions.

The GRH and BEA procedures, by way of contrast, were explicitly intended to reduce deficits. The former were widely regarded to be a failure, while the latter procedures are generally judged to be a significant success. A comparison of the two provides some insight into elements that may contribute to the success or failure of budget rules at the federal level.

GRH had six major deficiencies. First, it was little more than a promise to do something in the future backed up by a sanction system that lacked credibility. It represented an agreement about future fiscal outcomes, not an agreement over how those outcomes could or should be achieved. It did not specify how much taxes should be raised, the growth of mandatory programs curbed, or discretionary programs cut. But the problem policymakers faced was never that of getting the political system to agree on the desirability of reducing the deficit. Rather, it was that of obtaining agreement on how the deficit reduction should be accomplished.

Second, GRH had a very short time horizon, and this made it possible to postpone and evade the required fiscal discipline. The focus of GRH was on the budget year alone. Rosy economic and technical assumptions and gimmicks could be used to put the heavy lifting off to a future year.

A third deficiency of GRH was that when these evasive mechanisms had been exhausted and were no longer capable of delaying the required discipline, the size of the sanctions—the across-the-board cuts called sequestration—was so large as to be viewed as noncredible. The extreme example was the October 1990 sequestration order that preceded the budget agreement between President Bush and the Democrats in Congress. This order called for affected defense accounts to be cut by 34.5 percent across the board and nondefense accounts to be reduced by 31.6

percent. Cuts of these magnitudes would have had disastrous impacts on programs, people, and the economy, and so none of the participants in the budget process had any illusion that they would be imposed.

A fourth deficiency was that GRH provided no incentives for policy-makers to act responsible. Quite the reverse was the case. A large fraction of the budget was either protected completely or in large measure from the sanction mechanism. Savings from some of these favored programs, however, might have been logical components of a consensus deficit reduction package. Medicare, veterans' programs, and means-tested entitlement programs would be included on such a list. By derailing responsible efforts to pass a package of explicit program cuts and tax increases, advocates of these programs could guarantee that their favored programs would not be at risk even if the deficit were reduced.

Similarly, a committee that acted responsibly by expeditiously reporting out measures fulfilling the reconciliation instructions that called for cuts in programs under its jurisdiction ran a risk of having its programs hit twice. This could occur if other committees failed to produce their part of the overall deficit reduction package while the element reported by the responsible committee became law. In such a case, sequestration would be meted out to cover the remaining shortfall, and no credit would be given for spending cuts that had already been enacted. The result of this disincentive was that no committee wanted to act on its deficit reduction orders until it was sure all other committees would fulfill their orders. In short, nothing happened.

A fifth shortcoming of GRH was the widespread view that it was unfair because it held the political system accountable for forces over which it exercised no control. The targets were set as fixed levels of the deficit, not amounts of required deficit reduction. Although the level of the deficit is primarily the result of policy decisions, the strength of the economy, the weather, and external shocks also affect spending and revenues, and therefore the deficit. Under GRH, Congress could have enacted sufficient tax increases and spending cuts by July to reach the GRH deficit target for the upcoming year, only to be faced with a sequestration in October after good weather produced bumper harvests that caused CCC payments to explode and the deficit to rise.

GRH was also viewed as unfair because it concentrated the sanctions on a part of the budget, discretionary spending, that was not the source of the problem. Well over four-fifths of the across-the-board sequestration cuts were directed at discretionary accounts, which constituted only 44 percent of the spending side of the budget. Furthermore, spending on discretionary programs was a shrinking portion of the budget. Mandatory programs where the spending growth was concentrated were largely protected from sequestration, and revenues were asked to play no role.

A final deficiency with GRH was that it provided relatively little in the way of flexibility or wiggle room. Besides the $10 billion margin of error that was added in GRH-II, the GRH procedures constituted a rigid system attempting to impose discipline on a very fluid world.

The approach embodied in the BEA differs from that of GRH in three important respects that explain the BEA's relative success. First, it has a retrospective focus, at least in the areas of taxes and mandatory spending. It is designed to enforce deficit reduction that has already been enacted, not to require new actions. The PAYGO restraint is intended to prevent the Congress and president from backsliding by liberalizing mandatory spending programs or cutting taxes without paying for these actions. In the discretionary spending area, the budget authority and outlay caps represent a promise that future actions will be taken to curb spending. In this respect, it is similar to the GRH procedures, but the annual bites required by the BEA are of a more digestible size and are more specified than those required under GRH. During the first three years of the BEA, the promises were well defined in that separate caps were imposed for defense, international, and domestic discretionary spending.

Although Congress has complied with the discretionary caps for six years, the task was made relatively easy by the collapse of the Soviet Union. Between 1990 and 1995 all of the aggregate restraint was contributed by defense spending, which fell from 5.3 to 3.8 percent of GDP. Nondefense (domestic plus international) discretionary spending grew from 3.5 percent to 3.8 percent of GDP over this period. During the past two years, domestic discretionary spending has edged down a bit, but whether the political system can deliver the substantial reductions in such spending that are called for in the budget plans proposed by congressional Republicans and the president is an open question. Under these plans, by 2002, nondefense discretionary spending measured as a percentage of GDP would be less than at any other time since at least the early 1950s.

Second, the BEA is also a more flexible set of rules than was GRH. There are no binding deficit targets. If the deficit rises because the economy is hit by unexpected weakness, no further actions are required. If Congress and the president agree that additional spending or tax cuts are needed to meet some emergency, the limits can be breached. This escape hatch has been used quite sparingly over the past six years: for Desert Storm (most, if not all, of which was paid for with contributions from other governments), several natural disasters, and extended unemployment benefits during the previous recession. In addition, the discretionary spending caps are protected against unexpected surges in inflation. The discretionary caps are automatically adjusted to reflect deviations in the actual rate of inflation from the estimates of future inflation that were embodied in the BEA. To the surprise of most participants in the process, the caps were adjusted down during each of the first four years because actual inflation was below expectations.

A third important difference was that the BEA had a multiyear focus rather than the single-year focus of GRH. The original BEA covered fiscal 1991 through fiscal 1995. The omnibus reconciliation bill enacted in 1993 extended the duration to 1998. Additional Senate rules ensure that limits are not breached during the budget year, the first five years, and the second five years.

The battle to balance the budget or at least reduce the deficit substantially is far from over. New rules and institutions have made an important contribution to the effort. It seems inevitable that further procedural changes will be adopted. If they are crafted pragmatically to reflect the lessons learned over the past quarter of a century about what makes for effective procedural restraint, they can facilitate the effort. But if they are designed more to fulfill ideological dictates, they could prove to be counterproductive.

Comment

David Romer

Fiscal policy in many countries, including the United States, has exhibited a systematic tendency toward excessive deficits in recent decades. But although the adoption of specific measures to reduce deficits is politically difficult in these countries, there is considerable popular support for simple, broad antideficit provisions. For example, on several occasions a balanced budget amendment to the U.S. Constitution has come very close to obtaining the necessary two-thirds vote in both houses of Congress.

The fiscal record of the United States and other deficit-prone countries is sufficiently poor that it is reasonably clear that there are many simple antideficit rules that would be much preferable to current policy *if they were followed*. Consider a conventional balanced budget requirement that allows for explicit cyclical adjustment, permits a legislative override in recessions, or focuses on projected spending and receipts (and that can therefore be based on relatively normal economic conditions). If fiscal policy were set according to one of the these rules, there would be a tremendous improvement in long-run fiscal performance with at most a slight cost in terms of cyclical performance.

Thus, the only serious objection to a balanced budget requirement is that lawmakers would simply evade it, or that their attempts to evade it would lead to an avalanche of litigation and to the conduct of fiscal policy by the judiciary rather than by the legislature and the executive. The adoption of a balanced budget requirement that was ineffective would not be innocuous; it would be harmful in two ways. First, the inclusion in a country's constitution of a provision that was brazenly evaded would increase cynicism and weaken the rule of law. Second, most balanced budget requirements would not take effect for a considerable time; for example, the requirements currently under discussion in the United States would take effect only after seven years. In the meantime, by creating the illusion that fiscal problems were about to be solved, the requirements would postpone any serious efforts to deal with those problems.

Thus the key question about legislative and constitutional fiscal rules is whether they have important effects on budget outcomes. A large recent literature, to which James Poterba has been a leading contributor, examines the federal, state, and international evidence on this issue.

The international evidence is very limited and focuses more on such institutional features as the strength of the finance minister than on budget rules. Thus the most important evidence about the effects of budget rules comes from studies of the U.S. federal and state budgets.

Investigations of federal budget rules focus on two sets of legislation: the Gramm-Rudman-Hollings Act and its descendants, and the 1990 budget agreement and its offspring. The Gramm-Rudman-Hollings Act is one of the main sources of the perception that budget rules are easy to evade: lawmakers used asset sales, off-budget spending, unrealistic forecasts, shifts in spending among different fiscal years, and changes in the budget targets themselves to greatly relax the apparent constraints created by the act. According to Gramlich's (1990) and Reischauer's (1990) careful analyses, most of the apparent deficit reductions under Gramm-Rudman-Hollings came from accounting tricks like these. Gramlich argues further that essentially all of the remaining reductions came from policy changes that were largely unrelated to the act, such as lower defense spending with the ending of the cold war.

The effects of the 1990 budget agreement are less clear, for two reasons. First the agreement may just have reflected the emerging consensus in favor of reducing deficits; thus we do not know whether the apparent reductions in the wake of the agreement were the result of the agreement or of the consensus that gave rise to it. Second, the rules put in place by the agreement had the effect of encouraging actions creating deficit reductions in the short run, but deficit increases at horizons beyond the five-year period covered by standard deficit projections. Thus it is hard to know whether the apparent deficit reductions following the agreement were genuine. Auerbach (1994) finds evidence that at least some of the apparent reductions in fact merely shifted deficits from the near future to outside the budget window.

Studies of state budgets are generally much more supportive of budget rules. To begin with, it is rare for the rules to lead to judicial involvement in the budget process. This suggests that fears that a national balanced budget requirement would end up producing budget making by judicial opinion are overblown. In addition, the studies generally find that the rules do affect the level and content of state spending and receipts and their responses to shocks.

This difference in the results of the national and state-level studies is surprising. As Poterba makes clear, the state balanced budget requirements are generally much weaker than the rules embodied in Gramm-Rudman-Hollings and the 1990 budget agreement. The state requirements often exempt capital spending and various special funds, and they generally have no explicit enforcement procedures. Thus they have important additional margins for evasion. In other words, the evidence from the states suggests that you can do exactly what opponents of national balanced budget requirements say you cannot do: bring about a large change in budgetary outcomes simply by enacting a vague budgetary rule with no enforcement procedures.

One possible explanation of the puzzling difference between the national and state findings is that we have not yet delved deeply enough into the state-level data. The advantages of going from one observation to fifty are clear, but there is a disadvantage as well: it is much harder to undertake the kinds of detailed investigations that have been done of how the apparent deficit reductions under Gramm-Rudman-Hollings were achieved. Detailed investigations are particularly important in this area, where lawmakers' goal may be to make it look as if they have reduced deficits while the investigator's goal is to determine whether they are genuinely doing so. To exaggerate the potential problems, imagine sending out a survey to the states asking, "In response to budget shortfalls, do you: (a) Make genuine reductions in spending; (b) Enact genuine tax increases; or (c) Resort to gimmicks and tricks to blatantly evade your constitutional obligations?" Of course, this is not what these studies do. But they do rely on the states' own spending and revenue data. More generally, the fact that measured deficits are less common in states that prohibit them than in states that do not does not resolve the question of whether such rules have important effects on some economically meaningful concept of deficits. In short, one possible explanation of the seeming difference between the national and state findings is that the state findings will not hold up to closer scrutiny.

The second possible explanation of the different results is that they are genuine and that it takes a combination of budget rules and tradition to affect budget outcomes. Casual empiricism strongly suggests that states are less prone to persistent deficits than the national government is and that they are much more likely to take genuine measures to increase revenues and decrease expenditures in recessions. The reason may be that the history of roughly balanced budgets in the states, coupled with their antideficit rules, makes it politically much more costly for legislators and governors to use gimmicks and tricks to run large deficits.[1]

If this view is right, the adoption of a national balanced budget requirement in a previously deficit-prone country would not lead to the immediate adoption of genuinely balanced budgets but would lead to a gradual move in that direction. This suggests one possible explanation of why the 1990 budget agreement may have had more effect than Gramm-Rudman-Hollings: over time, the use of the kinds of devices that were used to evade Gramm-Rudman-Hollings has become increasingly politically costly, and thus there have been more moves to genuine deficit reductions.

I have suggested that the adoption of a balanced budget requirement could do anything from significantly worsening a country's fiscal problems to leading to their gradual solution. Determining where in this range of possibilities the truth lies is of great importance for public policy and social welfare. Let me therefore close by making the standard plea for more research. The international evidence on this issue has yet to be examined carefully, the local data are virtually untouched, and even the state-level evidence is only beginning to be examined. In sum, there is work to be done.

Note

1. Of course, there are reasons other than the states' antideficit rules that they are less prone to persistent, large budget deficits than the federal government is. But if the evidence that the specifics of the states' rules affects their responses to shocks holds up to scrutiny, this would strongly suggest that the rules themselves are important.

References

Auerbach, Alan J. 1994. "The U.S. Fiscal Problem: Where We Are, How We Got Here, and Where We Are Going." In S. Fisher and J. Rotenberg, eds., *NBER Macroeconomics Annual*, vol. 9. Cambridge, MA: MIT Press.

Gramlich, Edward M. 1990, May. "U.S. Federal Budget Deficits and Gramm-Rudman-Hollings." *American Economic Review* 80:75–80.

Reischauer, Robert D. 1990. "Taxes and Spending Under Gramm-Rudman-Hollings." *National Tax Journal* 43:223–232.

4 Work, Welfare, and Family Structure: What Have We Learned?

Hilary Williamson Hoynes

Welfare reform has once again made its way to the top of the domestic policy agenda. Although part of the motivation behind current reform efforts is fiscally driven, there is also an interest in making significant changes that address two prominent criticisms of the existing system of public assistance programs in the United States. First, the system has significant, adverse work incentives. It leads to low work effort among recipients, which contributes to long-term poverty. Second, the system discourages the formation of two-parent families and is responsible in a major part for the high, and rising, rates of female headship and out-of-wedlock birthrates. This chapter explores the validity of these criticisms using the empirical evidence and evaluates the impact of various reforms to the system.

Welfare most commonly refers to the Aid to Families with Dependent Children (AFDC) program, which provides cash assistance to low-income families with children. More broadly, welfare corresponds to the set of federal, state, and local means-tested transfer programs. The main goal of public assistance programs is to increase income and reduce poverty among the disadvantaged. The evidence based on comparisons of pre- with posttransfer income shows that these programs have had success meeting that goal (Danziger and Weinberg 1994). This transfer of income, however, generates potential efficiency losses though its distortions to individual behavior such as labor supply and family structure decisions. Although means-tested programs in the United States are also provided to the elderly and the disabled, the concern over adverse work and family structure incentives is directed primarily at programs serving low-income families with children.[1] In addition to cash benefits through the AFDC program, low-income families with children are eligible for in-kind benefits such as food stamps, medical coverage through the Medicaid program, and housing subsidies. Working-poor families can also receive earnings subsidies through the tax system with the earned income tax credit (EITC). While there are other smaller programs serving low-income families, this review will focus on the major programs.[2]

The disincentives toward work and family structure decisions are a direct result of the structure of benefit and eligibility rules for these programs. First, most programs are structured such that they provide a basic benefit level, called a *guarantee*, which is reduced as a family's earnings increases. The rate at which benefits are reduced, the benefit reduction rate (BRR), represents an implicit tax rate on earned income. Statutory tax rates in the AFDC program are 67 to 100 percent. When combined with other programs, cumulative tax rates can be over 100 percent. Static labor supply theory suggests that welfare benefits, with their combination of a guarantee and benefit reduction rate, lead unambiguously to lower levels of work effort than would exist in the absence of such a program. Second, welfare programs have historically restricted eligibility to single parents, and despite recent expansions for two-parent families, the system continues to favor single parents. The system therefore provides incentives to form single-parent families and have children out of wedlock.

Before evaluating the magnitude of these disincentive effects, I will provide some background on the system of public assistance programs in the United States and the population they serve. Section 4.1 describes the public assistance programs for low-income families and illustrates the magnitude of the cumulative tax rates faced by these families. Section 4.2 presents data on poverty, family structure, and the characteristics of welfare recipients. Section 4.3 discusses the expected effects of welfare programs on work and family structure decisions and sections 4.4 and 4.5 summarize what we have learned about the magnitude of these disincentive effects. Section 4.6 summarizes key elements of past and current efforts at reforming welfare and discusses the likely impact of various reforms.

4.1 Description of Major Public Assistance Programs

Eligibility and Benefits

Participation in most public assistance programs in the United States requires satisfying two types of eligibility conditions: resource restrictions (means tests) and categorical restrictions. Each of the programs considered here has an income test, and all programs except the EITC also have an asset test. In addition, there are categorical restrictions for many of the programs, often limiting receipt to single parents with children.

The AFDC program was established in 1935 as part of the Social Security Act, and eligibility and benefit determination and funding are shared between the federal and state governments. Eligibility for AFDC requires that the household contains at least one child who is less than eighteen years old, and has sufficiently low income and asset levels. The income test requires that family monthly income, after allowable deductions for work expenses and child care, fall below a state-determined maximum benefit level, which varies by family size.[3] Eligibility historically has been limited to single-parent (typically female-headed) families because of the additional requirement that the child be deprived of support due to the death, incapacity, or absence of a parent. Starting in 1961 with selected state expansions, and eventually mandated with passage of the 1988 Family Support Act (FSA), states have expanded eligibility to two-parent families by setting up AFDC Unemployed Parent (AFDC-UP) programs. However, the system still favors single parents because two-parent families must also satisfy a work history requirement and cannot work more than 100 hours per month while on welfare.[4] All AFDC recipients are categorically eligible for food stamp benefits and government-financed medical services under the Medicaid program.

AFDC benefits are calculated as the difference between the state-determined maximum benefit level and net family income. The benefit levels vary tremendously across states. For example, in 1993, monthly maximum benefits for a single mother and two children ranged from $607 in California and $658 in Vermont to $164 in Alabama and $120 in Mississippi (U.S. House of Representatives 1994). A standard amount for work expenses of $90 per month is deducted from earnings in calculating benefit payments. In the first four months of a recipient's working while on AFDC, an additional $30 plus one-third of remaining earnings is deducted from gross income. This is the so-called 30 and 1/3 rule. Thus for every $1 increase in earned income over the allowable deductions, benefits are reduced by 67 cents. After four months the one-third deduction is discontinued and benefits are reduced one-to-one with an increase in earnings. Thus the statutory tax rate on earned income, or BRR, for AFDC recipients is 67 or 100 percent.[5]

The EITC is a refundable tax credit that, when it was introduced in 1975, was designed to offset the social security tax for low-income families with children. In order to receive the credit, a family must contain a qualified child, have earnings below a specified level, and file a tax return.[6] In 1994, the EITC was available for families with earnings up to $23,755 for those with one child and $25,300 for those with two or more children. There is no difference in the generosity of the credit for one- and two-parent families and about 60 percent of recipients are single-parent families (Eissa and Liebman 1993). The amount of the EITC depends on whether earnings lie in the subsidy, flat, or phase-out range of the credit. Consider a family with two children in 1994. For this family, the subsidy range covers earnings up to $8,425, over which the subsidy equals 30 percent of earnings, generating a maximum credit of $2,538. In the flat range, covering earnings between $8,425 and $11,000, the family receives the maximum credit. In the phase-out range, the subsidy is reduced by 17.68 cents for each additional dollar in earnings such that the credit is fully phased out at earnings of $25,300. The credit is smaller for families with one child.

The federal food stamp program, which began in 1964, has uniform eligibility rules and benefits across the lower forty-eight states and the District of Columbia. This is the only program considered here that is extended to all needy families, regardless of the presence of children or other family structure requirements. Like AFDC, families must satisfy an asset test, and a net and gross income test. Net income must not exceed the poverty line, equal to $11,892 in 1994, for a single parent with two children, and gross income must not exceed 1.3 times the poverty line. Food stamp benefits are equal to maximum food stamp benefits, which varies by family size, less 30 percent of family net income. Net income includes AFDC benefits, and there are deductions for work expenses, child care expenses, and shelter expenses. Because AFDC income is taken into account in calculating food stamp benefits, families living in states with low AFDC benefits receive higher food stamp grants, thereby reducing the cross-state variation in combined benefits. In 1993, the maximum monthly food stamp benefit for a single mother and two children was $295. Food stamp benefits are adjusted each year for changes in the cost of food.

The Medicaid program, which was started in 1965 and is a joint federal-state program, is available primarily to recipients of cash assistance, including families with children receiving AFDC and the low-income aged, blind, and disabled receiving Supplemental Security Income (SSI). Benefits in most programs are phased out as income rises. Medicaid benefits, however, are typically provided in full or not at all. Tying Medicaid benefits to program recipiency leads to a "notch" whereby benefits are lost in their entirety when eligibility for cash benefits ends. However, recent expansions in the program have severed the link between cash benefit receipt and eligibility for Medicaid, thereby downplaying the importance of the notch. First, the FSA mandates transition benefits, whereby AFDC recipients losing eligibility because of increased earnings receive Medicaid for an additional twelve months. Second, beginning in 1984, Medicaid eligibility was expanded to pregnant women and children with income in excess of the AFDC limits. All states are now required to extend benefits to all children under the age of six with family income below 133 percent of the poverty line and to all children born after September 1, 1993, with family income below the poverty line. When the expansions are fully phased in, all poor children will be covered.[7]

All of the programs discussed above are *entitlement* programs. That is, a family that satisfies the eligibility conditions(s) for the program will receive benefits according to the appropriate benefit formula. Low-income housing benefits in the United States are not an entitlement. Although all AFDC recipients are categorically eligible, only about 30 percent receive benefits (U.S. House of Representatives 1994). Housing assistance typically takes the form of public housing or subsidized, private (Section 8) rental housing.[8] For both programs, families must satisfy both asset and income tests, with income tests set by the local housing authority. Once eligibility is determined, a family is placed on a waiting list. Queues can be quite long—more than two years in most urban areas (Painter 1995). For both types of housing aid, some contribution to rent is required from the family, and the subsidy is the difference between the fair market rent of the unit and the family's contribution.

Table 4.1 summarizes several key features of the main welfare programs covered in this review: AFDC, food stamps, Medicaid and the EITC. The table shows the variation in the level of finance, level of provision, and eligibility requirements across these programs. These figures show that Medicaid is the most expensive program for families with children, with a total expenditure of $32.1 billion dollars in 1993. AFDC is second, with $25 billion.

The last thirty years have encompassed great changes in our system of public assistance. Table 4.2 presents expenditures and participation in these programs for selected years, from 1960 to the present. The table consists of three panels. The first two present total participation and expenditures in these programs. The last panel presents figures on the percentage of benefits going to families with children for selected years during this period. The table shows that a major trend in welfare programs is the increased importance of in-kind benefits. In 1960, 85 percent of benefits were in cash, which decreased to 27 percent in 1975 and 18 percent in 1993. The real cost of the AFDC program reached a peak in the early 1970s and has remained fairly constant. Among the public assistance

Table 4.1
Description of public assistance programs for families with children, 1993 (current dollars)

	AFDC	Food Stamps[a]	Medicaid[a]	EITC
Year established	1935	1964	1965	1975
Level of finance	Federal and state	Federal	Federal and state	Federal
Level of delivery	State and local	Federal	State	Federal
Form of benefits	Cash	Food stamp coupons	Free medical services	Refundable tax credit
Nature of means test	Income, asset	Income, asset	Income, asset	Income
Groups covered	Families with children (primarily single parents)	All persons	AFDC recipients, poor children, elderly, disabled	Families with children
1993 expenditures for families with children	$25.2 billion	$12.9 billion[b]	$32.1 billion	$13,239 million (preliminary)
1993 participation for families with children	5 million families, 14 million persons	6.8 million families[c]	25.8 million persons	14 million families (preliminary)
1993 average benefit for families with children	$373/month (family)	$189/month (family)	$1,013/year for children; $1,813/year for adults	$945/year (family)
Statutory tax rate on earnings	67% or 100%	30%	Full benefits until eligibility point ("notch")	−30%, phase in; 0% flat; 18%, phase out

Source: U.S. House of Representatives (1994); Social Security Administration (1995); unpublished data from the Food and Nutrition Service.
[a] Program is not limited to families with children. The expenditure and participation figures reflect just those for the portion of the caseload comprising families with children.
[b] Calculated by multiplying total benefit payments by reported figures on the percentage of benefits going to AFDC recipients. This is an underestimate of the total cost of the food stamp program for families with children.
[c] Calculated from figures on the percentage of households with children in the food stamp unit.

Table 4.2
Expenditures and participation in selected public assistance programs, 1960–1993

	1960	1975	1980	1985	1990	1993
Program expenditures (millions of 1993 dollars)						
Cash programs						
AFDC	4,887	25,500	23,560	21,969	23,438	25,242
EITC[a,b]	0	3,357	3,483	2,804	7,659	13,239
In-kind programs						
Food stamps[c]	0	12,607	16,770	18,089	19,553	26,304
Medicaid	0	33,941	45,211	54,949	80,146	132,010
Housing[d]	864	30,189	29,554	25,167	20,940	20,535
Program participation (millions)						
Cash programs						
AFDC (families)	N.A.	3.3	3.6	3.7	4.0	5.0
AFDC (persons)	3.0	11.1	10.6	10.8	11.5	14.1
EITC (families)[b]	—	6.2	7.0	7.4	12.6	14.0
In-kind programs						
Food stamps (persons)[c]	—	16.3	19.2	19.9	20.0	27.0
Medicaid (persons)	—	22.0	21.6	21.8	25.3	30.9
Housing (households)[d]	N.A.	N.A.	4.0	5.1	5.4	5.6
Percentage of benefits for families with children						
Food stamps[e]	—	—	52.0%	51.5%	56.3%	54.7%
Medicaid	—	—	27.3%	24.4%	27.2%	29.8%

Sources: U.S. House of Representatives (1994); Social Security Administration (1995); Congressional Research Service (1993); unpublished data from the Food and Nutrition Service.
Notes: Many of these programs are also available to the elderly and childless families. Unless otherwise stated, the figures correspond to program totals, not just the benefits for the nonelderly. Expenditures include federal and state costs.
[a] Cost of EITC includes the tax expenditure associated with the credit and measures the decrease in individual tax receipts due to the credit, and the refunded portion.
[b] Figures for 1993 are projections.
[c] Does not include data for Puerto Rico, which operated a food stamp program from 1975 to 1982.
[d] Figures in the final column are for 1992.
[e] Includes percentage of benefits to AFDC recipients only.

programs considered here, the Medicaid program is both the largest and the one with the highest growth rate. Its cost, in 1993 dollars, increased from $54.9 billion in 1985 to $132 billion in 1993. However, although families with dependent children represent about 71 percent of all Medicaid recipients, expenditures for this group represent only 29 percent of the total expenditures (U.S. House of Representatives 1994). The cost of the EITC program has increased dramatically in the past ten years due to major expansions in 1986, 1990, and 1993. These expansions have increased the value of the credit as well as the range of incomes covered by the credit. The maximum credit for a family with two children, in current dollars, increased from $550 in 1986 to an expected $3,560 in 1996. During the same period, the upper limit on earnings increased from $11,000 to $28,524. After accounting for changes in prices, the maximum credit increased over 350 percent over this period, and the income limit increased by 86 percent. Table 4.2 shows that the number of families receiving the EITC is now about three times as large as the number of families receiving AFDC. Under current law, the cost of the EITC is expected to be over one and one-half times as large as federal spending on the AFDC program by 1996 (U.S. House of Representatives 1994). The food stamp caseload has grown fairly steadily over the past twenty years. Although the cost of the program is now about equal to the AFDC program, families with dependent children represent less than 60 percent of the food stamp caseload (U.S. House of Representatives 1994).

Figure 4.1 shows how total expenditures on public assistance programs have changed over time as a percentage of GNP.[9] Between the late 1960s and the mid-1970s resources on means-tested programs increased; since then they have remained very stable, at just under 4 percent of gross national product. The increase in cost of these programs in the past few years is primarily due to growth in Medicaid, where nonmedical means-tested programs increased only slightly at the end of the period. For comparison, the figure also presents the total cost of social insurance programs, such as social security, Medicare, and unemployment compensation, as a percentage of GNP. The cost of these programs is almost twice the amount spent on the poor.

Implicit Tax Rates Faced by Low-Income Families

Poor families with children are eligible for a patchwork of benefit and tax programs. In all programs except Medicaid, the benefit a family receives depends on its level of earnings, which in turn depends on its work effort.

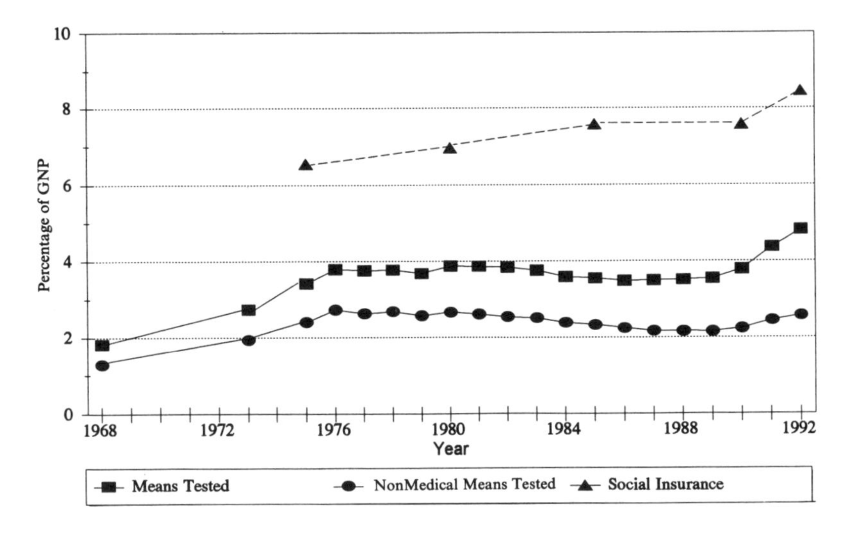

Figure 4.1
Government expenditures as a percentage of GNP (federal, state, and local). Source: Congressional Research Service (1993); Burtless (1994).

As a first step toward understanding the incentives to work for program participants, this section presents information on earnings, benefits, and income attainable at different wage rates and hours of work for representative welfare recipients. These incentives are summarized by implicit tax rates on earned income, which reflect by how much disposable income increases with an increase in work effort. Because a family may be participating in many programs simultaneously, one has to consider the taxes faced for the combined set of programs.

These implicit tax rates are relevant only for work reported to the case worker. In fact, high marginal tax rates for this group may increase the incentive to conceal earnings from the authorities. Although the evidence is somewhat anecdotal, it suggests that a large fraction of AFDC recipients are working and not reporting the income to the authorities (Edin and Jencks 1992).[10]

The earnings, income, and tax rates reported here are calculated using a benefit and tax simulation program that takes into account federal and state tax and transfer programs. In order to illustrate the magnitude of the tax rates faced by public assistance recipients, I have simulated benefits, taxes, and disposable income for representative families. The simulation model calculates payroll taxes, state and federal income taxes, and benefits received from AFDC and food stamps.[11] To do the calculation, we need to make assumptions about the hourly wage rate, the number of children, the state of residence, and the amount of child care and work expenses. Each of the simulations is calculated assuming that the family consists of a single mother with two children, where the mother incurs child care costs equal to 20 percent of earnings, and other work expenses amounting to 10 percent of earnings.[12] All taxes and transfers are calculated under 1993 law. Simulations are conducted under alternative assumptions concerning the woman's hourly wage, her state of residence, and which statutory BRR she faces in the AFDC program. These estimates are similar in construction and magnitude to others in the literature, such as recent analyses by Dickert, Hauser, and Scholz (1994) and Giannarelli and Steuerle (1995).

Table 4.3 presents the annual income, expenses, and average tax rates assuming that the woman lives in California, can earn $5 per hour, and is in the first four months of work and faces the 30 and 1/3 rule.[13] If she is not working, she has annual disposable income of $8,639, of which

Table 4.3
Annual income, expenses, and tax rates faced by a representative welfare recipient, 1993: California AFDC benefits with 30 and 1/3 rule

	No work	Part-time work[a]	Full-time work[b]
Income			
Earnings	$0	$5,200	$10,400
EITC	0	1,014	1,511
AFDC	7,284	5,817	3,391
Food stamp benefits	1,355	1,015	963
Expenses			
Child care	0	1,040	2,080
Work expenses	0	520	1,040
Other federal taxes	0	0	0
Payroll taxes	0	398	796
State taxes	0	0	0
Disposable income	8,639	11,088	12,349
Average tax rate, from no work[c]	—	52.9%	64.3%
Average tax rate, from part-time[c]	—	—	75.8%

Notes: The simulation is for a single mother living with two children in California earning $5 per hour. Child care expenses are 20 percent of earnings, and other work expenses are 10 percent of earnings. AFDC benefits are calculated using the 30 and 1/3 rule.
[a] Twenty hours per week.
[b] Forty hours per week.
[c] Tax rates calculated as one minus the change in disposable income over the change in earnings.

$7,284 comes from AFDC and the remainder from the food stamp program. If she chooses to work part time at $5 per hour, she has earnings of $5,200 but her disposable income increases by only $2,449. Increasing her work effort generates an EITC of $1,014, but she incurs child care expenses, work expenses, and a reduction in her AFDC payment of $1,467 and in her food stamp benefit of $340. This results in a tax rate for going from no work to part-time work of 52.9 percent.[14] The same woman considering full-time work would face a tax rate of 64.3 percent for going from no work to full-time work and a tax rate of 75.8 percent for going from part-time to full-time work.

There are several points to make in this table. First, the tax rates are very high. To put these in some perspective, in the absence of the implicit tax rates imposed by the AFDC and food stamp programs, tax rates for this woman would be about 18 percent for part-time work and 23 percent for full-time work. Second, they are somewhat lower than the statutory rate of 67 percent due to the allowable deductions. Third, the marginal tax rate (MTR) from going from no work to part-time work is lower than that going from part time to full time because of the standard deductions.[15] Finally, these tax rates are an underestimate of the actual rates because they do not take into account housing benefits and Medicaid. Until the recent expansions, losing AFDC eligibility would lead to a loss of Medicaid as well, adding to the already high tax rate. However, the transitional benefits and expansions in coverage for children together reduce the impact of Medicaid on tax rates, at least in the short run.

The presence of the 30 and 1/3 rule significantly reduces the tax rates faced by low-income families. Figure 4.2a presents disposable income as a function of hours worked for the case presented in table 4.3. Figure 4.2b recalculates disposable income for the identical family except we assume that the mother has been working for over four months and thus faces the 100 percent statutory tax rate in the AFDC program. The figures separate income into net earnings, EITC, AFDC, and food stamp benefits. Net earnings are gross earnings less all expenses and taxes other than the EITC. The difference between Figure 4.2a and 4.2b is striking. Without the 30 and 1/3 rule, in figure 4.2b, disposable income is almost unchanged between five and forty hours of work, and the tax rate for moving from no work to part-time work is 75 percent. The MTR of moving from part-time to full-time work is 99 percent. A woman contemplating leaving welfare to work full-time (at the $5 hourly wage) would see an increase in disposable income of only $1,400, representing a mere 16 percent increase over attainable income while not working.

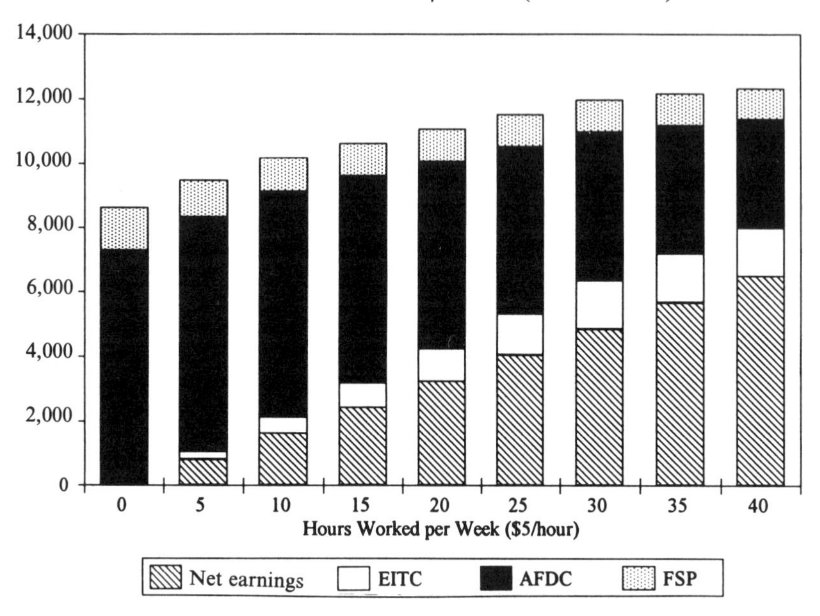

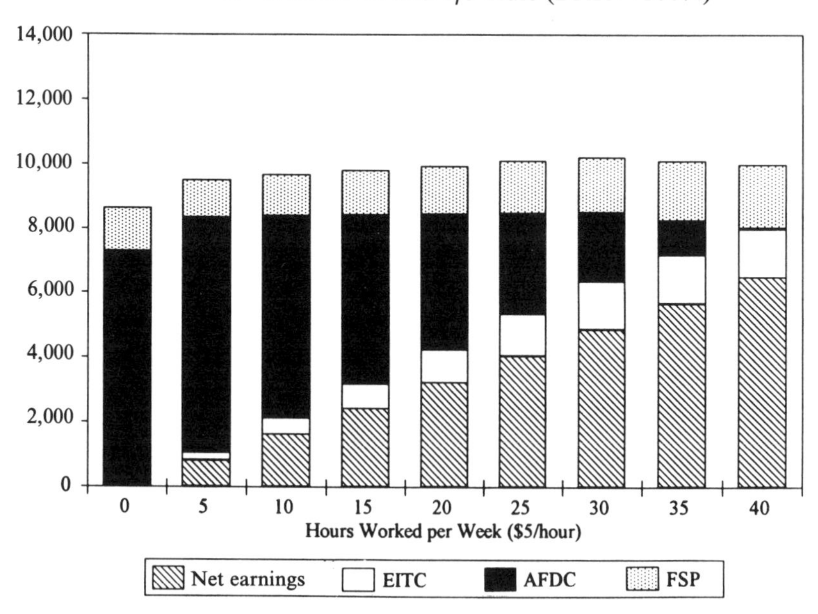

Figure 4.2
Disposable income as a function of hours worked and AFDC benefit reduction rate for a family of three in California.

California was chosen because it contains the nation's largest welfare population, accounting for about 17 percent of the AFDC caseload (U.S. House of Representatives 1994). California is unusual, however, because AFDC benefit levels are among the highest in the country. As shown in figure 4.2, the woman working full time for $5 per hour is still eligible for AFDC benefits, even when the BRR is 100 percent. These high implicit tax rates, however, are faced by recipients in all states, although the exact magnitude depends on many things, including the state's benefit level (and the amount paid for child care and other work expenses). To illustrate the possible differences between the states, figure 4.3 repeats the exercise assuming that the woman lives in Illinois. In 1993, our mother and two children could receive an AFDC grant of $367 per month in Illinois, which is about average for the United States, compared to $607 in California. A comparison of figures 4.2 and 4.3 shows that potential income is lower in Illinois, but a higher food stamp grant partially makes up for the lower AFDC grant. The same general pattern found in figure 4.2 also is evident in these figures. With the 30 and 1/3 rule, disposable income increases modestly with increases in earnings, and without the 30 and 1/3 rule, income is quite flat as a function of hours worked, until the family earns its way off AFDC, which in this case occurs at thirty hours per month.

To illustrate how tax rates vary for women with different wage opportunities, table 4.4 presents tax rates for our family in California at various wage levels. Increasing the wage generally leads to higher tax rates associated with part-time work but lower tax rates for full-time work. As wage rates rise, the break-even level of hours of work decreases, increasing the marginal tax rates at lower levels of hours. The table also shows the importance of the EITC. The top panel of the table presents tax rates based on the 1996 levels for the EITC, when the current expansions will be fully phased in. The lower panel presents tax rates in the absence of an EITC. The 1996 EITC (where the maximum wage subsidy is 40 percent) decreases tax rates by about 30 to 50 percent at the lower wage levels—significant reductions for low-wage workers.[16]

4.2 Facts on Welfare, Poverty, Work, and Family Structure

• ***Female-headed families are becoming increasingly more common.*** Figure 4.4 shows female-headed households as a percentage of all families with children over the period 1968 to 1993. In 1968, about 8 percent of white families with children were headed by a single mother; in 1993

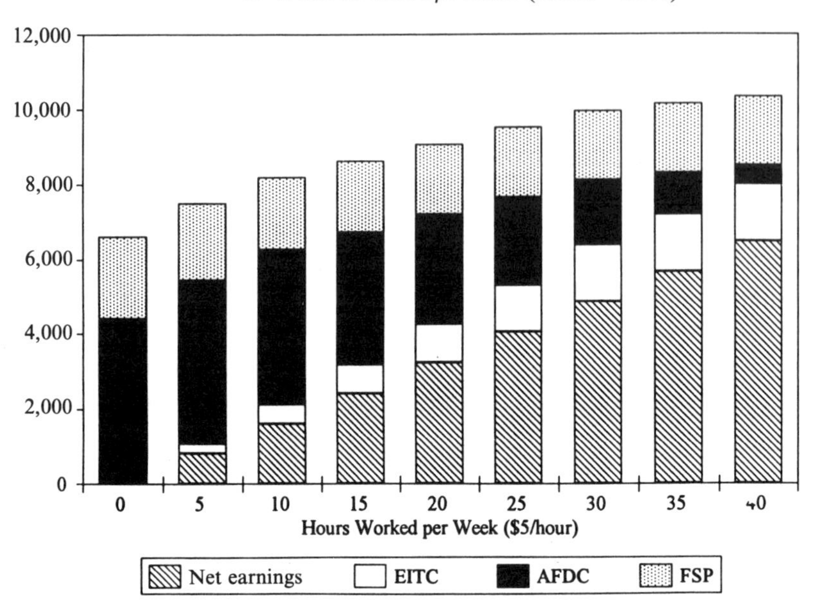

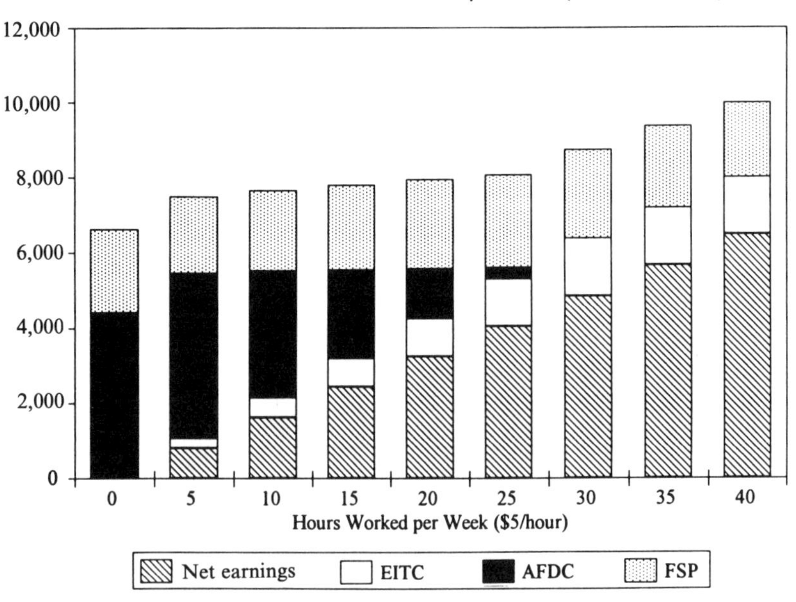

Figure 4.3
Disposable income as a function of hours worked and AFDC benefit reduction rate for a family of three in Illinois.

Table 4.4
Average tax rates for a representative welfare recipient in 1993, by wage rate and presence of EITC Program: California AFDC program with 30 and 1/3 rule

	Work transition		
	No work to part time	Part time to full time	No work to full time
Average tax rate with 1996 EITC			
Wage rate			
$5.00	32.4%	60.5%	46.5%
$7.50	36.7	91.3	64.0
$10.00	46.5	91.2	68.8
$12.50	56.9	78.0	67.5
Average tax rates without EITC			
Wage rate			
$5.00	72.4%	85.3%	78.9%
$7.50	76.7	82.1	79.4
$10.00	78.9	71.4	75.1
$12.50	79.6	56.9	68.3

Notes: The simulation is based on a single mother living with two children in California. Child care expenses are 20 percent of earnings, and other work expenses are 10 percent of earnings. AFDC benefits are calculated using the 30 and 1/3 rule. Part-time work is 20 hours per week, and full time is 40 hours per week. Tax rates are calculated as one minus the change in disposable income over the change in earnings.

almost 17 percent of white families with children were female-headed households. These trends are even more dramatic for black families, where the rate of female headship increased from about 30 percent in 1970 to over 50 percent in 1993.

Also significant is the dramatic increase in nonmarital birthrates, measured as the number of births to unmarried women per 1,000 unmarried women ages fifteen to forty-four. Figure 4.5 shows that the nonmarital birthrate has more than doubled over the period 1960 to 1992 from 20 to 42 per 1,000 unmarried women. These trends are occurring, to some degree, among women of all reproductive ages and in all racial and ethnic groups (Ventura et al. 1995). This steady increase in birthrates among unmarried women is particularly striking since overall birthrates for all women, as shown in figure 4.5, have shown only modest increases since the 1970s. In 1960 the birthrate of all women was almost six times the rate for unmarried women, yet that ratio has fallen to less than two-to-one by the end of the period. This increase is particularly striking for blacks, in 1993 fully 70 percent of all births were to unmarried mothers

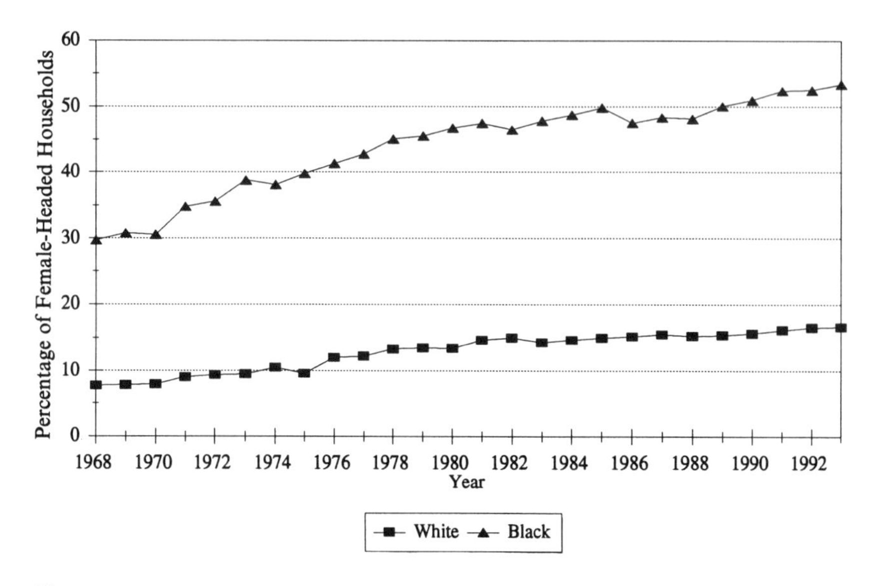

Figure 4.4
Female-headed households as a percentage of all families with children, 1968–1993 (by race). Source: U.S. Bureau of the Census, *Current Populations Reports*, Series P-20, *Household and Family Characteristics*, various issues.

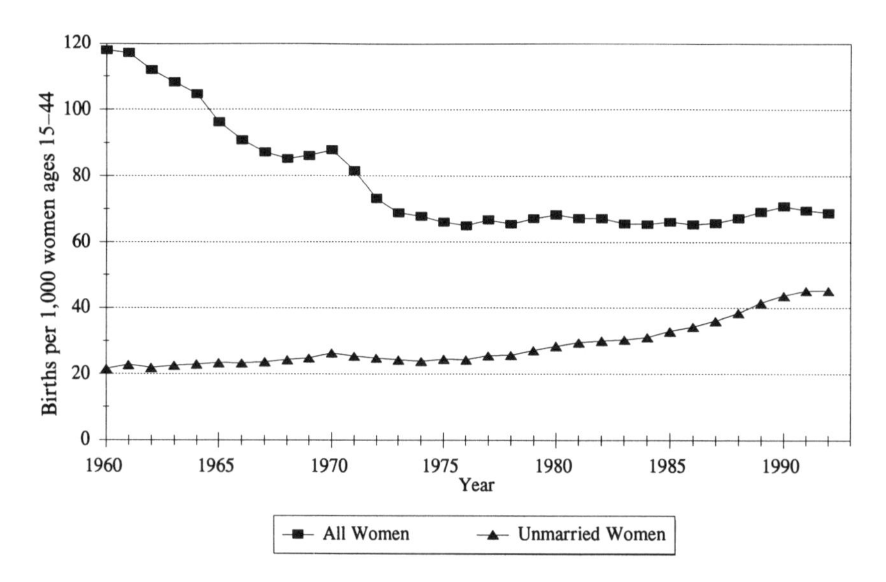

Figure 4.5
Birthrates by marital status, 1960–1992 (births per 1,000 women ages 15–44 in the specified group). Source: National Center for Health Statistics (1994); Ventura (1995).

Table 4.5
Percentage of families in poverty, by age of head of household and family type, 1993

	All	Head below age 65	Head age 65 or above
All families	12.2%	13.3%	6.9%
Families with children below age 18			
Husband-wife families	9.0	8.8	23.8
Female head	46.1	46.8	28.2
Male head	22.4	22.4	22.7
All	18.5	18.4	25.5
Families without children below age 18			
Husband-wife families	4.1	3.8	4.8
Female head	10.7	11.0	10.0
Male head	10.0	10.5	8.4
All	5.1	4.9	5.5

Source: Author's tabulation of March 1994 *Current Population Survey.*
Notes: Based on a sample of primary families only. Does not include secondary families or unrelated individuals. All results are weighted.

(Ventura 1995). Changes in the ratio of nonmarital births to all births (the nonmarital birth *ratio*) are a result of several demographic factors, such as nonmarital and marital fertility rates and marriage rates. Among whites, the increase in the nonmarital birth ratio is due to both increases in the nonmarital fertility rate and decreases in marriage. Among blacks, it is primarily the decrease in marriage that has driven up the nonmarital birth ratio (Ventura et al. 1995).

• ***Poverty rates are higher among female-headed households than any other group.*** Table 4.5 presents poverty rates among families by age of the head of household and family type in 1993, based on a tabulation of the March 1994 Current Population Survey (CPS). The poverty rate among female-headed households with children was about 46 percent compared to 9 percent among two-parent families. High poverty rates among female-headed households with children are not limited to minority groups: 41 percent of white, 58 percent of black, and 61 percent of Hispanic female-headed households are in poverty. Almost half of all families in poverty are now accounted for by female-headed households, yet they account for only about 13 percent of all families, reflecting the growing trend toward the feminization of poverty. The table also shows that poverty rates among elderly households are relatively low: 5.5 percent among families without children headed by an elderly individual.

• ***Public assistance programs reach poor families with children.*** Resources for public assistance programs in the United States are primarily spent on poor single-parent families with children and the elderly. This is reflected in table 4.6 which presents the percentage of nonelderly families in poverty who are participating in various public assistance programs. Among the 3.9 million female-headed households with children, 63 percent receive AFDC or general assistance, 87 percent receive some type of means-tested benefits, and 14 percent receive no benefits at all. In contrast, among the 2.3 million two-parent families with children in poverty, only 24 percent receive cash assistance and 40 percent receive no benefits. For the 1.1 million nonelderly families without children who are in poverty, fully 64 percent do not receive any of these means-tested benefits.

• ***Multiple program participation is the rule, not the exception.*** In-kind transfer programs have become increasingly important for welfare recipients. In 1992, 86 percent of all AFDC recipients received food stamps and 96 percent received Medicaid (U.S. House of Representatives 1994).

• ***Labor force participation rates among public assistance recipients are lower than among those not receiving benefits.*** Table 4.7 shows that among poor female-headed households with children receiving cash means-tested benefits during 1993, only 32 percent worked during 1993, compared to 71 percent among those not receiving any benefits and 87 percent among all female-headed households with children with incomes between 100 and 200 percent of the poverty line. Labor force participation rates are also low among poor two-parent families on public assistance: 43 percent of husbands and 23 percent of wives receiving cash assistance worked compared to 83 percent of husbands and 50 percent of wives who did not receive any benefits.[17]

4.3 Expected Effects of Public Assistance on Labor Supply and Family Structure

The standard model used to evaluate the work incentives of welfare programs is a static income-leisure model. In that model, individuals choose a level of work effort by maximizing the utility of income and leisure subject to a budget constraint, which takes into account the tax and transfer program(s) that are being examined. Figure 4.6 presents a simplified version of the budget constraint faced by an AFDC participant. In

Table 4.6
Percentage of poor families receiving public assistance benefits in 1993, by family type

		Percentage of poor families receiving benefits from:					
	Number in poverty (millions)	AFDC or General Assistance	Food stamps	Medicaid[a]	Subsidized housing	Any means tested[b]	No benefits[c]
Head below age 65 with children							
Husband-wife	2,268	23.6%	49.1%	45.2%	9.5%	60.1%	39.9%
Female head	3,941	62.6	76.5	77.0	36.7	86.5	13.6
Male head	338	41.1	53.8	60.0	16.2	65.6	34.4
Head below age 65, no children	1,065	9.4	30.1	31.4	11.7	45.0	55.0
All families with head below age 65	7,612	42.6	60.8	60.4	24.2	71.9	28.1

Source: Author's tabulation of March 1994 *Current Population Survey*.
Notes: Based on a sample of primary families only. Does not include secondary families or unrelated individuals. Receipt of benefits is determined at the household level. All results are weighted.
[a] At least one person in the household is covered by Medicaid.
[b] Includes receipt of AFDC, general assistance, food stamps, Medicaid, or subsidized housing.
[c] Not receiving any of the benefits listed in note b. Note that family can still be receiving other means-tested benefits such as school lunches and energy assistance.

Table 4.7
Labor force participation rates among parents in poor families, by family type and receipt of public assistance benefits in 1993: Nonelderly families with children

	Receipt of public assistance benefits			
	AFDC or General Assistance	Any means-tested benefits[a]	No benefits[b]	All families 100%–200% poverty
Female Head	32.8%	40.9%	70.8%	87.3%
Husband-wife family				
Husband	45.4	61.6	83.4	91.8
Wife	22.7	32.4	49.7	60.4

Source: Author's tabulation of March 1994 *Current Population Survey.*
Notes: Based on a sample of primary families only. Does not include secondary families or unrelated individuals. Receipt of benefits is determined at the household level. Nonelderly families are those headed by someone less than age sixty-five. All results are weighted.
[a] Includes receipt of AFDC, general assistance, food stamps, Medicaid, or subsidized housing.
[b] Not receiving any of the benefits listed in note a. Note that family can still be receiving other means-tested benefits such as school lunches and energy assistance.

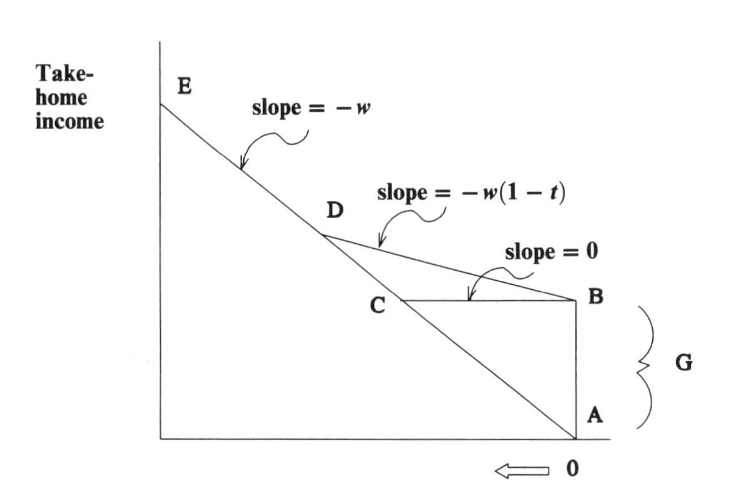

Figure 4.6
Sample budget constraint for an AFDC participant.

the absence of AFDC benefits, the person receives only his or her earned income, and the budget opportunities are represented by ACDE, with a slope equal to the wage rate w. The AFDC program provides a maximum benefit of G, called the guarantee, but introduces a BRR of t where for each additional dollar in earned income, the AFDC benefit is reduced by t dollars. Income opportunities in the presence of the AFDC program are then represented by ABDE, and the slope of the AFDC budget segment is $w(1 - t)$. The maximum benefit level and the tax rate combine to create a break-even level of income where benefits are zero. Below the break-even point, the household can receive positive benefits; above the break-even level, the household is not eligible.

The primary policy parameters are the guarantee and the BRR. Increasing the guarantee causes a reduction in labor supply, through a pure income effect. Changes in the tax rate, like changes in wages, generate both income and substitution effects, and the net effect is ambiguous. Figure 4.6 illustrates the effect of increasing the BRR to 100 percent, represented by ABCE. By reducing the net wage from $w(1 - t)$ to zero, the cost of leisure of is reduced and, hence, through the substitution effect, labor supply decreases. The income effect associated with an increase in the tax rate, by reducing income at a given level of hours, leads to lower levels of work effort. However, the total effect of a welfare program, by establishing a guarantee and tax rate, leads unambiguously to lower levels of work effort.

A change in the guarantee or tax rate not only changes the incentives for work for existing recipients; it also changes the composition of the recipient population through entry and exit, and it affects the labor supply of new entrants (Moffitt 1992a; Levy 1979). For example, a decrease in the BRR from 100 to 67 percent may increase work among current recipients. But reducing the BRR will increase the break-even level of income, which will lead to increases in entry into the program. Some new entrants will decrease their labor supply in response to the reduction in the BRR, and others will leave their labor supply unchanged but may be eligible due to the program expansion. Ashenfelter (1983) calls these two caseload effects the behavioral and mechanical effects. A third group of new entrants may have been eligible even before the program's expansion but were not participating due to lack of knowledge about the program or because of costs of participation (Moffitt 1983). This is a potentially important group, as the take-up rate is estimated to be between 45 and 65 percent for female heads of household (Moffitt 1983; Blank and Ruggles

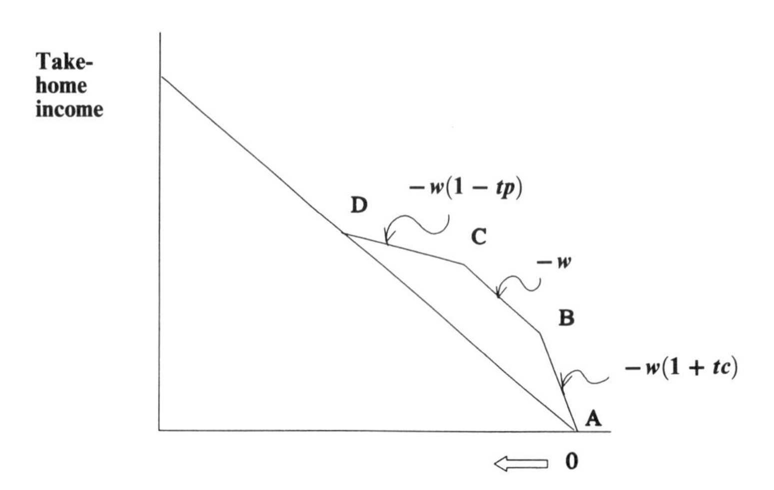

Figure 4.7
Sample budget constraint for an EITC participant.

1996). The overall change in the labor supply of female heads depends on the relative magnitudes of existing participants and new entrants.

The EITC program, in contrast to the AFDC program, is designed explicitly to subsidize employment. Figure 4.7 shows a stylized budget constraint for the EITC program. The main strength of the EITC is that, in contrast to AFDC, theory predicts unambiguous increases in labor force participation rates. For individuals out of the labor market, both the income and substitution effects of the EITC are positive and provide an incentive to enter the labor market. For those already in the labor market, the work incentives of the EITC program depend on which of the three segments of the budget constraint the family is on. In the subsidy region of the credit, over segment AB, the net wage increases to $w(1 + tc)$ where tc is the credit rate. In the flat region of the credit (segment BC), the net wage is w. In the phase-out region of the credit (segment CD), the net wage decreases to $w(1 - tp)$ where tp is the phase-out rate. For persons in the subsidy range of income, the substitution effect is positive, but the income effect is negative, leading to an ambiguous total effect. In the flat and phase-out ranges of the credit, work effort unambiguously decreases.[18] These negative effects on hours worked have the potential to be significant, as about 70 percent of recipients have incomes in the flat or phase-out ranges of the credit (Eissa and Liebman 1996).

Unfortunately, the world is much more complicated than that presented in the stylized figures. First, there are multiple programs that women are eligible for (and other taxes that they face), which complicate the budget constraint. For example, if Medicaid benefits are dropped when a family loses eligibility for AFDC, then a very high marginal tax rate is generated at this so-called Medicaid notch. Second, because of allowable deductions to earnings, the effective tax rate faced by these women will typically be lower than the statutory rate of 67 to 100 percent. Third, the static model does not take into account the long-term implications for current work effort, for example, through augmenting human capital and leading to higher future wages. Finally, although two-parent families represent a small fraction of AFDC participants (8 percent), they represent almost one-half of all EITC recipients (U.S. House of Representatives 1994; Eissa and Liebman 1993). The discussion here has presented the simple case of one potential earner in the family. The incentives of these programs are more complicated with two possible earners in the family.[19]

The theoretical justification for the adverse effects of the welfare system on family structure is straightforward. First, since the inception of the AFDC program, benefits for two-parent families have been nonexistent or limited. Because of unequal treatment of single- and two-parent families, the U.S. welfare system provides incentives to divorce, separate, and delay marriage and remarriage.[20] Second, for the same reasons, the welfare system provides an incentive for out-of-wedlock childbearing. Third, the benefit levels provided in most welfare programs increase with the size of the family. For example, in 1993, a single mother living in California with one child would receive an increase in her AFDC benefit of $117 (from $490 to $607) if she had an additional child.

Because the EITC provides benefits to both married and single-parent families, it appears to carry less of a marriage penalty compared to AFDC. But if both parents are working, there may be gains to splitting the family into two units if each can obtain the credit.[21]

The economic model underlying most studies of the impact of welfare programs on family structure is founded in work by Becker on marital formation and dissolution (Becker 1973, 1974, 1981). Becker's model is based on the proposition that a woman will choose marriage when the economic benefits (or utility) inside marriage exceed the economic benefits outside marriage. Implications of this model are that increases in the earnings or wages of the potential spouse will increase the probability of marriage, while increases in any benefits available outside marriage (such as welfare benefits) will decrease the probability of marriage. By the same argument, increases in benefits increase the probability of having another child or having a child out of wedlock.

4.4 Effects of Welfare on Labor Supply and Family Structure: Lessons from the Literature

The empirical literature on the incentive effects of welfare programs is largely based on evidence from three sources. The first source is differences in programs across states at a point in time. The second source is changes in programs over time. Empirical analyses using this type of variation can take the form of aggregate time-series analysis, pooled cross-section analysis, or studies using panel data. Examples used in the literature include changes in the BRR in the AFDC program in 1968 and 1981, changes in benefit levels over time, and expansions in the EITC and Medicaid programs. Studies using these two sources of variation are useful in determining how labor supply or family structure might change in response to changes in benefits or tax rates. Ultimately we are interested in not only these marginal effects but also how the existence of the programs themselves affects the outcomes of interest. We have very little program variation that allows us to observe such changes directly. Thus the existing studies are limited in their ability to make predictions about eliminating programs. These issues will be discussed in the context of welfare reform in a later section.

The third source is state-level demonstrations or experiments. State experimentation with welfare programs is typically done in a classical experiment setting, with random selection into treatment and control groups. The policy change in these cases is not limited to tinkering with benefit and tax rates but typically involves changing some other aspect of eligibility or participation. This section will concentrate on evidence from the first two sources. State experiments will be discussed in the next section.

Let us begin with a simple examination of the time-series trends in program generosity. Figure 4.8 presents trends in benefits in the AFDC, food stamps, and Medicaid programs over the past twenty-five years.[22] The most striking fact in this figure is the dramatic decline in AFDC benefits since the late 1960s. The real value of the AFDC guarantee dropped by almost 50 percent during this period, with benefits continually in decline, aside from the 1982–1988 period, when benefits were largely unchanged. The introduction of in-kind benefit programs in the late 1960s and early

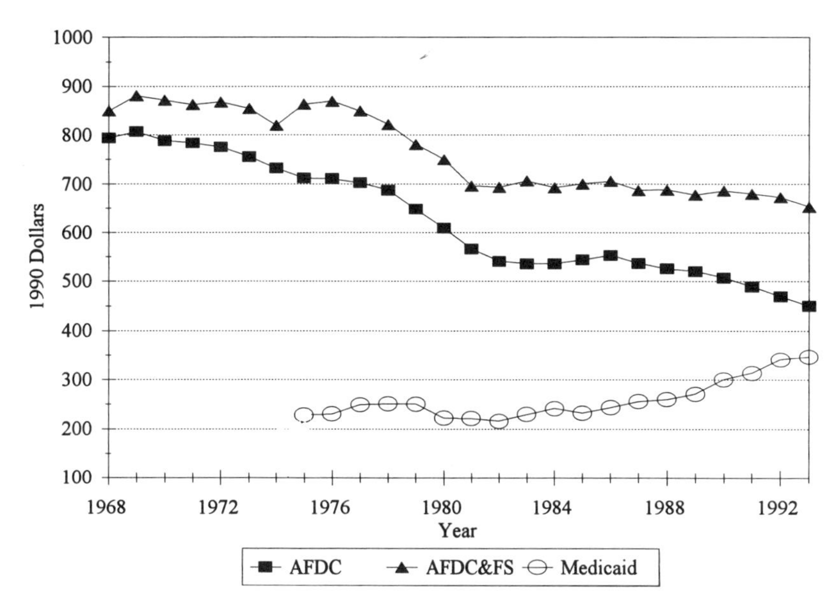

Figure 4.8
Maximum welfare benefits for a family of four, 1968–1993 (1990 dollars).

1970s moderated the decline in AFDC benefits in the early part of the period. The cash value of AFDC and food stamp benefits, as shown by the line labeled AFDC&FS, declined by about 30 percent over the period, in part due to the fact that food stamp benefits are adjusted annually for changes in food prices, whereas changes in AFDC have to be authorized by state legislatures. Despite the fact that real wages have also declined over much of this period, benefit-to-wage ratios exhibit similar trends to real benefits shown in figure 4.8 (Hoynes and MaCurdy 1994). Average state Medicaid expenditures for female-headed households have increased somewhat over the period, which, if valued by households as cash, would further moderate, but not reverse, the fall in AFDC benefits.[23]

If labor supply and family structure decisions are sensitive to the financial inducements of welfare programs, then one would expect the dramatic changes in benefits shown in figure 4.8 to be associated with changes in outcomes. Comparing the trend in benefits to the trends in female headship (figure 4.4) and nonmarital births (figure 4.5), it appears that benefits tracked these trends in family composition until the mid-1970s. Since then, real benefits have declined, while the headship rate and birthrates have continued to increase. In addition, time-series trends in labor supply and hours worked among female heads of household do not appear to track trends in AFDC tax rates or benefit levels (Moffitt 1992a). This approach is illustrative, not conclusive; there may be other factors that have changed over this time period, which, after taking them into account, may result in significant incentive effects of the welfare system. Further, comparing contemporaneous benefits with outcomes may not be appropriate, particularly for family structure decisions where welfare may affect these decisions with a significant lag, possibly through effects on long-run norms. This has not been addressed in the literature.[24]

The remainder of this section summarizes empirical studies on the effects of existing welfare programs on labor supply and family structure and will rely on existing reviews whenever possible. The vast majority of the literature has examined the incentive effects of the AFDC program, probably the result of many factors. First, in-kind programs were not introduced until the mid-1960s, some thirty years after the AFDC program and for some time were significantly smaller than the AFDC program. Second, AFDC benefits vary dramatically across the states, whereas food stamp benefits and, to a certain extent, Medicaid do not. Finally, examining in-kind benefits often requires making assumptions about how these benefits are valued by the household. Are they equivalent to cash and thus can enter directly in the budget constraint used in static labor supply analysis? Food stamp benefits are likely to be inframarginal and hence can be treated as cash transfers (Moffitt 1989). Medicaid benefits are much more difficult to value because of their insurance component.

Labor Supply

Static labor supply theory predicts that the existence of the AFDC program unambiguously leads to lower levels of labor supply among potential recipients. One of the main goals of the literature is to determine by how much labor supply is reduced among female heads of household. This is inherently difficult to measure since it requires out-of-sample prediction. Danziger, Haveman, and Plotnick (1981) and Moffitt (1992a) provide surveys of the literature and report that most studies find nontrivial disincentive effects. Overall, estimates show that the introduction of AFDC leads to a 10 to 50 percent reduction in labor supply from pretransfer levels. While the upper end of the disincentive effects is large, predicted levels of work effort among program participants in the absence of the program still remain very low compared to other female heads of household. The result is that in the absence of AFDC benefits, earnings would remain sufficiently low that fully 95 percent of previous participants would have incomes low enough to retain eligibility under the program and family income levels rarely are raised to the poverty level (Moffitt 1983). Hoynes (1996a) examines the effect of AFDC-UP on the labor supply of two-parent families and finds somewhat larger disincentive effects where husbands and wives reduce hours worked by about 80 percent from pretransfer levels. This may in part be explained by higher wage opportunities and greater work experience levels among these recipients. Page (1995) examines the effect of the FSA's expansion of AFDC-UP and finds labor supply effects consistent with Hoynes.

The evidence suggests that average levels of labor supply of female heads of household are not sensitive to changes in the BRR in the AFDC program. Although the studies find that increases in BRR lead to moderate and significant increases in labor supply among recipients, they are offset by decreases by new entrants responding to the increase in the break-even level of income (Danziger, Haveman, and Plotnick 1981; Moffitt 1992a; Hoynes 1996a). This does not necessarily imply that wage elasticities are low, but that entry effects may also be important. Because statutory levels of BRRs are constant across states, these studies typically identify the tax effect of differences in effective tax rates or wages. Examination of the time-series variation in BRR, through the reduction from 100 to 67 percent in 1968 and the increase back up to 100 in 1982, also shows no effect on labor supply (Moffitt 1992a).

The majority of welfare recipients receive not only AFDC payments but also food stamps, Medicaid, and, in about a third of the cases, subsidized housing. Only a handful of studies have taken into account these programs in estimating the work disincentives of welfare benefits. Overall, these studies show rather modest effects of in-kind programs. Fraker and Moffitt (1988) find that the food stamp program reduces labor supply among female heads of household by about 10 percent and that the combined impact of food stamps and AFDC reduces labor supply by about 21 percent. Blank (1989) and Winkler (1991) use cross-state variation in average Medicaid expenditures and find very small work disincentive effects. Moffitt and Wolfe (1992) estimate a family-specific value for Medicaid based on the health status of the family and find significantly larger effects on labor supply. Keane and Moffitt (1996) consider the combined impact of AFDC, food stamps, Medicaid, and public housing and find a modest work disincentive. In their analysis, however, they treat public housing as an entitlement. Painter (1995), accounting for rationing of public housing by controlling for average waiting times across public housing authorities, finds that ignoring housing benefits leads to an underestimate of the disincentive effects of 46 percent.

One of the most significant changes in in-kind programs is the severing of the link between AFDC receipt and Medicaid eligibility that has taken place in the past ten years. This has occurred through expanding Medicaid eligibility to children in families with incomes exceeding AFDC eligibility thresholds and providing up to one year of Medicaid coverage to families who leave AFDC for work. Yelowitz (1995) finds that expanding Medicaid coverage to children at levels above AFDc eligibility levels increased labor force participation rates by 1 percentage point among all female heads of household and reduced AFDC participation rates by 1.2 percentage points. The transitional benefits may not significantly influence welfare-to-work decisions because very few families have taken advantage of this program (Ellwood and Adams 1990).

In sum, the evidence suggests that welfare programs do create a modest work disincentive but that the existence of the programs does not completely explain the very low levels of work effort among welfare participants compared to nonparticipants. For example, Moffitt (1983) finds that AFDC benefits explain only about half of the difference in hours worked between female-headed participants and nonparticipants. Hoynes (1996a) finds that AFDC-UP benefits explain one-third of the difference among participating and nonparticipating married men and half of the difference among married women. This may be because the studies have not controlled adequately for recipients' poor work opportunities or other costs of going to work, or it may be explained by differences in tastes for work.

The empirical studies of work incentives of the EITC program have made use of the tremendous expansion of the program, in terms of both the size of the credit and the range of eligibility, which has take place over the past ten years. First, the expansion of the credit as part of the 1986 Tax Reform Act (TRA86) increased the credit rate from 11 percent to 14 percent and increased the maximum credit from $550 to $851 (U.S. House of Representatives 1994). Eissa and Liebman (1996) find that the TRA86 expansion led to a 2.8 percentage point increase in the labor force participation rate for single mothers, or a change of about 4 percent. As expected, the responses were concentrated among lower education groups, with an increase of 6 percentage points for those with less than a high school education. They found no significant effects of the EITC on hours worked for any group. They discuss several reasons that could explain the lack of an effect for hours of work. If the phase-out rate does not generate large distortions, then the deadweight loss associated with the program is potentially much lower than expected. Overall, however, Eissa and Liebman's estimated labor supply response was relatively small compared to the cost of the credit's expansion: about $23,000 per new worker.

Dickert, Hauser, and Scholz (1995) combined labor supply elasticities from the literature with their own estimates of the elasticity of labor force participation to examine the effects of the 1993 EITC expansion. Their results imply an increase in labor force participation rates of 3.3 percentage points, or 6 percent, for single mothers and 0.7 percentage point for primary earners in two-parent families. In contrast to Eissa and Liebman, they find the entry effect to be offset by significant reductions in hours of work among those already in the labor market. However, they find overall significant net positive effects of the credit on hours of work.[25] The cost of the expansion of the credit is paid for with a reduction in the AFDC caseload for single parents, but no cost savings occurs for two-parent families.

Family Formation

The early literature on the effects of AFDC on female headship is based primarily on state, Standard Metropolitan Statistical Area (SMSA), or city-level analyses. The results from this literature are mixed and find no strong evidence that AFDC has a significant effect on female headship decisions (Groeneveld, Hannan, and Tuma 1983). The more recent cross-sectional evidence, reviewed by Moffitt (1992a), shows a significant and positive but modest effect of welfare on female headship, remarriage, and divorce. These studies, however, are based on cross-state variation in welfare benefits and may be biased if there are omitted state characteristics correlated with welfare benefits. For example, a state that is more accepting of nontraditional family structures may favor a higher level of support for female-headed households. This positive correlation between benefits and unmeasured characteristics would lead to an upward bias in the estimated welfare effect. Moffitt (1994) and Hoynes (forthcoming) find that after controlling for state and individual fixed effects, the welfare effect is small and not statistically significant. Winkler (1995) finds that the FSA's expansion of AFDC-UP to all states did not lead to significant increases in marriage. Together this evidence suggests that marriage decisions are not sensitive to financial incentives.

The literature on the effect of welfare on out-of-wedlock births is also quite conclusive. Acs (1995) and Moffitt (1995) provide recent reviews of the literature on the effects of welfare on nonmarital births. Overall, these effects are often insignificant, and when they are not, they are small. Larger effects are found for whites, where, on average, a 10 percent increase in benefits leads to a 5 percent increase in the nonmarital birth rate (Acs 1995). All but one study found insignificant results for blacks. All but a few of these studies rely on cross-state variation, and the estimates are very sensitive to the other state controls that the included (Moffitt 1995). As with female headship, unmeasured state characteristics can potentially bias the estimated welfare effect. Ellwood and Bane (1985) and Jackson and Klerman (1995) look at changes over time within states and control for state characteristics and find no effect of welfare on nonmarital births for blacks or whites. Only a few studies examine the effects of welfare on subsequent births, and none of them has found a positive effect (Acs 1995).

4.5 Evidence from State Experiments

The studies discussed in the previous section use differences in policy across states or over time, or both, to estimate the effects of welfare programs on labor supply and family structure. An additional source of information, which is rising in importance, is the evidence based on the evaluation of state experimentation with AFDC programs—typically in the form of demonstration projects in selected localities within the state where a relatively small number of randomly chosen welfare recipients are randomly assigned to treatment or control groups. Within this classical experiment setting, the effects of the policy change or "treatment" is measured as the difference in the outcome of interest between the treatment and control groups (Hausman and Wise 1985). The policy changes considered within this setting are becoming increasingly diverse and include changes in participation requirements, eligibility, and benefit formulas.

The roots of state experimentation with the AFDC program are in the Social Security Act, the legislation that established the program. Although states have control over the setting of benefits and income eligibility rules, the act also gives authority to the secretary of the Department of Health and Human Services to "waive specified requirements of the Social Security Act pertaining to the AFDC program in order to enable a State to carry out any experimental, pilot, or demonstration projects that the Secretary judges likely to help in promoting the objectives of the program" (U.S. House of Representatives 1994, p. 364).

The modern use of state experiments began with the Reagan administration and has increased steadily throughout the Bush and Clinton administrations. The experiments of the 1980s and early 1990s were primarily welfare-to-work programs, with job search, work experience, job training, and education components. The Omnibus Reconciliation Act of 1981 (OBRA) had two major provisions aimed at reducing the AFDC caseload: it increased the BRR from 67 to 100 percent, and it provided guidelines for states to engage participants in employment and training programs. These guidelines were not mandates but provided an "OBRA toolbox" that states could use to innovate (Greenberg and Wiseman 1992). By the end of 1989, twenty-four evaluations were conducted on programs within nineteen states. Most of these programs took the form of mandatory job search programs for eligible adults in recipient families.[26] These programs were found to have a relatively small impact on earnings, employment, and the welfare caseload. The largest results were in the range of decreasing AFDC participation by 5 percentage points and increasing quarterly earnings by $100 (Greenberg and Wiseman 1992) and were concentrated among moderately disadvantaged recipients (Gueron and Pauly 1991).[27] Low-cost programs focusing on rapid placement generated greater cost-benefit calculations relative to higher-intensity, higher-cost programs focusing on training and education (Gueron and Pauly 1991).

Despite the rather modest impact of the OBRA demonstrations, they had a significant impact on welfare policy as reflected in the passage in 1988 of the Family Support Act (Wiseman 1991). The centerpiece of the FSA in the establishment of an employment, education, and training program for AFDC recipients, the Job Opportunities for Basic Skills (JOBS) program. While the FSA requires that all states implement a JOBS program, there is considerable freedom for the states in the design of a program. JOBS programs typically consist of some combination of education and training, job search and placement, and work experience. States have to decide, among other things, how to allocate resources between low-cost and high-cost programs and to whom the program will be targeted. Subject to available resources, however, participation is required among all nonexempt recipients.[28] In short, eligible recipients are expected to take jobs and participate in employment services, and the state is expected to provide services and the incentives to find employment.

Overall, participation in JOBS programs has increased dramatically such that in 1992, 23 percent of eligible adults were participating (U.S.

House of Representatives 1994). The evaluations of the state JOBS programs suggest that they have a modest impact on earnings, employment, and welfare participation. In order to illustrate the effect of JOBS programs, consider the case of the Greater Avenues for Education (GAIN) program, a California JOBS program that has been operating since the mid-1980s and is widely believed to be the most successful in the country. The most dramatic results among all major JOBS evaluations in the country have been found for Riverside County, a mixed urban-rural county located southeast of Los Angeles, which developed a low-cost program focusing on immediate job placement. Over a three-year period, the GAIN program increased employment rates by 14 percentage points, or 25 percent, and AFDC participation decreased by about 13 percent (Riccio, Friedlander, and Freedman 1994). The overall reduction in government expenses relative to the cost of the program was substantial: $2.84 per $1.00 invested. However, more resource-intensive programs, focusing on education and training of long-term recipients in urban areas, found much smaller results, yielding negative returns to the program.[29]

Beginning in the early 1990s, state demonstrations advanced far beyond employment and training programs. In January 1992, waivers had been approved for fifteen projects in nine states. At the Bush administration's encouragement, 1992 brought more than fifteen additional projects (Wiseman 1993).[30] Under the Clinton administration, more than twenty-five new or revised plans have been approved. The provisions being implemented as part of this waiver process affect nearly every facet of eligibility and benefit rules and include:

- Provisions concerning two-parent families, such as elimination of the 100-hour rule and work requirements for AFDC-UP participants.
- Changes in the benefit formula, such as reducing the benefit reduction rate, modifying allowable deductions, and implementing a two-tier benefit schedule, with benefits reduced after a fixed time on the program.
- Provisions for teenagers, such as establishing incentives for them to stay in school and live with their parents.
- Imposing a family cap, whereby benefits are not increased if an additional child is born while the family is on welfare.
- Establishing incentives for paternity identification.
- Imposing time limits on welfare receipt.
- Liberalizing asset tests.

Although the evaluations of these demonstrations will provide important information for reforming AFDC, the programs are in their infancy, and it is too early to include any information for this review.

The rise of experimentation at the state level is a significant trend in welfare policy. It is important, however, to keep in mind the limitations for their use in designing nationwide or even statewide welfare policy. First, state demonstrations are typically quite small in scale and take place in select communities in the state. The scale of the program limits the realization of possible macro or community feedback effects, such as the effect of the program on labor markets, social norms, and information diffusion (Garfinkel, Manski, and Michalopoulos 1992). If the sites for the program are not randomly selected, then the ability for wide-scale replication is uncertain (Greenberg and Wiseman 1992). Second, most of the current state demonstrations involve multiple changes to AFDC eligibility and benefits. For example, the Wisconsin Parental and Family Responsibility Initiative (PFRI) is aimed at teenaged recipients and simultaneously imposes a partial family cap, liberalizes the treatment of deductions against earned income, expands benefits for two-parent families by removing the 100-hour rule and the work history requirements, and increases the incentive for paternity establishment within one year of a child's birth (Wiseman 1993). In these demonstrations, recipients in the "treatment group" will experience all of these changes, and the evaluation of the program will show the net effect of all of them on employment and welfare outcomes. This multiple treatment approach will make it very difficult to determine the relative benefits of the various components of the law changes. Third, these demonstrations are typically of a limited duration. Since the recipients in the treatment group know this, they may be unlikely to make changes given uncertainty about future rules. This may be particularly true for long-term decisions, like marriage and having a child. Last, changes in eligibility and benefits will change the overall generosity of welfare, which may affect entry into the program. The demonstrations typically are based on a sample of recipients and thus will not measure the entry effect (Moffitt 1992b).

4.6 Welfare Reform, Work, and Family Structure

Current welfare reform proposals are motivated by a desire to achieve an overlapping set of goals: reducing dependency on the system, decreasing long-term dependence, reducing program costs and caseloads, encouraging work, encouraging the formation of two-parent families, and discouraging nonmarital childbearing. These goals are not new; in fact, they underlie reforms to the system that have been debated and to some extent implemented over the past twenty-five years. This section begins with a taxonomy of welfare reforms past and present. Some represent failed attempts at reform and others represent changes implemented at the state or nationwide level. This discussion is not meant to be a comprehensive history of welfare reform but presents the main measures aimed at strengthening the incentives to work and form two-parent families.

A Taxonomy of Welfare Reform

Let us begin with separating reforms into those inside welfare and those outside welfare (Ellwood 1988). Within those groups we will consider financial and nonfinancial measures.

Reforms Inside Welfare

Financial Incentives Over the history of the program, financial incentives have been the most common policy tool used in attempting to increase work and decrease welfare dependency. Changes to tax rates and benefit levels are the most prominent example of such a policy. The negative income tax experiments of the late 1960s and early 1970s represent the most significant, but unsuccessful, attempt at reforming the structure of benefit and tax rates.[31] Other examples are the decrease of the BRR in 1968 and its increase in 1982. Current state experiments reflect a renewed interest in affecting work incentives through changes in benefit rules. Many states have received waivers to implement decreases in tax rates, changes in the treatment of deductions in calculating benefits, and reductions in benefits.

Currently the use of financial incentives has expanded to encourage the formation of two-parent families and discourage nonmarital childbearing. Family cap provisions reduce or eliminate additional AFDC benefits if a child was born while the mother is on aid. Another example is the elimination of benefits for unmarried teenaged mothers unless they live with their parents or the provision of financial incentives to stay in school.

The justification for these reforms is simple. They place higher costs on undesirable behavior relative to desirable behavior, and their effectiveness depends on the sensitivity of individuals to these financial incentives, or disincentives.

Categorical Eligibility Rules Past reforms have expanded eligibility to two-parent families in order to encourage their formation. The FSA requires that all states provide AFDC benefits to two-parent families. In addition, many states are experimenting with eliminating the 100-hour work limit and work history requirements for the primary earner in the AFDC-UP family, which is an eligibility condition imposed on two-parent families but not single parents.

Current proposals limit eligibility in order to discourage nonmarital childbearing, such as prohibiting unmarried teenaged mothers from receiving AFDC. Another example of changing categorical eligibility is time-limiting benefits, thereby discontinuing eligibility after some fixed period of time on welfare. These proposals are also part of the state experiments now planned or in progress.

Transitional and Support Services Moving from welfare to work commonly results in two important sources of economic hardship in addition to losing AFDC benefits: the cost of child care and the loss of medical insurance through Medicaid. Both of these issues were addressed in the FSA. In order to make the transition to employment less costly, the FSA mandates twelve months of Medicaid coverage for the family after leaving AFDC for work and establishes programs to subsidize the cost of child care for working welfare recipients.

Welfare-to-Work Programs Welfare recipients have relatively low education levels and limited work experience and skills necessary to find employment. These shortcomings produce low earnings opportunities and, hence, small or no gains from seeking employment. These facts have motivated the reforms requiring participation of welfare recipients in mandatory work programs (often known as workfare), education and training programs, and job search and placement programs. The goal of each of these programs is to reduce the caseload through increased work effort. In workfare programs, this is achieved by providing work experience, while education and training programs expand wage opportunities through increasing human capital. Job search and placement programs reduce the costs associated with job search and build skills necessary for successful interviews and job performance. This reform, which has its roots in earlier legislation, culminated in the FSA, which included provisions requiring participation by all nonexempt adults in state-designed and -run welfare-to-work programs.

Reforms Outside Welfare

Financial Incentives Financial incentives have been used primarily to increase the returns to work. The most prominent, and most costly, of reforms implemented outside the welfare system is the expansion in the EITC over the past ten years. The EITC is advanced as a partial replacement of welfare by transferring income to poor families while minimizing the work disincentives associated with the program. Another example of this type of reform is increasing the minimum wage.

Health Care and Child Support When the Medicaid program was established, participation among families with children was linked to AFDC recipiency such that when a family earned enough to get off AFDC, it also lost Medicaid coverage. Recent expansions in Medicaid eligibility have severed the link between AFDC receipt and Medicaid coverage by providing coverage for poor children. In states with low AFDC benefit levels, the result has been significant expansions of eligibility. The effect of these expansions in the Medicaid program is to reduce both the cost of seeking employment and forming two-parent families.

The FSA contained provisions designed to reduce dependency on welfare by increasing the role of the absent parent. The first element provides incentives for paternity establishment, and the second establishes guidelines for setting child support payments and facilitating payment collection.

Expected Effects of Current Reforms

Summarizing decades of reform is not easy, but the conclusion that emerges from the evidence is that tinkering with the system is not likely to yield significant results. For example, changes in the BRR have not led to significant increases in work effort (Moffitt 1992a), and the introduction and expansion of welfare-to-work programs has had positive effects, but the results are modest and are not likely to generate huge reductions in the caseload (Gueron and Pauly 1991). On the other hand, reforms outside AFDC, such as expanding the EITC and Medicaid, may generate more sizable increases in labor supply (Dickert, Hauser, and Scholz 1995; Eissa and Liebman 1996; Yelowitz 1995). In the light of these findings, recent interest in reforming welfare focuses on more dramatic changes to eligibility and benefit rules. The current elements, focused on family structure, include eliminating benefits for additional children while on welfare, prohibiting or limiting the availability of benefits for unmarried teenaged mothers, and expanding benefits for two-parent families by eliminating additional work restrictions. Elements focused on decreasing dependency and increasing work include time-limiting benefits and liberalizing the benefit formula to increase the returns to work.[32]

The interest in welfare reform culminated in the fall of 1996 with passage of the Personal Responsibility and Work Opportunity Reconciliation Act of 1996. This sweeping welfare reform legislation ends the entitlement nature of the AFDC program by converting the program into a block grant to the states and giving the states greater flexibility in designing their own welfare programs. Some provisions in the new law include: prohibiting legal immigrants from receiving aid, requiring parents to work within two years, and imposing a five-year lifetime limit for receiving aid. It is likely that this reform will lead to additional changes in eligibility and benefit rules in many states. At this writing we do not know much about state implementation of the law. Instead let us consider possible reforms at the state level and the likely effects of these reforms on labor supply and family structure.

The available evidence suggests that family structure decisions are not sensitive to financial incentives. Thus provisions aimed at discouraging nonmarital births and female headship will have very small impacts. However, it is important to note that this conclusion is based on empirical evidence that uses cross-state differences or changes in benefit levels over time to estimate the program's effect on family structure. One should exercise caution when using studies to evaluate the effects of a change policy (e.g., eliminating a program for a subgroup) that has not been observed in previous data. Eliminating work requirements for two-parent families on AFDC-UP is not likely to lead to significant increases in marriage rates because the existing constraints are not binding for most couples (Hoynes 1996a) and the expansion of the AFDC-UP program as part of the FSA did not significantly affect family structure decisions (Winkler 1995).

Implementing time limits for AFDC receipt is likely to yield mixed results. With a five-year limit, 35 to 45 percent of new welfare entrants or three-quarters of the existing welfare population will be affected (Pavetti 1995; Ellwood 1986). Employment prospects for these long-term recipients are limited because over half enter welfare with no work experience and over 60 percent have less than a high school education (Pavetti 1995). Recent experience with eliminating Michigan's general assistance program also supports the claim that women may have difficulty finding employment. Two years after male general assistance recipients were removed from the roles, only 20 percent had found steady employment (Danziger and Kossoudji 1995).[33] Further, the employment outcomes of AFDC recipients may be very sensitive to local economic conditions (Hoynes 1996b). Together, this evidence suggests that family incomes could fall dramatically if time limits were implemented.[34] On the other hand, using evidence from France, Hanratty (1994) estimates that time-limiting benefits for single mothers has increased labor force participation rates by 11 percentage points, an increase of 25 percent. This is based on a means-tested program much like the AFDC program except that eligibility ends when the youngest child turns age three. These results may have limited applicability for the United States because France also provides universal medical care and high-quality free day care and preschool programs (Hanratty 1994).

Changing benefits formulas to increase work incentives is likely to generate minimal increases in labor supply. This is one area where we do have a significant body of evidence, and collectively it suggests that marginal changes to implicit tax rates faced by welfare recipients are not likely to have significant effects on labor supply (Moffitt 1992a). Increasing returns to work within welfare may increase labor supply for current recipients, but this is likely to be offset by reductions in labor supply among new entrants onto the program. Eliminating the 100-hour rule for two-parent families not only furthers the evening of the playing field between single- and two-parent families but also is designed to eliminate the inherent work disincentive that it creates. Hoynes (1996a), by estimating the structural parameters of household utility function, is able to examine the implications of elimination of the 100-hour rule and finds that it is likely to increase labor supply among AFDC-UP recipients without significantly increasing the program caseload. However, since participation in AFDC-UP is still very low, this is unlikely to have a significant impact on the income of the poor.

4.7 Summary and Policy Recommendations

This chapter has explored the validity of the claims that our welfare system causes low levels of work effort and high rates of female headship and nonmarital childbearing. Although it is true that the system provides adverse incentives for the formation of two-parent families, the empirical studies show conclusively that the magnitude of these disincentive effects is very small, such that the welfare system itself cannot explain the high rates of headship and illegitimacy. The estimated work disincentive effects of welfare programs are somewhat larger in size and show that public assistance programs explain about half of the difference in labor supply between participants and nonparticipants.

These results imply that current reforms aimed at reducing female headship and nonmarital births, such as family caps, eliminating benefits for teenagers, and equal treatment of two-parent families, are unlikely to generate large effects. Changes to implicit tax rates and benefit formulas may increase work among current recipients, but overall work effort may not be affected. Any changes should be accompanied by resources for job search and training, although these programs alone are not a panacea. These predictions should be accompanied by a word of caution. Many of the proposed changes have never been implemented at the state or federal level and require out-of-sample predictions. Current state experimentation may help fill this gap.

As the importance of in-kind benefits continues to rise, we need to continue to examine the implications of these programs on labor supply and family structure. In addition, as two-parent families become an increasingly large minority of welfare recipients, more research should focus on that group.

Notes

I thank Cindy Gustafson, Gabe Hanz, Patrick Wang, and Mark Wu for excellent research assistance. I also thank Alan Auerbach, David Cutler, Nada Eissa, Larry Katz, Jeff Liebman, and Robert Moffitt for helpful comments. Financial support was received from NICHD.

1. There is also a concern that the structure of benefits in programs for the disabled discourage work effort. These issues will not be covered here.

2. Other means-tested programs serving low-income families include school lunch programs; supplemental food program for women, infants, and children (WIC); energy assistance; Head Start; and various training programs. These programs are small compared to those mentioned in the text and have not received much attention in the literature. The other major public assistance programs in the United States are the Supplemental Security Income (SSI) program, which serves low-income elderly and disabled persons, and general assistance (GA) programs, which serve primarily single men. Low-income families also may receive social insurance benefits, such as unemployment compensation or social security.

3. In addition to the net income test, gross family income must be less than 1.85 times the need standard, which is also state determined and is typically lower than the maximum benefit level. The asset test limits real and personal property, excluding home equity and vehicle equity, to $1,000. Unlike income limits, this is set federally.

4. Two-parent families must satisfy two conditions not required of single parents. First, the primary wage earner in the family cannot work more than 100 hours per month. This hours

limitation is the origin for the term *unemployed* in AFDC-UP. Second, the primary wage earner must display previous "significant" attachment to the labor force. Significant attachment is typically satisfied if the worker was employed and earned at least $50 in at least six of the last thirteen calendar quarters, or was eligible to receive unemployment compensation sometime in the last year. Finally, the 1988 FSA mandates that states set up AFDC-UP programs, but it allows states to limit benefits to six months per year.

5. In addition to the standard deduction, one can also deduct child care expenses. In 1993 the maximum child care deduction was $200 per child per month for children less than two years old and $175 for children over two.

6. Starting in 1994, a small EITC was made available to childless workers ages twenty-five to sixty-four with earnings up to $9,000.

7. States can, and many do, cover children at higher income levels than required by Congress.

8. Other housing programs serving low-income households include rural housing programs, programs serving home owners, and farm programs.

9. Expenditures include the combined cost of federal, state, and local governments for a comprehensive set of means-tested transfer programs, including those in table 4.2 plus many other smaller programs such as school lunch programs, student loan programs, housing programs, and job training programs.

10. This information is based on Edin's in-depth interviews with fifty female-headed households receiving AFDC and living in Chicago. None lived on welfare alone; many worked off the books in legitimate jobs, and a few received income from drugs or prostitution. It is not clear whether these figures can be generalized to the entire AFDC caseload, which is very heterogeneous. Most states have developed tracking systems that link welfare case files to quarterly unemployment insurance earnings records. This catches unreported work in the covered sector but does not address work in the underground economy.

11. Because a minority of AFDC recipients receive housing benefits, they are not considered here. Including housing benefits would increase the estimated tax rates.

12. In 1990, 27 percent of working poor families paid for child care and spent, on average, 33 percent of family income on child care (Hofferth et al. 1991). Urban welfare recipients are more likely to have to pay for care (Mathematica Policy Research 1988).

13. Although the tax rate is set federally, California received permission from the Department of Health and Human Services to extend the 30 and 1/3 rule past the four-month limit. The lower tax rate was made permanent there in September 1993.

14. The tax rate is calculated as one minus the change in disposable income over the change in earnings.

15. The phase-out range of the EITC imposes a high MTR at high levels of work effort, but at the relatively low hourly wage in this simulation, the woman never reaches the phase-out range of the credit.

16. Note that in the top panel of table 4.4, the MTR of going from part-time to full-time work increases substantially between $5.00 and $7.50 per hour wage rate. This is because the worker earns enough to move into the phase-out range of the EITC, where the tax rate is over 20 percent.

17. These figures report what fraction worked at all last year among all those receiving welfare last year. Employment rates among current recipients are quite a bit lower. It is well recognized that these differences between recipients and nonrecipients should not be interpreted as a disincentive effect of welfare because families may be self-selected in the welfare recipient group (Moffitt 1983).

18. In the flat range there is only an income effect, leading to lower levels of work effort. In the phase-out range, the reduction in the net wage leads to lower work effort by decreasing the return to work (substitution effect) and increasing income, holding work effort constant (income effect).

19. For example, while the EITC encourages labor force participation for single parents, it is not necessarily valid for married couples. Depending on the income of the primary earner in the family, the incentives for the secondary earner may be to reduce hours (or earnings). The EITC may then be substituting for income that otherwise the secondary earner in the household would have contributed.

20. Actually AFDC provides disincentives to live with the natural father of the children, regardless of marital status. Cohabitating with an unrelated male is treated quite leniently in terms of eligibility and treatment of his income. Further, in many states, marrying a man unrelated to the children does not affect eligibility or benefit levels. The rules and incentives for cohabitation and marriage are discussed at length in Moffitt, Reville, and Winkler (1995).

21. For an illustrative example, see the comments to this chapter by Nada Eissa.

22. AFDC benefits are calculated as the weighted average of maximum benefit levels for a family of four in the fifty states, using the caseload as the weight. AFDC&FS is the combined value of AFDC and food stamp benefits and is equal to 70 percent of the maximum AFDC benefit plus the food stamp maximum benefit. The 70 percent results from AFDC income being "taxed" in calculating the food stamp benefit. Medicaid benefits are average benefits by state for a family of four. The AFDC data came from unpublished tables from the Family Support Administration, Department of Health and Human Services. The food stamp data came from unpublished tables from the Food and Nutrition Service, Department of Agriculture. The Medicaid data were provided by Robert Moffitt.

23. If the value of Medicaid to families is equal to the average expenditure, then the combined benefits in the three programs increased somewhat until the mid-1970s, declined until the late 1980s, and increased somewhat at the end of the period.

24. One exception is Murray (1993), who examines aggregate trends in nonmarital births and finds higher correlation with welfare benefits when a long lag is used.

25. In order to perform this calculation, Dickert, Hauser, and Scholz (1995) assume that new entrants in the labor market work twenty hours per week, for twenty weeks in the year.

26. Single parents with children under the age of six were usually excluded from the requirements.

27. These program effects, and all the other evidence in this section, are derived from comparisons of outcomes in the treatment group to outcomes in the control group.

28. Among the individuals who are exempt from participation in JOBS programs include those with a child less than three years old, those who are sick or are caring for a sick family member, or those residing in an area where services are not being provided (U.S. House of Representatives 1994).

29. The program in Alameda County, containing the city of Oakland, generated a return of $0.45 per $1.00 spent on the program while Los Angeles County generated a benefit-to-cost ratio of $0.26 (Riccio, Friedlander, and Freedman 1994).

30. As described in Wiseman (1993), Bush stressed the importance of innovation at the state level and promised that the waiver process would become more streamlined and less arduous for state welfare officials.

31. Like AFDC, a negative income tax program is characterized by two parameters: the benefit guarantee and the benefit reduction rate. The income maintenance experiments took place in four cities where several alternative combinations of benefit levels and tax rates were implemented. Many sources provide overviews of the experiments and the many outcomes studied; for example, see Munnell (1987).

32. One significant element in current welfare reform discussions is to convert the AFDC program into a block grant provided to the states to establish their own programs. If implemented, this is likely to cause many changes to the nation's welfare system as the entitlement nature of the program is eliminated. The potential implications for labor supply and family structure are difficult to discuss until we see how states respond. See Sawhill (1995) for a general discussion of the implications of block grants, and Quigley and Rubinfeld (1996) for a discussion of the likely state response.

33. This group may be more job ready than AFDC recipients because over three-quarters had some previous work experience, and all are childless. Their rates of disability were high, however, reflected by the fact that one-third of the group is now receiving disability benefits (Danziger and Kossoudji 1995).

34. Some plans for time-limiting benefits would provide for a public sector or subsidized job for those unable to find employment. This would act to lessen the impact of time-limiting benefits.

References

Acs, Gregory. 1995. "Do Welfare Benefits Promote Out-of-Wedlock Childbearing?" In Isabel Sawhill, ed., *Welfare Reform: An Analysis of the Issues*. Washington, DC: Urban Institute.

Ashenfelter, Orley. 1983. "Determining Participation in Income-Tested Social Programs." *Journal of the American Statistical Society* 78:517–525.

Becker, Gary. 1973. "A Theory of Marriage: Part I." *Journal of Political Economy* 81:813–846.

Becker, Gary. 1974. "A Theory of Marriage: Part II." *Journal of Political Economy* 82:511–526.

Becker, Gary. 1981. *A Treatise on the Family*. Cambridge: Harvard University Press.

Blank, Rebecca. 1989. "The Effect of Medical Need and Medicaid on AFDC Participation." *Journal of Human Resources* 24:54–87.

Blank, Rebecca, and Patricia Ruggles. 1996. "When Do Women Use Aid to Families with Dependent Children and Food Stamps? The Dynamics of Eligibility versus Participation." *Journal of Human Resources* 31(1):57–89.

Burtless, Gary. 1994. "Public Spending on the Poor: Historical Trends and Economic Limits." In Sheldon Danziger, Gary Sandefur, and Daniel Weinberg, eds., *Confronting Poverty: Prescriptions for Change*. Cambridge, MA: Harvard University Press.

Congressional Research Service. Library of Congress. 1993. *Cash and Noncash Benefits for Persons with Limited Income: Eligibility Rules, Recipient and Expenditure Data, FY 1990–92.* Washington, DC: U.S. Government Printing Office.

Danziger, Sandra, and Sherrie Kossoudji. 1995. "When Welfare Ends: Subsistence Strategies of Former GA Recipients." Mimeo. University of Michigan School of Social Work.

Danziger, Sheldon, Robert Haveman, and Robert Plotnick. 1981. "How Income Transfer Programs Affect Work, Savings, and the Income Distribution: A Critical Review." *Journal of Economic Literature* 24(3):975–1028.

Danziger, Sheldon, and Daniel Weinberg. 1994. "The Historical Record: Trends in Family Income, Inequality, and Poverty." In Sheldon Danziger, Gary Sandefur, and Daniel Weinberg, eds., *Confronting Poverty: Prescriptions for Change.* Cambridge, MA: Harvard University Press.

Dickert, Stacy, Scott Hauser, and John Karl Scholz. 1994. "Taxes and the Poor: A Microsimulation Study of Implicit and Explicit Taxes." *National Tax Journal* 47:76–97.

Dickert, Stacy, Scott Hauser, and John Karl Scholz. 1995. "The Earned Income Tax Credit and Transfer Programs: A Study of Labor Market and Program Participation." In James Poterba, ed., *Tax Policy and the Economy.* Cambridge MA: MIT Press.

Edin, Kathryn, and Christopher Jencks. 1992. "Reforming Welfare." In Christopher Jencks, ed., *Rethinking Social Policy: Race, Poverty, and the Underclass.* Cambridge, MA: Harvard University Press.

Eissa Nada, and Jeffrey Liebman. 1993. "The End of Welfare as We Know it? Behavioral Responses to the Earned Income Tax Credit." Mimeo. Harvard University.

Eissa Nada, and Jeffrey Liebman. 1996. "Labor Supply Response to the Earned Income Tax Credit." *Quarterly Journal of Economics* 111(2):605–637.

Ellwood, David T. 1986. "Targeting Would-be Long Term Recipients of AFDC." Prepared for the U.S. Department of Health and Human Services, Office of the Assistant Secretary for Planning and Evaluation. Princeton, NJ: Mathematica Policy Research.

Ellwood, David T. 1988. *Poor Support.* New York: Basic Books.

Ellwood, David T., and E. Kathleen Adams. 1990. "Medicaid Mysteries: Transitional Benefits, Medicaid Coverage, and Welfare Exits." *Health Care Financing Review* 11:119–131.

Ellwood, David T., and Mary Jo Bane. 1985. "The Impact of AFDC on Family Structure and Living Arrangements." In Ron G. Ehrenberg, ed., *Research in Labor Economics,* vol. 7. Greenwich, CT: JAI Press.

Fraker, Thomas, and Robert Moffitt. 1988. "The Effect of Food Stamps on Labor Supply: A Bivariate Selection Model." *Journal of Public Economics* 35(1):25–56.

Garfinkel, Irwin, Charles Manski, and Charles Michalopoulos. 1992. "Micro Experiments and Macro Effects." In Charles Manski and Irwin Garfinkel, eds., *Evaluating Welfare and Training Programs.* Cambridge, MA: Harvard University Press.

Giannarelli, Linda, and Eugene Steuerle. 1995. "The Twice Poverty Trap: Tax Rates Faced by AFDC Recipients." Mimeo. Washington, DC: Urban Institute.

Greenberg, David, and Michael Wiseman. 1992. "What Did the Work-Welfare Demonstrations Do?" In Charles Manski and Irwin Garfinkel, eds., *Evaluating Welfare and Training Programs.* Cambridge, MA: Harvard University Press.

Groeneveld, Lyle, Michael Hannan, and Nancy Tuma. 1983. *Final Report of the Seattle/Denver Income Maintenance Experiment*. Vol. 1: *Design and Results*. Washington, DC: U.S. Government Printing Office.

Gueron, Judith, and Edward Pauly. 1991. *From Welfare to Work*. New York: Russell Sage Foundation.

Hanratty, Maria. 1994. "Social Programs for Women and Children: The United States versus France." In Rebecca Blank, ed., *Social Protection Versus Economic Flexibility*. Chicago: University of Chicago Press.

Hausman, Jerry, and David Wise. 1985. *Social Experimentation*. Chicago: University of Chicago Press.

Hofferth, Sandra, April Brayfield, Sharon Deich, and Pamela Holcomb. 1991. *National Child Care Survey, 1990*. Report 91-5. Washington, DC: Urban Institute.

Hoynes, Hilary. 1996a. "Welfare Transfers in Two-Parent Families: The Case of AFDC-UP." *Econometrica* 64(2):295–332.

Hoynes, Hilary. 1996b. "Local Labor Markets and Welfare Spells: Do Demand Conditions Matter?" Mimeo. University of California, Berkeley.

Hoynes, Hilary. Forthcoming. "Does Welfare Play Any Role in Female Headship Decisions?" *Journal of Public Economics*.

Hoynes, Hilary Williamson, and Thomas MaCurdy. 1994. "Has the Decline in Benefits Shortened Welfare Spells?" *American Economic Review* 84(2).

Jackson, Catherine, and Jacob Klerman. 1995. "Welfare and American Fertility." Mimeo. Santa Monica, CA: Rand.

Keane, Michael, and Robert Moffitt. 1996. *A Structural Model of Multiple Welfare Program Participation*. Institute for Research on Poverty Discussion Paper 1080–96.

Levy, Frank. 1979. "The Labor Supply of Female Household Heads, or AFDC Work Incentives Don't Work Too Well." *Journal of Human Resources* 14:76–97.

Mathematica Policy Research. 1988. *Surveys of Child Care Supply and Needs*. Princeton, NJ: Mathematica Policy Research.

Moffitt, Robert. 1983. "An Economic Model of Welfare Stigma." *American Economic Review* 73(5):1023–1035.

Moffitt, Robert. 1989. "Estimating the Value of an In-Kind Transfer: The Case of Food Stamps." *Econometrica* 57:385–409.

Moffitt, Robert. 1992a. "Incentive Effects of the U.S. Welfare System: A Review." *Journal of Economic Literature* 30:1–61.

Moffitt, Robert. 1992b. "Evaluation Methods for Program Entry Effects." In Charles Manski and Irwin Garfinkel, eds., *Evaluating Welfare and Training Programs*. Cambridge, MA: Harvard University Press.

Moffitt, Robert. 1994. "Welfare Effects on Female Headship with Area Effects." *Journal of Human Resources* 29(2):621–636.

Moffitt, Robert. 1995. "The Effect of the Welfare System on Nonmarital Childbearing." In National Center for Health Statistics, *Report to Congress on Out-of-Wedlock Childbearing*. Hyattsville, MD: Public Health Service.

Moffitt, Robert, Robert Reville, and Anne Winkler. 1995. *Beyond Single Mothers: Cohabitation, Marriage and the U.S. Welfare System.* Institute for Research on Poverty Discussion Paper 1068–95.

Moffitt, Robert, and Barbara Wolfe. 1992. "The Effect of the Medicaid Program on Welfare Participation and Labor Supply." *Review of Economics and Statistics* 74:615–626.

Munnell, Alicia. 1987. *Lessons from the Income Maintenance Experiments.* Boston: Federal Reserve Bank of Boston and Brookings Institution.

Murray, Charles. 1993. "Welfare and the Family: The U.S. Experience." *Journal of Labor Economics* 11(p. 2):S224–S262.

National Center for Health Statistics. 1994. *Monthly Vital Statistics Report,* vol. 43, no. 5(S). Hyattsville, MD: Public Health Service.

Page, Marianne. 1995. "Welfare and Work in Two-Parent Families: The Effect of AFDC-UP on the Labor Supply of Husbands and Wives." Mimeo. The University of Michigan.

Painter, Gary. 1995. "Welfare Reform: Can We Learn from the Rationing of Housing Assistance?" Mimeo. University of California Berkeley.

Pavetti, LaDonna. 1995. "Who Is Affected by Time-Limits?" In Isabel Sawhill, ed., *Welfare Reform: An Analysis of the Issues.* Washington, DC: Urban Institute.

Quigley, John, and Daniel Rubinfeld. 1996. "Federalism as a Device for Reducing the Budget of the Central Government." Paper presented to the Conference on Fiscal Policy: Lessons from Economic Research, University of California, Berkeley.

Riccio, James, Daniel Friedlander, and Stephen Freedman. 1994. *GAIN: Benefits, Costs, and Three-Year Impacts of a Welfare to Work Program.* New York: Manpower Demonstration Research Corporation.

Sawhill, Isabel. 1995. *Welfare Reform: An Analysis of the Issues.* Washington, DC: Urban Institute.

Social Security Administration. 1995. *Social Security Bulletin, Annual Statistical Supplement.* Washington, DC: U.S. Government Printing Office.

U.S. Bureau of Census. Various years. Current Population Reports, Series P-20. *Household and Family Characteristics.* Washington, DC: U.S. Government Printing Office.

U.S. House of Representatives. 1994. *Background Materials and Data on Programs Within the Jurisdiction of the Committee on Ways and Means.* Washington, DC: U.S. Government Printing Office.

Ventura, Stephanie. 1995. *Births to Unmarried Mothers: United States, 1980–1992. National Center for Health Statistics. Vital and Health Statistics,* ser. 21, no. 53.

Ventura, Stephanie, Christine Bachrach, Laura Hill, Kelleen Kaye, Pamela Holcomb, and Elisa Koff. 1995. "The Demography of Out-of-Wedlock Childbearing." In National Center for Health Statistics, *Report to Congress on Out-of-Wedlock Childbearing.* Hyattsville, MD: Public Health Service.

Winkler, Anne. 1991. "The Incentive Effects of Medicaid on Women's Labor Supply." *Journal of Human Resources* 26:308–337.

Winkler, Anne. 1995. "Does AFDC-UP Encourage Two-Parent Families?" *Journal of Policy Analysis and Management* 14(1):4–24.

Wiseman, Michael. 1991. "Research and Policy: A Symposium on the Family Support Act of 1988." *Journal of Policy Analysis and Management* 10(4):588–666.

Wiseman, Michael. 1993. *The New State Welfare Initiatives.* University of Wisconsin, Madison, Institute for Research on Poverty, Discussion Paper 1009–93.

Yelowitz, Aaron. 1995. "The Medicaid Notch, Labor Supply and Welfare Participation: Evidence from Eligibility Expansions." *Quarterly Journal of Economics* 110(4):909–940.

Comment

Nada Eissa

Hilary Hoynes's chapter is centered around three issues. First, what is the structure of the current welfare system in the United States, and who does it serve? Second, what lessons have we learned from the empirical literature about the effects of welfare on work and marriage? Hoynes extends previous reviews of the literature to discuss more recent evidence. She concludes that welfare has a trivial effect on marriage, but nontrivial labor supply effects as measured by participation and hours. Finally, the chapter evaluates the expected impacts of current policy reform proposals.

I comment mainly on the empirical literature and then suggest a fourth issue that is implicit in the Hoynes discussion and in the policy debates but is not mentioned explicitly: how we should think more broadly about the design of income transfer programs. Much of what I have to say concerns labor supply, although some issues are applicable to family formation.

Basic Considerations

It is instructive to consider at the outset why we care about labor supply and marriage decisions. In each case, there are static and dynamic effects. First, lower labor supply and out-of-wedlock births increase welfare spending as both the caseload and spending conditional on the caseload increase. In each case, children are put in poverty. The dynamic effects include the fact that out-of-wedlock births have a strong intergenerational component: children born out of wedlock are more likely to have children as single parents and go on welfare (Case and Katz 1991). Also, sporadic attachment to the labor force reduces labor market skills and weakens the work ethic, leading to long-term poverty.

Empirical Literature

Methodology

The empirical literature on the incentive effects of the U.S. welfare system is extensive, and Hoynes's review justifiably relies on other reviews. I agree with Hoynes's summary of the literature. However, I would like to present a slightly different view of the empirical work in the area. As is well known, two main sources of variation in welfare variables have been used to estimate behavioral responsiveness from survey data: cross-state variation deriving from the fact that maximum benefits are determined at the state level (or cross-section variation, deriving partially from multiple program participation), and time variation, deriving from policy changes. I ignore here the work on the negative income tax experiments. The conclusion from this research is that welfare has nontrivial effects on labor supply, although the range of estimates is quite wide. As a result, there remains uncertainty about the size of the response to financial variables.

The work that examines the effects of policy changes is more recent and has not been extensively reviewed elsewhere. This work is generally based on quasi-experimental methods whereby program changes represent potentially exogenous shocks to variables of interest. Some of the important changes over the past two decades that have been analyzed with this methodology are the expansion of Medicaid availability for children and pregnant women (Yelowitz 1995), the expansion of the EITC (Eissa and Liebman 1996), and the extension of AFDC benefits to two-parent families (Page 1995). Overall these studies generate estimates that are similar to those in the literature: labor supply responses are nontrivial. One problem with these studies is that they estimate reduced form parameters that cannot be used to evaluate different reform proposals.

The earlier literature on welfare effects did estimate structural parameters from models that carefully incorporated the nonlinear budget constraint. The estimation procedure, however, relied on heavily parameterized models of labor supply that have been criticized for the sensitivity of the results. There probably exists a happy medium between the fully parameterized approach and the quasi-experimental methods than can better inform us about the parameters of interest. Future work in this area would be very useful.

Community Externalities

Much of the research on the behavioral responses evaluates standard variables, such as benefit levels and reduction rates. I suggest an alternative and relatively unexplored route through which welfare might have an important effect: neighborhood effects or community externalities.

The idea is that welfare, more specifically housing policy, creates a spatial concentration of recipients. If the behavioral model is one where individuals are influenced by the prevalent behavior in their reference group, then residence in a neighborhood in which a large proportion of other individuals exhibit a certain type of behavior increases the probability that a given individual exhibits that behavior. Therefore, high proportions of out-of-wedlock births increase the probability that any given individual has a child as a single parent. By focusing only on financial variables in the welfare system, we underestimate its effects on behavior.

Of course, spatial concentration may also affect individuals by limiting the flow of information from the larger community. This separation may alternatively affect the perceived returns to education and affect human capital accumulation.

Empirical work in this area is extremely difficult because of deep selection issues. However, recent work by Case and Katz (1991) and Cutler and Glaeser (1995) provides suggestive evidence. Case and Katz study neighborhood effects on disadvantaged youths in Boston using the 1989 NBER Boston Youth Survey. They find that peer influences operate in a manner such that like begets like and conclude that their results argue in favor of the importance of role models, emphasized by Wilson (1987). Cutler and Katz also find that segregating racial groups (specifically blacks) leads to poor schooling, employment, and single-parenthood outcomes. To the extent that neighborhood effects matter, altering the spatial concentration of the poor by integrating them more with the middle class may be one route for welfare reform.

Design of Income Maintenance Programs

It is important to recall that the ultimate goal of welfare policy is to alleviate poverty. This consideration brings up the major issue that needs to be addressed in the welfare reform debate: How should we think more broadly about the design of income maintenance programs? The traditional analysis of income transfer design focuses almost exclusively on labor supply decisions. Hoynes's review suggest that this focus may be the correct strategy to a first approximation.

Here I address the use of the tax system as a means of alleviating poverty. It is well known that economists have been recommending the use of the tax system to reduce poverty for more than three decades (Friedman 1962; Tobin 1965).[1] In *Capitalism and Freedom*, Friedman advocated the negative income tax as an alternative to the welfare system. The desirability of a negative income tax rests on its work incentives and low administrative costs.

The closest that the United States has come on a wide scale to a negative income tax as a policy for poverty alleviation is the earned income tax credit. Experience with the EITC has taught us two main lessons about the use of the tax system to transfer money to poor people.

First, as Hoynes notes, the evidence on the EITC has shown that the tax system does succeed in transferring money to the poor with less distortion to labor supply than welfare programs. The concern with the EITC is, of course, the high marginal rates in the phase-out region. In 1996, the EITC is phased out at a rate of 21.05 percent and is fully phased out at $28,495 for a family with two children. The evidence in Eissa and Liebman (1996) suggests, however, that higher phase-out rates will not adversely affect hours of work for those in the labor force. That brings up the question: What is the optimal phase-out rate? In the limit, the EITC could be phased out instantaneously (creating a notch) rather than gradually. The problem may then be that individuals respond to notches differently than they respond to very high marginal rates. More research needs to be done in this area.

Second, although the administrative costs of transferring money to the poor through the tax system are lower than through the welfare system, the compliance problem may be greater. Approximately one-third of all EITC recipients in 1988 were found to be ineligible for the EITC (Eissa and Liebman 1993). Liebman (1995) examines whether this noncompliance is due to error or fraud and argues that approximately one-third of ineligible recipients are committing fraud. His results come from a period where incentives for fraud were much lower than they are now (the maximum credit increased from $910 in 1989 to $3,556 in 1996), suggesting that fraud may be more prevalent now. On the other hand, most of the noncompliance in 1988 operated through falsely claiming dependents, which is unlikely to be important now that social security numbers for children are required.

Three caveats should be considered in evaluating income transfer programs such as the EITC. First, it does not address the problem of unemployable poor families. The EITC therefore cannot completely replace AFDC. It can, however, aid in the transition from welfare to work should we require employment by welfare recipients on a wide scale.

Second, the EITC and the tax system more generally can impose a heavy marriage penalty. As an example, consider the case of a married couple with two children, each spouse earning $11,900. Under 1996 rules, the couple would get an EITC of $990. If the couple divorces and each claims one child for the EITC, they get an EITC of $4,211 (imposing a marriage penalty of over $3,200). If the couple has four children and each claims two of the children on divorce, the couple is eligible for an EITC of $7,000.

Third, the EITC and all current welfare reform proposals require some form of employment by recipients with the idea it strengthens the work ethic and builds labor market skills. Although valid, these considerations are incomplete for evaluating the social welfare effects of employment by female heads since working mothers spend less time raising children. In fact, the optimal policy may be to subsidize nonemployment by female heads in this case. An observation with the EITC is that it encourages female heads to enter the labor force but generally discourages married women from doing so. As Hoynes concludes, evaluating the effects of the EITC and welfare programs more generally on family structure is indeed an important research agenda for the future.

Note

1. In fact, the literature includes references to a negative income tax dating as far back as 1946 to Stigler, who says that "there is great attractiveness in the proposal that we extend the personal income tax to the lowest brackets with negative rates in these brackets" (Green 1967).

References

Case, Anne, and Lawrence Katz. 1991. *The Company You Keep: The Effects of Family and Neighborhood on Disadvantaged Youths.* NBER Working Paper 3705.

Cutler, David, and Edward Glaeser. 1995. *Are Ghettos Good or Bad?* NBER Working Paper 5163.

Eissa, Nada, and Jeffrey Liebman. 1993. "The End of Welfare as We Know It? Behavioral Responses to the Earned Income Tax Credit?" Mimeo. Harvard University.

Friedman, Benjamin. 1962. *Capitalism and Freedom.* Chicago: University of Chicago Press.

Green, Christopher. 1967. *Negative Taxes and the Poverty Problem*. Washington, DC: Brookings Institution.

Liebman, Jeffrey. 1995. "Noncompliance and the EITC? Taxpayer Error or Fraud." Mimeo. Harvard University.

Page, Marianne. 1995. "Welfare and Work in Two-Parent Families." Mimeo. University of Michigan.

Tobin, James. 1965. "Improving the Economic Status of the Negro." *Daedalus* 94:878–898.

Yelowitz, Aaron. 1995. "The Medicaid Notch, Labor Supply and Welfare Participation: Evidence from Eligibility Expansions." *Quarterly Journal of Economics* 110(4):909–940.

Wilson, William Julius. 1987. *The Truly Disadvantaged: The Inner City, the Underclass, and Public Policy*. The University of Chicago Press: Chicago.

Comment

Robert A. Moffitt

Hilary Hoynes is absolutely correct to begin her excellent review of the research on welfare programs by noting the current resurgence of public interest in welfare reform. Unfortunately, the role of research in that resurgence is remote. Indeed, the public debate has never been more ideological and never more oblivious—almost deliberately so—of research than it is today. The last major piece of AFDC legislation, the Family Support Act of 1988, whose major provisions mandated employment and training programs for welfare recipients, was supported by a considerable body of research on the effects of work programs for welfare recipients. Even the 1967 Social Security Act Amendments, which lowered the AFDC benefit reduction rate from 100 percent to 67 percent, and the 1981 OBRA, which raised it back to 100 percent, were partly based on coherent behavioral assumptions that had some support in the research available at the time. But the public debate preceding the welfare legislation of 1996 was full of assertions that not only had little empirical support but also contradicted basic economic models of incentives. One can only hope that the role of analysis will reemerge and that work like that of Hoynes will contribute to that change.

Nevertheless, there are many interesting findings from economic research on the U.S. welfare system that are highly relevant to current debates, and Hoynes touches on almost all of them. There are also many strong implications of the research for the form that welfare reform should and should not take. Policymakers therefore have a great deal to learn from economic research on welfare if they wish to listen.

As Hoynes makes clear, there are several welfare reform topics that have been debated for thirty years—such as work incentives and tax rates, categorical versus universal programs, and antimarriage biases—where the economic framework for analysis is about the same as it has always been. Anyone who followed the debates of the late 1960s and early 1970s will find the issues essentially unchanged, although the conclusions that some economists have drawn from their framework, particularly about work incentives, have changed somewhat. Other topics are new to the last ten years or so: time limits, employment and training programs, the EITC, and child support reform. Much of the more recent economic research has been focused on these. However, the same simple economic model developed for the older reform topics is applicable to the new ones, and the time-honored concepts of incentives, equity, and efficiency that economic analysis brings to bear on these types of problems will seem familiar.

The ultimate goal of all welfare reform discussions is to determine good designs of welfare programs. I will focus on what economic research has to say about design issues, taking each of Hoynes's topics in turn.

Time Limits

Lifetime time limits on the number of years a woman can receive welfare is a reform that economists have little to say about beyond the obvious. Political rhetoric notwithstanding, hard time limits—that is, limits not followed by any other type of assistance—are equivalent to eliminating welfare beyond that point. It has been known for years and has been shown empirically repeatedly (as Hoynes notes) that welfare has work disincentives; consequently, it is easy to predict that labor supply will increase after women go off welfare. But it is also known that their money incomes and utilities will fall after welfare is eliminated. Although it is in principle possible for money income to rise, this requires a level of substitutability between leisure and consumption that is unsupported by the empirical literature. The only author to make the equivalent flip-side argument that welfare actually makes women worse off in terms of money income is Murray (1984), an argument equally unsupported by economic research. Hoynes is correct to recommend that time limits be tested and evaluated prior to full implementation given the predictions from this body of work; unfortunately, time limits have now been imposed by federal legislation, and we will have a full-dress "test" instead.

Little can be said beyond this. Time limits are merely a method of reducing redistribution, and this is a political decision ultimately up to the voters.

Work Incentives and Marginal Tax Rates

Following on this discussion of work incentives, mention should be made of a policy not emphasized by Hoynes, which is cutting the welfare tax rate (or benefit reduction rate), a policy associated by economists with the negative income tax. This policy is in fact still quite popular and is part of the reform plans in many states, California being one of the most prominent.

In her survey of the empirical research, Hoynes correctly notes that the available evidence suggests that there is little effect of benefit reduction rates on average labor supply, not because substitution effects are unimportant but because of the breakeven problem. A logical implication of this result is that we should have 100 percent tax rates in welfare because this maximizes benefits at the lower end of the income distribution. Lower tax rates merely increase both the caseload and welfare expenditures without doing anything for average labor supply, because lower rates encourage women to go onto the rolls and work part time or to fail to leave the rolls to work full time. A policy of 100 percent tax rates should have greater support among economists than it now has. The current state welfare reform efforts aimed at lower tax rates are misguided and are unlikely to produce anything in the way of significant work incentives.

Relatedly, there is no research basis for attempting to eliminate notches in the budget constraint such as those portrayed in Hoynes's figures and also created by the Medicaid program. Notches have no necessary negative effects on labor supply relative to the alternatives: either smoothing out the budget constraint (which would increase tax rates in other portions of the constraint) or extending the budget constraint upward to avoid sudden termination of benefits (which would increase the caseload and pull women onto the rolls, thereby reducing labor supply). This result is known from Blinder and Rosen (1985) and Moffitt and Wolfe (1990). Further, the provision of transitional child care and Medicaid benefits for a short period after leaving AFDC, discussed by Hoynes, is closely related to a reduction in the tax rate and a reduction in the notch, and therefore also has ambiguous effects on labor supply (Moffitt and Wolfe 1990).

Marriage and Family Structure

Hoynes is correct to emphasize the continued family structure biases in the current system, which discourages marriage between natural parents.

This continues to be the case despite expansions of the AFDC-UP program, that for which children living with both parents are eligible. This continued antimarriage bias has both incentive effects in discouraging marriage as well as undesirable (horizontal) equity effects, the latter arising because a child in a single-parent family receives more assistance than a child in a two-parent family even if resources available to the child are the same.[1]

My reading of the empirical evidence on marriage disincentives and incentives for out-of-wedlock childbearing is that there is considerable cross-sectional evidence for both. The fact that state fixed effects may eliminate those effects or reduce their magnitude does not answer the question of which form of evidence is correct. However, the question that currently concerns policymakers is a different one, for their question is whether the welfare system caused the increase in the out-of-wedlock childbearing rate in the United States in the 1980s, and the answer to that question is that it is almost impossible to ascribe that trend to the welfare system. There is no inconsistency with simultaneously holding the position that the welfare system may have deleterious effects on marriage and childbearing as well as the position that the welfare system has not been principally responsible for the trend in marriage and childbearing rates over a particular period of time.

The AFDC rules also have odd incentives for cohabitation and remarriage since the AFDC system is based on the traditional family law principle that only natural parents are legally responsible for children—not stepparents or live-in partners who are not biologically related to the child. Consequently, relative to marrying the natural father of her child, a woman has an incentive to cohabit with or marry a man who is not the natural father (Moffitt, Reville, and Winkler 1995).

Employment and Training (E&T) Programs

Mandatory E&T programs are still the most popular type of welfare reform. Such programs grew rapidly in the 1980s and were legislatively institutionalized in the Family Support Act of 1988. Economists should think of most of these programs not as workfare programs but as human capital investment programs (where human capital investment is meant to include job search) because most aim to reduce the caseload by raising individual earnings. Unfortunately, E&T programs for welfare recipients that are not available to nonrecipients violate principles of horizontal equity as well as provide incentives to go onto welfare if the E&T program provides a net utility gain, or to go off welfare if it provides a net utility loss (Moffitt 1996). As in the case of family structure, wider coverage for such programs would reduce the distortions, though not eliminate them entirely. It would not eliminate them entirely because a universal training program provided on the basis of income would provide incentives to reduce labor supply and to reduce private human capital investment.

Earned Income Tax Credit

The source of the popularity of the EITC among welfare experts arises because it is logically the antithesis to a negative income tax. Whereas an NIT subsidizes work while on the welfare rolls, the EITC subsidizes work off the welfare rolls.[2] The EITC constitutes "nonwelfare" reform instead of "welfare" reform (Ellwood 1988). The EITC is also popular because earnings and wage subsidies have stronger work incentives than does an NIT, a result known to economists for twenty-five years (Kesselman 1969).[3] However, these subsidies do not provide support to those without earnings, so some type of mixed system will always be necessary (Barth and Greenberg 1971; Kesselman 1973). An unfortunate implication of this direction of reform, also discussed in the early literature, is that it reintroduces categorization into the system by requiring a separation of those who "can" work—who might be denied eligibility for the income guarantee because the earnings and wage subsidy is available—from those who "cannot" work and are eligible for the guarantee. The distinction is difficult to make in an error-free way and in a way that does not provide incentives to change categories. Avoiding the necessity of categorical separation of workers from nonworkers was in fact one of the original motivations of the NIT, for the NIT is a universal program that attempts to provide work incentives and guarantees in a single system without categorization.

A Welfare Reform Design

Based on the economic research as I read it, a reasonable welfare program would be one with 100 percent tax rates, universally provided to all family types, and accompanied by a universal job training program and a universal earnings or wage subsidy. Both the training program and the subsidy programs should be kept administratively separate from the main welfare program, which should remain solely as a program to cut checks.

The level of the guarantee should be set based on a weighted average of the poverty line (for equity reasons) and the wage rate for unskilled workers (for efficiency reasons). Thus falling real wage rates for unskilled workers would pull down the guarantee. Mandatory work and training requirements, if vigorously supported by the voters, would be tolerable, but it would ultimately be better for the success of work and training programs for welfare recipients to have economic incentives to join them rather than being forced to.

Notes

1. It is worth noting that even a universal system that provides benefits to married parents as well as single parents would still distort marriage incentives unless individual benefits were paid to both adults and children independent of type of family or living arrangement. This is a reflection of the basic principle that only lump-sum transfers do not distort. This is not to say, of course, that the distortions could not be greatly reduced by universal coverage.

2. Or at least it would provide such a subsidy if the EITC were included by the welfare authorities in taxable income, which at present it is not.

3. Such subsidies must have disincentive effects as well because they must be phased out—at least if they are targeted on those with lower earnings or wages. See Hoynes's chapter and the Comments by Eissa.

References

Barth, M., and D. Greenberg. 1971, Spring. "Incentive Effects of Some Pure and Mixed Transfer Systems." *Journal of Human Resources* 6:149–170.

Blinder, A., and H. Rosen. 1985, September. "Notches." *American Economic Review* 75:736–747.

Ellwood, D. 1988. *Poor Support*. New York: Basic Books.

Kesselman, J. 1969, Summer. "Labor Supply Effects of Income, Income-Work, and Wage Subsidies." *Journal of Human Resources* 4:275–292.

Kesselman, J. 1973, Winter. "Incentive Effects of Transfer Systems Once Again." *Journal of Human Resources* 8:119–129.

Moffitt, R. 1996, Winter. "The Effect of Employment and Training Programs on Entry and Exit from the Welfare Caseload." *Journal of Policy Analysis and Management* 15:32–50.

Moffitt, R., R. Reville, and A. Winkler. 1995. "Beyond Single Mothers: Cohabitation, Marriage, and the U.S. Welfare System." Mimeo. Brown University.

Moffitt, R., and B. Wolfe. 1990. *The Effects of Medicaid on Welfare Dependency and Work*. Special Report 49. Institute for Research on Poverty, University of Wisconsin.

Murray, C. 1984. *Losing Ground*. New York: Basic Books.

5 Public Policy for Health Care

David M. Cutler

Government involvement in health care is on a scale virtually unrivaled in any other market. In most markets, the government has some regulatory authority and potentially an informational or monitoring role. Rarely does the government decide how much of the good people should buy or whom they should buy it from. Almost never does the government provide the good itself.

In health care, however, government involvement is much more extensive. Perhaps the largest role of the government is as a health insurer. The government provides insurance to the poor, the elderly, and the disabled through the Medicare and Medicaid programs. The government also insures veterans (the Veterans Administration, VA, system), active-duty military personnel and their families (the Department of Defense health system and Civilian Health and Medical Plan of the Uniformed Services [CHAMPUS]), and Native Americans (the Indian Health Service). The government provides implicit insurance to the poor with public hospitals and clinics, and insures mental illness with psychiatric hospitals. Governments pay for nearly half of health care services and supplies consumed in the United States.

In addition to providing insurance, the public sector also provides care directly to many people. Veterans, for example, receive care from government-paid providers at hospitals that are owned and operated by the VA system. Defense personnel receive care at Department of Defense hospitals, and state and local governments run public hospitals, clinics, and institutions for the mentally disabled. Even in the Medicare and Medicaid programs, the government is actively involved in setting reimbursement rates for providers rather than just contracting the insurance role to private insurers.

The public sector is also involved in financing research and monitoring public health. The National Institutes of Health spends over $10 billion annually on biomedical research, with another $5 billion or so on other government health research.

Governments are also involved in health care through tax policy. The most noticeable form of taxation is "sin taxes," levied on cigarettes, alcohol, and even snack foods in some states. More important budgetarily is the $70 billion annually or so that is not collected because employer spending on health insurance is not counted as income for tax purposes. This "tax expenditure" plays a major role in any discussion of public sector health reform.

Finally, the government is involved extensively in health care on the regulatory side. New drugs and medical devices, for example, must be approved by the Food and Drug Administration before they can be used clinically. Many state governments regulate the rates that hospitals can charge private sector payers, and nursing homes cannot expand their capacity without approval from state governments. Insurance companies are regulated by state insurance departments. And standards for malpractice litigation affect doctors and hospitals.

Yet even with this pervasive role of the public sector in health care—or perhaps because of it—fundamental issues about the appropriate role of the public sector in health care are still unsettled. The costs of medical care are rising two to three times as rapidly as the economy as a whole. Should the government limit spending on medical care? People are unhappy that their insurance may be canceled when they become sick or their rates may increase through no fault of their own. Should the public sector do anything about these practices? Fifteen percent of the population is uninsured, and that proportion is rising. Should the government intervene to guarantee health insurance to all? Some have called the 1980s the "tax decade" because tax policy consumed so much of the public agenda. Halfway through the 1990s, it seems fair to characterize this decade as the "health decade." Fundamental issues of health policy show every indication of being with us for years to come.

In surveying the economics of the public sector role in health care, I define the topic broadly. Discussion about health care often leaps immediately to the provision of medical services. It is certainly true that medical services influence health. But other factors as well, such as lifestyle and diet, influence health. I want to discuss the range of potential government involvement broadly.

Public intervention in private markets is typically justified on one of three grounds. In some cases, individuals may not make decisions about their individual behavior that are socially desirable, and these external effects should be rectified by government. Alternatively, the market mechanism itself may not work well, and governments may want to support or replace markets. Finally, society has preferences about the distribution of income or the consumption of specific goods, and the government may want to intervene to promote a fairer distribution of resources. All of these issues are prominent in the health care debate.

I begin by considering government intervention in individual lifestyle choices: smoking, drinking, and the range of other similar activities. The theory of public intervention is well developed here: the public sector should intervene if individuals do not accurately perceive the costs of their actions to themselves or if individual actions have effects on others that are not otherwise accounted for. For many goods, these problems are likely to be important. As a result, public action is appropriate, and economic theory suggests the magnitude of intervention. Increased taxation of tobacco and particularly alcohol finds broad economic justification.

The bulk of this chapter considers public involvement in markets for medical care and health insurance—the issues over which most of the public policy debate has occurred. Why have health costs increased so rapidly? Should we have public or private provision of insurance? Should receipt of health insurance be linked to employment? These issues are at the top of the public agenda.

I organize the discussion of medical care around three facts: the diffusion of technology is the source of increases in health costs over time, technology that has diffused widely is overused, and the financing of health insurance does not sufficiently pool risk. The first two facts are likely related; opportunities for technology to be overutilized create incentives for the more rapid innovation and diffusion of new technologies. The solution to this excessive utilization of care, and thus overly rapid growth of costs, is to create incentives for more cost-effective choice over insurance policies. Limiting excessive medical spending is largely a result of designing insurance policies that encourage or force individuals to receive less medical care. The trade-off between income and generosity of medical care has not been a central feature of health insurance markets, however, and thus the cost of medical care has become such a vexing issue.

The solution of increased competition in the insurance market is made difficult because of the third fact. Individual choices over insurance may lead to less rapid technological diffusion but certainly more segmentation by risk. Minimizing the incentives for risk selection is therefore likely to be a major concern of public policy.

Throughout this discussion, I focus very little on the redistributive aspects of medical care financing or insurance coverage. Medical care poses particularly tough questions for us as a society, in part because we feel differently about medical care than we do about most goods. Society does not feel that everyone has the right to a VCR, or even a telephone, as important as the latter may be in holding a job. We do feel that everyone should have the right to at least basic medical care.[1] Thus, the question about what is an appropriate base level of care is necessarily a public policy issue, and the cost of this care is necessarily a social cost. Considering this set of questions involves a host of other issues, however, such as the role of cash versus in-kind transfers in the welfare of the poor and the nature of our social guarantee. This goes beyond what I want to tackle here, and thus I largely omit this discussion.

I start by describing the potential role for the government in health care and then examine the role of the government in affecting individual lifestyles and organizing markets for medical care.

5.1 The Determinants of Health

Following Grossman (1972), it is helpful to think about the ultimate output of the health system as the health of the population. Individuals value health as well as consumption of goods, which together determine individual welfare.

Social welfare is a combination of individual welfares. Society may value the marginal welfare of some people (for example, the poor) more than it values the marginal welfare of others (for example, the rich). That is a statement about society's desire to transfer resources to the poor generally, however, not about society's desire to transfer medical resources to the poor. I want to separate issues of redistribution from issues of efficiency, so I ignore income differences across people.

There are a number of inputs into health. The first is lifestyle. Individuals decide how much to consume of different goods, whether to smoke or drink alcohol, whether to exercise, whether to own a gun, and a myriad of other issues directly affecting health. Lifestyle choices also affect utility directly, as a consumption item. Cigarettes provide direct utility even as they lower health. Jogging may be both pleasurable and good for health.

The second input is public health—factors such as air and water quality and overall sanitary conditions. Historically, public health measures were more important than they are now. A century ago, most of America's health problems were related to the lack of clean water, nonpasteurized milk, and poor sanitation. In 1900, life expectancy at birth was below fifty years. Today it is closer to eighty years, with a large share of this increase due to improvements in public health (Preston and Haines 1991).

The third input is medical care, which encompasses the range of acute care, mental health care, and long-term care. Some medical care may have independent consumption value, but most probably does not. Finally, there are random factors that affect health, such as the probability of coming down with a particular illness or the chance that a baby is born with a particular disease.

Two broad questions face the public sector. When, if at all, should the government intervene in these factors affecting individual health? And when the government does intervene in these factors, what are the results of this intervention?

5.2 Externalities and Individual Lifestyle Choices

Since Pigou in the 1920s, economists have recognized the role of the government in correcting externalities. Individual lifestyle choices—particularly smoking and drinking—are classic examples of this. If one person's smoking causes harm to others, society may want to intervene in this decision. This has been the traditional rationale for government taxation of sin—largely smoking and drinking. Currently, the federal government taxes cigarettes at $0.24 per pack, beer at $0.32 per six-pack, wine at $0.21 per 750-milliliter bottle, and 80-proof distilled spirits at $2.14 per 750-milliliter bottle. These taxes have increased in recent years as the need for revenue increased and the effects of these sins on health outcomes have become more apparent.

Of course, not all smoking or drinking is bad. Individuals will choose to engage in these activities if the consumption value to them is greater than the monetary and health costs of the behavior. Different people may feel differently about this trade-off. Some individuals, for example, will get more utility from smoking than from the current and future life years they would spend without smoking.

The public sector role here is twofold. A necessary condition for individuals to make appropriate lifestyle choices is that they correctly perceive the health consequences of their actions. If individuals do not have complete knowledge of the risks of smoking, for example, policy measures to provide this information or to raise the costs of smoking would be appropriate.[2]

Evidence on individual perceptions of risk is spotty. Viscusi (1992, 1995) shows that individuals, if anything, *overstate* the risk that they will get lung cancer from smoking.[3] These surveys are based on generic questions about a "typical" smoker, however. Schoenbaum (1996) shows that in response to a question about individual mortality expectations, moderate smokers correctly perceive their mortality risk, but heavy smokers underestimate the probability of near-term death. And recent evidence shows that children may be particularly susceptible to tobacco advertisements, suggesting that they may not accurately perceive the long-term consequences of smoking. The evidence on individual perceptions of smoking risk is thus mixed, with some sense that certainly for children and possibly for adults, public intervention can be justified on information grounds. I am aware of no information on individual perceptions of the health risks from drinking.

Beyond the issue of individual risk assessments, society has an interest in lifestyle choices if these choices have external effects beyond the individual involved. For example, smokers and drinkers use more medical expenses than do nonsmokers and nondrinkers. Since most Americans are insured, smokers and drinkers bear little of the additional medical costs resulting from their actions. Smokers and drinkers are also less productive than nonsmokers and nondrinkers, reducing tax revenue on their income. These two costs ought to be borne by individuals as they decide whether to smoke or drink. Taxing cigarettes and alcohol the amount required to pay for this care is therefore an appropriate policy.

A major issue of research has been estimating these external costs. There are factors in both directions. While the health and productivity externalities suggest increased taxation of sin, smokers and drinkers also die younger than do nonsmokers and nondrinkers, and thus receive less in the way of social security, Medicare, and Medicaid benefits. This would tend to lower optimal tax rates. Manning et al. (1991) estimated the external cost of smoking and drinking, accounting for the effects of these behaviors on medical costs, pensions, and forgone tax revenue. They concluded that current taxes on cigarettes were about right (because the savings in Medicare and social security are reasonably high) but that taxes on alcohol should be doubled.

This analysis of optimal taxation has received much attention (Grossman et al. 1993). Some arguments suggest that not all external effects should be counted as costs. For example, if I choose to ride in a car driven by a drunk driver and am hurt in an accident, is that an external effect, or did I internalize the cost in my decision to ride in the car? Most economists would say that was not an externality, but the Manning et al. analysis treats that as an external effect. Other effects would tend to argue for increased taxation. The Manning et al. analysis did not consider the health effects of second-hand smoke, a particularly contentious scientific issue. If one believes the evidence on adverse effects of environmental tobacco smoke, the optimal tax rate would be higher.

A related issue is the question of the decision-making unit. Women who smoke while pregnant put their fetus at increased risk of low birthweight, which has an extremely high personal and social cost. Are these costs internalized by the woman, or should they be counted as external effects? In the Manning et al. analysis, any effects within a family are treated as internal effects and thus not something that should contribute to increased taxation. Estimates that treat intrafamily health effects as externalities, however, produce optimal tax rates of as high as $5.00 per pack (Hay 1991).

A fair reading of the evidence is that, on net, economic research suggests very strongly that current taxes on alcohol should be doubled at the least, and that one could justify increases in cigarette taxes as well, although the case is less complete. Policies to limit adverse lifestyle behaviors for children are justified even more.

It is important to note that raising revenue is not the rationale for increased taxation of sin. Smokers and drinkers may respond to increased prices of these goods by cutting back on their consumption, and empirical evidence suggests they will (Grossman et al. 1993). The goal, instead, is to reduce the amount of excessive smoking or drinking. In this case, the more that people substitute out of these goods (and thus the less revenue that is raised), the more important it is to impose appropriate taxes.

Taxation of tobacco and alcohol has received most of the economic attention. I suspect that taxation of firearms and bullets is as important as taxation of tobacco and alcohol, but no comparable estimates for these goods have been made.

The same analysis involved in sin taxation is applicable to the case of public health measures as well. The key to efficient smoking decisions, for example, is that the marginal benefits to an individual from smoking equal the marginal costs to society of that individual's smoking. In the case of public health, efficient provision dictates that the sum of the marginal benefits to everyone from providing the public health measure equal the marginal cost of the good. Determining the valuation of public health for everyone is more difficult than determining the valuation for one person, but the principles in the analysis are the same.

Table 5.1
Trends in medical spending and income

	Spending ($1990)			Spending/GDP		
Country	1960	1990	Growth	1960	1990	Growth
Canada	$473	$1,770	4.4%	5.5%	9.5%	1.8%
France	326	1,532	5.2	4.2	8.8	2.4
Germany	425	1,486	4.2	4.7	8.3	1.8
Italy	223	1,236	5.7	3.3	8.1	2.5
Japan	117	1,171	7.7	2.9	6.7	2.7
United Kingdom	349	972	3.4	3.9	6.2	1.5
United States	621	2,566	4.7	5.2	12.2	2.8
Group of 7 (G-7) average	407	1,808	5.0	4.5	8.5	2.1
Ratio: US/G-7	1.53	1.42		1.16	1.44	
OECD average[a]	376	1,680	5.0	4.1	8.0	2.2
Ratio: US/OECD	1.65	1.53		1.27	1.53	

Source: Organization for Economic Cooperation and Development.
[a] The OECD average excludes Luxembourg, Portugal, and Turkey, for which data were not available in 1960.

5.3 The Organization of Medical Care Markets

Perhaps the most challenging public policy issue is the organization of markets for medical care. Medical care is an enormous industry in the United States, as it is in most other developed countries. Table 5.1 shows information on medical care spending in the United States and the member countries of the Organization for Economic Cooperation and Development (OECD). The United States spends close to $3,000 per capita on medical care, or about 12 percent of gross domestic product (GDP). The next highest country (Canada) spends about 10 percent of GDP on medical care, and the average in the OECD is about 8 percent of GDP. Spending in the United States is roughly 40 percent above the OECD average.

Spending on medical care is also increasing rapidly. Between 1960 and 1990, real per capita medical care spending rose at roughly 4.5 percent annually, far above the growth rate of GDP. As a result, medical spending as a share of GDP increased from 5 percent in 1960 to 12 percent in 1990. Increases in the share of GDP devoted to medical care are a characteristic of every OECD country.

Since medical costs are random to a large extent, it is natural and beneficial that people have health insurance. Table 5.2 shows the sources of

Table 5.2
Sources of health insurance coverage for the U.S. population (percentages)

Source	Groups insured	Share of total population	Share of total spending
Public			
Medicare	Elderly, disabled, end-stage renal disease	12	18
Medicaid	Elderly, blind and disabled, poor women and children	8	14
CHAMPUS/CHAMPVA[a]	Dependents of military personnel	1	12[b]
Private			
Employer sponsored	Workers and dependents	56	54
Nongroup	Families	7	
Uninsured		15	2

Source: Employee Benefit Research Institute (1994); U.S. Health and Human Services National Health Accounts.
[a] Civilian Health and Medical Plan of the Uniformed Services/Veterans Affairs.
[b] Includes all other public spending on health services and supplies.

health insurance in the United States.[4] About 20 percent of people are on public insurance programs. The largest public program is Medicare, which provides insurance for the elderly, the disabled, and those with end-stage renal disease. Medicaid is the second largest program, insuring the poor elderly (long-term care and Medicare cost sharing), the blind and disabled, and poor women and children. A small number of people are insured as dependents of military personnel or veterans. In total, the public sector accounts directly for nearly half of medical spending. Another two-thirds of Americans have private insurance, with 90 percent of this being employment-based policies. Spending by the privately insured accounts for roughly half of medical spending. Finally, 15 percent of the population is without health insurance. These people pay for about 2 percent of medical spending, although they use more resources than this (perhaps another 4 percent of medical spending). These additional costs are shifted to other payers and are thus reflected in the public and private sector spending in the earlier rows.[5]

A well-functioning medical care delivery system has two goals: to lead to the right amount of care being provided and direct that care to the right people and to spread the burden of financing care fairly. Many of the concerns about the organization of medical care in the United States are that it performs neither function well. The rapid increase in medical spending, for example, has led to enormous concern about whether we are wasting resources on too much medical care and whether costs are increasing too rapidly. Other fears have focused on the difficulty some people find in getting insurance and the fact that many people feel locked into their current job because they are uncertain if they will get equivalent insurance coverage on a new job.

The role of economic analysis is to provide some structure to analyze these concerns. I start with three facts about the amount of medical care provided and the financing of that care. The facts are not particular to the public sector; indeed, the issues in medical care delivery show up on the private ledger as much as the public one. Between 1970 and 1990, for example, real per capita spending on medical care increased by 4.1 percent in the private sector and 4.9 percent in the public sector. Given that the public sector programs expanded their benefits over this period and enrollment increases were more rapid in the public sector, these growth rates are remarkably similar. I thus state the facts as general for the medical sector as a whole:

Fact 1: The growth of medical care spending is a result of technological advance and the diffusion of existing technologies to new patients.

Fact 2: Technology that has diffused widely is overused.

Fact 3: The burden of financing medical care is not shared in a sufficiently widespread fashion.

5.4 Fact 1: The Diffusion of Medical Technology

The first issue in the analysis of medical care markets concerns the increase in spending on medical care over time. Continual increases in health costs have led to a series of public policy measures designed to limit cost growth. The first wave of action was in the 1970s. The perception at the time was that rising costs were due to haphazard investments in technology on the part of hospitals and the tendency of providers, once technology existed, to use it fully (Roemer's law). Thus, the solution was more appropriate system-wide planning of new facilities and services. By federal law, states implemented certificate of need (CON) programs in the 1970s, requiring hospitals to get approval for major capital purchases. Later analysis of CON programs found them to be essentially ineffective (Altman and Ostby 1991). As I explain below, this is not surprising, since the program did nothing to change the underlying incentives encouraging the diffusion of medical technology.

In the early 1980s, it was apparent that a new strategy was needed. The prevailing view became that the growth of medical costs was a result of the fee-for-service payment structure: providers performed too much care and charged too much for that care because they were paid retrospectively on a per-service basis. Thus, the way to limit costs was to bundle services into one price and limit the reimbursement for that bundle. The first manifestation of this was the prospective payment system (PPS) for hospitals, implemented in Medicare in 1984 and in many Medicaid programs shortly after. PPS set up roughly 470 diagnosis-related groups (DRGs) into which a patient was classified. Payment to the hospital is the product of the DRG weight and an "update factor." Since the implementation of PPS, the update factor has fallen in real terms as the need to limit Medicare spending increased. Continuing in this vein, the resource-based relative value scale (RBRVS) for physicians was implemented in 1992, which attempts to establish a similar pricing structure for physician services.

It is clear that PPS has not succeeded in limiting the growth of health costs. Figure 5.1 shows the growth of Medicare spending for hospitals

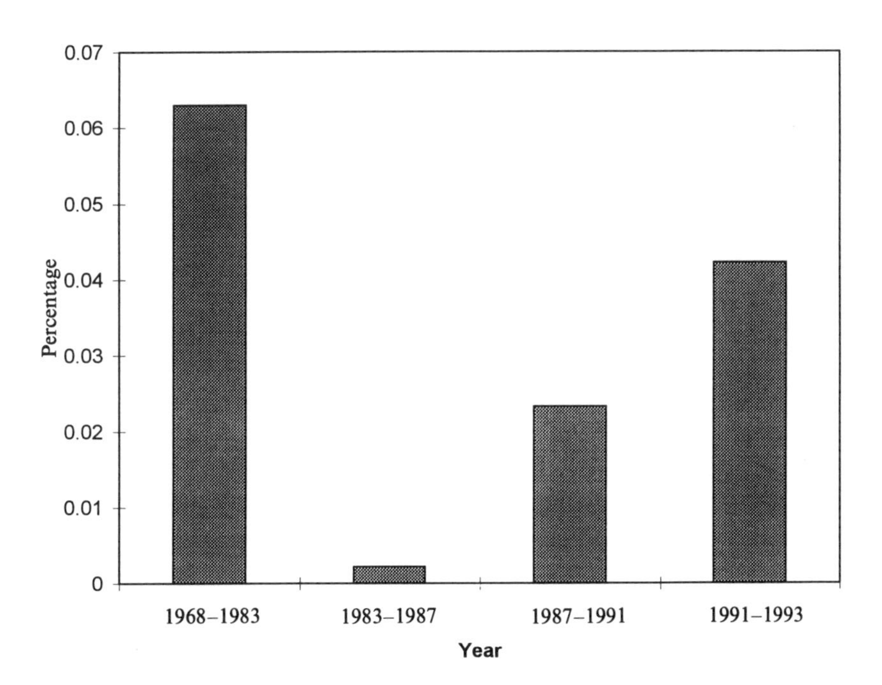

Figure 5.1
Growth in real spending per beneficiary of Medicare inpatient services. Source: Prospective Payment Assessment Commission (1994).

before PPS and in the years afterward (see Cutler and McClellan 1996a, 1996b for more details). For several years, PPS managed to lower the growth rate of hospital spending substantially, but cost growth has again increased, and official projections are for continuing rapid increases in Medicare expenditures. As a result, there is once again a search for public policy solutions to the rising cost of medical care. Before turning to these proposals, it makes sense to ask why health costs continue to increase. There are two ways to approach this question: at the level of medical spending as a whole and by considering particular types of care.

Aggregate Accounting for Health Costs

One way to approach the issue of rising health costs is at the aggregate level (Aaron 1991; Newhouse 1992). As the first row of table 5.3 shows, between 1940 and 1990, real per capita medical spending increased by 790 percent, or nearly 4.5 percent annually. There are seven potential explanations for this dramatic increase in spending.

A first explanation is demographics. The United States is older now than it was in 1940. Older people require more medical care than younger people, so some of cost growth is due to the natural aging of the population, but nowhere near as large as the increase in health costs noted in the table. As a quick calculation, the 1977 National Medical Expenditure Survey shows that children (up to eighteen years old) spend 37 percent of what nonelderly adults (aged nineteen to sixty-four) do, and the elderly (aged sixty-five and over) spend 165 percent of nonelderly adults (Fisher

Table 5.3
Accounting for the increase in health costs

Factor	Increase	Share of total
Total increase	790%	—
Static factors	399	51
Demographics	14	2
Income	37	5
Spread of insurance	100	13
Relative price change	147	19
Administrative expense	101	13
Factor rents	0	0
Residual	391	49

Source: Author's calculations as described in the text.

1980). Between 1940 and 1990, the share of the population over age sixty-five increased from 7 to 12 percent.[6] According to these data, population aging would be expected to explain an increase in medical spending of 14 percent, or 2 percent of the total increase from 1940 to 1990. Clearly, demographics does not explain much of the increase in medical costs over time.[7]

A second factor in the rise in health costs is income. Per capita income has increased dramatically since 1940. Since richer people demand more medical care than poorer people, it is natural that medical spending would increase along with income. Again, this explanation is economically sound but quantitatively unimportant. Estimates of the income elasticity of demand using microeconomic data (that is, holding the level of technology across people constant) typically find that a 10 percent increase in income leads to a 2 percent increase in medical spending, or an elasticity of .2 (Manning et al. 1987).[8] Between 1940 and 1990, real per capita income increased by 185 percent. Thus, income alone would predict an increase in spending of 37 percent, or 5 percent of the observed increase.[9]

A third factor is the spread of insurance. Americans are better insured for medical care now than they were in 1940. People demand more medical care when they are better insured; one of the purposes of insurance, after all, is to allow people to use care when they are sick. As insurance coverage has spread, we would naturally expect medical spending to rise. To evaluate the quantitative importance of this explanation, note that from 1940 to 1990, the average coinsurance rate for medical spending fell from 81 percent to 27 percent (U.S. Public Health Service 1990). Based on the Rand Health Insurance Experiment (Manning et al. 1987), a change in insurance of this magnitude *holding the level of technology constant* would be expected to increase spending by about 100 percent, or 13 percent of the observed increase.[10] Thus, this explanation too is theoretically correct but relatively unimportant quantitatively.

A fourth explanation is the "cost disease" of the services sector (Baumol 1988). Most services are labor intensive. Since productivity growth is typically associated with capital investment, services on average have less rapid productivity growth than do goods. This slower productivity growth translates into relative price increases over time for the service sector. In equilibrium, the price of medical care should increase at the difference in productivity growth rates between medical care and the rest of the economy.

Growth in the economy as a whole averages about 2 percent annually. What is uncertain is the rate of productivity growth in medical care. Since it is hard to measure the price of medical services, it is virtually impossible to know about the productivity of inputs into medical care. A worst-case assumption is that there is no productivity growth in medical care.[11] In that case, the relative price of medical services would be expected to grow by about 2 percent annually. With an elasticity of demand for medical care of about −.2 (Manning et al. 1987), roughly 80 percent of the increase in prices would be reflected in increased spending. Over fifty years, this would be a 147 percent increase in medical spending, or 19 percent of the observed amount. While this is high, it is important to remember that this is an upper bound.

A fifth factor explaining cost growth is administrative expense. Administrative costs are a central factor in medical care and other markets. Some administrative expense is necessary and helpful. Money spent monitoring what care doctors provide, for example, may cut back on the incentives for overprescription resulting from generous insurance. Other administrative expenses—for example, costs from nonstandard claims forms or from insurers seeking to screen out the best risks—are an unnecessary social cost. After all, someone must pay for the cost of those who are very sick, and money spent avoiding these people is a social loss. To the extent that these types of administrative costs have increased over time, unnecessary administration has contributed to the rise in medical spending.

The largest estimates are that avoidable administrative expense in 1983 was about 8 percent of medical spending (Himmelstein and Woolhandler 1986). If we assume that there was no avoidable administrative expense in 1940, then all of this spending on administration was a source of cost growth. If this were true, administrative costs would account for a 101 percent increase in spending, or 13 percent of the total rise in medical spending.[12]

A sixth explanation for increasing costs is inflation in factor prices, or what is often termed economic rents. The fact that medical treatments are often needed on an emergency basis and patients do not have time to search for the most efficient care means that doctors may induce additional care or may charge more than competitive levels for their services. If the ability to do this has increased over time, it might explain the growth in medical spending.

This supplier-induced-demand hypothesis has generated an enormous amount of controversy. On the issue of induced quantities of care, most economists believe that physicians induce more care than is optimal

(Fuchs 1996), although there is very little agreement on how large this is empirically or how it has changed over time (Cromwell and Mitchell 1986; Phelps 1992). There are also substantial differences in the price of medical services in different countries, which would be consistent with some economic rents. Fuchs and Hahn (1990), for example, show that doctors' fees in the United States are up to three times higher than fees in Canada.[13] Since net income of physicians is about 10 percent of total medical spending, these additional fees can explain about 3 percent of medical spending.

It is difficult to think of provider rents as an explanation for the rapid growth of costs, however. In the early postwar period, factor rents probably increased as the medical profession evolved into a major industry and the range of what doctors could do expanded. Indeed, doctors moved from an average profession in terms of income and status to one of the elite professions over this period. Recent changes in medical care markets have limited the ability of providers to extract rents, however. In the 1970s and 1980s, there was a wave of public regulation of prices and technology, including CON, all-payer rate regulation (APRS), PPS, and RBRVS. Although these programs were not uniformly successful, to the extent that they had any effect on medical spending, it is likely that they reduced factor rents. Finally, the late 1980s and early 1990s saw the advent of managed care. By negotiating for a group of patients, insurers can often cut fees below the levels providers would otherwise have set. This has surely reduced the amount of provider rents. I suspect that factor rents on net have been constant or declining in the 1940–1990 period. In the absence of better data, however, this is indicated in table 5.3 as having no contribution to the growth of costs.

The net effect of these six factors is to explain at most only half the growth of health costs in the past half-century. There is still a substantial residual of at least 50 percent of medical spending. The residual is almost certainly due to the introduction of new technologies—new and better treatments—and the diffusion of existing treatments to new patients. This conclusion is the one that essentially all health economists have reached (Fuchs 1996).

Indeed, the most striking observation about medical practice is how much it constantly changes.[14] Weisbrod (1991), for example, notes that about ten of the two hundred largest-selling drugs each year are new, and only 25 percent of the two hundred top-selling drugs in 1972 were top-selling drugs in 1987. In disease after disease, treatments now are substantially different than they were just a decade ago. This aggregate accounting suggests that this change in disease treatment is the source of most of the cost growth in medical care.

An Example: Acute Myocardial Infarction

An example of the impact of technology on costs is instructive.[15] Consider the case of heart attack treatments (acute myocardial infarction, or AMI) for the elderly. There are roughly 250,000 new heart attack cases in the Medicare population annually.[16] Medicare is a major payer for heart attacks. Indeed, if we add up hospital costs only in the year following a new AMI, Medicare spent $2.6 billion on heart attacks in 1984 (adjusted to 1991 dollars) and $3.4 billion in 1991, for an annual growth rate in real terms of 3.9 percent.[17] This is shown in the first row of table 5.4.

Table 5.4
Growth in spending for acute myocardial infarctions, 1984–1991

Measure	Year		Annual percentage change
	1984	1991	
Total reimbursement ($billion)	$2.6	$3.4	3.9%
Number of patients	233,295	227,182	−0.4
Average reimbursement per patient	$11,175	$14,772	4.0%
Average reimbursement			
Medical management	$9,829	$10,783	1.3%
Catheterization	15,380	13,716	−1.6
Angioplasty	25,841	17,040	−5.9
Bypass surgery	28,135	32,117	1.9
Treatments[a]			
Medical management	88.7%	59.4%	−4.2
Catheterization	5.5	15.5	1.4
Angioplasty	0.9	12.0	1.6
Bypass surgery	4.9	13.0	1.2
Share of cost increase			
Prices	24%		
Quantities	106%		
Covariance	−31%		

Source: Cutler and McClellan 1996b.
Note: Costs for 1984 are in 1991 dollars, adjusted using the GDP deflator.
[a] Growth is average percentage point change each year.

What accounts for this nearly 4 percent annual growth in spending on heart attacks? One potential explanation is an increase in the number of patients with heart attacks. In fact, however, as the second row of table 5.4 shows, the number of new heart attacks has been essentially constant.[18] In contrast, spending per heart attack, shown in the third row of the table, increased by 4.0 percent annually between 1984 and 1991.

To understand what is responsible for cost growth, it helps to know more about the treatment of a heart attack. The least invasive treatment for an AMI patient is medical management: drug therapy, monitoring, and intensive care interventions for heart failure or irregular heart rhythms, followed by counseling and treatment for reducing risk factors such as high cholesterol levels and smoking. There are important choices here—such as whether to use a drug to dissolve the clot and which drug to use—but this branch does not involve major surgical procedures.

An alternative to medical management of an AMI is to use one or more invasive cardiac procedures. Invasive treatment begins with a cardiac catheterization, a diagnostic procedure that detects areas of no or limited blood flow. If the catheterization procedure detects important blockages in the arteries supplying the heart, more intensive revascularization procedures may be used to treat the blockages. An older technology is coronary artery bypass surgery (CABG), a highly intensive, open heart surgical procedure that involves grafting arteries or leg veins to bypass occluded or near-occluded regions of the heart's blood flow. A more recent innovation in coronary revascularization, which is less intensive than CABG, is percutaneous transluminal coronary angioplasty (PTCA). In this procedure, a balloon-tipped catheter is inserted into the blocked artery and inflated, with the goal of restoring blood flow through the artery without having to undertake open heart surgery.

The importance of these major procedures in the treatment of AMIs is evidenced in the lower panels of table 5.4. In 1984, 11 percent of patients received a catheterization, with 5 percent of patients going on to receive bypass surgery and 1 percent receiving angioplasty. By 1991, 41 percent of patients received a catheterization, with 13 percent also receiving bypass surgery and 12 percent also receiving angioplasty.[19]

Naturally, Medicare pays much more for patients receiving intensive surgery than for patients not receiving intensive surgery. In 1991 bypass surgery was reimbursed at three times the rate of medical management, and angioplasty was reimbursed 60 percent more than medical management.

How much of the rise in costs is because of this explosion in the use of high-tech procedures, and how much is due to price changes? Arithmetically, the growth of per patient spending can be decomposed into the growth of prices, the growth of quantities, and a covariance term:

$$\Delta Spend = \sum_{i=1}^{T} \left[(P_{i,1} - P_{i,0}) \cdot q_{i,0} + (q_{i,1} - q_{i,0}) \cdot P_{i,0} + (P_{i,1} - P_{i,0}) \cdot (q_{i,1} - q_{i,0}) \right],$$

where $P_{i,t}$ is the price of treatment option i in year t (either 1984 or 1991), $q_{i,t}$ is the share of patients receiving that option in year t, and the sum is taken over the number of treatment options (four in this case).

As the last rows of table 5.4 show, most of the growth of costs stemmed from increases in the quantity of care. Indeed, quantity increases account for over 100 percent of cost growth. Price increases contribute a small amount to cost increases, and there was a reduction in costs as procedures being used more frequently on average fell in price. The inescapable conclusion is that *essentially all of the growth of costs for treatment of heart attacks is the result of the diffusion of new technologies. Price changes have played virtually no role in the growth of costs.*

The conclusion that spending growth is a result of increases in the amount of medical care provided is not necessarily bad. Spending more is worthwhile if we receive goods that are valued more than their cost. The important question is, What is the value of increased medical care?

5.5 Fact 2: The Low Marginal Value of Treatment

A key issue in analyzing the value of medical care is the heterogeneity of likely treatment effects. Some patients will benefit from intensive treatments a great deal. AMI patients with non-Q wave infarcts (heart attacks that are not severe) and with pain after the infarct, for example, will benefit a great deal from knowing the extent of the arterial blockage, which a cardiac catheterization can determine. Other patients will benefit substantially less from intensive technologies—for example, patients with an AMI but no pain after the infarct. There is likely to be a substantial difference between the average value of technology and the marginal value of technology. The average value of a technology will be high if some patients benefit from the technology a great deal. The marginal value of technology will be low if all care that has any value is applied.

In asking whether technological change is valuable on net, we care about the average value of care. In asking whether care is overprovided at any point, we care about the marginal value of medical care. I start by presenting evidence on the marginal value of care and later return to the question of the average value of care.

A substantial amount of research has examined the marginal value of medical care. This research almost uniformly suggests that *among those with insurance, the marginal value of medical care is low*. The Rand Health Insurance Experiment (Manning et al. 1987; Newhouse et al., 1993) is perhaps the best-known study. Individuals in it who were better insured used more medical care than those who had less generous insurance, but their health outcomes were no better. The demand for medical care is thus price elastic, but health is relatively unaffected by marginal amounts of care.

A second set of research has examined the implications of variations in the use of medical care in different areas of the country, in different types of institutional settings, or over time for health outcomes. People in Boston, for example, consume nearly twice as much medical care as people in New Haven, Connecticut, and yet health outcomes in Boston are no better than health outcomes in New Haven (Wennberg, Freeman, and Culp 1987). This type of area variation is quite common and has led to the widespread view that some areas provide too much medical care (Phelps 1992).

Garber, Fuchs, and Silverman (1984) looked at costs and outcomes for two groups of patients treated at the same hospital: one group seen by community-based physicians and the other seen by academic-based physicians. They found that patients seen by the academic physicians received over three times more care than patients seen by community-based physicians. These patients were also more likely to survive the hospital stay than patients treated by the community-based physicians. But by nine months postdischarge, both groups of patients had the same mortality rate. The benefits associated with dramatically more intensive care were thus limited to a few additional months of life.

Cutler and Staiger (1995) examined mortality rates after acute hospitalizations between 1974 and 1987. They found that mortality rates in the first fourty-five days after admission declined by 5 percentage points, but mortality rates at one year postadmission declined by only 40 percent as much. The implication is that about half of medical progress was directed at keeping people alive for several months but not as long as a year.

A third set of studies has examined the production function for health directly. McClellan and Newhouse (1995) used the distance between where a patient lives and the nearest hospital with high-technology care to estimate the value of intensive medical care for outcomes. The example they consider is cardiac catheterization after a heart attack. Patients who live farther from a hospital with catheterization are less likely to receive the procedure than those who live closer to a hospital with the technology, but they are only slightly more likely to survive in the next year. The implication is that catheterization does not substantially improve outcomes for those patients "rationed" by their distance to the technology.

A series of studies at the Rand Corporation also looked directly at the issue of the value of care (Chassin et al. 1987; Winslow et al. 1988a, 1988b; Greenspan et al. 1988). Those studies surveyed physicians about what constituted "appropriate care," "inappropriate care," and "care of equivocal value" and then determined how much of the care that was provided fell into each of these categories. For five common conditions in the elderly, the studies found that inappropriate care or care of equivocal value accounted for 20 to 30 percent of medical spending. These studies are controversial; recent evidence has found much less care that is inappropriate than these studies would indicate (Altman 1994). These studies also underestimated the amount of inappropriate care, however, because they considered only the health benefits relative to the risks to the patient, ignoring the costs to society of providing the care.

Finally, other research has focused on the effects of changes in payment policy on health outcomes. Kahn et al. (1990) looked at the health consequences of implementing prospective payment. Prospective payment led to substantial reductions in care provided: lengths of stay in the hospital fell, for example, by nearly 20 percent between 1983 and 1993. These authors found no significant effect of prospective payment on mortality in the first six months to one year.

In a related vein, Cutler (1995) and Staiger and Gaumer (1990) looked at the mortality experience in hospitals that received more money under prospective payment relative to hospitals that received less money. Both analyses found that in hospitals with payment reductions, more people died shortly after a hospital admission, but the share of people who survived a year did not change. The implication is that the marginal amount of medical care prolonged life by several months but not by as long as a year.

The common conclusion from all of these studies is that the marginal value of medical care is low or in many cases zero—or that care is being provided until it brings very little in the way of health benefits. I thus take the overprovision of technologically intensive care as a basic fact about the provision of medical services.

It is important to bear in mind that these findings refer to the marginal value of care among patients who are insured. They do not imply that additional care received by the uninsured would have little health benefit. Research has shown, for example, that the uninsured are substantially less likely to receive intensive treatments than the insured, and some research suggests that this results in materially better health outcomes (Weissman and Epstein 1994; Hadley, Steinberg, and Feder 1991; Currie and Gruber 1994). Designing insurance coverage for the uninsured, however, is not a subject that I shall explore at length.

5.6 Implications of the Overuse of Care

The observations that technology explains most of the growth of health costs and that technologies are overutilized once they diffuse are almost certainly related. Indeed, three types of explanations might be put forth to explain such a link.

The first explanation for these facts is a fatalistic one: new technologies develop because of advances in fundamental biological research. Once the technology exists, medical ethics make it hard to deny care to those in need—both those who would benefit a lot and those who would benefit only a little. Thus, the "culprit" behind rising costs and overuse of care is the inevitable march of technology. Indeed, with the genetic revolution and improved understanding of molecular biology, the future promises even more new knowledge and thus even more rapid cost increases (Schwartz 1994).

If the fatalistic view is correct, the only way to limit the growth of health costs is to limit research spending on medical care, limit the development of new technology, or limit the aggregate resources available for medical care. Thus, single-payer health systems draw support from those who believe that technological change is largely exogenous. Of course, in this scenario, there is no guarantee that limiting the growth rate of medical spending is a good policy. Indeed, if the new care provides large medical benefits on average, limitations on its use would be disadvantageous, and it would be far wiser to allow the new technology and develop appropriate revenue sources to pay for it. More generally, determinations would need to be made on a technology-by-technology basis about the appropriateness of new innovations.

Fundamentally this explanation is unsatisfying. Even if knowledge is uncontrollable, the decision to develop new technologies or apply them in particular cases is an economic one. Thus, other explanations for these findings have to be allowed.

The second explanation for these facts is a demand-side story (Feldstein 1971; Pauly 1986; Weisbrod 1991): patients are sufficiently well insured that they pay little for additional medical care. As a result, they consume medical services until the marginal value of services is essentially zero (the effective price they pay for the care).[20] Because patients demand technology so extensively, there is a bias toward excessive technological development. As a result, health costs increase at a rate greater than optimal. Thus, dynamic moral hazard causes both overuse of technology and overly rapid growth of medical costs.[21]

Of course, some amount of health insurance is optimal, and thus some moral hazard is unavoidable. What has drawn the most attention of economists is the subsidy to health insurance in the tax code. Income that is paid in the form of wages and salaries is taxed through federal income taxation, social security taxation, and state income taxation. Income that is paid in the form of health insurance premiums, in contrast, is untaxed. Thus, the price of consuming medical care through insurance is lower than the price of consuming medical care through out-of-pocket payments. Gruber and Poterba (1995) estimate that for the average person with health insurance, the tax code provides a subsidy of about 30 percent for the purchase of health insurance. This subsidy leads people to be over-insured, resulting in moral hazard, and thus cost growth, beyond what is optimal.

Three empirical assumptions are buried in this hypothesis: that the quantity of medical care consumed depends on the generosity of insurance, that the demand for health insurance is responsive to its price, and that technological innovation is driven largely by expected use once it is developed. That medical care responds to the price of care was demonstrated conclusively by the Rand Health Insurance Experiment.[22] The price elasticity of demand for medical care is relatively small (about −.2) but not zero. The elasticity of demand for health insurance has also been a subject of much research.[23] Most studies find a statistically significant response of health insurance coverage to price, with a demand elasticity on the order of −.2 to −1. I return to the evidence on the third question below.

The third explanation for these facts is a supply-side story: providers wishing to maximize their income induce medical consumption until the marginal amount of care has essentially no value. Because care is provided in excessive quantities, there are incentives for the excessive development and diffusion of new technologies, leading to cost growth above appropriate levels. This theory is similar to the demand-side theory, with the primary difference being that this hypothesis focuses on incentives for the excessive supply of medical care rather than incentives for the excessive demand for medical care.

There are several potential reasons that suppliers might induce more medical care than is optimal: to maximize their income (the supplier-induced-demand hypothesis noted above), attract more patients in a competitive environment (often termed the medical arms race; see Robinson and Luft 1985), or deter malpractice litigation (often termed defensive medicine; see Reynolds, Rizzo, and Gonzales 1987). There has been a great deal of debate over the importance of each of these theories. There is likely some truth to the supplier-induced-demand explanation, but the empirical importance of this view is relatively unknown. Most research suggests that malpractice is not particularly important in explaining the overuse of care, although recent research suggests that malpractice concerns can account for 5 percent or so of current medical spending (Kessler and McClellan 1996). Evidence on the medical arms race has been difficult to compile, and no consensus estimates are in the literature.

Both the demand- and supply-side explanations suggest that market structures cause a bias in the overall rate and composition of technological change. The rate of technological change is too high because too many procedures and devices are judged beneficial when some should not be. The composition of technologies is skewed because patients with generous insurance or providers will particularly value technologies that increase the range of what can be treated—even at a dramatic increase in cost—and will undervalue technologies that save money but result in slightly worse outcomes.

The composition effect is particularly important. In general, there is little economic presumption that private markets will lead to the right amount of new innovation. The inability to appropriate the returns from innovation fully and the importance of fixed costs in research typically suggest that there will be underinvestment in research and development. Allowing for greater reimbursement of new technologies, as generous health insurance has done, may be one way to alleviate this. The fact that the type of innovations is likely to be distorted, however, means that subsidizing innovation in this fashion may be inferior to subsidizing innovation through other means with less distortion in the type of innovation, for example, through increased direct funding of research efforts. The trade-off between these two sources of encouraging innovation has not been well explored.

Solutions to Overconsumption of Medical Care

Both the demand- and supply-side explanations of the overconsumption of medical care are really stories about imperfect insurance markets. The underlying problem in both of these theories is that individuals cannot contract ex ante to limit the care they will receive ex post. If patients and providers could agree on prices and agree to limit their care before they were sick, they would contract only for the socially desirable amount of care.[24] The fundamental problem is that the decision about appropriate medical care is separate from the one about insurance coverage.

This separation of insurance and provision of care is in large part due to the historical organization of the medical care sector: providers decided on appropriate treatments, and insurers paid the bills, with neither side interfering much with the operation of the other side. Increasingly, this situation is changing, with the insurance and delivery roles becoming more integrated. A broad range of insurance falls under the heading of managed care. Health maintenance organizations (HMOs) are the traditional form of managed care. They have a panel of approved providers; care received from those providers comes at little or no cost, while care received outside those providers is typically not reimbursed. Patients typically need approval from a "gatekeeper" before seeking specialty services. Preferred provider organizations (PPOs) are a looser form of managed care. PPOs typically have a network of physicians. Patients pay little when they use a network provider and pay more (but not the full amount) when they go out of the network. The popularity of PPOs has led to the creation of point-of-service plans (POSs), which are HMOs that have some reimbursement for patients who go outside the panel of physicians.

Managed care limits spending by controlling what services are performed, who performs the services, and how much the providers are paid. Moral hazard is typically limited by restricting the providers to whom individuals can go for care. Providers are generally not paid on a fee-for-service basis and thus do not have financial incentives to overprescribe care. Indeed, providers often bear a financial cost for providing additional care. And to get into the panels, doctors often agree to receive lower fees.

Indeed, the dominant fact about health insurance in the past decade in the United States is the increasing importance of managed care. As figure 5.2 shows, managed care enrollment has skyrocketed in just the past decade. In 1987, nearly three-quarters of the privately insured population was in conventional fee-for-service insurance, with few restrictions on the use of care. By 1993, less than half the privately insured population was in

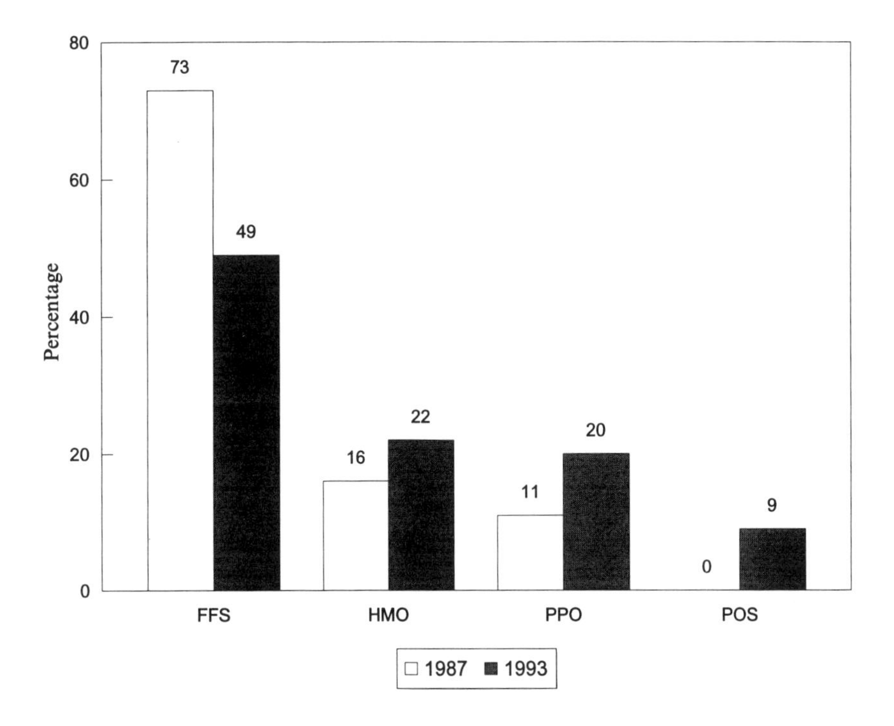

Figure 5.2
Growth of managed care, 1987–1993. Source: Health Insurance Association of America Surveys.

conventional insurance. About 30 percent of people were in an HMO or POS plan, and the remaining quarter were in PPOs.

These policies seem to many the most likely way to limit excessive utilization of medical care. To the extent that the overprovision of care leads to more rapid cost growth, encouraging use of alternative care arrangements will also limit the growth of health costs. Thus, the policy prescription that loosely draws the most support from economists is to *increase the choice that people have over different insurance policies, particularly policies that will limit the amount of care provided, and to increase the financial returns from choosing less expensive health insurance.* There is not one consensus choice-based approach to health care reform. Among the policies that have featured in many proposals are the following:

• *Encourage or require small firms to pool into larger groups and offer a choice of policies* (Enthoven 1993). Because of high administrative costs and fears by insurers of adverse selection, most small firms offer only one insurance policy. As a result, many proposals have called for increased pooling of small firms into large enough groups where multiple choices can be offered. Encouraging these purchasing groups has enjoyed widespread support; they were termed health insurance networks in the Bush plan, health alliances in the Clinton plan, and health insurance purchasing cooperatives in the Cooper plan.[25]

• *Convert Medicare into a choice-based system* (Cutler 1995; Aaron and Reischauer 1995). Medicare recipients are among the last major group of the population without substantial enrollment in managed care. Currently only 7 percent of Medicare enrolles are in managed care, compared to over half of privately insured people. Creating more efficient choice among this large segment of the population would increase substantially the cost sensitivity of the average insured person.

• *Limit the tax exclusion of employer-provided health insurance* (Feldstein 1995; Pauly 1986; Enthoven 1993). Tax policies that subsidize health insurance reduce the after-tax savings to individuals who choose less expensive health insurance plans because they reduce the other consumption that can be bought with less expensive insurance choices. Thus, many proposals eliminate the marginal tax subsidy to insurance. This does *not* imply that there should be no subsidy for health insurance, however. In the absence of universal health insurance coverage, it is desirable to provide an inframarginal subsidy to health insurance purchases as a means of countering the incentives to be uninsured. As a result, many proposals limit the exclusion of health insurance premiums from taxation to a fixed amount (for example, the cost of a abasic health insurance policy).

With several years of managed care experience, it is possible to develop a tentative view about how effective a choice-based system is likely to be in limiting the overuse of care and the rate of growth of costs. The evidence is mixed. Managed care plans do appear to reduce spending on medical care. Miller and Luft (1994) suggest that the reduction in spending is about 10 percent. In markets with more managed care penetration, costs grow more slowly for at least some period of time (Zwanziger and Melnick 1988), managed care premiums are lower (Wholey, Feldman, and Christenson 1995), and fee-for-service fees are lower (Baker 1994). Further, these reductions in spending do not appear to come at the cost of increased sickness (Miller and Luft 1994), although this finding is somewhat tentative since it is not clear that such effects could be measured in the short period for which we have data.[26]

What is particularly uncertain is whether these savings from managed care are one-time reductions in spending (for example, from reducing provider rents) or whether they represent longer-term reductions in the rate of cost growth from less rapid diffusion of technology. Historically, although managed care premiums have been lower than fee-for-service premiums, they have increased at the same rate over time (Newhouse 1985). And there has been no recent reduction in the growth of overall medical spending, even as managed care enrollment has skyrocketed (Huskamp and Newhouse 1994).[27] Thus, some argue that managed care will not have long-run effects on cost growth (Schwartz and Mendelson 1994).

If the diffusion of technology responds to the average level of insurance coverage, however, the fact that cost growth has not slowed with the increase in managed care enrollment would be expected. After all, managed care has not historically been a large enough share of the market to have much effect on the nature of technological change in aggregate, particularly given the lags between medical research and technological diffusion. Only recently has managed care assumed a more prominent role in health care delivery, and thus the best evidence on the long-run effects of managed care will not be known until more recent data are examined.

A fair synopsis of the literature on the cost and value of medical care is that the answer to this fundamental set of questions is uncertain. There is a great deal of evidence that care is overprescribed relative to efficient levels. Alternative insurance arrangements appear to limit the overuse of care and to reduce the fees paid for care, and these savings are valuable. But the important question is whether the growth of costs is inefficiently high. Economic theory suggests that it is, but there is not a great deal of evidence on the empirical determinants of this rate of cost growth or how to limit it. In the absence of such evidence, most economists support more choice in principle but remain skeptical about the size of any long-run effects.

5.7 Fact 3: Sharing the Burden of Medical Care Financing

If individuals are to have choice over insurance, the questions become at what price this choice will be offered and whether this choice will interfere with other decisions individuals need to make. In this section and the next, I examine these two issues.

As Rothschild and Stiglitz (1976) first pointed out, insurance markets are not like all other markets. Insurance works well when risks are large and neither individuals nor insurers know about the probability that an individual will experience any particular medical condition. People will be willing to buy insurance because the risk reduction is large; insurers will be willing to sell insurance because the pool will consist of a broad cross-section of the community.

What makes health insurance so problematic is that the likelihood of needing care is not unknown. Individuals certainly know something about their projected medical needs. People with a history of heart disease, for example, know they are at above average risk for a heart attack. When people know more about their medical risks than do insurers, the result is adverse selection. The sick will find generous health insurance more attractive than the healthy and will thus drive up premiums. The healthy will choose segregated policies, with less complete insurance but lower premiums.

Adverse selection is a key feature of many group health insurance policies (Newhouse 1994; Cutler and Reber 1996). Almost all health insurance systems where individuals are allowed choice over insurance have experienced adverse selection. Medicare enrollees who choose managed care, for example, are healthier than employees who do not (Hill and Brown 1990).[28] The Federal Employees Health Benefits Program, as a second example, has adverse selection between more and less generous policies. The spread in premiums between more and less generous policies is 68 percent greater than benefits alone would dictate (Price and Mays 1985). And almost every large organization that has encouraged employee choice has found that the cost of the most generous policies increases sufficiently rapidly that those plans are no longer viable (often termed a "death spiral").

Increasingly, however, adverse selection is being replaced by a second difficulty: the fact that insurers know as much or more about a person's expected spending as the person does. Knowledge about expected spending is readily available. If the group was insured in the previous year, the insurance company has direct estimates of medical resources used. If the group is applying for coverage, the insurer can administer detailed questionnaires on family background and likely health risks or can insist on medical screenings.

In competitive markets, insurers will then use this information in pricing: organizations with good risks receive low premiums; those with poor risks receive higher premiums. Pricing on the basis of expected cost is termed *experience rating*. The result is segmentation of insurance by risk. Table 5.5 presents evidence on the degree of premium variability by

Table 5.5
Distribution of benefit cost

		Number of employees				
Benefit cost (percentile)	Total	50 or below	51–100	101–500	501–1,000	Above 1,000
10	$831	$782	$925	$833	$1,017	$1,069
50	1,366	1,385	1,353	1,227	1,343	1,422
90	2,126	2,143	2,034	1,753	1,734	2,143
90/10	156%	174%	120%	111%	71%	100%

Source: Cutler (1994a).

company size.[29] For small organizations, premiums are extremely variable. Some firms pay up to three times more than others for roughly the same set of benefits. This difference declines as organization size increases, reflecting the lower variability of expected costs for larger groups. Among organizations with 500 to 1,000 employees, for example, high-end premiums are less than twice low-end premiums.[30]

At a point in time, experience rating allows more people to buy full insurance. The low-risk population can get insurance without having to pool with the more expensive high-risk population or can get more complete coverage than they otherwise could have. Over time, however, experience-rated health insurance reflects a substantial market failure: the inability of people to insure against future health status. In an experience-rated market, people have insurance in a given year but do not have insurance against the risk that they will learn they are high cost in the future—what might be termed *intertemporal insurance* (Cutler 1992; Cochrane 1995; Pauly, Kunreuther, and Hirth 1992).

The great worry about the future of health insurance is that insurers will get better at predicting who will be high cost and who will be low cost. Think about a future where DNA tests at birth indicate the probability that a person will die at a particular age or contract a particular costly disease. Individuals can be perfectly sorted on the basis of their expected costs, with those born less fortunate charged more for insurance throughout their lifetime. As knowledge about the biomedical link between genetics and health increases, this possibility becomes ever more likely, and the ability to achieve meaningful risk pooling will fall as well.

Risk selection is an extremely widespread concern among the public. The slogan for the Clinton health reform plan ("Health Care That's Always There") was in part a reference to problems in risk selection.

The potential for risk segmentation is the major drawback to increased choice in insurance markets. If price differences across plans reflect differences in the risk characteristics of enrollees in the plans rather than differences in efficiency or the social costs of increased choice, encouraging choice over health insurance policies will not result in an efficient outcome.

There are three potential solutions to problems of risk selection. The first is to contract for more than annual insurance. The further off is risk in the future, the less individuals are likely to know about their expected costs. Indeed, one could think about markets where individuals buy insurance against the possibility that they will learn this year that their future costs are likely to be high. Such policies have been proposed by Cochrane (1995) and Pauly, Kunreuther, and Hirth (1992) as solutions to risk selection problems. In practice, however, such insurance is rarely observed.[31]

The second solution is to group individuals into large pools on a basis other than risk. Diamond (1992), for example, proposed mandatory regional pools for health insurance. One insurance company would insure everyone but might offer multiple policies to the group. This solution would solve risk segmentation problems and still allow choice, although it might lead to regional monopoly insurance companies.

The third solution is to allow individuals choice over health insurance policies but adjust payments to insurers on the basis of expected health costs. Even if individuals pay the average cost for insurance, insurers do not need to receive the average price for each person they enroll. By "taxing" health plans that enroll healthier risks and "rebating" the money to plans that enroll sicker risks, the incentives to select health risks are minmized. Such a process is termed *risk adjustment*.

The prospects for effective risk adjustment are only mixed (Newhouse 1994). Easy-to-observe characteristics such as age and sex can explain only about 10 to 20 percent of the variability in health costs that can be explained with detailed clinical data. Indeed, the large share of medical expenses devoted to very highest cost cases (the top 10 percent of users account for 70 percent of medical spending; Berk and Monheit 1992) suggests that the incentives to risk-select, even with some risk adjustment, will be substantial. Thus, purely prospective risk adjustment is likely to leave substantial incentives for adverse selection and risk selection (Newhouse 1995). The search for ways to deal with these issues is just beginning.[32]

For some, the inability to risk-adjust perfectly inclines them against any form of choice-based insurance and often toward a single-payer system.

For others, the lack of perfect risk adjustment is a nuisance that gives some pause, but not much delay, to choice-based reform. One's weighing of these two choices is directly related to the weight one places on cost efficiency relative to distributional equity. As the efficiency costs of the current medical care system increase, however, more and more economists are willing to experiment with cost reforms and manage the risk problems to the best extent possible.

5.8 Health Insurance and the Labor Market

Beyond the implications of health insurance choice for health insurance markets is the effect of such choices on the labor market. Most private insurance is received through employment, with the employer (nominally) paying roughly 70 percent of the premium and the employee paying the remainder. Basic economic models suggest that this is beneficial: employment is a natural form of group coverage (avoiding the segmentation issues in individual markets), and such coverage is likely to be nondistortionary. The latter point is particular to economic reasoning. If employees value the insurance provided by employers at its cost, they should be willing to "buy" health insurance from their employer by accepting lower wages when the employer provides health insurance (Summers 1989). The employee will receive less cash income but the same total compensation. Indeed, empirical research suggests that this is in fact the case (Gruber 1994; Gruber and Krueger 1991; Sheiner 1994).

In practice, however, there are increasing strains in the employment relationship that appear due to the rising cost of health insurance. One is the effect of health insurance on job mobility. While wages may adjust so that the average worker is indifferent between receiving health insurance on a job or not, workers with preexisting conditions or high demand for continuous health coverage will not be indifferent between insurance and wages. As a result, these workers will be less likely to leave jobs with health insurance. An emerging body of empirical research documents the importance of "job lock" for labor market turnover (Madrian 1994; Buchmueller and Valletta 1994; Monheit and Cooper 1993; Gruber and Madrian 1994; Penrod 1994).[33]

A second strain results from the fact that not all workers are willing to accept wage reductions to pay for increased health insurance costs. Low-wage workers, for example, find it particularly hard to pay for health cost increases when their real incomes are falling. The response of employers has been increasingly to exclude these workers from coverage by expanding their use of contingent workers, temporary workers, and part-time workers, to whom benefits need not be provided. Anecdotal stories about the importance of these effects abound. And workers who are kept in the insurance pool are working longer hours, as the increase in the fixed costs of health insurance relative to the marginal costs of wages induces companies to substitute additional hours of work for additional numbers of employees (Cutler and Madrian 1996).

The effects of health insurance on the employment relationship are becoming increasingly apparent as health costs increase. When health insurance was a small part of total compensation, its effects on companies and workers was small. As costs have increased in importance and the wages of less-skilled workers have stagnated, health insurance has become a more significant determinant of employment relations. Almost certainly, the labor market distortions associated with employment-based health insurance will increase in the future.

The only long-run solution to these employment distortions is to remove the link to employment. This is consistent with the goal of giving employees more choice over health insurance, independent of the particular organization they work for. The salient question, however, is where people can go for coverage that is economically fair. The answer is not completely clear, making the discussion of employment-based health insurance that much more complicated.

5.9 Conclusions

My conclusions about public policy for health care can be summarized in three points. First, the public sector has an important role to play in affecting individual lifestyle choices. People do not bear the full cost of their lifestyle choices, and tax policy can be used to correct this. Taxes on alcohol, cigarettes, and probably firearms and bullets appear too low in light of their external effects.

Second, the medical care marketplace is driven by overuse of medical resources and the rapid development and diffusion of new technologies. The best hope for market-based cost containment is to provide individuals the ability and incentive to choose among alternative health plans with differing coverage and costs.

Third, choice-based systems must be used in conjunction with some method of risk adjustment. Choice-based systems have the potential for promoting cost reduction and can eliminate the inefficiencies associated with employer-provided insurance. They may also result in increased segmentation by risk, however, as adverse selection and risk selection are encouraged. Designing mechanisms to adjust for this risk selection is a substantial policy priority.

Public policy for health care is at a crossroads. The public did not support broad health care reform, yet nobody thinks that problems in health care markets will get better without some public action. The problem for economists is to design the sensible middle for reform.

Notes

I am grateful to Alan Auerbach, Ed Glaeser, Jon Gruber, Hilary Hoynes, Kim O'Neill, Richard Zeckhauser, and especially Henry Aaron and Joseph Newhouse for helpful discussions, and to the National Institutes on Aging for research support.

1. Victor Fuchs (1974, 1995) has termed this the choice between individual and social responsibility.

2. Information provision is the first response to misperceptions of health risks. Because such information has been widely available for years, however, if individuals do not correctly perceive these risks now, it may be that they are not capable of accurately processing this information, and therefore tax measures should be considered.

Richard Zeckhauser has pointed out that if tastes for cigarettes are random, people may want to insure against the risk that they will have a high demand for cigarettes. This point argues against using taxes to alter individual lifestyle choices.

3. The surveys do not indicate whether individuals understand the deterioration in physical functioning associated with smoking.

4. Individuals can have more than one source of insurance coverage. The table shows primary coverage.

5. National data do not indicate what share of spending is paid for by the privately insured relative to the uninsured, but a rough guess is that the 40 million uninsured pay about $500 annually on average for medical care (Cutler 1994b).

6. There is a second demographic issue that one would like to correct for but typically cannot. As medicine advances and more people are kept alive to older ages, the average healthiness of the surviors to any age will change. For example, policies that allow the least healthy forty year olds to survive an additional thirty years (perhaps through preventing death from infections disease) will increase the average sickness of the population thirty years in the future, and thus result in higher per capita medical spending at that time, even controlling for the subsequent age distribution of the population. Policies that improve the health of all forty year olds, in contrast, may increase the average health of the population thirty years in the future, even if the population at that point is composed of more "marginal survivors." There are no natural data on intrinsic healthiness, however, and thus such adjustments typically are not made. The evidence that is available (for example, Poterba and Summers 1987) does not suggest that such adjustments would be particularly important, and thus I suspect there is little bias from this omission.

7. Calculations using more detailed age breakdowns reach very similar conclusions (see Newhouse 1992).

8. Estimates of income elasticities based on macrodata are much larger (generally 1 or higher), but these estimates also include relative price differences and differences in technology across countries. Conceptually we want to hold these constant in evaluating the contribution of income alone to spending growth.

9. Note that this ignores any changes in the norms of care for poor people resulting from changes in average income. Such effects would be captured in the residual of this calculation.

10. Some extrapolation is needed to create this estimate. In the Rand Health Insurance Experience, the average coinsurance rate for the 95 percent cost-sharing plan was 31 percent, and spending on this plan was about 50 percent above the free care plan. Since the reduction in the average coinsurance rate between 1940 and 1990 was roughly twice the difference between the 95 percent cost-sharing plan and the free plan, I doubled the estimated inducement effect of moving to the free care plan from the 95 percent plan.

11. Calculating productivity in the medical care industry is particularly hard since the ultimate output (better health) does not show up directly in GDP. For purposes of relative price comparisons, the right measure of prices is the deflator for the physical output of the industry (the price of a surgery, a new drug, etc.) rather than a deflator for health. Even so, the computed consumer price index for medical care almost surely overstates the true value.

12. To put this in 1990 dollars, I assumed that the share of avoidable administrative expense in 1990 was the same as the share in 1983.

13. This estimate is not adjusted for any difference in physician quality between the two countries.

14. See Giljens and Rosenberg (1994) for an interesting discussion.

15. This example is taken from Cutler and McClellan (1996a, 1996b).

16. These figures exclude the elderly enrolled in managed care, a growing but still small share of the elderly population.

17. Total Medicare spending on inpatient care was $63 billion in 1991.

18. The demographic characteristics of heart attack patients have not changed greatly. In fact, since heart attack patients were on average older in 1991 than in 1984 and older patients are less likely to receive intensive treatments, demographic changes actually suggest a slight reduction in spending on heart attacks (see Cutler and McClellan 1996a).

19. Some patients may receive both bypass surgery and angioplasty. These patients are grouped with other bypass surgery recipients.

20. More generally, patients consume medical resources until the small amount that they pay plus the pain and suffering inherent in the consumption of the care are equal to the marginal benefit of the care.

21. As Blumenthal, Feldman, and Zeckhauser (1982) and Blumenthal and Zeckhauser (1984) put it, misuse of technology is a "symptom," not a "disease," of the problems in the health sector.

22. There is some controversy over whether the elasticity of demand estimated in the Rand Health Insurance Experiment is correct, particularly if insurance provisions are changed for the entire population rather than for just a few individuals, but the study certainly gives an appropriate lower bound.

23. In reality, there is not just one response of health insurance to price. In response to tax subsidies, companies may change the type of benefits offered, the generosity of the coverage, and the share of premiums paid by the employer. The first two of these would lead to incentives for greater provision of medical care; the latter would not. Unfortunately, the literature has not always separated these responses.

24. This assumes away cross-person externalities in medical care consumption.

25. Some want to set up regional purchasing arrangements so that later they can be used to limit spending on medical care through other means, if need be (Aaron 1995).

Jim Cooper is a former Democratic Representative from Tennessee. His health care plan had many elements similar to Clinton's although many of the aspects were more voluntary than the Clinton plan.

26. Indeed, it is not clear that doctors know exactly which care is marginal, even if they only wanted to eliminate marginal care. Some of the responses to the studies about appropriateness, for example, suggest that views about appropriate care differ from physician to physician.

27. Recent news reports have noted a reduction in the growth rate of employer spending on health insurance. No estimates have been made about how representative this finding is, whether it is true about total premiums or just employer-paid premiums, and whether it is explicable by changing numbers of people insured or changes in the generosity of insurance.

28. Indeed, they are sufficiently healthier that Medicare loses money when managed care enrollment rises.

29. The table actually shows the distribution of benefit costs. The benefit cost is the premium net of administrative load.

30. The distribution of benefit costs increases for the largest organizations. This likely reflects selection into the sample relative to self insurance.

31. One reason might be that in the longterm, a lot of the uncertainty in spending is about the average cost of care, not the cross-section distribution of costs across individuals. Risks to average costs, if they are serially correlated, are impossible for private firms to diversify. Cutler (1992) develops this point.

32. See Blumberg and Nichols (1995) for more discussion.

33. Not all studies have found evidence of job lock (Holtz-Eakin 1994).

References

Aaron, Henry. 1991. *Serious and Unstable Condition: Financing America's Health Care*. Washington, DC: Brookings Institution.

Aaron, Henry. 1995. "Health Care Reform: The Clash of Goals, Facts, and Ideology." In Victor Fuchs, ed., *Individual and Social Responsibility*. Chicago: University of Chicago Press.

Aaron, Henry, and Robert Reischauer. 1995. "Medicare: Where to from Here?" NBER, Mimeo.

Altman, Lawrence K. 1994, October 1. "Surgery Is Found to Fight Stroke." *New York Times*, p. 1.

Altman, Stuart, and Ellen Ostby. 1991. "Paying for Hospital Care: The Impact on Federal Policy." In Eli Ginzberg, ed., *Health Services Research*, Cambridge, MA: Harvard University Press.

Baker, Laurence C. 1994. *Does Competition from HMOs Affect Fee-for-Service Physicians?* NBER Working Paper 4920.

Baumol, William. 1988, Fall. "Containing Medical Costs: Why Price Controls Won't Work." *Public Interest*, pp. 37–53.

Berk, Marc L., and Alan C. Monheit. 1992. "The Concentration of Health Expenditures: An Update." *Health Affairs* (Winter) 145–149.

Blumberg, Linda J., and Len M. Nichols. 1995. *Health Insurance Market Reforms: What They Can and Cannot Do*. Washington, DC: Urban Institute.

Blumenthal, David, Penny Feldman, and Richard Zeckhauser. 1982. "Misuse of Technology: A Symptom, Not the Disease." In Barbara J. McNeil and Ernest G. Cravalho, eds., *Critical Issues in Medical Technology*. Boston: Auburn House.

Blumenthal, David, and Richard J. Zeckhauser. 1984. "The Artificial Heart as an Economic Issue." In Margery W. Shaw, ed., *After Barney Clark: Reflections on the Utah Artificial Heart Program*. Austin: University of Texas Press.

Buchmueller, Thomas C., and Robert G. Valletta. 1994. "Employer-Provided Health Insurance and Worker Mobility: "'Job-Lock' or Not?" Unpublished paper. University of California, Irvine (February).

Chassin, Mark et al. 1987. "Does Inappropriate Use Explain Geographic Variations in the Use of Health Care Services?" *Journal of the American Medical Association* 258:2533–2537.

Cochrane, John. 1995. "Time Consistent Health Insurance." *Journal of Political Economy* (June) 103(3):445–473.

Cooper, Philip F., and Alan C. Monheit. 1993. "Does Employment-Related Health Insurance Inhibit Job Mobility?" *Inquiry* 30:400–416.

Cromwell, Jerry, and Janet Mitchell. 1986. "Physician-Induced Demand for Surgery." *Journal of Health Economics* 5:293–313.

Currie, Janet, and Jonathan Gruber. 1994. *Saving Babies: The Efficacy and Cost of Recent Expansions of Medicaid Eligibility for Pregnant Women*. NBER Working Paper 4644.

Cutler, David M. 1992. *Why Doesn't the Market Fully Insure Long-Term Care?* NBER Working Paper 4301.

Cutler, David M. 1994a. *Market Failure in Small Group Health Insurance*. NBER Working Paper 4879.

Cutler, David M. 1994b. "A Guide to Health Care Reform." *Journal of Economic Perspectives* 8(3) pp. 13–27.

Cutler, David M. 1995. "The Incidence of Adverse Medical Outcomes Under Prospective Payment." *Econometrica* 63(1):29–50.

Cutler, David M., and Mark McClellan. 1996a. "What Determines Technological Change?" In D. Wise, ed., *The Economics of Aging*. Chicago: University of Chicago for NBER.

Cutler, David M., and Mark McClellan. 1996b. "The Determinants of Technological Change in Heart Attack Treatments." NBER Working Paper 5751.

Cutler, David M., and Brigitte C. Madrian. 1996, April. "Labor Market Responses to Rising Health Insurance Costs: Evidence on Hours Worked." NBER Working Paper 5525.

Cutler, David M., and Sarah Reber. 1996, October. "Paying for Health Insurance: The Trade-off Between Competition and Adverse Selection." NBER Working Paper 5796.

Cutler, David M., and Doug Staiger. 1995. "Measuring the Value of Medical Progress." Mimeo. Harvard University.

Diamond, Peter. 1992. "Organizing the Health Insurance Market." *Econometrica* 60 (November): 1233–1254.

Employee Benefit Research Institute. 1994. "Sources of Health Insurance Coverage, 1993." Washington, D.C. (January).

Enthoven, Alain. 1993. "Why Managed Care Has Failed to Contain Health Costs." *Health Affairs* 12(3):27–43.

Feldstein, Martin. 1971. "Hospital Cost Inflation: A Study of Nonprofit Price Dynamics." *American Economic Review* 61(5):853–872.

Feldstein, Martin. 1995. "Comment on Henry Aaron." In Victor Fuchs, ed., *Individual and Social Responsibility*. Chicago: University of Chicago Press.

Fisher, Charles R. 1980. "Differences by Age Groups in Health Care Spending." *Health Care Financing Review* 2:65–89.

Fuchs, Victor. 1974. *Who Shall Live?* New York: Basic Books.

Fuchs, Victor. 1995. *Individual and Social Responsibility*, Chicago: University of Chicago Press.

Fuchs, V. 1996. "Economics, Values, and Health Care Reform." *American Economics Review* 86(1):1–24.

Fuchs, Victor, and James Hahn. 1990. "How Does Canada Do It?" *New England Journal of Medicine* (27 September) 884–890.

Garber, Alan, Victor Fuchs, and James Silverman. 1984. "Case Mix Costs, and Outcomes." *New England Journal of Medicine* (10 May) 310:231–237.

Giljens, Annetine, and Nathan Rosenberg. 1994. "The Dynamics of Technological Change in Medicine." *Health Affairs* 13(3):29–45.

Greenspan, Allan M., et al. 1988. "Incidence of Unwarranted Implantation of Permanent Cardiac Pacemakers in a Large Medical Population." *New England Journal of Medicine* (21 January) 318:158–163.

Grossman, Michael. 1972. *The Demand for Health: A Theoretical and Empirical Investigation.* New York: Columbia University Press.

Grossman, Michael, Jody L. Sindelar, John Mullahy, and Richard Anderson. 1993. "Policy Watch: Alcohol and Cigarette Taxes." *Journal of Economic Perspectives* 7(4):211–222.

Gruber, Jonathan. 1994. "The Incidence of Mandated Maternity Benefits." *American Economic Review* 84(3):622–641.

Gruber, Jonathan, and James Poterba. 1995. *Tax Subsidies to Employer-Provided Health Insurance*. NBER Working Paper 5147.

Gruber, Jonathan, and Alan Krueger. 1991. "The Incidence of Mandated Employer-Provided Insurance: lessons from Workers' Compensation Insurance." In David Bradford, ed., *Tax Policy and the Economy*, vol. 5. Cambridge, MA: MIT Press.

Gruber, Jonathan, and Brigitte Madrian. 1994. "Health Insurance and Job Mobility: The Effects of Public Policy on Job Lock." *Industrial and Labor Relations Review* 48(1):86–102.

Hadley, Jack, Earl P. Steinberg, and Judith Feder. 1991. "Comparison of Uninsured and Privately Insured Hospital Patients." *Journal of the Americal Medical Association* (16 January) 265:374–379.

Hay, Joel W. 1991. "The Harm They Do to Others: A Primer on the External Costs of Drug Abuse." In Melvyn B. Krauss and Edward P. Lazear, eds., *Searching for Alternatives: Drug-Control Policy in the United States*, pp. 200–225. Stanford: Hoover Institution Press.

Hill, J. W., and R. S. Brown. 1990. *Biased Selection in the TEFRA HMO/CMP Program*. MPR 7786-503. Princeton: Mathematica Policy Research.

Himmelstein, David, and Steffie Woolhandler. 1986. "Cost Without Benefit: Administrative Waste in U.S. Health Care." *New England Journal of Medicine* (13 February) 441–445.

Holtz-Eakin, Douglas. 1994. "Health Insurance Provision and Labor Market Efficiency in the United States and Germany." In Rebecca M. Blank, ed., *Social Protection Versus Economic Flexibility: Is There a Tradeoff?* Chicago: University of Chicago Press.

Huskamp, Haiden A., and Joseph P. Newhouse. 1994. "Is Health Spending Slowing Down?" *Health Affairs* 13(5):32–38.

Kahn, Katherine L., et al. 1990. "Comparing Outcomes of Care Before and After Implementation of the DRG-Based Prospective Payment System." *Journal of the American Medical Association* 264 (17 October) 1984–1988.

Kessler, Daniel, and Mark McClellan. 1996. "Do Doctors Practice Defensive Medicine?" *Quarterly Journal of Economics* 111(2):353–390.

Madrian, Brigitte C. "Employment-Based Health Insurance and Job Mobility: Is There Evidence of Job-Lock?" *Quarterly Journal of Economics* 109:27–54.

Manning, Willard, et al. 1987. "Health Insurance and the Demand for Medical Care: Evidence from a Randomized Experiment." *American Economic Review*. 77(3):251–277.

Manning, Willard B., Emmett B. Keeler, Joseph P. Newhouse, Elizabeth M. Sloss, and Jeffrey Wasserman. 1991. *The Costs of Poor Health Habits*. Cambridge, MA: Harvard University Press.

McClellan, Mark, and Joseph P. Newhouse. 1995. "The Marginal Benefits of Medical Technology." Mimeo. Harvard University.

Miller, R., and H. Luft. 1994. "Managed Care Plan Performance Since 1980." *Journal of the American Medical Association*. (18 May). 1512–1519.

Monheit, Alan C., and Philip F. Cooper. 1993. "Does Employment-Related Health Insurance Limit Job Mobility?" *Inquiry* 30(4):400–417.

Newhouse, Joseph P. 1985. "Are Fee-for-Service Costs Increasing Faster Than HMO Costs?" *Medical Care* 23:960–966.

Newhouse, Joseph P. 1992. "Medical Care Costs: How Much Welfare Loss?" *Journal of Economic Perspectives* 6(3):3–22.

Newhouse, Joseph P. 1993. *Free for All? Lessons from the Rand Health Insurance Experiment*. Cambridge, MA: Harvard University Press.

Newhouse, Joseph P. 1994. "Patients at Risk: Health Reform and Risk Adjustment." *Health Affairs* 13(1):132–146.

Newhouse, Joseph P. 1996. "Reimbursing Health Plans and Health Providers." *Journal of Economic Literature* 34(3):1236–1263.

Pauly, Mark. 1986. "Taxation, Health Insurance, and Market Failure in Medical Care." *Journal of Economic Literature* 24:629–676.

Pauly, Mark, Howard Kunreuther, and Richard Hirth. 1992. "Guaranteed Renewability." Mimeo. Univ. of Pennsylvania.

Penrod, John R. 1994. "Health Care Costs, Health Insurance, and Job Mobility." Unpublished paper. Princeton University.

Phelps, Charles. 1992. *Health Economics*. New York: Harper Collins.

Poterba, James M., and Lawrence H. Summers. 1987. "Public Policy Implications of Declining Old Age Mortality." In G. Burtless, ed., *Work, Health, and Income Among the Elderly*. Washington DC: Brookings Institution.

Preston, Samuel H., and Michael R. Haines. 1991. *Fatal Years: Child Mortality in Late Nineteenth-Century America*. Princeton, NJ: Princeton University Press.

Price, James R., and James R. Mays. 1985. "Selection and the Competitive Standing of Health Plans in a Multiple-Choice, Multiple-Insurer Market." In R. Sheffler and L. Rossiter, eds., *Advances in Health Economics and Health Services Research*, vol. 6, Greenwich, CT: JAI Press.

Prospective Payment Assessment Commission. 1994. *Medicare and The American Health Care System* (June). Washington, DC.

Reynolds, Roger, John A. Rizzo, and Martin L. Gonzalez. 1987. "The Cost of Medical Professional Liability." *Journal of the American Medical Association (22/29 May) 2776–2781.*

Robinson J., and H. Luft. 1985. "The Impact of Hospital Market Structure on Patient Volume, Average Length of Stay, and the Cost of Care." *Journal of Health Economics* 4(4):333–356.

Rogowski, Jeanette A., and Lynn A. Karoly. 1993. "The Effect of Health Insurance on the Decision to Retire." Unpublished paper. Santa Monica, CA: Rand Corporation.

Rothschild, Michael, and Joseph Stiglitz. 1976. "Equilibrium in Competitive Insurance Markets: An Essay on the Economics of Imperfect Information." *Quarterly Journal of Economics* 90(4):629–650.

Schoenbaum, Michael. 1996. "Do Smokers Understand the Mortality Effects of Smoking? Evidence from the Health and Retirement Survey." Mimeo. University of California, Berkeley.

Schwartz, William B. 1994. "In the Pipeline: A Wave of Valuable Medical Technology." *Health Affairs* 13(3):70–79.

Schwartz, William B., and Michael Mendelson. 1994. "Eliminating Waste and Inefficiency Can Do Little to Contain Costs." *Health Affairs* 13(1):224–238.

Sheiner, Louise. 1994. "Health Costs, Aging, and Wages." Mimeo. Federal Reserve Board.

Staiger, Doug, and Gary Gaumer. 1990. "The Effect of Prospective Payment on Post-Hospital Mortality." Mimeo. Harvard University.

Summers, Lawrence H. 1989. "Some Simple Economics of Mandated Benefits." *American Economic Review Papers and Proceedings* 99:177–183.

U.S. Public Health Service. *Health United States*. Washington, DC: U.S. Government Printing Office, 1990.

Viscusi, W. Kip. 1992. *Smoking: Making the Risky Decision*. New York: Oxford University Press.

Viscusi, W. Kip. 1995. "Cigarette Taxation and the Social Consequences of Smoking." In James Poterba, ed., *Tax Policy and the Economy, 9*, 51–101. Cambridge, MA: MIT Press.

Weisbrod, Burt. 1991. "The Health Care Quadrilemma: An Essay on Technological Change, Insurance, Quality of Care, and Cost Containment." *Journal of Economic Literature* 24:523–552.

Weissman, Joel S., and Arnold Epstein. 1994. *Falling Through the Safety Net: Insurance Status and Access to Health Care*. Baltimore: Johns Hopkins University Press.

Wennberg, Jack E., J. L. Freeman, and W. J. Culp. 1987. "Are Hospital Services Rationed in New Haven or Over-Utilized in Boston?" *Lancet* 1 (23 May) 1185–1188.

Wholey, D., R. Feldman, and J. B. Christianson. 1995. "The Effect of Market Structure on HMO Premiums." *Journal of Health Economics* 14:81–106.

Winslow, Constance M., et al. 1988a. "The Appropriateness of Carotid Endarterectomy." *New England Journal of Medicine* (24 March) 721–727.

Winslow, Constance M., et al. 1988b. "The Appropriateness of Performing Coronary Artery Bypass Surgery." *Journal of the American Medical Association* (22 July) 505–510.

Yelowitz, Aaron S. 1995. "The Medicaid Notch, Labor Supply, and Welfare Participation: Evidence from Eligibility Expansions." *Quarterly Journal of Economics* 110(4):909–940.

Zwanziger, Jack, and Glenn Melnick. 1988. "The Effects of Hospital Competition and the Medicare PPS Program on Hospital Cost Behavior in California." *Journal of Health Economics* 7:301–320.

Comment

Henry J. Aaron

David Cutler covers an enormous range with virtuosity, summarizing a large literature and clearly laying out many issues with precision and with terseness. He paints with complete assurance, relying on broad but precise strokes to delineate the many topics he treats. None of the topics receives particular emphasis, however, so I feel rather as if I have been asked to comment on an orchard of many trees, each well formed but all about the same height.

My comments are divided into three parts. Each takes up one of the issues Cutler raises—not to disagree with him but to approach them from a somewhat different light.

I

My first comment concerns a finding of the health economics literature that has long stood as a minor puzzle. Estimates of the income elasticity of demand for health care based on cross-sectional data from the United States are all very low. Cutler cites Manning et al. that the elasticity, based on U.S. cross-section data, is only about 0.2. This estimate contrasts with elasticities from international cross sections, which invariably exceed 1.0 Cutler does not cite these studies. He uses the low intranational elasticity to calculate how much of the increase in health care spending the secular increase in incomes can explain.

The answer is "not much": about 5 percent of the observed increase between 1940 and 1990. In sharp contrast, Cutler shows that the increases in the relative price of health care services could account for as much as one-fifth of the increase in health care spending. This high estimate applies assuming Baumol's law regarding the relative increase in the price of goods produced by labor in sectors where labor productivity does not increase.

How can the differences between elasticity estimates based on intranational cross sections and those based on international cross sections be reconciled? The key is that international differences in incomes are systematically associated with differences in the price of health care.

Assume that at any given point in time, the productivity of labor in health care is identical internationally. This assumption is analogous to assuming that the intranational growth of productivity in health care is zero while productivity is rising elsewhere in the rest of the economy.

Labor accounts for about 60 percent of the cost of hospital services and probably a larger share of the cost of other medical services. Assume that, on the average, labor accounts for 70 percent of the cost of health care services. In most countries, tax-financed public systems insulate people from the price of health care when ill. Assume further that standards of care are set by professional norms and that these norms are uncorrelated with income. Under these assumptions, the estimated international income elasticity of demand for health care would be about 0.7, labor's approximate share in health care costs, even if the true intranational income elasticity of demand for health care were zero. Added to a measured intranational income elasticity of about 0.2—arguably, the "true" income elasticity—the observed international elasticity would be about 0.9, not much below actual estimates. This adjustment largely, but not entirely, eliminates the paradox, but it does reduce it to a negligible and probably statistically insignificant level.

II

A second issue, to which Cutler devotes considerable space, concerns the marginal value of health care services. He provides a clear and comprehensive review of the literature, but I find this literature troubling and unsatisfying. The issue is this: much of the literature uses the term "marginal value of health care" too casually. As a practical matter, it may be impossible to parse health care into marginal and inframarginal activities. If it is not possible in practice to identify marginal care at least some of the time, and if the literature on the ineffectiveness of care is correct, then the implications are more radical than Cutler or the authors of the literature he cites let on. In particular, either the studies are wrong or health care on the average is useless.

To begin with, one must define the term "marginal care" carefully. Novices sometimes refer to services or classes of services as marginal. With the exception of procedures that are universally ineffective or universally less effective than other less costly interventions, this usage is misleading. The practical question for an economist concerns which applications of a procedure yield sufficient benefits to be worth the cost. Not all uses of a particular service may pass muster, but not all will fail either. In this case, it makes no sense to speak of ineffective services. Services that yield net benefits but at excessive cost may properly be considered marginal.

This concept makes sense only if the cases in which a procedure is marginal can be distinguished from cases in which it is not. In addition, it is important to note that survival is not the only indicator of efficacy or quality; relief of pain, improvement of functioning in life, and simple amenities (lengths of stay of more than twenty-four hours for normal childbirth, for example) have value too, and they should not be disdained.

Several of the studies Cutler cites report evidence that curtailment of general spending has had little effect on health outcomes. In some cases, there is good reason to believe that the health care system was operating inside its production possibility frontier, however defined. The trend to reduced lengths of stay has coincided with improved hospital care because ambulation is curative after surgery and because hospitals are, to be blunt, rife with infection. Evidence that no adverse health outcomes occurred as a result of the DRG system is subject to this interpretation. It is also subject to another interpretation, however: service levels depend on per patient hospital revenues for all patients from all sources and DRG limits did not much change hospital service levels because hospitals managed to shift costs to private payers.

Studies regarding the provision of "inappropriate" care are even more unsatisfying. These studies consist of postaudits of case records by panels of physicians who evaluate case records to determine whether the use of particular procedure was "appropriate," "equivocal," or "inappropriate" in given cases. There is so much wrong with these studies that I hardly know where to begin. To begin, the terms *appropriate, equivocal,* and *inappropriate* are loosely defined and subjective. Second, as Cutler points out, these studies do not explicitly consider cost and, on that account, tend to underestimate the amount of inappropriate or equivocal care. And there is a much more serious problem: the model underlying these evaluations is that objective evidence exists ex ante on the basis of which highly competent scientist physicians can evaluate ex post the judgment of their less talented or more harried colleagues. There is something to this view. But some hard evidence exists that another more troubling interpretation is possible.

Studies of the appropriateness of care in different countries indicate that roughly the same proportions of care are inappropriate or equivocal, regardless of the level of spending or the use of a particular procedure. This finding calls several possible explanations to mind:

- It may be that the ex post jurors are no better than run-of-the-mill ex ante jurors, just different.
- It may be that if the ex post jurors had been forced to make judgments in real time with live human beings, they would not have made different decisions from those their colleagues in fact made ex ante.
- It may be that among physicians—as among physicists, economists, or violinists—talent and skill vary naturally, producing differences in performance that no practicable amount of training will eliminate.

In any of these cases, the term *marginal care* loses clear meaning—or any meaning at all. Although someone with God-like insight or judgment could eliminate marginal care, ordinary humans cannot. One is left to evaluate the average value of care, because the characteristics that might define the margin are unobservable in practice. To the extent that these alternative interpretations are correct, findings that marginal care is ineffective are really evidence that medical care on the average is ineffective. It is also possible that the difference between findings during post-audit and those made by attending physicians reflects facts relevant to the selection of care that are missing from the case files.

There is yet another possibility: the expert panels may be wrong. In fact, at least one may have been. RAND Corporation physician Robert Brook has coauthored a number of studies on the prevalence of inappropriate and equivocal care. Some of his most spectacular findings concern carotid endarterectomy, a procedure to ream out the carotid artery to reduce the likelihood of stroke. A study Brook coauthored reported that roughly two-thirds of the uses of this procedure in one selected population were inappropriate or equivocal. Some years ago, I shared a platform with Brook and heard him tell an audience that he thought carotid endarterectomy was almost never justified.

With this background, I was startled to read the 1994 *New York Times* story, which Cutler cites, reporting on a major randomized clinical trial of carotid endarterectomy. The managers of the trial felt compelled to suspend the trial because early findings so unambiguously showed that the procedure was beneficial in the population subject to study that failing to inform patients in the control group of those benefits could not survive standards of informed consent. The only ethical course available to the study mangers was to inform all participants, whether they were in the control group or not, of the medically and statistically significant benefits that were being observed, and terminate the study.

This outcome suggests that Brook should be embarrassed at least by his oral comments. The more interesting question is whether he should also be embarrassed by his written work. Perhaps so. General efficacy cannot be ruled out by the findings that led to suspension of the clinical trial. But it remains at least possible that carotid endarterectomy *is* inappropriately used on a massive scale, perhaps as widely as Brook's written work, if not his less temperate oral remarks, suggest. Now, however, it will be difficult, or perhaps impossible, ever to find out.

To understand why, consider what one would have to do to find out. Let us assume that the expert scientist model of medicine is correct; the top docs really know what is best. They believe that patients can be divided ex ante into N classes, based on expected benefits from the procedure. To test their hypotheses, they would like to assign presenting patients randomly in each of the N classes to receive the procedure or not to receive the procedure. Actually there are normally more, often many more, than two alternative ways to treat a given condition. As in agriculture, medicine has its "intensive," as well as its "extensive," margin. (This fact, incidentally, explains why the attempt in Oregon to rule treatment "in" or "our" of a fixed budget, using "condition-treatment" pairs, is analytically unacceptable.) As I have noted, however, we cannot be confident that the expert scientist model is correct.

The results of the trial whose suspension the *New York Times* reported forecloses this experimental course. Such an experiment cannot even begin because of the strictures, quite proper in my view, of informed consent. One might look for evidence to natural experiments created by resource constraints. Driven by cost competition or budget constraint, different medical groups might adopt different protocols for treatment. Although this source of variation holds out some potential, practical difficulties abound—achieving adequate sample size and controlling for other differences among groups, for example.

I have gone into the issue of marginal care and its detection at some length because I believe that we economists tend to invoke our professional comparative advantage with the concept of the marginal too facilely in the area of medicine. As the United States moves with seeming inexorability into an era of rationing, it is vitally important that we devise methods of ensuring that the benefits we forgo are indeed the marginal ones, arising from medical procedures that are costly but add little to survival, reduction of physical pain, improved functioning, or psychological comfort. Right now, I do not think we know how to do it. We can, and do, talk about medical care of marginal benefit, and anyone my age who studies the problem not only is aware of marginal care but has received it. Getting rid of it is another matter. Practical algorithms for doing so do not now exist. Devising them requires increased attention from economists, physicians, nurses, ethicists, and others.

III

The third topic I take up is the advance of medical technology. Cutler's analysis of the way in which technological advance has increased the cost of treating coronaries is fascinating, informative, and new. He agrees that it is the primary force behind rising real health care spending per capita. He points out that it is overused. Others have observed that the causation linking technology and spending also runs the other way. Not only has technology pushed up costs. Open-ended financing has fueled rapid growth of medical technology and provided little incentive to research on cost-limiting technologies.

Even if one accepts the probable correctness of all of these propositions—and I do—they leave two other questions. Was it a bad thing? And would there be any unintended side effects from successful efforts, private or public, to squeeze out excess spending arising from overuse of medical technology?

On the first question—whether the undisciplined system of health care spending was a bad thing—I think the only tenable answer is: Who knows? We have wasted welfare triangles galore by spending resources on health care that produce small benefits. But we may have purchased many welfare rectangles by supporting research that has yielded quite major benefits. It is quite possible that the big gains all came from publicly funded research or from private research that would have been done anyway. But the dominant fact is that the health care spending explosion is contemporaneous with a scientific revolution in medicine and molecular biology, a revolution that is intellectually at least as exciting as, and promises more far-reaching consequences for humanity than, the physics revolution of the early twentieth century. Would we have gained more from an efficient system of allocating spending to health care services than we would have lost from less rapid technical advance? I do not know. But I think it is the right question to ask. And asking it leads to my final observation, which is counterintuitive and may be a bit controversial. We are in the early stages of a national effort to slow the growth of health care spending. I hope that this effort succeeds. Let us assume that it does. Let us also assume that it succeeds in reducing low-benefit care disproportionately. In other words, let us assume that the concerns I just expressed about identifying marginal care turn out to be unfounded.

My question is this: What should be done about public support of medical research? One answer is that medical research should be curtailed because it is the primary engine driving health care spending. I think that answer is analytically wrong. If cost control selectively curtails those uses of any given medical technology that yield benefits less than cost and sustains uses of that same technology that yield benefits greater than cost, the net social benefit of any given technology increases. Nonetheless, cost control will lower private incentives to do research, because profits depend on total use, not just on efficient use. If there is a case for public support of research, and I think we all acknowledge that there is, successful cost control, public or private, would strengthen the case for sustaining, and possibly for increasing, public budgets for support of biomedical research.

Comment

Joseph P. Newhouse

David Cutler makes clear the many connections between health care and public policy. As a result, he had to take some care in choosing which connections to discuss. I think he has made wise choices. Although the bulk of his chapter takes up issues surrounding medical care services, he emphasizes that issues such as the level of sin taxes and the control of violence and injury are also important to the health of the population. I would like to take up two points he raised: the growth of health care costs, which may be inefficiently high, and managed care as a solution to the moral hazard present with traditional reimbursement or indemnity insurance.

The Optimal Growth Rate of Medical Care Costs

There is widespread agreement among American health economists that traditional insurance introduces a nontrivial amount of moral hazard or welfare loss at a point in time (Fuchs 1996). In other words, few would argue with Cutler's fact 2: the marginal value of treatment among the insured population is low.

Whether the growth rate of costs over time is too high, however, is less clear. Again, most American health economists agree with Cutler that the prime cause of the half-century health care cost increase has been the result of technological advances in medicine (Fuchs 1996).[1] Moreover, Cutler points out that the average and the marginal value of the new technology may differ substantially. These two facts suggest that consumers may have been willing to pay for much of the increase in costs.

I would like to sharpen the discussion of the welfare loss implied by the growth of medical care costs. I make two points: (1) arguments that any given technology is overused at a point in time because of insurance do not support the inference that the growth rate in spending is too high, and (2) even if insurance induces additional technological change, as is almost certainly the case, one cannot infer that there is a welfare loss.

The first point can be demonstrated with a simple arithmetic example. Suppose that there is an innovation each year and that because of moral hazard an insured population buys twice as much of it as an uninsured population. Assume for the sake of simplicity that in the base year, the insured population spent at twice the rate of the uninsured population. Then costs will grow at the same rate in the two populations.

Now suppose a magic bullet (managed care) passed through the insured population such that it started purchasing each new innovation at half its prior rate; in other words, it started acting as if it were uninsured. Suppose further that growth in both populations had been at a constant rate. With the advent of the magic bullet, growth rates of medical care costs in the insured population would fall, but this fall would be transitory; as total medical care costs (the denominator) grew at a slower rate than before, observed growth rates would increase and in the limit would approach the prior growth rate, as total spending approached the uninsured level. In short, the existence of insurance may not affect the steady-state growth rate, though without question it affects the level of spending.

The conclusion that the steady-state growth rate may not be much affected is consistent with the data in table 5.1, which show that the growth rate of U.S. medical spending between 1960 and 1990 was about the same as—actually slightly below—that of both the Group of Seven average and the OECD average (4.7 percent versus 5.0 percent), though the United States spends 40 percent more per person than Canada, the second highest spending country ($2,566 versus $1,770 in 1990). To be sure these other countries have insurance, but the traditional passive nature of U.S. insurance arrangements relative to, say, a government health budget is frequently thought to yield more moral hazard. Further, these data suggest that the U.S. tax subsidy may have a much larger effect on the level than on the growth rate of spending.

Suppose, however, that insurance does in fact raise the growth rate of health care costs, as it almost certainly does. Does that imply a welfare loss? Our intuition that any purchase induced by a subsidy has a deadweight loss associated with it assumes that income effects are small, but in many health care instances they are not. If the cost of a particular treatment for a rare disease is in the hundreds of thousands of dollars, the existence of modest fixed costs to develop the treatment could mean that the treatment would never come to market without insurance (formal or informal) simply because the size of the uninsured market might not be large enough to cover the fixed costs. Thus, the existence of technologies that would not have been on the market at all without insurance may increase welfare; the test is whether consumers would have been willing to pay ex ante for an insurance policy that covered the cost of the technology in specified states of the world (Goddeeris 1984a, 1984b). In other words, the second best may be to have the technology on the market with the associated moral hazard from insurance than not to have the technology at all. Of course, as the share of GDP in medical care rises, the opportunity costs of the resources in medical care also rise.[2]

For these reasons I would have reformulated Cutler's statement that economic theory suggests the growth of costs is inefficiently high to read as follows: both economic theory and empirical evidence suggest that the level of medical care costs in the United States is inefficiently high; theory, by itself, however, does not show that the growth rate is inefficiently high, though of course it may be.

Managed Care

Managed care, which I shall take to be a set of techniques for reducing moral hazard, is spreading rapidly, as figure 5.2 makes clear. In effect, the financing and delivery of care are being integrated. I wish to make three points about managed care, all of which open potential roles for the public sector. Managed care (1) raises the likelihood of a market failure in insurance for bad risks, (2) changes the incentives facing the physician, and (3) creates a contract ambiguity that makes the welfare economics difficult and will raise the demand for efficient dispute resolution mechanisms.

Market Failure for Bad Risks

Cutler makes the market failure case well at the end of his chapter, and there is no need to repeat it in my discussion. He cites my conclusion that purely prospective risk selection leaves substantial incentives for selecting good risks. Another way to put this is that increasing the degree of prospectivity increases incentives to select and to produce efficiently, and thus the optimal degree of prospectivity is not clear a priori (Newhouse 1996). I believe that determining the optimal degree of prospectivity will require some experimentation; although I have elsewhere proposed beginning with linear combinations of prospective payment (capiation) and fee for service, nonlinear combinations may well be better.

If one abandons purely prospective payment, there needs to be an agent to redistribute monies among insurance plans according to the use of their enrollees. The agent could be a government agency, which is reminiscent of the Clinton proposal for health alliances, or it could be a large employer or coalition of employers that redistribute monies among the several health plans that employees could enroll in.

The Incentives Facing Physicians

Managed care plans increasingly are offering physicians financial incentives to reduce use, the extreme version of which is to offer the primary care physician a fixed amount per patient (a capitation) and leave him or her responsible for the costs of all care. This, of course, poses the trade-off between selection and production efficiency in stark terms.

It is not that trade-off, however, that concerns me but rather the knowledge—or lack of it—of the consumer of these incentives. Indeed, policy should compel the disclosure of the nature of these incentives to the prospective plan purchaser.

The rationale for disclosure comes from the necessarily incomplete contract between the subscriber and the managed care company; all possible contingencies cannot be spelled out in advance, and even if they could, technical change in medicine would soon render any such contract obsolete. Thus, the language used in virtually all contracts requires plans to provide "medically necessary services."

Even if the contract cannot say exactly how the plan will treat the consumer in all the various states of the world—if she falls ill with breast cancer or has a heart attack or a rash—the consumer choosing a plan could potentially learn what incentives the gatekeeper physician will face in each situation and therefore infer the quantity of services she may expect to receive.

Knowledge of the financial risk on the physician is not sufficient for the consumer to judge plans; one would anticipate that the less the financial risk on the gatekeeper, the more the plan may substitute command-and-control management of moral hazard, and such mechanisms may be difficult or impossible to summarize for the consumer.[3] Indeed, even the financial incentives, such as the nature of bonus arrangements for reduced utilization, may be difficult to summarize in any straightforward way. Nonetheless, it would be useful to have information about the financial risk facing the physicians in the plan openly available to those considering enrollment.

Disputes Between Plans and Patients

In traditional insurance arrangements, physician's and patient's incentives are largely aligned; both desire the delivery of services with even modest benefits. Because of the financial incentives facing physicians in managed care plans, this congruence no longer holds. This outcome is not necessarily bad; supply-side cost sharing is a potential tool for reducing moral hazard (Ellis and McGuire 1986, 1993).

Economists' intuition, based on demand-side cost sharing, is that such supply-side cost sharing will reduce utilization of the lowest-valued services. But because consumers have no very obvious way to express their demand for any given service, this need not be the case.[4] A woman with breast cancer, for example, may have been willing to pay a premium ex ante for a policy that would have covered a bone marrow transplant; the health plan, however, may decide that the clinical benefit in her case is not sufficient to justify undertaking the procedure. There is no particular reason to think that the plan's perception of clinical benefit matches up with any individual consumer's willingness to pay.

Two consequences follow. The first is that managed care may not only reduce services whose benefit is less than their social cost but also services whose benefit (defined in an ex ante premium sense) actually exceeds social cost. To the degree this is the case, the welfare gains from managed care are clearly reduced. Second, there is a potentially large volume of disputes between consumers and plans over what benefits are to be provided, especially because the change for many insured consumers from the permissive traditional environment to the new environment is occurring quickly and consumers may believe their contract entitles them to all beneficial services. Processing such disputes through the civil justice system will surely incur high transactions costs. An alternative dispute resolution mechanism, perhaps patterned on the arbitration system for grievances over labor-management contracts, may well be preferable.

Notes

1. In other industries technological change tends to lower cost. Medical care may differ partly because of the presence of insurance (Weisbrod 1991), but some of it may simply be an arbitrary definition of industry. Medical care has come up with a large number of new lines of business, for example, renal dialysis, angioplasty, transplantation, and magnetic resonance imaging. Within each of the various new medical care product lines, technological change and learning by doing have tended to reduce costs and improve results, as has been the case in other industries.

2. This assumes approximately homothetic production possibility frontiers.

3. It seems difficult or impossible to summarize any merit-based incentives for salaried physicians.

4. I assume away under-the-table payments.

References

Ellis, Randall P., and Thomas G. McGuire. 1986. "Provider Behavior Under Prospective Reimbursement." *Journal of Health Economics* 5(2):129–151.

Ellis, Randall P., and Thomas G. McGuire. 1993, Fall. "Supply-Side and Demand-Side Cost Sharing in Medical Care." *Journal of Economic Perspectives* 7(4):135–151.

Fuchs, Victor R. 1996, March. "Economics, Values, and Health Care Reform." *American Economic Review* 86(1):1–24.

Goddeeris, John H. 1984a. "Insurance and Incentives for Innovation in Medical Care." *Southern Economic Journal* 51:530–539.

Goddeeris, John N. 1984b. "Medical Insurance, Technological Change, and Welfare." *Economic Inquiry* 22:56–67.

Newhouse, Joseph P. 1996, September. "Reimbursing Health Plans and Health Providers: Efficiency in Production versus Selection." *Journal of Economic Literature*. 34(3):1236–1263.

Weisbrod, Burton. 1991, June. "The Health Care Quadrilemma: An Essay on Technological Change, Insurance, Quality of Care, and Cost Containment." *Journal of Economic Literature* 29(3):523–552.

6 Privatizing Social Security in the United States: Why and How

Laurence J. Kotlikoff

Privatization of social security is spreading throughout the world. Chile, Peru, Argentina, England, Sweden, and Australia have already privatized, and Bolivia, Mexico, and Italy are likely to join them shortly. In the United States, there is growing interest among politicians, the public, and academics in privatizing social security.[1] Senators Alan Simpson and John Kerry have called for the partial privatization of the U.S. system, and former presidential candidate Steven Forbes has called for the complete privatization of the system.

Is privatizing social security a good idea? Is it something the United States should do? What would it mean for the economy? Who would benefit, and who would lose? Is there a simple way to privatize the U.S. system? This chapter attempts to answer these questions. It points out that privatizing social security has the potential for increasing economic efficiency, raising living standards, and improving the intra- and intergenerational distribution of resources. Whether it does so depends on the nature of the system being privatized and the manner in which privatization occurs.

To make this point clear, section 6.1 plays devil's advocate in arguing that privatizing social security may represent little more than a shell game in which the government simply relabels its fiscal receipts and payments, leaving underlying economic conditions unchanged. Chile's privatization is described here to illustrate the relabeling of fiscal variables, although the Chilean privatization appears to represent more than just a relabeling of existing fiscal arrangements.

Section 6.2 responds to section 6.1 by pointing out that at least in the United States, privatizing social security would represent not just a change in form but also a change in economic substance. This section also points out a number of fundamental economic problems associated with the U.S. social security system, all of which could be remedied through privatization. These problems include labor supply distortions, the capricious inter- and intragenerational distribution of resources, the lack of information and uncertainty surrounding individuals' future social security benefits, and the difficulty of sustaining the system through the demographic transition.

Section 6.3 examines one of these issues in more detail: the degree to which privatizing social security can reduce the distortion of labor supply and thereby improve economic performance and overall economic well-being. Specifically, I simulate the Auerbach-Kotlikoff dynamic life cycle simulation model (the AK model) to suggest the potential welfare changes and efficiency gains from privatizing a pay-as-you-go social security system in a stylized economy. The distinction between welfare changes and efficiency gains turns on whether initial generations are fully compensated for any economic injury associated with privatization. In the calculation of welfare changes, no compensation is provided, whereas full compensation is provided in the calculation of efficiency gains.

The results indicate that with the right initial conditions and the right choice of fiscal instruments during the transition, privatization can significantly reduce labor supply distortions and thereby raise economic efficiency. But if the initial conditions are not right or inappropriate fiscal instruments are used during the transition, privatization can end up lowering economic efficiency.

Section 6.4 considers the requirements for successful privatization of the U.S. social security system. It points out that a wholesale adoption of the Chilean formulation is not likely to work in the United States and offers instead a simple scheme for privatizing the U.S. system, called the Personal Security System. Section 6.5 considers its advantages and disadvantages.

6.1 Is Privatizing Social Security Just a Shell Game?

An evaluation of whether privatizing social security represents a fundamental change in policy or simply a relabeling of existing policy begins with the four features that typically arise in social security privatizations: (1) the replacement of payroll taxation with mandatory contributions to private pension accounts, (2) continued payment of social security benefits to current retirees (those collecting benefits at the time of the privatization), (3) the gradual phase-out of social security benefits for future retirees, and (4) a method of financing social security benefits during the transition to a completely privatized system.

Each of these elements is present in Chile's privatization, although not necessarily described in these terms. For example, existing social security beneficiaries continued to receive their benefits, but existing workers were given recognition bonds whose values were purported to equal the present value of the claims to future social security benefits that workers had accrued under the existing system.[2] The recognition bonds come due at retirement. Hence, although it used different language ("payment of principal plus interest on recognition bonds" rather than "social security benefits"), Chile in effect chose to provide social security income to existing workers that would phase out to zero for new workers who had accrued no benefits under the old system. Chile's method of financing social security benefits (including paying interest and principal of the recognition bonds) during the transition involves deficit finance (although no one in the Chilean government went out of his way to make this point clear). When it began to privatize, Chile was running large annual budget surpluses. With privatization, these surpluses were substantially reduced. The result was equivalent to Chile's leaving its budget surplus intact but explicitly borrowing to cover the payment of social security benefits during the transition.

At a quick glance, Chile's social security's privatization appears to represent simply a clever shell game. First, it left existing retirees in exactly their preprivatization position. Second, it transformed an implicit liability to pay existing workers their accrued social security benefits into an explicit liability to pay them principal plus interest on recognition bonds, all of which amounts, in the main, to simply a change in language. Third, it transformed the pay-as-you-go system's ongoing implicit tax on workers into an explicit tax. The implicit tax refers to the fact that compulsory contributions to a mature pay-as-you-go social security systems earn a below-market rate of return—the growth rate of the economy. In permitting workers to contribute to private pensions, Chile let them earn a market rate of return on their retirement contributions but hit them with higher explicit general revenue taxes to service the explicit debt issued to meet benefit payments to existing retirees and the recognition bonds provided to existing workers. Assuming initial older generations are not forced to share the burden of servicing the additional explicit debt as well as recognition bonds, the explicit tax hitting current and future workers will be just as large as the implicit tax would have been.

Following the money reinforces the impression of a shell game. Consider the money taken from young Chilean workers in the form of payroll taxes and handed to old retirees as social security benefits. Under privatization, the same money is taken from young workers but is placed in private pension funds. These pension funds, however, immediately hand back the money to the government in exchange for government bonds. The government then takes the money and hands it over to the old retirees as social security benefit payments. When workers retire, they receive principal plus interest payments from the pensions based on their pension's investment in government bonds. But they are forced to hand back some of this money to the government as taxes levied to pay interest on this same government debt. To a Martian observing from outer space the net flow of money from young workers and old retirees to the government, nonprivatized and privatized social security regimes would look identical.

Now one might object that certain elements of privatization, such as the fact that workers receive a variable rate of return on their private pension contributions, make the privatized system inherently different from its pay-as-you-go social security predecessor, which pays a potentially safer rate of return determined by the economy's growth rate. But such objections may not withstand close scrutiny. Under the Chilean system, workers do receive a random rate of return on their private pension contributions. But since these contributions are invested in government bonds, the variability in their return depends on the variability in the return paid on government bonds. Note that the workers also have to pay taxes to cover interest payments on the additional government bonds (including recognition bonds) issued in the course of privatization. If the interest rate paid on government bonds is high, taxes will be high; if they are low, taxes will be low. These variable taxes effectively represent a short position in government bonds in workers' portfolios that exactly hedge their increased holdings, through their pension funds, of risky government debt, leaving them in the privatized system exposed to no greater investment risk than under the original pay-as-you-go system. This argument assumes that workers will invest their additional pension contributions in government bonds or encourage their pension plans to do so. But this is precisely the outcome that should arise in equilibrium. Assuming workers were optimally investing their portfolios prior to the privatization, the postprivatization distribution of risks ends up identical to the preprivatization distribution of risks.

6.2 Substantive Aspects of Privatizing Social Security

First impressions notwithstanding, Chile's and other countries' privatizations of social security may produce fundamental economic changes along a number of dimensions. Privatization may reduce labor supply distortions, alter the inter- and intragenerational distribution of resources, leave households at greater risk of outliving their resources during their retirements, and alter the extent of intergenerational risk sharing.

Labor Supply Distortions

Suppose the preprivatized system provides social security benefits unrelated to a worker's past social security contributions (or perceived to be unrelated). Then social security's entire payroll tax will represent a distorting marginal tax on labor supply. Since privatizing social security eliminates the payroll tax, it eliminates this distortion.

Distortions of economic decisions rise with the square of the total effective marginal tax on the decision, so the contribution of the payroll tax to distorting labor supply depends on the size of marginal income taxes, as well as other effective marginal labor taxes. In the United States, workers who earn less than social security's covered earnings ceiling (currently $62,500) are subject to the full 15.3 percent marginal social security payroll tax.[3] Most of these workers are likely to be in the 15 percent federal marginal income tax bracket. They are also likely to face a 5 percent state marginal income tax and state sales taxes, as well as federal excise taxes, which together effectively tax their labor earnings at about 5 percent.

In combination, these non–social security marginal taxes total 25 percent. The 15.3 percent U.S. social security payroll tax rate raises the total effective marginal tax rate on labor supply from 25 percent to 39 percent once one takes into account the fact that half of the payroll tax contribution (the employer's contribution) is deductible from the federal income tax. Now 0.25 squared equals 0.0625, and 0.39 squared equals 0.1521. Since the distortion of labor supply is proportional to the square of the total effective marginal labor tax rate, the U.S. social security payroll tax may be raising labor supply distortions of low-income workers by 143 $(([0.1521/0.0621]-1)*100)$ percent even though it raises the total effective marginal labor tax rate by only 56 $(([0.39/0.25]-1)*100)$ percent.[4]

The Linkage at the Margin of Benefits to Earnings

This finger exercise is striking, but it may overstate social security's actual distortion of labor supply and the efficiency gains from privatization. One reason is that social security benefits are tied for many American workers to additional labor earnings. If such workers understand this linkage (a big if), their total effective marginal tax rate will be reduced by the size of this marginal subsidy.

In thinking about marginal benefit-tax linkage in unfunded social security systems, one's first inclination might be that this linkage is governed by the difference between the economy's real return to capital and its growth rate. Since pay-as-you-go social security pays, on average, a return equal to the economy's growth rate in the long run and since workers could otherwise receive a return equal to the economy's real return to capital if they could save their social security contributions on their own, it might seem impossible to provide workers with a dollar back in benefits (measured in present value) for each dollar they contribute in taxes—that is, to provide full benefit-tax linkage. But what social security pays out on average in exchange for additional social security contributions is not necessarily related to what it pays out on the margin, and it is marginal, not average, social security benefit-tax linkage that matters for understanding social security's contribution to labor supply distortions. Indeed, at the margin, one can potentially produce greater than dollar-for-dollar benefit-tax linkage with sufficiently high inframarginal taxation.

In the United States, marginal benefit-tax linkage varies enormously across the population. Many secondary earners in two-earner couples and all nonworking spouses in single-earner couples collect dependent retirement and survivor benefits based solely on their spouse's earnings histories. Consequently, they receive zero additional benefits in exchange for their marginal payroll tax contributions to social security.[5] The same is true for workers under age twenty-one since their earnings are not included in the calculation of average monthly earnings for purposes of determining retirement benefits. On the other hand, benefit-tax linkage for many primary earners in two-earner couples is significant.

Table 6.1 presents net marginal tax rates on social security contributions, taking into account benefit-tax linkage. These data were provided by Andrew Samwick based on a benefit-calculating program developed in Feldstein and Samwick (1992).[6] The calculations assume a 6 percent real rate of discount, a 1.2 percent rate of real wage growth, and a 3.5 percent rate of inflation and consider the net rate of social security benefit taxation arising from a permanent increase in monthly earnings by $1. The table considers six different cases: (1) a single very low-earning female who, at the margin, is in the 90 percent bracket of the social security benefit formula (a dollar more of average indexed social security monthly earnings leads to ninety cents more in social security benefits) and faces no federal income taxation of her benefits; (2) a single high-earning male who is in the 15 percent bracket of the social security benefit formula and pays federal income tax on 85 percent of his social security benefits at a

Table 6.1
Net marginal OASI tax rate on $1 rise in monthly wages (percentages)

Single female in 90 percent benefit bracket who faces no federal income tax

Age in 1995	Net Tax Rate
25	5
30	3
35	1
40	−1
45	−3
50	−5
55	−8
60	−12

Single male in 15 percent benefit bracket who faces 85 percent benefit taxation at a 33 percent rate

Age in 1995	Net Tax Rate
25	10
30	10
35	10
40	10
45	10
50	10
55	9
60	9

Husband in single-earner couple in 90 percent social security benefit bracket who faces no federal income tax

Age in 1995	Net Tax Rate
25	2
30	−0
35	−2
40	−6
45	−9
50	−12
55	−16
60	−23

Husband in single-earner couple in 15 percent social security benefit bracket who faces federal income taxation of 85 percent of benefits at a 33 percent rate

Age in 1995	Net Tax Rate
25	10
30	10
35	9
40	9
45	9
50	9
55	8
60	8

Secondary earner collecting benefits based solely on spouse's earnings record

Age in 1995	Net Tax Rate
25	11
30	11
35	11
40	11
45	11
50	11
55	11
60	11

Very high earner (earning above social security's earnings ceiling)

Age in 1995	Net Tax Rate
25	0
30	0
35	0
40	0
45	0
50	0
55	0
60	0

Source: Calculations by Andrew Samwick.

33 percent rate; (3) a married male in a single-earner couple who is in the 90 percent social security benefit bracket and faces no federal income taxation of his benefits; (4) a married male in a single-earner couple who is in the 15 percent marginal social security benefit bracket and pays federal income taxes in old age on 85 percent of his social security benefits at a 33 percent rate; (5) a secondary-earning spouse, whose earnings are sufficiently low that he will collect benefits based solely on his spouse's earnings record; and (6) a very high earner who earns more than the covered earnings ceiling.

The net tax rates reported in the table consider only old age and survivors insurance (OASI) benefits and should be compared with the 11.2 percent OASI payroll tax. Negative values refer to subsidies. The table shows three things. First, it confirms that marginal OASI net tax rates differ greatly across different Americans. For example, at age fifty, the table's low-earner, single-earner husband faces a 12 percent social security subsidy, whereas a high earner (in the 15 percent benefit bracket), single male age fifty faces a 10 percent marginal tax. Second, OASI net tax rates decline, often substantially, over the life cycle. Consider again the low-earner, single-earner husband. His net tax rate falls from 2 percent to −23 percent between ages twenty-five and sixty. The reason for the decline in net tax rates with age is that the closer one gets to collecting marginal benefits arising from additional labor earnings, the less severe is the discounting of those benefits.

Third, as one goes from low- to high-earner households earning less than social security's covered earnings ceiling, net marginal tax rates rise substantially. For example, there is a 15 percentage point spread between the 5 percent subsidy facing fifty-year-old low-earning, single males and the 10 percent tax facing fifty-year-old high-earning, single males. On the other hand, once one passes the covered earnings ceiling, the marginal OASI net tax drops to zero. Workers earning more than social security's covered earnings ceiling face zero marginal OASI payroll taxation and also receive no marginal social security benefits. For this large group of workers, social security does, however, represent a substantial inframarginal tax. Indeed, it is this large inframarginal tax on high earners that is used to provide low earners as a group with low or negative marginal OASI net tax rates and average rates of return on their contributions that exceed the economy's growth rate.

Do workers whose benefits are linked at the margin to additional earnings understand the linkage? We do not know. However, we do know that correctly assessing the linkage requires knowledge of intricate OASI benefit provisions and the ability to make sophisticated actuarial calculations. Since very few workers have such knowledge or actuarial background, the vast majority presumably are guessing about the degree to which their benefits are linked at the margin to their additional earnings. If they are over assessing the degree of linkage, the existing social security system may be less distortionary than it appears. On the other hand, if they are underassessing the degree of linkage, the opposite will be true. In this case, privatizing social security can be beneficial by simply making clear that the true rate of marginal taxation of labor supply is less than the perceived rate.

The Optimal Second-Best Tax Structure

A second reason that the simple efficiency calculation presented above may overstate the gains from privatization is that the tax used to finance transitional social security benefits (including the servicing of any additional debt issued in the course of privatization) may itself distort labor supply, as well as other economic choices. For example, if income taxes are used as the transition financing instrument, both labor supply and saving decisions will be distorted. Thus, whether privatization ends up, on balance, reducing tax distortions depends on whether privatization moves the economy closer to its second-best tax structure.

The second-best tax structure depends not only on the choice of what base to tax but also on the distribution of inframarginal and marginal taxes given the choice of tax bases. Although the literature on optimal redistributive taxation has not seemed explicitly to have considered social security net taxation, it is clear that this form of taxation can play an important role in achieving the optimum. It is also clear from table 6.1 that the current structure of marginal net social security taxation has a number of anomalous features that may be very hard to justify as part of an optimal second-best redistributive tax structure. From this perspective, social security's privatization can be viewed as an opportunity to the improve the structure of inframarginal and marginal taxation.

Privatization and the Intra- and Intergenerational Distributions of Resources

Table 6.2 reports lifetime net tax payments for different household types belonging to different cohorts. The table's data, provided by Gene Steuerle, differ from similar estimates reported in Steuerle and Bakija (1994) because they incorporate a 6 percent rather than a 3 percent

Table 6.2
Net lifetime OASI taxes (age 65 actuarial value, thousands of 1993 dollars, 6% discount rate)

								Couples					
		Single male			Single female			One earner			Two earners		
Year born	Cohort age 65	Low	Avg	High	Low	Avg	High	Low	Avg	High	Low/Low	Avg/Low	High/Avg
1875	1940	−7	−9	−14	−8	−12	−18	−11	−15	−23	−15	−18	−27
1885	1950	−13	−15	−16	−19	−22	−24	−25	−31	−36	−32	−35	−39
1895	1960	−16	−20	−15	−26	−34	−30	−40	−55	−54	−43	−53	−50
1905	1970	−13	−4	11	−27	−23	−10	−55	−64	−60	−46	−46	−23
1915	1980	8	40	74	−6	17	45	−52	−54	−44	−23	−6	59
1925	1990	45	123	183	34	106	160	−19	16	45	44	95	230
1935	2000	94	235	382	84	220	365	27	120	228	144	253	535
1945	2010	142	342	664	132	328	649	71	222	495	237	407	917
1955	2020	165	397	949	155	383	937	89	268	750	288	483	1240
1965	2030	194	463	1191	184	450	1180	112	323	971	339	570	1533
1975	2040	208	498	1278	196	483	1264	121	351	1047	364	618	1655
1985	2050	229	552	1411	216	533	1393	135	391	1160	406	687	1834

Source: Calculations by Gene Steuerle.

real discount rate.[7] The households under consideration are single males, single females, single-earner married couples, and two-earner married couples. Low, average, and high past and projected levels of earnings are considered. Average earnings refers to the average level of social security earnings. High earnings refers to social security's maximum level of covered earnings, and low earnings refers to a level of earnings equal to 45 percent of average earnings. For 1993, low, average, and high earnings were $11,000, $24,444, and $60,000, respectively.

As the table shows, pay-as-you-go social security has produced an enormous transfer of resources from current young and, by implication, future American cohorts to cohorts who are now old or are already deceased. The system also redistributes substantial sums from the lifetime poor to the lifetime rich, from males to females, from those who are unmarried to those who are married, and from two-earner couples and singles to single-earner couples. One caveat here is that the table ignores differences by income in survival probabilities. Since the poor have shorter life expectancies than the rich, the table overstates the extent of social security system's intragenerational redistribution.

Consider current forty year olds who were born in 1955 and will be age sixty-five in 2020. For males in this cohort with low earnings, the lifetime net loss from being forced to participate in pay-as-you-go social security is equivalent to arriving at age sixty-five with $165,000 less in assets—an enormous sum for someone who is now earning only $11,000 or so per year. For a high-earning single forty-year-old male, the net loss totals $949,000! For single females, the corresponding losses are about $10,000 smaller because females have longer life expectancies than do males. Next consider a forty-year-old single-earner couple whose single earner has low earnings. This couple's net tax is $89,000, which is $76,000 less than that of the low-earning single male who pays exactly the same taxes. It is less than one-third the $288,000 loss experienced by the same-aged two-earner couple in which both spouses are low earners, and it is less than a twelfth of the $1.24 million loss experienced by the same-aged two-earner couple in which one spouse is a high earner and one spouse is an average earner.

Would Privatization Alter the Inter- and Intragenerational Distribution of Resources?

The privatization of social security in the United States in all likelihood would significantly alter both the country's inter- and intragenerational distributions of resources. One reason the intergenerational distribution of resources would likely change involves the choice of the tax used to finance social security benefits during the transition. If, for example, a federal retail sales tax were used as the financing mechanism, those who were old at the time of the reform would, as a group, end up facing a higher remaining lifetime net tax burden than they would absent the reform.[8] Another reason involves deficit delusion. If, in the course of privatization, the implicit liability to pay social security benefits to existing retirees and current workers were made explicit through, for example, the issuance of recognition bonds, the level of official U.S. debt would roughly triple. The reaction of the general public, the financial markets, and the politicians to this change in fiscal nomenclature would likely be to adopt a more conservative course of fiscal policy than would have occurred with the preprivatization labeling of fiscal obligations. A more conservative course of fiscal policy would, in turn, likely mean that the initial elderly would face larger net taxes over the remainders of their lifetimes and that young and future generations would consequently face smaller net taxes over their course of their lives.

The intragenerational distribution of resources would almost surely be altered as well by privatization. Take, as an example, the Personal Security System proposed in section 6.5. This proposal features earnings sharing between spouses, that is, married workers' mandatory contributions to private pensions would be split fifty-fifty between themselves and their spouse and deposited in separate accounts—one for each spouse. Single-earner couples who receive dependent benefits free of any additional contribution under the current system would find they are no longer so advantaged. Rather than receiving roughly one and a half times the amount of retirement income per dollar contributed that single individuals as well as two-earner couples in which the spouses have roughly equal earnings receive, single-earner couples would receive the same total retirement income per dollar contributed.

Other capricious forms of intragenerational redistribution arising under the current system would also be eliminated. Consider two workers, A and B, who have the same present value of lifetime earnings, but A earns relatively more of his lifetime earnings when young. As table 6.1 indicates, the current social security system penalizes early earners relative to late earners because it fails to credit fully early earners with the fact that they pay their payroll taxes earlier and consequently pay more payroll taxes when measured in present value.[9] In a privatized system, contributions would earn the market rate of return, so that a dollar contributed at, say, age thirty would have more years to cumulate than a dollar contributed at, say, age forty-five, leaving contributors indifferent as to the timing of their contributions.

Another channel through which privatization would likely change the intragenerational distribution of resources involves bequests. If, as seems likely, privatization would reduce the degree of annuitization of the resources of the elderly, the elderly will end up leaving more bequests than would otherwise be the case.[10] The percentage increase in bequests would likely be greater for poor, low-income, and middle-income elderly households than it would for rich elderly households for whom social security benefits are small compared to their nonannuitized resources (their net wealth). Thus, privatization would reduce to some extent the inequality within a cohort in the receipt of inheritances.

Information

Another major problem with the current U.S. social security system is that workers receive no information about the size of their likely future social security benefits. In contrast, under a privatized system, workers would receive retirement account statements on a routine basis. Admittedly, workers can request a social security benefit calculation from the Social Security Administration, but few do so.

The failure of the social security system to provide benefit information may be changing. According to my understanding, the Social Security Administration is planning in the near future to distribute earnings statements and estimates of future benefits to the entire U.S. workforce annually. Unfortunately, this statement, like the current statement, will, it appears, contain assurances from the social security commissioner to the effect that workers can rely on receiving their benefits when they reach retirement. This badly misstates the facts. Social security's long-term finances are in worse shape now than prior to 1983 when the Greenspan Commission announced that it had resolved the system's long-term financing problem. According to the most recent *Social Security's Trustees' Report*, under intermediate assumptions, a 2.2 percentage point immediate and permanent increase in the payroll tax rate is needed to close the seventy-five-year social security old age and survivors disability insurance (OASDI) deficit. The comparable 1983 figure was 1.9 percentage points. Under pessimistic assumptions, a 5.7 percent point immediate and permanent OASDI tax increase is needed. (Recent experience suggests that the pessimistic projections may provide a better forecast of the future than the intermediate projections.)

Since social security has been declared off the table by our political leaders, it is not likely that payroll taxes will be raised any time soon. But the longer one waits, the higher is the requisite tax hike, assuming, that is, that tax increases, rather than benefit cuts, are ultimately used to shore up the system. Indeed, the *Trustees' Report* suggests that OASDI payroll taxes will need to rise by over 4 percentage points under intermediate assumptions and over 8 percentage points under pessimistic assumptions if the government waits until the Social Security Trust Fund is depleted before taking action. In considering the likelihood of such large future OASDI tax increases, one needs to take into account Medicare's long-term deficit. According to the Medicare Trustees, health insurance (HI) tax rate needs to rise immediately by roughly 5 percentage points under intermediate assumptions and by roughly 10 percent under pessimistic assumptions to achieve seventy-five-year actuarial balance. Is it likely that OASDHI payroll taxes will double at some point in the not-too-distant future without there being any cuts in social security benefits? The answer is surely no. Indeed, baby boomers could well experience sharp reductions in their social security benefits when they retire. Nothing in the soon-to-be issued social security benefit statements will, however, indicate that current workers' future social security benefits are threatened by the OASDI and HI long-term deficits.

Apart from providing workers misleading information that may lull them into a false sense of security and lead them to undersave, the U.S. government is leaving unresolved how it will deal with social security's long-term deficit. This uncertainty does not reflect aggregate risk, which cannot be diversified. On the contrary. The significant fiscal stress facing social security at the beginning of the next millennium is predictable. Leaving uncertain exactly who will be forced to deal with social security's pending fiscal crisis has a real economic cost. Today's workers presumably would be willing to pay a fair amount to find out right now whether they will suffer substantial social security benefit cuts when they reach retirement or whether their benefits will be fully paid, notwithstanding the likely need to levy sky-high payroll taxes on the next generation. Privatization offers a way of resolving this uncertainty, at least with respect to retirement income. In specifying the tax to be used to finance social security benefits during the transition, privatization lets everyone know today the amount they can expect to contribute to resolving this aspect of the nation's long-term fiscal problems. The act of privatization may also send a subtle but important message: that each of us must take personal responsibility for saving for and otherwise managing our retirements.

Life Span Insurance and the Annuitization of the Elderly

The privatization of social security is likely to reduce the resource annuitization of the elderly and, consequently, the degree to which they are insured against outliving their resources. The U.S. social security system provides benefits in the form of real annuities, and because it pools together virtually all members of each cohort, it implicitly provides its annuities at actuarially fair rates with respect to each cohort taken as a whole. A privatized social security system would find it difficult to match this performance for four reasons. First, since private insurance companies are unable to hedge the risk of unexpected inflation, they are unable to market real (indexed) annuities. Second, since private insurance companies cannot compel the public to purchase their annuities, they face the problem of adverse selection. Third, since private insurers need to market and advertise their annuity products and since they cannot capture the economies of scale associated with selling to the entire market, they would likely operate at higher administrative costs than the Social Security Administration. Fourth, unlike the government, which can adjust to unexpected increases in longevity by raising payroll taxes or making other fiscal adjustments that do not involve reducing social security benefits, private insurers need to maintain substantial reserves to deal with unexpected increases in the longevity of their annuitants. Their annuities typically involve a fairly low guaranteed rate of return with a variable dividend that depends on market conditions, including the insurers' actuarial experience.

The first of these concerns—the inability of insurance companies to market real annuities—could be avoided by having the government issue indexed debt, which insurance companies could then purchase to hedge their liabilities to pay real annuities. Indexed debt is issued by a number of countries. It does limit a country's ability to renege on its nominal debt and other nominal liabilities by inflating, but this should be counted as a plus.

The second concern—the problem of adverse selection—could be reduced in a privatized social security system by requiring all participants to spend their accumulated retirement accounts on annuities at a particular age, say, age sixty-five, and also by requiring insurers to sell annuities on equal terms to all those seeking to purchase them. Alternatively, the government could abandon the goal of annuitizing the elderly and simply ensure that the elderly do not spend down their retirement accounts at too fast a rate.[11] For example, the U.S. government could adopt the Chilean government's stipulation that a retiree can withdraw in a given year only one *n*th of those funds in his retirement accounts that are not annuitized, where *n* stands for the retiree's remaining life expectancy.

The third concern—administrative costs—is probably a somewhat smaller one for the United States than it would be in other countries. The reason is that the United States has a well-developed private defined contribution pension system (i.e., 401k, 403b, IRA, SRA, and Keogh accounts). The typical annual fees for managing these accounts appear to range from 0.5 to 1.5 percent of assets—fairly high. One way that the administrative fees for managing privatized social security accounts could be reduced would be to restrict the type of funds in which participants could invest. For example, the government could mandate that half of compulsory retirement contributions be invested in a U.S. equity index fund (e.g., the S&P 500), that one-quarter be invested in a foreign equity and bond index fund, and that one-quarter be invested in a U.S. government and private index bond fund. Competition to provide these standardized products presumably would lead to substantially smaller management fees since no real asset management would be required. Also, since the products being sold would be essentially identical, there would be little advantage in advertising.

The fourth concern—variable annuity returns with low guaranteed payouts—is more a concern about form than substance. The risk of unexpected increases in longevity confronts the existing social security system, just as it would confront a privatized system. The government's response to greater-than-expected longevity of its social security annuitants is, it appears, not to reduce the benefits of current retirees but rather to raise payroll and other taxes, including federal income taxation of social security benefits. Assuming the intragenerational and intergenerational distribution of the burden of the government's dealing with unexpected longevity is the same as that which would prevail under a privatized system, the government is, in effect, also providing the same low-guarantee, variable annuity that the private market would provide—just one that is packaged differently, as the combination of a certain annuity together with uncertain taxes.

Economic Uncertainty

Another way that privatization could substantively alter the economy is by changing the riskiness of old age consumption. Pay-as-you-go social security effectively introduces a new asset into the economy, one whose return equals, after a transition period, the growth rate of earnings in the economy. Even if the average growth rate of earnings is less than the average rate of return on capital, participants in social security may be better off because the variability of the growth rate of earnings is less than the variability of the return to capital.

To see this, consider the long run of a very simple model in which each generation lives for two period, works only when young, earning a wage W (which I will assume is invariant to the introduction of social security), and consumes only when old. Let r stand for the random rate of return on capital and g stand for the random population growth rate (labor productivity growth is assumed to be zero). In the absence of pay-as-you-go social security, old age consumption is given by $W(1+r)$. In the presence of pay-as-you-go social security, old age consumption is given by $(W-T)(1+r)+T(1+g)$, where T is the compulsory social security tax.

Clearly if the expected value of g is less than the expected value of r, the expected value of old age consumption will be reduced by social security. On the other hand, being able to invest in an asset paying g by making tax payments to social security when young permits participants to diversify their asset portfolio. The potential to use this asset to diversify the riskiness of consumption when old will, of course, be enhanced if r and g are negatively correlated. But the potential ability to diversify risk in this manner does not necessarily imply that pay-as-you-go social security raises the welfare of those living in the long run. The reason is that the disadvantage of being forced to invest in an asset with a lower expected return may outweigh the diversification advantage. In this regard, it is worth noting that in the United States, the average real rate of return to investing in capital appears to be roughly three times larger than the average growth rate of earnings.

If the growth rate of earnings were certain and the U.S. economy offered a safe asset in which to invest, one could compare the growth rate of earnings with the safe rate of return to determine whether pay-as-you-go social security would raise or lower the well-being of those alive in the long run (again ignoring general equilibrium effects on long-run factor prices). But those are two big ifs. Earnings growth is definitely not certain in the United States or any other country. Moreover, unlike some countries that issue indexed bonds, the United States does not issue a safe asset. The three-month U.S. Treasury bill rate is often referred to as a risk-free rate, but this ignores the fact that inflation, even three months ahead, is not perfectly predictable, making the real return on this security risky.[12]

Given the riskiness of the growth rate and the lack of a risk-free asset, there is no simple way to determine whether the diversification value of participating in pay-as-you-go social security is worth the price of receiving, on average, a lower return. And, unfortunately, there are not, to my knowledge, any empirical studies that have tried to address this question by specifying how households view risk and how the distribution of g compares and covaries with the distribution of r.

Intergenerational Risk Sharing

A final issue in considering the pluses and minuses of privatizing social security is the extent to which an existing pay-as-you-go social security system is part of a broader government scheme to share risks across generations.[13] If it is, the act of privatizing social security may alter the degree of intergenerational risk sharing. Consider again our model in which each person pays social security taxes when young. Now assume that there is no population growth, but that labor productivity each period is random, taking on either a high or a low value. Given a proportional social security tax rate, the amount of social security taxes collected each period depends on that period's labor productivity. Furthermore, since social security is, let us assume, a pay-as-you-go program, the level of benefits will be low if labor productivity is low and high if labor productivity is high. This means that social security helps the contemporaneous young and old share risk. When times are bad for the young and their wage earnings are low, the elderly receive smaller social security benefits, and vice versa when times are good. Indeed, we can describe this arrangement as one in which the young always pay the taxes associated with the high-productivity outcome to the contemporaneous old but receive a payment back from the elderly when productivity is low. This way of describing things views the elderly as providing the contemporaneous young with earnings insurance.

This example suggests that to evaluate the impact on the well-being of future generations of the elimination of pay-as-you-go social security requires understanding the nature and degree of risk-sharing arrangements in the existing system. Actually, there is a growing body of empirical evidence concerning intergenerational risk sharing in the United States (Abel and Kotlikoff 1994, Altonji, Hayashi, and Kotlikoff 1992; Hayashi, Altonji, and Kotlikoff 1996). As it turns out, this evidence provides remarkably little support for the proposition that social security or other fiscal institutions are pooling risks across generations.

6.3 Simulating the Macroeconomic Effects, Welfare Changes, and Efficiency Gains from Social Security Privatization

This section[14] reports the results of four social security privatization simulations of the AK model.[15] In these simulations, social security benefits are phased out slowly over time. However, the social security payroll tax is immediately permitting workers to save privately the money they would otherwise have contributed to social security. The simulations differ with respect to the method of financing social security benefits during the transition. Specifically, I consider paying for social security benefits during the transition through a consumption tax, raising the extant progressive income tax, or using deficit finance for five years and then raising either consumption or progressive income tax rates to pay not only for remaining annual social security benefits but also for interest on the accumulated government borrowing in the first five years of the transition.

The AK Model

The AK model calculates the time path of all economic variables in its economy over a 150-year period. The model has fifty-five overlapping generations. Each agent lives for fifty-five years (from age twenty to age seventy-five). There are three sectors: households, firms, and the government. Households (adult agents) decide how much to work and how much to save based on the after-tax wages and after-tax rates of return they can earn in the present and the future on their labor supply and saving, respectively. The work decision involves not only deciding how much to work in those years that one is working but also when to retire. The AK model's consumption and leisure preferences underlying these decisions were chosen in the light of evidence on actual labor supply and saving behavior.

As agents age in the model, they experience a realistic profile of increases in wages. This age-wage profile is separate from the general level of wages, the time path of which is determined in solving the model.

Fiscal policies affect households by altering their after-tax wages, after-tax rates of return, and, in the case of consumption taxes, after-tax prices of goods and services. The model is equipped to deal with income taxes, wage taxes, capital income taxes, and consumption taxes. It is also able to handle progressive as well as proportional tax rates. Finally, and most important for this study, the model includes a pay-as-you-go social security system in which the perceived linkage between taxes and benefits can be set at any desired value.

All agents are assumed to have the same preferences, so differences in behavior across agents arise solely from differences in economic opportunities. Since all agents within an age cohort are assumed to be identical, differences in economic opportunities are present only across cohorts. In this study, the model's population growth rate is set at a constant 1 percent rate, with the population of each new cohort being 1 percent larger than that of the previous cohort.

The AK model's production sector is characterized by perfectly competitive firms that hire labor and capital to maximize their profits. The production relationships that underlie firms' hiring decisions and their production of output are based on empirical findings for the United States. The government sector consists of a treasury that collects resources from the private sector to finance government consumption and an unfunded pay-as-you-go social security system that levies payroll taxes to pay for contemporaneous retiree benefit payments. There is no money in the model, and thus no monetary policy. There is, however, government debt, and the model can handle deficit-financed reductions in payroll and other taxes. It can also handle gradual phase-ins of one tax for the other. Finally, the model contains a lump-sum redistribution authority (LSRA)—a hypothetical governmental agency that can use lump-sum taxes and transfers to redistribute among generations alive at a point in time as well as those who will be born in the future. The LSRA can be used (switched on) to study the pure economic efficiency effects of particular policy changes.

Although the model handles a great number of complex processes, it leaves out large portions of reality. The model's agents are heterogeneous only with respect to their age. There are no welfare recipients or millionaires, whose saving and work behavior might differ dramatically from that of the model's agents. The model does not include saving for purposes other than retirement, such as bequests. Nor does the model incorporate uncertainty with respect to either individual or macroeconomic outcomes. These and other omissions suggest viewing the model's results cautiously.

Model Calibration

The preprivatization economy features a progressive income tax that finances government consumption equal to 20 percent of output, a 12 percent social security payroll tax, zero linkage between social security benefits and taxes, zero initial official government debt, a 1 percent population growth rate, zero technological change, a Cobb-Douglas production function, and a Consumer Expenditure Survey (CES) utility function in consumption and leisure with intertemporal and intratemporal elasticities of substitution of 0.25 and .8, respectively, and a time preference rate of 1.5 percent.

The simulation phases out social security benefits in a linear manner over a forty-five-year period. This phase-out period starts eleven years after the payroll tax is eliminated, thus permitting all beneficiaries at the time of the reform to collect all their benefits. Social security benefits during the transition are financed by a proportional consumption tax, a progressive income tax, or initial deficit finance coupled with subsequent increases in either proportional consumption tax rates or progressive income tax rates. For each case, we present results in which the welfare (utility) of initial generations is allowed to change in response to the privatization, as well as results in which the welfare of initial generations is held constant. In the latter simulations, the government uses lump-sum taxes and transfers to redistribute across generations during the transition so as to leave all generations alive at the time of the transition with precisely the same utility they would have enjoyed absent privatization and equalize the utility of all generations born after the policy is initiated.

Simulation Results

Figures 6.1 and 6.2 consider the case of using a proportional consumption tax to finance social security benefits during the transition. Figure 6.1's simulation does not compensate initial generations for any policy-induced changes in their welfare, whereas figure 6.2's simulation provides full compensation. The top panel of figure 6.1 (and all other figures) shows macroeconomic policy effects. The bottom panel shows welfare effects.

As the top panel in figure 6.1 makes clear, the privatization of social security can have major macroeconomic effects. In this simulation, there is a 50 percent long-run increase in the economy's capital stock, a 16 percent increase in output, and a 10 percent increase in the real wage. In addition, the real interest rate falls by almost 300 basis points. These

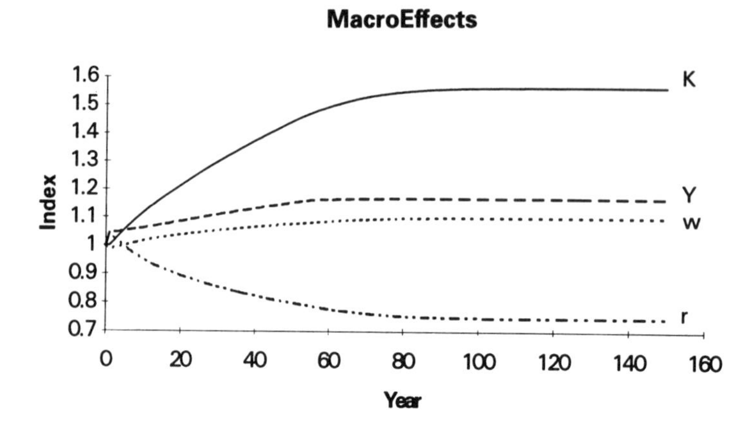

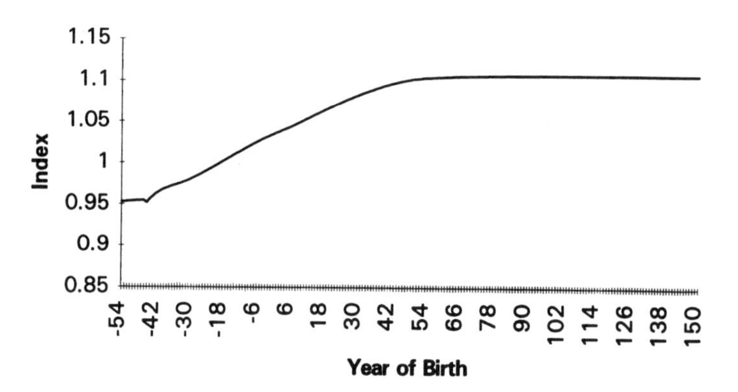

Figure 6.1
Proportional consumption tax finance of benefits, progressive income tax finance of general revenues.

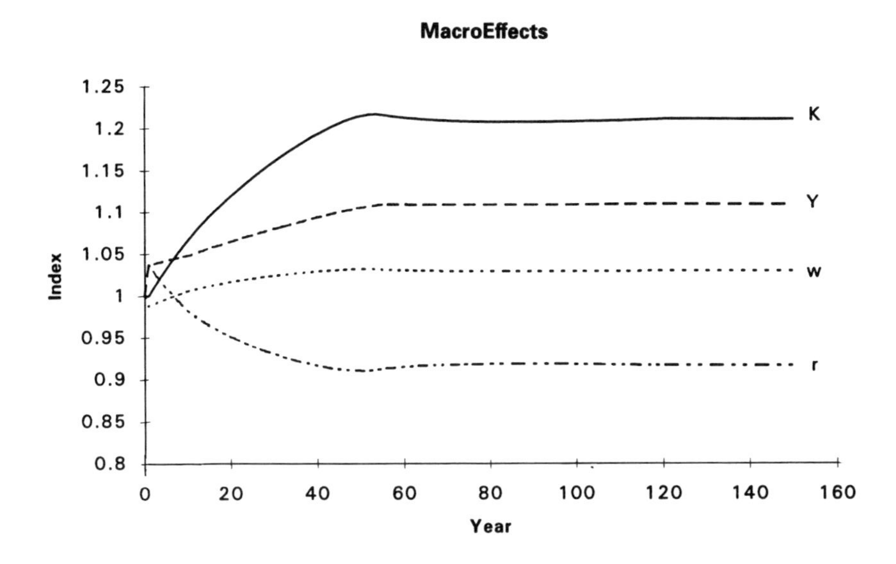

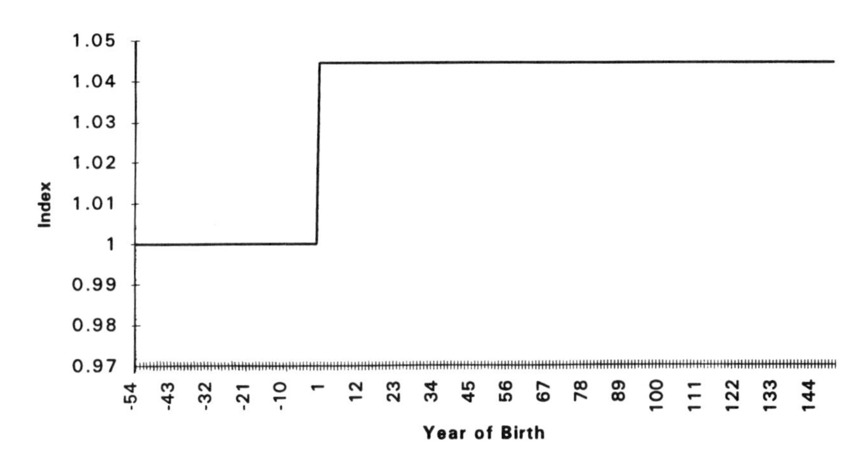

Figure 6.2
Proportional consumption tax finance of benefits, progressive income tax finance of general revenues, Welfare of Living Generations Constant.

macroeffects generate about a 10 percent increase in the welfare of generations born in the postprivatization long run. For older generations alive at the time of the reform, the story is different. Most of these generations lose as a result of privatization; they experience a decline in their remaining lifetime utility. For example, the oldest cohort alive at the time of the reform—the one born fifty-four years prior to the reform—experiences a 5 percent decline in remaining lifetime utility, where utility changes are measured in terms of the percentage change in remaining lifetime consumption and leisure needed, in the old steady state, to produce the same level of utility arising under privatization. The reason the initial elderly are made worse off is clear: they are forced to pay consumption taxes, which limits the amount of consumption they can finance out of their remaining lifetime resources.

As figure 6.2 shows, the gains to the long-run winners from social security are large enough to compensate the initial losers and consequently end up with a Pareto improvement in which all those initially alive are unaffected by the reform and all those born after the reform experience a 4.5 percent increase in their welfare compared with the status quo. Although 4.5 percent is less than 10 percent, it still represents a substantial improvement in the well-being of future generations. The compensated privatization produces not only smaller long-run welfare improvements but also smaller long-run macroeconomic effects. The intuition here is that compensating initial older generations permits them to consume more, which lowers national saving, capital accumulation, and transitional output growth.

Figures 6.3 and 6.4 raise progressive income tax rates, rather than consumption tax rates, to finance social security benefits during the privatization transition. The uncompensated simulation results are roughly similar to those arising when consumption taxation is used to finance transitional benefits. On the other hand, the compensated welfare gain to those alive after the reform is much smaller: only about 1.7 percent compared with 4.5 percent in the case of consumption tax finance. The reason is that progressive income tax finance entails much higher marginal tax rates during the privatization transition and therefore much greater economic inefficiency.

Figures 6.5 and 6.6 use consumption taxation to finance transitional social security benefits but delay raising consumption tax rates until the sixth year after the reform is implemented. Hence, during the first five years of privatization, the government borrows to pay for social security benfits. As a comparison of figures 6.1 and 6.5 shows, the additional

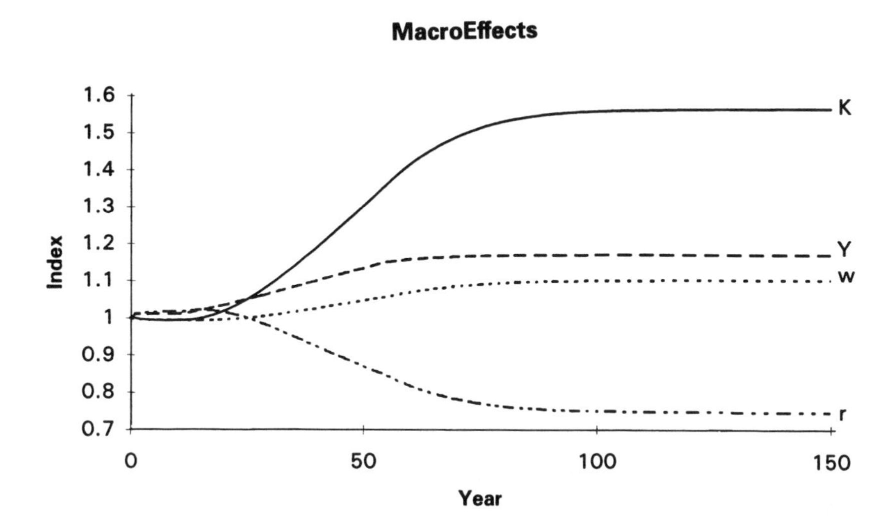

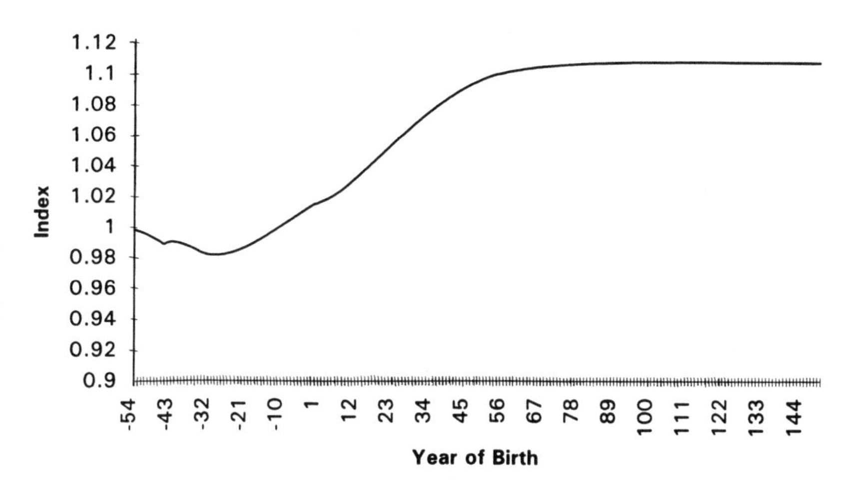

Figure 6.3
Progressive income tax finance of benefits.

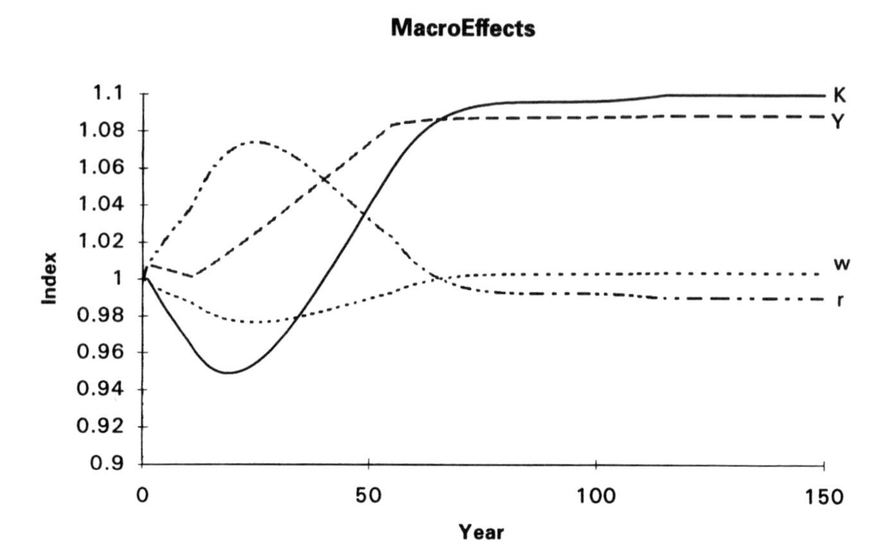

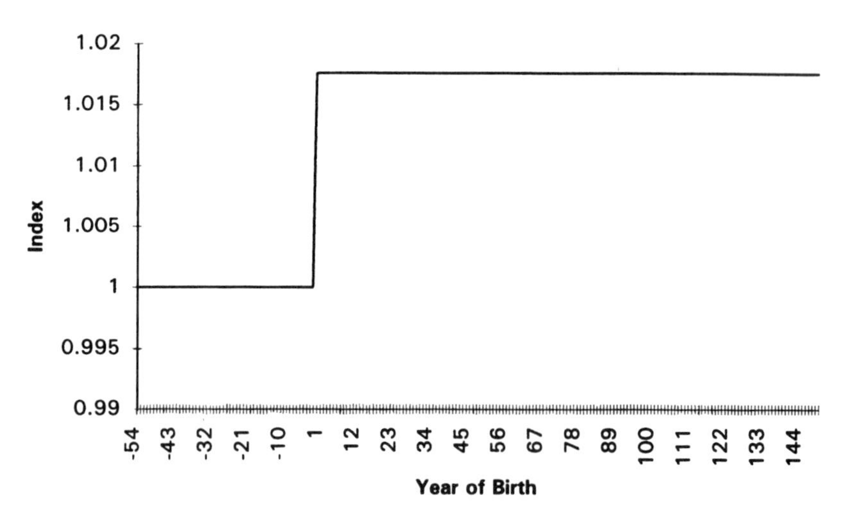

Figure 6.4
Progressive income tax finance of benefits, welfare of living generations constant.

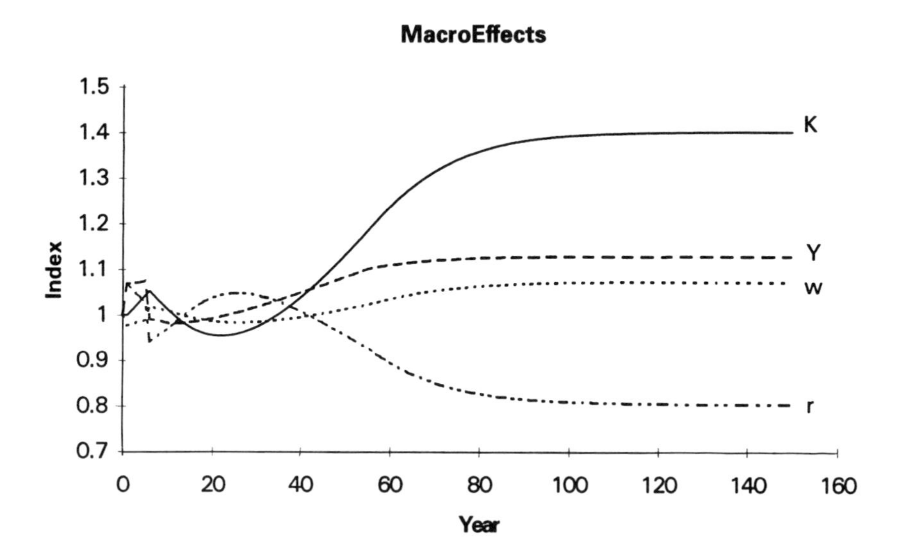

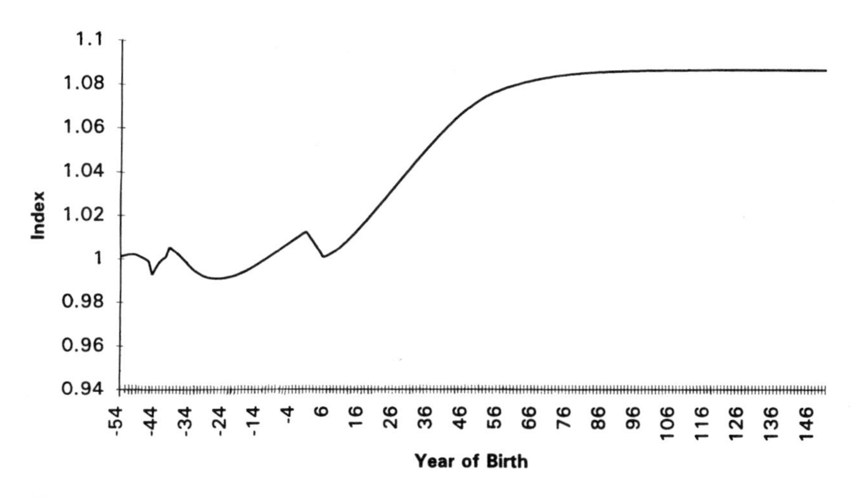

Figure 6.5
Proportional consumption tax finance of benefits, progressive income tax finance of general revenues, five-year debt finance.

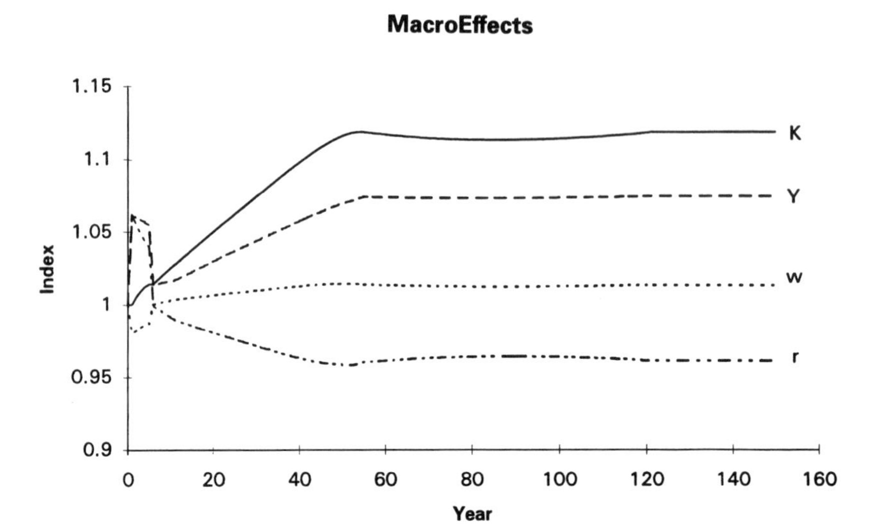

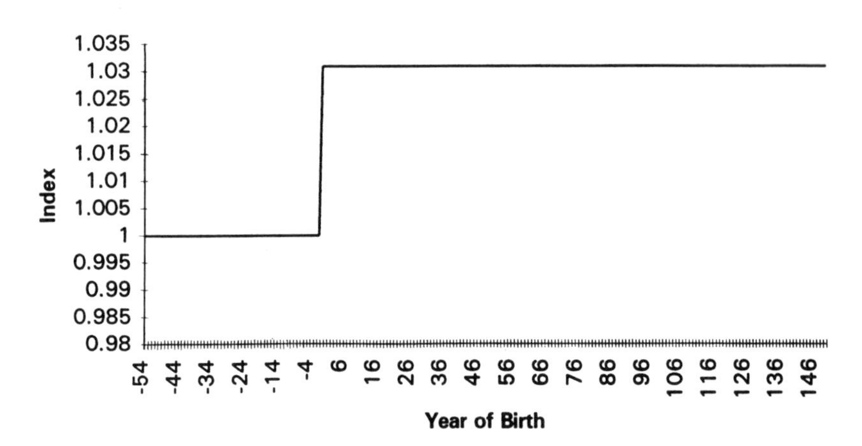

Figure 6.6
Proportional consumption tax finance of benefits, progressive income tax finance of general revenues, five-year debt finance, Welfare of living generations constant.

crowding out of saving arising from the short-term deficit finance in this transition leads to much smaller long-run increases in the capital stock, output, and real wage. The compensated long-run welfare gain is also smaller: about 3 percent rather than 4.5 percent. Note that in the uncompensated transition (figure 6.5), the use of deficit finance mitigates the reduction in welfare of initial older generations.

The final simulations, shown in figures 6.7 and 6.8, repeat the simulations of figures 6.3 and 6.4, in which progressive income taxation is used to finance transitional benefits but also incorporate five years of deficit finance. Again, both the long-run macroeconomic improvements and welfare gains are reduced by the deficit finance. On the other hand, the short-run loss in welfare for initial older generations is reduced in the uncompensated simulation. Indeed, the bottom panel of figure 6.7 indicates that using deficit finance plus progressive income taxation to finance transitional benefits generates close to a Pareto improvement.

Although these simulations are suggestive, much more detailed simulations are needed to evaluate the efficiency gains from privatizing the U.S. system. Such simulations would include income and demographic heterogeneity across households. They would also model the current system in sufficient detail to produce, as an initial condition, the structure of net marginal social security tax rates reported in table 6.1.

6.4 A Practical Guide to Privatizing Social Security in the United States

In my view, the key to successfully privatizing social security in the United States is to make it clear, simple, universal, and fair. Clarity and simplicity rules out much of the Chilean approach. To be precise, it rules out providing recognition bonds to existing workers because their calculation would entail using a complex formula that workers would not understand and consequently would likely mistrust. It also rules out using Chile's complicated and counterproductive method of regulating private pension funds. Finally, it rules out Chile's approach of privatizing not only retirement saving but also the purchase of life insurance and disability insurance.

The criterion of universality argues against Chile's choice of making privatization voluntary. In the United States, allowing the public to opt out of social security on a voluntary basis would lead to adverse selection in which the federal government would end up stuck with high-cost participants (those expecting to live longest). It would also require each

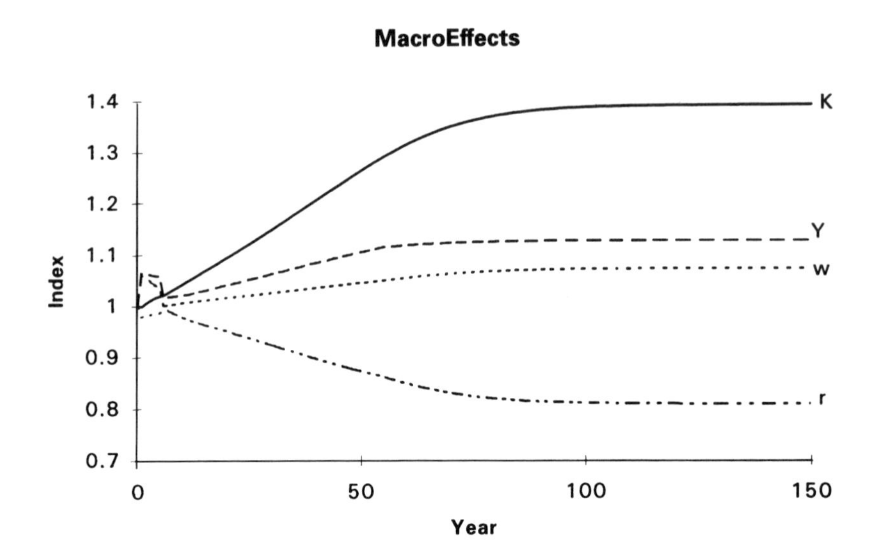

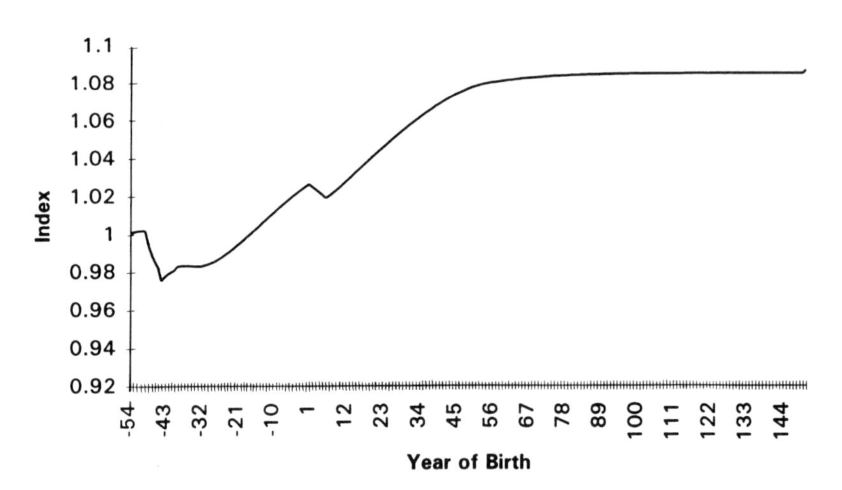

Figure 6.7
Proportional consumption tax finance of benefits, five-year debt finance.

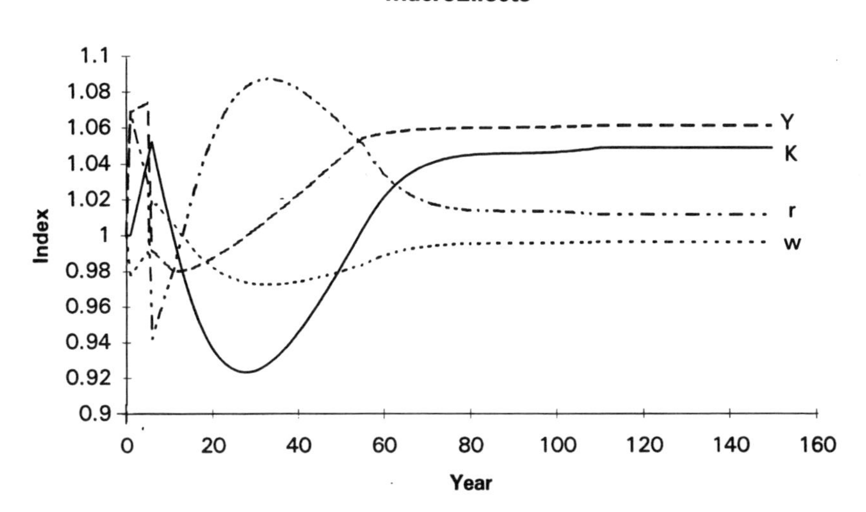

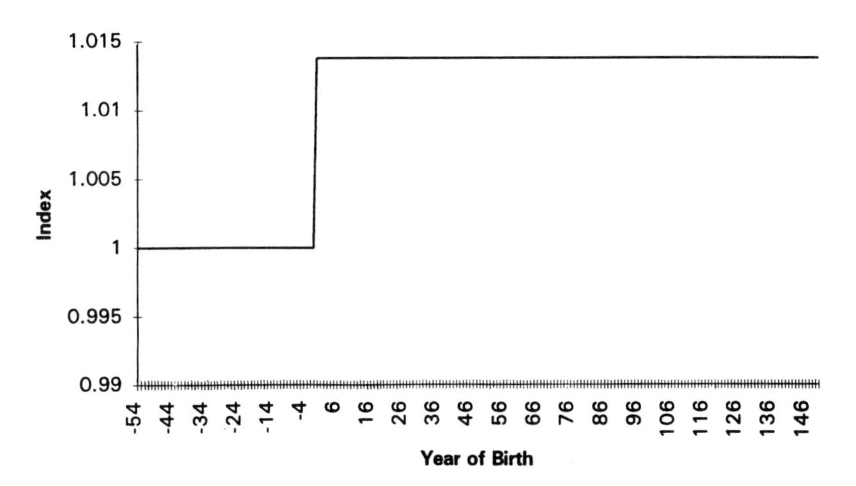

Figure 6.8
Proportional consumption tax finance of benefits, five-year debt finance, welfare of living generations constant.

worker to make a complicated actuarial decision concerning the advantages and disadvantages of opting out of the old system. Workers who chose not to switch would worry that they were making a mistake and were losing out to financially more sophisticated members of society. Workers who chose to switch would also wonder whether they had made the right choice or had been bamboozled out of their benefits by shrewd government officials.

Americans' perception of fairness also seems to rule out the Chilean approach to redistribution. This perception appears to require more progressivity in the provision of retirement income than simply providing all workers with a minimum guaranteed level of retirement income.

In contrast to the Chilean approach, the personal security system (PSS) is clear, simple, and universal. It is also fair in the way that most Americans apparently define the term. PSS has four features. First, it privatizes all contributions to old age insurance (the OAI part of OASDI), but *only* contributions to old age insurance. Thus it leaves unchanged those contributions made to and benefits received from the survivors and disability portions of social security. Second, for married workers, the OAI contribution (68 percent of the OASDI total) is split fifty-fifty between each spouse; that is, PSS has earnings sharing. These contributions are matched, on a progressive basis, with government contributions and are then invested by workers and their spouses in 401(k), 403(b), IRA, SRA, or Keogh accounts and are subject to the same tax treatment, survivor provisions, and investment regulations as these accounts. Third, after the reform begins, social security retirement (OAI) benefits are calculated by filling in zeros in the earnings records of all social security participants for years after the transition begins. This ensures that initial beneficiaries receive their full benefits, that existing American workers receive their full accrued benefits, and that young Americans entering the workforce end up with no OAI benefit claims.[16] The reduction in benefits across generations is smooth; they are are not "notch babies." Fourth, a federal retail sales tax or a value-added tax is used to finance transitional benefits.

The proposal would improve benefit-tax linkage, enhance survivor protection, eliminate, at the margin, the egregious subsidization of single-earner couples documented in table 6.2, offset somewhat the enormous ongoing transfer of resources from the young to the old (see Kotlikoff 1992), provide much better divorce protection to nonworking spouses, and eliminate the substantial uncertainty surrounding the manner in which we are going to resolve social security's long-term funding problem. It would also make the progressivity of the system transparent. All participants would understand the nature of the government's matching contribution and the fact that low contributors were being favored relative to high contributors.

The most serious concern with the proposal is its potential reduction in life span insurance. Because of adverse selection, it may prove quite difficult for households to purchase reasonably priced nominal annuities when they reach retirement, let alone real annuities. The size of this loss may, however, be offset by implicit family annuity arrangements (see Kotlikoff and Spivak 1981). The government could also ease the problem by issuing indexed debt and requiring the purchase of annuities at, say, age sixty-five. Another concern is that households would invest their PSS contributions poorly. One remedy here is financial education. Bernheim (1995) suggests that financial decisions may be highly responsive to financial education. Another remedy is forcing contributors to invest in large, diversified index funds. A third concern is the cost of administering PSS contributions. However, since PSS contributions can be made to existing accounts, marginal administrative costs may be smaller than the average costs examined by Diamond and Valdes-Prieto (1994). These costs may also come down over time in the light of competition to provide PSS participants with fairly homogeneous index funds. A fourth concern is that redistributing between workers based, in effect, on their annual earnings (since this determines their annual contribution) is less desirable than redistributing to them based on their lifetime earnings. True. But this seems a small price to pay compared with the value of being able to make transparent the system's actual method of redistribution.

6.5 Conclusion

At first glance, privatizing social security may seem to represent something of a shell game, but closer examination suggests that privatizing social security can have important real effects. In the United States, privatizing social security would tighten actual as well as perceived benefit-tax linkage and substantially reduce labor supply distortions. It would also eliminate significant intragenerational inequities, including the differential treatment of one- and two-earner couples. Finally, privatization would clarify, once and for all, how our nation will deal with social security's long-term financing crisis.

Although privatizing social security is a hot academic topic, its success in the policy arena will depend on its clarity, simplicity, inclusivity, and fairness. The Personal Security System is clear, simple, inclusive, and fair. Like all other policy proposals, it has its weaknesses. Nonetheless, it seems well worth a try.

Notes

This chapter benefited from discussions with Alan Auerbach, Peter Diamond, Martin Feldstein, Ned Gramlich, Andrew Samwick, and John Shoven. I also thank Andrew Samwick and Gene Steuerle for providing key data.

1. Recent academic work on privatization of social security includes Arrau (1990), Arrau and Schmidt-Hebbel (1993), Raffelheuschen (1993), Diamond and Valdes-Prieto (1994), Steuerle and Bakija (1994), the World Bank (1994), Feldstein (1995), Gustman and Steinmeier (1995), Imrohoroglu, Selahattin, Huang, and Sargent (1995), and Kotlikoff (1996b).

2. See Diamond and Valdes-Prieto (1994) for an excellent description of Chile's privatization of social security.

3. The 15.3 payroll tax rate includes the Medicare (HI) tax.

4. For low-income workers covered by the earned income tax credit, the payroll tax's marginal distortion is even larger. Such workers lose twenty cents of their earned income tax credit for every dollar that they earn. Hence, their total effective marginal labor tax rate is 45 percent absent the social security payroll tax and 59 percent with the payroll tax. For such workers, the payroll tax raises their total effective marginal tax rate by 31 percent but their labor supply distortion by 72 percent. Compared to workers who face the earned income tax credit, the incremental distortion from the payroll tax (proportional to the difference between .3481 and .2025) is 62.5 percent larger than the incremental distortion for workers who do not face the earned income tax credit (which is proportional to the difference between .1521 and .0625).

5. This discussion abstracts from disability benefits.

6. Boskin et al. (1987), an earlier study of the marginal net rate of social security taxation, reaches similar conclusions.

7. Since social security tax payments and benefit receipts are both risky, discounting them at a risk-adjusted discount rate seems more appropriate than, say, discounting at the real return on short-term government debt. It is also worth noting that the U.S. equity market has yielded at least a 6 percent real return over every thirty-year holding period since 1929.

8. Note that stince social security benefits are indexed, the real value of social security benefits would not be altered by the use of a retail sales tax or other form of consumption tax. Hence, those initial elderly whose consumption is solely financed by social security benefits would see no increase in their remaining lifetime net tax burden.

9. Note that the current system provides some crediting for early contributions through its wage indexation.

10. See Auerbach, Kotlikoff, and Weil (1992) and Auerbach et al. (1995) for a description of postwar changes in the resource annuitization of the elderly.

11. A recent study by Juster and Laitner (1994, September) using Teachers Insurance Annuity Association–College Retirement Equity Fund (TIAA-CREF) data and participants suggests

that the demand for annuities may be small even when they are fairly priced. However, their findings concern the residual demand for annuities given the receipt of social security benefits. Absent social security, the demand for annuities might be much greater.

12. After this Chapter was written, the U.S. Treasury did announce its plans to issue indexed debt.

13. The classic article on this issue is Merton (1983).

14. This section and the next draw heavily on Kotlikoff (1996b).

15. See Auerbach and Kotlikoff (1987).

16. The social security benefit formula is progressive, and workers with short earnings histories are, other things equal, treated as relatively poor. The reason is that social security benefits are based on the average of workers' indexed monthly earnings, where the average is taken over the worker's entire work span. Providing full accrued social security benefits as here proposed is, for this reason, more expensive.

References

Abel, Andrew, and Laurence J. Kotlikoff. 1994. "Intergenerational Altruism and the Effectiveness of Fiscal Policy—New Tests Based on Cohort Data." in Toshiaki Tachibanaki, ed., *Savings and Bequests*. Ann Arbor: University of Michigan Press, 1994.

Altonji, Joseph, Fumio Hayashi, and Laurence J. Kotlikoff. 1992, December. "Is the Extended Family Altruistically Linked? New Tests Based on Micro Data." *American Economic Review* 82(5):1177–1198.

Arrau, Patricio. 1990. *Social Security Reform: The Capital Accumulation and Intergenerational Distribution Effect*. Washington, DC: World Bank.

Arrau, Patricio, and Klaus Schmidt-Hebbel. 1993. *Macroeconomic and Intergenerational Welfare Effects of a Transition from Pay-as-You-Go to Fully Funded Pensions*. Washington, DC: Policy Research Department, Macroeconomics and Growth Division, World Bank.

Auerbach, Alan J., Jagadeesh Gokhale, Laurence Kotlikoff, John Sabelhaus, and David N. Weil. 1995, April. *The Annuitization of Americans' Resources: A Cohort Analysis*. NBER Working Paper 5089.

Auerbach, Alan J., and Laurence J. Kotlikoff. 1987. *Dynamic Fiscal Policy*. Cambridge: Cambridge University Press.

Auerbach, Alan J., Laurence J. Kotlikoff, and David N. Weil. 1992, October. *The Increasing Annuitization of the Elderly*. NBER Working Paper 4182.

Bernheim, B. Douglas. 1995, August. "The Determinants and Consequences of Financial Education in the Workplace: Evidence from a Survey of Households." Mimeo. Stanford University Dept of Economics.

Boskin, Michael J., Laurence J. Kotlikoff, Douglas J. Puffert, and John B. Shoven. 1987, March. "Social Security: A Financial Appraisal Across and Within Generations." *National Tax Journal* 40(1):19–34.

Diamond Peter, and Salvador Valdes-Prieto. 1994. "Social Security Reform." In Barry Bosworth, Rudiger Dornbusch, and Raul Laban, eds., *The Chilean Economy: Policy Lessons and Challenges*. Washington, D.C.: Brookings Institution.

Feldstein, Martin. 1995, August. "Would Privatizing Social Security Raise Economic Welfare?" Mimeo. Harvard University.

Feldstein, Martin, and Andrew Samwick. 1992, March. "Social Security Rules and Marginal Tax Rates." *National Tax Journal* 45(1):1–22.

Friedman, Benjamin, and Mark Wahrshawsky. 1990, February. "The Cost of Annuities: Implications for Saving and Behavior." *Quarterly Journal of Economics* 55(1):135–154.

Gokhale, Jagadeesh, Laurence J. Kotlikoff, and John Sabelhaus. 1996. "Understanding the Postwar Decline in U.S. Saving: A Cohort Analysis." *Brookings Papers on Economic Activity* 1:315–390.

Gustman, Alan L., and Thomas L. Steinmeier. 1995, September. "Privatizing Social Security." Mimeo. Dartmouth University.

Hayashi, Fumio, Joseph Altonji, and Laurence J. Kotlikoff. 1996. "Risk Sharing Between and Within Families." *Econometrica* 64(2):261–294.

Imrohoroglu, Selahattin, He Huang, and Thomas J. Sargent. 1996, March. "Two Computational Experiments to Privatize Social Security." Mimeo. University of Southern California.

Kotlikoff, Laurence J. 1992. *Generational Accounting*. New York: Free Press.

Kotlikoff, Laurence J. 1996a. "Privatizing Social Security: How It Works and Why It Matters." In James Poterba, ed., *Tax Policy and the Economy*. Cambridge, MA: MIT Press.

Kotlikoff, Laurence J. 1996b, May. "Privatizing Social Security at Home and Abroad." *American Economic Review* 84(2):368–377.

Kotlikoff, Laurence J., and Avia Spivak. 1981, April. "The Family as an Incomplete Annuities Market." *Journal of Political Economy* 89(2):372–391.

Laitner, John, and F. Thomas Juster. 1996, September. "New Evidence on Altruism: A Study of TIAA-CREF Retirees." *American Economic Review* 86(4):893–908.

Merton, Robert C. 1983. "On the Role of Social Security as a Means for Efficient Risk Sharing in an Economy Where Human Capital Is Not Tradable." In Zvi Bodie and John B. Shoven, eds., *Financial Aspects of the U.S. Pension System*, 325–58. Chicago: University of Chicago Press.

Raffelhueschen, Bernd. 1993. "Funding Social Security Through Pareto-Optimal Conversion Policies." In Bernhard Felderer, ed., *Public Pension Economics, Journal of Economics/Zeitschrift fur Nationalokonomie*, Suppl. 7:105–131.

Steuerle, C. Eugene, and Jon M. Bakija. 1994. *Retooling Social Security for the 21st Century*. Washington, DC: Urban Institute Press.

World Bank. 1994. *Averting the Old Age Crisis*. Oxford: Oxford University Press.

Comment

Edward M. Gramlich

Privatization of social security is in the air. A number of countries in South America, Europe, and Australia have already adopted partial privatization schemes. One now departed U.S. presidential candidate advocated privatization, several members of Congress have come out for partial privatization, and a majority of the Quadrennial Advisory Council on Social Security (which I chair) favors large- or small-scale privatization schemes.

Before getting into a discussion of the pros and cons of privatization, it should be noted that this word refers to a very big tent. In the present context, privatization of social security means loosely introducing mandatory individual defined contribution (DC) accounts into the present public defined benefit (DB) pension plan. Even among the set of compulsory programs, there are many ways in which this could be done:

- The individual accounts (IA) could complement or substitute for the existing payroll-tax-financed DB system. These IA could be added on top of the present system or carved out of the present payroll tax.
- The IA could be held inside or outside the social security trust fund.
- The IA could be small or large.
- The IA could be annuitized or not on retirement.

Larry Kotlikoff's privatization scheme has IA that largely substitute for the present DB system, are held outside, are large, and are not annuitized. In the council deliberations, I am suggesting a scheme that differs on each of these dimensions. The differences between the two approaches are extremely significant and well worth debating, but this is Kotlikoff's chapter, so for the most part I comment on his approach.

After establishing that the IA do not represent a mere shell game, Kotlikoff identifies several areas in which the IA are likely to have different efficiency or equity impacts from the present DB system.

Distortions

This is Kotlikoff's main argument for switching to IA. The existing payroll tax system distorts work-leisure choices and carries with it excess burden distortions. The simulation model he presents deals with these distortions.

But not so fast. For one thing, the DB system carries with it earned rights. Workers may pay in more in payroll taxes, but these same workers get more benefits in the end. Table 6.2 gives these huge values for lifetime OASDI taxes, but in fact the true cost of these taxes is much less if one considers the benefit side as well. In fact, one can compute the present value of expected social security benefits compared to the present value of expected employer and employee taxes, factoring in inflation indexing, disability protection, and survivor's protection. This ratio of the present value of benefits relative to the present value of taxes has come to be known as the *money's worth ratio*. The Advisory Council has done calculations of this sort (using the forecast real bond rate of 2.3 percent, unlike Kotlikoff's 6 percent) and shows that single workers born in 1950 with steady low earnings ($11,000 in 1995) get back about eighty-five cents per dollar of their and their employer's contribution in present value terms. Single workers born in 1950 with steady average earnings ($25,000) get back about sixty-five cents per dollar of their contribution in present value terms, and single workers with steady maximum earnings ($62,000) get back about forty-five cents per dollar of contribution in present value terms. Workers of each income class born before 1950 get better money's worth ratios, and workers born after 1950 will get worse ratios unless changes are made in the system. Workers with nonearning spouses in each category get money's worth ratios about twice as much as comparably situated single workers.

There are two implications of these types of calculations for Kotlikoff's chapter. First, the tax distortions he gives are substantially overstated; even high-wage single workers get back about half of their payroll tax, indicating that the distortion will be about half of the amount he gives (and the real distortion ratios are even less for other categories). Second, the tax drains he points to in table 6.2 are substantially overstated.

Kotlikoff himself could mention that there are further distortions within the retirement years. Until 1996, when the social security earnings test was largely eliminated, this earnings test was one such prominent distortion. On the other side, he does mention that if the country were to switch to an IA regime, there would need to be a transition tax that carries with it its own distortions. How all this comes out is a complicated issue, but I am less troubled by distortionary excess burdens than is Kotlikoff.

Intragenerational Redistribution

A second argument Kotlikoff gives for switching to a regime of IA is intragenerational redistribution. A large amount of that goes on now in the present DB system, and he views it as largely capricious.

It may not be optimal, but it is by no means entirely capricious. Most existing DB systems, and certainly that in the United States, have an explicit goal of social adequacy. For this reason there are internal subsidies to those with low-wage work histories, the disabled, the survivors of those who die early, and those who live a long time. These subsidies are clear and well known, and have been voted and revoted for sixty years now. There must be some sense in which society intends to support these classes of people. Moving to an IA regime would not inevitably remove their protection, because an IA scheme could be constrained in many different ways, but it could well remove some of these social protections.

Without specifying a complete social welfare function, it is hard to know how the intragenerational distributional calculus would come out. The differences could be surprisingly unimportant if the IA scheme has present-day social adequacy protections built into it. Kotlikoff seems to view any such social adequacy protections as capricious, while I in general view them as important and necessary. Here one's verdict on IA, both positive and normative, depends on one's social welfare function.

Intergenerational Redistribution

Kotlikoff poses this as an important reason for going to an IA regime, and I largely agree. But I would again point out that a country does not have to go an IA scheme to promote intergenerational redistribution.

One large problem with social security now is that it is not prefunded. The internal rate of return on a nonprefunded system is the economy's growth rate, which is now less than the real interest rate. This means that younger workers get a much worse return on their social security saving than did their parents and grandparents, causing an intergenerational equity problem. Were social security to be prefunded or were national saving to rise through social security, the new funds would return at least the real bond rate, and perhaps even the equity rate if a technique could be found to invest the fund in the equity market (and if the equity premium holds up). Prefunding then could solve, or partially solve, the intergenerational equity problem.

The Advisory Council has considered this issue and has come up with three different ways of prefunding. One is Kotlikoff's way: switch the system to large-scale IA and prefund through the transition tax. Another is the traditional way: just raise payroll taxes in advent of benefit rises, perhaps investing some of the funds in equities. A third is the way I favor: have small-scale IA on top of the present system, with the small-scale IA representing the new national saving. There are important differences in social security implicit in the three approaches, but for this point it is important to note that there are at least these three different ways of prefunding retirement saving and hence providing for a better rate of return on our children's pension saving. The IA may facilitate either prefunding or equity investment, but they are not logically necessary to bring about prefunding, or to improve intergenerational equity.

Information

Kotlikoff promotes this as an advantage to switching to regime of IA. I largely agree, though the IA are not the only way.

Under the present DB system, most people have a very poor idea of their likely social security benefits. Having IA would no doubt improve the situation, but the situation could also be improved by the simple expedient of having the Social Security Administration (SSA) provide to people their earnings records and their likely social security benefits. SSA is already in the process of doing that. Kotlikoff is aware of this new change and also makes the valid point that before any statements are mailed out, SSA must be sure the system has been brought into actuarial balance; if not, the SSA could generate a massive credibility problem.

If SSA is able to provide realistic DB information to people, that would largely eliminate this advantage of switching to IA. On the other hand, it may be intrinsically more difficult to provide this information in a DB plan, because SSA becomes responsible for all kinds of economic and demographic risks that affect likely benefits far in the future.

There is another advantage of switching to IA: it would permit individuals to make their own investment choices—stocks or bonds, index funds or not. Individuals could follow how their investments were doing, develop some ownership feelings, take their own risks, understand the value of saving, and in general understand the system better. To me, this is one of the strongest reasons for going to some form of IA.

Annuitization

Social security benefits are given in the form of indexed annuities with sizable survivor's benefits, and IA may not be. This sets up a potential advantage for the present system, in that there is less risk that people will outlive their retirement assets. Perhaps—but again there is no innate reason. If one is worried about people outliving their retirement assets in an IA world, the government could either force people to annuitize part or all of their accumulations, or at least force SSA to sell actuarially fair indexed annuities.

Risk Sharing

Present pay-as-you-go DB plans subject cohorts to wage growth risk: if wages do not grow at anticipated rates, there will be less there for retirees. Switching to IA subjects cohorts to investment risk: if bond or stock markets do not do well, there will be less for retirees. So far it is hard to see which is intrinsically better, except that investment risk has exceeded growth risk historically. But it strikes me that there is a further point. Principles of risk diversification would argue that perhaps retirees should have a little of both types of risk but not too much of either. In social security terms, this argues for a combined DB-DC system or for mandatory IA on top of the DB system.

Adding up all these points, one can favor or oppose the switch to IA. The real point is that the devil is in the details. One can design an IA scheme that more or less replicates the DB system or is very different. The evaluations of these schemes would differ substantially. Should a country privatize its social security system? It all depends.

Finally, I cannot resist a current policy point. Kotlikoff's evaluation framework convinces me more than ever that the best approach for the United States is a small-scale IA on top of the present DB system. Distortions would be moderated, the intragenerational redistribution could be whatever society chooses to make it, intergenerational equity is improved by the prefunding, the information would be clearer, the ownership responsibilities would be clearer, and retirees would have some diversification against both wage growth risk and investment risk.

Comment

John B. Shoven

Larry Kotlikoff's chapter is extremely useful in sorting out the real changes posed by privatizing social security from the changes that are simply relabeling cash flows. He emphasizes that the largest potential gain in economic efficiency from privatizing social security stems from sharply increasing the links between what participants pay into the system and what they can expect to get out of it. In a completely privatized system, the link is one for one. The entire system of social security becomes deferred compensation, like other defined contribution pension systems. In contrast, the link in the present social security system in the United States between contributions and benefits can be quite weak and uneven, as table 6.1 illustrates.

Kotlikoff does not make it entirely clear that most of the real advantages of a privatized system could be achieved without privatization at all. A pay-as-you-go (PAYG) system could be designed with much tighter links between contributions and benefits. Such a system would distort labor markets much less than the current U.S. social security program. Steps that could be taken include (1) counting all work years in the computation of benefits, rather than simply the highest thirty-five years, (2) lowering the forty-quarter minimum covered work history for the receipt of benefits, (3) making social security coverage universal in the economy, (4) reducing or eliminating the progressivity of the principal insurance amount formula use to calculate retirement benefits, (5) lowering or eliminating the spousal benefit, (6) instituting earnings sharing or community property with respect to social security entitlements, and (7) providing informative annual reports to all participants. Each of these steps would make the system appear more like a private pension program, but none of them actually requires privatization—highlighting that most of

Kotlikoff's paper is describing the potential benefits of linking benefits to contributions. Privatization is only one way to bring that about.

On a somewhat more technical note, I feel that the 6 percent real discount rate that Kotlikoff uses is far too high. He defends the number by discussing the uncertainty regarding future social security benefits, but raising the rate of time discount is generally not the appropriate way to adjust for risk. The preferred approach would be to assess the risks themselves, ascertain their covariance with other outcomes in the economy, convert uncertain social security outcomes into certainty equivalent amounts, and then use the risk-free real interest rate for discounting. It probably is fair to say that almost no one does this, but almost all previous studies use real interest rates in the 3 percent range rather than the 6 percent number. This makes comparing the results here with earlier work difficult. The 6 percent interest rate explains a number of the surprising results of table 6.2, which calculates the present value of lifetime net taxes (contributions less benefits) in 1993 dollars. Some of the numbers are staggeringly high (in excess of $1 million). The numbers for single women are often close to those for single men, even though the life expectancy of women at age sixty-five is 27 percent greater than for men. Clearly single women get far more benefits from social security than single men, so why are table 6.2 numbers so close? The explanation for these results is that with a 6 percent interest rate, the taxes early in life swamp in importance the benefits late in life. I find that the 6 percent real discount rate obscures some important factors, and this strengthens my conviction that it is way too high.

Kotlikoff discusses the issue of the transition from a PAYG system to a private system. One of the key matters is how to finance the massive promises of the existing system. Although Kotlikoff's simulations indicate the importance of this matter (he gets very different results if a consumption tax is used to finance the transition costs rather than an income tax), he does not mention the recent estimate of Feldstein (1996) that the present value of the net social security benefits for all adults alive today totals $11 trillion. That is, today's adults are being told by the Social Security Administration that they are entitled to benefits that have a present value of $11 trillion even after the present value of their future contributions is deducted. Just for reference, the assets in funded pensions in the United States total about $5 trillion. The Federal Reserve estimates that the tangible wealth in the country totals approximately $18 $20 trillion. Any way you look at it, U.S. social security "wealth" is enormous.

Kotlikoff spends some time discussing Chile, but Chile did not have a transition problem of remotely the same magnitude as we would face in the United States.

Kotlikoff ends by outlining a simple transition plan to a private social security system. Under it, the existing social security benefit structure would stay in place, but contributions to it would cease once the new plan is adopted. Future work years would not have covered earnings; zeroes would be entered for those years in calculating a worker's average indexed monthly earnings. The problem of this approach of simply adding zeros to the earnings record is that it enlarges the $11 trillion liability of the old system. Social security has always failed to distinguish between people with low lifetime earnings and those who have short covered careers. It treats people with short covered careers as if they are poor, even if they are not. This is a problem because of the sharply progressive structure of the primary insurance amount formula used in computing benefits. Kotlikoff's proposal not only does not correct this problem but amplifies it enormously.

The severity of this problem with Kotlikoff's Personal Security System is quite great. Consider a forty-year-old person who has been earning $1,820 per month for ten years. If she maintained that rate of pay for thirty-five years, she would qualify for a primary insurance amount (the amount that she would receive as a single person at age sixty-five) of $833 per month under current social security law. If social security is privatized when this worker is forty years old, one sensible thing to do would be to give her ten–thirty-fifths as much as she would have gotten form social security if it had not been changed (reflecting the ten years of contributions rather than thirty-five years). Thus, under this arrangement the worker would receive ten–thirty-fifths of $833, or $238 a month from the "old program." On top of that, she would have whatever the privatized plan provided. Kotlikoff proposes to be far more generous with benefits from the old plan, thus requiring more transitionary taxes. In this example, Kotlikoff's proposal would result in the worker's getting a primary insurance amount of $417 each month, a full 75 percent more than the proportional reduction suggested above. It seems to me that the transition problem of switching to a private system is so large that we cannot afford to consider a plan such as this Personal Security System, which makes it costlier than necessary.

My conclusion is that Kotlikoff raises a number of important issues and discusses them with great clarity. I certainly recommend his chapter to anyone trying to understand the debate about privatizing social security. On the other hand, the particular privatization proposal presented suffers from at least one important flaw, which in my mind eliminates it from serious policy consideration.

Reference

Feldstein, Martin. 1996, May. "The Missing Piece in Policy Analysis: Social Security Reform." *American Economic Review* 86(2):1–14.

7 Rethinking Saving Incentives

B. Douglas Bernheim

Low rates of saving in the United States have created widespread concern over investment, growth, the balance of payments, and the financial security of individual households. These concerns have prompted a variety of proposals designed to stimulate saving through tax incentives, ranging from narrowly focused tax-favored savings accounts to broad-based consumption taxation. Before attempting to weigh the advantages and disadvantages of these proposals, it is important to marshal the evidence and review the lessons that economists have learned about the relation (or relations) between tax incentives and personal saving.

This chapter undertakes a review of the existing academic work in this area. It both evaluates the evidence and identifies the important open questions. Although it does not provide a full evaluation of any particular saving incentive proposal, it does identify relevant implications.

The central conclusions of this review are as follows. First, the traditional life cycle hypothesis has had an excessive influence on the design and conceptualization of empirical investigations concerning the relation between taxation and saving. Although other behavioral hypotheses are mentioned in the literature with increasing frequency, this usually occurs in the course of explaining an anomalous result rather than at the stage of designing an empirical strategy or even at the stage of evaluating results that do not appear to be anomalous from a life cycle perspective. In part, this is no doubt attributable to the absence of sufficiently well-developed organizing principles for a compelling behavioral alternative. But even in the absence of an intellectually satisfying alternative, it is important to be aware of the potential for reaching misleading conclusions by imposing potentially false structure on the data.

Second, there is little reason to believe that households increase their saving significantly in response to a generic increase in the after-tax rate of return. Since the evidence is quite poor, there is still considerable uncertainty on this point. However, it is difficult to identify any robust empirical pattern suggestive of a high elasticity.

Third, the literature on the relation between Individual Retirement Accounts (IRAs) and personal saving is inconclusive. Studies that point to a large effect on personal saving contain identifiable biases that overstate this effect. Similarly, studies that find little or no effect on personal saving contain identifiable biases that understate the effect. Due to the nature of the IRA program and the characteristics of the available data, reliable estimation of the effect on personal saving may well be impossible. The IRA experience nevertheless does provide reasonably strong evidence that households' responses to narrowly focused tax incentives are governed, at least in part, by forces that are not considered in the traditional life cycle framework.

Fourth, the available evidence on 401(k) plans allows one to conclude with moderate confidence that, all else equal, eligibility for such a plan significantly stimulates personal saving. Econometric identification of this effect is facilitated by the fact that, in contrast to IRAs, there is considerable variation in 401(k) eligibility across the population, and some of this variation almost certainly arises from exogenous sources. Although no existing study corresponds to the ideal statistical experiment, at least one sensible approach concludes that 401(k)s do not displace other saving despite the fact that its primary shortcoming probably creates a bias in the opposite direction. In contrast, important biases obscure the interpretation of studies that reach the opposite conclusion.

Fifth, tax incentives probably have important effects on personal saving through third-party or institutional channels. Third parties are entities other than the households that benefit directly from the tax provisions, such as employers or vendors of tax-favored investments products. Examples of these effects include stimulation of pension provision, indirect encouragement of employer-based financial education, and the advertisement and promotion of opportunities for tax-favored saving. Since little is known about the relation between tax incentives and either the scope or characteristics of institutions that promote saving, this issue should be a priority for future research.

Sixth, there is, overall, considerable uncertainty about the effects of policies designed to promote saving. These uncertainties are greatest for policies that have the potential to induce significant institutional change, such as the implementation of a broad-based consumption tax. If, for example, the generic interest elasticity of saving is small (as the evidence seems to suggest) and if targeted tax incentives sustain vital pro-saving institutions (such as the pensions system), then consumption taxation could have disastrous implications for saving. In contrast, narrowly targeted incentives could bolster the institutional structures that encourage saving.

7.1 The Links Between Tax Policy and Personal Saving

The Life Cycle Hypothesis as an Organizing Framework

For more than fifty years, the framework of intertemporal utility maximization has dominated economists' thinking about saving incentives. The framework comes with an exceptional pedigree. It traces its roots to Irving Fisher (1930) and lies at the heart of the life cycle hypothesis (LCH) articulated by Modigliani and Brumberg (1954). In recent years, the validity of this framework has become controversial, and an increasing number of economists have expressed doubts concerning its general validity (see, e.g., Bernheim 1994a). Although various authors have suggested provocative alternative paradigms (Shefrin and Thaler 1988), no serious competitor for the attention and imagination of most professional economists has yet emerged. As a result, the LCH has remained the preeminent theoretical tool for analyzing saving incentives—in many cases, with serious reservations on the part of those who use it.

The evidence on the LCH is mixed. Although it would be rash to dismiss its many empirical successes and discard it unconditionally, it is equally rash (in the light of its empirical failures and well-founded skepticism about its underlying premises) to employ this theory as the sole organizing principle for understanding saving incentives. Any conceptual framework acts as a filter on reality. It shapes the questions that we pose and influences the manner in which we interpret evidence bearing on these questions. By treating the LCH as the universal maintained hypothesis, we run the risk of overlooking important evidence concerning the efficacy of saving incentives.

It is perhaps an exaggeration to say that economists studying saving incentives have been straightjacketed by the LCH. Yet references to alternative behavioral hypotheses are somewhat haphazard; they are usually mentioned in a rather ad hoc way as possible explanations for otherwise puzzling phenomena (Venti and Wise 1992; Feenberg and Skinner 1989). With rare exceptions, alternative behavioral hypothesis have not been used as frameworks for organizing lines of empirical inquiry concerning the effects of tax incentives or even for interpreting evidence that does not appear to be anomalous from the perspective of the LCH. The scarcity of well-developed organizing principles for these alternative hypotheses (aside form a few relatively imprecise notions such as "mental accounting" and "self-discipline") is a serious shortcoming of the existing literature.

Possible Links Between Tax Policy and Personal Saving

The traditional focus on the LCH has generated the perception that the task of evaluating the effects of saving incentives is fundamentally a matter of determining the extent to which these incentives affect the marginal dollar of saving, and of measuring the interest elasticity of saving. Consideration of alternative hypotheses broadens this line of inquiry considerably, to include all of the following concerns.

Perceptions of the Costs and Benefits from Saving

The field of psychology appears to offer relatively few organizing principles that are directly useful for evaluating the effects of saving incentives (see the discussion in chap. 9 of Furnham and Lewis 1986). One notable and pervasive exception is the principle of self-control (Ainslie 1975, 1982, 1984; Maital 1986; Schelling 1984; Thaler and Shefrin 1981; Shefrin and Thaler 1988; Hoch and Lowenstein 1991). Thaler and Shefrin equate the notion of self-control with the view that each individual has more than one set of preferences (or "selves") that conflict at a point in time and that individuals must expend energy and resources to restrict the kinds of behavior motivated by their shortsighted selves. In this view, aspects of the economic environment that tip the internal balance of power toward patient selves have the potential to stimulate saving.

One way to shift this balance of power is to alter the perceived costs and benefits of saving. Certain kinds of saving incentives have the theoretical capacity to precipitate such a shift through a variety of channels. When saving incentives are in place, individuals may be more likely to learn that others (including both "authorities" and peers) regard the benefits of saving as important.[1] By segmenting retirement saving from other forms of saving, certain kinds of tax-favored accounts also make it easier to monitor progress toward long-term objectives.[2] The existence of saving incentives may reinforce the notion that saving, as something worthy of encouragement, is an intrinsically desirable or virtuous activity, entirely apart from explicit consideration of future consequences (Scitovsky 1976; Katona 1975). Under certain circumstances, contributions to tax-favored accounts may also instill the perception that saving yields concrete short-run benefits, such as reductions in current-year tax liabilities (Feenberg and Skinner 1989).

Private Rules

The psychological literature on self-control also emphasizes the use of private rules (e.g., acting on some specific self-imposed principle, making promises to one's self, etc.) (Hoch and Lowenstein 1991). Saving incentives may facilitate the formation of effective private rules in two ways. First, they may provide a natural context for developing rules concerning the level of saving, such as "maxing out" on contributions. Certain plans, such as 410(k)s, actually provide participants with limited ability to commit themselves to these rules for short periods of time. Second, individuals may develop private rules regarding the allowable uses of funds that they have previously placed in tax-favored accounts. This phenomenon relates to the notion of mental accounting discussed by Shefrin and Thaler (1988). The existence of penalties for early withdrawal may help the individual establish and enforce barriers around tax-favored accounts.

Third-Party Activities

A uniform tax on all forms of capital income would create a neutral environment with respect to the form of saving. This neutrality would be preserved if all capital income taxes were eliminated (e.g., through the implementation of a consumption tax). In contrast, limited saving incentives are usually nonneutral, in the sense that they favor saving in certain forms. These nonneurtralities may stimulate activities by third parties—those other than the individuals who benefit directly from the tax provisions, such as employers or vendors of tax-favored investments products—and these activities may affect the level of personal saving through either life cycle or psychological channels. Perhaps the most obvious example of this phenomenon is the development of the pension system. Selective saving incentives may also have subtle effects on the choices that employers make in the context of pension plans. For example, Garrett (1995) argues that nondiscrimination requirements induce employers to take steps that stimulate 401(k) contributions among non–highly compensated employees (e.g., through matching contributions or retirement education). Selective incentives may also encourage the vendors of tax-favored savings vehicles to advertise and promote their products actively.

The Importance of the Nature of the Link

A pure (and somewhat narrow-minded) empiricist might dismiss the importance of the nature of the link between tax incentives and saving on the grounds that one can measure the quantitative effect of these incentives without identifying the underlying mechanism. But I believe that the nature of the mechanism is important, for three reasons.

First, the possible justifications for attempting to stimulate saving, and the manner in which we think about the social costs and benefit of saving incentives, differ across behavioral hypotheses. If, for example, profligacy results from a failure to understand financial vulnerabilities or an unintended breakdown of self-control, then the potential welfare gains associated with pro-saving policies are likely to be much larger than those implied by the LCH.

Second, the nature of the link between tax incentives and saving significantly affects our expectations concerning the likely effects of different kinds of pro-saving policies. As an example, consider the choice between broad-based and narrowly focused strategies for promoting saving. The widespread (though certainly not universal) support for consumption taxation among economists is almost certainly attributable to the influence of the LCH as the preeminent (if not exclusive) conceptual framework. From the perspective of a neoclassical maximizer of intertemporal utility, consumption taxation accomplishes the prime objective: it raises the marginal after-tax rate of return to saving, and reduces the tax wedge between the pretax return of investment and the after-tax return on saving. Yet psychological considerations generally suggest that narrowly focused tax incentives have the potential to be much more effective than broad-based measures. Narrow measures focus attention on the key issue, expose individuals to information concerning the importance of saving, provide a natural context for the development and enforcement of private rules, and promote the growth of pro-saving institutions. In contrast, a broad-based consumption tax could undermine the narrow focus on specific objectives that may be essential for the exercise of self-control. A true consumption tax would be institutionally neutral. It would remove one of the primary reasons for compensating workers through pension plans, and it would eliminate the special feature of particular financial instruments (such as IRAs and life insurance policies) that make them especially marketable. It would also eliminate the quirky aspects of the tax system that subtly promote activities such as employee retirement education.

Third, the nature of the links between saving incentives and behavior profoundly affects the lessons that we might be inclined to draw from a variety of possible empirical patterns. As an example, consider the generalizability of evidence on the interest elasticity of saving. Within the context of the LCH, all saving incentives motivate changes in behavior through the same fundamental mechanism: an increase in the after-tax rate of return. Measurement of the interest elasticity of saving therefore emerges as a central research priority. Alternative behavioral hypotheses allow for the possibility that the interest elasticity of saving may vary according to context and that households may respond (both positively and negatively) to aspects of tax incentive programs that are not directly related to the after-tax rate of return.

7.2 Direct Responses to Generic Changes in the After-Tax Rate of Return

Much of the literature on the relation between tax incentives and personal saving concerns the extent to which saving generally responds to a change in the after-tax rate of return. As is well known, the sign of the interest elasticity of saving is theoretically ambiguous in simple life cycle models, due to the existence of opposing income and substitution effects. Although certain kinds of life cycle simulations tend to generate substantial positive elasticities (Summers 1981), this result is highly sensitive to assumptions about utility (Starrett 1988) and uncertainty (Engen 1994), and it is easily reversed under alternative behavioral hypotheses (e.g., target saving behavior). Thus, the size of the interest elasticity of saving is fundamentally an empirical issue. Unfortunately, the existing methods of measuring the interest elasticity of saving are critically flawed. Despite these flaws, studies based on different approaches typically reach strikingly similar conclusions: evidence of a substantial elasticity is the exception rather than the rule. Based on this evidence, one is hard-pressed to make the case that saving is *in general* highly sensitive to the after-tax rate of return.

The Consumption/Saving Function Approach

The earliest approach to measuring the interest elasticity of saving involved the estimation of a consumption function or saving function featuring an interest rate among the list of explanatory variables. Since the initial work of Wright (1969), this approach has yielded a variety of elasticity estimates, ranging from essentially zero (Blinder 1975; Howrey and Hymans 1978; Skinner and Feenberg 1989) to 0.4 (Boskin 1978; Boskin and Lau 1978). This range is somewhat misleading, since the estimates tend to cluster near zero. There has been considerable discussion in the literature concerning the sources of the discrepancies between these various estimates (Sandmo 1985), with particular attention being given to the proper measurement of the real after-tax rate of return. The problems with this approach are more fundamental, however.

As Lucas (1976) noted, the relation between consumption (saving) and interest rates may depend on the wider macroeconomic context; consequently, there may not exist anything that one could properly regard as a stable saving or consumption function. Low elasticity estimates are largely attributable to developments during the 1970s (saving was relatively high and ex post real rates of return were very low). Since it is not at all obvious that the 1970s constitute a "clean" macroeconomic experiment for inferring the interest elasticity of saving, it is doubtful that these kinds of estimates have the potential to explain much about the likely response of saving to a change in tax policy.

The Euler Equation Approach

A second approach to estimating the interest elasticity of saving finesses the Lucas critique. This approach can be motivated as follows. To the extent that a change in the interest rate alters saving, this is accomplished by inducing the individual to revise consumption. We can decompose the change in consumption into two pieces: a change in shape of the age-consumption profile and a change in the overall level of this profile. The consumption/saving function approach makes no attempt to distinguish between these two effects. Yet it is conceivable that the level of consumption might be quite sensitive to aspects of the economic environment (through effects on expectations about future income, among other channels), whereas the relation between consumption growth and the interest rate might be stable. In that case, one could estimate this second relation reliably. Using the estimated relation along with the budget constraint, one could then infer the structural effect of the interest rate on the level of consumption or saving, thereby recovering the true interest elasticity of saving.

It is possible to justify this approach formally in the context of a standard life cycle planning model. Specifically, Hall (1988) notes that under appropriate parametric assumptions, the following Euler equation (governing the allocation between consumption in two consecutive periods, t and $t+1$) is a necessary condition for optimization:

$$\ln\left(\frac{c_t}{c_{t-1}}\right) = k + \sigma r + \varepsilon_t, \tag{7.1}$$

where k is a constant, σ is the elasticity of substitution in consumption, and ε_t is a random variable uncorrelated with information available prior to t. Estimation of this equation permits one to recover the key parameter of the utility function that governs intertemporal trade-offs rather than the parameters of a potentially unstable consumption function. The value of the estimated parameter is directly relevant to an analysis of the welfare effects of capital income taxation. Moreover, armed with a parameterized utility function and a budget constraint, one can infer the interest elasticity of saving. For example, $\sigma = 1$ corresponds to Cobb-Douglas utility, which in turn implies fixed expenditure shares. If one estimates $\sigma = 1$, then abstracting from the effect of changes in the interest rate on the present discounted value of wage income, the uncompensated interest elasticity of saving would be zero.

Hall demonstrates that the rate of change of consumption has been remarkably insensitive to changes in the rate of return. His estimates of σ are correspondingly small; he concludes that σ is almost certainly below 0.1 and possibly equal to zero (Leontief preferences). All of his estimates are well below unity, which corresponds to the Cobb-Douglas case. Thus, abstracting from the impact of the rate of return on the present discounted value of future earnings, one would infer from these results that the interest elasticity of saving (ε_{sr}) is negative. Although more recent research suggests that Hall may have underestimated σ due to aggregation problems and other concerns, most authors still place σ (as inferred from Euler equation estimates) significantly below unity, implying (for the case where the individual has no future earnings) $\varepsilon_{sr} < 0$ (Attanasio and Weber 1993).

Unfortunately, the interpretation of σ as the intertemporal elasticity of substitution is highly model specific. As Hall himself notes, the standard life cycle model makes an automatic connection between this intertemporal elasticity and the coefficient of risk aversion, whereas no connection appears to exist in practice. Although Hall exhibits one specification of utility that breaks this connection while still generating a Euler equation with an identical interpretation, there is no guarantee that Hall's result would remain valid under other specifications of utility. For example, a model with buffer stock saving might yield a Euler equation with a very different structural interpretation, and if one moves to other behavioral hypotheses, it is not obvious that an estimate of σ has any structural significance at all.

It is nevertheless possible to infer an interest elasticity of saving directly from estimates of equation 7.1 (the Euler equation) without specifying a behavioral hypothesis, provided that one is willing to assume the stability of the estimated relation. This is accomplished through a mechanical application of the budget constraint. Suppose in particular that

$$c_t = e^{g(r)t} c_0. \tag{7.2}$$

Imagine that a consumer lives for a total of T years, earning a wage flow of w_t through time R, and nothing from time R through time T. Let

$$W \equiv W_0 + \int_0^R w_\tau e^{-r\tau} d\tau,$$

where W_0 denotes initial wealth. Then the budget constraint requires

$$c_0 \int_0^T e^{[g(r)-r]t} dt = W. \tag{7.3}$$

Using equation 7.3, it is easy to verify that the interest elasticity of saving at time zero (defined as $s_0 = w_0 - c_0$) is given by

$$\varepsilon_{sr} = \left(\frac{rc_0}{s_0}\right)\left(\left[\frac{W - W_0}{W}\right] D(w, r) + [g'(r) - 1] D(e^T, r - g(r))\right), \tag{7.4}$$

where, for any income stream $y_t(t \in [0, \infty)), D(y, r)$ denotes the duration of y,

$$D(y, r) \equiv \int_0^\infty \tau \left[\frac{y_\tau e^{-r\tau} d\tau}{\int_0^\infty y_t e^{-rt} dt}\right], \tag{7.5}$$

and where e^T denotes a stream of income that is constant through time T. If one abstracts from the effect of the interest rate on the present discounted value of future earnings (i.e., assume $W_0 = W$), then for the case of $g'(r) = 1$, one obtains $\varepsilon_{sr} = 0$. This is intuitive since, in the context of the standard life cycle model, $g'(r) = \sigma = 1$ corresponds to Cobb-Douglas preferences.

Unfortunately, when one departs from the standard life cycle framework, the stability of the function $g(r)$ is no longer assured. With buffer stock saving, it is no longer obvious that the Euler equation approach successfully finesses the Lucas critique, since the expected desirability of next period's consumption depends on next period's resources (through the probability that the individual will run out of liquid wealth). The procedure described above may also yield misleading estimates of the interest elasticity of saving under other alternative hypotheses.

To illustrate, imagine that an individual follows a simple rule of thumb that specifies a constant level of consumption for each interest rate r, $c_w(r)$, throughout the preretirement period, and a potentially different constant level of consumption, $c_R(r)$, throughout the postretirement period. For simplicity, also assume that $W_0 = W$. Observing this individual either before or after retirement, one would conclude (based on the Euler equation approach) that $\varepsilon_{sr} = 0$. However, it is entirely possible that $c_R(r)$ and $c_W(r)$ are, respectively, increasing and decreasing in the interest rate. In that case, the actual interest elasticity of saving would be positive. The validity of the procedure for recovering ε_{sr} breaks down because the function $g(\cdot)$ depends on t as well as r.

Other Evidence

In the light of the difficulties associated with estimating interest elasticities through either of the two approaches already discussed, it is appropriate to seek out other evidence that could shed light on this issue. Ideally, one would like to find exogenous variation in the rates of return earned by different individuals and to relate this variation to differences in rates of saving. One obvious candidate for the source of this variation is eligibility to make contributions to a tax-favored savings account, such as an IRA or 401(k). I explore this possibility in the next section.

Another possibility is to identify the interest elasticity of saving by examining variation in the after-tax rate of return within a given class of tax-favored savings plans, such as 401(k)s. One impcrtant source of this variation arises from employer-matching provisions. Although an increase in the employer match is not mathematically equivalent to an increase in the after-tax rate of return, both have the effect of reducing the price of future consumption relative to current consumption. Indeed, since the mathematics of an employer match are easier to understand than the mathematics of compound interest, in seems doubtful that the interest elasticity of saving could be positive unless saving responds positively to employer-matching provisions within the context of 401(k)s.

Relatively few studies have attempted to relate 401(k) plan provisions, such as employer matches, to the choices of employees. Moreover, the existing studies focus exclusively on 401(k) contributions. Even if 401(k) contributions respond strongly to employer-matching provisions, conceivably this response could reflect asset shifting rather than new accumulation. Thus, a high elasticity of contributions with respect to the match rate would not necessarily establish that the interest elasticity of saving is also substantial. However, it would be very difficult to reconcile the existence of a substantial positive interest elasticity of saving with the finding that 401(k) contributions do not respond to employer-match rates.

The evidence on the effect of 401(k) match rates is mixed. Using survey data gathered by the General Accounting Office, Poterba, Venti, and Wise (1992) conclude that the existence of a match rate is correlated with higher participation but that the level of the match has little effect. Papke, Petersen, and Poterba (1993) survey a small sample of firms and corroborate this finding. Papke (1992) analyzes data drawn from IRS Form 5500 filings and finds that the effect of higher match rates is positive at low match rates but negative at high match rates. Her results are also somewhat sensitive to the introduction of fixed effects. Andrews (1992) studies household-level data from the May 1988 Current Population Survey and concludes that although the existence of a match increases participation, there is actually a negative relation between the match rate and contributions. Kusko, Poterba, and Wilcox (1993) analyze employee-level data for a single company and find that contributions and participation are relatively insensitive to changes in the matching rate through time. Scott (1994) argues that most of the negative results on the effects of matching provisions are attributable to the use of ex post rather than ex ante match rates. Using the 1985–1989 Employee Benefit Surveys (for which ex ante match rates are available), he finds some evidence that the size of the match matters; however, even Scott's results indicate that most of the effect is attributable to the existence of the match rather than to its magnitude.

The evidence on match rates is therefore somewhat puzzling. Within the context of the traditional life cycle hypothesis, it is difficult to imagine why employees would respond differently to match rate of 0 percent and 5 percent but behave almost identically with match rates of 5 percent and 100 percent. One possibility is that the existence of a match is correlated with the underlying preferences of the employees. This would occur if, for example, high-saving workers sorted themselves into plans with match rates or demanded that their employers provide matches. There are two problems with this explanation. First, it is hard to understand why the same considerations would not induce a correlation between contributions and the size of the match. Second, there is some reason to believe that matching provisions are adopted as remedial measures to stimulate contributions in instances where employees are predisposed against saving.

The evidence on matching provisions is more easily reconciled with alternative behavioral hypotheses. One can easily imagine that the availability of a match focuses employee attention on the 401(k) plan, authoritatively validates the importance of long-term saving objectives, undermines the resistance of impatient selves (due to its immediacy), and provides additional impetus for establishing a private rule. Although higher match rates might add to this impetus, one might well expect the observed discontinuity when match rates are introduced.

7.3 Direct Responses to Tax-Favored Savings Accounts

Even if saving does not in general respond significantly to changes in the after-tax rate of return, this does not necessarily imply that tax-favored savings accounts are ineffective. Certainly individuals may respond strongly to tax incentives in the context of certain institutional settings even if they do not respond more generally. However, to defend this position, one must be prepared to embrace the view that saving is driven in large part by psychological and institutional factors and not exclusively by pristine life cycle forces.

The literature on tax-favored savings accounts focuses primarily on IRAs and 401(k)s, and I will discuss the evidence on the efficacy of both. Before doing so, however, it is important to be clear about the nature of the question posed in this section. Specifically, I am attempting to determine whether the saving of individuals who contributed to IRAs and/or 401(k)s would have been lower had these programs not existed, *all else equal*. I am not attempting to learn whether these programs contributed to total personal saving. These are different issues, because the creation or elimination of tax-favored accounts need not leave all else equal. For example, it is conceivable that those with 401(k)s would, in the absence of statutes authorizing 401(k)s, have had other pensions. I take these kinds of issues up in section 7.4. For the moment, I am using IRAs and 401(k)s merely as opportunities to learn about the partial equilibrium response of individuals to focused tax incentives.

Individual Retirement Accounts

Individuals without pensions were first permitted to open IRAs in 1974. These accounts featured tax-deductible contributions up to a fixed limit, tax-free accumulation, taxation of principle and interest on withdrawal, and penalties for early withdrawal. Congress extended eligibility to all workers in 1981 and raised annual contribution limits to $2,000 for a single worker and $2,250 for a married couple with one earner. The Tax Reform Act of 1986 restricted eligibility for deductible contributions, based on adjusted gross income (AGI). Deductibility was phased out between AGI of $40,000 and $50,000 for joint filers and between $25,000 and $35,000 for single filers. Individuals with higher levels of AGI remained eligible to make nondeductible contributions up to the same annual limits and continued to benefit from tax-free accumulation.

Prior to the Tax Reform Act of 1986, IRAs had become quite popular. Annual contributions grew from roughly $5 billion in 1981 to roughly $38 billion in 1986, which represented approximately 20 percent of total personal saving. Contributions plummeted after 1986, falling to less than $10 billion in 1990. While it is indisputable that flows of saving through IRAs were substantial, there is considerable controversy concerning the extent to which these flows represented new saving. The existing evidence on the efficacy of IRAs falls into five general categories.

Direct Survey Evidence

One approach to measuring the effect of IRAs on saving is simply to ask people how they funded their contributions. In one such survey (Johnson 1985), about half of respondents said that they would have saved the money anyway, about 10 percent said that they would have spent all of it, and about 40 percent said that they would have saved some and spent some. Johnson concludes that, on average, individuals reduced consumption by roughly thirty-two cents to fund each dollar of IRA saving.

These finding should be regarded as at most vaguely suggestive. The relevant survey question asks individuals to imagine what they would have done in a counterfactual and purely hypothetical situation. This raises a variety of problems. Respondents may not think very hard about the hypothetical. If they think about it, they may assess the costs and benefits of various decisions differently than they would have in practice.

They may accurately report what their intention would have been in the hypothetical situation, but actions and intentions do not always coincide. They may also misrepresent their probable intentions in the hypothetical situation, particularly if they believe that some answer is more virtuous, or if they think that the interviewer is looking for a particular response.

Evidence on the Frequency of Limit Contribution

If one adopts a traditional life cycle perspective, then there is ample reason to be concerned about the efficacy of IRAs. Under this view, IRAs have the potential to stimulate saving only if they raise the after-tax rate of return earned on the marginal dollar of saving. But for individuals who save more than the IRA contribution limit, IRAs affect only the rate of return earned on inframarginal saving. This creates an income effect that increases consumption and decreases saving (under both the LCH and various alternatives), without an offsetting substitution effect. If, in addition, the interest elasticity of saving is small, then the increase in saving for those saving less than the IRA contribution limit will be modest. Conceivably the net effect of the program could be to reduce personal saving, particularly if a large fraction of the population saves more than the contribution limit. To make matters still worse, individuals would have an incentive to reach the limit by shifting existing savings or borrowing to fund their contributions.

In the light of this argument, many observers have been troubled by the fact that roughly three-quarters of all contributors saved at exactly the contribution limit (Burman, Cordes, and Ozanne 1990; Gravelle 1991). Others find comfort in the fact that only 30 percent of IRA contributors reached the contribution limit in each of three consecutive years (Hubbard and Skinner 1995).

In my view, this focus on the frequency with which IRA participants reached the contribution limit is misplaced, for two reasons. First, the existence of the contribution limit induces a kink in the individual's budget constraint. Many limit contributors may have been at the kink, in the sense that they did not undertake any other long-term saving for which IRA contributions would have been a good substitute. For individuals at the kink, the marginal after-tax rate of return is not well defined. It is entirely possible, even in the context of the LCH, that the long-term saving of these individuals would have been significantly less than the contribution limit in the absence of the IRA program.

Second, the pessimistic assessment of the data on limit contributors is predicated on the view that the LCH accurately depicts behavior. I have suggested a variety of behavioral channels through which IRAs may have affected saving besides changing the marginal after-tax rate of return. For example, IRAs may have increased awareness of the need for retirement saving or may have validated specific saving targets. Another possibility is that IRAs may have strengthened self-discipline. Even if they did not stimulate inflows into households' long-term savings, they may have deterred outflows (Thaler 1994).

Correlations Between IRA and Non-IRA Saving

A number of authors have attempted to measure the effects of IRAs on saving through more rigorous econometric analysis. Most of these studies have, with varying degrees of sophistication, examined the underlying correlations between IRA and non-IRA saving activity.

Before describing these studies, it is useful to describe an ideal experiment for assessing the effects of IRAs. The contrast between the ideal data and the available data explains why the measurement of IRA effects has proved so difficult. Imagine that we are given some large sample of individuals and randomly partition this sample into two subsamples. We treat the individuals in these subsamples exactly the same in all respects (identical initial assets, wages, fringe benefits, working conditions, and so forth) but permit the individuals in one subsample to contribute to IRAs (the experimental group), while withholding this opportunity from the other subsample (the control group). In this way, we create exogenous variation in IRA eligibility. We then compare the total saving of individuals in the two subsamples to determine the effects of IRAs.

Unfortunately, between 1982 and 1986, there is no exogenous variation in IRA eligibility. Instead we observe variations in participation. One could imagine attempting to mimic the ideal experiment by using this variation to identify new experimental and control groups—in effect, asking whether the saving or assets of IRA contributors are higher than, lower than, or the same as the saving or assets of noncontributors. Evidence based on this approach reveals that IRA contributors do not save less in other forms than noncontributors; in fact, they save a good deal more (see, e.g., Hubbard 1984).[3] Unfortunately, this finding conveys little about the extent to which IRAs displace other saving. Some households save a lot; some save little. The rates are presumably attributable to differences in preferences. Since the decision to contribute is endogenous, contributors probably consist of households with stronger preferences for saving. Therefore, one should not be surprised to discover that those who contribute to IRA accounts also save more in other forms than those who choose not to contribute.

In principle, one solution to this problem would be to identify some exogenous variation in IRA contributions that is unrelated to preferences toward saving. One could then use instrumental variables to estimate a specification explaining non-IRA saving or total saving as a function of IRA saving. Since eligibility was universal from 1982 to 1986, a potential source for this variation is difficult to imagine, let alone measure.

Rather than attempt to identify an instrumental variable, the literature has proceeded by reexamining the relation between IRA saving and non-IRA saving, controlling for initial wealth. This procedure is based on the assumption that two individuals with the same initial wealth must have the same underlying preferences toward saving; thus, the source of the spurious upward bias between IRA saving and total saving is supposedly removed. This approach has been followed in a study by Feenberg and Skinner (1989) and a series of studies by Venti and Wise (1986, 1990, 1991). Analysis of a variety of data sources (including the Michigan Tax Panel, the Survey of Consumer Finances, the Consumer Expenditure Surveys, and the Survey of Income and Program Participation) uniformly demonstrates that total saving is positively correlated with IRA saving, even controlling for initial wealth. The conditional correlation between IRA saving and non-IRA saving is typically nonnegative, which has been taken to indicate that IRA contributions are new wealth.

The central problem with this strategy is that initial wealth may be a relatively poor control for an individual's current underlying disposition toward saving. One problem is that wealth varies for reasons unrelated to tastes for saving (such as the receipt of unexpected inheritances). Another difficulty is that an individual's disposition to save may change through time due to fluctuations in income, household composition, perceived needs, or other factors; thus, the individual's disposition to save during any time period may differ from the dispositions that led to the accumulation of initial wealth at the start of the period. Even if wealth were perfectly correlated with the relevant aspects of tastes, it is well known that wealth is measured with a great deal of error. Any residual unobserved variation in the current inclination to save that is left after controlling for initial wealth will continue to bias the correlation between IRA saving and non-IRA saving upward: those who, for unobserved reasons, are inclined to save more overall will probably save more in both forms.

The underlying econometric justification for this procedure is also suspect. Suppose it were possible to control perfectly for all aspects of tastes that determine non-IRA saving. Even this would not allow one to calculate the extent to which IRA contributions displace other saving, unless there was some significant exogenous variation in IRA contributions independent of tastes for saving. But what is the source of this exogenous variation? Since eligibility was universal, it is hard to imagine any significant factor that would have affected IRA saving without also directly affecting non-IRA saving. And if there is no source of exogenous variation, it is difficult to see how the relation of interest could be identified.

In much of their work, Venti and Wise also place additional structure on the data. Specifically, they estimate the parameters of a model in which an individual maximizes a utility function defined over consumption, IRA saving, and non-IRA saving. The specification allows for a range of elasticities of substitution between the two forms of saving. Based on estimates of this model, Venti and Wise conclude that IRA contributions represented new saving, in the sense that they were funded almost entirely by reductions in consumption and income taxes.

The low estimates of the substitution parameter that emerge from estimation of the Venti-Wise model appear to be driven by two considerations. The first consideration is the nonnegative correlation between IRA saving and non-IRA saving, conditional on initial wealth (which appears in the Venti-Wise model through the budget constraint). For reasons that I have already discussed, this correlation is probably a poor barometer for the true degree of substitutability.

The second consideration has to do with a technical feature of the model. As formulated, the model implies that if IRA saving and non-IRA saving are perfect substitutes, then no individual would be willing to engage in non-IRA saving until reaching the IRA contribution limit. Since this prediction is manifestly false (many individuals who saved something did not contribute to IRAs), Venti and Wise's estimation strategy automatically guarantees the result that the two forms of saving are imperfect substitutes. This inference is unwarranted. Although it is evident that the IRA saving and non-IRA saving must not be perfect substitutes for savers who do not contribute to IRAs (perhaps due to differences in liquidity), it does not follow that these two forms of saving are poor substitutes for individuals who do contribute to IRAs. On the contrary, one could easily imagine that, among IRA contributors, IRA are quite good substitutes for other saving. This could occur if, for example, IRA contributors tend to save a lot in all forms and are therefore relatively unconcerned (on the margin) about liquidity.

Gale and Scholz (1994) estimate an alternative econometric model, in which they permit the parameters of the saving relation to vary according to whether an individual is an IRA contributor. This is intended to capture the possibility that those who do not contribute to IRAs may have different attitudes toward IRA and non-IRA saving than those who do contribute. In this way, Gale and Scholz avoid the automatic bias toward low substitution that is present in the analysis of Venti and Wise.

Intuitively, Gale and Scholz identify the degree of substitution between IRA and non-IRA saving as follows. Suppose we measure the marginal propensity to save (out of income) in IRAs ($MPS_{I,N}$), and the marginal propensity to save in other forms ($MPS_{O,N}$) for nonlimit contributors, as well as the marginal propensity to save in other forms ($MPS_{O,L}$) for limit contributors. If all IRA saving is new saving, then we should find $MPS_{O,L} = MPS_{O,N}$. One the other hand, if IRA saving simply displaces other saving dollar for dollar, we would expect to find $MPS_{O,L} = MPS_{O,N} + MPS_{I,N}$. On the basis of kind of comparison, Gale and Scholz conclude that a negligible fraction of IRA contributions represent new saving.

Gale and Scholz's analysis successfully demonstrates that the conclusions of Venti and Wise are highly sensitive to assumptions about the nature and distribution of unobserved preferences. This does not imply, however, that their particular procedure generates reliable estimates of the extent to which IRAs substitute for other forms of saving. On the contrary, this procedure probably has the effect of biasing their findings against the conclusion that IRAs represent new saving. The Gale-Sholz model is identified by the assumption that all IRA contributors have the same preferences toward saving, conditional on a list of covariates, regardless of whether they are limit contributors. This homogeneity assumption is distinctly odd in the light of the fact that their analysis is motivated by the observation that attitudes toward saving differ according to IRA participation status, even when conditioned on the same list of covariates. It is therefore natural to wonder whether this homogeneity assumption drives their results.

To understand the bias resulting from the Gale-Scholz homogeneity assumption, consider the following illustrative example. Suppose that there are three types of savers, with (respectively) low, medium, and high inclinations to save. Those with higher inclinations to save are assumed to have larger average and marginal saving propensities. Low savers never contribute to IRAs and are therefore of no further interest to us. As long as moderate savers are not constrained by the IRA contribution limit, they save five cents out of each dollar in IRAs and five cents in other forms. If they are constrained by the contribution limit, they still save five cents out of each dollar in other forms. As long as high savers are not constrained by the IRA contribution limit, they save ten cents out of each dollar in IRAs and ten cents in other forms. If they are constrained by the contribution limit, they still save ten cents out of each dollar in other forms. Our final assumption is that all moderate savers end up contributing less than the contribution limit, and all high savers turn out to be limit contributors.

Note that in this example, all IRA contributions represent new saving. However, applying the Gale-Scholz procedure, one would calculate that $MPS_{O,L} = 0.10 = 0.05 + 0.05 = MPS_{O,N} + MPS_{I,N}$, and infer incorrectly that IRA saving completely displaces other forms of saving. I have constructed this particular example to demonstrate that the bias could be quite large. Obviously hypothetical examples cannot establish the magnitude of the actual bias. However, the principle (and therefore the direction of the bias) generalizes: heterogeneity among those who contribute to IRAs typically implies that those who contribute more (and therefore have higher average propensities to save) will also tend to have higher marginal propensities to save. As a result, the data will appear to show that the marginal propensity to save in forms other than IRAs rises as contributions pass the allowable limit. But this is precisely the pattern that Gale and Scholz would interpret as evidence of displacement.

Some authors argue that correlations between IRA saving and non-IRA saving are particularly informative for new contributors. Using Survey of Income and Program Participation (SIPP) data from 1984 and 1985, Venti and Wise (1995) demonstrate that the inception of IRA contributions for a household does not coincide with a significant decline in other financial assets. They interpret this to mean that even new contributors engage in very little asset shifting to fund contributions and that these contributions must therefore represent new saving. Yet the observed patterns do not rule out the possibility that new contributors were simply new savers and that these new savers would have increased non-IRA savings in the absence of IRAs. Consequently, the evidence is consistent with significant asset shifting.

Attanasio and De Leire (1994) undertake a similar exercise but suggest that it is appropriate to evaluate the behavior of new contributors, treating old contributors as a control group. If new contributions come from consumption, then (it is argued) new contributors should exhibit slower consumption growth, and essentially the same growth in non-IRA assets, as old contributors. In contrast, if new contributions come from saving, then new contributors should exhibit the same growth in consumption but slower growth in non-IRA assets than old contributors. The authors implement this test using the Consumer Expenditure Surveys and find the second of these patterns. They conclude that IRA contributions primarily reflect asset reshuffling rather than new saving.

Unfortunately, there does not appear to be any compelling justification for using old IRA contributors as a control group. Without access to IRAs, new contributors might well have had higher consumption growth and slower growth of non-IRA assets than old contributors.[4] The availability of an IRA might then reduce the consumption growth of new contributors while leaving the growth of their non-IRA assets unaffected, thereby producing the observed pattern. Moreover, even if the control group were appropriate, the Attanasio–De Leire finding would at most establish that each household's initial IRA contributions are funded from asset shifting; it would be entirely consistent with the view that later IRA contributions reflect new saving.

Exogenous Changes in Eligibility

Another possible approach to mimicking the ideal experiment is to exploit the exogenous variation in IRA eligibility that existed prior to 1982 and after 1986. For example, one could imagine estimating a regression explaining non-IRA saving as a function of IRA contributions using eligibility as an instrument, or directly as a function of eligibility. There are two problems with this suggestion—one conceptual, the other practical. Conceptually a problem arises because, in contrast to the ideal experiment, IRA eligibility was nonrandom. Eligibility was triggered by the absence of pension coverage prior to 1982 and by a combination of pension coverage and AGI after 1986. Since both pension coverage and income are potentially important determinants of household saving, concerns about correlations with underlying preferences are still present. The practical problem arises because, with certain data sources, eligibility is difficult to assess. Information on pension coverage is sometimes unavailable, incomplete, or inaccurate, and one must extrapolate AGI from income.

The concern that IRA eligibility (prior to 1982 or after 1986) might have been correlated with preferences toward saving leads to a slightly more sophisticated suggestion. If the heterogeneity in preferences is captured by an individual-specific fixed effect, then it should be possible to eliminate this heterogeneity by differencing saving. One can then relate changes in saving to changes in eligibility, which differed across individuals in both 1982 and 1987. The impact of IRAs is then, in effect, inferred from differences in differences. For example, using panel data that cross 1982, one attempts to determine whether those who became eligible for IRAs increased their saving by more than those who remained eligible.

This is the general approach taken in Joines and Manegold (1995) and Engen, Gale, and Scholz (1994). Both studies make use of the Internal Reverive Service (IRS)–University of Michigan Tax Panel. Unfortunately, this data set contains no information on pension coverage and therefore provides no way to measure IRA eligibility prior to 1982. Of course, individuals who contributed to IRAs prior to 1982 must have been eligible. Joines and Manegold therefore propose using this as the control group. By defining the control group in this way, they tend to select individuals who have the highest predispositions to save among the eligible population. To counteract this selection effect, they use as their experimental group a sample of individuals who also contributed to IRAs (and therefore also have high predispositions to save) but who began to contribute after 1982.[5] Although this experimental group includes some individuals who were eligible prior to 1982, it also includes many who became eligible as of 1982. Therefore, allowable contributions increased on average by a larger amount for members of the experimental group than for members of the control group. Both studies nevertheless demonstrate that there is relatively little difference between the changes in saving across 1982 for the experimental and control groups. They conclude that IRAs had at most a moderate effect on saving (less than thirty cents on the dollar).

One difficulty encountered by Joines-Manegold and Engen-Gale-Scholz is that the IRS–University of Michigan Tax Panel does not contain measures of either saving or wealth. The authors are compelled to impute wealth from dividend and interest income. They then difference estimated wealth to obtain a measure of saving. This variable is the focus of their differences-in-differences analysis. Thus, their key results are based on third differences (twice across time and once across subgroups) of an imputed variable. One must seriously question how much "news" is left over after these operations. Not surprisingly, the key effects are generally estimated with large standard errors, and one typically cannot reject the hypothesis that a large fraction of IRA contributions represented new saving.

The selection criteria used to construct the control subgroup and the experimental subgroup are also potentially problematic. It is doubtful that these groups have comparable characteristics or similar dispositions to save. The differences-in-differences procedure is ostensibly designed to handle this problem, since it removes the fixed effect for each group. However, the validity of this solution depends critically on two assumption: that tastes enter the saving equation additively and that tastes do not affect the size of the response to a given change in the policy variable. In this context, the second assumption is objectionable.

To explore this point further, suppose that the saving of group i at time t is given by the following equation:

$$s_{i,t} = \mu_i + \alpha_t + \eta_i M_{it},$$

where μ_i and η_i are fixed group-specific coefficients, α_t is a time effect, and M_{it} is the IRA contribution limit applicable to this group. One would expect μ_i and η_i to be positively correlated, since higher savers are more likely to respond to an increase in the contribution limit. The differences-in-differences estimator is then

$$\Delta s_{et} - \Delta s_{ct} = [\eta_e \Delta M_{et} - \eta_c \Delta M_{ct}],$$

(where e indicates the experimental group and c indexes the control group). Note that one will correctly estimate the effect of the policy change on the experimental group as long as $\eta_e = \eta_c$ (if there is no heterogeneity in the response to a given change in policy) or if $\Delta M_{ct} = 0$ (the control group does not experience a change in the policy variable). In this instance, neither condition applies: it is likely that heterogeneity in preferences toward saving (as reflected in η_i) remains, and contribution limits were raised for the control group (albeit to a lesser extent than for the experimental group, so that $\Delta M_{et} > \Delta M_{ct} > 0$).

The resulting bias in the estimates depends on whether the control group is innately more inclined to save or less inclined to save than the experimental group. Suppose for the moment that the control group consists of particularly high savers, so that $\eta_c > \eta_e$. Then the sign of the differences-in-differences estimator becomes ambiguous, even if an increase in the contribution limit actually stimulates saving for both groups. To take an example, if a $2,000 increase in the contribution limit induces a $1,000 increase in the average IRA saving of the control group and a $250 increase in the average saving of the experimental group (because the control group largely consists of more highly motivated savers), then a $500 increase in the contribution limit for the control group (e.g., from

$1,500 to $2,000) and a $2,000 change in the contribution limit for the experimental group (e.g., for $0 to $2,000) will have the same total effect on saving ($250).

Unfortunately, with the available data, it is impossible to test whether the control group is more or less predisposed to undertake long-term saving than the experimental group. However, the following is suggestive. Prior to 1982, only a tiny fraction of those eligible for IRAs actually made contributions. Although these individuals had one characteristic that might be indicative of a predisposition for low saving (no employer pension), they were nevertheless a very highly selected subset of this population. This fact that they both discovered and took advantage of a little-known IRA provision suggests that they may have been exceptionally motivated to save for retirement. In contrast, since a much larger segment of the population contributed to IRAs after 1982 and since IRAs were more widely publicized, the experimental group may be less highly selected. If this is the case, then the differences-in-differences estimator understates the true effect on saving of an increase in the IRA limit. Of course, if the opposite proposition is true, then the differences-in-differences estimator overstates the effect.

As is well known, the differences-in-differences estimator may go awry for other reasons as well. One obvious possibility is that other changes in the economic environment may have affected the two groups differently. Since the changes in IRA eligibility were accompanied by other significant tax changes, as well as a variety of important macroeconomic developments (including large changes in inflation and interest rates, as well as business cycle effects), attributing the difference-in-difference of saving exclusively to relative changes in IRA eligibility is dicey.

Finally, it is important to realize that under some of the behavioral alternatives to the LCH, the procedure Joines-Manegold and Engen-Gale-Scholz used would be incapable of detecting certain kinds of links between IRAs on personal saving. Suppose, for example, that the expansion of the IRA program stimulated saving by raising awareness of retirement issues and triggering aggressive promotion of investment vehicles. If these developments affected members of the control group and the experimental group equally, the differences-in-differences estimator would falsely indicate no increases in saving.

Evidence of Psychological Effects

The chain of logical reasoning that leads one to doubt the efficacy of IRAs is largely predicated on the view that saving is a consequence of rational and deliberate life cycle planning. It is therefore possible to shed light on the key issue be asking whether other aspects of individuals' responses to IRAs are consistent with the predictions of standard life cycle theory. If they are not consistent, then one should be very cautious about drawing inferences concerning the efficacy of IRAs from anything but the most direct evidence.

The literature identifies a number of patterns in IRA contributions that appear to be anomalous from the perspective of the standard model. Four are particularly provocative.

First, it is difficult to account for the explosion of IRAs after 1982 and the collapse of IRA contributions after 1986, unless one credits the role of visibility and promotion (Long 1990; Venti and Wise 1992). Recall that only 1 percent of taxpayers made contributions to IRAs prior to 1982, despite the fact that roughly half were eligible to contribute up to $1,500. This figure rose to 15 percent by 1986. Recall also that many individuals remained eligible to make deductible IRA contributions after 1986 (those with sufficiently low AGIs or without pension coverage); moreover, all other individuals could still make nondeductible contributions and benefit from tax-free accumulation. Yet the fraction of taxpayers contributing to IRAs dropped to 4 percent by 1990. IRA contributions followed promotional activity (which exploded after 1982 and contracted after 1986) much more closely than actual economic incentives.[6]

Second, there has been a pronounced tendency for individuals to delay their IRA contributions until the end of a tax year (Summers 1986). This is puzzling because minimization of tax liabilities requires taxpayers to make these contributions as early as possible. To some extent, the tendency to delay contributions may result from the desire to maintain liquidity throughout the tax year (Engen, Gale, and Scholz 1994). But even allowing for the potential importance of liquidity, it is difficult to explain why more IRA contributors (particularly those with significant non-IRA assets) do not at least make a series of smaller contributions during the course of the tax year (Bernheim 1994b).

Third, individuals are significantly more likely to make IRA contributions if they owe the IRS money at the end of the tax year. Feenberg and Skinner (1989) interpret this as an indication that, psychologically, individuals would rather write a check to an IRA account than write a somewhat smaller check to the IRS. Conceivably this result could reflect spurious correlations of both underwithholding and IRA contributions with some third factor, such as income, tax filing status, or asset holding

(Gravelle 1991). However, the pattern is apparent even when Feenberg and Skinner include plausible controls for these factors.

Fourth, there is considerable evidence of focal point saving. Engen, Gale, and Scholz (1994) find that among those who could have contributed more than $2,000 but contributed less than the limit, 47 percent contributed exactly $2,000. This finding invites the interpretation that the well-publicized, "officially endorsed" $2,000 figure created a focal target for saving and that the very existence of this target may have influenced the behavior of many less serious savers (such as those contributing less than the limit).

One alternative explanation for this phenomenon concerns transactions costs. While single-earner married couples could contribute up to $2,250 per year, contributions in excess of $2,000 would have required them to open a second account. A contribution of $250 might seem insufficient to justify the effort. However, it is important to bear in mind that the one-time costs of opening the account must be weighed not against the benefits of a single $250 contribution but rather against the benefits of a $250 contribution that recurs for many year. Moreover, even among those with a $4,000 limit, 38 percent of those contributing less than the limit contributed exactly $2,000. The transactions cost hypothesis is therefore implausible.

Others have argued that the focal point saving phenomenon results from bargaining among spouses with conflicting objectives (Burman, Cordes, and Ozanne 1990). Yet it is hard to see how this would emerge in a formal model of household bargaining, without the introduction of significant transactions costs.

In summary, much of the evidence on IRA contribution patterns remains anomalous. This evidence raises serious concerns about the validity of logical inferences and statistical analyses predicated on the assumption that IRA contributions were motivated entirely by rational and deliberate life cycle planning.

401(k)s

Employers were originally authorized to establish 401(k) plans in 1978, but this option remained unpopular until after the Treasury issued clarifying regulations in 1981. In many ways, 401(k)s are similar to IRAs: contributions are tax deductible up to specified limits, the returns to investments are accumulated tax free, and there are restrictions on early withdrawals. There are also a variety of differences. A number of these differences lead one to suspect that 401(k)s might be more effective at stimulating personal saving than IRAs. Since contribution limits are much higher, they are less likely to bind. As a result, 401(k)s can increase the marginal after-tax rate of return for a much larger set of households. This effect is often reinforced through provisions whereby employers match employee contributions. The structure of a 401(k) plan also capitalizes more effectively on the psychology of saving. Since contributions occur through regular payroll deductions rather than through discretionary deposits, 401(k)s are more conducive to the exercise of self-discipline. Higher contribution limits may also provide authoritative validation for higher saving targets. Since 401(k)s are organized around the workplace, they may also create positive spillovers between employees (e.g., through conversations among employees and other peer group effects).

Form the perspective of econometric modeling, one of the most salient differences between IRAs and 401(k)s is that eligibility for 401(k)s is determined at the level of the employer. This has two implications. First, at all points in time there is substantial variation in 401(k) eligibility across households. Second, at least some of the variation in eligibility (and therefore in contributions) arises from sources that are plausibly exogenous to the individual. These considerations make it easier in principle to identify the effects of 401(k)s.

Studying 401(k)s in practice, however, is made considerably more difficult by the relative scarcity of good data. For example, none of the available waves of the Survey of Consumer Finances contains a clean measure of 401(k) eligibility. Of the standard public use data sources, only the SIPP contains good information on eligibility, participation, and asset balances for 401(k)s. Unfortunately, the SIPP does not provide longitudinal information that is useful for studying these plans. The literature has therefore treated the SIPP as a series of three cross-sections (1984, 1987, and 1991). An additional limitation of these data is that 401(k) plan balances were not available in 1984. Taken together, these limitations seriously handicap efforts to measure the behavioral effects of 401(k)s. Nevertheless, the literature has developed and explored two separate estimation strategies that attempt to finesse these limitations.

Exploiting Exogenous Variation in Eligibility

Imagine for the moment that each organization's decision to offer a 401(k) is completely random. Then 401(k)s would provide the perfect experimental setting for studying the effects of saving incentives. Eligibility is certainly not random, since it is demonstrably correlated with a variety of individual characteristics (such as income). But as long as variation in 401(k) eligibility is orthogonal to the unobserved individual characteristics that determine saving, the experiment is still a clean one.

Poterba, Venti, and Wise (1994, 1995) proceed from the assumption that 401(k) eligibility is exogenous to the process that determines saving. Using the 1987 and 1991 waves of the SIPP, they demonstrate that, controlling for other relevant factors, eligibility is significantly correlated with financial wealth. Indeed, eligibility has very little effect on non-401(k) financial wealth. They interpret this finding as an indication that virtually all 401(k) contributions represented new saving.

The central problem with this procedure is that 401(k) eligibility is probably not exogenous. On the contrary, there are several reasons to suspect that eligibility would be significantly correlated with the underlying predisposition to save (Bernheim 1994c; Engen, Gale, and Scholz 1994). First, employees with tastes for saving probably tend to gravitate toward jobs that provide good pension coverage, including 401(k)s. Second, employers frequently install 401(k) plans as a direct response to expressions of employee interest (Buck Consultants 1989).

Poterba, Venti, and Wise themselves provide convincing evidence of endogeneity. A careful reading of their tables reveals that differences in median financial assets between eligibles and noneligibles are often several times as large as 401(k) balances for eligibles (see also Engen, Gale, and Scholz 1994). Using a more recent cross-sectional household survey sponsored by Merrill Lynch, Bernheim and Garrett (1995) corroborate this finding. Thus, unless one believes that 401(k)s crowd in other forms of saving at the rate of four or five to one, the evidence must be construed as indicating that eligibility is strongly correlated with the innate inclination to save.

As in the case of IRAs, one could, in principle, attempt to control for the effects of tastes by estimating an equation explaining flow saving as a function of 401(k) eligibility, controlling for initial wealth. This approach would be far more coherent in the current setting: since there are identifiable, exogenous sources of variation in 401(k) eligibility, purging 401(k) eligibility of endogenous influences is actually a sensible objective.

Although the inclusion of wealth as an explanatory variable would not eliminate bias in the estimated coefficient of 401(k) eligibility, the direction of the bias would no longer be obvious. To understand this point, consider the partial correlation between eligibility and flow saving, controlling for initial wealth. Imagine two individuals who are the same in all observable respects (including initial wealth), except that one is eligible for a 401(k), and the other is not. Suppose for the moment that 401(k)s actually stimulate saving to some unknown extent. It is very likely (due to the presence of high serial correlation in eligibility) that the eligible individual was also eligible in past years. Thus, without eligibility, this individual's initial wealth would have been lower than that of the individual who is ineligible. The implications of this deduction are striking: under identical conditions (including eligibility), the eligible individual would have accumulated less wealth than the ineligible individual. This suggests that the ineligible individual is more inclined to save (given the observation that initial wealth is the same). If so, then assuming that 401(k)s stimulate saving, the estimated coefficient of eligibility would be biased downward. The same argument implies that if 401(k)s reduce saving, the estimated coefficient would have an upward bias; however, this is not particularly worrisome, since the primary focus of controversy concerning 401(k)s is the size of the effect rather than the direction.

In practice, the direction of the bias associated with the proposed estimation strategy is less clear-cut. The force of the argument in the preceding paragraph lessens if wealth varies for exogenous reasons (e.g., possibly the ineligible individual had the same initial wealth only because he or she had received an unexpected inheritance). In the extreme, if measured wealth is pure noise, controlling for wealth obviously cannot purge eligibility of endogenous variation. Nevertheless, evidence of this kind adds one more piece to the puzzle.

Bernheim and Garrett (1995) implement this strategy using the Merrill Lynch household survey data, which contain self-reported measures of flow saving (expressed as fractions of income), as well as categories of wealth. They find that 401(k) eligibility is associated with an increase in the retirement saving rate that exceeds the corresponding increase in the overall rate of saving. Thus, the use of wealth as a control for differences in tastes eliminates the anomalous finding that 401(k)s crowd in other forms of saving at an implausibly high rate. Unfortunately, their study does not permit drawing reliable inferences concerning the degree of crowding out.

Exploiting Transitional Effects

A second approach to measuring the effects of 401(k)s does not require assuming that eligibility is exogenous. Instead, this approach exploits the fact that the legislative authorization for 401(k)s was relatively recent. To understand this approach, first imagine two idealized worlds: one in which 401(k)s have always been available and one in which 401(k)s have never been available. Suppose for simplicity that each economy has converged to a steady state with a stable age-wealth profile. This profile may well be higher for the world in which 401(k)s have always been available, but this does not necessarily indicate that 401(k)s stimulate saving, since there may be other differences (such as tastes) between the two worlds. Now imagine a world in which 401(k)s have never been available in the past (so that this economy has also converged to a steady-state age-wealth profile) but where they are established unexpectedly at some point (without any change in tastes). At that point, each individual departs from his or her initial wealth trajectory and begins to move along some new wealth trajectory. Eventually the age-wealth profile will converge to a new steady state. But during the transition period, if 401(k)s stimulate saving, this profile should begin to shift upward relative to the profile from any world in which eligibility is unchanged.

In the ideal implementation of this strategy, one would identify a large group of workers who became eligible for 401(k)s relatively soon after the enabling legislation (say, before 1984) and remained eligible in all subsequent years, as well as a large group of workers who never became eligible. One would then follow these same individuals through time, estimating age-wealth profiles for each group every year. The relative amplitudes of these profiles in any particular year would prove nothing, since eligibility may be related to preferences. However, as time passes, the number of years of accumulated eligibility for the first group increases. Therefore, the cross-sectional age-wealth profiles for the eligible group should shift upward relative to the profile of the ineligible group.

Unfortunately, good panel data on 401(k)s are not available. Poterba, Venti, and Wise (1995) therefore implement this strategy for a series of cross-sections (1984, 1987, 1991) obtained from the SIPP. In each year, they compare the accumulated financial assets of those who are eligible for 401(k)s and those who are not eligible. The data unmistakably show the predicted upward shift in relative financial assets held by those who are eligible for 401(k)s. Indeed, there is no noticeable decline in the relative level of non-401(k) financial assets held by this group. This finding supports the hypothesis that individuals funded 401(k) contributions through a combination of reduced taxes and spending, not by diverting funds that they would have saved in any event.

Of course, Poterba, Venti, and Wise depart from the ideal strategy by using an unrelated sequence of cross-sections. It is important to consider how this deviation is likely to affect their results. If successive cross-sections of eligibles (and ineligibles) are simply random draws from the same population of eligibles (ineligibles), then there is no problem. A problem arises only if the composition of the population of eligibles (ineligibles) changes systematically through time.

It is virtually certain that some compositional changes occurred between the successive surveys used by Poterba, Venti, and Wise for the simple reason that new workers became eligible. One obvious implication is that as one moves forward in time by, say, four years, the average length of exposure to 401(k)s within the eligible population increases by less than four years. One can imagine cases in which this could create problem. For example, if 401(k)s pass through a period of sufficiently rapid growth, the average length of eligibility among eligibles could actually decline. Under more plausible assumptions, however, the effect would simply be to slow the observed rate at which the assets profile of the eligible population shifts relative to the profile of the ineligible population. The underlying logic of the exercise remains valid, as long as newly eligible workers are drawn from the same population as those who have been eligible for longer periods.

A serious issue arises because newly eligible workers are probably systematically different from those who have been eligible for longer periods. Eligibility for 401(k)s is almost certainly endogenous. It stands to reason that the most motivated, serious savers would have sought out employers who offered 401(k)s or encouraged their existing employers to provide 401(k)s, relatively soon after these plans became available. Less motivated, occasional savers would have been less likely to seek out or agitate for 401(k)s and more likely to drift into these plants slowly through time. Thus, as time passes, the eligible population becomes increasingly skewed toward less motivated savers. Bernheim (1994b) refers to this as the dilution effect. It is likely that the dilution effect became more severe after 1986, when more demanding nondiscrimination requirements were established for private pensions.

Dilution almost certainly biases the findings of Poterba, Venti, and Wise; however, the direction of the bias is critical. Since dilution creates a downward shift in the age-wealth profile, it has the potential to offset partially or completely or even reverse the upward shift due to the behavioral effect of 401(k)s. To see that this is more than a theoretical possibility, one can examine changes through time in the relations between 401(k) eligibility and variables that provide stable proxies for underlying tastes. One plausible proxy for the predisposition to save is ownership of an IRA. It is doubtful that this taste proxy is stable for the period of universal IRA eligibility (prior to 1987), since dilution probably affected the set of IRA participants in the same way that it affected the set of 401(k) participants. However, dilution of the IRA population probably declined significantly once eligibility for IRAs was restricted. It is therefore plausible that IRA ownership is a stable taste proxy for the 1987–1991 period. Notably, the fraction of individuals eligible for 401(k)s who owned IRAs declined significantly (relative to ineligibles) between 1987 and 1991, a good indication of the dilution effect.[7] Moreover, when one controls for IRA ownership, there is even stronger evidence that the financial asset profiles of eligible workers shift upward after 1987 (Poterba, Venti, and Wise 1995, 1996; Engen and Gale 1995). Thus, Poterba, Venti, and Wise may understate the extent to which 401(k)s stimulate saving.

Engen, Gale, and Scholz (1994) criticize Poterba, Venti, and Wise on the grounds that the eligible population differs significantly from the ineligible population. Although the conceptual framework of Poterba, Venti, and Wise allows for this possibility, the concern is nevertheless legitimate. To the extent the two groups are not comparable, their age-wealth profiles may have been shifting relative to each other for reasons that are entirely unrelated to 401(k)s. Although this does not provide a reason to believe that the findings of Poterba, Venti, and Wise are biased in any particular direction, it does reduce one's confidence in the validity of their results.

Engen, Gale, and Scholz propose and implement an estimation strategy that uses different experimental and control groups. Specifically, they restrict attention to 401(k) participants and compare them to individuals with IRAs who are ineligible for 401(k)s. The purpose of this strategy is to isolate groups of high savers who are more closely comparable than three groups considered by Poterba, Venti, and Wise. Although the authors do not present convincing evidence on the relative degree of comparability, their argument has at least the right of plausibility.[8] Since eligibility for IRA contributions was restricted in 1986, it is also argued that one would still expect to see an upward shift in the relative assets of 401(k) participants, provided that 401(k)s are effective. On the contrary, the authors find that the total financial assets of 401(k) participants actually declined between 1987 and 1991, whereas the total financial assets of the control populations actually increased. They interpret this as an indication that 401(k)s did not increase personal saving.

It is important to realize, however, that the approach Engen, Gale, and Scholz favor still suffers from the dilution problem and therefore is biased against the finding that 401(k)s stimulated personal saving. It is also apparent that by changing the selection criteria used to define the samples, the authors have probably altered the extent of dilution for the control group and the extent of reverse dilution for the experimental group (Bernheim 1994b). Therefore, one should not be too surprised that their findings differ from those of Poterba, Venti, and Wise.

The primary merits and drawbacks of these studies can be summarized succinctly as follows. Poterba, Venti, and Wise estimate that 401(k)s have a large effect on personal saving, and there is at least one good reason to believe that their estimate is biased downward.[9] Confidence in this result is limited by concerns about the comparability of the experimental and control groups. There is, however, no reason to believe that noncomparability biases their result in any particular direction, and the results are robust with respect to some efforts to improve comparability (controlling for IRA status). Engen, Gale, and Scholz estimate that 401(k)s have essentially no effect on personal saving. Their experimental and control groups are probably more closely comparable that 401(k) eligibles and ineligibles. However, there is at least one good reason to believe that their estimate is biased downward, and there is no reason to suspect that the magnitude of the bias is similar to that encountered by Poterba, Venti, and Wise.

It is noteworthy that the preceding discussion focuses almost entirely on financial assets. This is a limitation, since it is conceivable that 401(k)s may displace other forms of wealth as well. Engen, Gale, and Scholz present estimates based on broaded measures of wealth, and these exhibit similar patterns. In contrast, Poterba, Venti, and Wise focus exclusively on financial wealth. It is therefore natural to wonder whether the inclusion of other forms of wealth would undermine their conclusion.

Engen and Gale (1995) attempt to replicate the analysis of Poterba, Venti, and Wise, while at the same time extending it to broader measures of wealth. Alert to the dilution problem, they attempt to control for unobserved preferences by including a measure of IRA participation status. Their results indicate that mortgages grew and home equity fell in successive cross-sections (1987 and 1991) for the 401(k)-eligible population (both IRA participants and IRA nonparticipants), resulting in smaller overall wealth growth than for the control groups. They interpret this finding as an indication that 401(k) saving was offset almost completely by larger mortgages.

One difficulty with this interpretation of the Engen-Gale findings is that their results for total wealth are extremely imprecise. Typically they cannot rule out (at conventional level of confidence) the possibility that 401(k)s contributed significantly to total wealth accumulation. This raises the possibility that their finding might not be robust. In fact, Poterba, Venti, and Wise (1996) find exactly the opposite pattern when comparing 1984 and 1986. Conceivably some of the difficulties here could be linked to data problems, in which case the focus on financial wealth would be justified.

More important, Engen and Gale do not solve the dilution problem by controlling for IRA status. The trend in the probability that the typical 401(k) worker owns an IRA is properly regarded as a symptom of dilution rather than as the source of the underlying problem (Bernheim 1994b). It is highly unlikely that this single binary variable adequately controls for the full variation of preferences toward saving among eligibles and ineligibles. Because of the residual bias, the procedure is informative only as a one-tailed test: if the results indicate that 401(k)s stimulate saving *despite* dilution, then one can safely infer something about behavior; however, if the results indicate that 401(k)s do not stimulate saving, one cannot rule out the possibility that dilution has obscured a significant behavioral effect.

Engen and Gale attempt to bolster their contention that no dilution remains after controlling for IRA status by pointing to evidence on home values. Specifically they note that, conditional on IRA status, home values rose by virtually identical amounts for those eligible for 401(k)s and for those not eligible (in both cases, there was a small increase). It is, however, difficult to understand why this constitutes evidence against dilution. Homes are not like other assets, in that home ownership has an important consumption component, as well as an investment component. Those who are less inclined to save may stretch to buy larger homes and finance these purchases through greater leverage. Consequently, when Engen and Gale find no evidence of a decline in home values coupled with a 17.9 percent increase in median leverage for the 401(k) samples, it is entirely natural to construe this as further evidence of dilution.

Engen and Gale also defend their interpretation of the evidence by pointing out that the age-wealth profiles of 401(k)-eligible renters did not shift up relative to those of ineligible renters during the 1980s. Thus, according to Engen and Gale, there is no evidence that 401(k)s contribute to personal saving once one purges the sample of observations for which housing wealth is a potential contaminant. Although the results for renters are thought-provoking, their proper interpretation is unclear. Renters as a whole are a peculiar group in that they save practically nothing to begin with (Congressional Budget Office 1993). Those who are eligible for 401(k)s do accumulate significant financial assets (though significantly less than comparable home owners); however, the median net worth of those who are not eligible for 401(k)s is near zero. These observations have two implications. First, the sample of eligible renters appears to be more highly selected than the sample of eligible home owners. As a result, eligibility for 401(k)s may be more strongly related to underlying tastes among renters than among home owners. Sample selection biases and the associated effects of dilution should therefore play out differently in the two samples. It would not be surprising if eligible renters, being more highly selected to begin with, were subject to greater dilution with the passage of time. This would account for the Engen-Gale finding. Second, sample selection issues aside, the absence of significant wealth among ineligible renters can potentially invalidate the methodology used to draw inferences about the effects of 401(k)s. If economic forces were tending to depress saving by renters during the relevant time period, then the absence of a downward shift in the age-wealth profile for eligible renters would indicate that 401(k)s stimulated saving by this group. In theory, the Engen-Gale procedure would detect this by noting a downward shift in the age-wealth profile for ineligible renters. However, in practice, liquidity constraints would have prevented this downward shift from occurring.

It is apparent from this discussion that the evidence presented by Engen and Gale does not discriminate between the hypothesis that 401(k) accumulation displaced net housing wealth (primarily through larger mortgages) and the hypothesis that 401(k) contributions represented new saving. Other information, however, casts doubt on Engen and Gale's interpretation of this evidence.

To begin with, it is readily apparent that most individuals view and treat housing equity as a highly imperfect substitute for financial assets. In the past, retirees have proved extremely reluctant to downsize their homes or take reverse annuity mortgages for the purposes of using their home equity to finance normal living expenses during retirement (Venti and Wise 1989). Among younger workers (who are supposedly doing the substitution), roughly 60 percent say that they view their home equity primarily as a source of financial security, to be used in retirement only in the event of a major emergency (such as entering a nursing home); roughly 23 percent say that they think of it primarily as a method of passing wealth to their children through bequests; and only 14 percent say that they think of it primarily as a store of wealth of finance ordinary living expenses during retirement (Bernheim 1995a).

Another reason to doubt Engen and Gale's interpretation of the evidence on housing wealth is that 401(k) contributions are largely voluntary. We are asked to imagine that individuals choose to save through 401(k)s, only to undo this saving by borrowing more against their homes. One must wonder why these individuals would voluntarily undertake offsetting transactions.

One possibility is that 401(k) contributors rationally expect to benefit from tax arbitrage, borrowing at the posttax rate and investing at the pretax rate. However, further reflection suggests that efforts to conduct arbitrage might well prove unprofitable. It is not at all obvious that the appropriately risk-compensated rate of return on 401(k) investments exceeds the after-tax cost of borrowing on mortgages (which, aside from variations in the rate of inflation, are essentially riskless from the point of view of the borrower). Moreover, many strategies for borrowing against one's home (first mortgages, second mortgages, and refinancing) are inherently lumpy, whereas 401(k) contributions are generally made in rather smooth flows. If an individual used one of these devices to fund 401(k) contributions, he or she would be compelled to hold a substantial portion of the mortgage proceeds outside of the 401(k) for a significant period of time, earning the after-tax rate of return (which is certainly well below the after-tax cost of borrowing). It might be possible to avoid this problem through a home equity line of credit, which would allow the home owner to increase the size of his or her mortgage gradually. But the interest rates on home equity lines of credit are much higher than the rates on ordinary mortgages and may well exceed the appropriately risk-compensated, pretax rates of return on investments, even allowing for deductibility of mortgage payments.

The potential gains from arbitrage activities are certainly increased in the presence of employer-matching provisions. However, if this is an important motivation for 401(k) contributors, then we would expect to observe a strong positive relation between contributions and matching rates. On the contrary, there is little evidence that such a relation exists.

A second possibility is that 401(k) contributors irrationally expect to benefit from tax arbitrage. Although this is certainly conceivable as a matter of principle, the most obvious versions of the irrationality hypothesis are contradicted by the data. Suppose that individuals fail to understand the risks associated with equity investments and mistakenly compare the after-tax costs of borrowing with the pretax rate of return on the stock market. If this were the case, then one would expect 401(k) contributors to invest their plan balances heavily in equities. On the contrary, participants have tended to invest much more heavily in safe, fixed income securities, particularly during the period in question (see, e.g., Arthur D. Little 1993).

A third possibility is that myopic behavior leads 401(k) participants to take out larger mortgages. To illustrate this possibility, imagine that 401(k) contributors save less as renters, not because they rationally substitute one form of saving for another but because they have less disposable income. When these individuals begin to think about purchasing a home, they will have less money for a down payment. Conceivably they might buy the same house as in the absence of a 401(k) and take out a larger mortgage. This would produce a pattern of 401(k)-mortgage substitution, even if no arbitrage was intended. However, since it is quite common for households to borrow as much as possible against their first homes, one would also expect the reduction in resources available for down payments to induce many households to purchase smaller homes or to delay home purchase. One would then observe a downward shift in home values among eligibles, relative to ineligibles. But Engen and Gale's findings are inconsistent with this prediction.

A final reason to doubt Engen and Gale's interpretation of the evidence on housing wealth concerns the level of mortgage activity. Engen and Gale's figures show that as of 1991, only a little more than 14 percent of those eligible for 401(k)s had home equity loans. Based on other data in their paper, I would estimate that roughly 12 percent of those eligible for 401(k)s in 1991 extracted equity from their homes through refinancing during the previous four years.[10] According to Gale (private communication), 19 percent of those eligible for 401(k)s in 1991 purchased primary homes between 1987 and 1991. Given the likelihood of overlap between these groups, it is extremely doubtful that more than 30 to 40 percent of those eligible for 401(k)s behaved in ways that would have permitted them to extract any equity from their homes between 1987 and 1991.[11]

In the light of this discussion, it seems unlikely—though certainly not impossible—that the Engen-Gale results are attributable to substitution between 401(k)s and home mortgages. A more likely explanation is that 401(k)s increased personal saving significantly, and the apparent increase in mortgage debt reflects the effect of residual dilution. Confidence in this conclusion is, however, qualified by the continuing concern about the comparability of the experimental and control groups.

Other Evidence

In this section, I briefly touch on some additional sources of evidence on the efficacy of tax-favored savings accounts that do not specifically concern either IRAs or 401(k)s.

Comparisons Across Countries

The generosity of the incentives embodied in tax-favored savings accounts differs significantly across countries. It is doubtful that one could learn much from simple cross-country correlations between tax incentives and saving, since such correlations may exist for spurious reasons (e.g., people who like to save support tax systems that favor saving). However, if different countries implemented their tax incentives at different points in time, one might hope to learn something about the effect of tax incentives by examining whether the saving rates of different countries converged or diverged when incentives were introduced.

In this spirit, Carroll and Summers (1987) compare historical rates of saving for Canada and the United States. They demonstrate that these rates diverged when Canada expanded its system of Registered Retirement Saving Plans (RRSPs) during the mid-1970s. Although this pattern is interesting, an inference of causality requires an unusually large leap of faith, particularly since there are other possible explanations for the increase in Canadian saving during this period. Moreover, the adoption of tax incentives in the United States did not result in measurable convergence between the two countries.

Comparisons Across Cohorts

I have already discussed the manner in which transitional phenomena generated by the relative novelty of 401(k)s have been used to assess their effects. More generally, one could regard the 1980s as a grand experiment with several different types of tax-favored accounts and ask whether these accounts had the effect of shifting up the age-wealth profiles of entire cohorts. To take an example, if tax incentives were effective, then the typical individual reaching age sixty-five in, say, 1991 should have had more wealth than the typical individual reaching retirement in, say, 1984 (due to differences in years of eligibility for tax-favored saving).

Venti and Wise (1993) examine this hypothesis. Their analysis, which primarily relies on the SIPP, documents a substantial upward shift in financial asset profiles. More recent cohorts have greater wealth at the same ages as older cohorts, and the difference is roughly equal to accumulated balances in 401(k)s and IRAs. Although these patterns are interesting, it requires an unusually large leap of faith to ascribe all differences in saving between cohorts to tax incentives. The same pattern could emerge if, for example, younger cohorts are wealthier on a lifetime basis.

Simulations

The available evidence on 401(k)s and IRAs sheds some light on the relatively short-run effects of saving incentives. The long-run effects of these programs may differ significantly from their short-run effects. Conceivably, for example, contributions to these accounts could increasingly reflect net additions to saving with the passage of time as more households exhaust their ability to shift assets from other sources.

Unfortunately, since IRAs and 401(k)s were introduced in the relatively recent past, it is impossible to estimate their long-run effects empirically. One alternative is to build simulation models (Engen and Gale 1993; Engen, Gale, and Scholz 1994). The available simulations do indicate that tax incentives may have a substantial, positive influence on the long-run capital stock, even when the short-run response is dominated by asset shifting. However, simulation results do not constitute empirical evidence, and the simulations are only as good as the assumptions on which they are based. These assumptions generally include rational, far-sighted, and deliberate decision making in a complex environment with considerable uncertainly. It is dangerous and potentially misleading to adopt these assumptions unquestioningly, without exploring the implications of alternatives.

7.4 Indirect Third-Party Responses to Tax Incentives

Even if the interest elasticity of saving is low and households do not alter their behavior very much as a direct consequence of targeted tax incentives for saving, it might still be possible to influence personal saving through tax policy. I have argued that nonneutralities in the tax system may encourage various kinds of third-party activities that have the potential to affect the level of personal saving. Specifically, nonneutralities may encourage employers to adopt various kinds of pension plans or to substitute one kind of plan for another, and may influence the activities of employers in the context of these plans. The tax system may also create incentives for the vendors of tax-favored financial vehicles to market and otherwise promote their products.

Size and Scope of the Pension System

Since pensions provide a tax-favored mechanism for compensating employees, tax policy may have played an important role in stimulating the development of the pension system. To assess the ultimate impact on personal saving, one must answer two questions. First, to what extent is the size and scope of the pension system responsive to changes in tax rates? Second, to what degree does pension saving displace other forms of personal saving?

Incentives for Pension Saving

It is indisputable that there is a substantial tax incentive for pension formation. Ippolito (1986) estimates that the optimum exploitation of opportunities to defer compensation through pensions can reduce lifetime tax liabilities by 20 to 40 percent. However, this does not imply that the growth of the pension system is exclusively or even primarily attributable to the tax system. Pensions may enhance the productivity of the workforce in a variety of ways. They may bond the workforce against union activity, voluntary job turnover, or poor job performance.[12] Employers may use defined benefit plans to induce a desired pattern of retirement.[13] Mandatory pensions may also provide an effective device for overcoming the problems with adverse selection that characterize the market for private annuities.[14] Thus, it is conceivable that an extensive private pension system would exist even in the absence of tax incentives.

The evidence on the relative importance of these factors is sketchy at best.[15] The existing literature does not allow one reliably to infer the elasticity of pension coverage with respect to the magnitude of the tax breaks granted to pension plans.[16] I am therefore inclined to agree with Parson's (1995) conclusion that the quantitative importance of tax considerations and efficiency considerations remains unknown. However, it is difficult to account for observed behavior unless one attributes an important (though perhaps not preeminent) role to tax policy.

Do Pensions Crowd Out Other Personal Saving?

The extent to which pensions displace other forms of personal saving probably depends on the characteristics of the pension. For our purposes, it is important to distinguish between employer-controlled pensions that provide the employee with no choice concerning the level of participation and participant-controlled plans, such as 401(k)s, that permit the employee to determine contributions. I have already discussed the evidence on the extent to which contributions to participant-controlled plans crowd out other personal saving. Consequently, here I focus on employer-controlled plans.

The literature contains more than a dozen studies that attempt to measure the degree of substitutability between pensions and other saving. The usual approach is to estimate a cross-sectional relation between either saving or wealth and some measure of pension coverage. The two earliest studies on this topic (Cagan 1965; Katona 1965) conclude that pensions actually crowd *in* other forms of saving. Cagan rationalizes this finding by arguing that pensions induce workers to recognize the need for retirement planning; Cagan suggests that individuals may intensify their efforts to provide adequately for retirement because a pension renders this objective more feasible. Several subsequent studies corroborate the Cagan-Katona finding (Schoeplein 1970; Green 1981; Venti and Wise 1993; Bernheim and Scholz 1993a). More commonly, investigators have found either no effect, or a small effect (Munnell 1974; Kotlikoff 1979; Blinder, Gordon, and Wise 1980; King and Dicks-Mireaux 1982; Diamond and Hausman 1984; Hubbard 1986; Wolff 1988; Samwick 1995). Only a few studies have found substantial rates of crowding out (Munnell 1976; Dicks-Mireaux and King 1984; Avery, Elliehausen, and Gustafson 1986; Gale 1995), and most of these provide ranges of estimates that include relatively small effects. There is also some evidence that the rate of displacement rises with education (Bernheim and Scholz 1993b; Gale 1995).

Although there are many methodological concerns that bear on the reliability (both absolutely and relatively) of these various studies, three issues stand out as particularly salient. The first concerns the possibility that pension coverage is correlated with underlying tastes for saving. In contrast to the literature on 401(k)s, no study has come to grips with this issue. The direction of the resulting bias is ambiguous.[17] The second issue concerns the measurement of compensation. For the most part, the studies listed above control for income rather than total compensation (which would include the accrual of pension wealth). If the creation of a pension typically entails a shift in the form of compensation rather than incremental compensation, then this practice does not yield the appropriate displacement rate. Bernheim and Scholz (1993a) and Gale (1995) propose different solutions to this problem and obtain very different results. The final issue concerns the definition of wealth. Although one can point to a number of exceptions, there is some tendency, as in the 401(k) literature, to find higher rates of displacement when one uses a broader measure of wealth.

Although the extent of crowding out is not a settled issue, one is hard pressed to find convincing support in any study for the hypothesis that the rate of displacement is dollar for dollar. Indeed, there appears to be a significant likelihood that the true offset is much smaller. The importance of this finding becomes obvious when one considers that between 1980 and 1990, pension assets accounted for significantly more than 100 percent of the real change in national wealth (Shoven 1991). Thus, the effect of tax incentives on saving through the stimulation (or retardation) of pensions may be substantial, even if the rate of displacement is relatively low. This observation should give pause to those who favor the elimination of existing tax advantages for employer-controlled pensions, as well as those who support the removal of these advantages through the adoption of a consumption tax.

Employer-Controlled Pensions versus Participant-Controlled Pensions

In evaluating the extent to which 401(k)s contribute to personal saving, we have abstracted from the degree to which these plans substitute for other pensions. If the rate of substitution is low, then policies that stimulate 401(k)s will tend to increase saving if and only if 401(k) contributions are not fully offset by reductions in nonpension saving. In contrast, if the rate of substitution is high, then policies that stimulate 401(k)s may increase or decrease saving, depending on whether 401(k) contributions displace nonpension saving at (respectively) a lower or higher rate than other kinds of pensions.

Much has been written about the magnitude and probable causes of the shift from defined benefit to defined contribution pension plans in general, and 401(k)s in particular (see, e.g., Parsons 1995 or Papke, Petersen, and Poterba 1993 for selective reviews of this literature). The existence of this shift does not, however, establish that 401(k)s have substituted for more traditional plans, since aggregate trends could in principle be driven by changes in the composition and organization of economic activity.

Papke, Petersen, and Poterba (1993) examine data on individual firms and conclude that wholesale replacement of existing plans (particular defined benefit plans) occurs in a minority of cases. Although this evidence is informative, it does not resolve the central issue, since 401(k)s may displace other pension plans even if they do not directly replace these plans. For example, firms that adopt 401(k)s as supplementary plans may be less inclined to increase and more inclined to decrease the generosity of other pension plans. The evidence also indicates that changes in industrial composition and the structure of companies cannot fully account for the aggregate shift to defined contribution plans (Clark and McDermed 1990; Gustman and Steinmeier 1992; Kruse 1991). Since the unexplained component of the aggregate shift is large, 401(k)s may have substituted for other pension plans to a significant degree.

Other Activities Undertaken by Employers

Aside from encouraging employers to provide various kinds of pensions, tax policy may induce employers to engage in other activities that have the potential to influence saving. In some instances, this effect is indirect: by stimulating pensions, tax policy may encourage activities that are complementary to pensions. In other cases, subtle features of the tax code may directly affect the activity in question.

Employer-based investment and retirement education is an example of an activity that is complementary to the provision of a pension plan. Tax policies that stimulate pensions in general, and especially participant-controlled plans, may also stimulate complementary educational initiatives (Bernheim and Garrett 1995; Bayer, Bernheim, and Scholz 1996; Employee Benefit Research Institute 1995). Subtle features of the tax code, such as nondiscrimination requirements, may also encourage employer-based retirement education more directly (in addition to the preceding references, see Garrett 1995). Generally the impact of education is not subsumed in estimates of the relation between pensions and saving, since most of the growth of these offerings post-dates the most commonly used sources of data on household financial behavior.

There are sound reasons to expect that retirement education might have an important effect on household saving. Numerous studies have established that the level of financial literacy among adult Americans is extremely low. This phenomenon is accompanied by an apparently widespread failure to appreciate financial vulnerabilities (Bernheim 1995b). Although there is little direct evidence on the impact of educational programs, two recent studies conclude that employer-based offerings significantly stimulate both voluntary pension contributions and total household saving (Bernheim and Garrett 1995; and Bayer, Bernheim, Scholz 1996).

Marketing and Promotion of Financial Products

The expansion of IRA eligibility to all taxpayers in 1981 was accompanied by a great deal of media fanfare. Perhaps more important, the existence of these retirement saving vehicles created profit opportunities for financial institutions. Although the IRA tax incentive was targeted at households, it generated considerable impetus for private firms to promote saving through a blend of education and pure marketing. Similar phenomena occur in the context of other tax-advantaged savings instruments, such as long-term life insurance policies.

It is natural to wonder whether these promotional activities affect personal saving. Although there is virtually no direct evidence on this issue, there are two particularly interesting anecdotes. One concerns the introduction and subsequent scaling back of IRAs, which I have already discussed. The other concerns experience with saving promotion in Japan (Central Council for Saving Promotion 1981). After World War II the Japanese government launched a national campaign to promote saving. Promotional activities included monthly seminars that extolled the virtues of saving and provided workers with financial guidance, sponsorship of children's banks, the appointment of private citizens as savings promotion leaders, and the extensive dissemination of literature. The Japanese rate of saving rose precipitously over the relevant time period, but other factors were also at work, including strong tax incentives for saving and various aspects of postwar reconstruction. One can therefore only speculate about the extent to which the increase in saving was attributable to promotion.

7.5 A Concluding Lament

As an economist, I cannot review the voluminous literature on saving incentives without being somewhat humbled by the enormous difficulty of learning anything useful about even the most basic economic questions. Having been handed two grand experiments with tax incentives during the 1980s, it would seem that we ought to have learned a lot more and to have achieved greater consensus than we have. In our defense, it can be said that we have done our best with the information at our disposal. It is often easy to identify the kinds of data that would have allowed us to answer the pressing policy questions with much greater confidence. Unfortunately, we have had to make due with data that are, at best, a caricature of the ideal. Considering the budgetary costs of tax incentives and what is at stake in terms of economic growth and efficiency, it seems a shame that ongoing, comprehensive, microeconomic data collection has been such a low social priority.

Notes

I am grateful to the National Science Foundation, Grant SBR95-11321, for financial support. William Gale and Jonathan Skinner provided helpful comments.

1. There is considerable evidence that economic decisions in general are strongly affected by peer group effects. See Whyte (1943), Rainwater (1970), Stack (1974), or Jones (1984).

2. According to Thaler and Shefrin (1981), "Simply keeping track seems to act as a tax on any behavior which the planner views as deviant."

3. Hubbard's (1984) data are drawn from the 1979 President's Commission on Pension Policy and therefore include some noncontributors who were ineligible for IRAs. Thus, the sample selection problem discussed in the text is perhaps less pronounced that for estimates based on data collected between 1982 and 1986.

4. For example, imagine that, absent access to IRAs, new contributors would have consumed all of their disposable incomes (contributing nothing to non-IRA balances) and that their incomes would have been rising more rapidly than the consumption of old contributors.

5. Engen, Gale, and Scholz replicate this procedure but also estimate a fixed effects model using the full sample, treating all noncontributors prior to 1982 as if they were ineligible. This exaggerates the selection bias discussed below and thereby increases the likelihood that the resulting estimates will understate the true contribution of IRAs to personal saving. The fact that Engen, Gale, and Scholz significantly overstate the change in the contribution limit for individuals who were eligible for but did not participate in IRAs prior to 1982 exacerbates this bias. To understand this point, imagine for the sake of simplicity that all taxpayers file separately. In that case, the contribution limit for members of the group in question was increased by $500 (from $1,500 to $2,000) in 1982. Engen, Gale, and Scholz falsely assume that the contribution limit increased by $2,000 (from $0 to $2,000) for these individuals. Thus, their incremental saving per dollar increase in the contribution limit is biased downward by a factor of four. Since this group is large relative to the entire population, the resulting bias is likely to be substantial.

6. Engen, Gale, and Scholz (1994) argue that IRA contributions may have declined after 1986 because of reductions in marginal tax rates and limits on deductibility. But unless one believes that the interest elasticity of saving is enormous, this could not have accounted for the magnitude of the decline in contributions. The authors also attribute the decline in IRA saving to the increased availability of 401(k)s or the possible depletion of non-IRA financial assets. To my knowledge, there is no evidence that individual taxpayers replaced IRAs with 401(k)s or that IRA contributors as a group ran out of shiftable assets. It is also doubtful that either phenomenon can account for the sharpness of the decline in IRA contributions.

7. The fraction of individuals eligible for 401(k)s who owned IRAs rose (relative to ineligibles) between 1984 and 1987. However, this does not imply that reverse dilution occurred over this earlier period, for the simple reason that IRA ownership was not a stable taste proxy prior to 1987. IRAs were still universally available during this period, and participation was rising for the population as a whole. Even if the set of individuals eligible for 401(k)s had remained fixed between 1984 and 1987, one would have expected to see IRA ownership rise among eligibles (relative to ineligibles), since those with greater inclinations to save, including 401(k) eligibles, would have been more likely to open new IRA accounts.

8. To be clear, the issue here is not whether observable characteristics are comparable (a point which the authors do address). Rather, it is whether unobserved preferences are similar. Although the greater comparability of the experimental and control groups used by Engen, Gale, and Scholz seems intuitive, it does not follow purely as a matter of logic. In essence, the authors censor the distribution of preferences separately for the eligible population and the ineligible population. There is no guarantee that the truncation points are similar or that the upper tails of the preference distributions for the two samples have similar features. Thus, in principle, censoring could reduce comparability.

9. Engen and Gale (1995) argue for an upward bias because the total compensation of those with 401(k)s is understated in the data to a greater extent than the total compensation of those without 401(k)s. Even assuming that this is true (which is not at all obvious), the point is not relevant in the current context unless one believes that the authorization of 401(k)s had the effect of increasing the lifetime compensation of those who eventually received 401(k)s.

10. Engen and Gale report that as of 1989, only 20 percent of households with mortgages had ever refinanced and that equity had been extracted in only 57 percent of these cases. Other figures in their paper point to somewhat higher rates of equity extraction (upwards of 80 percent). As a rough approximation, assume that 20 percent of home owners covered by 401(k)s in 1991 refinanced their homes between 1987 and 1991 (probably an overestimate) and that 80 percent of these extracted equity. Since roughly three-quarters of those eligible for 401(k)s were home owners in 1991, this implies that roughly 12 percent extracted equity through refinancing between 1987 and 1991.

11. One might also defend Engen and Gale's interpretation by arguing that absent 401(k)s, eligible households would have accelerated repayment of their mortgages. However, under this view, the relative increase of mortgage debt among eligible households should be attributable, at least in part, to accelerated repayment by ineligible households (the control group). I doubt that this was the case.

12. See Ippolito (1985, 1986), Parsons (1986, 1995), or Williamson (1992).

13. See Burkhauser (1979, 1980), Lazear (1983), Fields and Mitchell (1984), Ippolito (1986), Lazear and Moore (1988), Kotlikoff and Wise (1990), Stock and Wise (1990), and Quinn, Burkhauser, and Myers (1990).

14. See Ippolito (1986). Kotlikoff and Spivak (1981) discuss the nature of market failure in private annuity markets.

15. A sampling of pertinent references includes Ippolito (1986), Bloom and Freeman (1992), Reagan and Turner (1995), Kruse (1993), Allen and Clark (1987), Clark and McDermed (1990), and Gustman and Steinmeier (1995).

16. There is, however, some evidence that fringe benefits do respond to variations in state-level income taxes, particularly for blue-collar workers. See Gentry and Peress (1994).

17. It is conceivable that the workers who are most inclined to save and who have the least problems with self-discipline sort themselves into jobs that are covered by pension plans with the greatest discretion, such as 401(k)s. Those who are interested in saving but have problems with self-discipline may prefer traditional employer-controlled plans. I know of no evidence that would allow one reliably to distinguish this hypothesis from various other alternatives, and thereby discern the direction of the resulting bias.

References

Ainslie, George. 1975, July. "Specious Reward: A Behavioral Theory of Impulsiveness and Impulse Control." *Psychological Bulletin* 82(4):463–496.

Ainslie, George. 1982. "A Behavioral Economic Approach to the Defense Mechanisms: Freud's Energy Theory Revisited." *Social Science Information* 21:735–779.

Ainslie, George. 1984. "Behavioral Economics II: Motivated, Involuntary Behavior." *Social Science Information* 23:47–78.

Allen, Steven G., and Robert L. Clark. 1987. "Pensions and Firm Performance." In Merris M. Kleiner et al., eds., *Human Resources and the Performance of the Firm*. Industrial Relations Research Association Series. Madison, WI: Industrial Reladition Research Association.

Allen, Steven G., Robert L. Clark, and Ann McDermed. 1993. "Pension Bonding and Lifetime Jobs." *Journal of Human Resources* 28:463–481.

Andrews Emily S. 1992. "The Growth and Distribution of 401(k) Plans." In J. Turner and D. Beller, eds., *Trends in Pensions 1992*. Washington, D.C.: U.S. Department of Labor.

Arthur D. Little. 1993, June. *America's Retirement Crisis: The Search for Solutions*. Final Report to Oppenheimer Management Corporation. Cambridge, MA: Arthur D. Little.

Attanasio, Orazio, and Thomas De Leire. 1994, October. *IRAs and Household Saving Revisited: Some New Evidence*. NBER Working Paper 4900.

Attanasio, Orazio, and Guglielmo Weber. 1993, July. "Consumption Growth, the Interest Rate and Aggregation." *Review of Economic Studies* 60(3):631–649.

Avery, Robert B., Gregory E. Elliehausen, and Thomas A. Gustafson. 1986. "Pensions and Social Security in Household Portfolios: Evidence from the 1983 Survey of Consumer Finances." In F. Gerard Adams and Susan M. Wachter, eds., *Savings and Capital Formation*. Lexington, MA: Lexington Books.

Bayer, Patrick J., B. Douglas Bernheim, and J. Karl Scholz. 1996. "The Effects of Financial Education in the Workplace: Evidence from a Survey of Employers." NBER Working Paper 5655.

Bernheim, B. Douglas. 1994a. "Personal Saving, Information, and Economic Literacy: New Directions for Public Policy." In *Tax Policy for Economic Growth in the 1990s*. Washington, DC: American Council for Capital Formation.

Bernheim, B. Douglas. 1994b. "Comments and Discussion." *Brookings Papers on Economic Activity*, pp. 152–166.

Bernheim, B. Douglas. 1994c. "Comments on Chapters 4 and 5." In David A. Wise, ed., *Studies in the Economics of Aging*. Chicago: University of Chicago Press.

Bernheim, B. Douglas. 1995a. "The Merrill Lynch Baby Boom Retirement Index: Update '95." Mimeo.

Bernheim, B. Douglas. 1995b. "Do Households Appreciate Their Financial Vulnerabilities? An Analysis of Actions, Perceptions, and Public Policy." In *Tax Policy and Economic Growth*, pp. 1–30. Washington, DC: American Council for Capital Formation.

Bernheim, B. Douglas, and Daniel M. Garrett. 1995. "The Determinants and Consequences of Financial Education in the Workplace: Evidence from a Survey of Households." Mimeo. Stanford University.

Bernheim, B. Douglas, and John Karl Scholz. 1993a. "Private Pensions and Household Saving." Mimeo. University of Wisconsin.

Bernheim, B. Douglas, and John Karl Scholz. 1993b. "Private Saving and Public Policy." *Tax Policy and the Economy* 7:73–110.

Blinder, Alan S. 1975. "Distribution Effects and the Aggregate Consumption Function." *Journal of Political Economy* 83:447–475.

Blinder, Alan S., Roger H. Gordon, and Donald E. Wise. 1980, December. "Reconsidering the Work Disincentive Effects of Social Security." *National Tax Journal* 33(4):431–442.

Bloom, David E., and Richard B. Freeman. 1992. *The Fall in Private Pension Coverage in the U.S.* NBER Working Paper 3973.

Boskin, Michael J. 1978. "Taxation, Saving, and the Rate of Interest." *Journal of Political Economy* 86:S3–S27.

Boskin, Michael J., and Lawrence J. Lau. 1978. "Taxation, Social Security and Aggregate Factor Supply in the United States." Mimeo. Standford University.

Buck Consultants. 1989, September. *Current 401(k) Plan Practices: A Survey Report.*

Burkhauser, Richard V. 1979. "The Pension Acceptance of Older Workers." *Journal of Human Resources* 14:63–72.

Burkhauser, Richard V. 1980, July. "The Early Acceptance of Social Security: An Asset Maximization Approach." *Industrial and Labor Relations Review* 33:484–492.

Burman, Leonard, Joseph Cordes, and Larry Ozanne. 1990, September. "IRAs and National Saving." *National Tax Journal* 43:259–284.

Cagan, Phillip. 1965. *The Effect of Pension Plans on Aggregate Saving: Evidence from a Sample Survey.* Occasional Paper 95. National Bureau of Economic Research.

Carroll, Chris, and Lawrence H. Summers. 1987, September. "Why Have Private Savings Rates in the U.S. and Canada Diverged?" *Journal of Monetary Economics* 20:249–280.

Central Council for Savings Promotion. 1981. *Savings and Savings Promotion Movement in Japan.* Tokyo: Bank of Japan.

Clark, Robert L., and Ann McDermed. 1990. *The Choice of Pension Plans in a Changing Regulatory Environment.* Washington, DC: American Enterprise Institute.

Congressional Budget Office. 1993. *Baby Boomers in Retirement: An Early Perspective.* Washington, DC: Government Printing Office.

Diamond, Peter, A., and Jerry A. Hausman. 1984. "Individual Retirement and Saving Behavior." *Journal of Public Economics* 23:81–114.

Dicks-Mireaux, Louis, and Mervyn King. 1984. "Pension Wealth and Household Savings: Tests of Robustness." *Journal of Public Economics* 23:115–139.

Doyle, Robert J., Jr., and Eric T. Johnson. 1991. *Readings in Wealth Accumulation Planning.* 4th ed. Bryn Mawr, PA: American College.

Employee Benefit Research Institute. 1995, April. "Can We Save Enough to Retire? Participant Education in Defined Contribution Plans." *EBRI Issue Brief*, no 160.

Engen, Eric M. 1994, June. "Precautionary Saving and the Structure of Taxation." Mimeo. Federal Reserve Board of Governors.

Engen, Eric M., and William G. Gale. 1993. "IRAs and Saving in a Stochastic Life-Cycle Model." Mimeo. Brookings Institution.

Engen, Eric M., and William G. Gale. 1995. "Debt, Taxes and the Effects of 401(k) Plans on Household Wealth Accumulation." Mimeo. Federal Reserve Board.

Engen, Eric M., William G. Gale, and John Karl Scholz. 1994. "Do Saving Incentives Work?" *Brookings Papers on Economic Activity*, 1:85–151.

Feenberg, Daniel R., and Jonathan Skinner. 1989. "Sources of IRA Saving." *Tax Policy and the Economy* 3:25–46.

Feldstein, Martin S. 1978, April. "The Welfare Cost of Capital Income Taxation." *Journal of Political Economy* 86(2), pt. 2:S29–51.

Fields, Gary S., and Olivia S. Mitchell. 1984. *Retirement, Pensions, and Social Security*. Cambridge, MA: MIT Press.

Fisher, Irving. 1930. *The Theory of Interest*. London: Macmillan.

Furnham, Adrian, and Alan Lewis. 1986. *The Economic Mind: The Social Psychology of Economic Behavior*. New York: St. Martin's Press.

Gale William G. 1995. "The Effects of Pensions on Wealth: A Re-evaluation of Theory and Evidence." Mimeo. Brookings Institution.

Gale, William G., and John Karl Scholz. 1994, December. "IRAs and Household Saving." *American Economic Review* 84:1233–1260.

Garrett, Daniel M. 1995. "The Effects of Nondiscrimination Rules on 401(k) Contributions." Mimeo. Stanford University.

Gentry, William M., and Eric Peress. 1994. *Taxes and Fringe Benefits Offered by Employers*. NBER Working Paper 4764.

Gravelle, Jane G. 1991, Spring. "Do Individual Retirement Accounts Increase Savings?" *Journal of Economic Perspectives* 5:133–148.

Green, Francis. 1981, March. "The Effect of Occupational Pension Schemes on Saving in the United Kingdom: A Test of the Life Cycle Hypothesis." *Economic Journal* 91:136–144.

Gustman, Alan L., and Thomas L. Steinmeier. 1992. "The Stampede Toward Defined Contribution Pension Plans: Fact or Fiction?" *Industrial Relations* 31:361–369.

Gustman, Alan L., and Thomas L. Steinmeier. 1995. *Pension Incentives and Job Mobility*. Kalamazoo, MI: W. E. Upjohn Institute for Employment Research.

Hall, Robert E. 1988, April. "Intertemporal Substitution in Consumption." *Journal of Political Economy* 96:339–357.

Hoch, Stephen J., and George F. Lowenstein. 1991, March. "Time-Inconsistent Preferences and Consumer Self-Control." *Journal of Consumer Research* 17(4):492–507.

Howrey, E. Phillip, and Saul H. Hymans. 1978. "The Measurement and Determination of Loanable Funds Saving." *Brookings Papers on Economic Activity* 2:655–685.

Hubbard, R. Glenn. 1984, March. "Do IRAs and Keoghs Increase Saving?" *National Tax Journal* 37:43–54.

Hubbard, R. Glenn. 1986, May. "Pension Wealth and Individual Saving." *Journal of Money, Credit, and Banking* 18(2):167–178.

Hubbard, R. Glenn, and Jonathan Skinner. 1995. "The Effectiveness of Saving Incentives: A Review of the Evidence." Mimeo. Columbia University.

Hubbard, R. Glenn, Jonathan Skinner, and Stephen P. Zeldes. 1995, April. "Precautionary Saving and Social Insurance." *Journal of Political Economy* 103:360–399.

Ippolito, Richard A. 1985. "The Economic Function of Underfunded Pension Plans." *Journal of Law and Economics* 28:611–651.

Ippolito, Richard A. 1986. *Pensions, Economics and Public Policy*. Homewood, IL: Dow Jones–Irwin.

Johnson, Alfred P. 1985. "Individual Retirement Accounts Help Boost Saving in the U.S." Testimony to the Committee on Finance, U.S. Senate, in Tax Reform Proposals (99–246, part XIII), pp. 129–149.

Joines, Douglas H., and James G. Manegold. 1995, February. "IRA and Saving: Evidence from a Panel of Taxpayers." Mimeo. University of Southern California.

Jones, Stephen R. G. 1984. *The Economics of Conformism*. Oxford: Basil Blackwell.

Judd, Kenneth L. 1987, August. "The Welfare Cost of Factor Taxation in a Perfect-Foresight Model." *Journal of Political Economy* 95(4):675–709.

Judd, Kenneth L. 1988, October. "Redistributive Taxation in a Simple Perfect Foresight Model." *Journal of Public Economics* 28(1):59–83.

Katona, George. 1965. *Private Pensions and Individual Saving*. University of Michigan Press.

Katona, George. 1975. *Psychological Economics*. Amsterdam: Elsevier.

King, Mervyn A., and Louis Dicks-Mireaux. 1982. "Asset Holdings and the Life Cycle." *Economic Journal* 92:247–267.

Kotlikoff, Laurence J. 1979, June. "Testing the Theory of Social Security and Life Cycle Accumulation." *American Economic Review* 69(3):396–410.

Kotlikoff, Laurence J., and Avia Spivak. 1981, April. "The Family as an Incomplete Annuities Market." *Journal of Political Economy* 89:372–391.

Kotlikoff, Laurence J., and David A. Wise. 1990. "The Wage Carrot and the Pension Stick: Retirement Benefits and Labor Force Participation." Kalamazoo, MI: W. E. Upjohn Institute for Employment Research.

Kruse, Douglas L. 1991. *Pension Substitution in the 1980s: Why the Shift Toward Defined Contribution Pension Plans?* NBER Working Paper. 3882.

Kruse, Douglas L. 1993. *Profit Sharing: Does It Make a Difference?* Kalamazoo, MI: W. E. Upjohn Institute for Employment Research.

Kusko, Andrea, James M. Poterba, and David W. Wilcox. 1993. "Tax Preferred Saving Vehicles and Personal Saving: New Evidence from the Behavior of 12,000 Participants in a 401(k) Plan." Mimeo. Federal Reserve Board of Governors.

Kusko, Andrea, James M. Poterba, and David W. Wilcox. 1994. *Employee Decisions with Respect to 401(k) Plans: Evidence from Individual Level Data.* NBER Working Paper 4635.

Lazear, Edward P. 1983. "Pensions as Severance Pay." In Zvi Bodie, John Shoven, and David Wise, eds., *Financial Aspects of the United States Pension System.* Chicago: University of Chicago Press.

Lazear, Edward P., and Robert Moore. 1988. "Pensions and Mobility." In Zvi Bodie, John Shoven, and David Wise, eds., *Pensions in the U.S. Economy.* Chicago: University of Chicago Press.

Long, James E. 1990. "Marginal Tax Rates and IRA Contributions." *National Tax Journal* 43(2):143–153.

Lucas, Robert E., Jr. 1976. "Econometric Policy Evaluation: A Critique." In Karl Brunner and Allan H. Meltzer, *The Phillips Curve and Labor Markets.* Carnegie-Rochester Conference Series on Public Policy, vol. 1, suppl., *Journal of Monetary Economics.*

Maital, Shlomo. 1986, July–September. "Prometheus Rebound: On Welfare-Improving Constraints." *Eastern Economic Journal* 12(3):337–344.

Modigliani, Franco, and Richard Brumberg. 1954. "Utility Analysis and the Consumption Function: An Interpretation of Cross-Section Data." In K. K. Kurihara, ed., *Post Keynsian Economics.* New Brunswick, NJ: Rutgers University Press.

Munnell, Alicia H. 1974. *The Effect of Social Security on Personal Saving.* Cambridge, MA: Ballinger.

Munnell, Alicia H. 1976. "Private Pensions and Saving: New Evidence." *Journal of Political Economy* 84(5):1013–1032.

Papke, Leslie E. 1992. *Participation in and Contributions to 401(k) Plans: Evidence from Plan Data.* NBER Working Paper 4199.

Papke, Leslie, Mitchell Petersen, and James M. Poterba. 1993, October. *Did 401(k) Plans Replace Other Employer Provided Pensions?* NBER Working Paper 4501.

Parsons, Donald O. 1986. "The Employment Relationship: Job Attachment, Work Effort, and the Nature of Contracts." In Orley Ashenfelter and Richard Layard, eds., *Handbook of Labor Economics,* vol. 2. Amsterdam: North-Holland.

Parsons, Donald O. 1995. "Retirement Age and Retirement Income: The Role of the Firm." Mimeo. Ohio State University.

Poterba, James M., Steven F. Venti, and David A. Wise. 1992. *401(k) Plans and Tax-Deferred Saving.* NBER Working Paper 4181.

Poterba, James M., Steven F. Venti, and David A. Wise. 1994. "401(k) Plans and Tax-Deferred Saving." In David A. Wise, ed., *Studies in the Economics of Aging.* Chicago: University of Chicago Press.

Poterba, James M., Steven F. Venti, and David A. Wise. 1995. "Do 401(k) Contributions Crowd Out Other Personal Saving?" *Journal of Public Economics* 58:1–32.

Poterba, James M., Steven F. Venti, and David A. Wise. 1996. "Do Retirement Saving Programs Increase Saving?" *Journal of Economic Perspectives*, forthcoming.

Quinn, Joseph F., Richard V. Burkhauser, and Daniel A. Myers. 1990. *Passing the Torch: The Influence of Economic Incentives on Work and Retirement*. Kalamazoo, MI: W. E. Upjohn Institute.

Rainwater, Lee. 1970. *Behind Ghetto Walls: Black Families in a Federal Slum*. Chicago: Aldine.

Reagan, Patricia B., and John A. Turner. 1995, June. "The Decline in Marginal Tax Rates During the 1980s Reduced Pension Coverage." Mimeo. Ohio State University.

Samwick, Andrew A. 1995, December. "The Limited Offset Between Pension Wealth and Other Private Wealth: Implications of Buffer-Stock Saving." Mimeo. Dartmouth College.

Sandmo, Agnar. 1985. "The Effects to Taxation on Savings and Risk Taking." In Alan Auerbach and Martin Feldstein, eds., *Handbook of Public Economics*, vol. 1. Amsterdam: North-Holland.

Schelling, Thomas C. 1984, May. "Self-Command in Practice, in Policy, and in a Theory of Rational Choice." *American Economic Review* 74(2):1–11.

Schoeplein, Robert N. 1970. "The Effect of Pension Plans on Other Retirement Saving." *Journal of Finance* 25(3):633–638.

Scitovsky, Tibor. 1976. *The Joyless Economy*. Oxford: Oxford University Press.

Scott, Jason. 1994, February. "The Determinants of Participation in Defined Contribution Pension Plans." Mimeo, Stanford University.

Shefrin, Hersh M., and Richard H. Thaler. 1988. "The Behavioral Life-Cycle Hypothesis." *Economic Inquiry* 26(4):609–643.

Shoven, John B. 1991, September. *Return on Investment: Pensions Are How America Saves*. Washington, DC: Association of Private Pension and Welfare Plans.

Skinner, Jonathan, and Daniel Feenberg. 1989. "The Impact of the 1986 Tax Reform on Personal Saving." In Joel Slemrod, ed., *Do Taxes Matter? The Effect of the 1986 Tax Reform Act on the U.S. Economy*. Cambridge, MA: MIT Press.

Stack, Carol B. 1974. *All Our Kin: Strategies for Survival in a Black Community*. New York: Harper & Row.

Starrett, David A. 1988. "Effects of Taxes on Saving." In H. Galper, H. Aaron, and J. Pechman, eds., *Uneasy Compromise: Problems of a Hybrid Income-Consumpion Tax*. Washington, DC: Brookings Institution.

Stock, James H., and David A. Wise. 1990. "The Pension Inducement to Retire: An Option Value Analysis." In David A. Wise, ed., *Issues in the Economics of Aging*. Chicago: University of Chicago Press.

Summers, Lawrence H. 1981, September. "Taxation and Capital Accumulation in a Life Cycle Growth Model." *American Economic Review* 71:533–554.

Summers, Lawrence H. 1986. "Summers Replies to Galper and Byce on IRAs." *Tax Notes* 31(10):1014–1016.

Thaler, Richard H. 1994, May. "Psychology and Savings Policies." *American Economic Review* 84:186–192.

Thaler, Richard H., and Hersh Shefrin. 1981, April. "An Economic Theory of Self-Control." *Journal of Political Economy* 89(2):392–406.

Venti, Steven F., and David A. Wise. 1986. "Tax-Deferred Accounts, Constrained Choice, and Estimation of Individual Saving." *Review of Economic Studies* 53:579–601.

Venti, Steven F., and David A. Wise. 1987. "IRAs and Saving." In Martin Feldstein, ed., *The Effects of Taxation on Capital Accumulation.* Chicago: University of Chicago Press.

Venti, Steven F., and David A. Wise. 1988. "The Determinants of IRA Contributions and the Effect of Limit Changes." In Zvi Bodie, John B. Shoven, and David A. Wise, eds., *Pensions and the U.S. Economy*. Chicago: University of Chicago Press.

Venti, Steven F., and David A. Wise. 1989. "Aging, Moving, and Housing Wealth." In David A. Wise, ed., *The Economics of Aging*. Chicago: University of Chicago Press.

Venti, Steven F., and David A. Wise. 1990, August. "Have IRAs Increased U.S. Saving: Evidence from Consumer Expenditure Surveys." *Quarterly Journal of Economic* 105:661–698.

Venti, Steven F., and David A. Wise. 1991. "The Saving Effect of Tax-Deferred Retirement Accounts: Evidence for SIPP." In B. Douglas Bernheim and John B. Shoven, eds., *National Saving and Economic Performance*. Chicago: University of Chicago Press.

Venti, Steven F., and David A. Wise. 1992. "Government Policy and Personal Retirement Saving." *Tax Policy and the Economy* 6:1–41.

Venti, Steven F., and David A. Wise. 1993, December. *The Wealth to Cohorts: Retirement Saving and the Changing Assets of Older Americans.* NBER Working Paper 4600.

Venti, Steven F., and David A. Wise. 1995. "Individual Response to Retirement Savings Programs: Results from U.S. Panel Data." *Recherche Economiche*. 49(3):235–54.

Whyte, William F. 1943. *Street Corner Society*. Chicago: University of Chicago Press.

Williamson, Samuel H. 1992. "U.S. and Canadian Pensions Before 1930: A Historical Perspective." In John A. Turner and Daniel J. Beller, eds., *Trends in Pensions 1992*. Washington, DC: U.S. Department of Labor, Pension and Welfare Benefits Administration.

Wolff, Edward N. 1988. "Social Security, Pensions and the Life Cycle Accumulation of Wealth: Some Empirical Tests." *Annales D'économie et de statistique* 9:199–226.

Woodbury, Stephen A., and Wei-Jang Huang. 1991. "The Tax Treatment of Fringe Benefits." Kalamazoo, MI: W. E. Upjohn Institute.

Wright, C. 1969. "Saving and the Rate of Interest." In A. C. Harberger and M. J. Bailey, eds., *The Taxation of Income from Capital*. Washington, DC: Brookings Institution.

Comment

William G. Gale

B. Douglas Bernheim provides an informative and intriguing review of theoretical models and empirical work on tax-based saving incentives. Although I do not agree with all of the conclusions, he makes a valuable contribution by bringing together many existing strands of thought and presenting several new analyses and directions for future research.

Theoretical Models of Saving

I regard the life cycle hypothesis more as a framework than a particular model. I find the framework useful for thinking about saving, but I find compelling Bernheim's claims that psychological considerations can be useful also. He discusses many ways that psychological or behavioral motives can influence saving.

One issue is the prevalence of psychological motives for saving. Bernheim describes several phenomena that he views as documenting an important role for psychological motives in saving behavior. One claim focuses on the rise in IRA contributions after 1981 and the fall after 1986. Although many other factors could have contributed to these changes (see Engen, Gale, and Scholz 1994, 1996), I agree that the visibility and promotion of IRAs likely affected contribution behavior.

Other claims are more difficult to accept. Bernheim argues, for example, that there is "considerable evidence of focal point saving" because among households that could have contributed more than $2,000 to an IRA but contributed less than the limit, 47 percent contributed exactly $2,000. However, these households represent only 15 percent of all contributors and less than 5 percent of all taxpayers.[1] An additional claim is that IRA contributions tend to bunch around April 15, the last day deductible IRA contributions can be made for the previous tax year (Summers 1986). My view is that this pattern provides little evidence about the prevalence of psychological motives, because the cost of the deviation from life cycle behavior (the forgone interest from contributing later rather than earlier) is small, especially given the illiquidity of IRAs and the transactions costs involved. Others assert that IRAs helped people get in a habit of saving (Thaler 1994). Skinner (1992) reports on the "surprising" persistence of IRA contributions from one year to the next. But Engen and Gale (1993) obtain the same persistence in a simulation model that posits fully rational choice.

As these examples show, it is difficult to identify saving patterns that can distinguish between realistic versions of life cycle and psychological models.[2] Thus, although it is plausible that psychological factors can affect saving, I do not see evidence that these factors typically dominate saving decisions.

A second issue is whether psychological models imply that saving incentives raise saving. Perhaps surprisingly, they do not. Bernheim (this volume, chap. 7) and Thaler (1994) note that a key element in psychological models of saving is the issue of self-control. If so, psychological models may be most applicable to people who do not save very much. But households with saving incentives tend to save substantial amounts overall. Thus, there could be many households with saving incentives and many that act mainly according to psychological motives, but the overlap between the two sets may not be very large. If so, the existence of psychological motives would have little impact on existing incentives.[3]

To the extent that psychological motives matter, they may have their primary impact on portfolio composition rather than the level of saving.[4] For example, many contributions for a given tax year are made in the following calendar year. People may be more likely to shift money into an IRA at the last minute if the money represents idle cash than if the money were destined to pay for some large consumption item, say, a family vacation. If so, then portfolios are affected, not saving. Advertising provides another example. Most IRA contributors have saved substantial amounts in other forms and so are aware of opportunities for saving. The information contained in advertising may be the presence of a tax deduction for doing what the household was already doing without a deduction. Again, portfolios would change, but saving would not rise.

What Bernheim describes as a "scarcity of well-developed organizing principles" means that many possible channels for psychological models need to be explored. He notes that a targeted tax subsidy may raise saving because it conveys information to people that authorities think saving is important. But people may instead receive the message that authorities think saving is such an unpleasant task that it deserves a tax break. In that case, those without saving incentive opportunities may reduce their saving, and those with such opportunities may reduce their taxable saving by as much as or more than their saving incentive contribution.

Alternative models of saving represent an important direction for future research, but distinguishing between the life cycle and psychological approaches need not be an either-or choice; saving behavior is likely to contain elements of both approaches.

The Interest Elasticity of Saving

I agree with Bernheim that the interest elasticity is unlikely to be positive and large, and it could plausibly be negative. Bernheim notes that target saving creates a negative elasticity. Target saving is a common explicit financial planning technique and may be implicitly behind many other people's retirement calculations as well. Of course, to the extent that people save to reach specific retirement targets, saving incentive programs will reduce overall private saving, since the plans offer a higher rate of return on a limited amount of contributions.

IRAs

Bernheim concludes that none of the IRA studies generates convincing evidence. Although I agree that most of the papers face very difficult econometric problems (see the discussion in Gale and Scholz 1994, pp. 1235–1240 or Engen, Gale, and Scholz 1996), two papers warrant further elaboration.

Gale and Scholz (1994)

These authors compare limit contributors to "interior" contributors (those who contribute less than the limit but more than zero to an IRA) and find that raising the IRA limits would have resulted in virtually no net new saving. Bernheim claims that if limit contributors have stronger unobservable preferences for saving than do interior contributors, the Gale-Scholz model is biased toward understating the effects of IRAs. Bernheim's example, however, does not show whether the bias is important quantitatively. My sense is that it is not. Gale and Scholz show that limit contributors on average have observable characteristics that imply more saving (e.g., they have higher income) than for interior contributors and the regressions in Gale and Scholz control for these observable differences.

Nor does Bernheim present evidence to support his assumption about unobserved preferences for saving. To provide information on this issue, Engen, Gale, and Scholz (1996) report the results of regressions using the 1983 Survey of Consumer Finances (SCF) sample of all limit and interior contributors. The regressions control for all of the covariates in the Gale and Scholz model except those relating to wealth. The results are that the coefficient on a dummy variable for limit contributors is negative and insignificant in an equation explaining 1983 wealth levels. If unobserved tastes for saving were higher among limit contributors than interior contributors, this coefficient would be positive and significant. The regression results are inconsistent with the idea that limit contributors have higher tastes for saving than interior contributors and suggest that the Gale and Scholz results do not suffer from the bias that Bernheim asserts.

Joines and Manegold (1995)

These authors estimate saving regressions that control for taxpayer-specific effects, period effects, and a variety of taxpayer characteristics. They conclude that between 19 and 26 percent of IRA contributions represented increases in national saving.

This estimate may overstate the effects of IRAs, however. First, the sample used in the formal estimates excludes elderly taxpayers. As discussed in Gale and Scholz, the elderly should find IRAs to be very good substitutes for other saving, and Joines and Manegold (table 2) show that this group accounts for 12 percent of IRA contributions in their overall sample. Second, the effects of IRAs are measured on only a narrow measure of assets. Any IRA contribution financed by an increase in consumer debt, investment debt, or mortgage debt, reduction in tax-exempt bond holdings, a shift from tangible assets, or a reduced contribution to a thrift, pension, or 401(k) plan is not captured. These considerations could plausibly reduce or eliminate the estimated impact of IRAs on saving.[5]

Bernheim raises an additional concern. He notes that only a small fraction of those eligible for IRAs before 1982 actually contributed and suggests that these households—the continuing contributors—had strong tastes for saving. He also suggests that this implies that the Joines and Manegold estimates understate the impact of IRAs on saving. The conclusion about bias, however, depends on Bernheim's assumption that, after a change in the IRA limit, the share of added IRA contributions that represents new saving is higher for high savers than for low savers. It seems to me, however, that the opposite is more likely to be true: high savers would find it easier to substitute other assets into IRAs and easier to shift current saving that would have been done anyway into IRAs. If so, the bias goes the other way: the Joines and Manegold estimate overstates the impact of IRAs.[6]

401(k) Plans

Bernheim notes that 401(k) plans capitalize more effectively than IRAs do on the psychology of saving. Thus, finding that 401(k) plans did not raise saving would be a sharper rebuke to psychological approaches than would a similar finding for IRAs. Bernheim concludes "with moderate confidence" that 401(k)s raise saving. I believe this conclusion is unwarranted.

Poterba, Venti, and Wise (1995)

These authors present two tests of the effects of 401(k)s. The first exploits cross-sectional variation in 401(k) eligibility. I agree with Bernheim that 401(k) eligibility is positively correlated with households' underlying tastes for saving, even after controlling for other factors. This implies these tests will overstate the impact of 401(k)s on saving.

The second set of tests is based on what Bernheim calls transitional effects.[7] These tests use random cross-sections of households in 1984, 1987, and 1991. Households eligible for 401(k)s in the later years have, on average, been exposed to 401(k)s for longer than eligible households in earlier years. Other things equal, if 401(k)s raise wealth, the wealth of cross-sections of eligible households should have risen over time. But other factors do affect wealth and may have changed over time. Thus, a cleaner test compares wealth patterns for eligible households relative to ineligible households (controlling for household characteristics). If 401(k)s raise wealth, wealth should rise more for cross-sections of eligible families than for cross-sections of ineligible families.

Poterba, Venti, and Wise implement tests along these lines and find that, relative to ineligible households, eligible households experienced an increase in financial assets, including saving incentives and no decline in financial assets other than IRAs and 401(k)s. They conclude that most 401(k) contributions represent net new saving. These findings represent an important advance in our understanding of 401(k)s but are not the complete story, due to two sets of biases.

The first bias arises because although the underlying issue is how 401(k)s affect household saving and wealth, Poterba, Venti, and Wise implement their test on financial assets. Financial assets are only a small part of total wealth.[8] Changes during the 1980s could have caused financial assets to rise without an increase in wealth and could have caused financial assets to rise more for eligible households than for ineligible households even if 401(k)s did not raise saving.

Consider shifts from nonfinancial to financial assets. The 1970s featured high inflation and high marginal tax rates. These conditions raise the attractiveness of tangible capital (in particular, housing) relative to financial assets. In the 1980s, inflation and marginal tax rates fell. This induced a shift toward financial assets and away from tangible capital.[9] The shift may have been larger for eligible households because they had greater access to tax-preferred financial assets and so would have found shifting into financial assets more attractive than did ineligible households.

In addition, mortgages and overall household debt rose relative to income or assets over this period. An increase in debt used to purchase financial assets is obviously not an increase in wealth. The increase in debt occurred disproportionately for eligible households relative to ineligible households between 1987 and 1991 (Engen and Gale 1995).

The second set of biases concerns the data, which overstate the increase in saving incentive balances for three reasons. First, saving incentives are pretax balances; taxes must be paid on withdrawals. In contrast, the entire balance in a conventional saving account can be consumed. Therefore, assuming a marginal tax rate of about 20 percent, 20 percent of the increase in saving incentive balances does not represent saving. Second, the data used by Poterba, Venti, and Wise contain no information on 401(k) balances in 1984. This means they understate 1984 wealth and overstate the increase in wealth from 1984 to 1991 for eligible households relative to ineligible households. This omission may create an important bias. Data from Form 5500s indicate that the average balance among 401(k) participants in 1984 exceeded $12,000. Third, the data used by Poterba, Venti, and Wise omit balances in after-tax thrift plans. Data from the 1983 Survey of Consumer Finances suggest that the median thrift balance among participants was $3,700 in 1983. Moreover, as these plans were converted into 401(k)s over the course of the 1980s, this would show up in the data as an increase in the reported assets of eligible households relative to ineligible households, though it would not represent an increase in wealth.

All of these factors impart biases in favor of finding that financial assets rose for eligible households relative to ineligible households even if 401(k)s did not raise wealth. Many of the biases appear to be large relative to the perceived increase over time in financial assets of eligible households relative to ineligible households. And the fact that the rise in financial assets occurred via saving incentives rather than fully taxable assets is not surprising either, given the tax advantages of saving incentives. Of course, none of these observations per se overturns the results of Poterba, Venti, and Wise; that requires additional evidence on the factors already noted. But the observations do serve as a caveat, and provide a framework within which to consider further work on the subject.

Engen and Gale (1995)

Engen and Gale address some of the issues raised above. They use the same comparison groups as Poterba, Venti, and Wise and measure the impact of 401(k) eligibility on narrow wealth measures, such as financial assets, as well as broader measures, such as net financial assets plus home equity (called "wealth" below). They avoid using data from 1984, due to the missing data on 401(k)s and thrifts.

Engen and Gale replicate broadly the main result of Poterba, Venti, and Wise: financial assets rose for eligible households relative to others over time. But they also show that among renters, being eligible for a 401(k) had little discernible impact on the accumulation of financial assets or net financial assets. Among home owners, being eligible for a 401(k) was associated with an increase in financial assets, but did not increase overall wealth. In short, controlling for other factors, 401(k) eligibility did not raise wealth for any group of eligible households relative to ineligible households.

Dilution

Bernheim claims that the results of Poterba, Venti, and Wise and of Engen and Gale understate the impact of 401(k)s due to dilution. Dilution occurs, according to Bernheim, if the average taste for saving among eligible households falls over time. The logic of this claim is that since 401(k) eligibility is positively correlated with tastes for saving, it is likely that the most dedicated savers became eligible for 401(k)s early on. Over time, additional savers, less dedicated than the original sample of eligibles, became eligible as 401(k)s spread through the workforce. This reduces the average tastes for saving among the sample of eligible households over time. Thus, by Bernheim's interpretation, the results of Poterba, Venti, and Wise and of Engen and Gale understate the impact of 401(k)s because the later samples of eligible households were more diluted with less dedicated savers than the earlier samples.

But the direction of the net bias caused by dilution is unclear. Over time, the most dedicated savers among ineligible households are the ones most likely to become eligible for 401(k)s, implying dilution in the group of ineligible households too. The key issue is the relative dilution of the two groups, not the absolute dilution in one group. The sample of eligible households could become diluted, but the ineligible sample could be diluted more. If so, the results of Poterba, Venti, and Wise and of Engen and Gale overstate the effects of 401(k)s.

Bernheim claims that trends in IRA participation are a "good indication" of dilution. But dilution is a statement about how unobservable characteristics (tastes for saving) changed, whereas changes in IRA participation are due to changes in observable as well as unobservable characteristics. Probit analysis using the SIPP indicates that between 1987 and 1991, controlling for household characteristics, the IRA participation rate of eligible households fell by only 1.3 percentage points relative to ineligible households. Therefore, changes in unobservable variables—the source of dilution—led to only a slight change in relative IRA participation rates.

A second empirical consideration is the 401(k) participation rate. If dilution among eligible families were empirically important, the proportion of eligible workers making contributions should have fallen over time. Instead, data from the Current Population Survey show that the proportion rose from 57 percent in 1988 to 65 percent in 1993 (Bassett, Fleming, and Rodrigues 1996).[10] Probit analysis using the SIPP indicates that between 1987 and 1991, controlling for household characteristics (including pension coverage), the 401(k) participation rate of eligible households *rose* by 8 percentage points, and the increase was statistically significant.[11] In this case, changes in unobservable variables led to increases in 401(k) participation, given eligibility.

Other factors raise additional questions about the magnitude and direction of dilution. Workers with low tastes for saving can and frequently do liquidate their 401(k) balance on departure from the firm. This serves to raise the average tastes for saving among eligible families and may reduce it among ineligible families. Ippolito (1993) presents a model of the productive benefits of 401(k)s. In this model, 401(k)s provide incentives such that average tastes for saving plausibly rise over time among the sample of workers at firms that provide 401(k)s. All of these factors work in the direction opposite to Bernheim's claim.

Dilution is a statement that an unobserved variable, tastes for saving, is changing over time. Although it is difficult to prove or disprove such an assertion convincingly, the empirical findings and other factors discussed above suggest that the bias created could work in the direction opposite to that indicated by Bernheim. More important, based on the considerations above, dilution is unlikely to be a major quantitative issue in interpreting the results of Poterba, Venti, and Wise and of Engen and Gale.

Other Criticisms

Bernheim raises many criticisms of Engen and Gale. I believe they are largely misplaced and will attempt to address most of them. Bernheim notes that the effects of eligibility on wealth are estimated imprecisely.[12] To address this concern, Engen and Gale also estimated the impact of eligibility on non-401(k) wealth. The estimates were uniformly large and negative and usually statistically significant. This is consistent with 401(k)s not raising overall wealth.

Bernheim claims that Poterba, Venti, and Wise (1996) find "exactly the opposite pattern" in an earlier time period. It is unclear from the text what pattern this refers to. These authors do claim that from 1984 to 1987, there was little relation between mortgage debt and the increase in saving incentive balances across age cohorts. This claim must be tempered by the fact that Poterba, Venti, and Wise do not have data on 401(k) balances in 1984, making it impossible to calculate the increase. But even if the claim is correct, it provides no evidence against Engen and Gale's results. These results suggest that whatever the trend in mortgage debt across cohorts (obviously many factors other than 401(k)s influence mortgage debt), eligible households used more mortgage debt or acquired less housing equity than ineligible households.

Bernheim claims there may be problems with the data on housing wealth. But data problems would have generated Engen and Gale's results only if the mismeasurement of housing equity became more negative from 1987 to 1991 for eligible families relative to ineligible families. This seems implausible, and Bernheim presents no evidence to back this claim. Moreover, problems in measuring housing wealth could not explain the results for renters.

Renters

Bernheim asserts that the sample of eligible renters appears to be "more selected" than that of eligible home owners. However, 401(k) participation rates conditional on income, age, and eligibility are slightly lower for renters than for home owners. This is not consistent with Bernheim's assertion. Bernheim suggests there could be greater dilution of eligible renters over time. Based on trends in IRA participation, the data do not support this claim.[13]

Bernheim claims that low wealth among ineligible renters could invalidate the results, because if economic forces were pushing down wealth in both groups of renters, ineligible renters may not have been able to reduce their wealth much, due possibly to liquidity constraints. However, if renters save almost nothing, as Bernheim notes, any increase in 401(k) balances should have shown up very clearly as an increase in wealth. Eligibility did raise financial assets in absolute terms among home owners, who have higher levels of wealth than eligible renters, so there is little reason to see why, if 401(k)s raise wealth, eligibility should not also have raised renters' financial assets.

Home Owners

Bernheim claims that past retirees have been reluctant to reduce housing equity and cites one study with that conclusion. But other studies reach different conclusions (see Hurd 1995), and all of these studies may suffer from an important sample selection bias: elderly people who reduce their equity (by selling their house and moving to another one, or into a nursing home, or in with relatives) may get dropped from subsequent waves of the survey.

Bernheim notes that many younger households say they view their home equity primarily as a source of financial security. The relevance of this observation is unclear. Bernheim has warned us earlier to be skeptical of surveys of people's intentions. And Engen and Gale measure people's actions, not their intentions. Finally, there have been several home equity lending booms in the 1980s and 1990s. Survey responses notwithstanding, some households are clearly removing equity.

Bernheim devotes several pages to questioning whether substitution between housing equity and 401(k)s is plausible or likely. Rather than respond to each point, some general remarks can address these issues. First, there are many ways to substitute between 401(k)s and housing equity. Bernheim seems intent on eliminating each possibility as *the* substitution mechanism, but there is no reason that the mechanism would have to be the same for everyone; different eligible households could substitute in different ways. Second, not everyone needs to substitute to obtain the Engen-Gale results. In fact, 401(k)s could raise wealth for some people, and these results would still hold. The Engen-Gale results refer only to how sample means and medians change. Third, the substitution does not have to be the result of rational and deliberate planning. Earlier, Bernheim embraces the notion that IRA behavior patterns are not fully consistent with rational and deliberate planning. But in discussing the plausibility of 401(k) substitution with debt, Bernheim frequently requires that households act purely rationally and deliberately. Fourth, the household need not be substituting intentionally and need not even be aware that such substitution occurs. These points are elaborated below.

Some ways to raise 401(k) balances and reduce home equity are obvious: finance the 401(k) contribution with a refinanced mortgage, a second mortgage, a home equity line of credit, or a smaller down payment on a house than would otherwise occur. About 14 percent of eligibles had home equity loans in 1991, about 19 percent of eligibles bought new homes between 1987 and 1991, and by Bernheim's estimate, about 12 percent of eligibles extracted equity from their home via a refinancing between 1987 and 1991. Thus, a substantial minority of eligible households clearly had direct access to one of these mechanisms.

Other ways to substitute 401(k)s and home equity are less obvious: finance the contribution by not accelerating mortgage payments or not trading up to a bigger house. It is important to keep these kinds of channels in mind when assessing the plausibility of substitution because they do not show up in surveys as a particular action taken.

Additional ways to substitute may be even more subtle. Consider different cohorts of new home owners who are observationally equivalent except that the new home owners in the later year have had longer exposure to 401(k)s and so have placed more funds in the 401(k) than did those in the younger cohort. Now suppose that households in the later cohort have smaller balances of liquid cash (because they have moved some of their liquid cash into 401(k)s) than those in the earlier cohort. Because they have less cash available, households in the later cohort might purchase the same size home as the earlier cohort but with a larger mortgage (less initial housing equity). A comparison of households in these two cohorts would reveal that households in the later cohort had less housing equity, more 401(k) wealth, but the same overall wealth compared to households in the younger cohort. As analysts, we can see that households in the later cohort were substituting 401(k)s for home equity relative to earlier cohorts, even if this substitution were completely unintentional and even if the household itself were unaware of the comparison.[14]

The last example raises an intriguing possibility: the later-year household could have taken funds from the 401(k) and raised the down payment but was assumed to choose not to. This is consistent with a mental accounting model where funds placed in a 401(k) are "off-limits." In this case, of course, psychological motives affect portfolio composition rather than saving.

Interactions between housing wealth and saving incentives are plausible and relevant for at least six additional reasons. First, 401(k)s and housing equity are both illiquid, tax preferred, and held for long terms. Such assets could clearly be substitutes. Second, because of employer matching, financing a 401(k) with borrowing can be lucrative. Indeed, simple calculations show that with high rates of employer matching, one should do everything possible to maximize one's 401(k) contributions up to the matching limit.[15] Third, most saving incentive account holders also own their own home and therefore have saved for a down payment and save regularly through monthly mortgage payments. Omitting these factors systematically understates how much saving these households have done and makes saving incentive accounts appear to be disproportionately important in household portfolios. Fourth, the budget constraint links all assets and consumption. Financial assets are a small part of most households' wealth portfolio. Omitting the effect of 401(k)s on other assets presents an incomplete and biased view. Fifth, much of the literature on social security and pensions examines the impact of such policies on broad measures of wealth.[16] Even in his own work, Bernheim (1987) finds fairly large amounts of substitution between social security wealth and broad measures of other wealth, a large part of which consists of housing. Sixth, the literature indicates that looking at broader asset definitions generates larger estimated offsets for pension wealth, consistent with Engen and Gale's results.[17] For all of these reasons, I am surprised that Bernheim does not embrace measuring the effects of policy on broad wealth measures.

Third-Party Responses

Pensions and Saving

The econometric literature on pensions and saving is in far worse shape than the literature on saving incentives. Gale (1995) identifies eight distinct econometric biases in the literature, each of which suggests that the estimated impact of pensions on nonpension wealth is more positive than the true impact. Therefore, although the literature taken at face value would suggest that pensions cause little or no reduction in nonpension wealth, these results may be severely biased. Gale (1995) suggests ways to adjust for several of the biases in principle and implements one set of tests in practice. He finds that correcting for the biases raises the estimated offset, in some cases substantially.

Bernheim questions whether eligibility for traditional pensions is correlated with tastes for saving. A number of theoretical studies suggest a positive correlation, and some evidence has been presented consistent with these views.[18] Bernheim argues that the sign of the correlation is ambiguous because those with the highest propensity to save may sort themselves into 401(k)s, while those with somewhat weaker but still strong interests in saving may choose traditional pensions. Those with low propensities to save would tend to have neither. Thus, those in traditional plans may be either more or less intense savers than average; the correlation is uncertain.

Two comments are warranted here. First, almost all of the studies of pensions cited by Bernheim use data from 1983 or earlier. During that period, 401(k)s were negligible, so traditional pensions would have attracted those with strong or intermediate tastes for saving, and there would be a positive correlation between pension coverage and tastes for saving. Thus, previous studies likely contain biases due to a positive correlation between pensions and tastes for saving. Second, 401(k) participants and eligibles currently have high traditional pension coverage rates relative to other observationally equivalent households. This suggests substantial overlap between the pension group and 401(k) group and thus that, even now, households with pensions have greater than average propensities to save.

Substitution Between 401(k)s and Other Pensions

Analysis of substitution at the firm level between 401(k)s and other pensions is crucial to understanding the impact of 401(k)s on overall wealth accumulation. The studies of the effects of 401(k)s on household wealth noted above do not include pension wealth. Thus, if a company converted its pension or thrift plan to a 401(k), observed "wealth" in the survey data would rise even though actual wealth did not.

Substitution between 401(k)s and pensions at the company level could occur in several ways. The company could convert previously existing plans to 401(k)s, terminate existing plans and replace them with 401(k)s, introduce 401(k)s and then cut back on existing pensions or not enhance them at the rate they otherwise would have. Or 401(k)s could replace other plans that would have been created in the absence of 401(k)s. It is difficult to obtain evidence on some of these factors.

Nevertheless, it seems clear that many 401(k) plans represented conversions of previously existing after-tax thrift saving plans. For example, tabulations of the Form 5500 data indicate that in 1985, 39 percent of existing plans, 65 percent of participants with nonzero balances, and 85 percent of asset balances in 401(k)s were in plans set up before 1982. Because 401(k)s did not become popular until 1982 and after, most of these earlier plans are thought to represent conversions of preexisting after-tax thrift plans. Even in 1991, the last year analyzed in Poterba, Venti, and Wise (1995), 62 percent of assets, 42 percent of participants, and 47 percent of contributions in 401(k)s were accounted for by plans created before 1982. Thus, it is plausible that a large proportion of 401(k) wealth would have existed as some other type of pension or thrift plan wealth if 401(k)s did not exist. If so, studies of the impact of 401(k)s on saving that omit this consideration (all studies to date) overstate the impact of 401(k) plans on saving.[19]

Worker Education

Bernheim and Garrett (1995) find that workers who received financial education have higher self-reported saving rates than those that did not. These results are encouraging, but some caveats are appropriate. People who have received retirement education may be aware of more of their saving than others. For example, they might include their employers' contributions to pensions and 401(k)s, as well as their own contribution. The questions referring to saving are vague and may have been difficult to interpret: no household reported a negative saving rate, which seems highly implausible.[20] If this occurred because households do not view borrowing as negative saving, then positive saving rate answers may be just as contaminated as the zero saving rate answers. Future work in this area is clearly warranted.

Conclusion

It may be useful to close by looking at the big picture. In thirteen years, from 1981 to 1994 saving incentive accounts accumulated balances of about $1.5 trillion, equivalent to about six years worth of personal saving as measured in the national income accounts. If saving incentives raised saving, accumulations of this magnitude may be expected to have a noticeable impact. However, the personal saving rate fell over that period. Of course, many factors affect aggregate saving, but confidently claiming that saving incentives are effective in raising saving seems unwarranted in my view based on either the microstudies or the macrodata.

Notes

The opinions expressed in this Comment should not be ascribed to the officers, staff, or trustees of the Brookings Institution.

1. See Engen, Gale, and Scholz (1994, pp. 135–136). Many of these families had combined limits below $4,000, indicating that one spouse earned less than $2,000. Such households may reasonably choose to contribute only $2,000, since the benefits of having a separate account for the spouse to make small and possibly sporadic contributions may not be worth the transactions, monitoring, and liquidity costs.

2. For example, the fungibility of assets is sometimes taken to be a primary implication of the life cycle model by advocates of psychological models (see Thaler 1990). But in the presence of real-world considerations such as transactions costs, illiquidity, and uncertainty, fungibility is no longer an implication of the life cycle approach.

3. However, it is not obvious that psychological models are most likely to apply to those that save very little. High-saving households could be those that have solved their self-discipline problems.

4. Browning and Lusardi (1995) make a similar point.

5. For example, Engen, Gale, and Scholz (1994), using a sample similar to Joines and Manegold, report that mean nonmortgage debt rose by $2,400 for IRA contributors over this period but by only $1,350 for noncontributors. Median nonmortgage debt rose by $2,350 for contributors compared to only $126 for noncontributors.

6. Bernheim specifies the saving of group i at time t as $s_{it} = \mu_i + \alpha_t + \eta_i M_{it}$, where μ_i measures the group's innate tastes for saving, α_t is a time-specific effect, M_{it} is the IRA limit, and η_i measures the share of added IRA contributions that represents new saving in response to a change in the IRA limit. Bernheim asserts that "one would expect μ_i and η_i to be positively correlated." However, there are good reasons why the two variables would be negatively correlated. Bernheim notes that "high savers are more likely to respond to an increase in the contribution limit"; that is, they are more likely to make additional IRA contributions. That much is not in dispute; the issue is the extent to which the increase in contributions represents new saving, (i.e., η_i). In particular, if continuing contributors have higher tastes for saving (more initial wealth controlling for other factors), I would expect that $\eta_c < \eta_e$, where the c and e subscripts correspond to the continuing contributors and newly eligible contributors,

respectively. This expectation is consistent with results in Gale and Scholz (1994) that indicate that, controlling for other factors, households with higher asset levels find IRAs to be better substitutes for other saving.

7. Poterba, Venti, and Wise refer to these as tests of "like families," while Engen and Gale (1995) and Engen, Gale, and Scholz (1996) call them tests based on "successive cross-sections." Each name emphasizes a different aspect of the test, but all refer to the same test.

8. Poterba, Venti, and Wise (1994) show that median financial assets of households aged sixty-five to sixty-nine in 1991 were $14,000. Median net worth was $261,000.

9. See Feldstein (1980), Summers (1981), and Poterba (1984) for further elaboration.

10. This increase is unlikely to be due to an increase in employer matching. In 1993, among eligible workers who did not receive a match, 60 percent contributed.

11. Participation in the SIPP refers to having a positive balance. Contributions are not observed. There is an obvious difference between making a positive contribution and having a positive balance. But SIPP "participation" data are very similar to the data from the Current Population Surveys in the level of participation and, in particular, in the increase in that participation rate over time.

12. It is worth noting, however, that almost none of the point estimates indicate any economically significant effect of 401(k) eligibility on wealth: of the eighteen estimates in tables 6 to 8 of Engen and Gale, only one is larger than $300, and many are negative.

13. In 1987, controlling for other factors, eligible renters were about 2.2 percentage points more likely to hold an IRA. In 1991, the corresponding figure was also 2.2 percentage points, indicating no symptoms of dilution of the sample of eligible renters compared to the sample of ineligible renters.

14. Engen and Gale discuss additional ways that unintentional substitution can occur.

15. Kusko, Poterba, and Wilcox (1994) report that about 75 percent of 401(k) participants in their sample at one company contributed at or above the match limit.

16. See Avery, Elliehausen, and Gustafson (1986), Blinder, Gordon, and Wise (1980), Diamond and Hausman (1984), Dicks-Mireaux and King (1984), and Hubbard (1986).

17. Avery, Elliehausen, and Gustafson, (1986) find that only 11 percent of pension wealth shows up as a reduction in liquid assets, but that 66 percent of pension wealth shows up as a reduction in other net worth. Engen, Gale, and Scholz (1994) and Gale (1995) obtain similar results.

18. The theoretical models include Allen, Clark, and McDermed (1993) and Ippolito (1993). For empirical work, see Ippolito (1993) and Johnson (1993).

19. For further discussion of these issues, see Engen, Gale, and Scholz (1996).

20. Sabelhaus (1993) carefully develops alternative measures of saving for U.S. households based on data from the 1989 Consumer Expenditure Survey and finds that 30 percent or more experience negative saving rates. The 1983 Survey of Consumer Finances contained a question that asked people whether, considering all of their accounts, they had put money in or taken more money out over the past year. Almost one-third said they had taken more money out.

References

Allen, Steven G., Robert L. Clark, and Ann A. McDermed. 1993. "Pensions, Bonding, and Lifetime Jobs." *Journal of Human Resources* 28(3):463–481.

Avery, Robert B., Gregory E. Elliehausen, and Thomas A. Gustafson. 1986. "Pensions and Social Security in Household Portfolios: Evidence from the 1983 Survey of Consumer Finances." In F. Gerard Adams and Susan M. Wachter, eds., *Savings and Capital Formation,* pp. 127–60. Lexington, MA: Lexington Books.

Bassett, William F., Michael J. Fleming, and Anthony P. Rodrigues. 1996, April. "How Workers Use 401(k) Plans: The Participation, Contribution, and Withdrawal Decisions." Mimeo. Federal Reserve Board of New York.

Bernheim, B. Douglas. 1987. "The Economic Effects of Social Security: Toward a Reconciliation of Theory and Measurement." *Journal of Public Economics* 33:273–304.

Bernheim, B. Douglas, and Daniel M. Garrett. 1995, August. "The Determinants and Consequences of Financial Education in the Workplace: Evidence from a Survey of Households." Mimeo. Stanford University.

Blinder, Alan S., Roger H. Gordon, and Donald E. Wise. 1980, December. "Reconsidering the Work Disincentive Effects of Social Security." *National Tax Journal* 33(4):431–442.

Browning, Martin, and Annamaria Lusardi. 1995, April. "Household Saving: Micro Theories and Micro Facts," Mimeo. McMaster University.

Diamond, P. A., and J. A. Hausman. 1984. "Individual Retirement and Savings Behavior." *Journal of Public Economics* 23:81–114.

Dicks-Mireaux, Louis, and Mervyn King. 1984. "Pension Wealth and Household Savings: Tests of Robustness." *Journal of Public Economics* 23:81–114.

Engen, Eric M., and William G. Gale. 1993, April. "IRAs and Saving in a Stochastic Life-Cycle Model." Mimeo. UCLA and the Brookings Institution.

Engen, Eric M., and William G. Gale. 1995, October. "Debt, Taxes and the Effects of 401(k) Plans on Household Wealth Accumulation." Mimeo. The Brookings Institution.

Engen, Eric M., William G. Gale, and John Karl Scholz. 1994. "Do Saving Incentives Work?" *Brookings Papers on Economic Activity* 1:85–180.

Engen, Eric M., William G. Gale, and John Karl Scholz. 1996, February. "Effects of Tax-Based Saving Incentives on Savings and Wealth: A Critical Review of the Literature." Mimeo. Brookings Institution.

Feldstein, Martin. 1980, December. "Inflation, Portfolio Choice, and the Prices of Land and Corporate Stock." *American Journal of Agricultural Economics* 62(5):910–916.

Gale, William G. 1995, June. "The Effects of Pensions on Wealth: A Re-Evaluation of Theory and Evidence." Mimeo.

Gale, William G., and John Karl Scholz. 1994, December. "IRAs and Household Saving." *American Economic Review* 84(5):1233–1260.

Hubbard, R. Glenn. 1986, May. "Pension Wealth and Individual Saving." *Journal of Money, Credit, and Banking* 18(2):167–178.

Hurd, Michael. 1995, November. "Mortality Risk and Consumption by Couples." Presentation at the Conference on the Microeconomics of Saving and Consumption Growth, Institute for Fiscal Studies and Bank of Portugal, Estori, Portugal.

Ippolito, Richard A. 1993, April. "Selecting and Retaining High-Quality Workers: A Theory of 401(k) Pensions." Unpublished paper. Washington, DC: Pension Benefit Guaranty Corporation.

Johnson, Richard W. 1993, December. *The Impact of Worker Preferences on Pension Coverage in the HRS.* Health and Retirement Study Working Paper Series, Paper 94-018.

Joines, Douglas H., and James G. Manegold. 1995. "IRAs and Saving: Evidence from a Panel of Taxpayers." Mimeo. University of Southern California.

Kusko, Andrea, James M. Poterba, and David W. Wilcox. 1994, February. *Employee Decisions with Respect to 401(k) Plans: Evidence from Individual Level Data.* NBER Working Paper 4635.

Poterba, James M. 1984, November. "Tax Subsidies to Owner-Occupied Housing: An Asset-Market Approach." *Quarterly Journal of Economics* 99(4):729–752.

Poterba, James M., Steven F. Venti, and David A. Wise. 1994, May. "Targeted Retirement Saving and the Net Worth of Elderly Americans." *American Economic Review* 84(2):180–185.

Poterba, James M., Steven F. Venti, and David A. Wise. 1995. "Do 401(k) Contributions Crowd Out Other Personal Saving?" *Journal of Public Economics* 58:1–32.

Poterba, James M., Steven F. Venti, and David A. Wise. 1996, January. "Do Retirement Saving Programs Increase Saving? Reconciling the Evidence." Mimeo. MIT.

Sabelhaus, John. 1993, September. "What Is the Distributional Burden of Taxing Consumption?" *National Tax Journal* 46(3):331–344.

Skinner, Jonathan. 1992, January 13. "Do IRAs Promote Saving? A Review of the Evidence." *Tax Notes.*

Summers, Lawrence H. 1981, May. "Inflation, the Stock Market, and Owner-Occupied Housing." *American Economic Review* 71(2):429–434.

Summers, Lawrence H. 1986, June 9. "Summers Replies to Galper and Byce on IRAs." *Tax Notes*, pp. 1014–1016.

Thaler, Richard. 1990, Winter. "Anomalies: Saving, Fungibility, and Mental Accounts." *Journal of Economic Perspectives* 4(1):193–205.

Thaler, Richard. 1994, May. "Mental Accounts and Household Saving." *American Economic Review* 84(2):186–192.

Venti, Steven F., and David A. Wise. 1986. "Tax-Deferred Accounts, Constrained Choice, and Estimation of Individual Saving." *Review of Economic Studies* 53:579–601.

Venti, Steven F., and David A. Wise. 1987. "IRAs and Saving." In Martin Feldstein, ed., *The Effects of Taxation on Capital Accumulation.* Chicago: University of Chicago Press.

Venti, Steven F., and David A. Wise. 1990, August. "Have IRAs Increased U.S. Saving? Evidence from Consumer Expenditure Surveys." *Quarterly Journal of Economics* 105:661–698.

Venti, Steven F., and David A. Wise. 1991. "The Saving Effect of Tax-Deferred Retirement Accounts: Evidence from SIPP." In B. Douglas Bernheim and John B. Shoven, eds., *National Saving and Economic Performance.* Chicago: University of Chicago Press and NBER.

Comment

Jonathan S. Skinner

Figuring out whether IRAs and 401(k)s are new saving or shuffled saving might appear to be an easy question. Economists have good data from the 1980s and early 1990s and were blessed with numerous natural experiments during that period. Yet determining whether retirement saving contributions are shuffled or new saving has proved to be difficult, as evidenced by the coexistence of studies showing that saving incentives are higly effective (Hubbard 1984; Venti and Wise 1988, 1990, 1992; Poterba, Venti, and Wise 1994, 1995, 1996), partially effective (Joines and Manegold 1995; Attanasio and De Leire 1994; Johnson 1985), and entirely ineffective (Gale and Scholz 1994; Engen, Gale, and Scholz 1994, 1996; Engen and Gale 1995).

In reviewing this tangled literature, Douglas Bernheim has provided a great public service in two ways. First, he has provided a readily accessible guide to the saving incentive debate, pointing out both the strengths and the weaknesses of each major study in nontechnical language. Second, he has recast the debate as one about issues larger than just whether saving incentives work. Instead, he has focused on larger question: Is the conventional life cycle model, with optimizing agents, the right paradigm for studying saving behavior? Targeted saving incentives do more than just vary the interest rate; they are often associated with up-front deductions, payroll contributions and education programs, and penalties discouraging early withdrawals, all factors that can affect saving behavior. By focusing on these factors, Bernheim has helped to turn the debate from one about the technical estimation of conventional life cycle models to a richer approach that links the economics of saving with factors, such as self-control, long considered obvious in the psychological literature. Accounting for self-control and confusion about saving may mean difficulty in modeling such behavior, but the payoff is likely to be a more accurate representation of saving choices.

I will not spend time commenting on specific aspects of the chapter, that job being already done with great fervor by Bill Gale. Instead, I will make three general points, focusing primarily on IRAs rather than on 401(k)s.[1] First, regarding the evidence on whether IRAs increase overall saving, Bernheim throws up his hand and concludes that we have no idea whether IRAs affect overall saving. I think that we can arrive at some consensus, albeit with wide confidence intervals. Second, one must look beyond that day when a consensus is reached on the saving effects of IRAs and 401(k)s[2] and ask how effective saving incentives must be to justify their revenue cost. For example, suppose we know with certainty that IRAs generate 30 cents of new saving per dollar of IRA contribution. Should IRAs be deemed a rousing success or an abject failure? To answer this question, we need to know a few more things than just how much saving is generated per dollar of IRA contribution. We need to know how much it costs in forgone revenue. Third, whether saving incentives such as IRAs or 401(k)s are a success also requires identifying the "market failure" they are designed to overcome. Only then, by comparing the revenue costs of saving incentive programs with the social benefits (if any) of the increased saving (if any), can one make an informed judgment as to whether saving incentive programs are worth the cost. Let us consider each issue.

First, IRAs were neither entirely new saving nor entirely no saving; my best guess is about 30 cents of new saving per dollar of IRA contribution. The best-known studies showing that IRAs consisted largely of new saving were by Venti and Wise, who in numerous studies compared the saving behavior of contributors to IRAs with the saving behavior of noncontributors. They concluded that IRAs were imperfect substitutes for other types of saving, so the marginal dollar contributed to an IRA came from reduced consumption rather than existing saving. Gale and Scholz (1994) tested for, and found, that IRA contributors had a much stronger taste for saving than noncontributors. If so, then (as Gale and Scholz suggest) the Venti and Wise results are probably biased upward. IRA contributors save more not because of the existence of an IRA program but because they like to save in both non-IRA vehicles.

On the other hand, the Gale and Scholz (1994) estimates that IRAs have no impact on saving are probably biased downward. Although their model is careful to address heterogeneity in saving, ultimately their conclusion—that IRAs do nothing for saving—is an exceedingly fragile one. A replication of the Gale and Scholz empirical analysis by Poterba,

Venti, and Wise (1996) is able to mimic the Gale and Scholz benchmark result that IRAs have a slightly negative impact on saving.

The Gale and Scholz benchmark result excludes households reporting more (in absolute value) than $100,000 in saving. However, when Poterba, Venti, and Wise reduced the saving limit to $90,000 or increased it to $110,000, thereby adding or subtracting a few limit contributors, the estimated coefficients in either case switch completely, implying that IRAs are entirely *new* saving![3] A number of other studies, such as Attanasio and De Leire (1994) and Joines and Manegold (1995), point toward partial effects of IRAs on saving. The upward bias in the Venti and Wise model, the downward bias in the Gale and Scholz model, and other studies showing an intermediate saving effect suggest to me that one can reasonably conclude IRAs were at least partially successful at generating new saving. And if econometrics fails to answer the question, then one can always just ask people, as did Johnson (1985): "About half of the respondents said they would have saved it anyway. About 10 percent said they would have spent it all, while about 40 percent said they would have spent some and saved some."

These numbers imply that IRAs yielded 32 cents in new saving per dollar of IRA contribution. Thirty-two cents is an upper limit since we do not know how respondents are accounting for their tax saving (and future tax liability) in answering the question. On the other hand, the survey questions about saving are short term, when the IRA program was just getting started. In the long term, the saving effects are likely to be larger (Engen, Gale, and Scholz 1994). For the reasons cited I am comfortable with a midpoint estimate of 30 cents in new saving per dollar IRA contribution, with a confidence interval ranging from about 18 cents to 42 cents.

Second, even adopting an assumption that IRAs generate just 30 cents of new saving per dollar of contribution yields a generous benefit-cost ratio of $2.70 in new private wealth accumulation per dollar revenue loss. The cost to the government of saving incentives is the lost revenue from offering the programs, and the gains are the (presumed) increased saving, whether for aggregate saving or the saving of specific target groups such as low-income or low-wealth retirees. Writing this as a benefit-cost ratio,

$$-\left[\frac{\Delta \text{ net capital accumulation per \$1 IRA}}{\Delta \text{ net government revenue per \$1 IRA}}\right]_t.$$

Both the numerator and denominator are stocks rather than flows and are defined for a particular time t after the initial IRA contribution. For example, suppose that the taxpayer is in the 36 percent tax bracket, and that 30 cents of the IRA contribution is drawn from new saving.[4] The ratio in the equation would therefore be 66 cents (36 cents saved through reduced tax liability plus 30 cents of new saving) divided by the revenue loss of 36 cents. The benefit-cost ratio for the first year after the IRA contribution is therefore 66/36, or a $1.83 increase in private saving per dollar in revenue loss in the first year. Were the IRA financed by deficit spending, the first-year net gain in the capital stock would be 83 cents per dollar of revenue loss. Over time, there is a gradual loss in tax revenue from the shuffled saving, although when the IRA is cashed out, even the shuffled saving yields additional tax revenue. Accumulating tax losses, wealth accumulation, and marker returns forward twenty-two years, the assumed date at which the IRA is cashed out, yields an estimate of $2.70 cents per dollar devoted to the IRA program (Hubbard and Skinner 1996). Again, for a deficit-financed IRA, the net capital stock would increase by $1.70. In other words, a relatively modest saving effect IRAs can translate into a quite substantial increase in capital per dollar of lost tax revenue. The estimates are substantially larger when the marginal saving effect is 40 cents per $1.00 IRA contribution (a $4.31 increase in the private capital stock) or when the incremental tax revenue from the corporate tax is included in the calculation ($8.32), as in Feldstein (1995). When IRAs increase saving by just 10 cents, the gains in private wealth accumulation are $0.81; a deficit-financed IRA program would reduce national saving by $0.19 per dollar of revenue cost.

To summarize, it does not take much, in terms of the extra saving per dollar of IRA contribution, to stimulate marginal increases in the capital stock per dollar of revenue loss. The intuition is that even if the aggregate effects of a given IRA program are not large—in terms of overall increases in new net saving—the revenue costs, once properly accounted for, are even smaller. This intuition is borne out by the simulation exercise in Engen, Gale, and Scholz (1994) that calculated the long-run impact of a general IRA program on the capital stock. In their model, the aggregate effects were quite modest, but the revenue losses were even more modest, leading to a benefit-cost ratio of about 5. They calculate a similar long-run benefit-cost ratio from a universal 401(k) program equal to 16, although it took many years to reach the long run.

Although these calculations allow us to focus better on the costs of IRAs and 401(k)s, we are still left with something of a problem: even the benefit-cost ratio calculated above does not answer the relevant question as to whether saving incentives are a good idea. The extra saving from IRAs comes from people's giving up consumption today for consumption (or bequests) in the future. Why is society better off if people defer consumption to the future?

Third, although there are a number of reasons that saving incentive programs could be socially valuable, the most plausible to me is that they are most valuable in overcoming myopia in planning for retirement. What is the "market failure" that causes people to spend too much today and not set aside enough for retirement? I consider four possibilities.[5]

1. *A high social value of capital accumulation.* To argue for substantial external effects of increased capital accumulation, one must appeal to models in which capital or investment yields positive external effects on productivity or output, as in the models of Romer (1986) or King and Rebelo (1990). Others have noted the close correlation between saving and investment rates, and between investment rates and Solow "residual" measures of productivity growth (Shultze 1992, p. 242). Hence the notion that a larger capital stock yields social external benefits is certainly a valid one, but it is difficult to quantify. One problem with appealing to capital stock externalities to justify saving incentives is that our current incentives are not particularly well suited to the job. They include restrictions on contributions and the forced withdrawal of assets after age seventy, mechanisms not designed to entice the wealthiest households—those that account for most of the nation's saving—to save much more.

2. *Reducing the distortion between current and retirement consumption.* Standard life cycle models predict that the tax on interest income distorts consumption at retirement years (e.g., Feldstein 1978). The consumer discounts future consumption at the net (after-tax) return, while at the social optimum, future consumption should be discounted at the gross (pretax) rate of return. Therefore shifting one dollar of current consumption to the future at the gross return should provide a first-order welfare gain approximated by the wedge between the gross and net return. However, the IRA and 401(k) program is a leaky bucket for effecting this transfer from current to retirement consumption since some revenue is lost because of partial shuffling. Calculations from Hubbard and Skinner (1996) suggest that one must either have a high saving effect of IRAs (about forty-six cents per dollar of contribution) or include the corporate income tax wedge before one can justify saving incentives *solely* on these grounds.

3. *Keeping the elderly off welfare programs.* Welfare programs such as Supplemental Security Insurance (SSI) and Medicaid are designed to assist elderly with limited assets and income. Encouraging people to contribute

money into IRAs and 401(k)s could save the government money in the long term by reducing the chance of people qualifying for means-tested welfare programs (see Hubbard, Skinner, and Zeldes 1995). It is difficult, however, to place a value of the incremental reduction in future government expenditures because people today participate in IRAs or 401(k)s. Another problem with this explanation for saving incentives is that the programs are typically voluntary rather than mandatory. Those most likely to end up on welfare at retirement are probably also those least likely to contribute to any pension or saving program.

4. *Myopia.* To this point, I have restricted our attention to individuals facing well-defined, dynamically consistent utility functions. As Bernheim emphasizes, there is considerable evidence that people stumble through their planning for retirement with little idea of what they require at retirement and little motivation to meet those requirements. For example, in earlier work, Bernheim (1994) suggests that saving rates on average are only one-third what they should be for households to consume during retirement at levels commensurate with their preretirement consumption patterns. If households made dynamically inconsistent plans (in the sense of Laibson 1994), there may be an intrinsic value to retirement saving programs that assist in self-control—the ability to plan ahead for one's retirement without the temptation of spending that money in the near term. Similarly, Posner (1995) distinguishes between one's "young self" and "old self," where the younger self does not care sufficiently for the older self to provide the latter with a retirement nest egg. In this case, encouraging people to forgo consumption today for consumption during retirement could well yield substantial social benefits, at least from the perspective of one's old self. Ultimately, I view this justification—the difficulty or inability of many Americans to save enough for their retirement—to be the most persuasive justification for encouraging saving incentives. The problem is that such benefits are difficult to quantify. If we cannot write down preferences in a dynamically consistent way, it makes it harder still to attach dollar-equivalent variation measures to capture the benefits of deferred consumption.

To sum up, I think there is good evidence that the saving effect of IRAs is about thirty cents of new saving per dollar of IRA contribution; probably the 401(k) saving effect is larger (although see Engen and Gale 1995). Whether this view means that saving incentives are socially useful or too expensive ultimately depends on whether one thinks that people do not save "enough" for retirement.[6] I find convincing the view, expressed by Bernheim, that people do not save enough for retirement because of problems with self-control and just plain confusion. If so, then saving incentives could play a role in meeting both market failures and individual failures that cause too little saving for retirement.

Notes

1. The discussion of these three points draws from Hubbard and Skinner (1996).

2. Probably not in our lifetime.

3. As noted above, Poterba, Venti, and Wise (1996) could not replicate the Gale and Scholz (1994) results exactly because of small differences in the sample size. So one cannot conclude that the Poterba, Venti, and Wise replicated saving coefficient for the $90,000 and $110,000 limits would be exactly the same as those that would arise from a similar exercise using the Gale and Scholz computer code.

4. See Hubbard and Skinner (1996) for technical details of these calculations.

5. This discussion again follows Hubbard and Skinner (1996). For a good exposition of the laissez-faire view of saving policy, see Lazear (1994).

6. The tricky part is determining how much is enough. Hubbard, Skinner, and Zeldes (1995) suggest that some people who save little for retirement do so optimally, because of means-tested welfare programs. But these people are probably still saving too little from a social standpoint.

References

Attanasio, Orazio, and Thomas De Leire. 1994, October. *IRAs and Household Saving Revisited: Some New Evidence.* NBER Wokding Paper 4900.

Bernheim, B. Douglas. 1994. "Personal Saving, Information, and Economic Literacy: New Directions for Public Policy." In *Tax Policy for Economic Growth in the 1990s.* Washington, DC: American Council for Capital Formation.

Engen, Eric M., and William G. Gale. 1995, October. "Debt, Taxes, and the Effects of 401(k) Plans on Household Wealth Accumulation." Mimeo. Brookings Institution.

Engen, Eric M., William G. Gale, and John Karl Scholz. 1994. "Do Saving Incentives Work?" *Brookings Papers on Economic Activity* 1:85–151.

Engen, Eric, William Gale, and John Karl Scholz 1996. "Effects of Tax-Based Saving Incentives on Saving and Wealth: A Critical Review of the Literature." *Journal of Economic Perspectives* 10(4) forthcoming.

Feldstein, Martin (1978). "The Welfare Cost of Capital Income Taxation." *Journal of Political Economy* 86:S29–S52.

Feldstein, Martin. 1995. "The Effects of Tax-Based Saving Incentives on Government Revenue and National Saving." *Quarterly Journal of Economics* 110:475–494.

Gale, William G., and John Karl Scholz. 1994. "IRAs and Household Saving." *American Economic Review* 84:1233–1260.

Hubbard, R. Glenn. 1984. "Do IRAs and Keoghs Increase Saving?" *National Tax Journal* 37:43–54.

Hubbard, R. Glenn, and Jonathan S. Skinner. 1996. "Assessing the Effectiveness of Saving Incentives." *Journal of Economic Perspectives* 10(4) forthcoming.

Hubbard, R. Glenn, Jonathan S. Skinner, and Stephen P. Zeldes. 1995. "Precautionary Saving and Social Insurance." *Journal of Political Economy* 103:360–399.

Johnson, Alfred P. 1985. "Individual Retirement Accounts Help Boost Saving in the U.S." Testimony to the Committee on Finance, U.S. Senate, in Tax Reform Proposals (99–246, p. XIII), pp. 129–149.

Joines, Douglas H., and James G. Manegold. 1995. "IRA and Saving Evidence from a Panel of Taxpayers." Mimeo. University of Southern California.

King, Robert G., and Sergio Rebelo. 1990. "Public Policy and Economic Growth: Developing Neoclassical Implications." *Journal of Political Economy* 98:S126–150.

Laibson, David. 1994. "Golden Eggs and Hyperbolic Discounting." Mimeo. Harvard University.

Lazear, Edward. 1994. "Some Thoughts on Saving." In David A. Wise, ed., *Studies in the Economics of Aging*. Chicago: University of Chicago Press.

Posner, Richard A. 1995. *Aging and Old Age*. Chicago: University of Chicago Press.

Poterba, James M., Steven F. Venti, and David A. Wise. 1994. "401(k) Plans and Tax-Deferred Saving." In David A. Wise, ed., *Studies in the Economics of Aging*. Chicago: University of Chicago Press.

Poterba, James M., Steven F. Venti, and David A. Wise. 1995. "Do 401(k) Contributions Crowd Out Other Personal Saving?" *Journal of Public Economics* 58:1–32.

Poterba, James M., Steven F. Venti, and David A. Wise. 1996. "How Retirement Saving Programs Increase Saving." *Journal of Economic Perspectives* 10(4) forthcoming.

Romer, Paul 1986. "Increasing Returns and Long-Run Growth." *Journal of Political Economy* 94:1002–10037.

Schultze, Charles L. 1992. *Memos to the President*. Washington DC: Brookings Instititution.

Venti, Steven F., and David A. Wise. 1988. "The Determinants of IRA Contributions and the Effect of Limit Changes." In Zvi Bodie, John B. Shoven, and David A. Wise, eds., *Pensions and the U.S. Economy*. Chicago: University of Chicago Press.

Venti, Steven F., and David A. Wise. 1990. "Have IRAs Increased U.S. Saving: Evidence from Consumer Expenditure Surveys." *Quarterly Journal of Economics* 105:661–698.

Venti, Steven F., and David A. Wise. 1992. "Government Policy and Personal Retirement Saving." In James M. Poterba, ed., *Tax Policy and the Economy*, vol. 6. Cambridge: MIT Press.

8 Tax Policy and Investment

Kevin A. Hassett and
R. Glenn Hubbard

The first ship to arrive in St. Petersburg in 1701, a Dutch vessel, received from Peter the Great the privilege of paying no custom duties for the rest of its physical life—a concession which had the effect of prolonging the ship's life for almost a century—three or four times the normal span."[1]

Just as Peter the Great's tax amnesty spurred substantial maintenance investment in that Dutch ship, many governments have apparently believed that tax policy can be used as an instrument to alter firms' capital investment decisions. Indeed, investment tax credits (ITCs), special investment reserve funds, or accelerated depreciation allowances have been the rule rather than the exception in more developed countries since World War II. Against this backdrop, however, economists have generally struggled to find a significant impact of tax policy on investment.

The empirical economic literature on investment finds its early roots in the work of Aftalian (1909), Clark (1917), and Fisher (1930). Aftalian and Clark observed that business investment is highly correlated with changes in business output, providing support for the early "accelerationist" school, while Fisher's neoclassical theory argued for the importance of marginal conditions. At the risk of oversimplifying, the literature subsequently divided into two camps. One side argued that the accelerator model performed so well empirically that it should be adopted as the standard model; the other side looked to neoclassical models relating investment to the user cost of capital. The neoclassical school may have had the theoretical high ground, but empirical implementations of neoclassical models have been generally disappointing. Indeed, while the time-series evidence has always revealed that lags of output are highly correlated with investment, interest rates have provided only limited additional explanatory power.[2] The debate between these two schools provides a useful introduction to our review of the literature relating tax policy to investment. Many observers even recently (e.g., Clark 1993) have argued that tax policy likely does not significantly affect investment, and the arguments inevitably harken back to the accelerationist debate.

Motivated by the hope that the simplest neoclassical models failed to explain investment fluctuations because they were too stylized, substantial energy was devoted to the task of extending these models to incorporate more realistic assumptions in the 1970s and early 1980s.[3] Chief among these was the incorporation of costs of adjusting the capital stock. According to these models, investment is forward looking and based on rational expectations of future variables. Because companies base their expectations of future variables in part on their observations of the past, researchers identified a link between lagged variables and current investment. Indeed, correlation of past output growth and future "fundamentals" could be used to rationalize a strong correlation between current investment and past values of the growth of output. When asked to explain the time-series movements of investment, however, these new models proved disappointing. Additional variables that were meant to capture the marginal cost or return to investment seemed to be of little use, over and above output, in predicting investment. Moreover, structural parameter estimates tended to be wildly implausible. It is at this point in the evolution of the literature that we begin this review.

8.1 Models of Investment in the Neoclassical Tradition

Models in the neoclassical tradition focus on the derived demand for capital by value-maximizing firms.[4] This intuition is typically transformed into models of investment by making assumptions about costs of changing the capital stock. For simplicity of exposition, consider the decisions of a price-taking firm. Absent taxes, in each period t, firm i's real net cash flow is given by

$$X_{i,t} = F(K_{i,t-1}, N_{i,t}) - w_t N_{i,t} - p_t I_{i,t} - C(I_{i,t}, K_{i,t-1}), \tag{8.1}$$

where $K(\bullet)$ is the capital stock, $F(\bullet)$ is the real revenue function of the firm, N is the variable factor, w is the price of the variable factor, p is the real price of investment goods, and $C(\bullet)$ is the function determining the cost of adjusting the capital stock. In the absence of taxes, then, the marginal cost of newly installed capital is $p_t + C_I(I_{it}, K_{i,t-1})$.

To study investment tax policy, we add to the net cash flow expression (8.1) a profits tax at rate τ, an investment tax credit at rate k, and the present value of a dollar's worth of depreciation allowances, z.[5] With these additions, the marginal cost of newly installed capital is

$$p_t(1 - \Gamma_{i,t}) + (1 - \tau_t)C_I(I_{i,t}, K_{i,t-1}),$$

where $\Gamma_{it} = k_t + \tau_t z_{it}$, and we can rewrite equation 8.1 as:

$$X_{i,t} = (1 - \tau_t)(F(K_{i,t-1}, N_t) - w_t N_{i,t} - C_I(I_{i,t}, K_{i,t-1})) - p_t(1 - \Gamma_{i,t})I_{i,t}.$$

Under the assumption of value maximization, the firm maximizes the present value of its future net cash flows. Letting β be the discount factor appropriate for the ith firm, the firm's value at time t is given by

$$V_{i,t} = \max E_{i,t} \sum_{s=t}^{\infty} \left(\prod_{j=t}^{s} \right) \beta_{i,j} X_{is}, \tag{8.2}$$

where E_{it} is the expectations operator for firm i conditional on information available at time t. The firm chooses the path of investment and employment of the variable factor, given the initial capital stock, to maximize firm value. The change in the capital stock—net investment—is given by $I_{it} - \delta K_{i,t-1}$, where δ is the (assumed constant) proportional rate of depreciation.

For investment, the solution to the problem requires that the marginal value of an additional unit of investment equals its marginal cost. Denoting the shadow value of an additional unit of investment by q,[6]

$$q_{i,t} = p_t(1 - \Gamma_{i,t}) + (1 - \tau_t)C_I(I_{i,t}, K_{i,t-1}). \tag{8.3}$$

The shadow price q must also obey

$$\Delta q_{i,t} = (r_{it} + \delta_i)q_{i,t} - (1 - \tau_t)F_K(K_{i,t-1}, N_{i,t}) + (1 - \delta_i)C_K(I_{i,t}, K_{i,t-1}), \tag{8.4}$$

where r is the instantaneous rate at which marginal cash flows are discounted.

We can now use this general setup to examine two conventional formulations of the neoclassical approach: one based on the user cost of capital and one based on q.

User Cost of Capital

Jorgenson (1963) and his collaborators suggested using a form of equation 8.4 to derive an expression for the user cost of capital. If we interpret q as the price at which a unit of capital can be bought or sold, we can consider the thought experiment of renting a unit of newly installed capital. The owner of this capital will levy a rental cost c such that the rate of return equals r, the return available on alternative (financial) assets. The owner's return from renting the capital equals the rental cost, c, plus the capital gain on the machine, $\Delta q_{it+1}/q_{it}$, less the depreciation of the machine, δq_{it}. Expressed as a rate of return and equating the rate of return with the available alternative yields

$$c_{i,t} = \left((1-\tau_t)(r_{it}+\delta_i)q_{it} - \frac{\Delta q_{it}}{q_{i,t}}\right). \tag{8.5}$$

We can substitute for q in equation 8.3 to express the user cost as a function of the price of investment goods, adjustment costs, and tax parameters. Jorgenson assumed that adjustment costs were zero, yielding the familiar user cost expression:

$$c_{i,t} = p_t\left(\frac{1-\Gamma_{i,t}}{1-\tau_t}\right)\left(r_{it}+\delta_i - \frac{\Delta(p_{t+1}(1-\Gamma_{i,t}))}{p_t(1-\Gamma_{i,t})}\right), \tag{8.6}$$

Returning to our derivation of q in equation 8.3, we can more generally express the user cost as equaling the marginal cash flow of an additional unit of capital:

$$(1-\tau_t)(F_K(K_{i,t-1},N_{i,t}) - C_K(I_{i,t},K_{i,t-1})) = c_{i,t}. \tag{8.7}$$

Jorgenson's interest centered on isolating the effects of the user cost on the desired capital stock and investment. He considered a special case in which the prices p, w, and r are constant and $I_{it} = \delta K_{i,t-1}$ in steady state (so that $C_I = C_K = 0$). Hence from equation 8.7,

$$(1-\tau_t)F_K(K_{i,t-1},N_{i,1}) = c_{i,t}.$$

Assuming a constant elasticity of substitution production function,

$$F(K,N) = A[bK^{-\theta} + (1-b)N^{-\theta}]^{-1/\theta},$$

where $A > 0$, $0 < b < 1$, and $\theta > -1$, one can express the marginal revenue product of capital as

$$F_K(K,N) = \left(\frac{b}{A^\theta}\right)\left(\frac{F}{K}\right)^{1+\theta}.$$

Returning to the Jorgensonian derivation in equation 8.7, the steady-state capital stock can be described as a function of the user cost of capital and the firm's real revenue,

$$K^* = \left(\frac{b}{A^\theta}\right)^\sigma F\sigma\left(\frac{c}{1-\tau}\right)^{-\sigma}, \tag{8.8}$$

where σ is the elasticity of substitution ($\sigma = 1/(1+\theta)$).

Equation 8.8 describes the steady-state capital stock, K^*. As we describe in more detail below, it is not an "estimating equation." To estimate investment, Jorgenson assumed that $\sigma = 1$ (Cobb-Douglas technology), so that $K^*_{i,t} = (b/A^\theta)[(1-\tau_t)F_{it}/c_{i,t}]$. He then assumed that the capital stock adjusted to the desired level at an exogenous rate dictated by, say, delivery lags. A substantial empirical debate ensued, with Eisner and Nadiri (1968, 1970) claiming on the one hand that the elasticity of substitution is nearer zero than unity, while Jorgenson and Stephenson (1969) claimed on the other hand that an elasticity of unity is more consistent with the data.[7]

More contemporary applications of the user cost model incorporate explicit adjustment costs as opposed to ad hoc mechanisms such as delivery lags. Auerbach (1989), for example, begins with the Euler equation for investment and assumes a production function with productivity shocks and adjustment cost function. He approximates the optimal solution for perturbations by solving a linearized version of the Euler equation. He then derives a relationship between the investment rate ($I_{i,t}/K_{i,t-1}$) and the user cost of capital, in which the user cost coefficient is a function of the steady-state average user cost and a root of the linearized difference equation in K (for applications, see Auerbach and Hassett 1991, 1992; and Cummins, Hassett, and Hubbard 1994, 1996).

The q Theory

Tobin's (1969) q theory of investment made more rigorous Keynes's (1936) idea that the incentive to add new fixed capital depends on the market value of capital relative to its replacement cost. Tobin represented by q the ratio of the market value of the firm to the replacement cost of its capital stock. One can easily incorporate adjustment costs and tax parameters in the q framework (see Hayashi 1982).

Returning to equation 8.2, we know that equilibrium *marginal* q is related to the price of investment goods, tax parameters, and adjustment costs. If we assume that the adjustment cost function is quadratic,

$$C(I_{i,t}, K_{i,t-1}) = \frac{\omega}{2}\left(\frac{I_{i,t}}{K_{i,t-1}} - \mu_i\right)^2 K_{i,t-1}, \tag{8.9}$$

where μ is the steady-state rate of investment and ω is the adjustment cost parameter, then equation 8.2 can be rewritten as an investment equation:

$$\frac{I_{i,t}}{K_{i,t-1}} = \mu_i + \frac{1}{\omega}\left[\frac{q_{i,t} - p_t(1-\Gamma_{i,t})}{(1-\tau_t)}\right]. \tag{8.10}$$

Equation 8.10 offers a convenient way of estimating the responsiveness of investment to neoclassical variables, including tax parameters, but there is a hitch: marginal q is unobservable. Following Hayashi (1982), if the firm is a price taker in input and output markets and the production function exhibits constant returns to scale, marginal q equals average q, defined for each firm as tax-adjusted q (denoted below by Q),

$$Q_{i,t} = \frac{V_{i,t} + B_{i,t} - A_{i,t}}{K^R_{i,t-1}}, \tag{8.11}$$

where V is the market value of the firms' equity, B is the market value of the firm's debt, A is the present value of depreciation allowances on investment made before period t, and K^R is the replacement value of the firm's capital stock (including inventories).

The Q formulation stresses a relationship between investment and the net profitability of investing, as measured by the difference between the value of an incremental unit of capital and the tax-inclusive cost of purchasing capital. As with the user cost approach, by making assumptions about costs of adjusting the capital stock, one can estimate effects of investment incentives on investment.

Foreshadowing Empirical Problems

Jorgenson (1963) investigated whether a version of equation 8.8 could be used to describe aggregate fluctuations in U.S. investment. Moving from this equilibrium relationship to an empirical model, however, required a few more steps. Because output is determined by the choice of K, equation 8.8 does not relate K to a set of exogenous variables.[8] Rather, it expresses a relationship between endogenous variables that holds in equilibrium. Indeed, equation 8.8 does not define an investment relationship, that is, the *flow* of capital, but rather describes only the equilibrium *stock* of capital.[9] Jorgenson moved to an "investment" specification by defining a firm's "desired" capital stock, K^*, as Y/c, and then assuming that the firm gradually approached this desired stock over time. He assumed that the rate at which the firm closed the gap between its actual and desired stocks was given exogenously and did not affect the level of the "desired" stock. These assumptions yielded the estimating equation:

$$I_{it} = \sum_{j=0}^{T} w_j(K_{i,t-j} - K^*_{i,t-1-j}) + \delta K_{i,t-1}. \tag{8.12}$$

Hall and Jorgenson (1967) originally used such a model to explain aggregate investment and concluded that it described the data well. Eisner and his collaborators later pointed out that the model they estimated—recognizing that K^* was the ratio of output to the user cost—could be capturing accelerator effects, which had long been known to be strong explanatory factors for investment. In particular, if one constrained the user cost to be a constant, one could rewrite equation 8.12

$$I_{it} = \sum_{j=0}^{T} w_j(Y_{i,t-j} - Y_{i,t-1-j}) + \delta K_{i,t-1}, \tag{8.13}$$

which is a form of an accelerator model. When critics of Hall and Jorgenson isolated the separate contribution of the user cost to explaining investment, they found it to be negligible (see Eisner 1969, 1970; Eisner and Nadiri 1968; Chirinko and Eisner 1983).

Nonetheless, by the late 1960s, the neoclassical model developed by Jorgenson and others had become the standard model for studying investment decisions, but empirical debates remained. On the one hand, the neoclassical approach offered a structural link between tax policy parameters—the corporate tax rate, the present value of depreciation allowances, and the investment tax credit—and investment through the user cost of capital.[10] On the other hand, the empirical evidence suggested that the more rigorous theory did not improve the econometrician's ability to explain aggregate investment fluctuations or the response of business investment to changes in tax policy.

Partially in response to this empirical concern, models based on the Q representation of the firm's investment problem occupied much of the empirical research by the 1980s.[11] A key appeal of the Q approach was that it related investment to a variable that was (under certain assumptions) easier to observe than the user cost of capital. However, early empirical adaptation of Q models did not fare well in explaining either time-series or cross-sectional (firm-level) variation in investment.

Despite such empirical frustrations, policymakers in the United States and other industrial economies, given the frequency with which they manipulate tax policy parameters, evidently believe that business fixed investment responds to tax changes. Hence it is disturbing that models emphasizing the net return to investing are defeated in forecasting "horse races" by ad hoc models and that structural variables are frequently found to be economically or statistically insignificant.[12] Recently the investment literature has begun to make a convincing case that the fundamentals are in fact key determinants of investment but that they appear to have little effect in the macro data because of several severe econometric problems.[13] To set the stage for the discussion of these problems in section 8.3, we first review key stylized facts about the time-series behavior of business fixed investment and "fundamental determinants of investment."

8.2 Some Stylized Facts About Business Fixed Investment

In figure 8.1, we plot aggregate U.S. equipment investment against several investment fundamentals. The top panel shows the comovement of investment and the Jorgensonian user cost. The series rarely move together in an obvious way, and the correlation since 1960 is a statistically insignificant −.11. The second panel illustrates the strong comovements between investment and corporate cash flow. The two series are roughly coincident, and the correlation over time is a highly significant .64. The bottom panel illustrates the accelerator effect, which relates changes in the growth rates of output and equipment spending. As with cash flow, the correlation is large and highly significant, and the coincidence of the series is visually striking.

Although one should be cautious interpreting such correlations formally, they nonetheless suggest clear patterns. Aggregate equipment investment varies significantly over the business cycle and neither lags nor leads the cycle; it is highly correlated with other variables that are also highly procyclical. The time-series correlation between investment and the user cost, on the other hand, is quite weak. Figure 8.1 can be though of as a visual summary of the early investment literature: accelerator effects are strong and obvious; user cost effects appear weaker and more subtle.

We focus on studies of equipment investment, in large part because empirical attempts to model investment in structures have been more disappointing. Figure 8.2, which repeats figure 8.1 with the relevant fundamentals related to the growth rate of investment in nonresidential structures, illustrates the problem. Structures investment is less clearly correlated with all of the fundamentals. The correlation with the user cost is insignificant and has the incorrect sign, the correlation with cash flow is

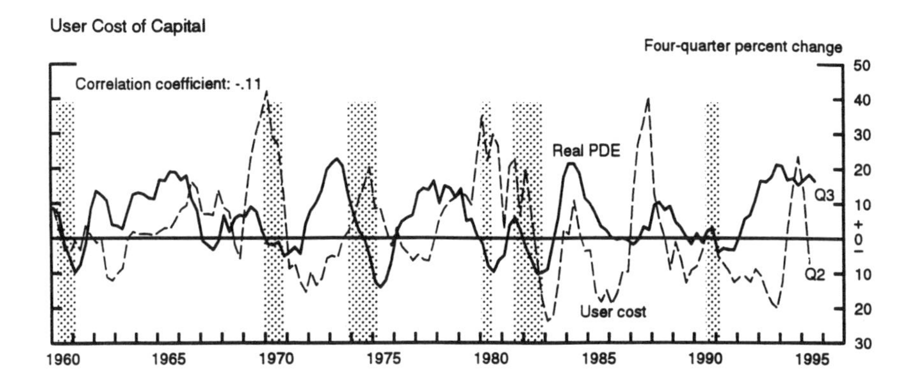

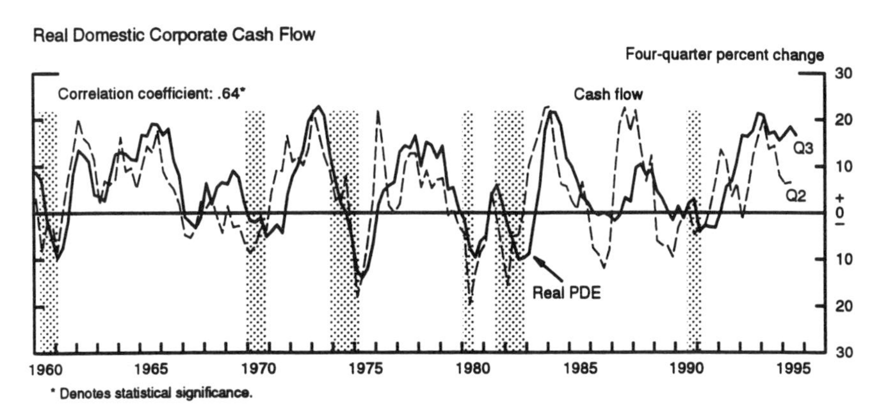

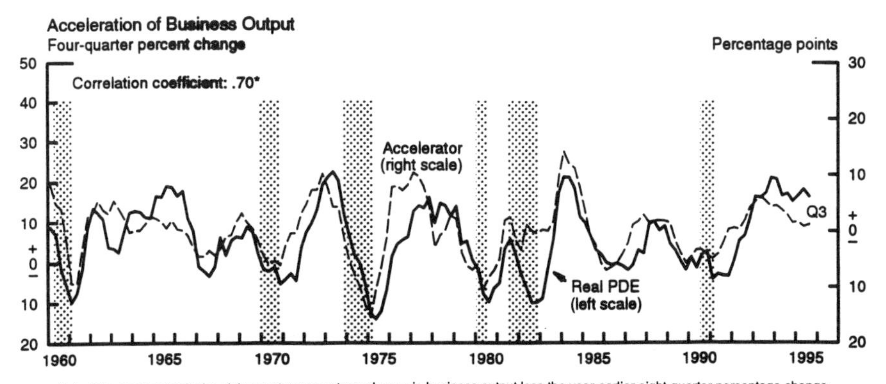

Figure 8.1
Fundamental determinants of equipment spending. Source: Bureau of Economic Analysis (BEA).

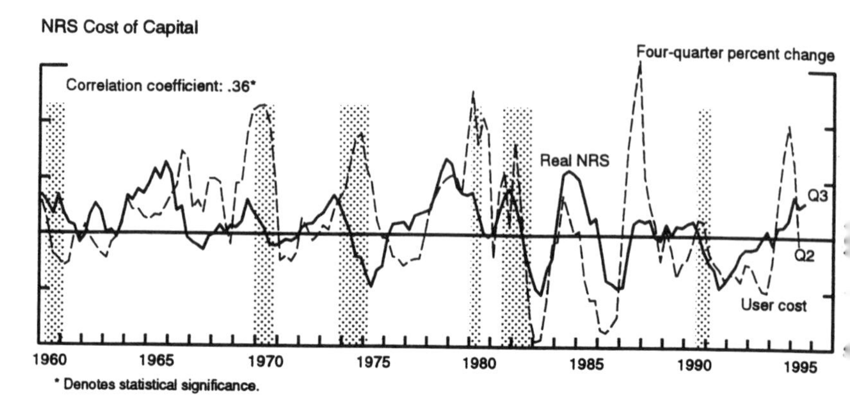

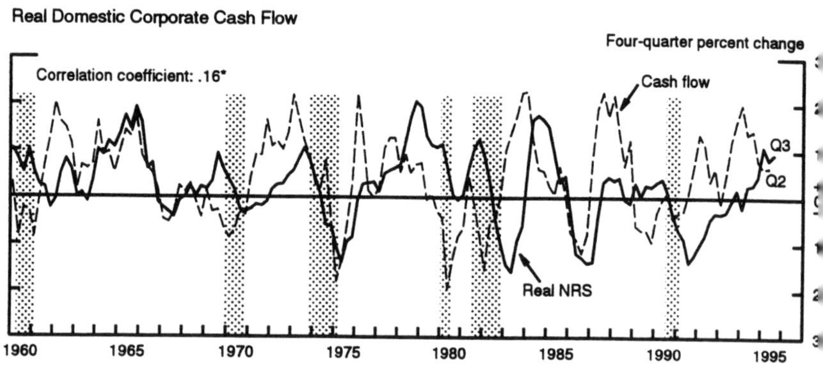

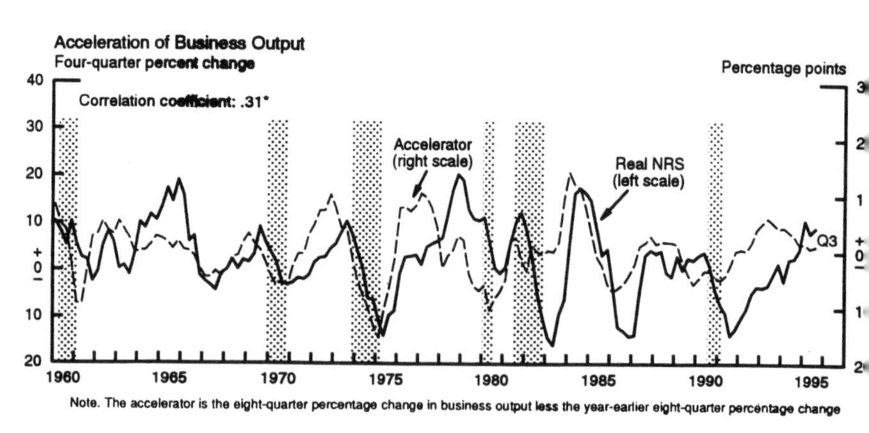

Figure 8.2
Fundamental determinants of nonresidential structures (NRS) spending. Source: BEA.

about one-fourth of that between cash flow and equipment investment, and the accelerator effect, still noticeable, is significantly weaker.

An alternative branch of the investment literature has followed the suggestion of Tobin (1969) that investment should be related to *Q*, the ratio of the market value of the firm to the replacement costs of its capital stock. Figure 8.3 depicts the correlation of aggregate business fixed investment with *Q*.[14] The top panel compares the level of real investment to the level of *Q*. Clearly the low-frequency movements in the two series are not highly correlated. The bottom panel relates the growth rates of these two series. Here it appears that growth in *Q* leads growth in investment somewhat, although the relationship is weak, and the contemporaneous correlation is actually negative.[15]

To summarize, the tendency for a number of aggregate variables to move together over the business cycle makes it difficult to isolate effects of individual fundamentals on investment. Hence a partial equilibrium investment demand approach might have very little power to explain aggregate investment fluctuations. Movements of the aggregate variables, including investment, are determined simultaneously, and disentangling the marginal impact of a single driving variable is difficult, if not impossible. For example, suppose that aggregate demand increases exogenously for some reason. This shift might lead firms to be more optimistic about their sales prospects and to purchase more investment goods; it might also be expected, at least in the short run, to lead to higher interest rates. If we then examine the correlation between investment and the interest rate, we might even find that the sign is the opposite of that predicted by the theory. While an instrumental variables procedure might allow us to overcome this simultaneity problem, the estimator is only as good as the instruments, and it is difficult to imagine an appropriate set of instruments for this application. Microeconomic data, however, provide a rich additional source of variation, and it is to the microdata studies that we now turn.

8.3 Estimating Effects of Tax Policy on Investment Using Microdata

Standard investment models emphasizing the net return to investment yield four empirical representations, each beginning with the firm maximizing its net present value. The first-order conditions lead to a Euler equation describing the period-to-period optimal path of investment. Abel

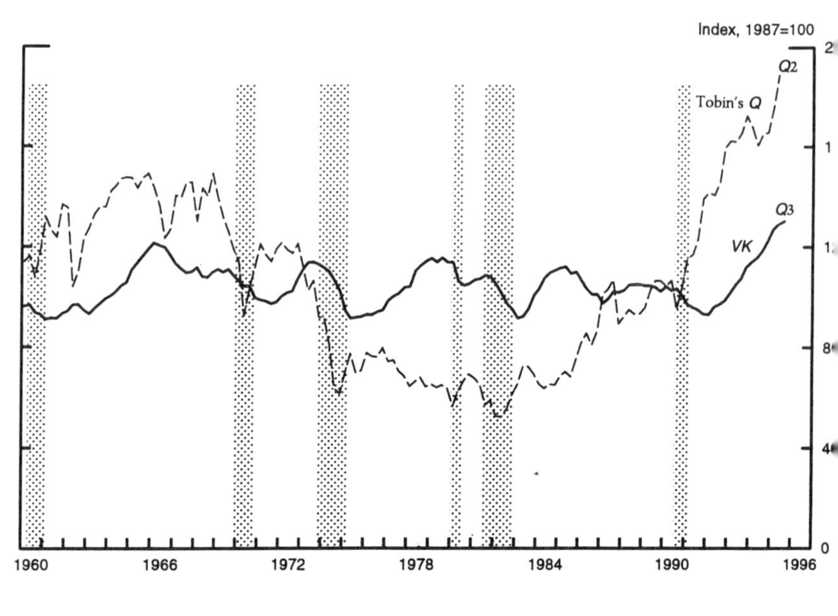

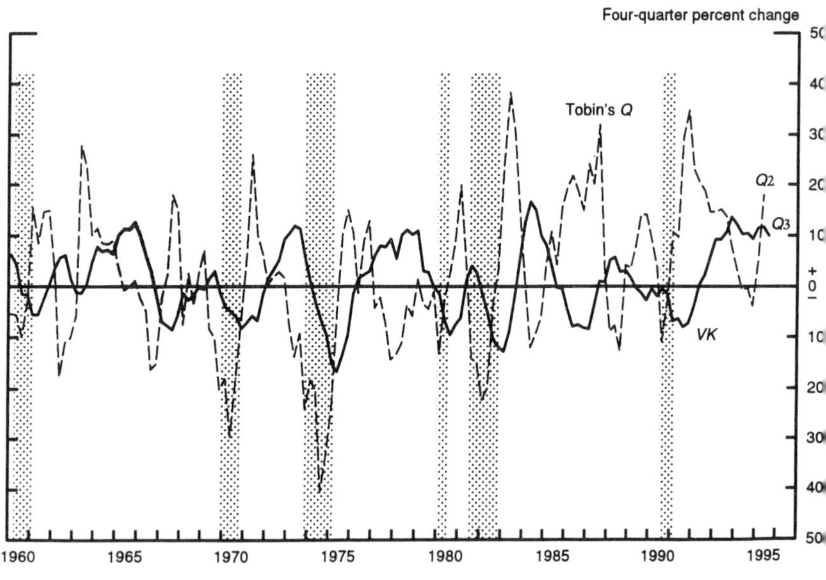

Figure 8.3
Tobin's Q and the I/K ratio. Source: BEA and Federal Reserve, Flow of Funds.

and Blanchard (1986) solved the difference equation that relates investment to its expected current and future marginal revenue products of capital; Gilchrist and Himmelberg (1995) apply a related forecasting approach to panel data. Alternatively, effects of tax parameters may be estimated from the Euler equation (see, e.g., Abel 1980; Hubbard and Kashyap 1992). As in Auerbach (1983b) and Abel (1990), investment can be expressed in terms of current and future values of the user cost of capital and, under some conditions, expressed in terms of average q. Again, this approach was suggested initially be Tobin (1969), with the necessary conditions supplied by Hayashi (1982).

The Basic Problem

To assess recent empirical work on tax policy and investment, we begin with the following general model of investment, which follows the discussion in section 8.1:

$$\frac{I_{i,t}}{K_{i,t-1}} = S_{i,t}\gamma + \varepsilon_{i,t}, \qquad (8.14)$$

where I and K denote investment and the capital stock, respectively; S is an underlying structural variable (e.g., the expected value of tax-adjusted Q or the user cost of capital) or set of variables; γ is a coefficient whose structural interpretation relates to assumptions about convex costs of adjusting the capital stock; and ε is a white-noise error term that reflects optimization error by firms.[16]

Researchers usually estimated such models using either ordinary least squares or generalized method of moments techniques with instrumental variables. Cummins, Hassett, and Hubbard (1994, 1996) note that conventional estimated values of γ in firm-level panel data for the United States or for other countries are very small, ranging from 0.01 to 0.05, implying marginal costs of adjustment of between one and five dollars per dollar of investment. Such estimates, which have emerged in many empirical studies (Summers 1981; Salinger and Summers 1983; Fazzari, Hubbard, and Petersen 1988a), imply very small effects of permanent investment incentives on investment.

Subsequently, empirical researchers have offered two general explanations of the failure to estimate significant tax effects on investment: (1) measurement error in fundamental variables and (2) misspecification of costs of adjusting the capital stock. Both research programs have contributed to our understanding of the responsiveness of investment to changes in the net return to investing and have reached similar conclusions about the likely effects of tax policy for some important cases.

Measurement Error in Fundamental Variables

A major problem in using equation 8.14 in order to recover estimates of marginal adjustment costs and the effect of tax changes on investment is that measurement error in Q or the user cost of capital may bias downward the estimated coefficient. A number of techniques have been suggested to address this measurement error, including statistical corrections, avoiding the use of Q or user cost representations, using new proxies for Q, focusing on periods or frequencies in which firm variation in fundamental variables is less subject to measurement error, and modifying assumptions about the financial frictions firms face. We consider each in turn and examine whether the techniques produce a consensus estimate of adjustment costs that can be used to forecast the effects of investment incentives on business fixed investment.

Statistical Approaches

There are at least two problems in measuring Q that might affect estimated adjustment costs. First, to the extent that the stock market is excessively volatile, Q might not reflect market fundamentals. Second, the replacement value of the capital stock in the denominator of Q is likely to be measured with error. Griliches and Hausman (1986) argue that measurement error will lead to different biases among potential estimators that are similar in that they control for firm-specific effects but differ in their signal-to-noise ratios, making it possible to place bounds on the importance of measurement error. Cummins, Hassett, and Hubbard (1994) estimate a model like equation 8.14 using first differences and longer differences (as opposed to the conventional fixed-effects, within-group estimator) to address measurement error problems. Their estimated adjustment costs decline significantly.

In a time-series setting, Caballero (1994) pursues an alternative estimation strategy, based on a suggestion by Stock and Watson (1993). Caballero argues that small sample biases of typically employed time-series estimation procedures are particularly severe when estimating adjustment cost models, and he shows that elasticities will generally be biased downward. Using the procedure of Stock and Watson for estimating the low-frequency relationships between variables in small samples, Caballero estimates a long-run elasticity of investment with respect to the user cost of approximately unity. This is much larger than the early estimates, but roughly consistent with the other studies summarized in this section.

Euler Equation Estimates

The second approach departs from the strategy of using proxies for marginal q and relies on the firm's Euler equation to model the investment decision. (As long as one makes the same assumption about technology and adjustment costs, the Euler equation can be derived from the same model as the conventional Q or user cost of capital models.) By not relying on the "investment function" representation, one can sidestep problems of measuring marginal q.

Tests following this approach have frequently used panel data on manufacturing firms to estimate the Euler equation (Pindyck and Rotemberg 1983; Shapiro 1986; Gilchrist 1991; Whited 1992; Bond and Meghir 1994; Hubbard, Kashyap, and Whited 1995). Studies using Compustat data for the United States are unable to reject the frictionless neoclassical model for most firms, and the estimated adjustment cost parameters are more reasonable than those found in estimates of Q models. For example, Hubbard, Kashyap, and Whited (1995) report estimated values of γ between 1 and 2.2. Very similar estimates are reported for European manufacturing firms by Cummins, Harris, and Hassett (1995) and for investment in overseas subsidiaries of U.S. multinational corporations in Cummins and Hubbard (1995).

Alternatives to Q

The measure of average Q used as a proxy for marginal q in most empirical studies is constructed as the ratio of the market value of the financial claims on the firm (equity and debt) to the replacement cost of the firm's capital stock. The third approach bypasses using financial variables as proxies for marginal q by forecasting the expected present value of the current and future profits generated by an incremental unit of capital—that is, the expected value of marginal q—an idea developed (in the time-series context) by Abel and Blanchard (1986) and extended for use in panel data by Gilchrist and Himmelberg (1995). One can extend this setup to a panel-data setting by constructing investment fundamentals using a VAR forecasting framework to decompose the effect of profits or cash flow on investment into two components: one that forecasts future profitability under the frictionless capital markets assumed in the neoclassical model (analogous to marginal q) and a residual component that may be attributable to financial frictions (analogous to the role played by cash flow in the imperfect-capital-markets approach of Fazzari, Hubbard, and Petersen 1988a). By including lags of cash flow in the vector of observed fundamentals in the forecasting equations, one can ensure that any information about future marginal profitability of capital contained in cash flow is reflected in the proxy for marginal q.

Using such an approach, Gilchrist and Himmelberg (1995) report estimates of γ that are roughly consistent with the Euler equation estimates discussed above. In addition, they test whether cash flow is an independent "fundamental" variable explaining investment and find that it is for a subset of firms that are likely to face financing constraints.[17] (We return to a discussion of this latter result below.)

Measuring Changes in Fundamentals Using Tax Reforms

One reason the data do not appear to favor neoclassical models over accelerator models is a simultaneous equations problem. If the data are dominated by exogenous increases or decreases in the real interest rate, then the user cost movements would lead investment to decrease or increase, respectively. But if investment rises with positive "animal spirits," then higher investment demand puts upward pressure on the real interest rate. Hence to the extent that data incorporate exogenous changes in both the real interest rate and the intercept of the investment function, the positive relationship between investment and the user cost of capital because of shifts in the investment function may dominate the hypothesized negative relationship between investment and the user cost of capital. In this case, the estimated coefficient on the user cost of capital will be "too small," leading to estimated adjustment costs that are "too large." Such simultaneity increases apparent accelerator effects, because positive shifts of the investment function raise both investment and output.

This simultaneity problem in the estimation of neoclassical models is remedied by the use of instrumental variables. Conventional instrumental variables (including lagged endogenous variables or sales-to-capital ratios) have not proved very helpful. Major tax reforms arguably offer periods in which there is exogenous cross-sectional variation in the user cost of capital or tax-adjusted q. Cummins, Hassett, and Hubbard (1994, 1996) demonstrate that major tax reforms are also associated with significant firm- and asset-level variation in key tax parameters (such as the effective rate of investment tax credit and the present value of depreciation allow-

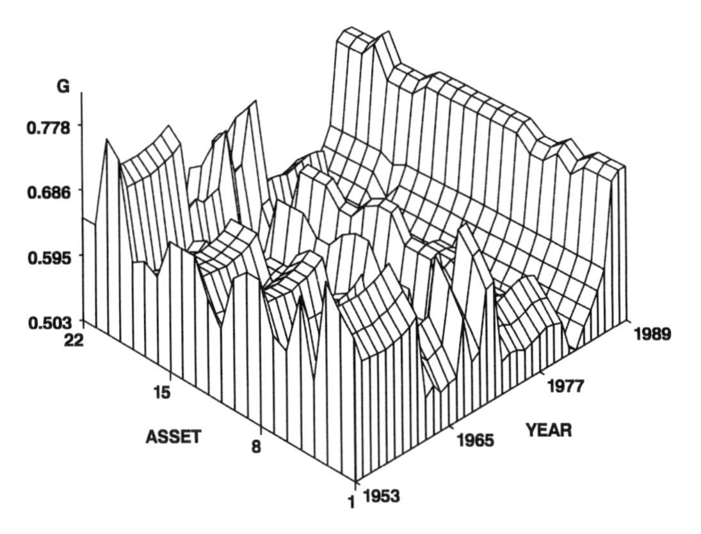

Figure 8.4
After-tax cost of one dollar of equipment investment, 1953–1989. Source: Author's calculations based on data from the BEA.

ances). Hence tax variables are likely to be a good instrument for the user cost or Q during tax reforms.

To indicate the significance of cross-sectional heterogeneity in incentives to invest, we emphasize variation across assets. Figure 8.4 plots the annual values of $(1 - \Gamma)$ for the twenty-two classes of equipment capital classified by the Bureau of Economic Analysis (BEA). The peaks and valleys along the year axis for a given asset reveal the time-series variation in the tax parameters, and those along the asset axis for a given year reveal the cross-sectional variation. For asset 8 (metalworking machinery), for example, the after-tax cost of investing falls in 1962, 1972, and 1981 and rises in 1986.

Figure 8.4 reveals that the variation across assets is large within most years in our samples, as is the time-series variation. In addition, the positions of the peaks and valleys change somewhat over time. For example, following the removal of the investment tax credit and the reduction of the corporate tax rate by the Tax Reform Act of 1986, the cross-sectional variation across assets fell, consistent with the act's stated goal to "level the playing field."

Cummins, Hassett, and Hubbard (1995) use vector autoregressions to forecast investment in the year following a tax reform and then compare the forecast errors for each of the assets to the changes in the user cost for

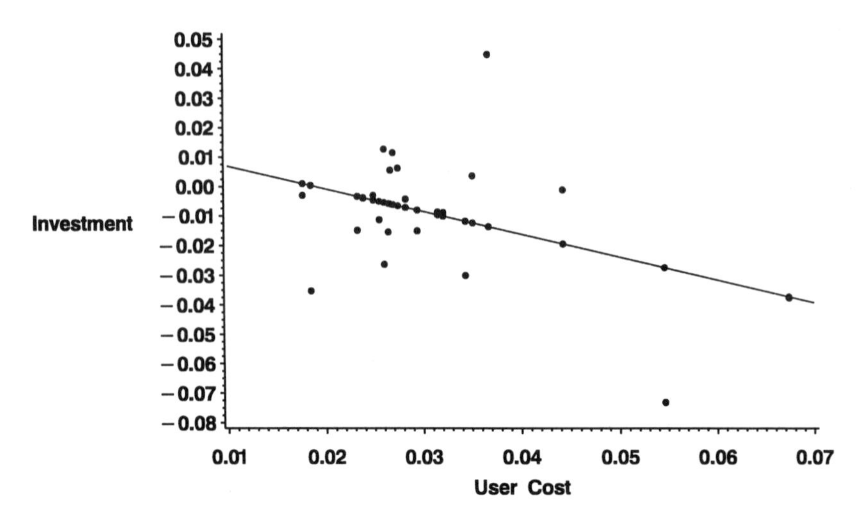

Figure 8.5
Cross-sectional relationship between investment and user cost forecast errors, 1987. Source: Cummins, Hassett, and Hubbard (1994, figure 3).

that asset. In figure 8.5, we repeat that experiment and for the Tax Reform Act of 1986, and provide a plot of the forecast errors constructed from models that exclude taxes against shocks to the user cost of capital for each of the twenty-two equipment asset classes tracked by the BEA. In addition, we draw a regression line through the scatterplot. The idea is that the forecast errors for investment should be negatively correlated with forecast errors for the user cost of capital. The downward-sloping line indicates a clear negative correlation.

We can now illustrate the effect of tax parameters on firm investment. Table 8.1 shows the significance of using exogenous tax changes to identify changes in Q.[18] Taken from Cummins, Hassett, and Hubbard (1996), it presents estimates of the investment equation (8.14) during major tax reforms in fourteen countries over the 1980s; firm-level data are taken from Compustat's Global Vantage. Using contemporaneous tax variables as instrument during major tax reforms, Cummins, Hassett, and Hubbard estimate γ to be 0.65 for the United States, compared with 0.048 under conventional estimates. They obtained similar estimates for each of the other major U.S. tax reforms in the postwar period using data from Compustat (Cummins, Hassett, and Hubbard 1994); focusing on the Tax Reform Act of 1986, Auerbach and Hassett (1991) found similar coefficients using asset-level data and cross-sectional variation in the user cost.

Table 8.1
Estimates of tax-adjusted Q model for fourteen countries

Country	Conventional panel data estimated coefficient on Q[a]	Estimated coefficient with contemporaneous tax instruments[b]
Australia	0.050	0.289
	(0.019)	(0.153)
Belgium	0.103	0.587
	(0.044)	(0.422)
Canada	0.041	0.521
	(0.009)	(0.127)
Denmark	0.104	0.765
	(0.085)	(0.308)
France	0.085	0.388
	(0.042)	(0.116)
Germany	0.095	0.784
	(0.040)	(0.296)
Italy	0.051	0.180
	(0.018)	(0.120)
Japan	0.029	0.086
	(0.008)	(0.035)
The Netherlands	0.069	0.633
	(0.044)	(0.150)
Norway	0.069	0.512
	(0.031)	(0.295)
Spain	0.044	0.404
	(0.028)	(0.233)
Sweden	0.051	0.293
	(0.047)	(0.169)
United Kingdom	0.062	0.589
	(0.013)	(0.078)
United States	0.048	0.650
	(0.006)	(0.077)

Source: Calculations in Cummins, Hassett, and Hubbard (1996) using Global Vantage data.
[a] See table 5 in Cummins, Hassett, and Hubbard (1996), GMM estimates. Instruments include twice- and thrice-lagged values of Q, (I/K), and the ratios of cash flow to capital.
[b] See table 7 in Cummins, Hassett, and Hubbard (1996), GMM estimates. Instruments include twice- and thrice-lagged values of (I/K) and the ratio of cash flow to capital, twice-lagged value nontax components of q, and contemporaneous values of tax parameters.

As table 8.1 shows, applying the Cummins-Hassett-Hubbard approach in tax reform periods in other Organization for Economic Cooperation and Development countries produces estimates roughly similar to those for the United States.[19]

Financial Frictions and the Neoclassical Model

In contrast to the frictionless capital markets in the standard neoclassical model, earlier applied research on investment, especially the work of Meyer and Kuh (1957), stressed the significance of financial considerations (particularly internal funds or net worth) for business investment. Since the mid-1960s, however, most applied research on investment isolated "real" firm decisions from "financing." The intellectual justification for this shift in approach drew on the seminal work by Modigliani and Miller (1958), who demonstrated the irrelevance of financial structure and financial policy for real investment decisions under certain conditions. The central Modigliani-Miller result, which facilitated the early development of the neoclassical model, was that a firm's financial structure will not affect its value in frictionless capital markets. As a result, if their assumptions are satisfied, real firm decisions, motivated by the maximization of shareholders' claims, are independent of financial factors such as the availability of internal funds.

The assumption of representative firms (in terms of trade on capital markets) is common to most research programs in the neoclassical tradition. That is, the same empirical model (e.g., equation 8.14) applies to all firms. Therefore, tests could not ascertain whether the observed sensitivity of investment to financial variables differs across firms and whether these differences in sensitivity explain the weak apparent relationship between the measured user cost and investment. Contemporary empirical studies of information and incentive problems in the investment process have moved beyond the assumption of representative firms by examining firm-level panel data in which firms can be grouped into high-net-worth and low-net-worth categories. For the latter category, changes in net worth or internal funds affect investment, holding constant underlying investment opportunities (desired investment).[20] Following Fazzari, Hubbard, and Petersen (1988a), empirical researchers have placed firms into groups as a priori financially constrained or financially unconstrained.

Two aspects of the findings of this research program are noteworthy in the context of measuring incentives to invest. First, numerous empirical studies have found that proxies for internal funds have explanatory power for investment, holding constant Q, the user cost, or accelerator variables (see the review of studies in Hubbard 1996). This suggests that tax policy may have effects on investment by constrained firms beyond those predicted by neoclassical approaches. (Indeed, returning to the accelerator analogy, Bernanke, Gertler, and Gilchrist 1996 argue that this literature describes a financial accelerator.) In particular, the quantity of internal funds available for investment is supported by the average tax on earnings from existing projects. In this sense, average as well as marginal tax rates faced by a firm affect its investment decisions.[21]

Second, empirical studies of financing constraints generally find that the frictionless neoclassical model is rejected only for the groups of firms that a priori are financially constrained (Calomiris and Hubbard 1995; Gilchrist and Himmelberg 1995; Hubbard, Kashyap, and Whited 1995). Hence, while the shadow value of internal funds may not be well captured for some firms in standard representations of the neoclassical approach, the neoclassical model with convex adjustment costs yields reasonable estimated values of marginal adjustment costs for most firms.

Measurement Error and Adjustment Costs: Nearing Consensus?
To summarize, a variety of empirical implementations of the neoclassical model with convex adjustment costs have attempted to mitigate measurement error and other econometric problems in conventional ordinary least squares and generalized method of moments (GMM) estimates of equation 8.14 in panel data. For Q models, the methods described generally yield estimated values of γ of .50 or higher, implying marginal costs of adjustment in the range of ten cents per dollar of additional investment (using the estimate in Cummins, Hassett, and Hubbard 1995 as a benchmark), and elasticities of investment with respect to the user cost of capital between -0.5 and -1.0.

An Alternative Interpretation: Misspecification of Adjustment Costs

The emphasis in many recent empirical studies of investment on sources of mismeasurement of explanatory variables acting as proxies for the net return to investing accepts the conventional belief that costs of adjusting the capital stock are convex. The Q, user cost of capital, and Euler equation approaches can all be derived from the same intertemporal maximization problem, given common assumptions about technology, competition, and adjustment costs. An important recent line of inquiry focuses on modeling and testing the effects of irreversibility and uncertainty on firms' investment decisions (see the excellent survey by Dixit and Pindyck 1994).[22] If this literature is correct, then there may be important regions wherein tax policy has little or no effect on investment, and knowledge of which region an economy is in is an important prerequisite to any policy analysis. Finally, these models can possibly explain a key remaining puzzle in the literature: why firms report in surveys that they use such high hurdle rates (Summers 1987).

Neoclassical models implicitly assume that there is an efficient secondary market for capital; hence irreversibility poses no problem. If a firm purchases a machine today and the output market turns sour in the future, the firm can recoup the purchase price of the machine at that time. But if investment is irreversible, the firm faces the chance that it cannot sell the machine in the future. In this setup, there is a gain to delaying investment and allowing the random price process to move either into a region far enough above the neoclassical "breakeven" point that the probability of the "bad state" becomes low enough, or into a region where it clearly does not make sense to purchase the machine. An investment extinguishes the value of the call option of delay, an option that has positive value when prices are uncertain. In this approach, the value of the lost option is a component of the opportunity cost of investment. In the terminology of the Q framework, the threshold criterion for investment requires that marginal Q exceed unity by the value of maintaining the call option to invest. As a consequence, high hurdle rates may be required by corporate managers who are making investment decisions.

Indeed, at least part of the interest in option-based investment models have been the problem raised in many time-series studies that indicated that the response of investment to changes in Q or the user cost of capital are implausibly small, implying, perhaps, that there are regions wherein Q varies but investment does not. In addition, it is not difficult to suggest examples of nonconvex adjustment costs, such as retooling in automobile plants or adopting more energy-efficient kilns in cement plants.

How Much Investment Is Irreversible?

Before turning to models with alternative adjustment cost specifications, we present a prima facie case that pure irreversibility may not be of overriding importance at the aggregate level.

A large literature (Hulten and Wykoff 1979; Jorgenson 1994; Fraumeni 1995; Oliner 1996) focuses on the estimation of economic depreciation rates for different types of machines. For the most part, researchers estimate rates of decay from the patterns of used machine prices. This literature is relevant to the debate concerning the form of adjustment costs

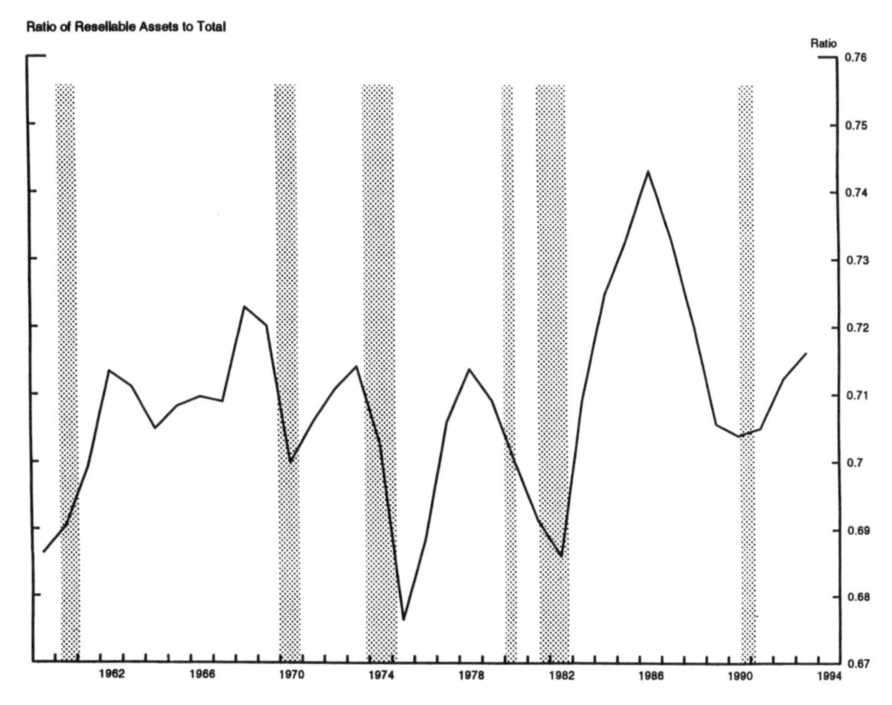

Figure 8.6
U.S. equipment investment. Source: Author's calculations based on data from the BEA.

because irreversibility results most plausibly from either the absence of resale markets or the presence of significant "lemons" problems in resale markets.

To examine the extent to which resale markets are limited, we surveyed the depreciation literature and cataloged types of equipment for which we could find an estimated economic depreciation rate. Using disaggregated data on investment by asset type, we then calculated the proportion of aggregate investment that is made up of assets with clearly identifiable resale markets. Figure 8.6 plots this proportion from 1960 to 1994. The proportion of investment in assets that have easily identifiable resale markets is about 0.7 over most of the period. This is not to say that the remaining assets are necessarily irreversible, of course; depreciation studies may not yet have found data for those assets.

Hence, in order to demonstrate that irreversibility is an important property of most investment goods, researchers must show that the market for used capital goods is plagued with lemons problems. To our knowledge, there is no existing evidence that lemons are important in markets for equipment goods. Indeed, Hulten and Wykoff (1981) argue that estimated secondary market prices in depreciation studies are inconsistent with a major role for lemons problems. One reason for this finding may be that the market for used capital good is one where the participants possess significant asset-specific expertise. The typical purchaser of a machine tool, for example, may have worked in a factory filled with machine tools for many years and would easily recognize a lemon. If this is the case, there is little asymmetric information, and the resale market functions well.

Models with More General Adjustment Costs

Abel and Eberly (1994) provide a general framework that encompasses irreversibility, fixed costs, and a wide array of alternative adjustment cost specifications. They show that, under certain conditions, the investment behavior of firms can be characterized by three distinct regimes: a regime in which gross investment is (1) positive, (2) zero, or (3) negative. The responsiveness of investment to fundamentals differs across regimes, and their more general model predicts a region in which gross investment will stay zero for a range of unfavorable values of Q. Because this model nests the more traditional q models, it provides a useful empirical framework, and we review attempts to estimate this model below.

Researchers are beginning to study the impact of alternative adjustment cost assumptions within structural investment models with panel data. Barnett and Sakellaris (1995) use Compustat data to investigate the implication of the model of Abel and Eberly (1995) that investment alternates between regimes of insensitivity to Q and regimes of responsiveness to Q. The region of inactivity should be close to the region for which the model predicts that investment is negative. Because the thresholds for these regions are unknown, conventional asymptotic distributions do not apply. Barnett and Sakellaris use a statistical framework that allows them to estimate the threshold points and the coefficients on Q simultaneously in the different regions given the threshold points. They find evidence of a nonlinear relationship between investment and Q; in particular, they estimate the largest responsiveness of investment to Q for low values of Q and the smallest for very high values of Q. On average, they estimate that the elasticity of investment with respect to Q is about unity but that the aggregate elasticity varies considerably over time, depending on the average level of Q. Barnett and Sakellaris argue that their results imply that adjustment costs may not be quadratic, though the most likely cause is not firms' inability to disinvest but, rather, their reluctance to make large changes.

Barnett and Sakellaris's results are not necessarily inconsistent with the measurement error story. Some firms in the Compustat universe have values of average Q that are astronomical (one firm actually has a Q of 40,000), presumably because the capital stock measure is missing important goodwill or human capital components. If one accepts that Q is a poor measure of fundamentals for these firms, then the result that investment does not respond as much to Q for these firms is not surprising. In the more normal range of Q values, the investment response seems to accord well with the predictions of the convex adjustment cost model.

Using firm-level data from Compustat, Abel and Eberly (1996a) estimate that the relationship between investment and fundamental determinants (Q and the tax-adjusted price of capital goods) is concave; that is, the response of investment to fundamental determinants is positive but monotonically declining. The results of Abel and Eberly suggest that the distribution of tax-adjusted Q or the user cost of capital may be a determinant of aggregate investment. However, the caution that applied to Barnett and Sakellaris conclusions applies here as well: large, observed values of Q may not coincide with high levels of investment because the high Q values reflect mismeasurement rather than extraordinary fundamentals.

Finally, Caballero, Engel, and Haltiwanger (1995) explore adjustment costs in a more general framework. Using a subset of 7,000 U.S. manufacturing plants from the Census Bureau's Longitudinal Research Database (LRD), they explore whether cross-sectional patterns of investment are consistent with symmetric, convex adjustment cost models or whether the data imply nonconvexities.[23] They proceed in two steps. First, they assume that there are no adjustment costs and that the Jorgensonian model adequately describes a firms' "desired" capital stock (K^*).[24] They then compare in each period a firm's beginning-of-period capital stock to its desired stock and call the difference ($K^* - K_{t-1}$) "mandated investment." Second, they explore how firms actually adjust their capital stocks. In this step, they find that the relationship between actual and mandated investment is highly nonlinear. If mandated investment is negative, then firms do not quickly adjust their capital stocks downward. If mandated investment is small and positive, then firms also do not respond very much. If mandated investment is very large, firms adjust their capital stocks quickly. They conclude that an (S, s) model, in which firms have a range of inaction and adjust their capital stocks to their desired levels only when the gap between current and desired capital stock is "large enough" offers a good description of the data.

Caballero, Engel, and Haltiwanger also illustrate how to construct aggregate implications from their microeconomic results. Integrating over the microeconomic distribution of plants, they calculate a predicted aggregate elasticity of investment with respect to the user cost of capital. The estimates of this elasticity vary considerably over time. If many plants are near the region for which mandated investment is very large, then small changes in the user cost can have large effects on aggregate investment. If, however, the bulk of the distribution of mandated investment is in the region of low responsiveness of investment to fundamentals, then changes in the user cost will have little impact. They concur with the main conclusion of Cummins, Hassett, and Hubbard (1994) that the aggregate elasticity of investment with respect to the user cost is between -0.5 and -1, and also conclude that tax reforms appear to have had generally large effects on investment. They caution, however, that the reforms have had large effects because they coincidentally occurred during periods in which the plant-level distribution of mandated investment was aligned in such a way to allow a large effect of changes in tax parameters. This would happen if, for example, investment tax credits were removed in booms, when mandated investment is very large, and an increase in the user cost can cause firms to cancel significant investment plans. As a consequence, Caballero, Engel, and Haltiwanger argue that researchers must consult the microdistribution of mandated investment before predicting the likely impact of future tax reforms on business investment.[25]

Alternatively, Cummins, Hassett, and Hubbard (1994, 1996) argue that recovering "reasonable" estimates of the response of investment to Q or the user cost of capital is easiest when large exogenous changes in the distribution of structural determinants occur, as during tax reforms. In response to the alternative interpretation that firms respond to changes in fundamentals only when these changes are large, Cummins, Hassett, and Hubbard use firm-level data to investigate whether there was evidence of bunching of investment around tax reforms. They estimate transition probabilities among various ranges of I/K over the year prior to, of, and after the tax reform and find no evidence that firms with large investment were likely to have lower investment in prior or subsequent years. Indeed, only a very tiny fraction of the sample was ever found to transit from high investment to low investment states.

In part, the conclusions of these studies may differ because of differences in the level of aggregation. At a sufficiently fine level of disaggregation, all investment looks lumpy. The plant-level evidence suggests that investment appears lumpy, but the firm-level evidence does not corroborate this. However, there may be interesting differences between the investment behavior of plants and firms, as might be the case if, for example, managerial attention is limited and only a fraction of a firm's plants adjust their capital in a given year. Clearly, reconciling the plant-level and firm-level results is an important topic for future research.

Summing Up: The Partial Equilibrium Effects of Investment Tax Policy

Recent studies appear to have reached a consensus that the elasticity of investment with respect to the user cost of capital is between -0.5 and -1.0. Indeed, recent studies using convex costs of adjustment and studies using nonconvex costs of adjustments agree that the long-run elasticity of investment to the user cost is high by the standards of the early empirical literature. This range of estimated responses of investment to tax parameters is well above the consensus of only a few years ago and suggests that investment tax policy can have a significant impact on the path of aggregate capital formation. One should be cautious, however, in moving from the microeconomic evidence to aggregate predictions. Caballero, Engel, and Haltiwanger demonstrate a technique for aggregating the microdistribution of firms to calculate aggregate investment demand, but very little continues to be known about the general equilibrium effects of major policy changes.

8.4 Arguments For and Against Investment Incentives

Thus far we have argued that tax incentives for investment are important components of the net return to investing and the short-term and long-term responses of investment to permanent tax incentives are large. We now turn to the deeper policy question of whether we should have permanent incentives for investment even if such incentives increase the stock of business fixed capital. (We then address the question of the desirability of short-run incentives.) Economists generally argue against intervention. Under what circumstances might one advocate distortionary investment incentives?

Do Investment Incentives Affect the Price of Capital Goods?

One scenario under which investment incentives might have an especially large impact on the quantity of investment without dissipation in prices of investment goods is one in which firms' demand for capital is responsive to changes in the user cost of capital and in which capital goods are supplied perfectly elastically. While it is implausible that the supply function for most individual capital goods manufacturers is perfectly elastic, the effective supply of capital goods to a given domestic market might well be highly elastic in the long run if the world market for capital goods is open. Investment incentives would raise prices of capital goods in the short run if the supply of capital goods is highly inelastic.

Using data for the United States and ten other countries, Hassett and Hubbard (1995) find that local investment tax credits have a negligible effect on prices paid for capital goods—indeed, they find that the capital goods prices for most countries are very highly correlated and that the movements of these over time are consistent with the "law of one price." In addition, using disaggregated data on asset-specific investment good prices and tax variables for the United States, they find that tax parameters have no effect on capital goods prices.[26] The conclusion that tax policy in the United States does not affect the world price of capital goods is especially meaningful, given the relative size of the U.S. economy. Taken together, these tests suggest that the effects of investment tax policy have not been muted in a significant way by upward-sloping supply schedules for capital goods.

Is the Capital Stock Too Small?

While it is instructive to ask how effective investment incentives are at increasing the fixed capital stock, a more important question remains: What is the social value of the increase in the fixed capital stock?

Theoretical research has demonstrated that perfectly competitive economies do not necessarily converge to the "correct" capital stock. Indeed, Diamond (1965) demonstrated that a competitive economy can reach a steady state in which there is "too much" capital, in the sense that the economy is investing more than it is earning in profit. In this case, individuals can be made better off if they are forced to consume a portion of the capital stock. When evaluating investment incentives, it is crucial for policy analysis to evaluate whether the economy is operating with "too much" or "too little" capital.

The classic "golden rule" literature offers benchmarks for guidance.[27] In the golden rule approach of Phelps (1961), the golden rule level of the capital stock relative to output is achieved when the marginal product of capital (R), net of depreciation (δ), equals the sum of the rate of growth of the labor force (n) and the rate of labor-augmenting technical change (g), or:

$$R = \delta + n + g. \tag{8.15}$$

Alternatively, in the optimal growth literature, Ramsey's (1928) golden rule levels require that the marginal product of capital net of depreciation equal the sum of the social rate of time preference (ρ) and the elasticity of marginal social utility with respect to per capita consumption (ϕ) or,[28]

$$R = \delta + \rho + \phi g. \tag{8.16}$$

Depending on the values of ρ and ϕ, the Ramsey golden rule levels of capital can be less than the Phelps golden rule levels.

Following the convention in neoclassical models of the capital stock, we assume a Cobb-Douglas technology, so that the ratio of the steady-state golden rule capital stock (K^*) to output (Y) equals the ratio of capital's share in output (α) to the marginal product of capital (R). Moreover, the golden rule level of net investment (I^*) relative to output equals $(n + g)$ times the capital output ratio. Hence:

$$\frac{K^*}{Y} = \frac{\alpha}{R} \tag{8.17}$$

and

$$\frac{I^*}{Y} = (n + g)\frac{K^*}{Y}. \tag{8.18}$$

One can account for different types of capital by noting that, in equilibrium, the net rates of return on the alternative types are equal. Hence one can substitute into equation 8.17 measure of α_k for each type of capital k and the relevant R (given differences in depreciation), and solve for the golden rule levels of the capital stocks.

Using a range of parameter values in the golden rule expressions in equations 8.17 and 8.18, Cohen, Hassett, and Kennedy (1995) compare golden rule and actual levels of the capital stock or net investment relative to output to their actual values over the period from 1980 to 1994. Table 8.2, which we excerpt from several tables in that study, indicates that for benchmark parameter values, equipment investment and capital stocks are below their golden rule levels (assuming 1980–1994 is sufficiently long to characterize a steady state), while residential investment and the residential capital stocks, which received significant tax subsidies over this time period, are near or above their golden rule levels. Cohen,

Table 8.2
Benchmark golden rule and actual levels of I^{net}/Y and K/Y

	Golden rule level		
Type of capital	Phelps	Ramsey	Actual level (1980–1994 average)
Net investment as a percentage of GDP			
Total fixed	8.3%	6.0%	4.2%
Business fixed	4.8	3.6	2.4
Producers' durable equipment	2.4	2.0	1.3
Nonresidential structures	2.0	1.3	1.2
Residential	2.7	1.6	1.8
Ratio of capital stock to GDP			
Total fixed	3.3	2.4	1.9
Business fixed	1.9	1.4	1.0
Producers' durable equipment	1.0	0.8	0.5
Nonresidential structures	0.8	0.5	0.5
Residential	1.1	0.6	0.9

Source: Cohen, Hassett, and Kennedy (1995, Table 2).
Note: Benchmark parameter values are: labor force growth rate = 0.01; rate of labor-augmenting technical change = 0.15; social discount rate = 0.12; and social intertemporal elasticity of substitution (Φ) = 3.
$\alpha_{\text{Total fixed}} = 0.30$; $\alpha_{\text{Business fixed}} = 0.24$; $\alpha_{\text{Equipment}} = 0.18$; $\alpha_{\text{Structures}} = 0.06$; $\alpha_{\text{Residential}} = 0.06$.

Hassett, and Kennedy also show that these conclusions are not changed if the key parameters are allowed to vary across a broad range of plausible values.

Alternatively, several authors have attempted to evaluate the optimality of the U.S. capital stock by relating various interest rates to the rate of economic growth. One the one hand, Tobin (1965), Solow (1970), and Feldstein (1977) argue that the marginal productivity of capital one obtains from accounting profits estimates is about 10 percent, and thus they conclude that the economy is dynamically efficient. On the other hand, Ibbotson (1987) calculates a mean return on U.S. Treasury bills from 1926 to 1986 of only 0.3 percent, suggesting dynamic inefficiency. The answer to the question using interest rates depends critically on assessing the impact of risk, of course.

Abel et al. (1989) pursue an alternative strategy for evaluating whether the U.S. capital stock is greater or less than the optimal level. In a stochastic setting with a very general production technology, they demonstrate that an economy is dynamically inefficient if it invests more than the returns from capital. They show that the economy is dynamically efficient—and hence in the range in which stimulative tax policy might have positive social returns—if the returns from capital exceed investment. Using their terminology, the key questions is whether the capital stock is, on balance, a "sink" or a "spout." This observation is a useful contribution because it allows one to base judgment about dynamic efficiency on readily observable cash flows. Abel et al. conclude that the economy is dynamically efficient. Thus, both capital stock data and cash flow data suggest that, by raising the stock of equipment capital, investment incentives have positive social returns.[29]

Should We Use Temporary Investment Incentives?

The discussion thus far pertains to permanent changes in investment incentives. Even a casual observation of the history of investment incentives since the 1950s suggests the usefulness of considering temporary investment incentives. Since 1962, the mean duration of a typical state in which an ITC is in effect has been about three and one-half years, and the mean duration of the "no-ITC" state has been about the same length. In 1992, President Bush advocated a modified ITC, known as the Investment Tax Allowance, and President Clinton proposed an incremental ITC in early 1993; neither of these measures was enacted. What is the likely impact on aggregate capital accumulation of temporary investment incentives?

Temporary investment incentives can have even larger short-run impacts on investment than permanent investment incentives (Auerbach 1989). Consider a temporary ITC known to last for one period. The expressions for the user cost of capital in equation 8.5 indicates that the ITC lowers the current user cost through both its effect on $\Gamma_{i,t}$ and the consequences of its removal on $\Gamma_{i,t+1}$. More generally, anticipated future changes in tax policy affect the current value of the user cost and investment.

The large potential effects of temporary tax incentives on investment do not imply that they are desirable tax policy—even if one believes that long-run investment incentives are sound tax policy. In the presence of uncertainty and adjustment costs, there is little reason to believe that policymakers can time investment incentives for the purposes of stabilization policy. Moreover, the use of temporary incentives increases uncertainty in business capital budgeting, making it more difficult for firms to forecast the path of the user cost of capital.

Does Uncertainty About Tax Policy Affect Investment?

What if firms do not know the exact timing of changes in investment incentives—that is, if tax policy is uncertain? A substantial literature evaluates the effects of price uncertainty on investment, and the lesson from this literature is that the sign of the effect of uncertainty on investment depends crucially on assumptions about adjustment costs and returns to scale. Hartman (1972) shows that uncertainty generally increases investment in a model with constant returns and convex adjustment costs. Abel (1983) derives a similar result in continuous time. Pindyck (1988), however, shows that uncertainty can significantly lower capital formation if investment is irreversible and returns to scale are decreasing. We described Pindyck's intuition earlier: in an uncertain world, there is a gain to delaying investment—the option value of waiting—and these gains are higher the higher is the variance in the output price.

Thus, one might be tempted to conclude from the early contributions to this literature that the predicted effect of tax policy uncertainty will depend on what we believe about the reversibility—or lack thereof—of capital investments. However, strictly speaking, tax policy uncertainty can increase investment in the models of Hartman, Abel, and even Pindyck (see Hassett and Metcalf 1994, 1995).

This difference arises because tax policy uncertainty is unlike price uncertainty in an important way. Researchers often introduced uncertainty by assuming that the price follows a continuous-time random walk (Brownian motion or geometric Brownian motion). When prices follow a random walk, the appropriate rational expectations forecast for the price at any time in the future is today's price, and the future path of the price is unbounded. Unlike most prices, tax parameters tend to remain constant for a few years and then jump to new values. In addition, jumps in the ITC tend to be mean reverting: when the credit is high, it is likely to be reduced in the future, and when the credit is low, it is likely to be increased in the future. Because of these properties, the normal gain to waiting in a model with irreversibility is reduced significantly when an investment tax credit is "on". Because the firm fears that the credit might be eliminated, it is more likely to invest today while the credit is still effective. Hassett and Metcalf demonstrate that this effect dominates the reverse effect in the state in which there is no investment tax credit, and they conclude that increasing tax policy uncertainty raises aggregate investment.

As with the case of temporary investment incentives generally, this result does not imply that random tax policy is desirable. Most existing studies analyze investment in a partial equilibrium setting wherein there are no utility costs to bunching capital formation. In a general equilibrium setting, Bizer and Judd (1989) show that welfare is reduced significantly by random investment tax policy. The randomness has a negative impact because consumers wish to smooth consumption, and fluctuations in investment credits make smoothing costly.

8.5 Policy Implications

Our finding of significant short-term and long-term effects of the user cost of capital on equipment investment suggests applications to current policy debates. In particular, we evaluate consequences for the user cost and investment of a reduction in inflation and a switch from an income tax to a broad-based consumption tax.

Low Inflation as a "Costless" Investment Subsidy

Many economists (see e.g., Feldstein 1976; King and Fullerton 1984) have argued that under fairly general assumptions, a reduction in the rate of inflation provides a relatively costless stimulus to business fixed investment by reducing the user cost of capital. Returning to the expression for the user cost, there are two channels through which expected inflation affects investment decisions. First, for given values of r and δ, the user cost varies positively with the level of expected inflation π because the present value of depreciation allowances—which is formed using the nominal rate, $r + \pi$, as a discount rate—varies inversely with inflation owing to historical-cost depreciation.[30] Second, inflation affects the real cost of funds, r. In this section, we briefly illustrate this second channel (following Auerbach 1983b) and calculate the extent to which lower inflation over the past decade led to a reduction in the user cost of capital.

In a small open economy, the real cost of debt would be determined in world capital markets and would be exogenously given to firms. If the capital market were closed, the marginal tax rate of the holder of debt would affect the interest rates that firms pay. That is, local debt holders require a fixed real after-tax return, r, where

$$r = i(1 - \tau_p) - \pi, \tag{8.19}$$

where i is the nominal interest rate on corporate debt, τ_p is the marginal personal tax rate on interest income, and π is the expected rate of inflation. The inflation premium component of interest income is taxable to bondholders. The firm's real cost of debt, ρ_d, depends on its own marginal income tax rate, τ_c,

$$\rho_d = i(1 - \tau_c) - \pi, \tag{8.20}$$

because under current U.S. tax law, nominal interest payments on corporate debt are fully deductible. Combining the two previous expressions relates the firm's, real cost of debt to the investor's required return and marginal tax rate:

$$\rho_d = (r + \pi)\frac{(1 - \tau_c)}{(1 - \tau_p)} - \pi. \tag{8.21}$$

Alternatively,

$$\rho_d = \frac{r(1 - \tau_c) + (\tau_p - \tau_c)\pi}{(1 - \tau_p)}. \tag{8.22}$$

The firm's real cost of equity finance, ρ_e, is defined as

$$\rho_e = D + E - \pi, \tag{8.23}$$

where D is the dividend-price ratio and E is investor's required ex-dividend nominal return to equity.

Note that for a given r, inflation has very little effect on the cost of debt finance if—as is likely the case in the United States—τ_c is approximately equal to τ_p. In this case, lower inflation reduces the nominal interest deduction but lowers the tax liability of bondholder by the same amount. Note also that the effects of inflation on the cost of debt finance depend crucially on the assumption that the marginal debt holder is taxable. If the marginal debt holder is a pension fund (whose income is not taxed under current law), then lower inflation unambiguously increases the cost of debt finance. Firms receive smaller interest deductions, and pension funds do not accrue an offsetting reduction in tax liability.[31]

Individuals receive the after-tax real return,

$$\rho_i = (1 - \tau_i)D + (1 - c)E - \pi, \tag{8.24}$$

where τ_i is the individual's marginal tax rate on dividend income and c is the individual's accrual equivalent tax rate on capital gains. Combining terms, the firm's real cost of equity finance is

$$\rho_e = \frac{(\tau_i - c)}{(1-c)} D + \frac{\rho_i}{(1-c)} + \frac{c}{(1-c)} \pi. \qquad (8.25)$$

Higher inflation unambiguously increases the cost of equity finance by the factor $c/(1-c)$. This term captures the "inflation tax" paid by shareholders who receive purely nominal gains; taxation of real capital gains would eliminate this effect.[32]

The total real cost of investment funds is simply the weighted average of the cost of equity and the cost of debt, where the weights are the share of each in marginal finance. Using this approach, one can examine the effect on investment of recent declines in expected inflation. Cohen, Hassett, and Hubbard (1996) calculate the marginal effects on the user cost of lowering inflation.[33] They estimate that under plausible assumptions, the current value of the user cost for equipment investment is about 0.22, and they conclude that a one-percentage-point permanent decrease in inflation lowers the user cost by about one-half a percentage point. In their calculations, the incremental effect of each additional percentage point reduction in inflation is approximately the same. Thus, if the annual inflation rate were reduced from 4 percent to zero, the user cost of capital would decline about two percentage points—proportionally by about 10 percent. Given the elasticity estimates reviewed in the previous section, this "tax cut" would provide a significant stimulus to investment.

Moving to a Consumption Tax

Under the income tax, the user cost of capital is influenced by the corporate tax rate, investment tax credits, and the present value of depreciation allowances (see equation 8.6). Under a broad-based consumption tax, firms pay tax on the difference between receipts and purchases from other firms. That is, there is no investment tax credit, and investment is expensed ($z = 1$). In this case (assuming that the corporate tax rate does not change over time), the user cost of capital simplifies to

$$c_{i,t} = p_t \left[r_{it} + \delta_i - \frac{\Delta p_{t+1}}{p_t} \right]. \qquad (8.6')$$

Comparing the user cost expressions in equations 8.6 and 8.6′ leads to two observations. First, under a consumption tax, taxes do not distort business investment decisions; investment decisions are based on nontax fundamentals. Second, given current U.S. tax policy, the user cost is lower under a consumption tax than under an income tax.

By how much? Under current law, and assuming that the output price and the capital goods price are both equal to unity, then for assets with seven-year lives (assuming that the expected real interest rate is 4 percent, the expected inflation rate is 3 percent, and the marginal machine is financed half with equity and half with debt), the value of $(1-\Gamma)/(1-\tau)$ under 1996 U.S. tax law is 1.148, and the user cost of capital is equal to 0.234. The move to the consumption tax would lower the value of the user cost to 0.205, a reduction that would lead, ceteris paribus, to about a 10 percent increase in equipment investment given the consensus estimates of γ in equation 8.14.

Of course, other aggregate variables are also likely to change if such a large change to the tax code were adopted. For example, nominal interest rates and the supply of savings are likely to change. While it is difficult to say how large the net stimulus to investment would be, the consensus of the recent investment literature suggests that the partial equilibrium impact on investment may be quite large.

8.6 Conclusions

Economists and policymakers have long been concerned about the effects of business taxation and investment incentives on the equilibrium capital stock and the timing of investment. Such concerns figure prominently in research programs (1) identifying impacts of tax parameters on fundamental determinants of investment, (2) describing links between fundamentals and the capital stock or investment, and (3) testing models of those links. Studies within the neoclassical tradition offer rigorous applications of the first two, but until recently have not produced reasonable empirical estimates of effects of fundamentals on investment. Indeed, the poor empirical performance of neoclassical factors led some researchers to conclude that "taxes don't matter" and still others to question assumptions of the neoclassical paradigm.

Our principal conclusions are four. First, neoclassical models that use convex costs of adjusting the capital stock to derive investment equations yield economically important short-run and long-run effects of tax policy on investment. This result reflects recent research that, through a number of complementary approaches, demonstrates that measurement error in fundamentals biases downward conventional estimates of tax effects. Second, at least for data on firm-level investment, predictions of models with nonconvex adjustment costs are no more consistent with observed links between fundamentals and investment than those of models with convex adjustment costs. Third, recent studies conclude that U.S. business investment is below its golden rule level. Finally, consensus estimates of the impact of the user cost of capital on investment indicate that two current policy suggestions—pursuing a monetary policy that would reduce expected inflation and switching from an income tax to a consumption tax—would significantly stimulate investment.

The current state of research on business investment decisions suggests the desirability of developing tests to distinguish among alternative models of costs of adjusting the capital stock. Different adjustment cost specifications imply different time paths of the response of the capital stock to tax policy, making such tests useful for policymakers. Nonetheless, most recent studies imply a high long-run elasticity of the capital stock to the user cost of capital, so that tax policy clearly has the potential to have a powerful effect on equipment investment and the capital stock in the long run.

Notes

We are grateful to Josh Gillespie for excellent research assistance and to Alan Auerbach, Darrel Cohen, Jason Cummins, Bronwyn Hall, Charlie Himmelberg, Jim Kennedy, Sandy Struckmeyer, John Taylor, and conference participants for helpful comments and suggestions. The opinions expressed here are not necessarily those of the Board of Governors of the Federal Reserve System.

1. See Braudel (1992, p. 241).

2. We update the time-series stylized facts in section 8.2.

3. Eisner and Strotz (1963) offer an early discussion of adjustment costs. The theory was developed and extended by Lucas (1967, 1976), Gould (1968), Treadway (1969, 1970), Uzawa (1969), Mortensen (1973), Abel (1980), and Hayashi (1982). Researchers have generally assumed convex costs of adjusting the capital stock—the idea that it is more costly to implement a given increment to the capital stock quickly rather than gradually. We discuss alternative assumptions about adjustment costs in section 8.4.

4. For a more detailed discussion of the models introduced in this section, see Abel (1990).

5. For the sake of simplifying the discussion, we focus here on the U.S. tax system. For a parallel analysis that employs a more general tax formulation nesting that of many countries, see Sinn (1987) and King and Fullerton (1984). Sweden, in particular, has had one of the more complicated and interesting tax codes in the postwar period. For a discussion relating its code to this model, see Taylor (1982), Södersten (1989), and Auerbach, Hassett, and Södersten (1995).

6. Implicit in this derivation is the idea that firms can remove capital goods and sell them subject to an adjustment cost.

7. It may be important to allow the ex ante and ex post values of σ to be different, the argument being that the labor needed for a given piece of capital in place is fixed. This is the "putty-clay" hypothesis, put forward by Bischoff (1971). In some cases, these models have been shown to perform well empirically (see Struckmeyer 1983).

8. To be more specific, Jorgenson assumed that the revenue function of the firm was Cobb-Douglas and that the firm set marginal revenue (with respect to capital) equal to the user cost in order to maximize profits.

9. For example, Haavelmo (1960) writes, "The demand for investment cannot simply be derived from the demand for capital.... I think the sooner this naive, and unfounded theory of the demand for investment schedule is abandoned, the sooner we shall have a chance of making some real progress in constructing more powerful theories to deal with the capricious short-run variations in the rate of private investment" (quoted in Jorgenson 1967, p. 133).

10. In an alternative representation, Feldstein (1982) explored the effects of effective tax rates on investment in reduced-form models; for a critique of this approach, see Chirinko (1987).

11. As we noted earlier, Hayashi (1982) provided the conditions required to equate marginal q with average Q, which is observable because it depends on the market valuation of the firm's assets. Summers (1981) incorporated additional tax parameters in the Q model.

12. See e.g., Bosworth (1985), Bernanke, Bohn, and Reiss (1988), and the survey in Chirinko (1993). The often poor empirical performance of Q models has led some researchers to abandon the assumptions of reversible investment and convex costs used in testing neoclassical models in favor of approaches based on lumpy and "irreversible" investment. See e.g., the discussions and reviews of studies in Pindyck (1991), Dixit and Pindyck (1994), and Hubbard (1994).

13. Taylor (1993) does find, however, that aggregate fixed investment is significantly negatively related to the real interest rate in every one of the Group of 7 countries.

14. The measure of Q plotted here is constructed from data from the Federal Reserve's Flow of Funds Accounts.

15. If we regress the growth rate of business fixed investment on many lags of the growth rate of Q, the sum of the coefficients is about 0.1, implying that a 20 percent increase in the growth rate of Q would lead to a prediction of about a 2 percent higher growth rate of business fixed investment. Cochrane (1991) finds significantly larger effects of the growth of Q on the growth of total private investment. The results differ because Cochrane's measure of investment includes residential investment, which is—perhaps surprisingly—more highly correlated with stock market fluctuations.

16. One could, of course, incorporate more complex error structures. We make this simplifying assumption for ease of exposition.

17. This is a test of the restricted model against the alternative model that current profits have explanatory power for investment beyond their ability to predict future profits. Gilchrist and Himmelberg find that cash flow is an independent fundamental and that excess sensitivity of investment to cash flow is a characteristic of firms they identify as constrained—measured by size, bond rating, commercial paper rating, or dividend payout.

18. Cummins, Hassett, and Hubbard (1994, 1995) also use this approach in a user cost model. For U.S. data, they estimate a user cost coefficient of about -0.65.

19. Tax reforms are not the only plausible reform that can be used to estimate adjustment costs. A large body of evidence suggests that union power to expropriate returns is significant and that the "union tax" adjusts as the return to capital changes. If union wage demands vary with the return to capital, then the union rent share is—in part at least—a tax on capital, distorting the level of investment when it is introduced. Fallick and Hassett (1995) explore whether a change in the union status of the firm is another type of large, identifiable shock that affects purchases of capital. Using firm-level panel data, they document a large negative response of investment to union certification elections. For most of the firms that experience union certification elections in their sample, net investment turns significantly negative in the year immediately following the election, with the mean response to union certification being roughly the same size as that which would occur—given the responsiveness of investment to the user cost in Cummins, Hassett, and Hubbard (1994)—if the corporate tax rate were increased by 35 percentage points. This set of firms, at least, is not burdened by an ability to adjust their capital stock downward when a negative shock to profitability occurs.

20. For reviews of the theoretical literature, see Bernanke, Gertler, and Gilchrist (1996) and Hubbard (1990, 1996).

21. Fazzari, Hubbard, and Petersen (1988b) and Gertler and Hubbard (1988) illustrate this point in examining the effect of the investment tax credit on investment. Calomiris and Hubbard (1995) focus on a tax experiment in which retained earnings are taxed more heavily than distributed profits. In frictionless capital markets, firms would take advantage of the incentive to change their payout policies. Working against this response for some firms is the potential difference in the cost of internal and external funds. To the extent that the marginal cost of external funds is high, a growing firm with profitable investment opportunities might choose to pay the undistributed profits tax and invest its internal funds rather than distribute funds and then reacquire them in the capital market. The U.S. undistributed profits tax of 1936–1937, which imposed a graduated surtax on corporate retention, offers a useful experiment. Because the maximum marginal tax rate on corporate retention was 27 percent, most firms had large incentives to alter their payout policies. Using firm-level panel data from the 1930s, Calomiris and Hubbard find that a neoclassical investment model with no explicit capital market frictions is rejected only for firms with high ex ante surtax margins.

22. The seeds of this literature are much older. For example, Rothschild (1971) writes: "Convex cost-of-adjustment functions may help to explain why Rome was not built in a day. However, there is no clear saving and may be some loss to spreading the work of installing a button on a shirt over several weeks." His "bang-bang" model of investment provides an early example of a "lumpy investment" model.

23. In earlier work, Doms and Dunne (1994) report that plant-level investment data exhibit skewness and kurtosis that is consistent with investment's being somewhat lumpy.

24. To calculate the desired capital stock for each firm, Caballero, Engel, and Haltiwanger use plant-level output data and two-digit Jorgensonian user costs constructed from the tax data used in Cummins, Hassett, and Hubbard (1994) and Goolsbee (1996).

25. Because their mandated investment measure is the same as that in a frictionless neoclassical model, their tests, although suggestive, neither confirm nor reject the presence of convex adjustment costs. First, mandated investment itself depends on adjustment costs. Second, if adjustment costs were present, mandated investment also depends on future values of tax parameters.

26. Using a different approach, Goolsbee (1996) finds evidence that U.S. tax shocks are positively correlated with capital price movements. He argues that the elasticity of investment demand with respect to the user cost is likely greater than unity (in absolute value), but that an upward-sloping short-run supply curve for capital goods likely dampens mildly the effects of tax policy.

27. Another argument for subsidies to equipment investment has been advanced by Judd (1995), who concludes that the optimal tax on equipment investment is negative. He argues that to the extent that capital-goods-producing industries are imperfectly competitive (owing, say, to the presence of patents), equipment prices contain significant markups. Hence to return firm's input mix to the optimal level, the government should design an investment subsidy that equates the price paid for equipment to its marginal cost.

28. See, e.g., the analysis in Blanchard and Fischer (1989).

29. Because the golden rule models are developed for a closed economy, it is difficult to extend the comparison to domestic versus foreign fixed capital.

30. That is, the present value of depreciation allowances is given by:

$$\sum_{s=t}^{\infty}(1 + r_{is} + \pi_s)\tau_s DEP_{is}(s - t),$$

where $DEP(a)$ is the depreciation allowance permitted an asset of age a, discounted at a nominal rate that includes the expected inflation rate π.

31. There is no clear consensus regarding the effects of marginal tax rates on domestic real interest rates or on the question of whether the "Fisher effect" implicit in equation 8.21 holds. This is an important area for future research in this context.

32. For the calculations described below, we do not include the first term reflecting the tax on dividends. In effect, we adopt the "tax capitalization" view of equity taxation (summarized in Auerbach 1983b), which suggests that the relevant tax rate is the effective capital gains tax rate, regardless of the amount of dividends paid. This view assumes that marginal equity funds come primarily from retained earnings rather than from new share issues and that earnings distributions to shareholders are primarily through dividends rather than share repurchases.

33. Earlier empirical studies of the effect of inflation on real business tax burdens include Feldstein and Summers (1979) and Auerbach (1983b). Cohen, Hassett, and Hubbard (1996) also allow for inflation to increase taxes paid because of the effects of inflation on the cost of carrying inventories.

References

Abel, Andrew B. 1980, Spring. "Empirical Investment Equations: An Integrative Framework." *Journal of Monetary Economics* 12:39–91.

Abel, Andrew B. 1983, March. "Optimal Investment Under Uncertainty." *American Economic Review* 73:228–233.

Abel, Andrew B. 1990. "Consumption and Investment." In Benjamin M. Friedman and Frank H. Hahn, eds., *Handbook of Monetary Economics*, vol. 2. Amsterdam: North-Holland.

Abel, Andrew B., and Olivier J. Blanchard. 1986, March. "The Present Value of Profits and Cyclical Movements in Investment." *Econometrica* 54:249–273.

Abel, Andrew B., and Janice C. Eberly. 1994, September. "A Unified Model of Investment Under Uncertainty." *American Economic Review* 84:1369–1384.

Abel, Andrew B., and Janice C. Eberly. 1995. "The Effects of Irreversibility and Uncertainty on Capital Accumulation." NBER Working Paper 5363.

Abel, Andrew B., and Janice C. Eberly. 1996a, January. "Investment and *q* with Fixed Costs: An Empirical Analysis." Mimeo. Wharton School.

Abel, Andrew B., and Janice C. Eberly. 1996b, April. "Optimal Investment with Costly Irreversibility." Review of Economic Studies 63:581–594.

Abel, Andrew B., N. Gregory Mankiw, Lawrence H. Summers, and Richard J. Zeckhauser. 1989. "Assessing Dynamic Efficiency: Theory and Evidence." *Review of Economic Studies* 56:1–20.

Aftalian, A. 1909. "La reálité des surproductions générales, essai d'une théorie des crises générales et periodiques." *Revue d'Economie Politique.*

Auerbach, Alan J. 1983a. "Corporate Taxation in the United States." *Brookings Papers on Economic Activity* 2:451–513.

Auerbach, Alan J. 1983b, September. "Taxation, Corporate Financial Policy, and the Cost of Capital." *Journal of Economic Literature* 21:905–940.

Auerbach, Alan J. 1989. "Tax Reform and Adjustment Costs: The Impact on Investment and Market Value." *International Economic Review* 30:939–962.

Auerbach, Alan, J., and Kevin A. Hassett. 1991, Autumn. "Recent U.S. Investment Behavior and the Tax Reform Act of 1986: A Disaggregate View." *Carnegie-Rochester Conference Series on Public Policy* 35:185–215.

Auerbach, Alan J., and Kevin A. Hassett. 1992. "Tax Policy and Business Fixed Investment in the United States." *Journal of Public Economics* 47:141–170.

Auerbach, Alan J., Kevin A. Hassett, and Jan Södersten. 1995, July. "Taxation and Corporate Investment: The Impact of the 1991 Swedish Tax Reform." NBER Working Paper 5189.

Barnett, Steven A., and Plutarchos Sakellaris. 1995, October. "Nonlinear Response of Firm Investment to Q: Testing a Model of Convex and Nonconvex Adjustment Costs." Working Paper 95-11. University of Maryland.

Bernanke, Ben, Henning Bohn, and Peter C. Reiss. 1988, March. "Alternative Nonnested Specification Tests of Time-Series Investment Models." *Journal of Econometrics* 37:293–326.

Bernanke, Ben, Mark Gertler, and Simon Gilchrist. 1996. "The Financial Accelerator and the Flight to Quality." *Review of Economics and Statistics* 78:1–15.

Bischoff, Charles. 1971. "Business Investment in the 1970s: A Comparison of Models." *Brookings Papers on Economic Activity* 1:13–63.

Bizer, David, and Kenneth Judd. 1989, May. "Taxation and Uncertainty." *American Economic Review* 79:331–336.

Blanchard, Olivier Jean, and Stanley Fischer. 1989. *Lectures on Macroeconomics.* Cambridge: MIT Press.

Blundell, Richard, et al. 1992. "Investment and Tobin's *Q*." *Journal of Econometrics* 57:233–257.

Bond, Stephen, and Costas Meghir. 1994. "Dynamic Investment Models and the Firm's Financial Policy." *Review of Economic Studies* 61:197–222.

Bosworth, Barry P. 1985. "Taxes and the Investment Recovery." *Brookings Papers on Economic Activity* 1:1–38.

Braudel, Fernand. 1992. *The Wheels of Commerce.* Berkeley: University of California Press.

Caballero, Ricardo J. 1994. "Small Sample Bias and Adjustment Costs." *Review of Economics and Statistics,* 52–58.

Caballero, Ricardo J., and John V. Leahy. 1995, December. "Fixed Costs: The Demise of Marginal *q*." Mimeo. MIT.

Caballero, Richard J., Eduardo M. R. A. Engle, and John C. Haltiwanger. 1995. "Plant-level Adjustment and Aggregate Investment Dynamics." *Brookings Papers on Economic Activity* 2:1–54.

Calomiris, Charles W., and R. Glenn Hubbard. 1995, October. "Internal Finance and Investment: Evidence from the Undistributed Profits Tax of 1937–1938." *Journal of Business* 68:443–482.

Chirinko, Robert S. 1987. "The Ineffectiveness of Effective Tax Rates on Business Investment: A Critique of Feldstein's Fisher-Schultz Lecture." *Journal of Public Economics* 32:369–387.

Chirinko, Robert S. 1993, December. "Business Fixed Investment Spending: Modeling Strategies, Empirical Results, and Policy Implications." *Journal of Economic Literature* 31:1875–1911.

Chirinko, Robert S., and Robert Eisner. 1983. "Tax Policy and Investment in Major Macroeconometric Models." *Journal of Public Economics* 20:139–166.

Clark, J. M. 1917, March. "Business Acceleration and the Law of Demand." *Journal of Political Economy* 25:217–235.

Clark, Peter K. 1993. "Tax Incentives and Equipment Investment." *Brookings Papers on Economic Activity* 1:317–339.

Cochrane, John. 1991, March. "Production-Based Asset Pricing and the Link Between Stock Returns and Economic Fluctuations." *Journal of Finance* 46:209–237.

Cohen, Darrel, Kevin A. Hassett, and R. Glenn Hubbard. 1996, December. "Inflation and the User Cost of Capital: Does Inflation Still Matter?" Mimeo. Columbia University.

Cohen, Darrel, Kevin A. Hassett, and James Kennedy. 1995. *Are U.S. Investment and Capital Stocks at Their Optimal Levels?* FEDS Working Paper 9532. Board of Governors of the Federal Reserve System.

Cummins, Jason G., Trevor S. Harris, and Kevin A. Hassett. 1995. "Accounting Standards, Information Flow, and Firm Investment Behavior." In Martin Feldstein, James R. Hines, and R. Glenn Hubbard, eds., *The Effects of Taxation on Multinational Corporations.* Chicago: University of Chicago Press.

Cummins, Jason G., Kevin A. Hassett, and R. Glenn Hubbard. 1994. "A Reconsideration of Investment Behavior Using Tax Reforms as Natural Experiments." *Brookings Papers on Economic Activity* 2:1–74.

Cummins, Jason G., Kevin A. Hassett, and R. Glenn Hubbard. 1995. "Have Tax Reforms Affected Investment?" In James M. Poterba, ed., *Tax Policy and the Economy*, vol. 9. Cambridge: MIT Press.

Cummins, Jason G., Kevin A. Hassett, and R. Glenn Hubbard. 1996. "Tax Reforms and Investment: A Cross-Country Comparison." *Journal of Public Economics*. 62:237–273.

Cummins, Jason G., and R. Glenn Hubbard. 1995. "The Tax Sensitivity of Foreign Direct Investment: Evidence from Firm-Level Panel Data." In Martin Feldstein, James R. Hines, and R. Glenn Hubbard, eds., *The Effects of Taxation on Multinational Corporations*. Chicago: University of Chicago Press.

Diamond, Peter A. 1965, December. "National Debt in a Neoclassical Growth Model." *American Economic Review* 55:1126–1150.

Dixit, Avinash, K., and Robert S. Pindyck. 1994. *Investment Under Uncertainty*. Princeton: Princeton University Press.

Doms, Mark, and Timothy Dunne. 1994. *Capital Adjustment Patterns in Manufacturing Plants*. Discussion Paper 94-11. Washington, D.C.: Center for Economic Studies, U.S. Bureau of the Census.

Eisner, Robert. 1969, June. "Tax Policy and Investment Behavior: Comment." *American Economic Review* 59:379–388.

Eisner, Robert. 1970, September. "Tax Policy and Investment Behavior: Further Comment." *American Economic Review* 60:746–752.

Eisner, Robert, and M. Ishaq Nadiri. 1968. "Investment Behavior and Neoclassical Theory." *Review of Economics and Statistics* 50:369–382.

Eisner, Robert, and M. Ishaq Nadiri. 1970, May. "Neoclassical Theory of Investment Behavior: A Comment." *Review of Economics and Statistics* 52:216–222.

Eisner, Robert, and Robert H. Strotz. 1963. "Determinants of Business Investment." In *Impacts of Monetary Policy*, studies prepared for the Commission on Money and Credit. Englewood Cliffs, NJ: Prentice Hall.

Fallick, Bruce C., and Kevin A. Hassett. 1995, September. "Union Certification and Investment." Mimeo. Board of Governors of the Federal Reserve System.

Fazzari, Steven M., R. Glenn Hubbard, and Bruce C. Petersen. 1988a. "Financing Constraints and Corporate Investment." *Brookings Papers on Economic Activity* 1:141–195.

Fazzari, Steven M., R. Glenn Hubbard, and Bruce C. Petersen. 1988b, May. "Investment, Financing Decisions, and Tax Policy." *American Economic Review* 78:200–205.

Feldstein, Martin S. 1976, June. "Inflation, Income Taxes, and the Rate of Interest: A Theoretical Analysis." *American Economic Review* 66:809–820.

Feldstein, Martin S. 1977, May. "Does the United States Save Too Little?" *American Economic Review* 67:116–121.

Feldstein, Martin S. 1982, July. "Inflation, Tax Rules, and Investment: Some Econometric Evidence." *Econometrica* 50:825–862.

Feldstein, Martin S., and Lawrence H. Summers. 1979, December. "Inflation and the Taxation of Capital Income in the Corporate Sector." *Notional Tax Journal* 32:445–470.

Fisher, Irving. 1930. *The Theory of Interest*. New York: Macmillan.

Fraumeni, Barbara M. 1995, January. "The Measurement of Depreciation in the U.S. National Income and Wealth Accounts." Mimeo. National Science Foundation.

Gertler, Mark, and R. Glenn Hubbard. 1988. "Financial Factors in Business Fluctuations." In *Financial Market Volatility: Causes and Consequences*. Kansas City: Federal Reserve Bank of Kansas City.

Gilchrist, Simon. 1991. "An Empirical Analysis of Corporate Investment and Financing Hierarchies Using Firm-Level Panel Data." Mimeo. Board of Governors of the Federal Reserve System.

Gilchrist, Simon, and Charles P. Himmelberg. 1995. "Evidence on the Role of Cash Flow in Reduced-Form Investment Equations." *Journal of Monetary Economics* 36:541–572.

Goolsbee, Austan. 1996. "Investment Tax Incentives and the Price of Capital Goods." Mimeo. University of Chicago.

Gould, John P. 1968. "Adjustment Costs in the Theory of Investment of the Firm." *Review of Economic Studies* 35:47–55.

Griliches, Zvi, and Jerry A. Hausman. 1986, February. "Errors in Variables in Panel Data." *Journal of Econometrics* 31:141–154.

Haavelmo, Trygve. 1960. *A Study in the Theory of Investment*. Chicago: University of Chicago Press.

Hall, Robert E., and Dale W. Jorgenson. 1967, June. "Tax Policy and Investment Behavior." *American Economic Review* 57:391–414.

Hartman, Richard. 1972 "The Effects of Price and Cost Uncertainty on Investment." *Journal of Economic Theory* 5:258–266.

Hassett, Kevin A., and R. Glenn Hubbard. 1995, December. "The World Market for Capital Goods: Does Local Policy Affect Prices?" Mimeo. Columbia University.

Hassett, Kevin A., and Gilbert E. Metcalf. 1994, June. *Investment with Uncertain Tax Policy: Does Random Tax Policy Discourage Investment?* NBER Working Paper 4780.

Hassett, Kevin A., and Gilbert E. Metcalf. 1995. *Random Taxes and Continuous Investment*. Working paper. Tufts University.

Hayashi, Fumio. 1982, January. "Tobin's Marginal q and Average q: A Neoclassical Interpretation." *Econometrica* 50:213–224.

Hayashi, Fumio. 1985. "Corporate Finance Side of the Q Theory of Investment." *Journal of Public Economics* 27:261–280.

Hayashi, Fumio, and Tohru Inoue. 1991, May. "The Relation Between Firm Growth and q with Multiple Capital Goods: Theory and Evidence from Panel Data on Japanese Firms." *Econometrica* 59:731–753.

Himmelberg, Charles P. 1991. "A Dynamic Analysis of Dividend and Investment Behavior Under Borrowing Constraints." Mimeo. New York University.

Hubbard, R. Glenn. 1990. Introduction to R. Glenn Hubbard, ed., *Asymmetric Information, Corporate Finance, and Investment*. Chicago: University of Chicago Press.

Hubbard, R. Glenn. 1994, December. "Investment Under Uncertainty: Keeping One's Options Open." *Journal of Economic Literature* 32:1816–1831.

Hubbard, R. Glenn. 1996, July. "Capital-Market Imperfections and Investment." Mimeo. Columbia University.

Hubbard, R. Glenn, and Anil K. Kashyap. 1992, June. "Internal Net Worth and the Investment Process: An Application to U.S. Agriculture." *Journal of Political Economy* 100:506–534.

Hubbard, R. Glenn, Anil K. Kashyap, and Toni M. Whited. 1995, August. Internal Finance and Firm Investment." *Journal of Money, Credit, and Banking* 27:683–701.

Hulten, Charles R., and Frank C. Wykoff. 1979, July. *Tax and Economic Depreciation of Machinery and Equipment: A Theoretical and Empirical Appraisal*. Working Paper. U.S. Treasury Department, Office of Tax Analysis.

Hulten, Charles R., and Frank C. Wykoff. 1981. "The Measurement of Economic Depreciation." In Charles R. Hulten, ed., *Depreciation, Inflation, and the Taxation of Income from Capital*. Washington, DC: Urban Institute.

Ibbotson, R. G. 1987. *Stocks, Bonds, Bills, and Inflation: Market Results for 1926–1986*. Chicago: Ibbotson and Associates.

Jorgenson, Dale W. 1963, May. "Capital Theory and Investment Behavior." *American Economic Review* 53:247–259.

Jorgenson, Dale W. 1967. "Theory of Investment Behavior." In Robert Ferber, ed., *Determinants of Investment Behavior*. New York: Columbia University Press.

Jorgenson, Dale W. 1971, December. "Econometric Studies of Investment Behavior: A Survey." *Journal of Economic Literature* 9:1111–1147.

Jorgenson, Dale W. 1994, December. *Empirical Studies of Depreciation*. Working Paper 1704. Harvard Institute of Economic Research.

Jorgenson, Dale W., and Calvin D. Siebert. 1968, September. "A Comparison of Alternative Theories of Corporate Investment Behavior." *American Economic Review* 58:681–712.

Jorgenson, Dale W., and James A. Stephenson. 1969. "Issues in the Development of the Neoclassical Model." *Review of Economics and Statistics* 51:346–353.

Jorgenson, Dale W., and Martin A. Sullivan. 1981. "Inflation and Corporate Capital Recovery." In Charles R. Hulten, ed., *Depreciation, Inflation, and the Taxation of Income from Capital*. Washington, DC: Urban Institute.

Judd, Kenneth L. 1995, April. "The Optimal Tax Rate for Capital Income Is Negative." Working Paper. Hoover Institution.

Keynes, John Maynard. 1936. *The General Theory of Employment, Interest, and Money*. New York: Harcourt Brace.

King, Mervyn A., and Don Fullerton, eds. 1984. *The Taxation of Income from Capital: A Comparative Study of the United States, United Kingdom, Sweden, and West Germany*. Chicago: University of Chicago Press.

Lucas, Robert E., Jr. 1967, August. "Adjustment Costs and the Theory of Supply." *Journal of Political Economy* 75:321–334.

Lucas, Robert E., Jr. 1976. "Econometric Policy Evaluation: A Critique." In Karl Brunner and Allan Meltzer, eds., *The Phillips Curve and Labor Markets, Carnegie-Rochester Conference Series on Public Policy* 1:19–46.

Meyer, John R., and Edwin Kuh. 1957. *The Investment Decision.* Cambridge: Harvard University Press.

Modigliani, France, and Merton H. Miller. 1958, June. "The Cost of Capital, Corporation Finance and the Theory of Investment." *American Economic Review* 48:261–297.

Mortenson, Dale T. 1973. "Generalized Costs of Adjustment and Dynamic Factor Demand Theory." *Econometrica* 41:657–667.

Nickell, Stephen J. 1978. *The Investment Decisions of Firms.* Cambridge: Cambridge University Press.

Oliner, Stephen D. 1996. "New Evidence on the Retirement and Depreciation of Machine Tools." *Economic Inquiry* 34:57–77.

Phelps, Edmund S. 1961. "The Golden Rule of Accumulation: A Fable for Growth Men." *American Economic Review* 51:638–643.

Pindyck, Robert S. 1988, December. "Irreversible Investment, Capacity Choice, and the Value of the Firm." *American Economic Review* 78:969–985.

Pindyck, Robert S. 1991, September. "Irreversibility, Uncertainty, and Investment." *Journal of Economic Literature* 29:1110–1148.

Pindyck, Robert S., and Julio J. Rotemberg. 1983. "Dynamic Factor Demands Under Rational Expectations." *Scandinavian Journal of Economics* 85:223–238.

Ramsey, Frank P. 1928. "A Mathematical Theory of Saving." *Economic Journal* 62:543–559.

Rothschild, Michael. 1971. "On the Cost of Adjustment." *Quarterly Journal of Economics* 85:605–622.

Sakellaris, Plutarchos. 1995. "Investment Under Uncertain Market Conditions." *Review of Economics and Statistics.* 77:455–469.

Salinger, Michael A., and Lawrence H. Summers. 1983. "Tax Reform and Corporate Investment: A Microeconomic Simulation Study." In Martin Feldstein, ed., *Behavioral Simulation Methods in Tax Policy Analysis.* Chicago: University of Chicago Press.

Shapiro, Matthew D. 1986, August. "The Dynamic Demand for Capital and Labor." *Quarterly Journal of Economics* 101:513–547.

Sinn, Hans-Werner. 1987. *Capital Income Taxation as Resource Allocation.* Amsterdam: North-Holland.

Södersten, Jan. 1989, December. "The Investment Funds System Reconsidered." *Scandinavian Journal of Economics* 91:671–687.

Solow, Robert. 1970. *Growth Theory.* Oxford: Oxford University Press.

Stock James H., and Mark W. Watson. 1993, January. "A Simple MLE of Cointegrating Vectors in Higher Order Integrated Systems." *Econometrica* 61:111–152.

Struckmeyer, Charles S. 1983. "Capital, Energy, and Economic Growth: A Vintage Approach." Ph.D. dissertation, Yale University.

Summers, Lawrence H. 1981. "Taxation and Corporate Investment: A *q*-Theory Approach." *Brookings Papers on Economic Activity* 1:67–127.

Summers, Lawrence H. 1987. "Investment Incentives and the Discounting of Depreciation Allowances." In Martin Feldstein, ed., *The Effects of Taxation on Capital Accumulation.* Chicago: University of Chicago Press.

Taylor, John B. 1982. "The Swedish Investment Funds System as a Stabilization Policy Rule." *Brookings Papers on Economic Activity* 1:57–101.

Taylor, John B. 1993. *Macroeconomic Policy Design in a World Economy: From Econometric Design to Practical Operation.* New York: W. W. Norton.

Tobin, James. 1965. "Economic Growth as an Objective of Government Policy." In *Essays in Economics,* Vol. 1: *Macroeconomics.* Amsterdam: North-Holland.

Tobin, James. 1969, February. "A General Equilibrium Approach to Monetary Theory." *Journal of Money, Credit, and Banking* 1:15–29.

Treadway, A. B. 1969. "On Rational Entrepreneurial Behavior and the Demand for Investment." *Review of Economic Studies* 36:227–239.

Treadway, A. B. 1970. "Adjustment Cost and Variable Imports in the Theory of the Competitive Firm." *Journal of Economic Theory* 2:329–347.

Uzawa, H. 1969. "Time Preference and the Penrose Effect in a Two-Class Model of Economic Growth." *Journal of Political Economy* 77:628–652.

Whited, Toni M. 1992, September. "Debt, Liquidity Constraints, and Corporate Investment." *Journal of Finance* 47:1425–1460.

Comment

Bronwyn H. Hall

During the past several decades, few areas of economics research have received as much empirical attention as the demand for investment. That this has occurred is due primarily to two factors: (1) the perceived importance of investment for both the cyclical behavior of the economy and its long-term growth and (2) The relative lack of success of conventional modeling approaches in explaining investment and the creativity of economists in responding to this lack of success. Kevin Hassett and R. Glenn Hubbard attempt to produce a coherent whole out of our progress to date and to reconcile the often conflicting results found in the literature. The focus is on the lessons learned from this research for the formation of investment policy, specifically on the effectiveness of tax policy in promoting investment.

This topic is enormous, and Hassett and Hubbard have focused their attention on a representative, although not comprehensive, area: equipment investment in the United States. Clearly this leaves out evidence from the rest of the world, as well as investment in structures and intangibles. In addition, although they allude to other strands of research, they direct their survey mainly toward modeling and estimation that is derived from an (expanded) neoclassical model of the firm. This is their term for the modeling strategy. I prefer to think of it as a modeling strategy whose central principle is supply and demand, whether or not the firm is a strictly neoclassical one. That is, the focus is on the estimation of models where the demand for investment is determined by its price, whether that price is a conventional user cost of capital or a proxy for the marginal shadow value of capital.

I am sympathetic to the goal of the authors, which is to reconcile apparent conflicting evidence on the validity or usefulness of structural models of investment for empirical application and policy analysis, and to argue that these models, correctly used, yield meaningful estimates. I agree with them that this area is in some ways a success story for econometric analysis rather than a failure. This discussion looks at the development of the neoclassical investment model (including the q model) from a slightly different perspective, focusing on the traditional supply and demand view, which is the natural way to discuss the econometrics. This is followed by a few minor quibbles and comments on the microeconomic evidence that the authors cite. The discussion focuses on Hassett and Hubbard's evaluation of the econometric evidence (their primary contribution) and leaves to John Taylor the larger macroeconomic questions of whether a specific policy toward investment is desirable.

Their chapter has four major sections: a survey of modeling strategies, with an emphasis on neoclassical models; a set of stylized macroeconomic facts about investment; an extended discussion of the problems inherent in microeconomic estimation of investment demand and discussion of results; and a discussion of whether investment incentives are a good thing from an economic point of view. The survey of microeconomic results is well done, if not completely comprehensive, and the authors make a strong case that microeconomic models of investment demand, when correctly estimated, indicate a strong response of investment to changes in its price. From this responsiveness, they conclude that tax policy has and will have an impact on investment. The only remaining question is whether tax policy of any kind is desirable (they seem to answer yes).

Hassett and Hubbard see the history of research on the determinants of investment as having evolved from early nonstructural accelerator-type models through Jorgensonian models that include a user cost of capital to the present-day models that use various proxies for Tobin's q as the "price" of investment. In my view, it is more correct to see the Jorgensonian and Q models of investment as two sides of the same coin: one focusing on the demand side for investment (the user cost of capital as the price) and one on the supply side (marginal q as the price). Neither model will be very useful in the aggregate without some identifying assumptions, since the only data points one is likely to see are equilibrium data points.

Hassett and Hubbard begin their discussion of the econometric evidence on investment with the following generic model:

$$\frac{I_{it}}{K_{it-1}} = \gamma S_{it} + \varepsilon_{it}, \tag{1}$$

where S_{it} is the underlying price variable (tax-adjusted Q or the user cost of capital). In order to understand what has been estimated in the past, it is necessary to relate this equation more precisely to the underlying structural model from which it is derived. The Q model implies the following form for the equation (1):[1]

$$E_t\left(\frac{I_t}{K_{t-1}} - \mu - \frac{1}{\omega}\frac{q_t - p_t(1-\Gamma_t)}{(1-\tau_t)}\right) = 0. \tag{2}$$

The Jorgensonian cost of capital model with expectations implies the form:

$$E_t\left(\frac{I_t}{K_{t-1}} - \mu - \sum_{i=0}^{T}\frac{\omega_i}{K_{t-1}}\left(\frac{Y_{t-i}}{C_{t-i}} - \frac{Y_{t-i-1}}{C_{t-i-1}}\right)\right) = 0, \tag{3}$$

where c_t is given by

$$c_t = p_t\frac{(1-\Gamma_t)}{(1-\tau_t)}\left(\frac{(r_t+\delta)}{(1+r_t)} + \frac{\Delta[p_t(1-\Gamma_t)]}{p_t(1-\Gamma_t)}\right).$$

It is obvious that either model can be used to estimate the response of investment to the tax parameters τ and Γ_t, but it is equally obvious that regression will be inappropriate for either model. Even if prices and tax parameters are exogenous, in the Q model q_t will be simultaneously determined with investment, and in the Jorgensonian model, Y_t will be simultaneously determined. At the macro level, we would also expect that the price of investment p_t and the required rate of return r_t are not exogenous.

Although this is by no means the first time the point has been made, it cannot be emphasized too strongly that much of the prior empirical literature on investment demand has ignored the presence of the supply curve for investment, in the sense that equation 1 has been estimated using data from the supply-demand equilibrium rather than data from the demand curve itself. A second difficulty with estimation is also present in equations 2 and 3: under uncertainty, the expected investment rate equals the expectation of some function of the supply cost of capital. Estimation is done with the realized values of these quantities, and surprises that affect the realizations of both sides of this equation will produce spurious correlations.

Investment demand estimation thus confronts two problems: the usual problem of identification and the difficulty of measuring the price of demand for a good that is inherently intertemporal. The second difficulty has focused attention on finding proxies for the shadow price of capital that incorporate expectations about its future profitability.

Given these considerations, Hassett and Hubbard spend little time on the macroeconomic evidence on investment, summarizing the evidence only to show that neither demand model has much predictive power, which is not surprising given the amount of simultaneity in equations 1 and 2. They then move on rather quickly to the microeconomic version of equation 1, and discuss a variety of approaches to the consistent estimation of γ when investment and S are simultaneously determined and S is measured with error. They divide their discussion of the estimation of equation (1) into several issues: measurement error in S, simultaneity, the form of the adjustment costs used to derive equation 1, and the type of uncertainty embodied in E[.]. I have a few specific comments on their survey results.

Measurement Error in Fundamentals (and Simultaneity)

In the case of Q, it is hard to argue that measurement error is of the random nonserially correlated (white noise) variety considered by Griliches and Hausman (1986), so the comparison of first-differenced and long-differenced estimates is not appropriate. It is likely that marginal Q is below average Q for most firms, that this gap is correlated at least over short time periods (due to adjustment costs), and that the relationship is somewhat nonlinear. Some of these factors will tend to overturn the simplistic conclusion that long differences are more accurate than first differences.

The Euler equation corresponding to equation 2 is the following:

$$E_t\left(\frac{I_t}{K_{t-1}} - \beta(1-\delta)\frac{I_{t+1}}{K_t} - \mu' - \frac{1}{\omega}\left(\frac{\beta(1-\delta)p_{t+1}(1-\Gamma_{t+1})}{(1-\tau_{t+1})} - \frac{p_t(1-\Gamma_t)}{(1-\tau_t)} + \frac{\partial X_{t+1}}{\partial K_t}\right)\right) = 0. \quad (4)$$

Identification of the responsiveness of investment to its price in this equation is based on the intertemporal shifts of investment in response to expected intertemporal price differences and the expected marginal product of capital. Given this fact, it is perhaps surprising that this approach has yielded fairly reasonable estimates for ω. The explanation undoubtedly lies in the fact that the marginal product of capital is usually proxied by a cash flow or profits variable, which is known to be strongly positively correlated with investment growth. Once again, the importance of using instrumental variable estimates that are free of the demand shock effect of cash flow is clear.

Measuring Changes in Fundamentals Using Tax Reforms

This approach, which has been pioneered by Auerbach and Hassett (1991) and Cummins, Hassett, and Hubbard (1994, 1996), seems very promising. The basis of the method is to use the cross-sectional variation in the tax-adjusted price of investment that comes from the variations in tax positions of individual firms (see Hall 1993 for the use of similar methodology for R&D investment), but the real novelty in the method is the use of innovations to equation 1 rather than equation 1 itself for estimation. In a sense, this approach turns the standard instrumental variable approach to estimating investment demand on its head, since it focuses on the effects of the nonpredictable component of the cost of capital on investment rather than the effects of the predictable component, as in conventional IV.

In the context of identifying a standard supply-demand model, however, the method makes perfect sense. The textbook solution to identifying the demand curve in figure 1 is to find instruments that are correlated with the supply curve (the cost of capital or supply price q facing the firm) but not the demand curve. The conventional microeconomic estimates use the past history of the firm itself as these instruments by conditioning on a time t information set; such instruments may indeed be uncorrelated with the supply of funds, at least after one or two lags, but they are also likely to be weak predictors of the cost of capital. The approach by Auerbach and others essentially uses changes to the tax law as instruments for the price of investment, assuming that these changes were known to the firm in the period before they are introduced. The method is somewhat complicated by the fact that some components of the investment price are still endogenous, leading to a hybrid two-stage estimation rather than conventional instrumental variable estimation. It would be interesting to explore the results of simply adding these tax changes to the instrument set in the conventional approach.[2] In any case, according to Hassett and Hubbard, this method has yielded estimates of the elasticity of investment to changes in its price of approximately 0.5 to 1.0.[3]

Are there any drawbacks to this methodology for identifying investment demand? From my own work on the R&D investment tax credit, I can suggest two possible reasons that this approach might not always be appropriate. First, the tax rate faced by firms on their investment program is to some extent endogenous to the firms, in the sense that there is a wide range of tax planning activities (leasing rather than buying or vice versa, selective acquisition, avoidance of the alternative minimum tax, income shifting over time, the timing of repatriation of foreign income, and so forth) that may affect the marginal tax rate on investment. It is probable that major changes in the tax treatment of investment dominate these factors in firms' tax planning, but this fact by itself will tend to diminish the cross-sectional variation for identification of the response.

Second, the presence of adjustment costs for investment will make the long-run response to tax changes different from the short run and will also make the response dependent on expectations about future tax changes. Conceptually, the traditional cost of capital model assumes away the second problem, but the Q model allows for both differences between the long run and the short run and expectations about the future course of tax parameters. The problem is that both of these factors are buried in the shadow price q_t, which contains both the effects of the expected investment trajectory after period t and the effects of changes in the tax regime this period on future expectations.[4] Solving for the long-run response of ivestment to changes in tax parameters may therefore involve making sufficient assumptions on the dynamic program of the firm so that it can be solved to give the future path of investment as a function of changes in today's price. To a certain extent, this difficulty can be mitigated either by investigating the role of lagged investment in the equation, in order to obtain an ad hoc long-run estimate, or by noting that firms do indeed appear to move investment somewhat easily from one period to another (adjustment costs based on the microeconomic estimates are about 1 to 2 percent on investment). More careful study of the intertemporal implications of this style of investment demand estimation seems a fruitful area for future research. However, neither the endogeneity of tax prices nor the focus on the short-run response of investment is likely to be a flaw major enough to overturn the results achieved using this methodology.

Financial Frictions and Liquidity Constrains

Hassett and Hubbard go on to discuss the enormous, if somewhat inconclusive, literature on the role of financial frictions in investment. In equation 1, this typically will imply

$$\frac{I_{it}}{K_{it-1}} = \frac{\gamma}{\alpha_t} S_{it} + \varepsilon_{it}, \qquad (1')$$

where α_t is the shadow price of the flow of funds constraint in a model with taxes and where external finance is more costly than internal.[5]

Usually $\alpha_t < 1$ for internal finance ("trapped" equity), $\alpha_t = 1$ for some level of debt finance, and $\alpha_t > 1$ if the firm has to issue lots of debt or new equity (the lemons premium). This implies a reduced response of investment to changes in q or the price of investment for firms that are more financially constrained, which contaminates the relationship. In addition, it implies that tax changes that shift a firm from an $\alpha_t > 1$ regime to an $\alpha_t < 1$ regime may have inframarginal effects on investment.

Although it is beyond the scope of this discussion to go into details, evidence to date on the importance of liquidity constraints in investment is somewhat inconclusive. In many cases conflicting results have been found using essentially the same data sets, and the modeling has proceeded in a somewhat ad hoc manner due to the difficulties with fully implementing a dynamic programming model that incorporates financial frictions. Sorting out the demand side effects (increased marginal product of capital) in cash flow shocks from supply side effects (liquidity) has proved extremely difficult. The most compelling evidence is that of Calomiris and Hubbard (1995), admittedly on an earlier historical period, and Lamont (1995), where the effects of cash windfalls are evaluated. There is room for a critical econometric survey of the evidence, which Hassett and Hubbard do not supply in this paper.

Misspecified Adjustment Costs and Aggregation

Adjustment costs can be misspecified because they are truly asymmetric or nonconvex and/or because the intertemporal nature of investment returns means that it behaves like an option. Certainly some kinds of investment are lumpy, and the serial correlation with firms of investment rates is strongly negative from year to year. Asymmetry must be a factor for certain kinds of investment. Evidence on the existence of resale markets is inconclusive because it ignores the ex ante cost of the ex post sunk adjustment costs faced by firms undertaking investment. That is, before firms sink the adjustment costs, they will include them in their decision process, and they cannot be recovered on a resale market. Thus the existence of resale markets for most capital goods does not completely dispose of the idea that adjustment costs may be asymmetric.

Hassett and Hubbard are anxious to dismiss the possibility that nonconvex adjustment costs are clouding the estimation of models like equation 8.14, and they could be right, but the survey here is somewhat less than comprehensive. The most interesting results seem to be due to Caballero, Engel, and Haltiwanger (1995), who do find what appears to be both asymmetry and lumpiness in investment. The most important implication of their work, however, is that aggregating investment responses of this kind produces elasticities with respect to user cost that change over time as the average gap between desired and actual capital stock changes. Further work of this kind seems desirable, because the current state of research on investment appears to be that aggregate models in general have performed poorly, while micromodels, correctly estimated, yield plausible results. To say anything about policy, eventually we need to aggregate, but in an intelligent way that accounts for the heterogeneity of individual firm behavior. A research agenda that extends the Caballero, Engel, and Haltiwanger approach to other investment models would seem to be indicated.

Notes

1. Although Hassett and Hubbard derive these two models, they do not make explicit the connection between equation 1 (their equation 8.14) and the investment demand implied by the models.

2. This would have the advantage of simplifying the standard error computation; the current approach does not necessarily take account of estimation error in the first stage, although this will not matter if the dependent variable is a true "surprise" in investment rates (Pagan 1984).

3. The estimates of γ (0.5 to 0.8) that Hassett and Hubbard give seem consistent with a much higher elasticity, at least at normal investment rates of 10–15 percent. I am not sure how to reconcile these two sets of figures.

4. This fact is another argument for using instrumental variable techniques with the tax parameters as instruments rather than imposing the precise functional form implied by the formula for the current year's tax-adjusted q, because the full effects of changes in tax parameters on q may not take exactly that form.

5. Such models are much more difficult to derive and work with empirically since they involve more than one state variable (because the Miller-Modigliani propositions no longer hold in this setting, there will be state variables describing the current capital structure of the firm along with the capital stock), and models with more than one state variable no longer generate an observable proxy for q except under very strong conditions on the aggregation implicit in the value function.

References

Auerbach, Alan J., and Kevin A. Hassett. 1991, Autumn. "Recent U.S. Investment Behavior and the Tax Reform Act of 1986: A Disaggregate View." *Carnegie-Rochester Conference Series on Public Policy* 35:185–215.

Caballero, Richard J., Eduardo M. R. A. Engel, and John C. Haltiwanger. 1995. "Plant-level Adjustment and Aggregate Investment Dynamics." *Brookings Papers on Economic Activity* 2:1–54.

Calomiris, Charles W., and R. Glenn Hubbard. 1995, October. "Internal Finance and Investment: Evidence from the Undistributed Profits Tax of 1937–1938." *Journal of Business* 68:443–482.

Cummins, Jason G., Kevin A. Hassett, and R. Glenn Hubbard. 1994. "A Reconsideration of Investment Behavior Using Tax Reforms as Natural Experiments." *Brookings Papers on Economic Activity* 2:1–74.

Cummins, Jason G., Kevin A. Hassett, and R. Glenn Hubbard. 1996. "Tax Reforms and Investment: A Cross-Country Comparison." *Journal of Public Economics* 62:237–273.

Griliches, Zvi, and Jerry A. Hausman. 1986, February. "Errors in Variables in Panel Data." *Journal of Econometrics* 31:141–154.

Hall, Bronwyn H. 1993. "The R&D Tax Credit During the 1980s: Success or Failure?" *Tax Policy and the Economy* 7:1–51.

Lamont, Owen. 1995. "Cash Flow and Investment: Evidence from Internal Cash Flow and Investment: Evidence from Internal Capital Markets." NBER Working paper 5499.

Pagan, Adrian. 1984. "Econometric Issues in the Analysis of Regressions with Generated Regressors." *International Economic Review* 25:221–247.

Poterba, James, and Lawrence H. Summers. 1985. "The Economic Effects of Dividend Taxation." In Edward J. Altman, and Marti G. Subrahamanyam, eds., *Recent Advance in Corporate Finance*. Homewood, IL: Richard D. Irwin.

Comment

John B. Taylor

Kevin Hassett and Glenn Hubbard provide an excellent review of the empirical research on the effects of changes in the user cost of capital on investment decisions. The long-term perspective of the review—starting with the original empirical studies using macroeconomic data and ending with the more recent panel data studies—reveals an enormous amount of progress and, even more intriguing, an emerging consensus that the user cost has a large and statisically significant impact on business fixed investment.

Until recently there has been considerable skepticism about the significance of the user cost of capital for investment behavior. The neoclassical investment model, originally formulated by Hall and Jorgenson (1967), implicitly tied the user costs variable together with the accelerator variable: user costs and output entered multiplicatively. Hence, critics of the neoclassical model attributed the evidence reported in favor of strong user costs impacts to the well-known accelerator effects observed over the business cycle. When one separated out the accelerator and user costs variables, most of the variation appeared to be explained by the accelerator. The effects of changes in user costs were much smaller and frequently insignificant. Changes in output and investment are highly correlated over the business cycle (see figure 8.1).

This view that user costs effects were small carried over to the macroeconomic literature on the impact of monetary policy on investment. If changes in the user costs had a small impact, then changes in interest rates—a component of the user costs variables—would also have a small impact. The implication that interest rates have a small effect on investment gave credence to the view that the monetary transmission mechanism—the process through which monetary policy affects real GDP and inflation—could not work through interest rates. The interest rate elasticities were viewed as too small and insignificant to matter for the monetary transmission mechanism. This perceived problem with the "interest rate view" of the monetary transmission mechanism gave impetus to the alternative "credit view."

In my own empirical work on the effects of interest rates on investment—also using macroeconomic investment aggregates—the finding of significant interest rate effects has been more common than in the other macroeconomic literature Hassett and Hubbard cite (see Taylor 1993). In all of the Group of 7 countries and for most categories of investment, I found significant effects of changes in real interest rates on investment. One reason may be the greater use of rational expectations estimation methods, which may give better estimates of real interest rates. Another reason may be that interest rate effects are examined separately rather than as part of a user cost variable.

In any case, Hassett and Hubbard are correct to emphasize that more recent research has moved away from macroeconomic aggregates and toward individual firm data on investment. Recent panel data studies show user cost elasticities about ten times larger than the previous macroeconomic estimates. The results are robust to various specifications and sample periods.

Although I have no disagreement with this survey of the evidence that Hassett and Hubbard present, I believe that they could do more to illustrate why the panel data yield these large effects while the macro–time series data in figure 8.1 seem to be so dominated by the accelerator effects. Some analogous charts showing the effects of large one-time changes in the cost of capital on individual firms would provide some useful illustrations. For example, consider the repeal of the investment tax credit in 1986. This repeal was effective on January 1, 1986, but was anticipated by the end of 1985. Not surprisingly, aggregate investment soared by 20 percent in the fourth quarter of 1985 and then declined by 20 percent in the first quarter of 1986. This change in the user cost of capital brought on by the change in the investment tax credit thus had huge and statistically significant effects on aggregate investment. This was clearly an episode where the user cost was not correlated or tied in with the accelerator, and the direct effects were huge. Examining how some of the individual firms that make up the aggregate responded would add to our sense of what is going on in the panel.

In addition to this suggestion I have some small disagreements. First, Hassett and Hubbard's demonstration of the favorable welfare effects of a reduction in the inflation rate, an increase in the investment tax credit (ITC), or a switch to a consumption tax seems to be entirely dependent on a "dynamic efficiency" argument showing that the capital stock in the United States is not so high that lowering it would lead to an unambiguous gain. Unfortunately, this approach does not result in quantitative estimates of the size of the effects. Other studies using more complete dynamic general equilibrium models, such as those of Kotlikoff and Auerbach, have given explicit numerical estimates and do not rely on an either-or dynamic efficiency argument.

Second, I was disappointed not to see greater discussion of the pros and cons of the ITC as a countercyclical device. Short-run and long-run issues are important in practice. Recall that the ITC was originally proposed in the 1960s for short-run countercyclical reasons. And both President Bush and President Clinton proposed temporary ITC changes as a means to stimulate the economy after the last recession. Thus the ITC seems to be alive and well as a discretionary countercyclical instrument.

The ITC should not be used in this discretionary way; the uncertainty and the lags are too great. Although there are instances where an ITC could be operated as a systematic policy rule (see Taylor 1982), in reality the policy would most often be used in a discretionary fashion.

References

Hall, Robert E., and Dale W. Jorgenson. 1967, June. "Tax Policy and Investment Behavior." *American Economic Review* 57:391–414.

Taylor, John B. 1982. "The Swedish Investment Funds System as a Stabilization Policy Rule." *Brookings Papers on Economic Activity* 157–101.

Taylor, John B. 1993. *Macroeconomic Policy in a World Economy: From Econometric Design to Practical Operation.* New York: W. W. Norton.

9 Tax Policy and the Activities of Multinational Corporations

James R. Hines, Jr.

It is an uncommon American presidential election in which at least one of the major party candidates does not promise to overhaul the tax system if elected (or reelected). The hardiness of this campaign issue suggests three nonexclusive possibilities: that the electorate has an insatiable thirst for tax reform rhetoric, that Congress has a chronic inability to draft popular tax laws, and that evolving economic conditions necessitate frequent tax changes.

The changing position of the United States in the world economy is consistent with the third of these possibilities (which is not to rule out the first two). The basic structure of federal income taxation was in place long before the American economy acquired the kind of international position it has in the last few decades; as a consequence, international considerations are afterthoughts in its design. This aspect of tax policy is slowly changing. Recent U.S. legislation devotes considerable effort to modifying the foreign provisions of U.S. tax law.[1] International tax issues attract popular attention as well; it is noteworthy that as obscure (from the standpoint of the general public) and technical an issue as the transfer pricing practices of foreign investors in the United States became a major topic of discussion during the 1992 presidential election campaign. Unfortunately, not all of the public discussion reflects the latest thinking and evidence on the economic behavior of firms subject to international taxation.

This chapter examines quantitative studies of the impact of international tax rules on the financial and real behavior of multinational firms.[2] The evidence, much of it recent, indicates that taxation significantly influences the financing of multinational corporations and their allocation of factors and products around the world. As a consequence, foreign tax rules can be expected to affect the performance of foreign economies;

these tax rules also affect the U.S. domestic economy, doing so through at least three channels. The first channel of influence reflects the interdependence of operations within U.S. firms: a firm's foreign and domestic activities affect each other through productivity spillovers and by competing for resources. The second way in which foreign tax rules affect the American economy is by influencing the level and composition of foreign-owned business activity in the United States. The third effect is more subtle, stemming from the way that the United States taxes foreign income together with domestic income, thereby often indirectly modifying the incentives firms have to undertake domestic activities.

It is useful to distinguish the sources of increased U.S. attention to international tax issues in order to identify the role that quantitative analysis can play in enlightening the development of U.S. tax policy. The growing recognition of the importance of foreign direct investment (FDI) in the lives of modern economies is clearly one factor. The importance of FDI implies in turn that tax policies that once made sense may no longer do so, since resources appear to be more internationally mobile than ever before. Furthermore, the magnitude of FDI suggests that the penalties for mistaken or inefficient international tax rules are far greater than they were in the past.

The tax policies of other countries also contribute to the U.S. attention to its own international tax policy. Together with the expanding role of FDI, foreign tax changes put pressure on the United States to make its own tax environment competitive with those available in other locations. Other countries typically pay greater attention than does the United States to the international consequences of tax policies, and although the United States traditionally felt little inspiration to respond to the tax policies of other countries, this attitude appears to be changing.[3]

The complexity of international tax rules may also contribute to the perceived desirability of reform. Not that simplicity per se is thought to be a critical attribute. Many of the recent U.S. reforms complicate rather than simplify the tax treatment of international transactions. Instead, the complexity of the U.S. system of taxing international income serves to convince observers that the tax system may have undesirable and previously unknown effects that could be removed through reform. Due in part to their complexity, the economic implications of the international provisions of U.S. tax law were for many years probably the least studied of any of the major parts of the Internal Revenue Code. But these issues have attracted considerably more attention in recent years.

9.1 The Tax System

Throughout the world, governments tax economic activity that occurs within their boundaries, typically including any income earned locally by foreign firms and individuals.[4] In addition, some countries (including the United States) attempt to tax the foreign incomes of their residents. Since international transactions typically entail income-generating activity in more than one country, it is necessary for tax systems to identify in which countries income is attributed for tax purposes and (in many cases) to distinguish various types of income, deductions, and credits for purposes of calculating tax liabilities. This section outlines some of the important features of U.S. taxation of foreign income, both to illustrate worldwide taxation and to provide some background for the empirical studies reviewed in later sections.

The United States taxes income on a residence basis, meaning that American corporations and individuals owe taxes to the U.S. government on all of their worldwide income, whether earned in or outside the United States. In order to avoid subjecting American multinationals to double taxation, U.S. law permits firms to claim foreign tax credits for income taxes (and related taxes) paid to foreign governments.[5] The U.S. corporate tax rate is currently 35 percent. Under the foreign tax credit system, a U.S. corporation that earns $100 in a foreign country with a 15 percent tax rate pays a tax of $15 to the foreign government and $20 to the U.S. government, since its U.S. corporate tax liability of $35 (35 percent of $100) is reduced to $20 by the foreign tax credit of $15.

Deferral of U.S. Taxation

Under U.S. law, Americans must pay tax to the U.S. government on their worldwide incomes, with the exception that a certain category of foreign income is temporarily excluded from U.S. taxation. The excluded category is the unrepatriated portion of the profits earned by foreign subsidiaries; taxpayers are permitted to defer any U.S. tax liabilities on those profits until they are paid as dividends to the United States.[6] This deferral is available only on the active business profits of American-owned foreign affiliates that are separately incorporated as subsidiaries in foreign countries. The profits of unincorporated foreign businesses, such as those of U.S.-owned branch banks in other countries, are taxed immediately by the United States.

To illustrate deferral, consider the case of a U.S-owned subsidiary that earns $500 in a foreign country with a 10 percent tax rate. This subsidiary pays taxes of $50 to the foreign country (10 percent of $500) and might remit $100 in dividends to its parent U.S. company, using the remaining $350 (500 – $50 of taxes – $100 of dividends) to reinvest in its own, foreign, operations. The U.S. parent firm must then pay U.S. taxes on the $100 of dividends it receives (and is eligible to claim a foreign tax credit for the foreign income taxes its subsidiary paid on the $100).[7] But the U.S. firm is not required to pay U.S. taxes on any part of the $350 that the subsidiary earns abroad and does not remit to its parent U.S. company. If, however, the subsidiary were to pay a dividend of $350 the following year, the firm would then be required to pay U.S. tax (after proper allowance for foreign tax credits) on that amount.

U.S. tax law contains provisions designed to prevent American firms from delaying the repatriation of lightly taxed foreign earnings. These tax provisions apply to controlled foreign corporations, which are foreign corporations owned at least 50 percent by U.S. corporations holding stakes of at least 10 percent each. Under the Subpart F provisions of U.S. law, some foreign income of controlled foreign corporations is deemed distributed and therefore immediately taxable by the United States, even if not repatriated as dividend payments to American parent firms. This Subpart F income consists of income from passive investments (such as interest and dividends received from investments in securities), foreign base company income (that arises from using a foreign affiliate as a conduit for certain types of international transactions), income that is invested in U.S. property, money used offshore to insure risks in the United States, and money used to pay bribes to foreign government officials. American firms with foreign subsidiaries that earn profits through most types of active business operations and subsequently reinvest those profits in active lines of business are not subject to the Subpart F rules and can therefore defer U.S. tax liability on their foreign profits until they choose to remit dividends at a later date.

Excess Foreign Tax Credits

The U.S. government permits American firms to claim foreign tax credits, with the understanding that this policy reduces the tax revenue collected by the United States on any given amount of foreign source income. The foreign tax credit is intended to reduce the problems created by international double taxation, since, in the absence of some kind of correction, the combined tax burdens of host-country and home-country taxation might effectively prohibit most international business transactions. Consequently, the U.S. government attempts to design the foreign tax credit in a way that prevents American firms from using foreign tax credits to reduce U.S. tax liabilities that arise from profits earned *within* the United States.

The government imposes limits on the foreign tax credits that U.S. firms can claim; a firm's foreign tax credit limit equals the U.S. tax liability generated by the firm's foreign source income. For example, with a U.S. tax rate of 35 percent, an American firm with $200 of foreign income faces a foreign tax credit limit of $70 (35 percent of $200). If the firm pays foreign income taxes of less than $70, then it would be entitled to claim foreign tax credits for all of its foreign taxes paid. But if the firm pays $95 of foreign taxes, it would be permitted to claim no more than $70 of foreign tax credits.

Firms described by this second case, in which foreign tax payments exceed the foreign tax credit limit, are said to have excess foreign tax credits; the excess foreign tax credits represent the portion of their foreign tax payments that exceeds the U.S. tax liabilities generated by their foreign incomes. Firms described by the first case, in which foreign tax payments are smaller than the foreign tax credit limit, are said to have deficit foreign tax credits. Under American law, firms can, under some circumstances, use excess foreign tax credits in one year to reduce their tax obligations for other years. They are allowed to apply any excess foreign tax credits against their U.S. tax obligations in the two previous years or in any of the following five years.[8]

In practice, the calculation of the foreign tax credit limit entails many complications not reviewed here. However, one major feature of the calculation should be noted: U.S. law requires firms to use all of their worldwide foreign income to calculate the foreign tax credit limit. Firms then have excess foreign tax credits if the sum of their worldwide foreign income tax payments exceeds this limit.[9] This procedure is known as worldwide averaging.

9.2 The Impact of Taxation on Foreign Direct Investment

There is a great deal of deal of interest in and concern about the possible impact of tax policy on FDI. High tax rates are naturally thought to discourage foreign investment, though there is some controversy over this point. Older time-series studies indicate a great responsiveness of

FDI to tax differences, though the infrequency of major tax changes and the correlation of tax changes with movements in important omitted variables may make this evidence inconclusive. Recent research is more cross-sectional in nature than earlier studies and offers more convincing evidence of a smaller but important and statistically significant effect of taxation on the location and volume of investment.

Before examining the existing evidence on the impact of taxation on FDI, it is worth considering why this issue receives the kind of attention that it does. Clearly if all other considerations are held constant, international investors would prefer to avoid taxes than to pay them, so there must be some situations in which tax differences significantly influence investment. The question driving empirical work is the extent to which these situations arise in practice. International investments are influenced by a host of considerations, of which taxes are just one. The complexity of international investment planning, given the uncertainty firms face in forecasting future economic and political conditions, convinces some observers (such as Vernon 1977) that tax differences are too small to have anything other than trivial effects on investment location. Alternatively, if multinational firms can costlessly structure their finances to relocate taxable income, tax rates would not influence investment because firms would pay little or no taxes in jurisdictions with high rates. A third possibility is that governments imposing high tax rates indirectly compensate firms with difficult-to-measure investment incentives, such as worker training and infrastructure. These possibilities make it difficult to predict the responsiveness of FDI to taxation, though this responsiveness is measurable with available information.

American Direct Investment Abroad

Most models of the investment process imply that capital is attracted to activities and locations in which it earns the greatest after-tax returns. A number of empirical studies report positive correlations between investment levels and after-tax returns to foreign direct investment.[10] The idea underlying these studies is to use the correlations to infer the effect of taxation on foreign direct investment; this is a legitimate inference under the assumption that higher tax rates reduce after-tax rates of return. These inferences are subject to some well-know limitations, however, since rates of return are endogenous to investment levels and are likely to be influenced by omitted variables that also influence investment.

Table 9.1 summarizes a small literature that examines the effect of taxation on U.S. direct investment abroad. Hartman (1981) estimates the responsiveness of aggregate U.S. direct investment abroad over the 1965–1979 period to after-tax rates of return available in foreign countries and in the United States. This study distinguishes investment financed out of retained foreign earnings from investment financed out of new transfers of funds from the United States. For investment financed out of retained earnings, Hartman reports the expected positive effect of foreign after-tax rates of return (investment elasticity of 1.4) and negative effect of domestic U.S. after-tax rates of return (investment elasticity of −0.66). Investment financed by transfers of funds does not exhibit a consistent correlation with after-tax returns.

Studies by Boskin and Gale (1987) and Newlon (1987) extend and update Hartman's findings, confirming that the patterns Hartman identified are present over longer periods of time and are robust to definitional changes in the underlying data. The time-series evidence seems to indicate strongly that years in which U.S. direct investment abroad is most profitable are those in which Americans invest the most abroad through retained foreign earnings. It is difficult to say whether this relationship represents the effect of investors responding to incentives, rule-of-thumb behavior in which firms finance their foreign affiliates with fixed fractions of after-tax profits, or the effects of omitted variables. Alternatively, this correlation could be a purely statistical phenomenon stemming from the fact that FDI is measured as fund transfers plus foreign profits minus repatriations, implying that any independent measurement error in foreign after-tax profits is by construction correlated with measured direct investment abroad. More generally, the primary limitation of aggregate time-series studies is that they are identified by yearly variations in taxes or profitability that may be correlated with any of a number of omitted nontax factors.

Frisch and Hartman (1983) investigate the impact of host-country taxation on the cross-sectional distribution of subsidiary assets in 1972, as reported in tax returns. They pool aggregate data for fifteen industries in sixteen countries, reporting an elasticity of −0.26 with respect to local tax rates. Although many variables of potential importance are also omitted from these regressions, the cross-sectional strategy they embody is more robust than are time-series models to measurement error and to minor specification issues (such as the choice of lag length). In pooling their data, Frisch and Hartman treat different industries as separate, and therefore

Table 9.1
Studies of investment patterns: U.S. direct investment abroad

Study	Method (Data)	Estimates
Hartman (1981)	Time series, aggregate U.S. investment financed by retained earnings, 1965–1979 (BEA annual; 15 years)	1.4 elasticity with respect to after-tax earnings, and −0.66 elasticity with respect to domestic after-tax returns
Bond (1981)	Responses to Puerto Rican tax holidays, SIC 2342, 1949–1972 (Labor Department survey; 152 firms)	Significant effect of losing tax holiday on firm's decision to exit the industry
Frisch and Hartman (1983)	Cross section, U.S. investment aggregated by 15 industries, 1972 (SOI aggregates, 16 countries)	−0.26 elasticity of subsidiary assets to local tax rates
Boskin and Gale (1987)	Time-series estimates of aggregate FDI out of the United States, 1965–1984 (BEA annual; 20 years)	1.2 elasticity with respect to after-tax return for FDI financed by retained earnings
Newlon (1987)	Time-series estimates of aggregate FDI out of the United States, 1953–1984 (corrected BEA data; 32 years)	U.S. and foreign after-tax returns influence FDI financed by retained earnings
Grubert and Mutti (1991)	Capital demand by U.S. affiliates in cross section, manufacturing only, 1982 (BEA benchmark; 33 countries)	−0.11 elasticity of capital demand with respect to local tax rate
Harris (1993)	Foreign investment as fraction of total investment by U.S. multinationals, 1984–1990 (Compustat; 36 firms)	Firms with higher cost of capital in United States after 1986 shift investment significantly toward foreign countries
Hines and Rice (1994)	Capital demand by U.S. affiliates in cross-section, 1982 (BEA benchmark; 73 countries)	1 percent higher tax rates reduce capital demand by 3 percent
Grubert and Slemrod (1994)	Demand for affiliates located in Puerto Rico (tax data; 4,099 firms)	Firms with greater intangible assets more likely to have Puerto Rican affiliates
Cummins and Hubbard (1995)	Investment Euler equations for unbalanced panel of foreign subsidiaries of U.S. firms, 1980–1991 (Compustat; 1,047 firms)	1 percent higher after-tax cost of capital reduces annual investment by 1–2 percent

Note: BEA: Bureau of Economic Analysis; SOI: Statistics of Income; SIC: Standard Industrial Classification independent, observations, however, which is difficult to justify and suggests that their estimated standard errors may be too small.

Grubert and Mutti (1991) and Hines and Rice (1994) estimate the effect of national tax rates on the cross-sectional distribution of aggregate U.S.-owned property, plant, and equipment (PPE) in 1982. These studies use a somewhat different concept of capital ownership than does the Frish-Hartman study, since PPE in American-controlled foreign affiliates is not the same as gross American-owned assets; of the two, PPE probably more closely corresponds to capital that enters production functions and for which derived demand is a function of tax rates. Grubert and Mutti analyze the distribution of PPE in manufacturing affiliates in thirty-three countries, reporting a −0.11 elasticity of PPE with respect to local tax rates. Hines and Rice consider the distribution of PPE in all affiliates in seventy-three countries, reporting that 1 percent lower tax rates (such as the difference between tax rates of 37 percent and 36 percent) are associated with 3 percent greater PPE; this corresponds to an elasticity of about −1. The much higher elasticity that Hines and Rice report reflects differences in industrial coverage (Hines and Rice examine the determinants of investment in all industries, while Grubert and Mutti consider only manufacturing investment), as well as their inclusion of data from U.S. operations in many more countries—particularly tax havens—than those analyzed by Grubert and Mutti.

Two studies analyze firm-level information on the impact of taxation on U.S. direct investment abroad. Harris (1993) investigates whether companies whose costs of capital in the United States rose most dramatically after passage of the Tax Reform Act of 1986 respond by investing more abroad. The Tax Reform Act of 1986 removed the investment tax credit and accelerated depreciation for investments within the United States, expanded the coverage of the alternative minimum tax, and made other changes; Harris finds that firms concentrating their investment in equipment (which was particularly hard hit by the act) respond by expanding their investment abroad. Cummins and Hubbard (1995) estimate investment equations for foreign subsidiaries of U.S. firms under two alternative scenarios: one in which it is assumed that firms simply ignore taxes, and a second in which it is assumed that firms incorporate taxation in their decision making (and therefore reduce investment in response to higher tax rates). They report that the data fit the second specification better than the first, suggesting that taxes influence direct investment by affiliates.

Further evidence on the effect of taxation on direct investment abroad is provided by the experience of Puerto Rico. Under U.S. law (section 936 of the Internal Revenue Code), American companies investing in Puerto Rico and other U.S. possessions (such as Guam and American Samoa) treat their U.S. possession income as foreign income on which U.S. federal income tax can be avoided altogether by the use of foreign tax credits. This very favorable tax treatment is intended to encourage local economic development and to provide a tax base for Puerto Rican authorities. The government of Puerto Rico taxes local business profits, but frequently attempts to attract new investment by offering firms tax holidays of roughly twelve years, during which no local taxes are due. Bond (1981) finds the tax holiday to be an important determinant of business activity among the firms in the garment industry he studies: exit from the industry closely coincides with expiration of a firm's holiday from Puerto Rican taxes. Grubert and Slemrod (1994) analyze the factors that determine whether an American firm has a Puerto Rican affiliate. The favorable tax treatment of income earned in Puerto Rico gives firms incentives to shift profits from operations in the mainland United States to affiliates located in Puerto Rico. (The theory and practice of such income shifting is discussed in section 9.3.) Grubert and Slemrod argue that firms whose domestic assets are largely intangible (the product of activities such as research and development or advertising) will find it easier than other firms to shift profits to Puerto Rico and should therefore have the greatest demand for Puerto Rican affiliates. Tax return data are consistent with this prediction.

Foreign Direct Investment in the United States

Empirical investigations of foreign direct investment into the United States closely parallel those of U.S. direct investment abroad, in both approach and the type of results they report. There is, however, an important distinction between the two types of studies beyond the obvious difference in their coverage. U.S. direct investment abroad is subject to a single home-country tax regime and multiple host-country tax regimes; foreign direct investment in the United States is subject to multiple home-country tax regimes and a single U.S. federal tax system. Consequently, studies of U.S. direct investment abroad are generally more capable of identifying the effect of host-country taxes on FDI, and those of foreign direct investment in the United States more capable of identifying the effect of home-country taxes on FDI.

Table 9.2 summarizes a number of the studies of FDI in the United States. Hartman (1984), Boskin and Gale (1987), Newlon (1987), and Young (1988) all estimate time-series equations of aggregate foreign investment in the United States. Hartman and Boskin and Gale report than FDI financed by retained earnings is positively correlated with after-tax rates of return available in the United States; Newlon and Young confirm that FDI financed by retained earnings responds negatively to U.S. tax rates. These studies examine slightly differing periods, use similar but not identical econometric specifications, and employ BEA data that are periodically revised and may warrant the special treatment afforded them by Newlon and by Slemrod (1990),[11] but their empirical conclusions are very similar: the relevant behavioral elasticities do not differ greatly from unity. Of course, these findings are subject to the same limitations as are those of the studies of U.S. direct investment abroad.

Slemrod (1990) extends the time-series approach by distinguishing FDI in the United States by the tax regime of its country of origin. Foreign firms investing in the United States fall into two broad categories. The first category includes investors from countries (of which Slemrod considers Australia, Canada, France, Germany, and the Netherlands) that do not tax—or tax very lightly—the American profits of their resident multinationals. The second category includes investors from countries (of which Slemrod considers Japan and the United Kingdom) that do tax the American profits of their firms but provide foreign tax credits for the federal and state income taxes these firms pay. To investors from Canada and Germany, U.S. corporate income taxes represent costs of doing business; to investors from Japan and the United Kingdom, corporate income taxes also represent costs, but these costs are—at least in part—compensated by their own government's provision of foreign tax credits. Consequently, investors from Canada and Germany have stronger incentives to avoid locating their businesses in the United States during periods of high tax rates than do investors from Japan and the United Kingdom, even if the businesses are otherwise identical. Slemrod does not find consistent timing differences between the two groups of investors that correspond to the incentives created by their home-country tax regimes. He does, however, report that higher U.S. taxes appear to discourage FDI financed by transfers of new funds.

Auerbach and Hassett (1993) and Swenson (1994) examine the correlation between the industrial and asset compositions of foreign-owned businesses in the United States and incentives created by the interaction of host-country and home-country tax systems. The starting point for

Table 9.2
Studies of investment patterns: Foreign direct investment in the United States

Study	Method (Data)	Estimates
Hartman (1984)	Time-series estimates of aggregate FDI into the United States, 1965–1979 (BEA annual data; 15 years)	FDI financed by retained earnings responds negatively to higher US taxes
Boskin and Gale (1987)	Time-series estimates of aggregate FDI into the United States, 1956–1984 (BEA annual data; 29 years)	−1.7 elasticity with respect to relative tax rates for FDI financed by retained earnings
Newlon (1987)	Time-series estimates of aggregate FDI into the United States, 1956–1984 (corrected BEA data; 29 years)	1.1 elasticity with respect to after-tax return for FDI financed by retained earnings
Young (1988)	Time-series estimates of aggregate FDI into the United States, 1953–1984 (revised BEA data; 32 years)	1.7 elasticity with respect to after-tax return for FDI financed by retained earnings
Slemrod (1990)	Estimates of aggregate FDI into the United States distinguished by investing country, 1962–1987 (adjusted BEA data; 7 countries)	Higher U.S. taxes significantly reduce FDI financed by new fund transfers; no effect of home-country repatriation taxes
Auerbach and Hassett (1993)	Cross-sectional estimates of capital composition of U.S. firms acquired by foreigners, 1980–1990 (Compustat; 243 acquired firms)	Acquirers eligible to claim FTCs exhibit no shift of demand toward equipment-intensive firms after 1986
Swenson (1994)	Time-series estimates of tax effects on new investments by industry, 1979–1991 (BEA data; 18 industries)	1.13 elasticity of investment with respect to tax changes around 1986
Coughlin, Terza, and Arromdee (1991)	Location of new manufacturing plants within the United States, 1981–1983 (Commerce survey; 736 plants)	Insignificant tax effects
Ondrich and Wasylenko (1993)	Location of new plants within the United States, 1978–1987 (Commerce survey; 1,184 plants)	−0.57 elasticity of location probability with respect to state corporate tax rates
Hines (1996b)	Location of FDI within the United States, distinguishing investments by tax regime of investing country, 1987 (BEA benchmark; 7 countries)	1 percent higher state tax rates reduce investment by 10 percent

Note: BEA: Bureau of Economic Analysis

these studies is the observation of Scholes and Wolfson (1992) that the U.S. tax changes introduced by the Tax Reform Act of 1986—in particular, the removal of the investment tax credit and accelerated depreciation—raised the attractiveness of U.S. assets to foreigners whose home countries tax the foreign profits of their resident multinationals while providing foreign tax credits for taxes paid to foreign governments. For American investors, the inability to claim investment tax credits or to take accelerated depreciation in the years after 1986 greatly reduced the after-tax returns to new investments, while for foreign investors from Japan or the United Kingdom, the loss of tax advantages after 1986 is less consequential, since their higher U.S. tax liabilities in many cases generate offsetting credits against home-country taxes. Consequently, one might expect to observe a shift in the ownership of assets located in the United States away from Americans and toward certain foreigners; on this basis, Scholes and Wolfson hypothesize that the Tax Reform Act of 1986 is responsible for the FDI influx of the late 1980s.

Swenson (1994) analyzes aggregate FDI in eighteen industries over the years 1979 through 1991. Her time-series estimates suggest that the higher U.S. after-tax cost of capital after 1986 is correlated with greater foreign investment, which conforms to the predictions of Scholes and Wolfson. Other studies report evidence that is not consistent with the Scholes-Wolfson hypothesis. Auerbach and Hassett (1993) find that, in acquiring American firms, investors from foreign tax credit countries do not exhibit preferences for equipment-intensive firms or industries, as would be predicted by the Scholes-Wolfson hypothesis, and they go on to describe other inconsistencies between the implications of the Scholes-Wolfson model and aggregate behavior of foreign investors after 1986. Collins, Kemsley, and Shackelford (1995) report that the relative tax advantages realized by British and Japanese acquirers are small relative to acquisition purchase prices in the period after 1986. As they note, however, FDI is influenced by expected tax considerations, which differ from realized tax considerations if subsidiaries have unanticipated negative profitability. Willard (1994) argues that the removal of accelerated depreciation in the United States should discourage rather than encourage FDI from foreign tax credit countries. She notes that their tax systems typically contain provisions that automatically adjust home-country taxation of foreign profits to host-country tax bases, implying that the removal of accelerated depreciation raises home-country taxation of foreign income. Willard offers evidence that investors from foreign tax credit countries were in fact the least inclined to expand their American operations after 1986.

Several studies examine the extent to which taxation influences the geographic distribution of foreign-owned business activity within the United States. Coughlin, Terza, and Arromdee (1991) estimate the determinants of new manufacturing plant location over the 1981–1983 period, reporting that state corporate income tax rates do not have significant effects on plant location after controlling for other state characteristics. Ondrich and Wasylenko (1993) examine new plant location over a longer period of time (1978–1987), finding instead that state corporate tax rates do influence the sites that foreign investors choose. The effects of state corporate tax rates are difficult to identify, however, since states do not choose their fiscal polices randomly. Omitted variables that influence investment may also be correlated with state corporate tax rates, since wealthy states with particularly active business sectors (such as California or New York) are the most likely to impose high tax rates to finance their public sectors.

Hines (1996b) addresses the omitted variable problem by comparing the interstate distribution of foreign investments in the United States from foreign tax credit countries with the distribution of investments from other countries. If omitted variables (such as those that make Manhattan a desirable investment location) have the same impact on German investors as they do on British investors, then these effects can be captured by state fixed effects, permitting one to test whether the fact that British investors receive home-country credits for taxes paid while German investors do not means that British investors are more willing than Germans to locate their investments in high-tax American states. There is a significant difference: 1 percent state tax rate differences are associated with 10 percent differences between foreign tax credit and exemption investors in amounts of manufacturing capital owned in 1987, and 3 percent differences in numbers of firms owned. The estimates imply an elasticity of capital ownership with respect to state taxes of approximately −0.6, which is consistent with some of the more recent studies of the effect of state taxes on the location of domestic American businesses.[12]

Evaluation of FDI Research

The bulk of the literature surveyed in this section addresses a quite straightforward, almost rudimentary, question: To what extent does taxation influence foreign direct investment? The answer that emerges in a variety of contexts and from a variety of approaches is that, in spite of all the other economic and political considerations that are clearly very important, taxation exerts a significant effect on the magnitude and location of FDI. While it is somewhat unscientific to summarize the results of so many different studies in a single number, they appear to be generally consistent with a unit elasticity of investment with respect to after-tax returns. At prevailing tax rates, this corresponds roughly to a −0.5 elasticity of investment with respect to tax rates.

In spite of their mutual consistency, there are several unsatisfying elements in existing studies of the effect of taxation on FDI. One is the general disregard most studies have for the complex ways in which multinational firms are organized and financed. Authors of FDI studies are aware of these omissions, but data limitations, along with a desire to answer the very basic question of whether taxation influences FDI, motivate the specifications used in practice. Financing alternatives influence investment not only by affecting the cost of capital but also by changing the timing and form that investments take. As a consequence, small differences between countries in the ease with which firms can borrow in local debt markets can have dramatic consequences for measured FDI, completely independent of the taxation of these transactions. (These issues are considered further in section 9.3.)

A second limitation of the methods used to evaluate the effects of taxation on FDI stems from the way in which tax regimes are described by the small number of parameters used in most studies. The resulting imprecision can be responsible for misleading inferences about incentives created by tax policies. One such tax-specification issue receiving recent attention is that of tax base definitional differences between countries. Hines (1988) observes that accelerated depreciation, or other similar investment incentives can raise the cost of new FDI by firms with ongoing operations by reducing the foreign tax credits they can apply against home-country tax liabilities on inframarginal dividend repatriations. Leechor and Mintz (1993), Hines (1994a), and Mintz and Tsiopoulos (1994) analyze the importance of this consideration to effective tax rates in practice. Other important but often omitted tax features include the treatment of foreign income under the U.S. alternative minimum tax, analyzed by Lyon and Silverstein (1995).

Another limitation of existing FDI studies is that their very general econometric specifications do not easily provide tests of theoretical predictions of subtle economic responses to incentives created by—in particular—home-country taxation. One example of such an economic response is the time profile of investment by parent firms that stand to benefit from deferral of home-country taxation of their foreign subsidiaries' profits. If significant home-country tax liabilities are triggered by dividend repatriations, then firms undertaking new investments are encouraged to undercapitalize their subsidiaries initially in order to preserve profitable opportunities for future reinvestment of profits. This incentive is strongest in countries with low tax rates. As a consequence, American firms may undercapitalize their initial investments in countries with low tax rates, even though they plan to accumulate quickly and maintain large steady-state capital stocks in those countries. These incentives, which are analyzed by Newlon (1987), Sinn (1993), and Hines (1994a), may generate behavior that appears, in aggregate FDI estimation, to imply that low tax rates do not influence investment—while in fact the opposite is the case. A second example of economic response to home-country taxation is the way in which tax rules may affect the organizational form of foreign business operations, as analyzed by Desai and Hines (1996).

The fourth and perhaps most important limitation of existing FDI studies is their general inability to incorporate the general equilibrium effects of taxation. When governments change tax policies, they affect not only the after-tax returns earned by firms but also equilibrium product prices, interest rates, wages, and exchange rates. The considerable difficulty of incorporating such considerations in empirical analyses does not itself justify their exclusion, particularly when drawing policy conclusions from existing research.

One general equilibrium consideration is the potential substitutability between different business operations. The magnitude and even the direction of the effect of foreign tax rates on levels of American investment may depend on this consideration. If American-owned affiliates compete little with local businesses, then high tax rates should discourage U.S. investment by raising associated tax costs. If, instead, U.S. affiliates compete strongly with local firms or with affiliates of multinationals headquartered in exemption countries, then high local tax rates offer American companies, which can claim tax credits for foreign taxes, competitive advantages over their fully taxed rivals. The FDI evidence is generally consistent with the first of these possibilities, but the data have not been subjected to subtle tests that might fully distinguish them.

Similar issues arise in drawing implications for the effects of tax policies on local business activity. If the relatively high California tax rate discourages German investment more than it does British investment, it does not necessarily follow that the high tax rate reduces total foreign investment in California, since British investors might simply replace German investors on a one-for-one (or better) basis. Such an outcome might be unlikely on prior grounds but cannot be dismissed without further investigation.

A different type of general equilibrium consideration is one of the substitutability of complementarity of foreign and domestic business activities. The operating assumption of many policy activists (such as McIntyre 1989) is that foreign and domestic factors of production are substitutes. There exists the alternative possibility that lower foreign tax rates stimulate domestic investment by encouraging the accumulation of foreign capital and thereby enhancing the profitability of domestic operations. The negative effect of after-tax rates of return in the United States on outbound FDI in the time series estimates is consistent with mild substitutability between foreign and domestic capital. Feldstein (1995) reports more direct evidence in his cross-sectional analysis of the performance of Organization for Economic Cooperation and Development (OECD) economies over the 1970–1989 period. He finds that direct investment abroad reduces investment levels, while foreign direct investment increases domestic investment. The coefficient estimates imply that in spite of the considerable extent to which the foreign operations of American multinational firms are financed by local borrowing, each dollar of foreign investment reduces the domestic capital stock by between twenty and forty cents. Devereux and Freeman (1995) come to a different conclusion in their study of bilateral flows of investment funds between seven OECD countries from 1984 through 1989, in which they find no evidence of tax-induced substitution between domestic and foreign investment.

The firm-level evidence reported by Lipsey (1995) and Stevens and Lipsey (1992) offers a similarly mixed picture of the interdependence of foreign and domestic operations. Lipsey provides evidence of a mild positive relationship between production by overseas affiliates of U.S. firms and employment levels in the United States. But Stevens and Lipsey find that greater demand for output by foreign affiliates of U.S. firms is associated with reduced investment in the United States. Of course, the joint determination of foreign and domestic operations makes this type of evidence difficult to interpret. Harris's (1993) firm-level study of reaction to the 1986 U.S. tax change offers sharper identification and is also consistent with substitutability between foreign and domestic operations.

New methods of analyzing foreign and domestic operations may be necessary to obtain consistent indicators of the degree of complementarity or substitutability between them. There are many reasons that this is a difficult issue to resolve, not the least of which is that the own-price elasticities of foreign (and domestic) investment are still imprecisely measured. In addition, economic changes that influence demands for foreign and domestic assets typically also influence their costs. In the absence of a complete general equilibrium model, it is impossible to predict with certainty the impact of tax changes on capital demand throughout a multinational firm. The available FDI evidence is suggestive, and further evidence is provided by studies of the ways in which multinational firms are financed.

9.3 The Impact of Taxation on the Financing of Multinational Firms

Multinational firms have considerable discretion in arranging their own financing, and tax policy influences the choices they make—hardly surprising in the light of the FDI evidence, since financing is likely to be more responsive to taxation than is investment, which appears to respond sharply to tax incentives. In fact, the real and financial operations of firms are closely connected, and the tax consequences of this connection carry important implications for policy.

Taxation influences several aspects of financial policy that warrant at least somewhat separate treatment: leveraging, transfer pricing policy, dividend payout policy, and others as well.

Use of Debt Finance

Multinational firms finance their foreign affiliates with debt and equity provided by parent firms, other foreign affiliates, and unrelated parties. Tax systems treat these financing alternatives quite differently, which is important to firms and often more important to governments that tax them.

To illustrate the tax consequences of financing decisions, consider the difference between financing the foreign subsidiary of a U.S. firm with equity from the parent and financing the same subsidiary with debt from the parent. If the subsidiary is financed with equity, then its profits are taxable in the host country and no taxes are owed the U.S. government until the profits are repatriated to the United States. But if the subsidiary is financed with debt, then interest paid by the subsidiary is taxable foreign source income of the American parent, and the interest is usually deductible in host countries. In addition, host-country governments often impose withholding taxes on cross-border interest, dividend, and royalty payments. Firms from foreign tax credit countries are eligible to claim foreign tax credits for withholding tax payments, and withholding tax rates are often reduced by the terms of bilateral tax treaties.

Simple tax considerations appear to make debt the preferred form of finance in high-tax countries and equity that in low-tax countries. The financing of U.S. multinationals is at least partly consistent with this implication. Hines and Hubbard (1990) find that the average foreign tax rate paid by subsidiaries remitting nonzero interest to their American parent firms in 1984 exceeds the average foreign tax rate paid by subsidiaries with no interest payments; the reverse pattern holds for dividend payments. Grubert (1995) estimates separate equations for dividend, interest, and royalty payments by 2,200 foreign subsidiaries of U.S. firms in 1990, finding that high statutory corporate tax rates and low interest withholding tax rates are correlated with greater interest payments (normalized by subsidiary assets). The opposite pattern holds for dividend payments.

If the formal distinction between related-party debt and equity is immaterial to multinational firms, then a simple tax arbitrage explanation is difficult to reconcile with the observed simultaneous use of both debt and equity to finance many foreign affiliates of U.S firms. Various legal restrictions imposed by host governments, including "thin capitalization" rules that limit allowable debt-to-equity ratios, may be responsible for some of the observed behavior. There are other explanations as well. Hines (1994a) notes that firms have incentives to underinvest in subsidiaries located in low-tax countries in order to provide opportunities to reinvest subsequent profits, thereby deferring home-country taxes that would be triggered by repatriation. This underinvestment raises the marginal productivity of debt-financed investment by the same subsidiaries. As a consequence, tax-avoiding behavior can, over some ranges, carry the paradoxical implication that lower tax rates are associated with greater use of debt finance. More generally, the model implies that the relationship between tax rates and subsidiary leverage should be quadratic, which is what Hines (1994a) finds in aggregate tax return data for fifty-seven countries in 1984.

The financial policies of parent firms and those of their foreign subsidiaries are connected in many ways, including through the tax treatment of interest payments and interest receipts. American firms with foreign income are generally not permitted to deduct all of their interest costs in the United States against their U.S. taxable incomes.[13] Instead, U.S. law requires firms to allocate their interest expenses between domestic and foreign income based on the relative sizes of domestic and foreign assets. The intention of the law is to retain full deductibility of interest expenses against taxable U.S. income, but only for that part of interest expense generating income subject to U.S. taxation. From the standpoint of taxpaying firms, the law's distinction between domestic and foreign deductions is potentially quite important, since if interest expense is deemed to be domestic, then it is deductible against the taxpayer's U.S. taxable income, and if it is deemed to be foreign, then the interest expense reduces foreign taxable income *for the purposes of U.S. income taxation only*. Foreign governments do not use U.S. methods of calculating interest deductions and generally do not permit U.S. firms to reduce their taxable incomes in foreign countries on basis of interest expenses incurred in the United States. Consequently, interest expenses allocated against foreign income are valuable to a U.S. firm only if it has deficit foreign tax credits. If it does, then some of its foreign income is subject to U.S. tax, and any additional dollar of interest expense allocated against foreign income reduces the firm's U.S. taxable income by a dollar.

The Tax Reform Act of 1986 is responsible for the current U.S. tax treatment of interest expenses; pre-1986 U.S. law affords opportunities for adeptly structured American multinational firms to deduct all of their domestic interest expenses against their U.S. taxable incomes. Table 9.3 first summarizes three studies of the impact of the 1986 change in the deductibility of interest expenses. Collins and Shackelford (1992) examine preferred stock issuances. Since firms can structure preferred stock dividends to mimic interest payments on debt, preferred stock is a natural substitute for debt among firms whose after-tax costs of using debt rise due to a tax change. Collins and Shackelford find that among the Fortune 100, firms with higher ratios of foreign to domestic assets—for which higher fractions of interest expense are allocated against foreign income—are more likely than are other firms to issue preferred stock after 1986.

Altshuler and Mintz (1995) report evidence of firms using different substitutes for domestic debt in response to the 1986 tax change. Their study of eight American multinational firms finds a high correlation between tax costs imposed by interest expense allocation and propensities to borrow abroad after 1986. These results are quite consistent with those reported by Collins and Shackelford, since both suggest that firms for which the 1986 tax change made domestic borrowing more expensive react by expanding their uses of substitutes for domestic debt. These findings do not indicate the extent to which domestic borrowing responds to the tax

Table 9.3
Studies evaluating effects of specific incentives and penalties

Issue/Study	Method (Data)	Estimates
Debt finance		
Collins and Shackelford (1992)	Preferred stock issuances by U.S. multinationals subject to interest allocation (Fortune 100), 1982–1989 (Compustat plus 10-Ks; 100 firms)	Significant effect of foreign assets on proclivity to issue preferred stock after 1986
Altshuler and Mintz (1995)	Location of borrowing by U.S. multinationals subject to interest allocation, 1988–1992 (survey responses from 8 firms)	1.7 elasticity of foreign indebtedness to interest allocation rate
Froot and Hines (1995)	Borrowing and investment by U.S. multinationals subject to interest allocation, 1986–1991 (Compustat; 416 firms)	50 percent interest allocation reduces annual debt accumulation by 5 percent and capital accumulation by 3 percent
Hines (1994a)	Loans by U.S. parent firms to foreign subsidiaries, 1984 (aggregate tax data; 57 countries)	Nonlinear effect of tax rates on parent loans to subsidiaries; strongest at low tax rates
R&D		
Hines (1993)	R&D by U.S. multinationals subject to expense allocation, 1984–1989 (Compustat; 116 firms)	0.8–1.8 elasticity of R&D to after-tax cost (as affected by cost allocation)
Hines (1995a)	R&D by U.S. and foreign firms subject to withholding taxes on royalties; 1987 and 1989 (BEA benchmarks; 43 countries)	0.1–0.3 cross elasticity of R&D with respect to royalty withholding taxes
Exports		
Kemsley (1995)	Exports as a fraction of total foreign sales by U.S. multinationals, 1985–1992 (Compustat; 544 firms)	Foreign sourcing of export earnings generates additional $70 million of exports for firms with excess FTCs
Bribery		
Hines (1995b)	Location of aggregate U.S. business activity after tax and criminal penalties imposed on bribe payments, 1977–1982 (BEA benchmark; 41 countries)	Reduced U.S. activity in corrupt countries equivalent to 6 percent annual declines in GDP

Note: BEA: Bureau of Economic Analysis

change, and they leave open the possibility that substitution between domestic debt and other alternatives is so complete that the tax change had little impact on costs of capital.

Froot and Hines (1995) find that firms most affected by the 1986 tax change do the least borrowing (as a fraction of assets) after 1986. The behavior of their sample of 416 U.S. multinationals implies that firms with excess foreign tax credits and half of their assets abroad borrow 5 percent less annually than do firms with unchanged borrowing costs after 1986. Affected firms also accumulate plant and equipment at 3 percent slower relative annual rates after 1986. These firms may not actually reduce their *use* of capital after 1986, since Froot and Hines also find evidence of increased plant and equipment leasing by firms affected by the interest allocation changes. Lease payments are fully deductible against U.S. taxes, so leasing rather than owning capital is an attractive option for firms that are unable to deduct all of their interest expenses. Unless leased capital substitutes perfectly for capital owned and used by the same firms—which is unlikely given the moral hazard problem associated with lease contracts—the use of leases by firms subject to interest allocation and their unwillingness to accumulate plant and equipment after 1986 together indicate that the interest allocation rules raise the capital costs of affected firms.

Transfer Pricing

Ordinary business operations of multinational firms typically entail numerous transactions between entities located in different countries but within the same controlled group. The prices attached to these transactions are known as transfer prices, about which there need be noting nefarious in spite of their unwholesome reputation. Of course, there are numerous situations in which firms have incentives to adjust transfer prices in order to reduce their tax liabilities or avoid capital controls. Multinational firms typically can reduce their total tax liabilities by lowering the prices changed by their affiliates in high-tax countries for items sold to affiliates in low-tax countries.

Governments, aware of these incentives, attempt to prevent firms from adjusting transfer prices to avoid taxes. This effort is complicated by the existence of many situations in which appropriate transfer prices are difficult to identify. The standard used by most countries, particularly OECD members, is that appropriate transfer prices equal the prices that would have been paid in transactions between unrelated parties. The difficult valuation cases arise when outside markets for comparable goods do not exist—which is often the case, since valuable items, such as patent rights, can have unique attributes that make them costly to trade in markets subject to problems of asymmetric information. The problem of valuing such goods for tax purposes is generally thought not to have a single answer. In part as a concession to this ambiguity, the U.S. tax regulations provide three alternative methods to use in valuing intangible goods for which market prices are unavailable.

The ambiguity of appropriate standards, in combination with the usual problems of tax enforcement, make it difficult for governments to prevent firms from adjusting transfer prices to reduce their tax liabilities at least to a moderate extent. Table 9.4 describes several studies of the magnitude of tax-induced transfer price adjustment. All but the first of the studies listed in the table use indirect indicators of the behavior of U.S. multinationals. Lall (1973) is the exception: he identifies the incentives created by Colombian tax and regulatory policies and confirms, on the basis of Colombian audits of pharmaceutical firms, that multinationals respond to the incentives by overinvoicing exports to their Colombian affiliates.[14]

Jenkins and Wright (1975) examine the distribution of the profitabilities of foreign affiliates of U.S. oil companies in 1966 and 1970, finding that affiliates are considerably more profitable if located in countries with low tax rates. Their aggregate calculations suggest that U.S. firms avoid two-thirds of the taxes that they would otherwise pay to oil-consuming countries in those years. Bernard and Weiner (1990) also consider the behavior of U.S. oil companies, in their case comparing oil transaction prices to spot market prices of comparable petroleum products. Bernard and Weiner do not find evidence of transfer prices that systematically deviate from spot prices in the direction implied by tax-avoiding behavior.

Kopits (1976) analyzes royalty payments by foreign subsidiaries of U.S. firms to their American parents in 1968. He finds that royalty payments as fractions of sales are negatively correlated with differences between the tax costs associated with paying royalties and those associated with paying dividends, which he interprets as evidence that firms manipulate royalty rates in order to reduce their tax liabilities. Kopits reports a royalty elasticity of −0.56 with respect to this tax difference on the basis of the aggregate behavior of U.S. firms in twelve industries in fourteen developed countries. There are some minor statistical problems with this study, including its treatment of the many missing or zero observations on country-industry cells[15] and its inclusion of different industries as

Table 9.4
Transfer pricing studies

Study	Method (Data)	Estimates
Lall (1973)	Pharmaceutical imports in Colombia (government audits; 14 firms)	Significant underinvoicing of imports in response to taxes and capital controls
Jenkins and Wright (1975)	Profit rates of U.S. oil affiliates, aggregate, 1966 and 1970 (BEA data; 10 country groups)	Tax payments by U.S. firms to oil-consuming countries only one-third of predicted
Kopits (1976)	Royalties paid by U.S. subsidiaries in developed countries, aggregated by country and industry, 1968 (SOI data; 14 countries)	1 percent higher tax rate on royalties relative to dividends reduces royalties by 0.56 percent
Bernard and Weiner (1990)	Differences between third-party prices and within-firm transfer prices for oil, 1973–1984 (EIA transaction data; 77 country-year observations)	No significant effect of tax rates on price differences
Grubert and Mutti (1991)	Profit-to-equity and profit-to-sales ratios for U.S. manufacturing affiliates, 1982 (BEA benchmark; 29 countries)	1 percent higher tax rates reduce after-tax profit/equity by 0.26 percent
Harris et al. (1993)	U.S. tax liabilities of American multinationals with tax haven affiliates, 1984–1988 (Compustat; 469 firms)	Significant dummy variables indicate firms with haven affiliates have lower domestic tax liabilities
Grubert, Goodspeed, and Swenson (1993)	U.S. tax liabilities of foreign-owned affiliates in the United States, 1987 (tax returns; 600 foreign firms)	Observable variables explain only half of profit disparities between foreign-owned and U.S.-owned firms in the United States
Klassen, Lang, and Wolfson (1993)	Return on equity in the United States and six foreign regions, 1984–1990 (Compustat; 191 firms)	10 percent higher U.S. pretax profitability of multinationals after 1986 tax reduction
Hines and Rice (1994)	Profitability of U.S. affiliates, controlling for capital and labor inputs, 1982 (BEA benchmark; 59 countries)	1 percent higher tax rates reduce profitability by 2 percent

Note: BEA: Bureau of Economic Analysis; SOI: Statistics of Income independent observations. But Hines (1995a) reports a similar elasticity (−0.40) in his investigations of royalty payments by U.S. affiliates in forty-one countries in 1989, and Grubert (1995) also finds significant effects of withholding and statutory tax rates on the propensities of 2,200 U.S.-owned subsidiaries to pay royalties in 1990.

The fact that royalty payments are negatively correlated with associated tax liabilities need not imply that firms illegally manipulate their transfer prices to reduce tax liabilities. Estimated royalty equations by necessity omit many important characteristics of the royalty-paying operations of U.S. multinationals, leaving open the possibility that the estimates simply reflect that royalty-intensive operations are attracted to locations in which associated tax burdens are lower. Furthermore, a negative correlation between taxes and transfer prices may imply that firms simply select more favorable transfer prices within the (rather broad) acceptable range created by current regulations. Of course, it is also possible that royalty payments are extensively used to avoid taxes.

Grubert and Mutti (1991) and Hines and Rice (1994) analyze the aggregate profitabilities of U.S. affiliates in different foreign locations in 1982. Grubert and Mutti examine profit-to-equity and profit-to-sales ratios of U.S.-owned manufacturing affiliates in twenty-nine countries, and Hines and Rice regress the profitability of all U.S.-owned affiliates in fifty-nine countries against capital and labor inputs and local productivities. Grubert and Mutti report that high taxes reduce the after-tax profitability of local operations, while Hines and Rice find considerably larger effects (1 percent tax rate differences are associated with 2.3 percent differences in before-tax profitability) in their data.

One of the more interesting transfer pricing issues from the standpoint of American policymakers is the extent to which firms adjust transfer prices to raise or lower the profits they report earning in the United States. There are periodic media reports of meager U.S. tax payments by foreign-owned firms in the United States, typically accompanied by the suggestion that these firms use aggressive transfer pricing to reduce their U.S. tax obligations. This issue received considerable attention during the 1992 presidential election campaign, in spite of the complicating factor that since the home-country tax rates of foreign investors in the United States typically exceed the 1992 U.S. corporate tax rate of 34 percent, foreign investors often face incentives to overreport U.S. profits at the expense of profits in their home countries.

Grubert, Goodspeed, and Swenson (1993) use firm-level tax return data to compare the tax liabilities of foreign-owned firms in the United

States with the tax liabilities of otherwise-similar American-owned firms in 1987. They report that approximately 50 percent of the variation in reported U.S. tax obligations can be explained by observable variables such as firm sizes and ages. This information does not firmly resolve this issue, since the remaining 50 percent may represent either the impact of other omitted variables or the particular proclivities of foreign investors to adjust transfer prices to avoid U.S. taxes. Even if observable variables could explain little of the difference between the profitabilities of foreign-owned and American-owned businesses in the United States, it would be difficult, on the basis of the profitability data, to reject the hypothesis that foreign investors in the 1980s made unwise business decisions or undertook investments that they did not anticipate would pay off over the short term—in neither case making recourse to a transfer-pricing explanation. There is a separate issue about whether the behavior of American-owned firms is an appropriate benchmark for foreign-owned firms, since American-owned multinational firms might also use transfer pricing to adjust the profits they report earning in the United States.

Harris et al. (1993) examine firm-level evidence of the transfer-pricing practices of a pooled sample of American multinationals over the period 1984 through 1988. They find the U.S. tax liabilities of American firms with tax haven affiliates to be significantly lower than those of otherwise-similar U.S. firms, which they take to be indirect evidence of aggressive transfer pricing by firms with tax haven affiliates. As they note, however, variable omissions make it impossible to rule out other, more benign explanations for this pattern. And it is probably incorrect to attach structural interpretations to variables indicating ownership of tax haven affiliates, since firms endogenously select the locations of their foreign operations.[16] Collins, Kemsley, and Lang (1996) analyze a pooled sample of U.S. multinationals over 1984–1992, finding a similar pattern of greater reported foreign profitability (normalized by foreign sales) among firms with foreign tax rates below the U.S. rate. This result is consistent with those of Harris et al., and Collins, Kelmsley, and Lang present additional evidence on stock market valuations that conforms to their profitability results. Klassen, Lang, and Wolfson (1993) consider the responses of American multinational firms to the U.S. corporate tax rate reductions after 1986. They find that during the period around 1986, reported returns on equity in the United States rose by 10 percent relative to those reported by the foreign operations of the same companies. Klassen, Lang, and Wolfson note that since the U.S. statutory corporate tax rate fell after

1986 relative to the tax rates of other countries, firms had incentives to adjust (or unadjust) their transfer prices to augment the reported relative profitability of their American operations.

Dividend Payments

Foreign subsidiaries with after-tax profits can reinvest the profits abroad or use them to pay dividends to their parent companies; tax differences may influence this choice. Table 9.5 summarizes the recent evidence on the impact of taxation on dividend payments by American multinational firms. The phraseology is potentially confusing, since profit remittances from foreign subsidiaries to their parent companies are called dividend payments, as are the payments that the parent companies make to their

Table 9.5
Studies of dividend payments

Study	Method (Data)	Estimates
Kopits (1972)	Dividends from foreign subsidiaries to U.S. parents, 1962 (SOI cross-section; 18 countries)	−0.4 elasticity of dividends to host-country tax rate
Mutti (1981)	Dividends from foreign subsidiaries to U.S. parents, ordinary least squares, 11 countries, 1972 (tax returns; 4,446 firms)	1 percent higher U.S. tax rate on repatriated dividends reduces dividends by 0.75 percent
Hines and Hubbard (1990)	Dividends from foreign subsidiaries to U.S. parents, Tobit, 1984 (tax returns; 10,606 firms)	1 percent higher tax cost of dividend repatriation reduces dividends by 4 percent
Altshuler and Newlon (1993)	Dividends from foreign subsidiaries to U.S. parents, Tobit, 1986 (tax returns; 3,116 firms)	1 percent higher tax cost of dividend repatriation reduces dividends by 1.5 percent
Altshuler, Newlon, and Randolph (1995)	Dividends from foreign subsidiaries to U.S. parents, unbalanced panel, 1980–1986 (tax returns; 22,906 firms)	1 percent higher transitory cost of repatriation reduces dividends by 0.3 percent; no effect of higher permanent tax costs
Hines (1996a)	Dividends from U.S. multinationals to shareholders, 1984–1989 (Compustat; 505 firms, also aggregate time series, 37 years)	Foreign profits have three times the effect of domestic profits on payouts to shareholders

Note: SOI: Statistics of Income

shareholders. The literature summarized in table 9.5 investigates correlations between propensities to pay dividends from foreign subsidiaries to parent firms and associated tax costs. There are two important features of dividend payments by U.S.-owned foreign subsidiaries to their American parent firms. The first is that such payments are generally optional, since firms have the alternative of reinvesting after-tax profits in their foreign operations. The second feature is that U.S. taxation of foreign profits earned by separately incorporated affiliates is generally deferred until profits are repatriated as dividends.

Kopits (1972) examines country-level aggregate tax return data on dividend payments from U.S.-owned foreign subsidiaries to their American parents in 1962. He reports that subsidiaries located in countries that heavily tax undistributed profits are the most likely to remit dividends to their American parents; the elasticity of dividend repatriation with respect to the tax cost of retaining earnings in subsidiaries is approximately −0.4. Mutti (1981) uses tax return microdata to analyze dividend payments from foreign subsidiaries located in eleven different countries in 1972 to their American parents. Mutti reports that 1 percent higher U.S. taxation of repatriated dividends is associated with 0.75 percent fewer dividends paid that year.

Mutti's study offers valuable subsidiary-level evidence to complement the country-level study by Kopits but is limited by two aspects of the dividend repatriation process. The first limitation is statistical, stemming from the nature of dividend payout behavior: most subsidiaries pay zero dividends to their parent firms each year. Hines and Hubbard (1990) report that 84 percent of the active U.S.-controlled foreign subsidiaries paid zero dividends to their American parents in 1984; Altshuler, Newlon, and Randolph (1995) report similar findings for 1980, 1982, and 1986. This behavior is probably rational in the light of the incentives firms have to reduce their tax liabilities through selective repatriations but from a statistical standpoint, since dividend payments are so often zero, ordinary-least-squares estimation of dividend payout rates (as in Mutti's study) is inappropriate.

The second limitation of Mutti's analysis concerns its implicit model of the dividend process. Multinational firms with deficit foreign tax credits have no particular incentive to delay repatriating profits earned by their subsidiaries located in low-tax foreign jurisdictions, in spite of the immediate U.S. tax liability that accompanies repatriation. The reason, as Hartman (1985) notes, is that the repatriation tax is unavoidable: deferral delays payment of the repatriation tax, but since the tax is proportional to the amount repatriated, deferral reduces the present value of the tax only if it also reduces the present value of repatriations—in which case it would reduce the present value of after-tax receipts by the parent. Firms that maximize after-tax profits do so by maximizing the present value of repatriations, which is the same rule that profit-maximizing firms would follow in the absence of repatriation taxes. Consequently, repatriation taxes—if unavoidable and proportional to receipts—should not influence repatriations. On the other hand, transitory conditions of parent companies, such as excess foreign tax credits that are expected to be temporary, affect the cost of current dividend repatriations from subsidiaries located in certain countries. Mutti's study omits information on the foreign tax credit status of parent companies.

Hines and Hubbard analyze the repatriation behavior of a sample of all large U.S. multinationals filing tax returns for 1984. Their study finds three notable patterns in the data. First is the infrequency with which subsidiaries remit dividends to their parents (only 16 percent did so in 1984), which is suggestive of either considerable heterogeneity among subsidiaries of very active tax planning. The second pattern is that a subsidiary is more likely to remit dividends to its parent if the combined effect of its own tax situation and its parent's tax situation makes the cost of repatriation low. The results imply that 1 percent differences in the tax cost of repatriation are associated with 4 percent differences in dividend payout rates. The third pattern reported by Hines and Hubbard is that payments of dividends from subsidiaries to parent firms are correlated with propensities of the U.S. parents to pay dividends to their common shareholders in the United States. Since both types of dividend payments —those from foreign subsidiaries to American parents and those from American parents to their shareholders—are determined simultaneously, it is difficult to attribute causality, but the evidence suggests that foreign subsidiaries may serve as sources of cash with which to pay domestic dividends.

Altshuler and Newlon (1993) estimate a similar model of the dividend-payment behavior of U.S. multinationals in 1986. They use tax return data that differ in two ways from the 1984 information that Hines and Hubbard use: first, the coverage is limited to a smaller number of (the largest) subsidiaries, and second, Altshuler and Newlon use detailed country-specific information to measure more precisely the tax costs of dividend repatriations. The results are qualitatively similar to those Hines and Hubbard report for 1984, though the estimated elasticity of dividend payments with respect to the tax cost is half as large.

Altshuler, Newlon, and Randolph (1995) analyze dividend payments by an unbalanced panel of subsidiaries over the years 1980, 1982, 1984, and 1986. Their goal is to distinguish the effects of permanent and transitory differences in the tax costs associated with dividend repatriations, since Hartman's (1985) theory predicts that only transitory tax costs should influence dividend payments. Altshuler, Newlon, and Randolph define a subsidiary's permanent tax cost of repatriation to be the component of tax cost that is predictable by either the average tax cost for subsidiaries in its country or the country's statutory withholding tax rate on dividends. On the basis of this breakdown, it appears that higher transitory tax costs discourage dividend payments, while permanent tax costs do not, which is consistent with Hartman's view of the dividend process and with the tax-timing interpretation of the dividend results reported by Hines and Hubbard and by Altshuler and Newlon. These results offer valuable information, although it may not be possible to identify completely the distinction between permanent and transitory tax costs in such a short panel and without using firm fixed effects (Gentry 1995).

Hines (1996a) analyzes the determinants of corporate dividend payments to shareholders in an effort to extend Hines and Hubbard's finding of a correlation between dividends received from foreign subsidiaries and dividends paid to shareholders. Hines reports that foreign profits (whether or not repatriated) not only influence dividend payments to shareholders but do so with triple the impact of domestic profits. The finding that one dollar of foreign profits has the same effect on dividends as does three dollars of domestic profits appears in annual cross sections of 500 large U.S. multinationals, in panel estimates of dividend payments by 300 firms in the mid-1980s, and in aggregate time-series estimates of U.S. dividend payments over the period 1950 through 1986. This result suggests that firms may feel it necessary to offer the market credible signals of their reported foreign profits, which they do by paying dividends; if so, then it implies that the tax costs of foreign operations include the additional personal tax liabilities triggered by dividends used to signal foreign profits. Hines's estimates imply that the foreign activities of American firms generate as much U.S. tax revenue through the personal income taxation of dividends received as they do through corporate taxation of foreign source income.

Evaluation

The evidence indicates that the financial behavior of multinational corporations is quite sensitive to tax considerations, though not completely determined by them. Since much of the literature concentrates on identifying the effects of tax provisions on capital structure, transfer pricing, and dividend payments, it is worth bearing in mind that considerations other than tax avoidance also appear to influence multinational firms' financial activities. Measured elasticities, while large, seldom approach the infinite values implied by simple tax-arbitrage models. Important nontax considerations in financing multinational operations include political and regulatory climates, incentive structures within firms, needs for flexibility in deploying cash to different locations, and relations with creditors and shareholders. The interactions between tax and nontax factors that influence financial policy are likely to have important consequences in some cases, through they receive relatively little explicit attention.[17] In some instances it may be less valuable to test the standard hypothesis that taxes influence financial behavior than to test the alternative hypothesis that *only* taxes influence financial behavior. Although neither is generally correct, deviations from tax arbitrage positions reflect nontax considerations of considerable interest.

Evidence of the impact of taxation on financial behavior has four features that should influence, and possibly broaden, its interpretation. The first feature is that much of the evidence is indirect. Studies of parent loans to foreign subsidiaries use interest payments as proxies; transfer pricing studies usually examine reported profitability and tax obligations instead of transfer prices; and studies of dividend payments analyze dividend receipts of American parent companies (which may not own 100 percent of their foreign affiliates). Although there is nothing necessarily wrong with drawing inferences from indirect indicators, there is always the possibility that other considerations influence the observed patterns.

The second feature of the financial evidence is that interpretations of the data typically rely to a significant degree on fine distinctions in timing. Under U.S. law, excess foreign tax credits can be carried backward two years or forward five, making the tax consequences of observed distinctions between excess and deficit foreign tax credit positions potentially very subtle. In addition, some financial responses to tax differences may take time to develop, since financial contracts (such as bonds) often have long horizons; as a consequence, estimated short-run elasticities may miss longer-run effects.

The third feature of the financial evidence is the incompleteness of available data. Multinational firms are heterogeneous in numerous unobserved ways, making it impossible to isolate the effects of taxation from other variables that are correlated with tax rates. Since subsidiaries are not randomly assigned to different countries or industries or parent companies, their tax situations are likely to be endogenous to other operating conditions and to their parent companies' tax situations. This unobserved heterogeneity need not invalidate many of the measurements of financial responsiveness to taxation, but it does suggest that observed differences in financial policies reflect these endogenously chosen characteristics as well as financial policies.

The fourth feature of the financial evidence is the close connection between financing and investment decisions that makes it difficult, if not impossible, to distinguish them completely. New investments require financing; at the other end of the life cycle, mature subsidiaries must either invest their after-tax profits or repatriate them as dividends. Furthermore, the ability to use advantageous financing, such as favorable transfer pricing, enhances the desirability of locating investments in certain countries.[18] As a result, tax considerations influence financing and investment decisions in tandem, and a complete analysis treats them as joint decisions.

9.4 The Impact of Taxation on Specific Activities

International tax provisions influence numerous activities of multinational firms other than FDI or financing: research and development (R&D), export activity, foreign bribery and other prohibited actions, and the choice of home country by tax-avoiding firms.

Research and Development

Multinational firms frequently undertake R&D in one country in the hope of generating revenue in many countries. As with interest expenses, governments then face the problem of deciding whether all or part of a multinational firm's expenditures on R&D represent deductible expenses in the location in which they are incurred.

The U.S. tax treatment of the R&D expenses of multinational firms mirrors its treatment of their interest expenses. Between 1981 and 1986, multinational firms could deduct all of their U.S. R&D expenses against their U.S. taxable incomes; since 1986, a portion must be allocated against foreign income. The fraction allocated against foreign income is a function of the firm's ratio of foreign to domestic sales (or, in some case, assets). As a consequence, after 1986, the tax cost of performing R&D in the United States is a complicated function of a firm's foreign tax credit status and the fraction of its sales and assets located abroad.

Hines (1993) uses firm-specific changes after 1986 in tax costs of undertaking R&D in the United States to estimate the responsiveness of R&D spending to its after-tax cost. The study analyzes two samples of large firms over the 1984–1989 period: (1) a sample of 40 firms that experience no merger activity between 1984 and 1989 and (2) a sample of 116 firms that includes those with minor merger activity. In both samples, the R&D expenditures of firms with significant foreign sales and excess foreign tax credits grow systematically more slowly after 1986 than do the R&D expenditures of other firms. The implied price elasticity of R&D is −1.8 in the 40-firm sample and −0.8 in the 116-firm sample; given the omission of variables to control for merger effects in the larger sample, the true elasticity is probably closer to −1.8 than to −0.8. An own-price elasticity of R&D in that range is much larger than those reported by earlier studies but is consistent with Hall's (1993) firm-level study of responses to incentives created by the Research and Experimentation Tax Credit. Hines (1994b) argues that such a large elasticity is also consistent with pre- and post-1986 trends in the fraction of R&D that American firms perform abroad.

One of the issues of interest to both capital-importing and capital-exporting countries is whether imported technology is a complement or a substitute for technology produced by local R&D. Hines (1995a) investigates this question by estimating the effect on R&D of royalty withholding taxes. Since foreign subsidiaries are required to pay royalties to their parent companies for imported technology, higher royalty taxes, even if partly avoided by adept transfer pricing, raise the cost of technology imports. Higher costs of imported technology stimulate local R&D if the two are substitutes and discourage R&D if they are complements. Cross-sectional estimates of R&D intensities of the foreign operations of U.S. firms in 43 countries in 1989 indicate a cross-elasticity of 0.16, suggesting that R&D and imported technology are substitutes. Cross-sectional estimates of the R&D activities of foreign-owned firms in the United States in 1987 indicate a somewhat larger cross-elasticity, 0.30, which also suggests that imported technology and locally produced technology are substitutes.

Export Activity

The taxation of export earnings raises many of the same issues as does the taxation of royalties or other foreign source income, with the difference that governments are so often eager to subsidize export activity that there are specific General Agreement on Tariffs and Trade prohibitions against doing so. The U.S. tax system nevertheless offers American exporters the choice of two favorable treatments of export income: tax deferral by routing exports through foreign sales corporations or treatment of a portion (typically 50 percent) of export profits as foreign source income. For firms with excess foreign tax credits, any export profits treated as foreign source income are effectively untaxed, making the second option quite attractive. Kemsley (1995) compares changes in ratios of U.S. exports to foreign sales by a panel of U.S. multinationals over the 1985 through 1992 period, finding that firms moving into excess foreign tax credit positions are more likely than others to substitute exports for foreign production. His estimates imply that the ability to treat export profits as foreign source income raises exports by $70 million for a typical firm with excess foreign tax credits.

Prohibited Activities

International tax policy occasionally is used to promote foreign policy or other government goals, often accompanied by debate about the ability of tax policy to induce behavior that furthers noneconomic objectives. One example is provided by the U.S. Tax Reform Act of 1976, which, with the Foreign Corrupt Practices Act of 1977, imposes tax and criminal penalties on American firms and individuals caught paying bribes to foreign government officials. Hines (1995b) finds that the business activities of American firms in bribe-prone foreign countries fell sharply after these acts took effect in 1977. In a cross-section of forty-one countries, local bribery propensities are negatively correlated with post-1977 growth rates of U.S. FDI, capital-to-labor ratios of American-owned affiliates, U.S. joint venture activity, and U.S. aircraft exports. This reduction in American business activity corresponds to a much higher post-1977 cost of doing business in countries in which official bribery is common, implying that the U.S. tax and criminal legislation significantly influences the practices of American firms.[19]

Choice of Home Country

U.S. taxation of the repatriated foreign earnings of American corporations makes it more expensive for a firm with foreign earnings to be incorporated in the United States than for the same firm to be incorporated in certain other countries (such as the Netherlands Antilles) that exempt foreign earnings from taxation. The ease with which multinational firms can relocate between countries carries with it the potential to undermine governments' abilities to tax them. Hines (1991) documents the case of one firm, McDermott, Inc., that changed its site of incorporation from the United States to Panama in 1982 in order to avoid U.S. taxation of its foreign source income. Collins and Shackelford (1995) measure the relative tax costs of residence in four different home countries, finding that American multinational firms would face lower tax liabilities if resident in Canada but higher tax liabilities if resident in Japan or the United Kingdom. Various tax costs associated with reincorporating, particularly the taxes due on any previously unrealized capital gains, prevent international movement from becoming common, though a small number of firms may find it in their interest to relocate. Start-up firms owned by Americans could incorporate in tax havens in the hope of someday earning significant untaxed foreign profits, but the U.S. tax treatment of accumulated earnings and personal holding companies limits severely the attractiveness of this option. Consequently, in spite of their potential mobility, tax laws constrain corporations sufficiently that there is little reason to anticipate an imminent demise of the U.S. corporate tax base.

Evaluation

There are numerous specific U.S. tax provisions that appear to influence the activities of American firms. These include the tax treatment of R&D expenses, export profits, and royalty income received from abroad, the tax penalties for foreign bribery and foreign boycott participation, and the tax costs triggered by corporate relocation. In some cases the tax provisions have the effect Congress intends—for example, when foreign-sourcing rules encourage exports by American multinationals. (This is a provision that may, from the standpoint of its drafters, work too well, in that it provides export incentives that differ sharply *between* firms.) In other cases, the tax provisions have undesired effects, as is probably true of the 1986 reform that raises the tax costs of R&D performed by firms with excess foreign tax credits. Still others lie between these extremes: Congress sought to eradicate foreign bribery by American firms with its legislation in the 1970s but did so in the hope that American business activity would not be thereby adversely affected.

The evidence of strong behavioral response is subject to most of the same limitations as is the FDI and financial evidence, stemming from the omission of important variables, the time-sensitive nature of its interpretation, and the need to include both FDI and financial considerations. Furthermore, measured behavioral responses typically represent reported responses, and the transfer-pricing evidence suggests that behavior may deviate from reports in ways that are correlated with tax incentives. It would be helpful to incorporate endogenous reporting to distinguish real from apparent effects of taxation on specific activities.

It would also be helpful to consider the general equilibrium effects of specific international tax provisions, which empirical studies enlighten but do not address directly. Tax changes that influence the costs of R&D by half of the firms in an economy will, in general, change the average prices of R&D, other factor inputs, and final products. Panel studies omit these effects in order to focus on firm-specific differences, thereby producing estimates that cannot be used without appropriate modification to gauge the effect of tax policies on aggregate behavior.

Many of the activities affected by specific international tax provisions, such as investment or R&D, also receive special domestic tax treatment. The response elasticities of multinational firms to international tax provisions may offer valuable, if indirect, evidence of the impact of purely domestic tax provisions. Similarly, research on the effects of domestic taxation provides information that is relevant to international behavior but is seldom incorporated in studies of international taxation. The activities of multinational firms influence each other jointly; given the limited available information with which to analyze the effects of taxation, this interdependence can be used to advantage by applying evidence and lessons drawn from one set of activities to others.

9.5 Implications

One clear implication of the quantitative evidence is that the investment, financing, and other activities of multinational corporations are quite sensitive to their tax treatment. This sensitivity carries numerous implications for tax policy, including the standard incentive for governments to compete with each other to offer firms ever-lower tax rates to attract activities that are believed to be beneficial to their economies. An alternative to tax competition is to form supranational agreements to harmonize tax rates and tax bases, but such attempts are notoriously ineffective and quickly abandoned.

There is another approach to designing international tax policy in an environment dominated by very mobile multinational operations: tax rules that sufficiently constrain the activities of firms that it becomes possible to apply moderate levels of taxation without driving economic activity abroad. This is the method used by the United States and other large OECD countries. It entails many costs, not the least of which are the compliance and enforcement burdens borne by firms and governments, which must apply a very large and cumbersome set of rules and regulations.[20] Complex structures of taxes and incentives inevitably contain sections that embody mistaken reasoning and lead to inefficient outcomes, particularly if the tax treatment of financial and real activity is not properly coordinated. The strategy of using tax rules to discourage tax avoidance can be successful, but since it is often necessary for governments to observe tactics before developing remedies, this method inevitably leads to policies that are somewhat behind the latest practices used to avoid taxation.

The responsiveness of governments to the behavior of taxpayers is in part responsible for the tax reforms that make it possible to measure the impact of taxation. Some of the evidence that comes from tax reforms suggests that governments can use the responsiveness of multinational firms to further their own objectives in ways that might otherwise be more difficult or costly. As an example, countries eager to encourage local R&D can do so through both purely domestic policies (such as local credits) and policies designed to change the relative attractiveness of locating R&D elsewhere. Similarly, governments influence local investment in plant and equipment directly through its tax treatment and indirectly through the tax treatment of foreign activities that may substitute or complement domestic investment. Governments that choose to do so can also use tax policies to pursue various noneconomic objectives.

International mobility also affects the revenue consequences of tax policies. The ability of American firms to adjust transfer prices (within limits) may help U.S. tax collections, since many foreign tax rates currently exceed the U.S. rate, and firms have incentives to report their profits in the United States. In addition, U.S. multinationals that transfer reported profits from subsidiaries located in high-tax foreign countries to those located in low-tax foreign countries reduce their own foreign tax liabilities and reduce the foreign tax credits they are eligible to apply against their U.S. tax liabilities. In reducing foreign tax credits claimed by American firms, transfer pricing augments U.S. tax revenue.

Existing empirical studies offer consistent evidence that multinational firms respond to international tax incentives. Unfortunately, these studies generally do not provide enough information to test subtle distinctions of different theories of the effect of taxation on multinational firms. The somewhat rudimentary state of the literature reflects the recency of much of the quantitative work on international tax issues as well as the incompleteness of the theory of multinational firms and foreign direct investment. Since almost all of the evidence implies that response elasticities are large, the efficiency costs associated with misguided tax policies are also likely to be large. Consequently, reliable and sophisticated quantitative information has the potential to enlighten tax policy development in a way that significantly enhances the efficiency of resource allocation. Current studies of the effect of tax policy on the activities of multinational corporations suggest promising directions for the next generation of empirical work.

Notes

I thank Jeffrey Frankel and Joel Slemrod for helpful comments on a draft of this chapter.

1. The Joint Committee on Taxation (JCT) of the U.S. Congress provides elaborate explanations of major U.S. tax legislation. One way to gauge the significance of individual items in large tax bills is to measure the attention they receive in the accompanying JCT explanation. Of 1,341 pages explaining the revenue provisions of the Tax Reform Act of 1986 (U.S. Congress 1987), 276 pages, or 21 percent of the total, are devoted to its foreign provisions. While the primary purpose of the 1986 act was to reform domestic taxation, Congress apparently felt that it had extensive unfinished business in the foreign tax area as well.

2. International tax rules affect returns to many other activities, such as worker migration and the allocation of financial investments by individuals. This chapter does not consider those issues in the interest of concentrating on multinational corporations. Of course, it is not possible to separate completely the effects of tax policies on firms and individuals, since individuals own firms and may also work for them. See, for example, Gordon and Jun (1993), who analyze the way that taxes influence substitution between individual ownership of foreign equity and direct investment by multinational corporations.

American multinational corporations typically perform many more international transactions than do American individuals. Individual Americans report $29 billion of foreign source income for 1991 (Redmiles 1994), while American corporations report $90 billion of foreign source income for 1990 (Nutter 1994). Even if individuals are more likely than corporations to underreport their foreign incomes, these figures reveal a large difference between the magnitudes of the foreign activities of American individuals and corporations, a difference that would be much larger still if measured by value-added rather than income.

3. For example, the JCT offers its analysis of other countries' recent experiences with value-added taxes (U.S. Congress 1991, 321–333) as a guide to the formation of U.S. policy.

4. Some parts of this brief description of international tax rules are excerpted from Hines and Hubbard (1995).

5. The U.S. government is not alone in taxing the worldwide income of its resident companies while permitting firms to claim foregian tax credits. Other countries with such systems include Greece, Italy, Japan, Norway, and the United Kingdom. Under U.S. law,

firms may claim foreign tax credits for taxes paid by foreign affiliates of which they own at least 10 percent, and only those taxes that qualify as income taxes are creditable.

6. Deferral of home-country taxation of the unrepatriated profits of foreign subsidiaries is a common feature of systems that tax foreign incomes. Other countries that permit this kind of deferral include Canada, Denmark, France, Germany, Japan, Norway, Pakistan, and the United Kingdom.

7. If the parent firm does not have excess foreign tax credits (on which more shortly), it is eligible to claim a foreign tax credit of $11.11, representing the product of foreign taxes paid by its subsidiary and the subsidiary's ratio of dividends to after-tax profits [$50 × ($100/$450) =$11.11].

8. Foreign tax credits are not adjusted for inflation, so are generally the most valuable if claimed as soon as possible. Barring unusual circumstances, firms apply their foreign tax credits against future years only when unable to apply them against either of the previous two years. The most common reason that firms do not apply excess foreign tax credits against either of the previous two years is that they already have excess foreign tax credits in those years.

Firms paying the corporate alternative minimum tax (AMT) are subject to the same rules, with the added restriction that the combination of net operating loss deductions and foreign tax credits cannot reduce AMT liabilities by more than 90 percent. It is noteworthy that since the AMT rate is only 20 percent, firms subject to the AMT are considerably more likely to have excess foreign tax credits than are firms that pay the regular corporate tax.

9. Not all countries that grant foreign tax credits use worldwide averaging. For example, although Japan uses worldwide averaging, the United Kingdom instead requires its firms to calculate foreign tax credits on an activity-by-activity basis. The United States used to require firms to calculate separate foreign tax credit limits for each country to which taxes were paid; the current system of worldwide averaging was introduced in the mid-1970s.

10. FDI is often used as a measure of foreign investment, but it is noteworthy that changes in FDI need not correspond to new investment in plant, equipment, or inventories. U.S. direct investment abroad is the (annual) change in the value of American claims on foreign businesses owned significantly by Americans. If an American company that owns 90 percent of a foreign subsidiary spends $1 million to increase its ownership share to 92 percent, then the $1 million is treated as FDI. An otherwise-similar transaction that increases an American firm's ownership share from 2 percent to 4 percent is not treated as FDI. See also note 11.

11. The data on which these FDI studies are based are produced by the Bureau of Economic Analysis (BEA) of the U.S. Department of Commerce as part of its effort to construct the national income and product accounts. FDI is one of the most difficult economic variables to measure in practice, which is why the BEA conducts periodic benchmark surveys of U.S. direct investment abroad and foreign direct investment in the United States in order to correct cumulative errors in its annual measurement of FDI. Furthermore, the definition of FDI changes over time (prior to 1974, BEA defined FDI in the United States to be investment by an entity in which a foreigner owns at least a 25 percent stake; starting in 1974, the required foreign ownership share is only 10 percent). Newlon and Slemrod correct some inconsistencies in the historical BEA series and add dummy variables and time trends around years of data revisions to remove mechanical patterns created by revisions.

12. See, for example, Bartik (1985) and Papke (1991).

13. See Froot and Hines (1995) for a more extensive description of the tax rules governing interest expenses and receipts by multinational firms, from which the following is drawn.

14. Similar evidence appears in the occasional studies (such as Wheeler 1988) of the (high) profit rates of individual tax haven affiliates of American multinational companies.

15. Kopits uses ordinary least squares to analyze the fifty-two nonzero royalty observations out of the set of $14 \times 12 = 168$ country-industry cells.

16. The magnitudes of the estimated tax haven dummy variables are perhaps too large to correspond to the effects of transfer pricing alone, as Mutti (1993) notes. Also, the pooling of multiple annual observations of the same firms (over the 1984–1988 period) may not be appropriate, as Harris et al. (1993) acknowledge.

17. Exceptions include Wilson (1993) and Cummins, Harris, and Hassett (1995).

18. The ability to adjust (within limits) transfer prices will generally make American firms more willing than they would be otherwise to invest in very low tax and very high tax locations. For an elaboration of this point, see Hines and Rice (1994), Grubert and Slemrod (1994), and Gordon and MacKie-Mason (1995).

19. American firms are also subject to tax and criminal penalties for participating in unsanctioned international boycotts (such as the Arab countries' boycott of Israel). Redmiles (1992) offers evidence that American firms refuse most boycott requests, and Hines (1996c) finds that these refusals are positively correlated with the tax costs of boycott compliance. This evidence again suggests the ability of U.S. policy to restrict the foreign behavior of U.S. multinationals.

20. Blumenthal and Slemrod (1995) provide estimates of the costs of complying with the foreign provisions of U.S. tax law.

References

Altshuler, Rosanne, and Jack M. Mintz. 1995. "U.S. Interest-Allocation Rules: Effects and Policy." *International Tax and Public Finance* 2:7–35.

Altshuler, Rosanne, and T. Scott Newlon. 1993. "The Effects of U.S. Tax Policy on the Income Repatriation Patterns of U.S. Multinational Corporations." In Alberto Giovannini, R. Glenn Hubbard, and Joel Slemrod, eds., *Studies in International Taxation*. Chicago: University of Chicago Press.

Altshuler, Rosanne, T. Scott Newlon, and William C. Randolph. 1995. "Do Repatriation Taxes Matter? Evidence from the Tax Returns of U.S. Multinationals." In Martin Feldstein, James R. Hines Jr., and R. Glenn Hubbard, eds., *The Effects of Taxation on Multinational Corporations*. Chicago: Unversity of Chicago Press.

Auerbach, Alan J., and Kevin Hassett. 1993. "Taxation and Foreign Direct Investment in the United States: A Reconsideration of the Evidence." In Alberto Giovannini, R. Glenn Hubbard, and Joel Slemrod, eds., *Studies in International Taxation*. Chicago: University of Chicago Press.

Bartik, Timothy J. 1985. "Business Location Decisions in the United States: Estimates of the Effects of Unionization, Taxes, and Other Characteristics of States." *Journal of Business and Economic Statistics* 3:14–22.

Bernard, Jean-Thomas, and Robert J. Weiner. 1990. "Multinational Corporations, Transfer Prices, and Taxes: Evidence from the U.S. Petroleum Industry." In Assaf Razin and Joel Slemrod, eds., *Taxation in the Global Economy*. Chicago: University of Chicago Press.

Blumenthal, Marsha, and Joel B. Slemrod. 1995. "The Compliance Cost of Taxing Foreign-Source Income: Its Magnitude, Determinants, and Policy Implications." *International Tax and Public Finance* 2:37–53.

Bond, Eric. 1981. "Tax Holidays and Industry Behavior." *Review of Economics and Statistics* 63:88–95.

Boskin, Michael, and William G. Gale. 1987. "New Results on the Effects of Tax Policy on the International Location of Investment." In Martin Feldstein, ed., *The Effects of Taxation on Capital Accumulation*. Chicago: University of Chicago Press.

Collins, Julie H., Deen Kemsley, and Mark Lang. 1996. "Cross-jurisdictional income shifting and earnings valuation." Working paper. University of North Carolina.

Collins, Julie H., Deen Kemsley, and Douglas A. Shackelford. 1995. "Tax Reform and Foreign Acquisitions: A Microanalysis." *National Tax Journal* 48:1–21.

Collins, Julie H., and Douglas A. Shackelford. 1992. "Foreign Tax Credit Limitations and Preferred Stock Issuances." *Journal of Accounting Research*, supplement 30:103–124.

Collins, Julie H., and Douglas A. Shackelford. 1995. "Corporate Domicile and Average Effective Tax Rates: The Cases of Canada, Japan, the United Kingdom, and the United States." *International Tax and Public Finance* 2:55–83.

Coughlin, Cletus C., Joseph V. Terza, and Vachira Arromdee. 1991. "State Characteristics and the Location of Foreign Direct Investment Within the United States." *Review of Economics and Statistics* 68:675–683.

Cummins, Jason G., Trevor S. Harris, and Kevin A. Hassett. 1995. "Accounting Standards, Information Flow, and Firm Investment Behavior." In Martin Feldstein, James R. Hines Jr., and R. Glenn Hubbard, eds., *The Effects of Taxation on Multinational Corporations*. Chicago: University of Chicago Press.

Cummins, Jason G., and R. Glenn Hubbard. 1995. "The Tax Sensitivity of Foreign Direct Investment: Evidence from Firm-level Panel Data." In Martin Feldstein, James R. Hines Jr., and R. Glenn Hubbard, eds., *The Effects of Taxation on Multinational Corporations*. Chicago: University of Chicago Press.

Desai, Mihir A., and James R. Hines Jr. 1996. "'Basket' Cases: International Joint Ventures after the Tax Reform Act of 1986." NBER Working Paper 5755.

Devereux, Michael P., and Harold Freeman. 1995. "The Impact of Tax on Foreign Direct Investment: Empirical Evidence and the Implications for Tax Integration Schemes." *International Tax and Public Finance* 2:85–106.

Feldstein, Martin. 1995. "The Effects of Outbound Foreign Direct Investment on the Domestic Capital Stock." In Martin Feldstein, James R. Hines Jr., and R. Glenn Hubbard, eds., *The Effects of Taxation on Multinational Corporations*. Chicago: University of Chicago Press.

Frisch, Daniel J., and David G. Hartman. 1983. "Taxation and the Location of U.S. Investment Abroad." NBER Working Paper 1241.

Froot, Kenneth A., and James R. Hines Jr. 1995. "Interest Allocation Rules, Financing Patterns, and the Operations of U.S. Multinationals." In Martin Feldstein, James R. Hines Jr., and R. Glenn Hubbard, eds., *The Effects of Taxation on Multinational Corporations*. Chicago: University of Chicago Press.

Gentry, William M. 1995. "Comment." In Martin Feldstein, James R. Hines Jr., and R. Glenn Hubbard, eds., *The Effects of Taxation on Multinational Corporations.* Chicago: University of Chicago Press.

Gordon, Roger H., and Joosung Jun. 1993. "Taxes and the Form of Ownership of Foreign Corporate Equity." In Alberto Giovannini, R. Glenn Hubbard, and Joel Slemrod, eds., *Studies in International Taxation.* Chicago: University of Chicago Press.

Gordon, Roger H., and Jeffrey K. MacKie-Mason. 1995. "Why Is There Corporate Taxation in a Small Open Economy? The Role of Transfer Pricing and Income Shifting." In Martin Feldstein, James R. Hines Jr., and R. Glenn Hubbard, eds., *The Effects of Taxation on Multinational Corporations.* Chicago: University of Chicago Press.

Grubert, Harry. 1995. "Royalties, Dividends, and R&D." In *Proceedings of the Eighty-Seventh Annual Conference on Taxation.* Columbus, OH: National Tax Association.

Grubert, Harry, Timothy Goodspeed, and Deborah Swenson. 1993. "Explaining the Low Taxable Income of Foreign-Controlled Companies in the United States." In Alberto Giovannini, R. Glenn Hubbard, and Joel Slemrod, eds., *Studies in International Taxation.* Chicago: University of Chicago Press.

Grubert, Harry, and John Mutti. 1991. "Taxes, Tariffs and Transfer Pricing in Multinational Corporation Decision Making." *Review of Economics and Statistics* 73:285–293.

Grubert, Harry, and Joel Slemrod. 1994. "The Effect of Taxes on Investment and Income Shifting to Puerto Rico." NBER Working Paper 4869.

Hall, Bronwyn H. 1993. "R&D Tax Policy During the 1980s: Success or Failure?" In James M. Poterba, ed., *Tax Policy and the Economy,* vol. 7. Cambridge, MA: MIT Press.

Harris, David G. 1993. "The Impact of U.S. Tax Law Revision on Multinational Corporations' Capital Location and Income-Shifting Decisions." *Journal of Accounting Research,* supplement 31:111–140.

Harris, David, Randall Morck, Joel Slemrod, and Bernard Yeung. 1993. "Income Shifting in U.S. Multinational Corporations." In Alberto Giovannini, R. Glenn Hubbard, and Joel Slemrod, eds., *Studies in International Taxation.* Chicago: University of Chicago Press.

Hartman, David G. 1981. "Domestic Tax Policy and Foreign Investment: Some Evidence." NBER Working Paper 784.

Hartman, David G. 1984. "Tax Policy and Foreign Direct Investment in the United States." *National Tax Journal* 37:475–487.

Hartman, David G. 1985. "Tax Policy and Foreign Direct Investment." *Journal of Public Economics* 26:107–121.

Hines, James R., Jr. 1988. "Taxation and U.S. Multinational Investment." In Lawrence H. Summers, ed., *Tax Policy and the Economy,* vol. 2. Cambridge, MA: MIT Press.

Hines, James R., Jr. 1991. "The Flight paths of Migratory Corporations." *Journal of Accounting, Auditing, and Finance* 6:447–479.

Hines, James R., Jr. 1993. "On the Sensitivity of R&D to Delicate Tax Changes: The Behavior of US Multinationals in the 1980s." In Alberto Giovannini, R. Glenn Hubbard, and Joel Slemrod, eds., *Studies in International Taxation.* Chicago: University of Chicago Press.

Hines, James R., Jr. 1994a. "Credit and Deferral as International Investment Incentives." *Journal of Public Economics* 55:323–347.

Hines, James R., Jr. 1994b. "No Place Like Home: Tax Incentives and the Location of R&D by American Multinationals." In James M. Poterba, ed., *Tax Policy and the Economy*, vol. 8. Cambridge, MA: MIT Press.

Hines, James R., Jr. 1995a. "Taxes, Technology Transfer, and the R&D Activities of Multinational Firms." In Martin Feldstein, James R. Hines Jr., and R. Glenn Hubbard, eds., *The Effects of Taxation on Multinational Corporations*. Chicago: University of Chicago Press.

Hines, James R., Jr. 1995b. "Forbidden Payment: Foreign Bribery and American Business After 1977." NBER Working Paper 5266.

Hines, James R., Jr. 1996a. "Dividends and Profits: Some Unsubtle Foreign Influences." *Journal of Finance* 51:661–689.

Hines, James R., Jr. 1996b. "Altered States: Taxes and the Location of Foreign Direct Investment in America." *American Economic Review* 86:1076–1094.

Hines, James R., Jr. 1996c. "American Participation in Unsanctioned International Boycotts." Working paper, Harvard University.

Hines, James R., Jr., and R. Glenn Hubbard. 1990. "Coming Home to America: Dividend Repatriations by U.S. Multinationals." In Assaf Razin and Joel Slemrod, eds., *Taxation in the Global Economy*. Chicago: University of Chicago Press.

Hines, James R., Jr., and R. Glenn Hubbard. 1995. Appendix to Martin Feldstein, James R. Hines Jr., and R. Glenn Hubbard, eds., *Taxing Multinational Corporations*. Chicago: University of Chicago Press.

Hines, James R., Jr., and Eric M. Rice. 1994. "Fiscal Paradise: Foreign Tax Havens and American Business." *Quarterly Journal of Economics* 109:149–182.

Jenkins, Glenn P., and Brian D. Wright. 1975. "Taxation of Income of Multinational Corporations: The Case of the United States Petroleum Industry." *Review of Economics and Statistics* 57:1–11.

Kemsley, Dean. 1995. "The Effect of Taxes on the Choice Between Exports and Foreign Production." Working paper. Columbia Business School.

Klassen, Kenneth, Mark Lang, and Mark Wolfson. 1993. "Geographic Income Shifting by Multinational Corporations in Response to Tax Rate Changes." *Journal of Accounting Research*, supplement 31:141–173.

Kopits, George F. 1972. "Divdend Remittance Behavior Within the International Firm: A Cross-Country Analysis." *Review of Economics and Statistics* 54:339–342.

Kopits, George F. 1976. "Intra-Firm Royalties Crossing Frontiers and Transfer-Pricing Behaviour." *Economic Journal* 86:791–805.

Lall, Sanjaya. 1973. "Transfer Pricing by Multinational Manufacturing Firms." *Oxford Bulletin of Economics and Statistics* 35:173–195.

Leechor, Chad, and Jack Mintz. 1993. "On the Taxation of Multinational Corporate Investment When the Deferral Method Is Used by the Capital-Exporting Country." *Journal of Public Economics* 51:75–96.

Lipsey, Robert E. 1995. "Outward Direct Investment and the U.S. Economy." In Martin Feldstein, James R. Hines Jr., and R. Glenn Hubbard, eds., *The Effects of Taxation on Multinational Corporations*. Chicago: University of Chicago Press.

Lyon, Andrew B., and Gerald Silverstein. 1995. "The Alternative Minimum Tax and the Behavior of Multinational Corporations." in Martin Feldstein, James R. Hines Jr., and R. Glenn Hubbard, eds., *The Effects of Taxation on Multinational Corporations*. Chicago: University of Chicago Press.

McIntyre, Robert S. 1989, March 27. "Tax Americana," *New Republic*, pp. 18–20.

Mintz, Jack M., and Thomas Tsiopoulos. 1994. "The Effectiveness of Corporate Tax Incentives for Foreign Investment in the Presence of Tax Crediting." *Journal of Public Economics* 55:233–255.

Mutti, John. 1981. "Tax Incentives and Repatriation Decisions of U.S. Multinational Corporations." *National Tax Journal* 34:241–248.

Mutti, John. 1993. "Comment." In Martin Feldstein, James R. Hines Jr., and R. Glenn Hubbard, eds., *The Effects of Taxation on Multinational Corporations*. Chicago: University of Chicago Press.

Newlon, Timothy Scott. 1987. "Tax Policy and the Multinational Firm's Financial Policy and Investment Decisions." Ph.D. dissertation, Princeton University.

Nutter, Sarah E. 1994. "Corporate Foreign Tax Credit, 1990: An Industry Focus." *Statistics of Income Bulletin* 13:78–106.

Ondrich, Jan, and Michael Wasylenko. 1993. *Foreign Direct Investment in the United States: Issues, Magnitudes, and Location Choice of New Manufacturing Plants*. Kalamazoo, MI: W. E. Upjohn Institute.

Papke, Leslie E. 1991. "Interstate Business Tax Differentials and New Firm Location." *Journal of Public Economics* 45:47–68.

Redmiles, Lissa. 1992. "International Boycott Participation, 1990." *Statistics of Income Bulletin* 12:88–89.

Redmiles, Lissa. 1994. "Individual Foreign-Earned Income and Foreign Tax Credit, 1991." *Statistics of Income Bulletin* 14:113–122.

Scholes, Myron S., and Mark A. Wolfson. 1992. *Taxes and Business Strategy: A Planning Approach*. Englewood Cliffs, NJ: Prentice Hall.

Sinn, Hans-Werner. 1993. "Taxation and the Birth of Foreign Subsidiaries." In H. Heberg and N.V. Long, eds., *Trade, Welfare, and Economic Policies: Essays in Honor of Murray C. Kemp*. Ann Arbor, MI: University of Michigan Press.

Slemrod, Joel. 1990. "Tax Effects of Foreign Direct Investment in the United States: Evidence from a Cross-Country Comparison." In Assaf Razin and Joel Slemrod, eds., *Taxation in the Global Economy*. Chicago: University of Chicago Press.

Stevens, Guy V. G., and Robert E. Lipsey. 1992. "Interactions Between Domestic and Foreign Investment." *Journal of International Money and Finance* 11:40–62.

Swenson, Deborah L. 1994. "The Impact of U.S. Tax Reform on Foreign Direct Investment in the United States." *Journal of Public Economics* 54:243–266.

U.S. Congress. Joint Committee on Taxation. 1987. *General Explanation of the Tax Reform Act of 1986*. Washington, DC: U.S. Government Printing Office.

U.S. Congress. Joint Committee on Taxation. 1991. *Factors Affecting the International Competitiveness of the United States*. Washington, DC: U.S. Government Printing Office.

Vernon, Raymond. 1977. *Storm over the Multinationals: The Real Issues*. Cambridge, MA: Harvard University Press.

Wheeler, James E. 1988. "An Academic Look at Transfer Pricing in a Global Economy." *Tax Notes*, pp. 87–96.

Willard, Kristen Leigh. 1994. "Essays on International Taxation." Ph.D. dissertation, Princeton University.

Wilson, G. Peter. 1993. "The Role of Taxes in Location and Sourcing Decisions." In Alberto Giovannini, R. Glenn Hubbard, and Joel Slemrod, eds., *Studies in International Taxation*. Chicago: University of Chicago Press.

Young, Kan H. 1988. "The Effects of Taxes and Rates of Return on Foreign Direct Investment into the United States." *National Tax Journal* 41:109–121.

Comment

Jeffrey Frankel

International taxation is a field that international economists have for the most part defaulted on, leaving it to public finance economists, who have more patience for the details of tax law. Jim Hines's survey of the research, to which he has been a major contributor, is extremely clear. It will be my bible on this subject in the future.

The Topics Surveyed

The topics Hines surveys fall into three categories: (1) the impact of taxation on foreign direct investment (FDI), (2) the impact on financing of multinational corporations (MNCs), and (3) the impact on other specific activities of MNCs.

The first category includes studies of U.S. direct investment in various foreign countries and studies of FDI coming into the United States from various source countries. Hines notes that the former set of studies are naturally suited to studying differences in host-country tax systems and the second to differences in the source country. My first question is: Are there no tax studies of bilateral FDI among a set of countries? I am well aware that there are data problems, including many missing pairs, that are even more severe than those in the studies surveyed here. But it can be done. There are a few studies of bilateral FDI motivated by a desire to test for regional blocs; Shang-Jin Wei and I have been doing one on a data set that we cobbled together, with twelve source countries and fifty-four host countries. The closest we get to public finance considerations is a dummy variable for whether there exists a bilateral tax treaty between the pair in question. (We find a statistically significant effect of 30 percent.) There are simultaneity problems, to be sure. Furthermore, our data are cruder than those used here, and perhaps the audience for this book is interested only in behavior that involves the United States, as either source country or host. But it seems to me there might be something to be learned from studying a larger cross-section of experience.

The second category includes implications of tax policy for leveraging, transfer pricing, and dividend payments. The third includes implications for R&D spending, exports, bribery of foreign officials, and choice of home country.

In almost all cases, firm behavior is found to respond significantly to tax incentives in the direction hypothesized. I find this quite impressive—even amazing. Apparently the typical procedure runs as follows. The researcher figures out what the incentive influencing some decision is, a priori, from reading the tax code (itself quite an impressive feat, given the complexity of the code), then finds the right data set for the question (or one that is close enough), tests for the hypothesized response, and finds effects that are significantly greater than zero statistically. Hines even deems it worth noting that the estimated elasticities are not infinite; corporate behavior is governed by a trade-off in which nontax factors enter along with tax factors.

Can Things Really Be This Clear-cut?

I said at the outset that Hines's chapter was very clear. But I am now going to suggest (mischievously) that it seems almost *too* clear. My question is: Is there any selection going on here (whether by the authors in reporting their results, the journals in publishing them, or Hines in choosing to include them in his survey)? Or, at a minimum, do the authors consult with tax lawyers and their clients to find out directly the aspects of the tax code that are operationally governing behavior, before formulating their hypotheses?

It occurs to me to be suspicious because things never work out this neatly in the research I am accustomed to. Part of this may be because in my fields of specialization—international trade and macroeconomics—we have a hard time getting significant results. One would expect behavioral response to direct tax incentives to be relatively easier to find.

Consider the field of finance, however. Incentives in financial markets should be clear, and arbitrage should be powerful. But the norm in finance is to fail to reject market efficiency, which is generally the null hypothesis, and here I am talking about the *successful* papers. To repeat, a successful paper must *fail* to get significant results. Sometimes the finance people fail to fail to reject the efficient markets hypothesis. Then they get very upset and call it an "anomaly." Familiar examples include the January effect, the small firm effect, the initial public offering effect, the term structure bias, the forward discount bias, and the home-country bias. The finance people do not calm down until someone comes up with an explanation for the anomaly—usually a tortured one, in terms of a tax effect that nobody had thought of before or a risk premium. Then that explanation becomes the new efficient markets hypothesis, which people can then fail to reject. Of course, it is generally much easier to fail to get significant results than to succeed in getting significant results, which is why we macroeconomists over the last decade or so have gone over to the system used by the finance people.

To put my reaction to Hines's chapter in a positive manner, it is refreshing to see so many researchers looking for and finding statistically significant evidence in support of their hypotheses instead of either rejecting or failing to reject their hypotheses.

Transfer Pricing

One place where Hines deviates a bit from the pattern of explaining the incentive first and then the test is the issue of transfer pricing. As he notes, it has been alleged, particularly during the 1992 election campaign, that Japanese and other foreign-owned corporations set transfer prices so as to reduce their U.S. tax obligations. This section of the chapter deviates from most of the rest, first in the respect that the evidence is not especially strong and second in that Hines does not explain the incentive up front. I think the right answer is that the corporate tax rate is higher in Japan and some European countries than in the United Sates; thus the incentive is to *overstate* artificially U.S. earnings and thus U.S. tax payments, and to reduce them elsewhere, just the opposite of what one would think from listening to the campaign rhetoric.

Missing Topics

One kind of research study that seems to be missing is studies of the simultaneous determination of the various decisions made by the MNC: whether and where to undertake FDI, how and where to finance it, how much profits to remit, and in what form. Hines mentions that these decisions should in principle be simultaneous, but I wonder, if indeed nobody has done it, then why not. Is it data limitations? The data apparently exist to address each of these questions independently, so why not together? Or is the problem that if too much is made endogenous, then there are not enough exogenous variables to identify the equations?

Trying to think of topics that might be missing from the chapter, I have come up with another two. A relatively minor one, perhaps, is taxation of multinational corporations at the state level, particularly the unitary tax that has been such a big issue here in California.

Differences in the Cost of Capital

A bigger topic is the effect of international tax differences on the corporate cost of capital. This is one area of the literature that I am familiar with, particularly the hypothesis that the cost of capital facing Japanese corporations is—or, more accurately, was (in the 1980s)—lower than that facing their American competitors. This issue is the origin of some of my surprise that the lessons from the research described in this survey seem relatively clear.

Consider that the Japanese corporate tax rate during most of the 1980s, at 42 percent, was higher than the U.S. rate of 34 percent. You might think that the implications for the relative after-tax cost of capital in the two countries would be clear or that the implications of Japan's reduction of its corporate tax rate at the end of the decade, from 42 percent to $37\frac{1}{2}$ percent, would be clear. But the leading public finance authorities are divided on how to think about this.

Some authors, including Ando and Auerbach (1988), reach the intuitive conclusion that "it is Japanese, not American, firms that are taxed more heavily" and have a higher after-tax cost of capital. Others, however, notably Bernheim and Shoven (1987) and Shoven (1989), reach the conclusion that the high average corporate tax rate in Japan worked to reduce the effective marginal rate on new investment. The reason is that the high corporate tax rate increased the value to the corporation of borrowing to finance investment and deducting the interest payments from taxable income (an effect that is especially powerful for Japanese firms, because they are more highly indebted than American firms). Shoven (1989) thus finds that Japan's decision to reduce the average corporate tax rate in 1988 raised the effective tax rate on investment (by 9 percentage points).

Now this is the kind of directly conflicting conclusions to which I am accustomed. Ando and Auerbach were well aware of the tax advantages of borrowing in Japan but put an upper bound on its size, and so claimed to be able to "rule out" the claim that the corporate tax system gave firms there a cost-of-capital advantage.

Incidentally, the economists writing on this subject tended to agree that tax differences between the United Sates and Japan, however they are interpreted, are much less important than differences in the before-tax real interest rate in determining the relative cost of capital. Low real interest rates did indeed produce a low cost of capital for Japanese firms in the 1980s, but this changed abruptly in 1990, when real interest rates were raised sharply and stock market values collapsed.[1]

Returning to Hines's chapter, a good literature review of this sort can be put to several uses. I can think of four. First, it can be used to confirm our belief in the maximizing behavior of firms. Second, and most successfully in my view, the chapter can be used to verify what are the important international attributes of the tax law, distinguishing those that do not seem to affect behavior, either because they are minor in magnitude or are not binding, from those that do. Third, one can take away various specific parameter estimates, such as Hines's interesting estimate that one dollar of foreign profit has the same effect on dividends paid to shareholders as three dollars of domestic profit.

Finally, one might use what one has learned, in the light of the internationalization of the economy, to pass judgment on policy reforms. The chapter does very little of this.

I will put one possible policy recommendation on the table. In 1986, the law was changed so that a portion of firms' R&D spending must be allocated to foreign income, reducing the tax advantage for some firms, particularly those with foreign sales but without excess foreign tax credits. Hines (1993) finds that R&D subsequently grew more slowly for those firms than for others. My final question is: Was this an undesirable policy change? Many economists, whether working in the fields of growth theory, international trade, labor, or income distribution, have concluded that R&D has positive spillovers within the country where it is undertaken. If this is right, shouldn't we be encouraging MNCs to undertake R&D in the United States, regardless whether it supports their sales abroad or domestically?

Note

1. I survey this literature in Frankel (1993).

References

Ando, Albert, and Alan Auerbach. 1988. "The Corporate Cost of Capital in the U.S. and Japan: A Comparison." In John Shoven, ed., *Government Policy Towards Industry in the United States and Japan*, 21–49. New York: Cambridge University Press.

Bernheim, Douglas, and John Shoven. 1987. "Taxation and the Cost of Capital: An International Comparison." In C. E. Walker and M. A. Bloomfield, eds., *The Consumption Tax: A Better Alternative?* pp. 61–85. Cambridge, MA: Ballinger.

Frankel, Jeffrey. 1993. "The Evolving Japanese Financial System, and the Cost of Capital." In Ingo Walter and Takato Hiraki, eds., *Restructuring Japan's Financial Markets*, pp. 235–285. New York: Irwin Press and New York University.

Hines, James. 1993. "On the Sensitivity of R&D to Delicate Tax Changes: The Behavior of US Multinationals in the 1980s." In Alberto Giovannini, R. Glenn Hubbard, and Joel Slemrod, eds., *Studies in International Taxation*. Chicago: University of Chicago Press.

Shoven, John. 1989. "The Japanese Tax Reform and the Effective Rate of Tax on Japanese Corporate Investments." In *Tax Policy and the Economy*, Lawrence Summers, ed., Cambridge, MA: MIT Press.

Comment

Joel Slemrod

Jim Hines's thorough and careful review of how taxes affect multinational corporations (MNCs) concludes that "taxation exerts a significant effect on the magnitude and location of foreign direct investment (FDI)," of a magnitude that is "generally consistent with a unit elasticity with respect to after-tax returns." Furthermore, he adds, "the evidence indicates that the financial behavior of MNCs is quite sensitive to tax considerations." Although he perceives a fair degree of consensus in his extremely valuable cataloging of the results of empirical studies in this area, in the end he offers only fairly vague policy prescriptions, concluding by asserting that "the goal of tax policy should be to design a system that is as responsive as possible to the very great ability of multinational firms to modify their activities in response to taxation."

I fully agree that we should be circumspect in drawing firm policy conclusions from the empirical literature, for two reasons. One is that the welfare economics of international taxation is very much an unsettled issue, among other reasons because the objective itself—national or global welfare—is unsettled. The second reason, which is more pertinent here, is that the empirical elasticities do not provide adequate information about the structural parameters of the choice problems faced by MNCs and therefore are not well suited to gauging the impact of particular policy changes.

In other areas of economics we adopt parsimonious enough models so that the estimated parameters map directly into particular structural parameters. For example, under certain assumptions, labor supply elasticities correspond to characteristics of utility functions, and investment demand elasticities inform us about capital-labor substitutability and adjustment cost functions. But what does an FDI elasticity inform us about? To answer this question, we need to refer back to the prevailing theory of the nature of a multinational enterprise, coined the "eclectic theory" by Dunning (1985). According to this theory, the firm controls certain intangible assets that have a public good aspect to them, in that they can be exploited extensively with low marginal cost; the intangible asset is often thought of as information about product or process. To take full, meaning global, advantage of this intangible, the firm could produce its product domestically and export goods that embody the intangible asset, could license the intangible asset to foreign firms and received a royalty, or could create controlled foreign subsidiaries to produce and distribute the product abroad. As Dunning puts it, FDI by firms of country A in country B is more likely if A's firms possess ownership-specific advantages relative to B's firms in sourcing markets, find it profitable to use these advantages themselves rather than leave them to B's firms, and find it profitable to utilize these ownership-specific advantages in B rather than A. Which choice is taken depends on an array of factors, including transportation costs, tariffs, the expropriability of the intangibles via licensing arrangements, export subsidies, and the tax rules that apply to foreign direct investment.

Leamer's (1996) terminology is evocative. He contrasts the "mutual fund" model of MNCs, in which the firm allows investors access to foreign equity markets that are otherwise inaccessible, to the idea of a MNC as a kind of "safe-deposit box" that keeps trade secrets from being used by foreign businesses and facilitates the deployment of intangible assets in foreign locations of production; the latter is closer to Dunning's eclectic theory.

Within this conceptual framework it is undoubtedly true that, ceteris paribus, a lower effective tax rate on FDI makes it more attractive and thereby should increase its volume. But what does the measured elasticity of FDI to its after-tax rate of return inform us about? The responsiveness of cross-border capital movements? Not likely, as FDI can be financed largely by local borrowing or local sales of shares, so that increased FDI need not mean increased capital movement. Capital-labor substitutability? Also unlikely, as FDI tells us about who controls a given investment. Certainly the elasticity of who controls the shoe industry in the United States is different from the elasticity of the size of the U.S. shoe industry, regardless of ownership.

The distinction makes a difference not only for how we interpret empirically estimated elasticities but also for the evaluation of policy. Consider the question of optimal tax policy toward inward FDI of a small, open economy. The standard result, discussed in Gordon (1986), is that such a country should, ignoring foreign tax credits offered by the capital-exporting country, impose no distortionary tax on the income earned by capital imports; taxes like the value-added tax that do not provide a disincentive to investment are allowable. The model generating this standard result conceives of inward FDI as a capital investment. But if capital movement is not involved but rather the spread of intangibles, what policy is optimal? If pure profits are at issue, the rate of a tax that is nondistortionary on physical capital investment may matter a lot. Economists are only beginning to deal with such questions.

The real world is messier that Leamer's two-tiered classification suggests, because some MNCs do not fit neatly into either of Leamer's categories. They are neither safe-deposit boxes nor mutual funds. Consider the Cook Island corporations set up to accept the funds of New Zealand residents, to be invested back into New Zealand—the so-called Cook Island runaround. Many such firms are simply conduits designed to suck in taxable profits from other relatively high-tax jurisdictions and as such are neither mutual funds nor safe-deposit boxes, but rather tax shell games. There are tax haven countries that are in the business of facilitating MNC tax avoidance, for a fee. The presence of tax havens and the opportunities for avoidance and evasion they provide are a key reason that the tax regimes governing MNCs are so complex. They make a nod toward efficient allocation of resources by offering schemes to avoid punitive double taxation, but often in large part are antitax avoidance devices.

Recognizing the opportunities for income shifting puts a new slant on what is appropriate policy. Consider the example of a country that decides to stimulate domestic investment by lowering its effective tax rate. It has two choices: keep its current statutory corporate tax rate at 35 percent and introduce a generous investment tax credit or lower the statutory rate to 25 percent, or even to 10 percent, as Ireland has done. Presume that both policies provide equal Hall-Jorgenson-King-Fullerton effective tax rates. Will the two policies have the same impact on domestic investment? The answer is no, because only the low statutory rate regime has the attraction that, once operations are located in the country, taxable income can be shifted in from other high-tax locations to lower the MNC's worldwide tax burden. To capture this distinction requires the construction of what Grubert and Slemrod (1994) refer to as an income-shifting-adjusted cost of capital (ISACC). The ISACC measures the true cost of capital for real investment because it accounts for the possibility that real investment facilitates income shifting.[1]

The next generation of empirical studies must be based on structural theoretical models that lay out both the "real" choices involved, such as the location of real investment or research and development operations, and also the array of other choices an MNC faces, including financing, income-shifting opportunities, and, in some contexts, retiming opportunities. The interaction among these choices will certainly be critical. For example, are avoidance opportunities independent of real choices, or facilitated by some real choices? In at least some contexts, the latter is certainly true. Grubert and Slemrod (1994) find that U.S. real investment in Puerto Rico is primarily driven by the income-shifting opportunities that Puerto Rican operations afford, as evidenced by the predominance of high-margin production located there.

As Hines notes, another complicating factor is the need to embed the information about the behavioral elasticities of particular participants into a general equilibrium framework. He asserts, "in the absence of a complete general equilibrium model it is impossible to predict with certainty the impact of tax changes on investment demand throughout a multinational firm." A good example of the considerations introduced by a general equilibrium perspective is the hypothesis (Scholes and Wolfson 1990) that an increase in U.S. effective tax rates would make investment in the United States more attractive to MNCs resident in certain countries, those for which U.S. tax liabilities may at the margin be credited against home-country tax liability.

Although the empirical support for this hypothesis at it relates to the Tax Reform Act of 1986 has been successfully challenged by Auerbach and Hassett (1993) and Collins, Kemsley, and Shackelford (1995), it stands as an excellent example of how unintuitive outcomes can, at least in theory, be generated within the complex patchwork of international tax regimes.

Is this any different from the importance of a general equilibrium perspective for studying investment in a purely domestic context? After all, in understanding the effect of investment tax credits on the volume of domestic investment, we need to be cognizant of the impact on interest rates and the relative price of capital goods. It is especially important in the context of multinational corporations because the ISACCs will differ across potential investors for the same investment. For this reason, the equilibrium outcome is likely to feature tax clienteles, so that the attractiveness of investment A to potential investor B will crucially depend on the tax treatment of other investors and other investments.

Providing clear policy advice in this environment is certainly difficult, even if we put equity issues aside and concentrate on efficient tax policies. There are efficiency costs due to the misallocation of resources, to be sure.

There are pharmaceutical plants in Puerto Rico that, absent tax (in this case, tax shifting) considerations, would never be there. There are high-priced lawyers operating out of the Cayman Islands who would not be there either. There are, moreover, substantial compliance costs associated with FDI, as documented in Blumenthal and Slemrod (1995), as well as administrative costs as governments struggle to protect their revenues.[2] From a global welfare point of view, one must be concerned about a fiscal race to the bottom, which results ultimately in no tax being collected on resources mobile across countries.

Jim Hines has written thoughtfully on these normative issues in his other work, and empirical research is needed to sharpen our understanding of the policy questions. Hines offers some tentative policy conclusions but recognizes that there is much more we need to know before we can be more confident about any advice.

Hines demonstrates that the first generation of empirical research on MNCs has established conclusively that the answer to the question—Do taxes matter?—is yes. A new generation of research, based on structural models of the joint decisions regarding real decision and tax avoidance, is required to answer the next question: How do taxes matter? This question presents a fascinating intellectual challenge of integrating models of the nature of the multinational enterprise and opportunities for tax avoidance into normative models of tax policy. It is an important challenge because the international tax system is gaining prominence as economies integrate, MNCs expand, and traditional barriers to trade fall.

Notes

1. This point applies much more broadly than to MNC investment (Slemrod 1994). For example, if the increased income from more labor supply facilitates more tax avoidance, then its true marginal tax rate lies below the statutory marginal tax rate. In this case estimated labor supply elasticities do not directly reveal information about utility functions, but instead a mixture of information about utility functions and the tax avoidance technology.

2. From any one country's perspective, it makes sense to devote one dollar of resources to prevent a dollar of revenue from being remitted to a foreign government, but the same marginal condition certainly does not hold for determining optimal enforcement of taxes in a purely domestic context, as in that case the dollar collected is simply a transfer from private to public hands.

References

Auerbach, Alan, and Kevin Hassett. 1993. "Taxation and Foreign Direct Investment in the United States: A Reconsideration of the Evidence." In A. Giovannini, R. G. Hubbard, and J. Slemrod, eds., *Studies in International Taxation*. Chicago: University of Chicago Press.

Blumenthal, Marsha, and Joel Slemrod. 1995. "The Compliance Cost of Taxing Foreign-Source Income: Its Magnitude, Determinants, and Policy Implications." *International Tax and Public Finance* 2:37–53.

Collins, Julie H., Deen Kemsley, and Douglas A. Shackelford. 1995. "Tax Reform and Foreign Acquisitions: A Microanalysis." *National Tax Journal* 48:1–21.

Dunning, John H., ed. 1985. *Multinational Enterprises, Economic Structure, and International Competitiveness*. Clichester: Wiley.

Gordon, Roger. 1986. "Taxation of Investment and Saving in a World Economy." *American Economic Review* 76:1086–1102.

Gordon, Roger, and Joosung Jun. 1993. "Taxes and the Form of Ownership of Foreign Corporate Equity." In A. Giovannini, R. G. Hubbard, and J. Slemrod, eds., *Studies in International Taxation*. Chicago: University of Chicago Press.

Grubert, Harry, and Joel Slemrod. 1994, September. *Tax Effects on Investment and Income Shifting to Puerto Rico*. NBER Working Paper 4869.

Leamer, Edward E. 1996. "What Do We Know About the Impact of Offshore Investment on the U.S. Economy?" In J. Slemrod, eds., *Studies in the Taxation of Multinational Corporations*. New York: Kluwer Academic Press.

Scholes, Myron, and Mark A. Wolfson. 1990. "The Effect of Changes in Tax Laws on Corporate Reorganization Activity." *Journal of Business* 63:5141–5164.

Slemrod, Joel. 1994. "A General Model of the Behavioral Response to Taxation." Mimeo. University of Michigan.

Index